World War I

The International Library of Essays on Military History
Series Editor: Jeremy Black

Titles in the Series:

Warfare in Europe 1650–1792
Jeremy Black

Warfare in the Middle East since 1945
Ahron Bregman

The English Civil War
Stanley Carpenter

Warfare in Latin America
Miguel A. Centeno

United States Military History 1865 to the Present Day
Jeffrey Charlston

Medieval Warfare 1300–1450
Kelly DeVries

Medieval Warfare 1000–1300
John France

Warfare in the Dark Ages
John France and Kelly DeVries

Naval History 1500–1680
Jan Glete

Byzantine Warfare
John Haldon

Warfare in Early Modern Europe 1450–1660
Paul Hammer

Naval Warfare 1680–1850
Richard Harding

Warfare in Europe 1919–1938
Geoffrey Jensen

Warfare in Japan
Harald Kleinschmidt

Naval History 1850–Present
Andrew Lambert

African Military History
John Lamphear

Warfare in China to 1600
Peter Lorge

World War I
Michael Neiberg

The Army of Imperial Rome
Michael F. Pavkovic

The Army of the Roman Republic
Michael F. Pavkovic

Warfare in South Asia from 1500
Douglas Peers

The American Civil War
Ethan Rafuse

The British Army 1815–1914
Harold E. Raugh, Jr

The Russian Imperial Army 1796–1917
Roger Reese

Medieval Ships and Warfare
Susan Rose

Warfare in Europe 1792–1815
Frederick C. Schneid

The Second World War
Nick Smart

Warfare in China Since 1600
Kenneth Swope

Warfare in the USA 1775–1861
Samuel Watson

The Vietnam War
James H. Willbanks

Warfare in Europe 1815–1914
Peter Wilson

World War I

Edited by

Michael Neiberg

University of Southern Mississippi, USA

Routledge
Taylor & Francis Group

LONDON AND NEW YORK

First published 2005 by Ashgate Publishing.

Reissued 2018 by Routledge
2 Park Square, Milton Park, Abingdon, Oxon, OX14 4RN
605 Third Avenue, New York, NY 10017

First issued in paperback 2021

Routledge is an imprint of the Taylor & Francis Group, an informa business

© Michael Neiberg 2005. For copyright of individual articles please refer to the Acknowledgements.

All rights reserved. No part of this book may be reprinted or reproduced or utilised in any form or by any electronic, mechanical, or other means, now known or hereafter invented, including photocopying and recording, or in any information storage or retrieval system, without permission in writing from the publishers.

A Library of Congress record exists under LC control number: 2004066021

Notice:
Product or corporate names may be trademarks or registered trademarks, and are used only for identification and explanation without intent to infringe.

Publisher's Note
The publisher has gone to great lengths to ensure the quality of this reprint but points out that some imperfections in the original copies may be apparent.

Disclaimer
The publisher has made every effort to trace copyright holders and welcomes correspondence from those they have been unable to contact.

ISBN 13: 978-0-815-39914-8 (hbk)
ISBN 13: 978-1-351-14280-9 (ebk)
ISBN 13: 978-1-138-35802-7 (pbk)

DOI: 10.4324/9781351142809

Contents

Acknowledgements vii
Series Preface ix
Introduction xi

PART I   EASTERN FRONT

1 Stephen J. Cimbala (1996), 'Steering Through Rapids: Russian Mobilization and World War I', *Journal of Slavic Military Studies*, **9**, pp. 376–98. 3
2 D.J. Dutton (1979), 'The Balkan Campaign and French War Aims in the Great War', *English Historical Review*, **94**, pp. 97–113. 27
3 Josh Sanborn (2000), 'The Mobilization of 1914 and the Question of the Russian Nation: A Reexamination', *Slavic Review*, **59**, pp. 267–89. 45
4 Dennis E. Showalter (2002), '"The East Gives Nothing Back": The Great War and the German Army in Russia', *Journal of the Historical Society*, **2**, pp. 1–19. 69
5 Glenn E. Torrey (1966), 'Rumania and the Belligerents 1914–1916', *Journal of Contemporary History*, **1**, pp. 171–91. 89
6 Ulrich Trumpener (1962), 'Turkey's Entry into World War I: An Assessment of Responsibilities', *Journal of Modern History*, **34**, pp. 369–80. 111

PART II   HOME FRONTS

7 Keith Allen (1998), 'Sharing Scarcity: Bread Rationing and the First World War in Berlin, 1914–1923', *Journal of Social History*, **32**, pp. 371–93. 125
8 P.E. Dewey (1984), 'Military Recruiting and the British Labour Force During the First World War', *Historical Journal*, **27**, pp. 199–223. 149
9 Keith Grieves (1989), 'Improvising the British War Effort: Eric Geddes and Lloyd George, 1915–18', *War and Society*, **7**, pp. 40–55. 175
10 Nicoletta F. Gullace (1997), 'White Feathers and Wounded Men: Female Patriotism and the Memory of the Great War', *Journal of British Studies*, **36**, pp. 178–206. 191
11 Jon Lawrence, Martin Dean and Jean-Louis Robert (1992), 'The Outbreak of War and the Urban Economy: Paris, Berlin, and London in 1914', *Economic History Review*, **45**, pp. 564–93. 221
12 Tyler Stovall (1998), 'The Color Line Behind the Lines: Racial Violence in France During the Great War', *American Historical Review*, **103**, pp. 737–69. 251

PART III   WESTERN FRONT

13 Robert B. Bruce (1998), 'To the Last Limits of Their Strength: The French Army and the Logistics of Attrition at the Battle of Verdun, 21 February – 18 December 1916', *Army History*, **45**, pp. 9–21.   287
14 David French (1988), 'The Meaning of Attrition, 1914–1916', *English Historical Review*, **103**, pp. 385–405.   301
15 John Horne and Alan Kramer (1994), 'German "Atrocities" and Franco-German Opinion, 1914: The Evidence of German Soldiers' Diaries', *Journal of Modern History*, **66**, pp. 1–33.   323
16 Timothy K. Nenninger (1987), 'Tactical Dysfunction in the AEF, 1917–1918', *Military Affairs*, **51**, pp. 177–81.   357
17 William Philpott (2002), 'Why the British Were Really on the Somme: A Reply to Elizabeth Greenhalgh', *War in History*, **9**, pp. 446–71.   363
18 Charles Rearick (1992), 'Madelon and the Men – in War and Memory', *French Historical Studies*, **17**, pp. 1001–34.   389
19 Hew Strachan (1998), 'The Battle of the Somme and British Strategy', *Journal of Strategic Studies*, **21**, pp. 79–95.   423
20 Ulrich Trumpener (1975), 'The Road to Ypres: The Beginnings of Gas Warfare in World War I', *Journal of Modern History*, **47**, pp. 460–80.   441

PART IV   OTHER FRONTS

21 C.M. Andrew and A.S. Kanya-Forstner (1978), 'France, Africa, and the First World War', *Journal of African History*, **19**, pp. 11–23.   465
22 Lal Baha (1970), 'The North-West Frontier in the First World War', *Asian Affairs*, **57**, pp. 29–37.   479
23 T.R.H. Davenport (1963), 'The South African Rebellion, 1914', *English Historical Review*, **78**, pp. 73–94.   489
24 Albert Grundlingh (1985), 'Black Men in a White Man's War: The Impact of the First World War on South African Blacks', *War and Society*, **3**, pp. 55–81.   513
25 Geoffrey Hudson (1969), 'The Far East and the End of the First World War', *Journal of Contemporary History*, **4**, pp. 165–79.   541
26 James K. Matthews (1982), 'World War I and the Rise of African Nationalism: Nigerian Veterans as Catalysts of Change', *Journal of Modern African Studies*, **20**, pp. 493–502.   557
27 Richard Rathbone (1978), 'World War I and Africa: Introduction', *Journal of African History*, **19**, pp. 1–9.   567
28 Ann-Louise Shapiro (1997), 'Fixing History: Narratives of World War I in France', *History and Theory*, **36**, pp. 111–30.   577

Name Index   597

Acknowledgements

The editor and publishers wish to thank the following for permission to use copyright material.

American Historical Association for the essay: Tyler Stovall (1998), 'The Color Line Behind the Lines: Racial Violence in France During the Great War', *American Historical Review*, **103**, pp. 737–69.

Blackwell Publishing Ltd for the essay: Dennis E. Showalter (2002), '"The East Gives Nothing Back": The Great War and the German Army in Russia', *Journal of the Historical Society*, **2**, pp. 1–19.

Cambridge University Press for the essays: P.E. Dewey (1984), 'Military Recruiting and the British Labour Force During the First World War', *Historical Journal*, **27**, pp. 199–223. Copyright © 1984 Cambridge University Press; C.M. Andrew and A.S. Kanya-Forstner (1978), 'France, Africa, and the First World War', *Journal of African History*, **19**, pp. 11–23. Copyright © 1978 Cambridge University Press; James K. Matthews (1982), 'World War I and the Rise of African Nationalism: Nigerian Veterans as Catalysts of Change', *Journal of Modern African Studies*, **20**, pp. 493–502. Copyright © 1982 Cambridge University Press; Richard Rathbone (1978), 'World War I and Africa: Introduction', *Journal of African History*, **19**, pp. 1–9. Copyright © 1978 Cambridge University Press.

Copyright Clearance Center, Inc. for the essay: Timothy K. Nenninger (1987), 'Tactical Dysfunction in the AEF, 1917–1918', *Military Affairs*, **51**, pp. 177–81.

Duke University Press for the essay: Charles Rearick (1992), 'Madelon and the Men – in War and Memory', *French Historical Studies*, **17**, pp. 1001–34. Copyright © 1992 Society of French Historical.

George Mason University for the essay: Keith Allen (1998), 'Sharing Scarcity: Bread Rationing and the First World War in Berlin, 1914–1923', *Journal of Social History*, **32**, pp. 371–93.

Hodder Arnold for the essay: William Philpott (2002), 'Why the British Were Really on the Somme: A Reply to Elizabeth Greenhalgh', *War in History*, **9**, pp. 446–71. Copyright © 2002 Arnold.

Houghton Library, Harvard University for the image: In the Fall of 1918 war-weary *poilus* are shown singing the now famous 'La Madelon' as they march through a liberated, battle-damaged village. *La Baïonette*, 3 October 1918. Drawing by Gus Bofa. Shelfmark H 796.822.10*F. By permission of Houghton Library, Harvard University.

Le Musée d'histoire contemporaine-BDIC for the image: An illustrated postcard from the war era highlighting an officer's marriage proposal and Madelon's (negative) reponse. This part of the story was of particular interest to the civilian population towards the end of the war and in the immediate postwar period (the date 1919 is handwritten on the back of the card). Courtesy of Le Musée d'histoire contemporaine-BDIC. Illustrator anonymous. All rights reserved.

Oxford University Press for the essays: D.J. Dutton (1979), 'The Balkan Campaign and French War Aims in the Great War', *English Historical Review*, **94**, pp. 97–113; David French (1988), 'The Meaning of Attrition, 1914–1916', *English Historical Review*, **103**, pp. 385–405; T.R.H. Davenport (1963), 'The South African Rebellion, 1914', *English Historical Review*, **78**, pp. 73–94. By permission of Oxford University Press.

Sage Publications Ltd for the essays: Glenn E. Torrey (1966), 'Rumania and the Belligerents 1914–1916', *Journal of Contemporary History*, **1**, pp. 171–91. Copyright © 1966 Sage Publications; Geoffrey Hudson (1969), 'The Far East and the End of the First World War', *Journal of Contemporary History*, **4**, pp. 165–79. Copyright © 1969 Sage Publications.

Taylor and Francis for the essays: Stephen J. Cimbala (1996), 'Steering Through Rapids: Russian Mobilization and World War I', *Journal of Slavic Military Studies*, **9**, pp. 376–98; Hew Strachan (1998), 'The Battle of the Somme and British Strategy', *Journal of Strategic Studies*, **21**, pp. 79–95; Lal Baha (1970), 'The North-West Frontier in the First World War', *Asian Affairs*, **57**, pp. 29–37.

The University of Chicago Press for the essays: Ulrich Trumpener (1962), 'Turkey's Entry into World War I: An Assessment of Responsibilities', *Journal of Modern History*, **34**, pp. 369–80; Nicoletta F. Gullace (1997), 'White Feathers and Wounded Men: Female Patriotism and the Memory of the Great War', *Journal of British Studies*, **36**, pp. 178–206. Copyright © 1997 The North American Conference on British Studies; John Horne and Alan Kramer (1994), 'German "Atrocities" and Franco-German Opinion, 1914: The Evidence of German Soldiers' Diaries', *Journal of Modern History*, **66**, pp. 1–33. Copyright © 1994 University of Chicago; Ulrich Trumpener (1975), 'The Road to Ypres: The Beginnings of Gas Warfare in World War I', *Journal of Modern History*, **47**, pp. 460–80.

US Army Center of Military History for the essay: Robert B. Bruce (1998), 'To the Last Limits of Their Strength: The French Army and the Logistics of Attrition at the Battle of Verdun, 21 February – 18 December 1916', *Army History*, **45**, pp. 9–21.

War and Society for the essays: Keith Grieves (1989), 'Improvising the British War Effort: Eric Geddes and Lloyd George, 1915–18', *War and Society*, **7**, pp. 40–55; Albert Grundlingh (1985), 'Black Men in a White Man's War: The Impact of the First World War on South African Blacks', *War and Society*, **3**, pp. 55–81.

Every effort has been made to trace all the copyright holders, but if any have been inadvertently overlooked the publishers will be pleased to make the necessary arrangement at the first opportunity.

Series Preface

War and military matters are key aspects of the modern world and central topics in history study. This series brings together essays selected from key journals that exhibit careful analysis of military history. The volumes, each of which is edited by an expert in the field, cover crucial time periods and geographical areas including Europe, the USA, China, Japan, Latin America, and South Asia. Each volume represents the editor's selection of the most seminal recent essays on military history in their particular area of expertise, while an introduction presents an overview of the issues in that area, together with comments on the background and significance of the essays selected.

This series reflects important shifts in the subject. Military history has increasingly taken a cultural turn, forcing us to consider the question of what wins wars in a new light. Historians used to emphasise the material aspects of war, specifically the quality and quantity of resources. That approach, bringing together technological proficiency and economic strength, appeared to help explain struggles for mastery within the West, as well as conflicts between the West and non-West. Now, the focus is rather on strategic culture – how tasks are set and understood – and on how resources are used. It involves exploring issues such as fighting quality, unit cohesion, morale, leadership, tactics, strategy, as well as the organisational cultural factors that affect assessment and use of resources. Instead of assuming that organisational issues were driven by how best to use, move and supply weapons, this approach considers how they are affected by social patterns and developments.

Former assumptions by historians that societies are driven merely by a search for efficiency and maximisation of force as they adapt their weaponry to optimise performance in war ignored the complex process in which interest in new weapons interacted with the desire for continuity. Responses by warring parties to firearms, for example, varied, with some societies, such as those of Western Europe, proving keener to rely on firearms than others, for example in East and South Asia. This becomes easier to understand by considering the different tasks and possibilities facing armies at the time – when it is far from clear which weaponry, force structure, tactics, or operational method can be adopted most successfully – rather than thinking in terms of clear-cut military progress.

Cultural factors also play a role in responses to the trial of combat. The understanding of loss and suffering, at both the level of ordinary soldiers and of societies as a whole, is far more culturally conditioned than emphasis on the sameness of battle might suggest, and variations in the willingness to suffer losses influences both military success and styles of combat.

Furthermore, war is not really about battle but about attempts to impose will. Success in this involves far more than victory on the battlefield; that is just a pre-condition of a more complex process. The defeated must be willing to accept the verdict of battle. This involves accommodation, if not acculturation – something that has been far from constant in different periods and places. Assimilating local religious cults, co-opting local élites, and, possibly, today, offering the various inducements summarised as globalisation, have been the most important means of achieving it over the years. Thus military history becomes an aspect of total history; and victory in war is best studied in terms of its multiple contexts.

Any selection of what to include is difficult. The editors in this series have done an excellent job and it has been a great pleasure working with them.

JEREMY BLACK
Series Editor
University of Exeter

Introduction

This volume of the *International Library of Military History* focuses on the First World War, a conflict that has recently witnessed a resurgence of interest from both popular and scholarly communities. The war remains a captivating episode in modern history owing to several factors, including: the immense disconnect between the war's causes and its effects; the futility and enormous casualties of most military operations, symbolized by the static trench warfare of the Western Front; the global extent of the war; and the family connections that virtually all Europeans (as well as many Americans) have to combatants in one or more of the armies.

As Brian Bond (2002), Gary Sheffield (2001), Hew Strachan (2001) and others have noted, this complex international war has presented those interested in it with numerous challenges of interpretation. Drawing conceptual links, explaining connecting patterns and giving meaning to the war remains as difficult and almost as controversial as ever. Scholars still lack a consensus on such critical issues as the war's causes and the reasons for the stalemate that characterized combat on the Western Front for the better part of four years. Popular and scholarly understandings alike therefore remain dominated by facile explanations that include an image of generals who were somehow exponentially more incompetent than those of other wars, a battlefield so dominated by technology that men became irrelevant to combat operations, and a generation of naïve young men unsure of why they were fighting and, in the words of one recent popular song, were 'dying in waves'.[1]

For all we know about the patterns of this 'world' war, however, our understandings remain dominated by the Western Front. The enormous battles of the Eastern Front are still largely unknown, despite a few notable books.[2] Even when other theatres appear prominently in works on the war, they most commonly do so through Western eyes. Thus, for many, the war in the Middle East remains the war of the eccentric British officer, T.E. Lawrence, better known as Lawrence of Arabia. Similarly, the war in Africa is most commonly remembered in Europe as the war of the German commando leader Paul von Lettow-Vorbeck. That his army contained three times as many Africans as Europeans seems far less important than the image of a European who eluded his European-led enemies until the very end of the war. The impact of the war on Africans themselves remains understudied and little appreciated.[3]

The essays collected in this volume together reflect two growing trends in the study of the First World War. First, they are global in nature. Although half the essays concern the Western powers, one section is dedicated to the Eastern Front, including a focus on Romania, and one section is dedicated to Africa and Asia. The focus in so much of the historical literature on Britain, France, Germany and the United States reflects more than ethnocentrism. Studying the 'lesser powers' (for lack of a more appropriate term) and the colonial empires of the great powers presents numerous challenges. Language, of course, is one such challenge, but of greater concern for most historians, archival records for the nations of Eastern Europe, Asia and Africa are less comprehensive and, during the period of the Cold War, those in Eastern Europe were often closed to Western researchers. Thus much of our understanding of these facets of the war rest in journal essays like those presented here. This volume does not pretend to close all of the gaps in our understanding of the war outside France and Belgium. Nor does it presume to offer a complete catalogue of the experiences of all groups affected by the war. Rather, it brings together essays on parts of the world on which the historical literature remains notably thin.

The essays collected here follow a second trend in First World War studies, that of interdisciplinary studies. Recently, scholars have worked to move beyond the front lines and develop a holistic approach to understanding the war (see especially Macleod and Purseigle, 2003). In many ways, studies of the First World War have blazed new trails in this direction for all periods of military history. The enormous efforts of groups on the home front during four years of total war, plus the revolutionary changes that the war brought about, led to an unprecedented role for the home front, and civilians more generally, in the course of the war. Because the soldiers of the war were socially, economically and politically indistinguishable from their peers who did not serve, the linkages between armies and societies were as tight as they have ever been in the history of warfare.

Many of the studies in this volume are highly specialized and deal with topics not covered by larger monographs. The great strength of this series lies in its ability to bring these studies together in one volume. The works presented here are divided into four parts, beginning with the Eastern Front, a choice that may strike some readers as unusual, given the emphasis on Western studies in the historical literature. Nevertheless, Eastern Europe was the fulcrum of the July crisis of 1914. The tensions between Austria-Hungary and Serbia, especially the former's delivery of an ultimatum to the latter late in the month, created the immediate spark that led to war.

The Eastern Front

Even before the Archduke Franz Ferdinand and his wife entered Sarajevo, Eastern Europe had been an especially volatile tinderbox. Before leaving office in 1890, German Chancellor Otto von Bismarck had famously warned that 'some damn foolish thing in the Balkans' would start the next great European War (cited in Tuchman, 1962, p. 71). In the years following Bismarck's exit from the continent's diplomatic stage, the decline of the Ottoman empire, Russian humiliation in the Russo-Japanese War of 1904–1905, and the growth of irredentist nationalism all contributed to the instability of Eastern Europe.

For most contemporaries, the 1903 revolution in Serbia that overthrew the pro-Austrian Obrenovich dynasty hardly seemed like an event likely to influence their lives in the near future. Even today the historical literature pays scant attention to it. But the Karadjordjevićs who, with support from the army, seized power were much closer to the Russians and quickly worked to dismantle the pro-Austrian policies of the Obrenovichs. The new regime emphasized common Russo-Serbian religious and ethnic links while at the same time highlighting the plight of Slavic peoples living under Austrian oppression. On an economic level, the Karadjordjevićs and the much larger Austro-Hungarian empire engaged in the so-called 'pig war', a trade imbroglio that caused Balkan tensions to rise and seemingly underscored Karadjordjević notions of Austro-Hungarian perfidy. Austrian refusal to purchase Serbian pork caused economic dislocations in Serbia and led the Serbians to sell their goods in Bosnia and Herzegovina, two provinces officially under Ottoman control but under heavy Austrian influence.

In order to stop what they saw as Serbian aggression in their own backyard, the Austro-Hungarian empire formally annexed Bosnia and Herzegovina in 1908. The move infuriated Serbia, whose nationalists began to increase their already shrill calls for a political union of Serbs and Croats, a clear threat to the internal integrity of the Austro-Hungarian empire. Russia, too, was angry at the annexations, but, still reeling from the Russo-Japanese War and unable to challenge German diplomatic and military support for Austria, the Russians had little choice but to accept what was presented to them as a *fait accompli*. True to Bismarck's prediction, the Balkans were rapidly becoming the most unstable part of an increasingly unstable continent.

Two diplomatic crises in Morocco in 1905 and 1911 temporarily pulled the eyes of European diplomats westwards, but the Balkans remained the continent's main crisis region. In 1911 Italy seized Libya and the Dodecanese Islands from the overextended Ottoman empire, leading Serbia, Bulgaria, Greece and Montenegro to conclude that the time was ripe to eliminate Ottoman presence in Europe once and for all. Loosely banded together as the Balkan League, they declared war and drove the Ottomans to the gates of Constantinople itself. The Ottomans kept the Gallipoli peninsula, the region around their capital and a few scattered fortresses. Otherwise, the period of Ottoman suzerainty in Europe was over.

The military prowess of Serbia, whose 200 000-man army had fought well in what became known as the First Balkan War, unnerved the Austrians. When Bulgaria turned on its former allies in the Second Balkan War (1912) Serbia once again fought with a determination and a skill that created tremendous concern in Austrian circles (see Hall, 2000). By 1913 Serbian politicians, who just a scant decade earlier had been reliably pro-Austrian, were calling for territorial adjustments that would give landlocked Serbia an outlet to the sea. More importantly, Serbian military success added weight to calls for a greater Slav state under Serbian leadership. Such a state could only gain power at the expense of the polyglot Austro-Hungarian empire. General Franz Conrad von Hötzendorff, the chief of the Austrian general staff, warned Archduke Franz Ferdinand that any concessions to the Serbians 'would relegate the [Austro-Hungarian] Monarchy to the status of a small power' (quoted in Henig, 1989, p. 21). Conrad repeatedly urged Emperor Franz Joseph to fight a pre-emptive war against the Serbians, eliminate the Karadjordjevićs and annex Serbia.

The assassinations of Austrian Archduke Franz Ferdinand and his commoner wife Sophie on 28 June 1914 can only be understood in this context. In modern parlance, the Austrian ruling elite, most of whom disliked both Franz Ferdinand and Sophie, saw the assassinations as acts of state-sponsored terrorism. The Austrian government had evidence connecting the assassin, a Bosnian teenager named Gavrilo Princip, to a secret organization called the Black Hand with known ties to Serbian intelligence officers. With international sympathy for the dead couple on their side, Conrad and others now saw a long-sought-after opportunity to punish Serbia without seeming to be an unwarranted aggressor.

Thus it was in the east that the critical chain of events leading to war in 1914 began, although the assassination itself need not have led to war. It soon became clear to European diplomats, however, that the Austro-Hungarian government intended to use the assassination as a pretext for war and that the German government intended to provide full support to its Austrian ally, adding fuel to already unpredictable wildfire. All eyes turned again to the east as the danger of the situation belatedly became apparent. The degree of Russian support for Serbia would probably determine the intensity of the coming conflict. If Russia reneged on its historical connections to Serbia and allowed Austria to conduct a punitive war, then the war might well be the Third

Balkan War – small, localized, and with a minor direct impact on the great powers of Europe. If, on the other hand, Russia, with its alliance ties to France and Britain, intervened, a much larger conflict became a realistic possibility.

For their part, Russian leaders saw little choice but to defend Serbia. To do otherwise would fatally undermine Russian influence in the Balkans. A satisfactory outcome to the crisis, on the other hand, would erase the humiliations of the Russo-Japanese War and, not coincidentally, bolster the tarnished claims of the tsar and the nobility to leadership of Russian society. The very size of Russia forced the great powers to take it seriously, even if the Germans largely denigrated both Russian culture and the ability of the Russian army which was then still in the process of reform and rebuilding.

Despite their rather blithe dismissal of Russian military prowess, German and Austro-Hungarian military leaders soon realized, much to their shock and horror, that neither had adequately planned for Russian intervention. Relations between the two allies' general staffs had been lukewarm at best in the years before the war, leading to an astonishing disconnect in their plans for war. German war plans, hard-wired for almost a decade into fighting and defeating France before engaging with the Russians, expected the Austrians to hold the Russians in check. Burning with a desire to punish Serbia, however, the Austrians planned to march the bulk of their forces to the south against Belgrade. Even an exclusive focus of Austro-Hungarian fighting strength could not have held off the much larger Russian force, especially in faraway East Prussia, the traditional seat of the German elite.

Incredibly, then, neither side was fully prepared to fight the largest land army in Europe at a time when the perfect coordination of both would have been necessary. In another of his works, one of the authors in this collection, Dennis Showalter, cleverly likens the situation to a married couple leaving for vacation with each mistakenly assuming that the other has turned off the gas in the stove (Showalter, 2004, p. 143). The spark of the war led that powerful gas to explode, destroying within four years not just the German and Austrian royal houses, but the Russian and Ottoman royal houses as well.

The one saving grace for Germany and Austria lay in the fact that the strength of the Russian army lay in its size, not in its finesse. To stand a reasonable chance of survival, the Germans would need to take care of their business in France and the Austrians to take care of theirs in Serbia before the massive Russian giant awoke and loaded his guns. Administratively primitive, with a fragile transportation system and mobilization centres spread out across an enormous expanse of space, the Russians might indeed stumble and bumble enough in the early months of the war to keep German and Austrian hopes alive. Certainly nothing in Russian performance in the war with Japan had indicated any special competence in military affairs.

Nevertheless, as Stephen Cimbala indicates in 'Steering Through Rapids: Russian Mobilization and World War I' (Chapter 1), the Russians performed admirably in the war's mobilization phase. From 1912 the Russians had begun to develop aggressive war plans predicated on an early offensive against Germany in East Prussia, both to fulfil alliance commitments to France and to keep Germany off-balance. The Russian plan aimed to mobilize in stages in order to deploy large numbers of soldiers at the front quickly and to ease the stress on Russian transportation and supply. The Russian plan required a total mobilization as early as possible, dashing the tsar's hopes of mobilizing against Austria-Hungary only and thereby using the army to deter an Austrian attack on Serbia without simultaneously threatening Germany. War planning, Cimbala argues, played a central role in leading the continent to war, and not just in Germany.

In addition to efficiency, notes Josh Sanborn in 'The Mobilization of 1914 and the Question of the Russian Nation: A Reexamination' (Chapter 3), the Russian elite also had to worry about Russian subjects responding to mobilization calls. The Russian military elite had no special confidence that disaffected peasants would in fact report as ordered. Russian political leaders recalled that the stresses of war in 1905 had led to revolution and major political change. The Russian experience in 1914 is typically understood as a success story because the overwhelming majority of Russians did respond to calls to arms. Sanborn modifies this view by reminding us of the anti-draft riots and the vast sadness that greeted news of the war's outbreak. One does not have to take literally his assertion that in July, 1914 '[t]he most common sound in Russia was that of men, women, and children weeping' (p. 50) to accept his argument that most Russians expected to gain little from the war.

The speed and strength of the Russian response was not the only wild card in Eastern Europe in that critical month. Ulrich Trumpener, in 'Turkey's Entry into World War I: An Assessment of Responsibility' (Chapter 6), gives us an appreciation for what Turkish entry into the war meant both to the ailing Ottoman empire and to the larger patterns of the war. One of the foremost historians of Turkey in this period, Trumpener used this 1962 essay to underscore Turkish agency in the empire's decision to go to war. The obvious benefits of Turkish entry to Germany traditionally led historians to see the Ottoman empire as a 'toy' of the more powerful Germans. Germany did indeed benefit from Turkish entry because it forced Russia to leave troops in the Caucasus region and the British to be concerned with the security of India. Turkish battlefield performance in the war belied the abysmal reputation its army had acquired from the two Balkan Wars and the war with Italy (Erickson, 2001). Turkey's decision to enter the war, based on its own self-serving logic, contributed greatly to the global nature of the war, symbolized in 1915 by Australian and New Zealand troops fighting for the British on the Gallipoli peninsula in an operation designed in part to assist the Russians.

The war in the east in 1914 and 1915 settled into a general pattern of Russian armies defeating the Austrians but being in turn defeated by the Germans. The titanic twin German victories in the early weeks of the war at Tannenberg (26–31 August) and the Masurian Lakes (9–14 September) guaranteed that Russia would not be able to take advantage of the collapse of German war plans in the west. The following spring, the Germans caved in the entire Russian line during the Gorlice-Tarnow Offensive (2 May–27 June) and obliged the Russians to abandon Poland. The glaring contrast between German military efficiency and Austrian blundering led to the unification of the German and Austrian command structures under the dominance of the former.

Shattering German triumphs notwithstanding, Russia remained able to call on its vast spaces and seemingly endless manpower resources to not only survive, but launch a successful offensive of its own in summer 1916 under General Alexei Brusilov. Dennis Showalter's '"The East Gives Nothing Back": The Great War and the German Army in Russia' (Chapter 4) analyses German frustrations with the inability to knock the Russians out of the war. He underscores the cold reality that even a succession of lopsided battlefield victories cannot always yield results commensurate with their costs – a lesson a future generation of German military leaders refused to grasp before it was too late. Showalter, one of this generation's most eminent military historians, explores the ways in which the German army reacted to these frustrations, foreshadowing, in many ways, the much more brutal Russo-German War of 1941–1945.

The Eastern Front also merits study as a corrective to the image of the war as a series of static trenches. With lower force-to-space ratios and less dominant quantities of machine guns and artillery pieces, the Eastern Front experienced rapid and expansive shifts, most often to the south and east. War on this front also experienced widespread 'demodernization', meaning that traditional problems like disease, lack of supplies and terrible exposure to the elements often caused more casualties than combat. As a result, while the Western Front often foreshadowed the highly technical war of 1939–1945, the Eastern Front just as often recalled the relative primitiveness of the Crimean War of 1854–1856.

Caught between Germany and Russia in both world wars in the east sat Rumania. Glenn Torrey, in 'Rumania and the Belligerents, 1914–1916' (Chapter 5), discusses the tensions between the elites and the masses in a nation with deep and abiding hatreds for both Austria-Hungary and Russia. Torrey reminds us of the roles that family connections played in a Europe dominated for a little while longer by royal and family ties. He also reminds us of the roles of propaganda, influence-peddling and bribery in settling the Rumanian elite upon war against the central powers. Rumania, whose elite tried to fight a cabinet war in an era of people's war, found to its great tragedy that it had made a bad decision for bad reasons.

The interest of the western powers in the Balkans became manifest when the British and French opened a front in Greece in Salonika in 1915. Done in part to assist the beleaguered Serbians, the motives for the sustenance of this front is the subject of D.J. Dutton's 'The Balkan Campaign and French War Aims in the Great War' (Chapter 2). Largely a French idea and always commanded by a French general, the mostly inactive 'gardeners of Salonika' have long been a subject of historical controversy. Dutton explores this controversy and highlights the difficulty of alliance warfare. Indeed it was at Salonika that French General Maurice Sarrail allegedly said that, now he had seen alliances at work, he had lost some of his admiration for Napoleon.

Home Fronts

From the Eastern Front this volume moves to Part II, 'Home Fronts'. Modern, total war in the twentieth century required much greater sacrifices from civilians than had previous wars. Those states whose populations either could not endure these sacrifices or determined that the sacrifices had become futile lost the domestic cohesion needed to prosecute the war with maximum efficiency. The collapse of domestic consensus may have played a greater role in the defeat of Austria-Hungary and Russia than any losses on the battlefield. Similarly, states like Bulgaria and Rumania that had an increasingly diminished capacity to produce weapons, uniforms and food for their soldiers created the conditions for disaster.

The ability of Britain and France to develop ways of negotiating domestic conflict during the war played no small role in their ultimate victory. Part of the answer lies in the emergence of two dynamic, purposeful prime ministers, David Lloyd George and Georges Clemençeau. The allies' links with the industrial and financial capabilities of the United States also provided tremendous flexibility and strength, although it also indebted the victors to the Americans. All of the home fronts experienced tensions and conflicts; the states that found ways to manage them and compensate for them stood the greatest chance of success. The essays in Part II explore these home fronts in all of their complexity.

The outbreak of the war led to an initial outpouring of patriotism in the political arenas of all of the great powers. The kaiser's famous call that he no longer recognized political parties, only Germans, marked a critical step towards the creation of the *Burgfrieden*, a civil truce in domestic political squabbling. Its complement in France, the *Union Sacrée*, also brought together monarchists, socialists and centrist politicians in a political alliance designed to show that politicians would speak with one voice through the course of the war. Although Sanborn, for Russia, Adrian Gregory (2003), for Britain, Jeffrey Verhey (2000), for Germany, and others (Becker, 1977, 1993) correctly caution against the presumption of war enthusiasm, there was, at the very least, little organized resistance to the outbreak of the war.

In Chapter 11 Jon Lawrence, Martin Dean and Jean-Louis Robert offer us a comparative look at how the beginning of the war affected the capital cities of Paris, Berlin and London in their essay 'The Outbreak of War and the Urban Economy'. None of these cities had made adequate preparations for the outbreak of war on such an enormous scale. Paris sat in a particularly vulnerable position, facing a German invasion, having to prepare for the government's evacuation to Bordeaux, and beginning the process of mobilizing large numbers of essential workers for military service. Normal civilian life in the French capital virtually ended on the first day of mobilization, in sharp contrast to London, where the war still seemed far away and the effort to recruit men was still in an embryonic state.

Nevertheless, London, and England more generally, faced its own unique challenges. Alone among the great powers, Britain had no conscription. Thus the outbreak of the war forced Britain to engage in a massive programme to recruit men into the armed forces voluntarily. As Britain's small pre-war regular army suffered terribly in the war's first weeks, the need for volunteers grew. P.E. Dewey's 'Military Recruiting and the British Labour Force During the First World War' (Chapter 8) seeks to explore the impact of the recruitment process on British workers across economic sectors. As the Americans did in 1917, the British had to balance their need for military manpower with the equally pressing need to ensure that men with vital economic skills did not enlist. This process, Dewey argues, interacted with wages and the demographic structure of various professions to produce diverse patterns in British recruitment. Echoing those scholars who warn against trusting the myth of war enthusiasm, Dewey concludes that patriotism played only one part in the vast complex of factors that led men to enlist in 1914.

Nicoletta Gullace explores another motivation for British recruitment in her essay, 'White Feathers and Wounded Men: Female Patriotism and the Memory of the Great War' (Chapter 10). She is interested in the ways in which British society used female sexuality, and images of femininity more generally, to bully men into enlisting. Her work explores the White Feather campaign wherein British women tried to shame men into enlisting by presenting men in civilian clothes with feathers. The essay reaches deeper, however, also examining the use of feminine images in recruitment posters and classified ads placed in British newspapers. Associating cowardice with femininity, of course, also associated bravery with masculinity by contrast.

Gender studies form a central component of the new research on World War I. In all the belligerent states the exigencies of war brought unprecedented numbers of women into the workforce in order to compensate for the large numbers of men who enlisted. France also tried to augment its industrial workforce by bringing in workers from its empire – some from as far away as Indochina. Tyler Stovall's 'The Color Line Behind the Lines' (Chapter 12) examines the racism experienced by these workers and connects that prejudice to the conditions of the war. His essay is both an analysis of one of the most unpleasant aspects of the home front and a reminder of the abiding racism of European society in the years before the war's outbreak. Stovall's work also cautions historians not to take at face value the perceptions of African-American soldiers that French society was less pathologically racist than American society.

French racism thus appears here as a variable affected by many factors – most notably the war as experienced on the home front. Although Stovall's work is not explicitly comparative, he offers insights into the nature of that racism, notably as it contrasted to the warm reception French civilians gave to African-American soldiers. That reception stands in the minds of many scholars as evidence of the more cosmopolitan and tolerant attitudes of the French. However, Stovall suggests another explanation. While colonial workers became associated in the French popular mindset with strike-breaking and depressed wages, African-American soldiers became quickly associated with the American force of arms that had crossed the ocean to expel the German invaders from French soil. Seen in this light, the differing reception French civilians gave to colonial workers and African-American soldiers appears less as a manifestation of French egalitarianism and more as an expression of the war and the many tensions it produced.

In Chapter 7 Keith Allen tackles one of the most controversial discussions of the home front and its meaning for the larger war. Images of hunger and scarcity in German cities dovetailed nicely in the post-war years with proponents of the belief that the German army had not really been defeated in battle. Taken together, they allowed the blame for the loss of the war and the harsh peace that followed to be transferred to enemies on the home front, thus leaving untarnished the reputation of German arms. In 'Sharing Scarcity: Bread Rationing and the First World War in Berlin, 1914–1923' Allen shows us a voluntary food distribution system that worked well enough to provide food to the civilians at home, and even allowed civilians to send food to the men at the front.

Allen's work helps us rethink what remains a persistent element of the explanation for the German defeat. The focus on the alleged failures of the German home front not only disguises the battlefield efficiency of the allies in 1918 in driving the Germans back, but also places an undue emphasis on the suffering of the German people. All civilians suffered during the war, and the starvation and malnutrition of children stands as one of its particularly vile aspects. Nevertheless, a focus on the particular suffering of the German population obscures the suffering caused by the German army when it took millions of tons of food from Belgium, Rumania, Poland, Russia and the Ukraine. We lack a definitive series of studies on the extent of the civilian food crisis in these countries.

Finally, Keith Grieves's 'Improvising the British War Effort: Eric Geddes and Lloyd George' (Chapter 9) focuses on two of the most dynamic civilian leaders of the war. Working closely together, they changed the Asquith government's policy of fighting the war while simultaneously engaging in 'business as usual'. The system developed by Lloyd George and Geddes depended on improvisation and changing the mentality of British industrial and political leaders. In a modern war that swallowed guns, ammunition and other materiel at a prodigious rate, economics came to centre stage. Like his French counterpart, Albert Thomas, Geddes reformed and adapted British industry and transportation to provide the right quality and quantity of weapons to the men at the front.

The Western Front

Grieves's essay helps to transition the volume to the section that will be most familiar to readers, the Western Front. The stasis of the Western Front and the squalid conditions of the front lines themselves created images that have become the ultimate symbol of the war in the eyes of many post-war commentators. In reducing the Western Front to simple stereotypes, these images lose the nuances and complexities of a war that was, at times, dynamic. Thus while historians still argue about the strategic wisdom of operations and the relative capabilities of commanders, they do not see the Western Front as four years of more or less identical failures of military operations. The essays in Part III, written by many of the war's most perceptive historians, reveal the Western Front in all of its many forms.

John Horne's and Alan Kramer's study, 'German "Atrocities" and Franco-German Opinion, 1914' (Chapter 15) – part of a much larger study on this subject – tackles another common motif of the war (see also Horne and Kramer, 2001). The 'Rape of Belgium' contributed to the British decision to intervene in the war and fed allied propaganda machines for four years. Allied journalists and trigger-happy propagandists unnecessarily embellished these stories, creating a generation of cynics when the most lurid tales proved to be unfounded. The revelation of so much exaggeration and intentional lying in wartime propaganda led many in the inter-war period to discount all German war crimes, even those that obviously did occur. Horne and Kramer analyse the issue of German army atrocities in Belgium from the perspective of diaries written by German soldiers themselves. Their conclusions are surprising and present a scholarly treatment of a subject still very much alive in the historiography of the war (see also Zuckerman, 2004).

Some of the same Germans who participated in the invasion of Belgium might well have been present at Ypres in April 1915 when the Western Front saw its first large-scale use of poison gas. In his second essay in this collection, Ulrich Trumpener details the origins of gas weapons in his 'The Road to Ypres: The Beginnings of Gas Warfare in World War I' (Chapter 20). The novelty of gas and the horrific ways it caused men to die led to charges from all sides that the weapon was both inhumane and counterproductive to winning the war because the side that used it would also have to defend against it. The politicians and future Nobel laureates who developed and defended the use of gas weapons argued that they were no less humane than artillery (a defensible argument) and that the proscriptions on poison gas belonged to a more chivalrous and humane period in the history of warfare.

In part because of the limitations of gas weapons, the massive German assault on Verdun that began in February 1916 relied much more on heavy artillery. Verdun soon became the largest and most important battle fought by the French army. By the time it ended in December, the French had sustained 377 000 casualties and the Germans another 337 000. In 'To the Last Limits of Their Strength: The French Army and the Logistics of Attrition at the Battle of Verdun' (Chapter 13) Robert Bruce studies the logistical efforts that allowed the French army to fight on at Verdun. In this mammoth battle of attrition, fighting on meant continuing to feed what the men on both sides called the 'slaughterhouse' of Verdun. As Bruce notes, attrition warfare, aiming to kill the enemy at acceptable ratios to one's own losses, changed the rationale of military operations from seizing ground to mass murder on an unprecedented scale.

Attrition as a part of British strategy is the subject of David French's 'The Meaning of Attrition, 1914–1916' (Chapter 14). Contrary to the image of attrition as the Germans used it at

Verdun, French sees it as a logical extension of British strategy. The British, moreover, saw attrition as a way of saving lives, not as a way to have one more soldier alive at the end of the war than the enemy. Attrition, he contends, was in place as a central part of British strategy well before Field Marshal Sir Douglas Haig launched his 'wearing out' battles at the Somme in 1916 and Passchendaele in 1917.

The Battle of the Somme, launched in midsummer 1916, remains one of the most studied and most controversial campaigns of the war. Originally conceived in late 1915 as a coalition battle to be launched by coordinated British and French armies, it became a largely British campaign as French resources moved south to keep Verdun out of German hands. British tactical and strategic failures led to the bloody repulse of 1 July 1916, still the most costly single day in the history of the British army. To many Britons, the tragedy seemed multiplied because the casualties were felt disproportionately by the enthusiastic volunteers of the New Armies.

Ever since, the Somme has been criticized as a needless offensive fought with improper tactics by simplistic officers. Journalist Philip Gibbs and Winston Churchill were among the first post-war critics to lambast Haig and his staff for wasting the lives of the 'flower' of British youth. Defenders of the battle point to the enormous German casualties at the Somme and the description of the battle by one German veteran as 'the muddy grave' of the German army. They argue that the battle played a critical role in wearing down the Germans, thus making the success of 1918 possible.

William Philpott's essay 'Why the British Were Really on the Somme' (Chapter 17) addresses another controversy sparked by this battle. Philpott argues here that the demands of coalition warfare restricted British freedom of action and led the British army to take French needs into account when planning their offensive. Nevertheless, the decision about exactly where and when to attack remained in Haig's hands. The massive bloodletting at Verdun obviously played on the minds of British generals, leading Haig to become despondent about the future offensive power of the French army. Philpott's position that the restraints of alliance impaired the development of an independent British strategic line has been challenged, as the debate in *War in History*, from which this essay has been taken, reveals.

Hew Strachan's 'The Battle of the Somme and British Strategy' (Chapter 19) analyses yet another aspect of this battle. The Somme witnessed the first introduction of the tank to warfare. That innovation, combined with airpower and the awesome power of British artillery, led the Germans to coin a new phrase, *Materialschlacht*, or war of machines. In this essay Strachan, probably the most influential historian of the war writing today, connects *Materialschlacht* to British planning before the Somme and to the belated British decision to introduce conscription in 1916. The end result was a battle that forever changed the nature of land warfare.

Attrition warfare, of course, depended on the victors having greater resources than the vanquished. The 1917 entry of the United States into the war gave the allies those resources as the fresh, large divisions of the American Expeditionary Forces contributed to victory. Nevertheless, as Timothy Nenninger shows in 'Tactical Dysfunction in the AEF, 1917–1918' (Chapter 16), the Americans had much to learn. Utilizing a flawed doctrine and operating under false presumptions about the nature of warfare on the Western Front, the eager and anxious American doughboys fought with more élan than skill. The crisis of spring 1918, when the Germans launched a massive offensive, forced the Americans to enter into combat before they were fully prepared to do so. Perhaps the most remarkable feature of the Americans was their ability to recover from their own misconceptions and hastily improvised solutions to become a solid fighting force by the time of the armistice.

A study of the culture of men at war provides a constrast with discussions of strategy. Using the most popular song of the war among French soldiers, Charles Rearick's 'Madelon and the Men – in War and Memory' (Chapter 18) analyses French mindsets during the war and after it. The song 'Quand Madelon' revealed the desparate homesickness of the soldiers at the front and their quest for the female companionship that all but disappeared from their lives once they entered the trenches. Rearick concludes with an examination of what the song meant to men after the war.

Other Fronts

Part IV covers the war outside Europe. Although combat in these theatres was less regular and less central to the overall course of the war, virtually all of the colonies of the great powers were involved in the war in one way or another. White colonialists understood that their homelands might very well end up as bargaining chips in a post-war peace settlement, giving them a motivation to fight or support others who fought. We know much less about the beliefs of Africans and Asians towards the war, although the essays here offer some insight.

The impact of the war on colonialism more generally remains a subject of some debate. The post-war peace settlement transferred former Ottoman and German colonies to the control of the victors, most notably Britain, France and Japan. On the surface, then, the war seemed to extend the colonial holdings of the victors, even if the veneer of the mandate system had been added. But the immediate post-war years witnessed a resurgence in violent opposition to imperialism as witnessed by the Anglo-Irish War (1916–1921); the Third Afghan War (1919–1921); the Armistar Massacre in India (1919); the Kurdistan Revolt (1922–1924); the French war against the Druze in Lebanon (1925–1927) and the Franco-Spanish War against the Riff in Morocco that lasted until 1925.

Sub-Saharan Africa, however, remained relatively calm. This region occupied a greater place in the French imagination than in the British or German, but all three powers fought for control of it. French general Charles 'The Butcher' Mangin's idea of creating a 'Force Noire' composed of black soldiers to compensate for a declining French birth rate gives an indication of French desires to exploit their African colonies. During the war, the French used Senegalese soldiers on the Western Front as shock troops; these units soon acquired a reputation among German soldiers for a particular ruthlessness, although whether that reputation derived from their combat performance or from German racial stereotypes remains an open question.

Richard Rathbone's 'World War I and Africa: An Introduction' (Chapter 27), designed as a preface to a collection of published papers from a 1977 symposium on World War I in Africa, introduces several important conceptual and analytic themes. Stressing the diversity of the continent, Rathbone underscores the reality that no one war existed for Africa. Nevertheless, he offers some conclusions and generalizations, including the notion that the war accelerated changes already underway in Africa and that the overall impact of the war for most Africans was decidedly negative.

The role of African veterans in promoting change is the focus of 'World War I and the Rise of African Nationalism: Nigerian Veterans as Catalysts for Change' by James Matthews

(Chapter 26). His essay, influenced by modernization theory, argues that the war brought Africa into the twentieth century by introducing medicines, technology, currency and new cultural exchanges. He also argues that the war led to a greater Nigerian consciousness and to a greater level of self-governance. Nevertheless, the Nigerian regiment of the British army had difficulty in overcoming its image as a tool of the British government and an oppressor of Africans, indicating the abiding tensions and contradictions of imperialism.

C.M. Andrew and A.S. Kanya-Forstner offer similar a conclusion for the French African empire in their essay, 'France, Africa, and the First World War' (Chapter 21). They see the war as representing the apex of formal French influence in Africa, despite the general increase in metropolitan investments on the African continent in the post-war years. They emphasize the differing French views of the African empire in 1914, with a sharp division between Sub-Saharan Africa – largely tangential to the imaginations of Frenchmen – and Algeria which was considered a central part of French identity. This bifurcation had tremendous consequences not only in the 1954–1962 Franco-Algerian War, but also in the 1914–1918 war.

T.R.H. Davenport's 'The South African Rebellion, 1914' (Chapter 23) introduces one of the most complex African situations. Since the end of the Boer War in 1902 some South African leaders, most importantly Louis Botha and Jan Smuts, had advocated accommodationist practices with the British. Thus, on the outbreak of the war they supported the dispatch of white South African soldiers to the Western Front where they became best known for the attack on Delville Wood during the Somme campaign. Others saw the war as a chance to attain independence from Britain with help from German South-West Africa. The year 1914 thus saw two wars in South Africa – a war between a German colony and a British one plus a civil war between pro-British and anti-British Afrikaaners.

Those two conflicts largely concerned South Africa's minority whites. Albert Grundlingh offers insights about the war's meaning for the majority black population in 'Black Men in a White Man's War: The Impact of the First World War on South African Blacks' (Chapter 24). More than 20 000 blacks went to the Western Front as labourers in the South African Native Labour Contingent which constituted farmers motivated by poverty, criminals hoping to erase their records and elites raised in British schools who believed in the British cause. Once in France they were often treated as little better than enemy prisoners of war and generally kept apart from the civilian population. Their experiences offer interesting comparisons with the treatment of French colonial workers presented by Stovall in Chapter 12.

Lal Baha's perceptive 'The North-West Frontier in the First World War' (Chapter 22) concerns Afghanistan, long an area of competition between Britain and Russia, although by the First World War the greatest security concerns came from within. Although the Amir of Afghanistan remained loyal to the British (in large part owing to increases in his 'allowance' from the government of India), concerns about Afghanis heeding the Ottoman empire's call for jihad never disappeared. German efforts to undermine British military strength by inciting rebellion among the British empire's Muslim subjects further accentuates the global nature of this war.

The instability that the war created at the other end of Asia is discussed by Geoffrey Hudson in 'The Far East at the End of the First World War' (Chapter 25). With Germany, France and, to a lesser extent, Great Britain in relatively weaker positions in the Far East at the conclusion of peace in 1919 than they had been in 1914, change in East Asia became inevitable. Chinese frustrations led to the May 4th movement, still recalled as the birth of modern Chinese nationalism and commemorated by a monument in Beijing's Tiananmen Square. The power vacuum that resulted from the relative decline of the European powers in East Asia also contributed to the emerging rivalry for influence in East Asia between Japan and the United States.

The volume ends with a postscript of sorts – Ann-Louise Shapiro's 'Fixing History: Narratives of World War I in France' (Chapter 28). Using the French case as an example, this essay wrestles with the delicate, and still controversial, question of how people tried to make sense of the war and comprehend the meaning of the death and destruction. This debate over memory and commemoration focuses not so much on the war itself as on how individuals and communities processed the war (see, further, Fussell, 1975; Winter, 1995). Shapiro's focus, appropriately for this volume, is on the teaching of history and how the war interacted with France's traditional views of itself.

Conclusion

This volume makes no pretence at complete coverage. Regrettably, India, Australasia, Canada and Latin America are not represented. The United States, moreover, is the subject of only one contribution. These omissions, of course, do not suggest that these regions are unworthy of study. Rather, they reflect the choices an editor must always make in a volume such as this one. Indeed, the omissions of such important subjects highlight how wide and deep the impacts of the war ran. Its global reach, its complex legacies and its multi-layered meanings merit still further examination. The essays presented here offer some starting points for such research.

Notes

1 Sting, 'Children's Crusade' from *Dream of the Blue Turtles* (A & M Records, 1985).
2 The two best-known English-language books on the Eastern Front are Showalter (2004 [1991]) and Stone (1975). There is no book-length scholarly study in English of either Gorlice-Tarnow or the Brusilov Offensive. Herwig (1997) is not exclusively dedicated to the east, but offers important insights.
3 For an essay on the dearth of literature on Africa in the war and an introduction to what does exist see Moyd (2003).

References

Becker, Jean-Jacques (1977), *1914: Comment les Français sont entrées dans la Guerre*, Paris: Presses de la Fondation des Sciences Politiques.
Becker, Jean-Jacques (1993), *The Great War and the French People*, trans. Arnold Pomerans, Oxford: Berg. First published 1985.
Bond, Brian (2002), *The Unquiet Western Front: Britain's Role in Literature and History*, Cambridge: Cambridge University Press.
Erickson, Edward J. (2001), *Ordered to Die: A History of the Ottoman Army in the First World War*, Westport, CT: Greenwood Press.
Fussell, Paul (1975), *The Great War and Modern Memory*, Oxford: Oxford University Press.
Gregory, Adrian (2003), 'British "War Enthusiasm" in 1914: A Reassessment', in Gail Braydon (ed.), *Evidence, History, and the Great War*, New York: Berghahn, pp. 67–85.
Hall, Richard C. (2000), *The Balkan Wars, 1912–1913: Prelude to the First World War*, London: Routledge.
Henig, Ruth (1989), *The Origins of the First World War*, London: Routledge.

Herwig, Holger (1997), *The First World War: Germany and Austria-Hungary*, London: Arnold.

Horne, John and Kramer, Alan (2001), *German Atrocities, 1914: A History of Denial*, New Haven, CT: Yale University Press.

Macleod, Jenny and Purseigle, Pierre (eds) (2003), *Uncovered Fields: Perspectives in First World War Studies*, Amsterdam: Brill Academic Publishers.

Moyd, Michelle (2003), 'Africa', in Robin Higham and Dennis Showalter (eds), *Researching World War I: A Handbook*, Westport, CT: Greenwood Press, pp. 279–92.

Sheffield, Gary (2001), *Forgotten Victory: The First World War, Myths and Realities*, London: Headline Press.

Showalter, Dennis (2004), *Tannenberg: Clash of Empires* (new edn), Dulles, VA: Barnsey's Press. Originally published Hamden, CT: Archon Books, 1991.

Stone, Norman (1975), *The Eastern Front, 1914–1917*, New York: Scribner.

Strachan, Hew (2001), *The First World War: To Arms!*, Oxford: Oxford University Press.

Tuchman, Barbara (1962), *The Guns of August*, New York: Ballantine Books.

Verhey, Jeffrey (2000), *The Spirit of 1914: Militarism, Myth, and Mobilization in Germany*, Cambridge: Cambridge University Press.

Winter, Jay (1995), *Sites of Memory, Sites of Mourning: The Great War in European Cultural History*, Cambridge; Cambridge University Press.

Zuckerman, Larry (2004), *The Rape of Belgium: The Untold Story of World War I*, New York: New York University Press.

Part I
Eastern Front

[1]

Steering Through Rapids: Russian Mobilization and World War I

STEPHEN J. CIMBALA

The recreation of Russia out of the ashes of the former Soviet Union calls for a restudy of Russia's security dilemmas as they existed prior to Sovietization. Russia remains a great power bordering on many of the most sensitive areas in Eurasia, including those former Soviet republics now surrounding it. Russia has been through the problem of managing its security dilemmas while ringed by potential adversaries before. In fact, Russia's war planning experience from the 1870s until the outbreak of the First World War is a case study in the balancing of military preparedness against military provocation.

Russia was prevented from striking an ideal balance between the avoidance of provocation and the preparedness for attack by some forces beyond its control and others within its compass. This discussion first revisits some of the international context within which Russia's mobilization planning had to take place, especially what was known about German military planning in the later nineteenth and early twentieth centuries. Then Russia's planning in the years immediately prior to the outbreak of World War I is gone into in greater detail. Because Russia's mobilization system was organizationally unlike that of any other great power, its strength lay in a strategy based on the strategic defensive. But Russia deviated from this strategy on account of alliance commitments and inept policy guidance. Misperceptions of Russia's fighting power, as formidable rather than fragile for large scale offensives in the initial period of war, led Germany to join Austria in taking provocative measures that contributed to its own unnecessary haste into battle.

Military-Strategic Planning and the Prelude to World War I

It became obvious to the powers of Europe well before the turn of the twentieth century that mobilization planning for future war would become more administratively complex, strategically significant, and more closely tied to deterrence than in past wars. There were many reasons for this, but four most generally explain the changed assumptions about the character of future war which motivated General Staffs, foreign offices and their civilian political leaders from 1870 to 1914. First, the scientific spirit of the age led people to believe that war, including the operational as well as the logistical aspects of it, could be reduced to a science and denuded of all indeterminacy. Second, larger armies, made possible by the industrial revolution and the beginnings of mass politicization, included many reservists. Unprecedented numbers of civilians would have to be trained and deployed rapidly during a threatening period preceding war, and this training and deployment would have to proceed on the basis of standard operating procedures and programs. Third, the importance of railroads for strategic deployment increased the emphasis on the observance of strict timetables for mobilization and concentration of forces. Fourth, a generalized peace in Europe from the end of the Franco-Prussian War until the outbreak of the Balkan Wars in 1912–13 contributed to optimism about the controllability of local wars and the containment of escalation.[1]

Imperial Germany's Schlieffen Plan, although subsequently modified in application by Schlieffen's successor as head of the German General Staff, Helmuth von Moltke (the Younger), called for a massive battle of annihilation against the French in a campaign of six weeks or so.[2] The Germans would fight a holding action against Russia in the east until the French were rapidly defeated; then the bulk of the German armed forces would swing eastward to dispose of the Russian armies, presumably held in check in the meantime by fighting against Austro-Hungarian forces. The Schlieffen Plan has probably absorbed more historical criticism than it deserves as a result of the emphasis placed by the 'Fischer school' on Germany's responsibility for the outbreak of World War I.[3] The responsibility for the causation of World War I is complex, and by no means are historians agreed on a principal culprit. The Schlieffen Plan has also been faulted by historians, and with justification, on the grounds that it required the violation of Belgian neutrality in the initial period of war, ensuring Britain's immediate commitment to a European war on the side of the Entente powers.

However, neither alleged German responsibility for the outbreak of war nor the violation of Belgian neutrality embodied in the Schlieffen Plan is the major concern here. The aspect of the Schlieffen Plan that is of most interest for the present discussion is its assumption that a rapid campaign of annihilation in the west was Germany's only feasible war plan.[4] The assumption may be regarded as a strong or as a weak one: it depended for its success on the quickness of the knockout blow against the French, on the slowness of Russian mobilization in the east, and on the ability of Austria-Hungary to keep the Russians at bay to forestall an invasion of East Prussia. The assumption of a *rapid* campaign of annihilation against France was very important.[5] In theory, Germany might have sought to defeat France in a slow campaign, withholding more forces for defensive actions on the Eastern Front against Russia. Germany might also have chosen, along the lines of the planning guidance laid down by Helmuth von Moltke (the Elder) in the Bismarckian era, to fight an offensive war in the east and a defensive war in the west.

But Germany chose the Schlieffen Plan (modified), and pursuant to this the General Staff committed itself to a prompt and massive strategic Cannae in which French and allied defenders would be enveloped by the strong right wing of the German armies. The implications of this plan for the timing of mobilization prior to war were very significant. The powers had surmounted various crises prior to 1914 on the assumption that mobilization, while threatening, was not necessarily tantamount to war. The Balkan crisis of 1912 had been a virtual warmup for the eventual outbreak of war that did occur in 1914. The assumption that armies could mobilize for the purpose of crisis bargaining and threat was one shared by most of the powers, but for Germany it was a luxury. Faced with the prospect of a two front war if French and Russian prewar commitments held firm, Germany had to beat Russian mobilization to the punch by sufficient weeks to allow for the rapid defeat of France.[6]

Germany's assumption that mobilization was tantamount to war had grave consequences in view of the closer association between Russian and French military plans that grew up after 1912. Prior to 1912, Russian plans for mobilization and concentration of forces were in a state of considerable flux, as explained below. After 1912, rethinking of Russia's geostrategic threat perception and pressure from their French allies led the Tsar and his advisors to develop plans which were much more dependent on early offensives against Germany.[7] Russia would not have the option, as some of her officials such as Foreign Minister Serge Sazonov might have hoped, to announce a partial mobilization in the military districts facing Austria-Hungary but not in those districts most relevant to a war against Germany.[8] Sazonov and other civilian leaders of Russia failed to appreciate how constrained military options were in July 1914, as a result of previously taken decisions and uncertainty within the High Command from 1906–12 about whether the main threat to Russia lay in the East or in the West. And both military and civilian leaders failed to consider the potential contribution of Russian partial mobilization to crisis instability. From the standpoint of her potential adversaries, especially the Germans, there was little difference between a Russian partial mobilization and a general one, since the

Schlieffen Plan dictated that German mobilization must beat Russian mobilization by a large lead time.[9]

Russia's Security Dilemmas

From the conclusion of the Russo-Japanese War until the approval of war plans in 1912 which would carry Russia over the threshold to war in August 1914, Russia's foreign policy left open the question as to the identity of the major threat to its security. Divided into 'Easterners' who thought that a future war against Japan was most likely, and 'Westerners' who considered that the Dual Alliance of Austria-Hungary represented the major threat, Russian military planners were caught on the horns of a dilemma. In December 1909 War Minister General V. A. Sukhomlinov, whose sympathies lay with the Eastern view, proposed a series of military reforms. These proposed reforms included the shifting of large numbers of forces eastward, away from the western military districts and toward the center of the empire. His plan was influenced by a proposal put forward the previous year by General Iu. N. Danilov of the General Staff. Impressed by the speed with which Germany and Austria could probably mobilize their forces compared to Russia, Danilov recommended that Russia cede large tracts of territory to the Austrians and Germans in the initial period of war while Russian forces safely mobilized and concentrated in the center of the country. Once Russian forces had been safely mobilized and concentrated they would launch a decisive strategic counteroffensive to defeat their opponents.[10]

The mobilization Plan 19 approved by the Tsar in 1910 was based on the plan first devised by Danilov in 1908. Danilov's plan was based on assumptions very congenial to Sukhomlinov, who became War Minister in 1909. Danilov doubted that Russia could conduct a very successful defense of its western border districts in the initial period of war against a determined German offensive, and Sukhomlinov fretted a great deal about the weakness of Russian defenses in the east against a renewal of Japanese aggression.[11] Plan 19 in its 1910 version provided that large territories in Russian Poland would be conceded to Germany and Austria while Russian forces mobilized and concentrated in safety. The plan thus provided for reassurance against the possibility of a two front war, should Japan take advantage of Russia's difficulties in the west to attack her in the east. The 1910 version of mobilization Plan 19 also allowed for the possibility that Germany or Austria-Hungary might not immediately assume the offensive against Russia once war began. Germany in particular might launch the bulk of its forces against its enemies in the west and fight a strategically defensive action in the east, at least initially. Thus, if the first stages of war proceeded according to the guidelines of Plan 19 and if the Germans and Austrians were limited by their entanglements on other fronts, Russia would have time to mobilize and to concentrate its superior numbers of forces against its western enemies.[12]

By 1912 this version of Plan 19 was obviously out of date, for several reasons. First, the military leadership now acknowledged that the probability of war with Japan was virtually nonexistent. Second, the Bosnian crisis of 1908–09 and more recent turbulence in the Balkans meant that a future war would take place mainly on Russia's western and southern fronts. Third, the French leadership wanted reassurance that Russian armies would invade East Prussia at the earliest possible moment in order to draw off German forces which might otherwise promptly crush French defenses in the west.[13] However, this French demand presented Russian military planners with a dilemma: they could not ignore their front with Austria, for an Austrian attack into Poland might stir Polish nationalism and lead to a breaking apart of the western empire. Therefore, to relieve the potentially beleaguered French and to contain the possibility of Austrian invasion, Russian military planning had to provide for prompt offensives in two directions: against Austria-Hungary into Galicia, and against Germany into East Prussia.[14]

As a result of these contrasting strategic appreciations, the Russians in 1912 developed two variatons of Plan 19, revised, and the two were permitted to co-exist. Variant 'A' was the main variant, for the case in which Germany directed its main blow westward against France. In Variant 'A', Russian First and Second Armies deployed against Germany formed the Northwestern Front. First Army, commanded by General P. K. Rennenkampf, included 6½ infantry divisions and 5½ cavalry divisions. Second Army under General A. V. Samsonov included eleven infantry and three cavalry divisions. Altogether, the Northwestern Front under variant 'A' at the beginning of war disposed of 17½ infantry and 8½ cavalry divisions, including 1,104 field guns and some 250,000 troops.[15] On the Southwestern Front, for a major offensive planned according to variant 'A' against Austria-Hungary in Galicia, Russia deployed four armies (Fourth, Fifth, Third and Eighth), for a total at the outset of war of 34½ infantry and 12½ cavalry divisions, roughly 600,000 troops.[16] However, only about 75 per cent of these forces were successfully mobilized according to the time schedule laid down in General Staff plans.[17]

Variant 'G' was the back-up plan, for the case in which Germany chose to throw the bulk of its offensive forces eastward against Russia. General Danilov indicates quite clearly that variant 'A' was to be activated automatically once the order for mobilization was received; 'G' variant required the receipt of a special order.[18] In this case First, Fourth and Second

RUSSIAN MOBILIZATION AND WORLD WAR I

TABLE 1

CORRELATION OF FORCES ON THE EAST EUROPEAN THEATER AT THE BEGINNING OF MILITARY OPERATIONS, 1914

Fronts, armies	Russia		
	Infantry div.	Cavalry div.	Field guns
North-Western Front			
1st Army	6.5	5.5	402
2nd Army	11.5	3	702
TOTAL (North-Western Front)	18	8.5	1104
South-Western Front			
4th Army	6.5	3.5	426
5th Army	8	3	516
3rd Army	12	3	685
8th Army	8	3	472
TOTAL (South-Western Front)	34.5	12.5	2099
Total Forces, East European Theatre of Operation	52.5	21	3203

Armies	Germany and Austria-Hungary		
	Infantry div.	Cavalry div.	Field guns
North-Western Front			
8th Ger. Army	15	1	1044
TOTAL	15	1	1044
South-Western Front			
Corps Voirsha	2		72
Corps Kummer	3	1	144
1st Aus. Army	9	2	480
4th Aus. Army	9	2	474
3rd Aus. Army	6	3	318
Keves Group	8	3	366
TOTAL	37	11	1854
Total Forces East European Theater of Operations	52.5	11	2898

Source: I.I. Rostunov, *Russkii front pervoi mirovoi voiny* (Moscow: 'Nauka' 1976) p.110.

Armies were to be deployed against the front with Germany, while Fifth and Third Armies were to bear the brunt of first action against Austria.[19] Variant 'G' called for a larger proportion of Russian forces, fighting against both Austria and Germany on the defensive, to complete their deployment and concentration toward the interior of the country. The assumption by Danilov with regard to variant 'G' was that Germany and Austria could easily have enveloped the Russian forces forward deployed in the Polish salient. Russian strategy against variant 'G' therefore had to have a defensive character initially, awaiting the arrival of fresh troops rushed to the front from Siberia, Turkestan and the Transcaucasus.[20]

During staff conversations in 1912 and 1913, the Russians had attempted to assuage French fears by promising an offensive against Germany by the 15th day of mobilization with some 800,000 troops.[21] However, the revised war plans of 1910 had created a gap between capabilities and expectations with which Russia would be crippled when war did break out in 1914. The eastward shifting of forces in 1910 and the neglect of funding for railway modernization in the western military districts meant that neither the smooth operating procedures nor the infrastructure for a rapid mobilization westward could be counted on in 1914 to the extent that French military planners had hoped for.[22] The inability of Russian planners to shift rapidly from a strategically defensive to a strategically offensive footing was ironical in view of Germany's conclusion that an early Russian offensive into East Prussia was almost certain. Germany expected to hold off any Russian offensive with a small fixing force until the decisive battles in the west had been fought, after which German troops would be transferred from the west to the east for a decisive counteroffensive. Ironically, Germany's actual mobilization planning for war with Russia in 1914 was thus very similar to Russia's mobilization planning of 1910 for war with Germany: initially defensive operations followed by a later and decisive counteroffensive.

Partial and General Mobilization

Political leaders in Germany and Russia during the crisis months of June and July 1914 did not know or fully appreciate the extent to which existing war plans, and military expectations based on those plans, would constrain the crisis management options of Kaiser and Tsar. I do not mean this argument in a literal or simplistic sense. Political leaders were aware of hostile alliances, of offensively oriented military doctrines, and of the expectations held by their General Staffs that the speed of mobilization might make the difference between victory and defeat in a short war.[23] In short, political leaders were not kept in the dark about the significance of war plans in general.[24] However, neither political leaders nor military advisors in Germany and in Russia sufficiently appreciated the significance of a change in context, from general to immediate deterrence, as early as 28 June. The condition of immediate deterrence that obtained from 28 June to 23 July (Austria's ultimatum to Serbia) was muted by complacency about Austria's willingness to push a local crisis into war. After 23 July states' priorities and expectations shifted: the avoidance of war became less important for policy makers and for military planners compared to the prevention of defeat in the early stages of a war, should it occur. War plans and signals of diplomatic resolve which had appeared merely necessary and expedient prior to the last eight days of July took on entirely different meanings. Instead of deterring an outbreak of war, mobilizations and signals of resolve provoked escalation and war.

What is most significant about the primary source documents that political leaders and military planners of the time have left historians and political scientists is the subtle change of tone that occurs between 23 July and 1 August. Leaders more and more frequently use the term 'inevitability' to refer to the likelihood that war will erupt. This fatalistic attitude is not something that the heads of state or their principal advisors entered the July crisis with. Instead, it develops out of their interactions in a hothouse environment which is first created by the tension between Austria and Serbia over the assassination of Archduke Ferdinand and his spouse, and then exacerbated by the ultimatum and declaration of war against Serbia by Austria (23 and 28 July, respectively). Leaders' references to the 'inevitability' of war in July 1914 sound like expressions which avoid their own responsibility for breaking the peace. A fairer appreciation is that statements of inevitable war reflect leaders' genuine frustration when additional measures of deterrence fail to prevent escalation, and instead, provoke it. One could with justification divide the period of immediate deterrence preceding the outbreak of World War I into two separate phases: an earlier and relatively more stable phase, and a later and less stable one. The earlier phase began with the assassination of Archduke Ferdinand on the 28 June and ended with the Austrian ultimatum to Serbia on 23 July. The second phase began with the Austrian ultimatum and ended with the outbreak of war. Measures designed to preserve the peace through deterrence were especially likely to be construed as provocative challenges during this second and less stable phase of the crisis. Table 2 provides a chronology of the steps taken by the major powers during this crucial second phase of the July crisis.

German political leaders, including three successive Chancellors, were familiar with the Schlieffen Plan in general, but they were largely unaware of the implications of planning precision and detail for limitation of leaders' viable political options during the latter stages of a crisis.[25] The Russian military leadership was relatively more concerned with avoiding delayed mobilization in case of war than it was with providing bargaining ballast to the Tsar or to Foreign Minister Sazonov during the July crisis. On 25 July a meeting of the Russian Imperial Council presided over by the Tsar decided to introduce at once the 'Period Preparatory to War' throughout European Russia, taking all the steps necessary for an immediate mobilization should the Tsar authorize such a step.[26] There is significant evidence that some Russian military leaders regarded this step, not as a way to buy additional time for negotiation or for coercive diplomacy to influence Austro-Hungarian decision making, but, instead, as a green light for war.

TABLE 2
SECOND PHASE OF JULY 1914 CRISIS (INCLUDING OPENING STAGES OF WAR)

Date	Russia, Serbia	France	Britain	Germany	Austria-Hungary
24 July			First Lord of the Admiralty orders Royal Navy to remain mobilized after maneuvers		
25 July	Mobilization in Serbia; Russian troops return to permanent duty stations	French forces in Morocco receive changed plans, alerting them for possible use in Europe; general railway alert in metropolitan France	Change of naval command	Squadron of battleships is called back from Norway	2130: partial mobilization against Serbia
26 July	Beginning of premobilization in all of Russia; fortresses on war footing	Leaves cancelled; persons on leave recalled; civilians provide railroad security	Naval maneuvers end; Navy remains mobilized		Corps on Serbian border is placed on war footing
27 July		All military units return to permanent duty stations; security for railroads	Replenishment of Royal Navy stockpiles	XVI Army Corps cancels leaves to Bavaria on local orders; some soldiers given harvest leave return to Metz	
28 July		Measures 'in time of tension'		Some units return to permanent duty stations	First day of mobilization against Serbia
29 July	Daytime: partial mobilization		First line fleet to Scapa Flow; warning telegrams to Army and Navy as signal of threat of war	Evening: all units return to permanent duty stations; all return from leave; order to build positions for mobilization period	Evening: corps begin movement to Serbian front

RUSSIAN MOBILIZATION AND WORLD WAR I

Date	Russia	France	Britain	Germany	Austria-Hungary
30 July	1800: general mobilization ordered	establishment of border security by mobilization of 11 inf. divs and 10 cav. divs		partial border security in east by discretion of local command; mobilize forts on eastern border; Navy on war footing;	
31 July	First day of mobilization	various additional measures of mobilization according to schedule (Carnet B)		1300: threat of war issued; 1500: rail and telegraph links cut at French border	1130: general mobilization; war footing on Russian front
1 August		1640: mobilization of Army and Navy	1415: mobilization of the Royal Navy	1700: mobilization of Army and Navy; declaration of war on Russia	first day of war footing on Russian front
2 August	Russian 4th Cav. Div. crosses German border	first day of mobilization	0215: order to mobilize reserve navy	First day of mobilization	
3 August		morning: cover transports completed	1200: decision to mobilize ground forces; 5 Aug. designated as first day of mobilization	declaration of war on France; German cav. crosses border into Belgium	units begin to reinforce covering forces in Galicia
4 August		mobilization transports conclude		infantry brigades (six) cross Belgian border opposite Liége	first day of mobilization against Russia
5 August		beginning of concentration transport		evening: main assault on Liége begins	
6 August	First actions on Austrian border				Austro-Hungarian declaration of war on Russia

Source: A.A. Svechin, *Strategiya* (Strategy) 2nd ed. (Moscow: Voennyi Vestnik 1927) pub. in English and ed. by Kent D. Lee (Minneapolis, MN: East View Publications 1991) pp.202–3.

The meeting of the Imperial Council on the 25th had approved in principle a proposal presented to the Council on the preceding day by Sazonov and Ianushkevich for partial mobilization of the Odessa, Kiev, Moscow and Kazan military districts, although implementation of mobilization measures was suspended pending further review.[27] Several important Russian military leaders, especially General Dobrorolsky (responsible for mobilization) and Quartermaster-General Danilov, sought to have general mobilization ordered instead. Both of these key leaders (Danilov was, despite his innocuous-sounding title, the principal Russian war planner and a prominent commander of forces on the Eastern Front in World War I) thought that partial mobilization would endanger general mobilization.[28] This was to some extent a fair critique of Sazonov's plan but from a different perspective: that of fighting an all out war against the Central Powers, not of using military force for bargaining purposes.

Professional military skepticism toward partial mobilization had to do with the way in which Russian personnel were mobilized for the various military districts into which the country was divided. Each military district drew personnel from regions outside its own territory. The multi-racial nature of the Russian empire required sensitivity to nationality distributions within military units and regions: rules existed that military units should be three-fourths Slav and, wherever possible, one-half Great Russian.[29] Skilled cadres were not randomly distributed throughout Russian territory, but concentrated in a few urban centers.[30] Therefore, under partial mobilization many reservists from the Moscow and Kazan military districts would eventually be assigned to units deployed against Germany, not Austria-Hungary. And the Kiev and Odessa military districts drew some of their reserve personnel from areas outside the four regions included in partial mobilization. Most crucial and problematic in a partial mobilization scenario was the Warsaw Military District, facing both Austria-Hungary and Germany. A bogging down of troop trains or other timely mobilization measures in this crucial district would, according to Russian General Staff appreciations, jeopardize Russian defenses against the expected Austrian attack from Galicia.[31]

For no apparent reasons other than inexperience and deference to superior authority, Russian Chief of Staff Ianuskevich had not objected to Sazonov's plan for partial mobilization proposed on the 24th and approved in principle by the Tsar on the 25th.[32] However, the plan was not immediately implemented, for Quartermaster General Danilov and other members of the General Staff objected to it. Ianuskevich, who had gone along with Sazonov's idea of partial mobilization on the 25th and 26th, was persuaded by Danilov and others to support general mobilization on the grounds that partial mobilization now would complicate any attempt later to institute general mobilization.[33] The extent to which this assessment was a strategic appreciation as well as the result of bureaucratic politics is open to genuine debate. Ianushkevich had, notwithstanding the complaints of his staff, prepared a plan for partial mobilization in response to the Council decision of the 24th and the approval of the Tsar on the 25th.

Regardless of the grounds for General Staff objection, it carried the day, and by the 27th Ianuskevich, now converted to the predominant view of his staff that partial mobilization would make an effective general mobilization impossible, began to urge Sazonov toward general mobilization.[34] Danilov contended that any partial mobilization was 'nothing more than an improvisation' and could only introduce 'germs of hesitation and disorder in a domain in which all must be based on preestablished calculations of the greatest precision'.[35] In his memoirs published in 1927, Danilov maintained his position that partial mobilization was not possible against Russia's likely enemies in the west without compromising her ability for general mobilization.[36] He bases this claim on two technical points and one political argument. The technical points are the limitations of Russian railways in moving troops from interior districts to the frontiers in time of war, and the absence of a territorial district system for mobilizing manpower. One could not mobilize an army corps or another large formation only by drawing on manpower in the local region, leaving other regions undisturbed.[37] The political reason was the indissoluble linkage (as Danilov saw it) between Germany and Austria that the option of taking them on separately was effectively ruled out. Moreover, according to Danilov and presumably reflecting the judgments of most General Staff planners, 'each of these two countries represented by itself such a considerable military power that our security interests required, in case of conflict with one of them, a concentrated effort of the totality of our armed forces'.[38]

Danilov's arguments about the dysfunctional relationship between partial mobilization and general mobilization, as the Russian general staff understood both options at the time, has face validity. However, it leaves unanswered the larger question whether, if the Russians had planned with more concern for the relationship between crisis management or deterrence and options for mobilization, Sazonov and Ianuskevich would have had additional options below the level of general mobilization. As the highly regarded Russian military theorist A. A. Svechin, who chaired the Soviet military historical commission following World War I that investigated Russian performance in that conflict, noted in his major work on strategy in 1927:

> The need for mobilization plans to be flexible stems from the need to subordinate mobilization to the political situation at the time of

mobilization. In 1914 Russia had a general mobilization plan, but the political situation required only a mobilization directed against Austria...the mobilization of some military districts proved to be technically careless: the districts were tied together by extensive transfers of reserves and so forth, and the avoidance of a general mobilization planned out in all its details forced the Russian army to improvise. Hence the *military command used all means possible to obtain an order for general mobilization, which they succeeded in getting. Politics was subordinated to a clumsy inflexible mobilization. The means triumphed over the end.*[39]

This criticism is not entirely fair, in view of the strategic commitments made by Russia's War Ministry and General Staff planners to their French counterparts, with the approval of the Tsar, in 1912 and 1913. General Palitsyn, Chief of the General Staff from 1905 to 1908, held that Russia should attempt to deal a decisive blow to the southwest against Austria, while assuming a defensive posture to the northwest against Germany. This sensible course of action was rejected as a planning parameter after Sukhomlinov became War Minister and the General Staff was made subordinate to him. Sukhomlinov and Zhilinski as Chief of the General Staff agreed in conversations with their French counterparts that Russia would launch simultaneous offensives in two directions against both Austrian and German forces. These revisions in General Staff thinking were incorporated into the 'Instructions' to Military Districts of May 1912 and with minor revisions in the subsequent 'Considerations' approved by the Tsar in September 1913. In addition, Russia committed itself to commence offensive operations on the 15th day of mobilization, which meant well before the required forces had been properly assembled, trained and equipped. According to Lt General N. N. Golovine in his careful study of Russia's prewar and early war experiences, only by the 24th day of mobilization should Russia have reasonably have expected to take the offensive, and then only on a single front.[40] Although individual divisions or corps might be ready sooner, the thorough preparedness of entire armies required between 24 and 29 days. In addition, the 'Instructions' of 1912 failed to take into account that corps from the more remote Russian provinces could only reach the Russian frontier in the second month of mobilization. The required times for completing the concentration of Russian armies according to main variant plan 'A' according to the 1912 'Instructions' were as indicated in Table 3.

Table 3 suggests to General Golovine that War Minister Sukhomlinov and the General Staff 'must have undertaken the obligation to commence a resolute offensive upon the 15th day of mobilization lightly and without due

RUSSIAN MOBILIZATION AND WORLD WAR I

TABLE 3
REQUIRED TIME FOR CONCENTRATION OF RUSSIAN ARMIES PLAN 'A', 1912 INSTRUCTIONS

	50 per cent of force	70 per cent of force	100 per cent of force
First Army (German front)	15 days	20 days	36 days
Second Army (German front)	10	15	40
Third Army (Austro-Hungarian front)	15	22	40
Fourth Army (Austro-Hungarian front)	20	30	41
Fifth Army (Austro-Hungarian front)	20	27	38
Sixth Army (Independent army securing flanks)	20	27	36
Seventh Army (Independent army securing flanks)	10	15	20

Source: Lt Gen. Nicholas N. Golovine, *Russian Campaign of 1914* (note 40) p.71, with interpretive modifications by author.

consideration'.[41] Elsewhere in the same study he refers to the decision by Sukhomlinov and Zhilinksi to begin offensive operations on the 15th day of mobilization as 'fatal' and literally a *'crime against their own country'*.[42] Russia's commitment to hasty offensives in two directions with unprepared forces certainly contributed to her early reverses on the northwest front at Tannenberg and Masurian Lakes.

Faced with General Staff skepticism and angered by Austria's declaration of war against Serbia on 28 July, Foreign Minister Sazonov ordered Ianushkevish on 28 July to prepare two ukases for the Tsar's signature: one for partial and one for general mobilization.[43] Nicholas vacillated on 29 July by first ordering general mobilization and then cancelling it. The cancellation was decided upon by his own initiative and after receiving a telegram from the Kaiser urging restraint.[44] As their military organizations put into motion the procedures which they themselves had, with some ambivalence, authorized earlier, the German and Russian heads of state and chefs de cabinet now sought to draw back from the brink of catastrophe. Russian military advisors maneuvered to reinstate the order for general mobilization, and the Chief of Staff asked Sazonov on the morning of 30 July to see the Tsar, in order to persuade the Emperor to reverse his decision. Ianushkevich urged that Sazanov telephone him immediately with news of the Tsar's consent. 'After this', said Ianushkevich, 'I will retire from sight, smash my telephone, and generally take all measures so that I cannot be found to give any contrary orders for a new postponement of general mobilization'.[45] Ianuskevich was not to be disappointed. At 1 p.m. on the same day, Ianushkevich was called to the telephone by Sazonov, who declared that the Tsar, after receiving the latest news from Berlin, had decided to decree general mobilization of the Army and the Fleet.[46] According to Dobrorolsky, Sazonov then told the Russian

Chief of Staff: 'Give your orders, my general, and then ... disappear for the rest of the day'.[47]

Rationality, Motivation and Doctrine

German, French and Russian military planning prior to World War I, according to Jack Snyder, was influenced by organizational ideology, based on three components: rational calculation; motivational biases; and doctrinal simplification.[48] Although the domestic conditions under which French military planning took place were different from those in Germany in the decade or so before 1914, some similarities existed in military and political decision-making behavior in the two countries. In both cases, military planners had strong motivational biases to discount the risks of offensive operations, despite substantial evidence that technology and tactics would favor the defense in a future European war. The experiences of the American Civil War, the Russo-Japanese War and the Boer War showed the difficulty of frontal attacks on fixed and fortified positions. Such fortifications could not be breached by frontal assaults in good time; attackers would wear out their best forces, allowing the defender to hold back until the culminating point of the attacker's offensive had been reached. Then, the defender's counteroffensive would strike a decisive blow against the retreating attacker, or, equally as bad, the war would be prolonged into an inconclusive war of attrition.

As alliances solidified and leaders began to take more seriously the possibility of war between 1910 and 1914, their fears of a disrupted offensive spent against formidable defensive barriers and entrenched firepower did not suggest to them the abandonment of offensive military strategies. Instead, French and German planners moved more insistently toward an emphasis on the offensive as the key to victory. In the French case, doctrines supported by leading theorists such as Colonel de Grandmaison and commanders such as Foch and Joffre argued for the ability of elan and offensive spirit to compensate for any technology or tactics apparently favorable to the defense.[49] French military planners also assumed that any delay in mobilization would be fatal to their efforts to establish a coherent defense against German attackers. Every 24 hours of delay would, according to French prewar estimates, allow the Germans to advance an additional 15 to 20 kilometers.[50]

The French professional officer corps also had a motivational bias against the ideas of outsiders, including military critics in Parliament, who had attempted to impose their own notions of doctrine and recruitment policy on the armed forces leadership. Attempts to 'civilianize' the French armed forces in order to break the hold of professional military ethnocentrism became especially intense after the Dreyfus affair, and professional resistance to perceived threats to organizational autonomy marked the behavior of the French armed forces leadership down to 1914. One way of keeping external critics at bay was to establish a doctrine based on assertions of military principle which were not falsifiable by external standards (such as those asserting the importance of moral qualities and offensive spirit). Another way was to espouse offensive military doctrines which required well trained regular forces and deemphasized the role of short term reservists, along with the civilianized perspectives these new recruits might bring with them.[51]

Following the Prussian victory over France which established the German Reich in 1871, the German General Staff under the leadership of Helmuth von Moltke (the Elder) undertook to plan for future wars which Germany might have to fight. The revenge-minded French were obvious candidates (over the annexation of Alsace and Lorraine) and so were the Russians. Von Moltke the elder took little comfort from Prussia's rapid victory over the French main forces in 1870; the heady battlefield victories were followed by a period of protracted insurrection by Frenchmen under the direction of Leon Gambetta which only terminated in January 1871 after two weeks' bombardment of Paris.[52] Moltke had also observed the growing importance of firepower and the likelihood that future attacks on frontal positions could be more expensive for the attacker.

Partly for these reasons, the elder Moltke gradually became less enchanted with the potential of strategic offensive operations. A new French fortification system had been developed sufficiently by 1879 to add to Moltke's doubts about the chances for any quick German victory based on an attack westward, and the same fortification system might have provided a suitable base for early French offensives against Germany. Moltke therefore urged Bismarck toward an alliance with Austria, which was signed in 1879 and depended on plans for an initial concentration of German and Austrian forces to the east against Russia.[53] An alternative plan was prepared, however, in which the major concentration and deployment of German forces would be against France, in case of changes in the political environment for military planning.

The flexibility planning of von Moltke the Elder and the diplomatic skills of Chancellor Otto von Bismarck were both missing once the Kaiser had dismissed Bismarck and Schlieffen had taken over as Chief of the German General Staff. Germany planned for one war and one war only. This was not at all illogical. German planners assumed that their first objective was to defeat France in a short campaign, and that their subsequent objective was to turn east and to defeat Russia. There was some vagueness about the postwar political situation once Russia's military forces were defeated or stalemated. Von Moltke the Elder recognized that any attempt to pursue Russian forces far into the interior of that country would probably use up too much of the German army, and his successors concurred to the extent that an initial offensive against France, not Russia, was deemed advisable.

German war planning was based on some confusion between the conduct of a war and the fighting of a campaign. A military campaign is a series of battlefield engagements taking place within a certain geographical theater of operations. Campaigns are intended by each side to defeat the armed forces of their opponents. A war includes not only the results of campaigns, but also the policy objectives for which those campaigns are being fought. Germany's objectives for war in the First World War were formulated much less clearly than those of Russia or France. The Kaiser and his military planners somehow supposed that they could wage a war for the occupation of conquest of France without the participation of Britain, and they further supposed that France having been subdued and Britain disinterested, Germany could go on to crush the armies of Russia and to occupy part of her territory. The clarity and singlemindedness of German military planning was in drastic contrast to the plural confusion of Germany's political objectives for war.

In Russia and in France, the reverse was true. Russia and France knew with much greater precision than Germany what they wanted to get out of this war. France wanted to expel any German invader from its territory, to recover the lost provinces of Alsace and Lorraine, and to inflict on Germany a military defeat which would preclude future aggression against France. Russia wanted to accomplish the same first and third objectives: expulsion of the invader and its ultimate defeat by virtue of a decisive counteroffensive. However, neither Russia nor France gave sufficient consideration to the stability of a postwar power structure in Europe if Germany's regime should change its character from autocracy to something else. Nor did they give adequate consideration to the probable instabilities in postwar Europe if military technology changed to favor offensive instead of defensive warfare, as it did during the 1920s and 1930s. Finally, they failed as did the Germans to think through the consequences of dissolving the Austro-Hungarian and Ottoman empires simultaneously. One can understand the reluctance of German and Russian planners to act on the assumption of their own demise, and one can also appreciate the difficulty they had in foreseeing the relationship between war and the end of their empires. But both Russia and Germany, with strong interests in the Balkans and in Turkey's political and military status from the onset of the twentieth century, should have considered what would happen if Turkey and Austria left the chessboard as major players.

Had they applied such geostrategic logic to the forecasting of war outcomes and their implications, the leaders of Germany and Russia in 1914 might have concluded that the logical winner of World War I was Britain. Notwithstanding the upheavals in British domestic politics following the war and the incredible losses she suffered on the battlefields from Flanders to Gallipoli, Britain's imperial reach throughout the Middle East and southwest Asia expanded enormously between 1914 and 1922.[54] The Kaiser's personality occasionally drove him to fitful remonstances against British duplicity, and Germany's military planners prior to World War I worried for obvious reasons about the status of the naval arms race between England and Germany. But the basis of German planning for World War I remained largely fixated on the military-operational campaign or theater strategy of conquering France, ignoring for the present the problem of what to do if the French could not be defeated in a shorter campaign and if Germany were forced into a longer one.

The preceding discussion sets up a significant point about the July crisis of 1914 and other failed efforts at international crisis management. Mobilization plans embody expectations that interact during a crisis with the expectations included in the plans of other states. For example, one problem in prewar crisis management in 1914 was that Germany's strategy for a short war, based on a militarily coherent but politically incoherent planning guidance, interacted with Russia's planning guidance, which was militarily incoherent but politically coherent. That is: Russia had a more or less consistent grand strategy after 1910 but a complicated, confusing and scenario driven system for operational war planning. Germany had the world's best system for operational war planning, but a confused notion of its wartime and postwar political objectives. Each of the two states most crucial for preventing or for unleashing European war in July 1914 was unable to resolve the trade-off between deterrence and nonprovocation of potential opponents. As a result, they got less deterrence and more provocation than they expected.

Conclusion

Russian participation in the failed crisis management system of July 1914 teaches an important lesson. One cannot take the decision for war readiness without opening the door to war. This is so in two senses. First, one state's own preparations for war may encourage other states to believe that the first state is acting from offensive, not defensive, motives. Second, even if the motives of a state with regard to mobilization are transparently defensive, the crisis behavior of its constituent organizations may foreclose options of war prevention or delay. States can be locked into mobilization systems not only by the normal peacetime procedures to which planners remain wedded, but also by the inexpedient disruption of *any* order subsequent to last minute changes. A crisis is by definition unexpected: but organizations must deal with it by standardized, and therefore potentially maladapted, means.

Russian mobilization planning from the era of the Miliutin reforms until about 1910 was patterned on the assumption that Russia would assume the strategic defensive in the initial period of war. From 1910 until the outbreak of World War I, Russia drifted into a tighter coupling with French mobilization planning, demanding of Russia's mobilization planners a delivery system for the supply of timely prompt offensives against Germany's Eastern Front. Ironically, had Germany realized Russia's inability to fulfill the requirements of an offensive strategy and Russia's advantage in fighting on the defensive, Germany might not have felt as threatened by Russia's 'measures preparatory to war' subsequent to Austrian mobilizaton. In addition, Germany's misperception of Russia's mobilization planning fed into the insistence by the German General Staff on a one variant strategy for rapid overthrow on the Western Front.

NOTES

The author is grateful to Jack Levy for extensive comments and suggestions on an earlier review of this article, and to William C. Fuller, Jr. for clarifying issues pertinent to this study. Others who provided important references or contributed to the author's knowledge of this subject include Tom Christensen, Jacob Kipp, Ned Lebow and Jack Snyder. This article includes some material from the author's *Military Persuasion: Deterrence and Provocation in Crisis and War* (University Park, PA: Penn State Press 1994).

1. The trends are summarized in Martin Van Creveld, *Command in War* (Cambridge, MA: Harvard 1985) Ch.5, esp. pp.150-1.
2. There is a large literature on the Schlieffen plan. See Gerhard Ritter, *The Schlieffen Plan: Critique of a Myth* (London: Oswald Wolff 1958) esp. pp.134-48 for text of Schlieffen's 'great memorandum' of Dec. 1905; L.C.F. Turner, 'The Significance of the Schlieffen Plan', Ch.9 in Paul M. Kennedy (ed.) *The War Plans of the Great Powers, 1880-1914* (London: Allen & Unwin 1979) pp.199-221; and Holger M. Herwig, 'The Dynamics of Necessity: German Military Policy during the First World War', Ch.3 in Allan R. Millett and Williamson Murray, *Military Effectiveness, Vol.I: The First World War* (Boston: Unwin Hyman 1988) pp.80-115.
3. See e.g. Fritz Fischer, *War of Illusions: German Policies from 1911 to 1914*, trans. from the German by Marian Jackson (NY: Norton 1975) esp. pp.389-92 on the Schlieffen Plan. (Published in Germany as *Krieg der illusionen* (Dusseldorf: Droste Verlag und Druckerei GmbH 1969).
4. Historian Dennis Showalter argues that Germany's strategy, based on traditions dating from Prussia's military-strategic predicament in the seventeenth century, was one of 'total war for limited objectives'. By this he means that German military thinking emphasized prompt and significant battlefield victories followed by a negotiated peace. See Showalter, 'Total War for Limited Objectives: An Interpretation of German Grand Strategy', in Paul Kennedy (ed.) *Grand Strategies in War and Peace* (New Haven, CT: Yale 1991).
5. Schlieffen's plan is related to precedent and subsequent developments in German military

theory in Jehuda L. Wallach, *The Doctrine of the Battle of Annihilation: The Theories of Clausewitz and Schlieffen and Their Impact on the German Conduct of Two World Wars* (Westport, CT: Greenwood 1986).

6. The case that German mobilization was unique and tantamount to war is argued by Paul Kennedy in his intro. to *War Plans of the Great Powers* (note 2) pp.15–16. German planning for World War I might fit very well Graham T. Allison's Model II ('organizational process') on account of the wide latitude which was given to the General Staff to work out war plans, almost entirely indepenent of any outside influence. In such cases organizational ethos and standard operating procedures will be highly resistant to any changes in the surrounding political and military environment. Bismarck had run into this with von Moltke, the elder, and succeeded in forcing his policies on sometimes reluctant military leaders by force of personality and perseverance. Bismarck's successors were unable to do so.

    On the 'organizational process' model of decision making, see Graham T. Allison, *Essence of Decision: Explaining the Cuban Missile Crisis* (Boston: Little, Brown 1971) pp.78–96. The author would like to acknowledge Jack Levy for suggesting this comparison.

7. Sukhomlinov's 1910 deployment plan, embodied in mobilization schedule Plan 19 and largely the work of Iurii Danilov, Quartermaster General, called for eastward redeployment of the Russian Army to allow the secure mobilization and concentration of Russian Army to allow the secure mobilization and concentration of Russian troops away from the frontiers. The assumption underlying this plan was that war with Japan was as likely, or more likely, than war in the west. However, this plan became controversial because it conceded almost ten provinces of russian Poland at the oubreak of war and because it called for razing obsolete western fortresses that certain elements in therussiain elite held dear. See pertinent references in note 11, below. Thomas J. Christensen and Jack Snyder suggest that the phenomenon of 'chain ganging', or chaining a state's fate to allies in order to preserve the balance of power, was characteristic of the powers' behavior in the years immediately preceding the outbreak of World War I. They also note that, in a multipolar system, this phenomenon is more likely to occur when states perceive offensive doctrines and military technologies to be advantageous compared to defensive ones. See their discussion of this in Christensen and Snyder, 'Chain gangs and passed bucks: predicting alliance patterns in multipolarity', *Int. Org.*, 2 (Spring 1990) pp.137–68, esp. p.155 with regard to France and Russia.

8. For a discussion of Sazanov's role in Russian deliberations about partial and general mobilization during the July crisis, see Sidney Bradshaw Fay, *The Origins of the World War, Vol. II*, 2nd ed., revised (NY: Free Press 1966) pp.446–81. Fay contends that the Russian decision to order general mobilization on 30 July was tantamount to war, ibid. p.479. He is also doubtful that Sazanov really expected anything to come of partial mobilization, other than protective diplomatic cover so that Britain would be certain to place the blame for general mobilization and war on Germany. On the other hand, the Russian decision making system required that the Tsar resolve all matters in dispute among his civilian and military advisors, and this system produced a great deal of wig-wagging in Russian decisions on mobilization between 25 July and 30 July. On 28 July Russia ordered partial mobilization of the military districts of Kiev, Odessa, Moscow and Kazan along with increased readiness for war in the Baltic and Black Sea fleets. On 29 July the Tsar ordered general mobilization, but later revoked it and insisted upon a reversion to partial mobilization (which, according to War Minister Sukhomlinov, Chief of the Gen. Staff Ianushkevish and Quartermaster Gen. Danilov, was not militarily feasible anyway). See D.C.B. Lieven, *Russia and the Origins of the First World War* (NY: St Martin's 1983) Ch.5, pp.144ff. and chronology, pp.155–62.

9. L.C.F. Turner, 'The Russian Mobilization in 1914', Ch.II in Kennedy (note 2) pp.252–68 argues that the distinction between Russian partial and general mobilization was essentially meaningless in view of the interpretation Germany would place on either. According to Turner, Sazanov sought to use partial mobilization against Austria-Hungary as a coercive measure short of war, but 'he did not understand that a partial mobilization involving 13 Russian army corps along her northern border would compel Austria to order general mobilization, which in turn would invoke the Austro-German alliance and require general mobilization by Germany'. (Ibid. p.260). Turner also doubts that Russian partial

mobilization would have caused confusion making later general mobilization impossible: see Turner, *Origins of the First World War* (NY: Norton 1970) p.104, although he acknowledges that it would have caused some delay, Ibid., fn. 16. Interesting arguments about Russian partial mobilization and its impact on Germany appear in Marc Trachtenberg, *History and Strategy* (Princeton UP 1991) pp.80–7 and pp.94–5. Trachtenberg suggests that Russian partial mobilization softened the stance of German Chancellor Bethmann-Hollweg on the evening of 29–30 July, prior to the adoption of Bethmann of a more fatalistic attitude toward war later that same day. Albertini refers to the plan for partial mobilization as 'this bright idea of Sazonov's' and comments that the Russian General Staff had never worked up a plan for mobilization against Austria alone. Luigi Albertini, *The Origins of the War of 1914*, Vol.II, trans. and ed. by Isabella M. Massey (London: OUP 1953) pp.292–3.

10. I am grateful to Dr William C. Fuller Jr for clarification of issues pertinent to this section and for the opportunity to read a draft chapter of his manuscript in progress on Russian war planning and mobilization. He is not responsible for any arguments here.
11. See William C. Fuller Jr, *Strategy and Power in Russia 1600–1914* (NY: Free Press 1992) pp.430–45. Nonetheless, Sukhomlinov failed to spend credits made available by the Finance Ministry to improve the eastern fortifications. Gen. Unterberger, Gov.-Gen. of the Amur region, feared that the Japanese would soon attack Russia along its Vladivostok front, and in 1909 he sent numerous warning telegrams to that effect to the Minister of War, the Foreign Minister and to others. Sukhomlinov agreed with Unterberger and blamed the Finance Ministry for not appropriating the necessary credits for improving the Vladivostok fortifications. Fortunately, Japanese policy called for friendly relations with Russia: Russia's defenses in the Far East were in deplorable shape, and the Tsar was not amused to be informed of this state of unpreparedness in 1909 by the Japanese ambassador. H.H. Fisher, (ed.) and Laura Matveev, translator, *Out of My Past: The Memoirs of Count Kokovtsov* (Stanford UP 1935) pp.229–33.
12. Fuller, draft MS (note 10) p.47.
13. In addition to sources cited below, see Christensen and Snyder, 'Chain gangs and passed bucks', (note 7) p.151 for the argument that France concluded after the Moroccan crisis of 1911 that the risk of entrapment in any Russian war in the Balkans was less than the risk of abandonment of France by Russia in a future crisis between France and Germany. The Christensen-Snyder argument in favor of French fear of abandonment receives support from the related argument that it was fear of alliance commitments not being honored that drove the powers toward war in 1914, and not fear of being entangled in unnecessary commitments (fear of 'buck passing' more than 'chain ganging'). See Charles S. Maier, 'Wargames: 1914, 1919', in Robert I. Rotberg and Theodore K. Rabb (eds.) *The Origin and Prevention of Major Wars* (Cambridge, MA: Cambridge UP 1988) pp.249–80.
14. See Norman Stone, *The Eastern Front* (NY: Scribner's 1975) pp.33–6 and Jack Snyder, *The Ideology of the Offensive: Military Decision Making and the Disasters of 1914* (Ithaca, NY: Cornell UP 1984), Chs.6 and 7 for pertinent background.
15. I.I. Rostunov, [Doctor of Historical Science and ed.], *Istoriya pervoi mirovoi voiny* (Moscow: Izdatel'stvo 'Nauka' 1975) pp.196–7; 251–2. See also idem. *Russki front pervoi mirovoi voiny* (ibid. 1976), pp.92–4; Iu.N. Danilov, *La Russie dans la Guerre Mondiale (1914–1917)* pp.134–6; and A.M. Zaionchkovskii, *Podgotovka Rossii k imperialisticheskoi voine* (Moscow 1926) p.257 and *passim*. Implications of the reorganization of 1910 are noted in Rostunov, *Russkii front pervoi mirovoi voiny*, p.58, table six, and the same source discusses the evolution of army organization in the context of developing war plans, pp.42–59. On the correlation of forces in the E. European theater of operations at the beginning of military operations, see ibid., p.110, table 13, and Rostunov, *Istoriya pervoi mirovoi voiny*, p.254.
16. Rostunov, ibid. p.252.
17. Ibid. p.253.
18. Danilov, *La Russie dans la Guerre Mondiale* (note 15) p.147.
19. Rostunov, *Russkii front pervoi mirovoi voiny* (note 15) p.94.
20. Danilov (note 15) p.145.
21. Fuller, draft MS (note 10) p.58.
22. Ibid. pp.58–9.

23. Oddly, few if any political leaders or military planners at the time seemed to appreciate that mobilization capacity for a long war would be even more critical than the speed of 'surge' mobilization for a short war. Demonstrating to a prospective attacker that he faces, even if successful in the initial period of war, a prolonged and destructive war of attrition thereafter is an effective way to contribute to deterrence without raising the risks of crisis instability and provocation. The Russians could certainly have followed this strategy in July 1914, refusing the option of partial mobilization against Austria and emphasizing their staying power for a long war in diplomatic exchanges between 24 July and 30 July. Such a stance would have abandoned Serbia to Austrian coercion, which Russia was reluctant to do. Russian management of the tension between deterrence and provocation was complicated by the tension between the requirements for localizing the Austro-Serbian conflict and for deterring its escalation into a wider war. The risks of the strategy I am recommending here for Russia prior to World War I were acceptable so long as the Schlieffen Plan hurled Germany's main forces westward against France, and not eastward against Russia.
24. This is effectively demonstrated in Trachtenberg, *History and Strategy* (note 9) Ch.2, *passim*.
25. Turner, 'Significance of the Schlieffen Plan' (note 2) p.205 emphasizes this point. The German government also apparently understood that the Schlieffen Plan would probably entail the violation of Belgian and Dutch neutrality. The governments in question were headed by Chancellors Hohenlohe, von Bulow and Bethmann, resp. Logistical weakness inherent in the Schlieffen Plan may have been its undoing: see Theodore Ropp, *War in the Modern World* (Durham, NC: Duke UP 1959) p.208.
26. Turner, 'Russian Mobilization in 1914' (note 9) p.262.
27. Turner suggests that the partial mobilization proposed in July 1914 for Sazonov was not originally or necessarily his own idea, but was based on partial mobilization plans laid down during the autumn of 1912, pursuant to the events of the First Balkan War and a deterioration of relations between Austria and Russia. Ibid. p.260. However, the point remains that Sazonov had different expectations about the contribution of this measure to crisis management than did military leaders.
28. Fay, *The Origins of the World War* (note 8) pp.450–1.
29. Lieven, *Russia and Origins of the First World War* (note 8) p.150.
30. Ibid.
31. Ibid.
32. Inter-service, intra-service and other political rivalries surrounding the high command resulted in the development of factional struggles for the control of military policy in prewar Russia. Grand Duke Nikolai Nikolaevich and future war minister Sukhomlinov, for example, each served as a magnet for the expression of views by officers who were sympathetic to their (opposed) perspectives. In 1908 the Tsar appointed Sukhomlinov as Chief of the Gen. Staff and in 1909 the latter was raised to Minister of War. The War Ministry was charged by the Tsar to establish an independent perspective from the Gen. Staff, and Sukhomlinov sought to ensure that no rival would emerge from the Gen. Staff in the future. One result was that, from 1909 to 1914, the Russian General Staff had four chiefs of staff; Germany (including Prussia) had had four chiefs in the preceding 53 years. See David R. Jones, 'Imperial Russia's Forces at War', Ch.8 in Millett and Williamson Murray (eds.) *Military Effectiveness* (note 2) pp.249–328, esp. pp.255–6.
33. Danilov (note 15) pp.32–3.
34. Albertini, *Origins of the War of 1914* (note 9) p.542 contends that additional pressure in favor of general mobilization and against partial mobilization came from the Grand Duke Nikolai Nikolaevich, Russian C.-in-C. and a political opponent of War Minister Sukhomlinov.
35. Danilov (note 15) p.33.
36. He acknowledges that plans for partial mobilization in the Far East had been developed, for in that theater one could foresee situations where it was necessary 'to mobilize only a small number of troops and that without great haste'. Ibid. p.35.
37. According to Danilov, the 'immensity of (our) territory and the insufficient development of our railroads obligated us to concentrate our troops principally on the western frontier, whereas the most important sources for completion (of mobilization) – in men as in horses – were located, to the contrary, in the provinces of the east and the south'. Ibid. p.34.

38. Ibid. p.33.
39. A.A. Svechin, *Strategiya* (Strategy), (see source of Table 2) p.200. Italics supplied.
40. Nicholas N. Golovine, *The Russian Campaign of 1914: The Beginning of the War and Operations in East Prussia* (Ft Leavenworth, KS: Command and Gen. Staff School Press 1933) English ed. Gen. Golovine was professor of military history at the Russian Imperial War College prior to WWI and served in command posts during that conflict. His documentary archives were unique and his access to prominent persons equally so.
41. Ibid.
42. Ibid. p.59.
43. Albertini, Vol. II (note 9) p.544.
44. Fay, *Origins of the World War,* p.465; Albertini, ibid. pp.555–61.
45. Ianuskevich, quoted in Fay (note 8) p.470.
46. S. Dobrorolsky, 'La mobilisation de l'armee russe en 1914', *Revue d'Histoire de la Guerre Mondiale* 1 (1923) pp. 144–65 here p.150.
47. Ibid.
48. Snyder, *Ideology of the Offensive* (note 14) p.200 and *passim*.
49. Stefan T. Possony and Etienne Mantoux, 'Du Picq and Foch: The French School', Ch.9 in Edward Mead Earle (ed.) *Makers of Modern Strategy: Military Thought from Machiavelli to Hitler* (Princeton UP 1943) pp.206–33; S.R. Williamson, 'Joffre Reshapes French Strategy, 1911–1913,' Ch.6 in Kennedy (note 2) pp.133–54; Michael Howard, 'Men Against Fire: The Doctrine of the Offensive in 1914', Ch.18 in Peter Paret (ed.) *Makers of Modern Strategy: From Machiavelli to the Nuclear Age* (Princeton 1986) pp.510–26.
50. Barry R. Posen, *The Sources of Military Doctrine: France, Britain and Germany between the World Wars* (Ithaca, NY: Cornell UP 1984) p.22.
51. For further discussion, see Snyder (note 14) Ch.3, esp. pp.70–97.
52. Col. T.N. Dupuy, USA, Ret. *A Genius for War: The German Army and General Staff, 1807–1945* (Englewood Cliffs, NJ: Prentice-Hall 1977) pp.107–8.
53. Ibid. p.120.
54. See David Fromkin, *A Peace to End All Peace; Creating the Modern Middle East, 1914–1922* (London: André Deutsch 1989).

[2]

The Balkan campaign and French war aims in the Great War

It is now more than a decade since the late Professor Renouvin produced his pioneer article on French war aims in the Great War.[1] The difficulties of documentation which Renouvin noted remain a factor in efforts to add to his contribution in this field of research. In particular the opening of the ministry of foreign affairs archives has revealed just how depleted are the diplomatic files relating to war aims.[2] Renouvin's arguments were limited to the basic theme of French war aims in relation to Germany. The primary instrument to achieve these would necessarily be military victory on the western front and it is no surprise that the greatest part of France's war effort was concentrated there. There was, however, a second theatre to which at least some sections of the political and military hierarchy appeared almost equally devoted. The paradox must be faced that for three years France maintained a large army in the Balkans, whose military activity was severely limited until the last few months of the war, while many of her national provinces were under constant enemy occupation and when German forces were on occasion within striking distance of Paris. France stuck steadfastly to a Balkan campaign while half her coalfields and the iron ore of Briey and Longwy had fallen into the clutches of Germany. The close interaction between French domestic politics and the developing course of the Salonica campaign has now been examined,[3] but the purpose of the present paper is to suggest that the basis of French enthusiasm for this largely abortive expedition lies deeper than the struggles within the parliamentary chamber.[4]

Certainly British observers gradually concluded that some sinister territorial, strategic or economic motivation must underlie French persistence in the campaign. But often their suspicions were ill-defined and based more on instinct than concrete evidence. Typically

1. P. Renouvin, 'Les buts de guerre du gouvernement français, 1914–1918', *Revue Historique*, ccxxxv (1966).
2. The foreign ministry documents for the Great War were divided from the outset into two basic categories: those concerned with the prosecution of the war itself and those appertaining to war aims and the question of the future peace. Approximately 80 per cent of the second category (Série A-Paix) was destroyed in the course of the Second World War. But the very fact that two such categories were devised perhaps suggests a greater interest in France than in England in the early stages of the conflict with war aims and the conditions upon which France would be prepared to make peace.
3. See for example, J. K. Tanenbaum, *General Maurice Sarrail 1856–1929* (North Carolina, 1974), *passim*.
4. The present account differs substantially from that in J. K. Tanenbaum, pp. 155–8. Tanenbaum places emphasis upon military necessities in the determination of French policy in the Balkans.

Sir William Robertson, the chief of the imperial general staff, had felt since the beginning of the expedition that there was 'something behind the French mind in regard to their policy in that part of the world'. What it was he had never been able to discover,[1] but he had learnt that there was 'a great deal of Finance as well as Politics mixed up in this French enterprise', which explained why the French would not come away from Salonica if they could help it.[2] As Lord Robert Cecil told the members of the imperial war cabinet in May 1917, there seemed to be 'a section in France which aimed at utilising the war in order to secure for France some special political or financial position in Greece'.[3] Both the vagueness of Cecil's charge and the uncertainty with which it was directed merit attention. They reflect the inadequate understanding with which Englishmen viewed the French political structure in the course of the war. No one was really sure where the direction of French policy lay. As late as July 1918 Maurice Hankey, the secretary to the war cabinet, could only confide to his diary that 'there are and always have been subtle influences, possibly of a financial character, behind the French attitude towards the Salonica expedition'.[4]

One very clear opinion of the long-term aims of French diplomacy in the eastern Mediterranean was enthusiastically conveyed to the foreign office in March 1917 by Sir Francis Elliot, the British minister in Athens, from the British intelligence officer in Greece, Compton Mackenzie. Searching for the French rationale Mackenzie argued[5] that it was not surprising that when General Sarrail, the commander of the allied Armée d'Orient, had secured the military safety of Salonica and realized the impossibility of a serious advance, the French brain should have looked around for something to do. The reproach often cast against Sarrail of being too political a general accorded, Mackenzie thought, with the lazy English way of thinking that he was 'up to something', without trying to find out what it was, yet it might be assumed that the whole of Sarrail's policy, after the English refusal to consider a military advance, had been dictated by nothing but political considerations. Sarrail, however, had always been clever enough to mask French political ambitions under the plea of military necessity. The safety of the Armée d'Orient had been the excuse for any action the French had taken and it was only now being realized that French policy in Greece had nothing whatever to do with the army's well-being. Yet even now, Mackenzie complained, the explanation of French policy in the near-east was either

1. Robertson to A. J. Balfour 26 Aug. 1916, Liddell Hart Centre for Military Archives, King's College, London, Robertson MSS 1/35/5.
2. Robertson to General Murray 5 Apr. 1916, *ibid.* 1/32/19.
3. Imperial War Cabinet 2 May 1917, P[ublic] R[ecord] O[ffice], London, CAB 23/40/IWC14.
4. M. Hankey, *The Supreme Command 1914–18* (London, 1961), ii. 821.
5. Memorandum by Compton Mackenzie 5 Mar. 1917, P.R.O., F.O. 371/2865/60223.

that Sarrail, as a member of the 'Financial Democratic Party', was engineering a scheme for French Jews to make money, that his personal dislike of King Constantine had unreasonably coloured his attitude, or even that he aimed at a military *coup d'état* in France, after the style of Boulanger. It was generally assumed that it was Sarrail who dictated policy and that, if Sarrail were removed, the policy would change. Mackenzie, however, believed the contrary view – that Sarrail was but the agent of his government's schemes – to be equally possible.[1]

Mackenzie argued that political schemes of a far-reaching nature had been behind the arrival of the French naval mission under Commandant de Roquefeuil in January 1916.[2] As early as February the Greek Liberal leader, Venizelos, had been approached with a view to creating a revolution and by April the occupation of the country by French forces had been definitely envisaged. De Roquefeuil's ambition was 'to make Greece the halfway house to a French domination of the Levant'.[3] Any action the French wished to take in Greece had been facilitated by the attitude of the English government, which, throughout 1916, steadily allowed them to take the lead in Greek politics. They now wished to occupy Greece to interfere with Italian aspirations in the near-east. Probably the reason why they hung on so ardently to Salonica was their nervousness over Syria. 'Salonica was the expression of their aspirations in the near-east.'[4] It was, Mackenzie concluded, time to prevent English policy being any longer the rubbing rag of the ill-considered aspirations and unreasonable ambitions of two rival Latin nations.

Suspicions of a French intrigue to bring about revolution in Greece appear to have been in the hands of one member of the British government over a year before Mackenzie produced his memorandum. Indeed Lord Kitchener, secretary of state for war until his death by drowning in June 1916, appears to have decided that French enthusiasm for Salonica masked more sinister intentions long before any of his colleagues did so. On 21 March 1916 he mysteriously informed the war committee of his belief that the French were following out part of a general scheme and were using the war for purposes of future expansion in the east,[5] and a week later he suggested to Douglas Haig that they were aiming at the development of their dominions in the eastern Mediterranean and would not now fight actively to beat the Germans in France.[6] The editor of Haig's papers, analysing this 'remarkable conversation', has concluded that 'Kitchener was wrong'. The French refusal to withdraw their army from Salonica was based 'neither on strategy nor a subtle foreign policy; it was based on the character of General

---

1. *Cf.* C. Mackenzie, *Greek Memories* (London, 1939), p. 75.
2. *Ibid.* pp. 74–75.
3. *Ibid.* p. 336.
4. *Ibid.* p. 66.
5. CAB 42/11/6.
6. R. Blake (ed.), *The Private Papers of Douglas Haig* (London, 1952), p. 137.

Sarrail... Therefore despite its normal reluctance to countenance eastern diversions the French government was most unwilling to withdraw the army from Salonica in case such action would be interpreted as an attack on General Sarrail.'[1] Yet Kitchener was probably basing his analysis not on France's refusal to contemplate evacuation but on information received from his liaison officer in Paris, General Yarde Buller. In January and February 1916 the latter had reported on the 'Briand-Buonaparte intrigue' in Greece, designed apparently to change the ruling royal family in Athens. By the beginning of February a new factor had arisen in the shape of a Russian counter-intrigue to put up Prince Nicholas of Greece for the throne in the event of 'a development of the revolutionary scheme'. Yarde Buller considered that this might prove a 'serious obstacle to M. Briand's aims'.[2] There is no evidence of Kitchener having shared this information with his governmental colleagues. Such behaviour is consistent with the contempt in which he held the politicians. The previous September Hankey had let Kitchener know the strength of feeling in the Cabinet at his giving them so little information – a practice that was causing discontent. Kitchener replied that he could not tell them everything because they were 'so leaky'. But he added that 'if they will only all divorce their wives I will tell them everything!'[3]

As regards the sort of empire-building in the near-east which Kitchener so feared, evidence exists to suggest that Aristide Briand, French prime minister from October 1915 to March 1917, was alive to the possibilities of furthering French interests. When David Lloyd George had visited France in February 1915 he had received indications of the motivation behind Briand's enthusiasm for a Balkan campaign – at a time moreover before the whole idea became bound up with the political position of General Sarrail. As Lloyd George told foreign secretary Grey, the French were very anxious to be represented in any expeditionary force. Briand thought it desirable that France and England should establish a right to a voice in the final settlement of the Balkans by having a force there. He did not want Russia to feel that she alone was the arbiter of the fate of the Balkan peoples.[4] In a future more or less near when Russia might become too powerful, it was important that the peoples should realize that Russia was not the only state to interest itself in their welfare. They should be constituted as a barrier to Russian omnipotence and possession of Constantinople and to all the exclusive advantages which such a possession would give to Russia.[5] In part

1. *Ibid.* p. 52.
2. Yarde-Buller to Kitchener 6 Feb. 1916, P.R.O., W.O. 159/12.
3. Hankey, i. 221.
4. Lloyd George to Grey 7 Feb. 1915, House of Lords Record Office, London, Lloyd George MSS, E2/15/4; D. Lloyd George, *War Memoirs* (London, 1933–6), i. 409.
5. Note by Bertie of talk between Lloyd George and Briand 5 Feb. 1915, P.R.O. Bertie MSS, F.O. 800/172/Gr/15/5.

Briand appears to have been responding to pressure groups within and outside the Chamber, which clamoured for the protection of French interests, largely economic, in the Mediterranean. One historian has gone as far as to say that Briand conceived the Salonica enterprise 'predominantly as a French bid for power in the near-east'.[1]

Relatively early in the war the Chamber of Deputies voiced its concern at the Mediterranean situation. When the question of Italian participation was discussed, Georges Leygues, a future president of the Chamber Foreign Affairs Commission, reminded his colleagues of France's vital interests in the Mediterranean. When the war was over France would need a period of economic reconstruction. This could only occur if she now acquired and protected bases and lines of communication without which industrial and commercial prosperity were impossible. Such considerations would have to be borne in mind in diplomatic negotiations with Italy concerning the Mediterranean,[2] and the government's attention was constantly brought to the defence of the sea's vital eastern basin.[3] Similar concern was expressed at the damage resulting to French interests if Germany were allowed to pursue her political and economic ambitions 'en Orient' and so create an immense economic domination from Hamburg to the Persian Gulf by way of Constantinople, and from the North Sea to the Indian Ocean.[4] Indeed members of the Commission saw the supplanting of German economic predominance in both allied and neutral countries as a primary war aim.[5]

Briand soon revealed that his diplomatic strategy was largely determined by the sort of considerations influencing the parliamentary commission. In the first secret session of the war he argued that the government had recognized the Balkans as an essential theatre and that he and his colleagues had not been acting for the present but with an eye to the future. States like France did not, he suggested, have the right to allow their prestige to be lost in the countries of the east, and the decision to remain at Salonica had averted such a catastrophe.[6] Then, while appearing before the Foreign Affairs Commission to give an account of the Balkan expedition, Briand revealed the overriding importance which he attached to this area when he said that the age-old Eastern question, in its widest sense, would remain the vital issue even after the war was over. Moreover, the countries which had secured a

---

1. W. W. Gottlieb, *Studies in Secret Diplomacy during the First World War* (London, 1957), p. 82.
2. Meeting of the Chamber Foreign Affairs Commission 26 Apr. 1915, A[rchives] N[ationales] Paris, C 7488.
3. See, for example, Leygues to Briand 20 June 1916, C 7490.
4. Chamber F.A. Commission, ordre du jour 20 July 1915, C 7488.
5. *Ibid.* speech by M. Cruppi 17 Nov. 1915, C 7490.
6. Secret session 20 June 1916, C 7647.

preponderant voice in its solution would be the masters of the world.¹

As the war progressed the propaganda agency established under Briand's influential *chef de cabinet*, Philippe Berthelot, became increasingly concerned with economic expansion in the Balkans.² From Bucharest his agent, Edouard Tavernier, reported that if Roumania entered the war it would be necessary to direct French propaganda to the replacement of the Central Powers by France in the Roumanian market for the post-war years.³ As Tavernier noted 'notre influence politique [doit] être dans l'avenir fonction de notre influence économique'.⁴ If after defeating the enemy in battle France found herself vanquished on the economic plane, it would be as if nothing had been achieved: 'Nous sortirions, au contraire, de ce terrible conflit, complètement diminués et appauvris.'⁵ Within the Quai d'Orsay de Margerie gave his backing to the idea of a campaign of economic and political propaganda in Roumania, which would become for France an outpost of Latin civilization, protecting her against German and Slav expansion, and at the same time providing a counter-weight to the growing Italian influence in the area.⁶ The conclusion is inescapable that the development of French propaganda in the Near-East, encouraged by parliamentary agitation, assumed a deeper significance than merely winning the confidence of native peoples so as to defeat the Central Powers in the current war. It was inextricably bound up with the preparation of France's position in the post-war world – a position in which the eastern Mediterranean was seen to occupy a crucial role. In the light of this the continued survival of the Armée d'Orient takes on a new importance.

France's interest in the Near-East was, of course, no new phenomenon. 'Constantinople... was the heart of an Empire enmeshed by immense French political interests and financial investments amounting to 3,000 million francs.'⁷ Organizations interested in the affairs of the Near-East had proliferated in France and were constantly alert to anything that might undermine French predominance there. It was their apprehensions which were voiced in the Chamber in 1915 and 1916 and to which Briand and others proved responsive. In this general Mediterranean strategy Greece occupied an important but not overriding position for France. Her trade with Greece had

1. F.A. Commission 26 Oct. 1916, C 7490.
2. The economic sphere has been noted as one of the first areas in which France consciously formulated war aims. From the very beginning of the war enquiries were made to determine how French industrial products could be made to replace German competition in foreign markets. (Renouvin, p. 8; Briand to Diplomatic, Consular and Commercial Agents 1 Jan. 1916, Quai d'Orsay, Paris, M[inistère des] A[ffaires] E[trangères], Série A-Guerre, vol. 1499.)
3. Tavernier to Perroy 11 July 1916, Quai d'Orsay, Berthelot MSS (Propaganda), Carton 6. 4. Report by Tavernier 3 Oct. 1916, *ibid*.
5. Gabriel Doumergue to Ministry of Commerce 18 July 1916, *ibid*.
6. Undated note of visit of M. Perroy to de Margerie, *ibid*.
7. Gottlieb, p. 98.

increased steadily since the end of the nineteenth century and stood at the outbreak of war at around 24 million francs per annum. Nonetheless France occupied only the fifth place amongst Greece's trading partners and her export trade to Greece had remained almost static since 1906.¹ France, then, possessed interests in Greece which she understandably enough sought to safeguard and augment during the conflict with the Central Powers. As the war progressed, however, Greece came to assume for France an importance out of all proportion to her pre-war interests there or indeed to the fact that allied troops were based in Greece's northern provinces. By a secret arrangement of March 1915 the Allies agreed to the acquisition of Constantinople by Russia, providing the war was fought to a successful conclusion – the first step towards the possible dismemberment of the Ottoman Empire. And for Russia possession of Constantinople and the Straits might be the prelude to ultimate supremacy in the Near-East and naval power in the Mediterranean.² Thus a cardinal principle of French foreign policy had been breached – but with only the very reluctant approval of her government. Bertie, the British ambassador in Paris, noted that the Quai d'Orsay had suggested that the French government would have been quite ready to take a firm line towards Russia if the British had shown any disposition to support them, but the latter had on the contrary hastened to yield everything to Russia.³ In addition the Chamber Foreign Affairs Commission showed signs of dissatisfaction with any formal engagements to Russia. Many public figures in France hoped that the British and French forces would get to Constantinople before the Russians.⁴

France had long tried to check the slow disintegration of the 'sick man of Europe', for there existed in Paris a genuine fear that, should the Turkish Empire collapse, the relative strength of France in the Near-East might be reduced. As Delcassé stressed at the opening of the Dardanelles operation, the aim of France was not fatally to destroy the Ottoman Empire. Evidently the taking of Constantinople would probably involve some loss of territory by Turkey, but Delcassé hoped that this would be compatible with the maintenance of the Turkish Empire, desirable for 'la sauvegarde des intérêts politiques et économiques français'.⁵ In arrangements made after the treaty of March 1915, however, the break-up of Turkey became well-nigh accepted as an allied war aim. When the question of

1. Report in 1916 by Lefeuvre-Méaulle, Attaché Commercial de la France en Orient, M. A. E. Nouvelle Série, vol. 53.
2. Gottlieb, p. 65.
3. Lord Bertie, *Diary of Lord Bertie of Thame*, ed. Lady A. G. Lennox (London, 1924), i. 132.
4. *Ibid.* pp. 132, 134–5, 141.
5. Delcassé to Millerand 28 Apr. 1915, Service historique de l'Armée, Vincennes, A[rchives] de G[uerre], 7N 1344.

Constantinople was first mooted, President Poincaré stressed that France could not sacrifice her own interests to the satisfaction of Russia. The possession of the Straits would enable Russia to become a great naval power and introduce her for the first time to the Mediterranean. Everything would thus be changed in the European equilibrium and France could not acquiesce in such annexations without extracting equivalent compensations for herself. 'Tout est donc forcément lié!' concluded Poincaré. 'Nous ne pourrons seconder les désirs de la Russie que proportionellement aux satisfactions que nous recevrons nous-mêmes.'[1] In reply France's ambassador in St Petersburg blamed England for his country's present situation, for as early as November 1914 George V had intimated to the Russian ambassador in London that his government considered that Constantinople should be attributed to Russia.[2] At all events France now found her concept of the Mediterranean balance of power in the post-war settlement overturned because the linchpin of her existing policy had fallen away. Naturally she was anxious to compensate herself elsewhere in the area. So France secured inclusion in her adherence to the Russian agreement of a clause to the effect that the attribution of Constantinople was dependent on France and Britain realizing their own aims in the Near-East and elsewhere. In the first instance this meant securing for France absolute rights over Syria and Cilicia – which were no more than 'la contre-partie et la légitime compensation des droits et intérêts considérables dont nous faisons la sacrifice à la Russie'.[3] But it also meant that France looked again at the whole question of her standing in the eastern Mediterranean. Greece and the Balkan peninsula in general therefore assumed a new importance. The conclusion was reached at the Grand Quartier Général that France's Mediterranean policy now demanded that she should be able to rely on a strong and friendly Greece. France could no longer count on Turkey and if, after the war, she occupied Syria side by side with English, Italian and Russian influences in the Levant, she would need an additional point of support.[4] Thus when England and France began tentatively to discuss the future peace, Berthelot reminded Paul Cambon, French ambassador in London, that the Balkans were of direct interest to France and that their settlement was entirely a function of the cession of Constantinople to Russia.[5]

The promise made to Russia in March 1915 helped to lessen

1. Poincaré to Paléologue 9 Mar. 1915, Pichon MSS, Institut de France, Paris, 4397; quoted in R. Poincaré, *Au Service de la France* (Paris, 1926–33), vi. 94.
2. Paléologue to Poincaré 16 Apr. 1915, Quai d'Orsay, Paul Cambon MSS, vol. 5.
3. Berthelot to Barrère, No. 1367, 21 Sept. 1916, M.A.E., A-Paix, vol. 130. A. Ribot, *Letters to a Friend* (London, 1926), p. 130; M. S. Anderson, *The Eastern Question 1774–1923* (London, 1966), p. 325.
4. Note on French policy towards Greece 31 Aug. 1916, A. de G., 16N3057.
5. Berthelot to Cambon 12 Jan. 1917, Berthelot MSS (in possession of M. Daniel Langlois-Berthelot).

French enthusiasm for the Dardanelles Campaign. It was scarcely congenial to many French minds determined to use the war for the construction of French spheres of influence. Even before the attribution of Constantinople the Senate Foreign Affairs Commission had expressed its anger at the French government's secondary role in a region where France possessed the right of command.[1] Clemenceau termed English command of the Dardanelles expedition 'l'abandon par nous de notre maîtrise dans la Méditerranée'.[2] In any case, French interest in the operation soon waned. As the Salonica expedition got underway the Grand Quartier Général urged that a French presence should be maintained at Gallipoli – but only because of the undesirability of leaving England in total control of the situation.[3] In fact France preferred Salonica as a base for the sphere of influence she now sought in the Balkans and as the main stage overland to the Golden Horn.[4] Thus there was perhaps more than nominal significance in the order of 7 October 1915 announcing the formation of Sarrail's Armée d'Orient. The Corps Expéditionnaire d'Orient at Gallipoli was now renamed Corps Expéditionnaire des Dardanelles. The Salonica army thus became the expression of France's aspirations 'en Orient', while that of the Dardanelles, now pursuing an essentially Russian goal, was symbolically reduced in status.[5] Not surprisingly, therefore, France struggled throughout the Salonica campaign to maintain her own direction of it.

Developments in relation to Russia and the Ottoman Empire were not the only factors affecting France's standing in the Near-East during the Great War. After being wooed by both sides, Italy renounced her allegiance to the Triple Alliance and concluded the Secret Treaty of London with the Allies on 24 April 1915. As a result of the promises contained in this treaty she would emerge at the end of the war as an Adriatic and Mediterranean power of the first magnitude. France's own growing interest in the Balkans made her wary of too great an Italian expansion. From Rome the French ambassador, Barrère, warned that Italian motives for participation in the Balkan expedition were far from disinterested. Italy hoped by raising her standard in the Near-East to stake her claim to rights and compensations commensurate with her military effort.[6] French agents in Greece soon reached similar conclusions and from Salonica, the Director of the Mission Laïque, Lecoq, argued that France had to erect a strong Greece as a barrier against further Italian ambitions.[7] The existence of Greece was indispensable, argued

1. Speech by de Freycinet 22 Feb. 1915, transcript in Pichon MSS 4398.
2. Speech by Clemenceau 30 Apr. 1915, *ibid*.
3. Erased extract from Joffre to Millerand 3 Oct. 1915, A. de G. 16N1678.
4. Gottlieb, p. 103.
5. Note by War Ministry 7 Oct. 1915, M.A.E. A-Guerre, vol. 1030.
6. Barrère to Briand no. 560, 9 Aug. 1916, *ibid*. vol. 1038.
7. Lecoq to Léon Bourgeois 7 Sept. 1916, Quai d'Orsay, Bourgeois MSS, vol. 9.

de Fontenay, former French minister in Albania, for the equilibrium of the Mediterranean. She was the obvious counterpoise to Italy and her ever-growing appetite for territorial expansion.[1] Was France, he asked, going to sacrifice her vital Mediterranean interests in order to satisfy her friends of the day, who, in the not too distant future, would become her rivals? With Serbia in need of a long period of reconstruction at the end of the war, only Greece could provide France with the support she required.[2] The Balkans thus focused a power struggle between France and Italy for the right to assert a preponderant voice in the post-war situation. Despairingly Sir Francis Elliot noted that both constantly looked to the future and to the partition which would come after the war, while Britain alone was devoting her 'whole faculties to the one object of winning it'.[3]

The ambitions of two of France's allies – Russia and Italy – thus had a marked effect upon the way in which she examined her own position in the Near-East – one which had been materially altered by the claims and aspirations of these two powers. French policy in the Balkans was, however, also determined by her appreciation of the war aims of her greatest enemy, Germany. In no sense was France's understanding of the situation restricted to her desire to recover Alsace-Lorraine. Both Britain and France were conscious of the underlying expansionist push eastwards which fashioned German war strategy – the age-old *Drang Nach Osten*. For Britain this obviously threatened her continued presence in Egypt, her interests in the Near and Middle East and her route to the Indian Empire. The British mind, however, never really saw the Balkan campaign as a barrier against German expansion. It was appreciated that the Salonica expedition might make it harder for Germany to draw upon the resources of the Ottoman Empire, but the British military and political hierarchy never saw the Balkans as the cockpit in which the future destinies of the great powers in the Near-East were being determined. The same, however, was not true of France. As the Grand Quartier Général concluded, the Berlin–Constantinople rail link was of vital importance to Germany and represented 'le gage le plus précieux qu'elle puisse obtenir en vue des négociations futures, en attendant qu'il devienne entre ses mains, la paix conclue, son plus puissant instrument de domination sur la Turquie d'Asie'.[4] German aspirations in the Near-East forced France to defend her own interests there. By remaining in Macedonia, therefore, France was not merely seeking to defeat the Central Powers but to nullify specific German ambitions for the post-war settlement, which ran directly counter to her own. The danger was that if France did not

1. de Fontenay to Bourgeois 28 Nov. 1916, *ibid.* vol. 8.
2. *Ibid.* 22 Dec. 1916, *ibid.*
3. Elliot to Hardinge 9 Apr. 1917, Lloyd George MSS, F/55/3/2.
4. 2ᵉ Bureau, Note on the situation on the Eastern Front 2 Nov. 1916, M.A.E., A-Guerre, vol. 1040.

act decisively while the war was still in progress, Germany could, with the advent of peace, renew her push to the east with Greece as a base. What ends would then have been served, de Fontenay rhetorically enquired, by the Salonica campaign and the great sacrifices which it had involved?[1]

For a variety of reasons, therefore, the war obliged France to re-examine the bases of her authority and influence in the Eastern Mediterranean and made her realize that the balance of power in the post-war world would not closely resemble that to which she had grown accustomed. Greece, in particular, acquired a totally new importance for France – one which she had never previously enjoyed. It is against this background, moreover, that the presence of a French army in northern Greece must be viewed. The Armée d'Orient inevitably became as much an instrument of French strategic and diplomatic as of military policy. No one was more conscious of this than the chief agent of French policy in the Near-East, General Maurice Sarrail. Writing when the war was over, Sarrail disclaimed all intentions beyond what were proper in a military commander: 'J'étais en Orient non pour édifier l'après-guerre mais pour arriver par la guerre à un résultat de guerre.'[2] His line of conduct was simple – to carry out the policy of the Allies not for the 'after-war', but for the war itself. Sarrail's activities at Salonica reveal, however, that the General's ingenuous behaviour extended no further than the pages of his memoirs. Ineffective as a military commander he may have been, but as the leading architect of a planned invisible French Empire in the post-war world he proved singularly adept. Moreover, it was this use of a war-time military occupation to carve out for France a sphere of influence which would exclude enemy and ally alike which was so abhorrent to France's allies and particularly to England. Whereas the British probably realized that for strategic reasons France could not simply ignore Greece, they resented the subordination of the military aspects of the Macedonian campaign to the fostering of France's post-war influence.

It was above all in financial and commercial affairs that Sarrail was most active. Supported perhaps by backers on the Paris Bourse, the French commander proved not uninterested in the economic well-being of Salonica and its hinterland. Salonica certainly offered a base for French commercial penetration and expansion. Its crucial geographical position meant that it inevitably dominated the economic life of the Balkans and its influence radiated throughout the eastern Mediterranean. Furthermore the Society of the Port of Salonica, responsible for its construction and exploitation, though Turkish in name, was, in practical terms, French.[3] In addition, the Bank of

1. de Fontenay to Bourgeois 14 Aug. 1917, Bourgeois MSS, vol. 8.
2. M. Sarrail, *Mon Commandement en Orient* (Paris, 1920), p. 271.
3. Delcassé to Millerand 1 Oct. 1915, M.A.E. A-Guerre, vol. 1030.

Salonica, whose capital was overwhelmingly French, was closely connected with the great French financial houses and as the French consul noted, 'son concours nous sera précieux pour l'expansion commerciale qui ne manquera pas de se produire à la suite des événements en cours'.[1]

Lecoq noted with satisfaction that Sarrail had a clear understanding of the role of his army in the extension of French influence. It was, for example, entirely within the orbit of the Armée d'Orient, Lecoq argued, for it to assist in the founding of schools, which would spread the French language and, by extension, French influence. Undoubtedly it had a primary military task to accomplish when circumstances permitted, but in the meantime the army should not forget its duty to leave behind it other traces in Macedonia than those of blood. It would bequeath something permanent and durable in terms of increased economic activity with France. At the time Lecoq wrote, the army was drawing up a commercial dossier to put French and Macedonian merchants and businessmen in touch with one another. Special contacts had already been established with Lyons through the enthusiasm of its radical-socialist mayor, Edouard Herriot, with the result that Macedonian industrialists would be represented at the next Lyonnaise trade fair. Under the influence of his officer, Intendant Bonnier, moreover – 'un des esprits les plus ouverts et les plus précis de l'Armée d'Orient et dont l'activité égale la lucidité d'esprit' – Sarrail had approved a proposed circular to be signed by himself and widely distributed among commercial organizations in France. Lecoq hoped that France would continue to interest herself in the Salonica market, which offered a potential outlet for commerce, of whose extent people in France had as yet no conception.[2] Sarrail's thinking was entirely in line with these sentiments. The task of the Armée d'Orient was self-evident: 'Là encore... nous aurons à préparer l'après-guerre par l'introduction immédiate de nos produits et de nos marques sur les places reconquises par nos armées... Ainsi seraient sauvegardés... les intérêts des populations qu'il nous appartient de gagner à l'influence française et l'avenir du commerce et de l'industrie français dont l'expansion doit suivre en Orient plus que partout ailleurs la victoire de nos armes.'[3]

On 1 August 1916 the General addressed a circular to the Presidents of the Chambers of Commerce in France, setting out the organization at Salonica of the 'Commercial Bureau for French Importations'. He was convinced that they would wish to be associated with an enterprise whose aim was to create immediately an outlet for French industry which would greatly expand after the

---

1. Graillet to Briand no. 24, 19 Feb. 1916, *ibid.* vol. 252.
2. Lecoq to Bourgeois 26 July 1916, Bourgeois MSS, vol. 9.
3. Sarrail to Briand no. 164, 3 Aug. 1916, M.A.E. A-Guerre, vol. 302.

war. 'Développer à l'heure présente l'exportation française, c'est préparer la victoire et s'en assurer d'avance tous les fruits.' Sarrail explained that the creation of the Commercial Bureau under Bonnier reflected the unique situation of the Macedonian market – devoid of goods and with French suppliers having no serious competition. Sarrail would therefore act as liaison between French producers, who would write to inform him of the nature of their goods and the quantities available, and potential buyers in Salonica. Once contact had been established the two parties could conduct their business directly. A certain and stable clientele would thus be built up for French manufacturers, assuring for France 'sur ce marché, pour l'après-guerre, la première place'.[1] As Berthelot noted, Sarrail was preparing for the economic conquest of Macedonia by profiting from the exceptional situation which resulted from France's military occupation.[2] At all events the response in France to Sarrail's initiative was encouraging. Lecoq reported on 20 August that the last mailbag had contained thirty letters from French merchants wishing to start trading with Salonica,[3] while after less than three months an increase in business in the order of 600,000 francs was noted. Such organizations as the Salonica Commercial Bureau thus represented a 'precious hope for the future', and were a model to be copied elsewhere.[4] Bonnier found the success of the new enterprise heartening. In a fortnight he had received 300 letters from French industrialists, whom he had put in touch with business houses in Salonica. He regretted only that the administrative authorities in France had sometimes been intransigent over export permits. Bonnier hoped that such restrictions would be removed for all goods unrelated to warfare. All the efforts of France should be united to facilitate the extension of her economic interests in the area as the basic prerequisite of French influence in the Near-East.[5] Indeed by the end of January 1917 Bonnier noted that permits were now granted by the Customs Offices in Marseilles instead of the Derogations Commission in Paris. This would speed up considerably the administration involved in the export of goods to Salonica and reflected 'l'intérêt que témoigne le Gouvernement de la République au développement des relations... qui unissent la France au grand port de la Mer Egée'.[6]

By the beginning of the new year Bonnier sensed that a fresh spirit was animating French businessmen and industrialists. The Chambers of Commerce had responded splendidly to Sarrail's initiative, giving their fullest support. Herriot's example in creating a permanent

1. Sarrail to Presidents of French Chambers of Commerce 1 Aug. 1916, M.A.E. Nouvelle Série, vol. 53.   2. Note by Berthelot on above.
3. Lecoq to Bourgeois 20 Aug. 1916, Bourgeois MSS, vol. 9.
4. Report by the deputy Meunier-Surcouf 25 Oct. 1916, A.N., Painlevé MSS, 313 AP 109.   5. Bonnier to Péan 7 Sept. 1916, M.A.E. A-Guerre, vol. 302.
6. *Ibid.* 30 Jan. 1917, *ibid.* vol. 304.

Lyons–Macedonia Committee had been followed in Dijon, Grenoble and Marseilles.[1] In addition the Chambers of Commerce in Bordeaux, Rouen, Toulouse, Beauvais, Orléans, Angoulême, Nancy, Belfort, Besançon and Limoges were organizing regional committees, to be grouped in Paris. The initial results by which seventy-five per cent of goods arriving at Salonica were French were such as to promise the widest extension of French economic power in Macedonia and, as a result, throughout the Near-East.[2] Apart from putting the two sides in touch with one another, the Commercial Bureau offered several more specific services. By building up a collection of French samples and catalogues open for inspection by local merchants, the Bureau could supply potential buyers in Macedonia with accurate information necessary to complete their orders. Secondly, by tapping the information provided by banks and private informers, the Bureau had built up a file on 1200 firms in Macedonia, which was at the disposal of French traders. Bonnier guaranteed to provide information within three days on any Salonican firm about which he had received an enquiry from France. Then the Bureau published a monthly Commercial Bulletin which contained studies on the natural resources of Macedonia and the needs of the area in manufactured goods.[3]

In all this preparation for 'l'après-guerre' Sarrail himself was deeply committed. British observers noted that Sarrail was a political general, not a military one, and that he knew that financial and economic success would better please his political supporters than military progress.[4] Sarrail passed or refused, and signed with his own hand, every single application for a permit to export goods from the district. This was 'hardly the work for a Commander-in-Chief of allied armies in the field'.[5] Sarrail also used the postal censorship to learn which local merchants sent their orders to France and which to other countries. The latter were not infrequently the objects of thinly veiled threats and persecutions inflicted with a view to persuading them to change their ways.[6] With pride Sarrail informed the then war minister, Paul Painlevé, in April 1917, that of a total monthly value of 22 million francs in imports to Salonica 16 millions were French.[7]

The extent of France's strategic, political and commercial interests

---

1. Interestingly enough the Marseilles and Lyons Chambers of Commerce had campaigned for the establishment of a French protectorate in Syria as early as 1915. C. M. Andrew and A. S. Kanya Forstner, 'The French Colonial Party and French Colonial War Aims 1914–18', *Historical Journal*, xvii (1974), 98.
2. Note by Bonnier on Circular of National Association of Economic Expansion 25 Jan. 1917, M.A.E. Nouvelle Série, vol. 53.
3. Note on the Commercial Bureau 24 Oct. 1917, A. de G. 5N287.
4. Stead to Lloyd George 12 Mar. 1917, CAB 24/8/249.
5. Granville to Lloyd George 6 Feb. 1917, Lloyd George MSS, F55/3/1.
6. L. Villari, *The Macedonian Campaign* (London, 1922), p. 59.
7. Sarrail to Painlevé no. 657, 2 Apr. 1917, A. de G. 5N153.

in the Near-East in general and of her more specific concerns in particular regions should now be apparent. The war served to magnify and accentuate these in their wider context and in certain cases afforded France the opportunity to develop them. In both instances, moreover, the Armée d'Orient became the expression of French aspirations. Its value extended, therefore, beyond what it might offer towards the winning of the war (which was of only limited importance) to the area of determining what sort of victory France was likely to win. Sarrail's army focused above all the determination of Frenchmen to ensure that the peace settlement would represent, not only the defeat of Germany, but also the victory of France – and a victory which would be expressed in tangible gains, territorial, strategic, commercial and political. The abandonment of the Salonica campaign was thus unthinkable on the basis of purely French considerations, leaving aside whatever might have been desirable for the total allied war effort. 'Si nous rembarquons nous perdons de ce fait à tout jamais notre action en Orient. L'abandon de Salonique... serait la fin de la France dans le bassin oriental de la Méditerranée.'[1]

The problem crystallizes the different attitudes towards the Great War of France and her British ally. For France the struggle against Germany was essentially to decide whether Germany could establish her own hegemony in central and eastern Europe and the Near-East. This was an issue in which France was immediately and vitally involved. But while the prevention of an over-strong power on the continent of Europe was a long-standing principle of British foreign policy, such a consideration affected Britain less centrally than it did France, and she could not share the latter's overriding concern at the outcome of the war in the eastern Mediterranean. British war aims inevitably reflected her status as the world's leading naval power and centred on her desire to protect her existing Empire. The defence of Egypt naturally entered into such calculations, but Britain never saw in the Salonica campaign a means of defending her post-war interests in the Near-East and the route to India. These would be guaranteed, as always, by the Royal Navy. The belief existed in France, on the other hand, that only through the maintenance of the Armée d'Orient could she secure her right to a say in the post-war arrangements of the Near-East. Sheer physical, military presence was seen to bestow on a power the right to a commanding voice at the final settlement. Moreover, because of the ambitions and encroachments of France's rivals, it came to be seen that the Armée d'Orient was based on a country where France would need to interest herself much more than in pre-war days. The war increased the importance of Greece for France just as her military presence

---

1. Parliamentary report on the Armée d'Orient by de Chappedelaine and others 1 June 1917, M.A.E. A-Guerre, vol. 1042.

there magnified the temptation to use this country as a foothold for her own Mediterranean ambitions.

France obviously had certain territorial designs in the eastern Mediterranean: in the first instance this involved the possession of Syria and Cilicia, and included, at least in the first half of the war, Palestine.[1] But the possession of Syria merely reflected a deeply-held conviction that France's future was inextricably bound up with her standing in the Near-East. It masked, therefore, a much broader aim to carve out as wide a sphere of influence as possible in the whole area. Thus while campaigns on the western front might help France win the war, those in the east would play as important a role in aiding her to win the peace. In a strategic sense, then, the Salonica expedition was a lever for French ambitions in a wide area. More immediately, however, it was used as the vehicle by which France would acquire direct economic and hence political influence in the area closely affected by the presence of her army. French industry at the end of the war would be in a difficult position. The vast plant employed in the manufacture of armaments would need to be converted to peace-time production if serious unemployment were to be averted. But to cope with the inevitable increase in production France would need new markets and the Balkans, which would have great need of agricultural equipment and manufactured goods, were ideally suited to fill this role.[2] The Armée d'Orient therefore fought a commercial war in addition to the efforts it made on the battlefield and its opponents in the two struggles were not necessarily the same, since that for economic supremacy involved 'une lutte pacifique contre nos alliés'.[3]

All of these factors made it most unlikely that France and England would be able to co-operate fully in the Salonica venture, especially when there were few in England who even favoured the continuation of the campaign. France's underlying strategic motivation inevitably cut across British interests in the Mediterranean balance of power, while her commercial and political aspirations in Greece and Macedonia ran counter to British policy, which in this part of the world at least, was more concerned with winning the war as soon as possible. What is difficult to determine is the extent to which what have been seen as 'French ambitions' permeated the whole of the French governmental hierarchy – whether in fact they represented governmental policy rather than the sectional and vested interests of pressure groups in France and of French agents in Athens and Salonica.[4] What seems unquestionable is that French agents on the

---

1. Note by Berthelot 27 Aug. 1915, M.A.E. A-Paix, vol. 130.
2. Note on commercial relations between France and Macedonia, 3 Dec. 1917, A. de G. 5N287.   3. Report by de Chappedelaine, *op. cit.*
4. 'Only Clemenceau, the strongest prime minister of the Third Republic, possessed the power and determination to shape Middle East policy according to his own design.' Andrew and Kanya Forstner, p. 106.

spot, and in particular those closely associated with the Armée d'Orient, appreciated and championed at least some of the non-military advantages deriving from France's participation in the eastern theatre. While no coherent and precise governmental policy ever seems to have emerged, this understanding of the situation was apparently shared, to varying degrees, by the changing governments in Paris. Not surprisingly it appears that Paris and its agents were most closely in accord on this matter during the ascendancy in 1917 of those politicians most sympathetic to General Sarrail himself.

University of Liverpool   D. J. DUTTON

[3]

The Mobilization of 1914 and the Question of the Russian Nation: A Reexamination

Josh Sanborn

Sir George Buchanan, Great Britain's ambassador to Russia during World War I, published his widely read memoirs in 1923. In those pages, he provided an influential account of the response of the Russian people to Germany's declaration of war:

> During those wonderful early August days Russia seemed to have been completely transformed. The German Ambassador had predicted that the declaration of war would provoke a revolution. He had even declined to listen to a friend who had advised him, on the eve of his departure, to send his collection of art to the Hermitage for safe keeping, as the Hermitage would, he foretold, be one of the first buildings to be sacked. Unfortunately for him, the only act of mob violence throughout the whole Russian Empire was the wholesale looting of the German Embassy on August 4. Instead of provoking a revolution, the war forged a new bond between Sovereign and people. The workmen proclaimed a truce to strikes, and the various political parties laid aside their grievances.[1]

Buchanan's assessment of Russia's response to the war was seconded by his compatriot Sir Alfred Knox, Britain's military attaché in Russia:

> Mobilisation went smoothly and the number of men called up in comparison with the partial mobilisation of 1904 caused general astonishment. The spirit of the people appeared excellent. All the wine shops were closed and there was no drunkenness—a striking contrast to the scenes witnessed in 1904. Wives and mothers with children accompanied the reservists from point to point, deferring the hour of parting, and one saw cruel scenes, but the women cried silently and there were no hysterics. The men generally were quiet and grave, but parties cheered one another as they met in the street. The war was undoubtedly popular with the

---

Earlier versions of this essay were presented at the 1997 annual convention of the American Association for the Advancement of Slavic Studies in Seattle and at the conference entitled "Rossiia v pervoi mirovoi voine" held in St. Petersburg in June 1998. I would like to thank the participants and audience members at those panels, in particular Geoffrey Hosking and Bill Rosenberg, who were the designated discussants, for their comments. In addition, I would like to thank Sheila Fitzpatrick, Ron Suny, Michael Geyer, Peter Holquist, Troy Davis, and the anonymous reviewers for *Slavic Review* for their input and bibliographical advice. Finally, I would like to express my deep gratitude to the Center for the Advancement and Study of Peace and International Cooperation and the John D. and Catherine T. MacArthur Foundation for the funds necessary to conduct the research that led to this article.

1. Sir George Buchanan, *My Mission to Russia and Other Diplomatic Memories* (Boston, 1923), 1:213.

middle classes, and even the strikers, who Russians believed had been subsidised with German money, at once on mobilisation returned to work.[2]

Both of these men placed Russia's experience firmly within the dominant European paradigm of the Great War. The Russian throngs cheering their soldiers on to victory fit quite nicely with the image of Europe marching proudly, innocently, and unanimously to war in 1914. This picture of glorious enthusiasm made the ensuing horror and social collapse all the more dramatic. World War I became Act V of the "long" European nineteenth century, turning morality play into tragedy.

Buchanan and Knox also provided the general outline of the western account of "Russia's" response to the declaration of World War I.[3] On the one hand, we have Buchanan's description of unity, the "bond between Sovereign and people" that supposedly existed throughout the land in this moment of crisis. On the other, we have Knox's slightly more subtle analysis, which contrasted the war's popularity in urban areas with the "quiet and grave" response in rural ones.

This composite description of urban patriotic enthusiasm and rural resignation has dominated nearly every account written since, as writers focusing on urban areas have sought to explain the end to the 1914 strikes, while those looking at the countryside have usually fallen back on the assumption that obtuse Russian peasants, locked in primitive localism, had no conception of the nation as a whole and could not begin to comprehend the events that were taking them from their dirty huts.[4] Thus Richard Pipes claimed that during World War I the *muzhik* (peasant man) had little sense of "Russianness." He thought of himself not as a "Russkii," but as a "Viatskii" or "Tulskii"—that is, a native of Viatka or Tula province—and as long as the enemy did not threaten his home territory, he had no quarrel with him.[5]

In these accounts, Russia entered the war with a burst of patriotism that masked the ultimately fatal flaws of class division in the cities and brutish ignorance in the countryside. When the war turned sour and the patriotism dwindled, those flaws became apparent, leading to the collapse of the old regime.

---

2. Sir Alfred Knox, *With the Russian Army, 1914–1917* (London, 1921), 1:39.

3. These are not the only foreign observer sources that have been widely cited in the western literature. Other influential works include Maurice Paleologue, *An Ambassador's Memoirs*, vol. 1 (London, 1923), and Bernard Pares, *The Fall of the Russian Monarchy: A Study of the Evidence* (London, 1939).

4. See, for instance, Leopold Haimson, "The Problem of Social Stability in Urban Russia, 1905–1917," *Slavic Review* 23, no. 4 (December 1964): 619–42 and *Slavic Review* 24, no. 1 (March 1965): 1–22; W. Bruce Lincoln, *Passage through Armageddon: The Russians in War and Revolution, 1914–1918* (New York, 1986), 41–45; Richard Pipes, *The Russian Revolution* (New York, 1990), 203–10; Orlando Figes, *A People's Tragedy: The Russian Revolution, 1891–1924* (London, 1996), 251–52; Martin Gilbert, *The First World War: A Complete History* (New York, 1994), 31; Allan K. Wildman, *The End of the Russian Imperial Army: The Old Army and the Soldiers' Revolt (March–April 1917)* (Princeton, 1980), 76–77.

5. Pipes, *Russian Revolution*, 203.

The Mobilization of 1914 and the Question of the Russian Nation 269

This picture was bolstered by influential accounts by Russian émigrés. Pipes, in the passage printed above, was quoting General Nikolai Golovin, who in turn was citing General Iurii Danilov. Both Danilov and Golovin were reformist General Staff officers who were involved in the military preparations for World War I and survived the war to write accounts of why the war had been lost. Both ultimately turned to the explanation that Russian peasants, the bulk of the soldiers, had been insufficiently imbued with national consciousness and hence were not the citizen-soldiers that armies required to win modern wars. This was a soothing justification, for it shifted blame away from military leaders and patriotic progressive politicians onto the legacy of Russian backwardness and onto those conservative political figures who had resisted the modernizing nation-building effort spearheaded by military reformers like Golovin and Danilov prior to the war.[6]

The mixture of foreign observations and reformist justifications combined to produce a historiographical juggernaut in western scholarly circles that began soon after the war and continues to hold sway today. There are two basic problems with the standard interpretation. The first is empirical: practitioners of the dominant model have simply not bothered to research the actions and thoughts of reservists and their families in 1914. The fact that historians have not used one of their stocks-in-trade is befuddling, for though library shelves are not overflowing with Russian World War I memoirs, letters, and diaries, many such sources have been published and are available both in Russia and abroad.[7] Archival sources such as police reports, manuscripts of personal narratives, and letters of normal soldiers and rural families to state institutions have also been almost completely ignored. As a result, certain major events, such as the 1914 draft riot in Barnaul that claimed as many lives as the 1863 draft riot in New York City, are virtually unknown to western readers, despite the fact that the Barnaul uprising was mentioned in nearly every Russian military account of the war.[8]

---

6. Pavel Miliukov indicted Russian peasants for a lack of patriotism in nearly the same words that Golovin and Danilov did. See Paul Miliukov, *Political Memoirs, 1905–1917,* ed. Arthur P. Mendel, trans. Carl Goldberg (Ann Arbor, 1967), 300.

7. For an excellent bibliography of such sources, along with Russian-language secondary sources, see *Pervaia mirovaia voina: Ukazatel' literatury 1914–1993* (Moscow, 1994). Additional mention should be made of a handful of primary sources written by soldiers that are not covered in this bibliography and are not normally cited by historians. I. M. Gordienko, *Iz boevogo proshlogo, 1914–1918 gg.* (Moscow, 1957); V. I. Gurko, *War and Revolution in Russia, 1914–1917* (New York, 1919); A. A. Ignatyev, *A Subaltern in Old Russia,* trans. Ivor Montagu (London, 1944); Vladimir S. Littauer, *Russian Hussar: A Story of the Imperial Cavalry, 1911–1920,* reprint ed. (Shippensburg, Penn., 1993); E. A. Vertinskii, *Pamiatnye dni: Iz vospominanii gvardeiskikh strelkov* (Tallinn, 1932); A. Vavilov, *Zapiski soldata Vavilova* (Moscow, 1927); Boleslav Vevern, *6-ia batareia, 1914–1917 gg. Povest o vremeni velikago sluzheniia rodine* (Paris, 1938).

8. Lieutenant-General Nicholas N. Golovin(e), *The Russian Army in the World War* (New Haven, 1931), 204; Golovin, *Voennye usiliia Rossii v mirovoi voine* (Paris, 1939), 2:121; Iurii N. Danilov, *Rossiia v mirovoi voine, 1914–1915 gg.* (Berlin, 1924), 111; Sergei Dobrorolski, *Die Mobilmachung der russischen Armee 1914* (Berlin, 1922), 33.

The omission of draft riots is minor, though, compared to the more basic conceptual problem of the literature on the social response to mobilization. Historians have sought an answer to an impossible question: how did Russia respond to the war? Even in its less egregious (and more pernicious) manifestation, scholars have had few qualms about seeking to discover what "peasants," "workers," or the "middle classes" thought about the war. In both guises, these questions, by presupposing unitary social groups, have rather naturally lent themselves to monolithic answers.

The Soviet historiography on the 1914 mobilization depended on different sources and used a different interpretive framework than the western historiography did, but in the end it too failed to provide a convincing analysis of public activity and public attitudes upon the outbreak of the war. In contrast to western scholars, many Soviet historians included accounts of draft riots and popular unhappiness with the war in their narratives, but their fixation with labeling violent outbursts against the state as either "revolutionary" or "anarchic" blinded them to the quite novel modes of rhetoric and practice used by the demonstrators, both patriotic and unpatriotic, who surged into the streets during the massive upheaval that followed Germany's declaration of war on Russia.

The earliest Soviet interpretation of the mobilization relied on the proposition that Vladimir Lenin and the Bolsheviks were the only ones to truly understand the nature of the war and the opportunity it presented for liberation. Other socialist parties were condemned for their blind patriotism, while regular peasants and workers were pitied for the fact that they had been duped by their tsarist masters. In the first systematic scholarly work devoted to the war, for instance, A. M. Zaionchkovskii claimed that the patriotic front presented by all other opposition parties "allowed the tsarist government to mobilize painlessly and then to drive millions of nearly unarmed men to slaughter over the course of the next three years."[9]

This position was tempered in the early 1960s by the introduction of evidence of unrest during the war. D. V. Verzhkhovskii and V. F. Liakhov cited the draft riots as evidence that Russian workers had been the only ones in Europe to resist their government's attempts to "hide the true goals of the war" and had "actively demonstrated against it." The Bolsheviks, they claimed, had been the only political party to heed the voice of the working class.[10] Meanwhile, A. M. Anfimov, writing about the response to the war in the countryside, also noted unrest, but he argued that peasant unhappiness could only take the form of an "anarchic and uncoordinated struggle."[11] In the multivolume history of the war published in 1975, these analyses were combined in the claim that, though the Russian bourgeoisie had responded to the war with enthusiasm, both workers and poor peasants protested the war in "all the major cities of Russia" but had failed

---

9. A. M. Zaionchkovskii, *Mirovaia voina 1914–1918*, 2d ed. (Moscow, 1931 [1924]), 14.

10. D. V. Verzhkhovskii and V. F. Liakhov, *Pervaia mirovaia voina, 1914–1918 gg.: Voenno-istoricheskii ocherk* (Moscow, 1964), 39–40.

11. A. M. Anfimov, *Rossiiskaia derevnia v gody pervoi mirovoi voiny (1914–1917 g.)* (Moscow, 1962), 347–48.

to make an impact on policy because the outbursts were "anarchic attempts of the populace" to stop the war.¹² Revolution awaited the organizing hand of the Bolsheviks.¹³

Unfortunately, despite the upsurge in interest in World War I and the reevaluation of Russia's past that has occurred since the fall of the Soviet Union and the opening of Russian archives, post-1991 analyses of 1914 have been quite traditional, both in Russia and abroad. Thus one Russian author, throwing off the yoke of Bolshevik interpretations of popular mood, parroted Buchanan's "patriotic" position in a 1994 article:

> World War I ... what do we know about it? A few phrases from school primers, "annexationist," "imperialist," "crisis of elites," "revolutionary situation." The war is perceived as a prologue to two revolutions—February and October—and, by comparison with them, the events are barely important and even less significant. But that is how it is for us, the offspring, schooled not in the history of the Fatherland, but in the history of the revolutionary movement. For contemporaries it was different, and now that we are opening the yellowed archival folders, we learn with surprise that among the people [*narod*] it was called a Fatherland war and that the patriotic spirit in Russia in the first two years was unusually high.¹⁴

Hubertus Jahn, in his fine 1996 study of patriotic culture during the war, also arrived at the conclusion that there was an "initial outburst of flag-waving enthusiasm" that soon dissipated. Despite this outburst, Jahn argued, "Russia was not a nation during World War I" because Russians only understood whom they were fighting and not who they were.¹⁵

The problems that plagued earlier accounts of the war have not gone away. Scholars still rely on thin source bases when considering the 1914 mobilization and consider only parts of the public's response without placing manifestations of patriotism and dissent within a broader political context. Given the richness of that source base and the scale of the events that took place in 1914, it is impossible to describe and to analyze the World War I mobilizations in a single article. Instead, it is my desire in this article to provide a brief catalog of the many responses to the outbreak of the war and to argue that historians need to reconceptualize their notions of political community and political action in late imperial Russia in order to make sense of those responses.

The Mobilization of 1914

The declaration of mobilization and war in July 1914 brought about three basic responses from the Russian populace. The first was by far the most

---

12. I. I. Rostunov, ed., *Istoriia pervoi mirovoi voiny, 1914–1918* (Moscow, 1975), 1:228.

13. Some authors, however, remained unaffected by this attempt to portray the laboring masses of Russia as instinctively opposed to imperialist wars and continued to assert the standard position that the outbreak of war had intoxicated all of Europe and that "hurrah-patriotism" reigned throughout Russia as surely as it did in England. See, for instance, Nikolai Iakovlev, *1 avgusta 1914*, 3d ed. (Moscow, 1993 [1974]), 28–29.

14. Elena Seniavskaia, "Kornet bezhit na voinu," *Pogranichnik*, no. 3 (March 1994): 61.

15. Hubertus F. Jahn, *Patriotic Culture in Russia during World War I* (Ithaca, 1996), 171–73.

prevalent: a private response to the danger and disruption of the war. Most men spent the one-day grace period before they were due to appear arranging for ways to fulfill their obligations in their absence and spending time with their families. The most common sound in Russia was that of men, women, and children weeping. The other common sound was silence, not the "eternal silence" of the Russian countryside that Russian urbanites, too deaf to rural noises to know the difference, generally heard, but a stunned silence.[16] Rural men themselves recalled the eeriness of buzzing villages falling silent as families quietly grieved.[17]

A typical situation was described by a noncommissioned officer in his unpublished memoirs written as he lay in a military hospital in early 1915.[18] Ivan Kuchernigo lived in a village near the district center of Aleshka and received the news as most rural Russians did, at a village assembly:

> On 17 July, a policeman who had never been to our village before arrived and went door to door calling everyone to a meeting, and so I went.
> "What's going on?" the peasants asked each other, but no one responded because no one knew what was going on, and how could we have known...?
> Suddenly, the village elder appeared and made a sign with his hand to be quiet. Everyone became silent, straining their ears and wanting to hear exactly what our elder would say...
> "Here's what's afoot boys! An enemy has turned up! He has attacked our Mother Russia [*Matushku Rossiiu*], and our Father-Tsar needs our help, our enemy for now is Germany."
> "It's the Germans! The Germans!" spread through the crowd...
> "Quiet! Quiet!" boomed the voice of the elder. "OK boys, in order not to lose time messing with lists, whoever feels healthy and able to serve the Fatherland should all show up at 9 o'clock on the 18th in the office of the District Military Commander in Aleshka, and I advise you to bring with you two pairs of underwear, and they'll give you everything else there, just do it quick."

At this point, the crowd dispersed to their huts, "forgetting about their field work." The heartbreaking family scenes he described in his village were played out all over Russia:

> My God, how many tears were spilled when we had to go. My five-year-old daughter sat in my arms and, pressing against me, said "Daddy, why are you going? Why are you leaving us? Who's going to earn money and get bread for us?" Her little arms clasped me about the neck and tightly, tightly hugged me. I heard the beating of her little heart, and heard her lips begin to kiss my neck. I couldn't answer her questions, and couldn't hold back my own tears, and just answered "I'll be home soon, baby."

---

16. The quote that the Russian countryside responded to the declaration of war with "eternal silence" comes from Kadet leader Pavel Miliukov. Miliukov, *Political Memoirs*, 300.

17. O. I. Gorodovikov, *Vospominaniia* (Moscow, 1957), 34.

18. "Zapisi starshego unter-ofitsera kom. 253 pekhotnogo Cherekopnogo polka Ivan Vasil'evich Kuchernigo," Gosudarstvennyi arkhiv Rossiiskoi Federatsii (GARF), f. 6281, op. 1, d. 173, ll. 1–3.

Throughout the village the only thing you could hear were prayers, and curses thrown at the Germans.

Khristina Semina, living in an area of Transcaucasia populated mostly by Armenians and Azeris, had similar recollections of the general response to the news that war had been declared:

Among the Armenians the whole family lived only on the labor of the male. . . . Therefore, when it was demanded that husbands, fathers, and brothers go to the induction point and they said that it was war—there arose such crying and wailing among the women and children that it immediately became horrible. The din of this weeping prevailed throughout the city both night and day.

The sorrow was not, of course, limited to Armenians. Semina herself was overcome by tears and could not stop crying as her husband both prepared to leave and brought home tales of the "awful scenes" that were occurring at the induction point as families were split apart.[19] The same sounds resonated in Anna Akhmatova's ears. "Soldiers' wives are sobbing for the boys," she wrote on 20 July 1914, "the weeping of widows is ringing throughout the countryside."[20]

The second response has received far more attention than it deserves in proportion to its prevalence. This was vocal public support. It has received undue attention because a disproportionate number of people who got their remembrances of Russia's response to war published witnessed that response on Palace Square in St. Petersburg, the site of a truly substantial patriotic demonstration of about a quarter of a million people, moving and singing in unison in response to the tsar. Needless to say, the scale of the event and the presence of the Petersburg elite made the demonstration atypical, but the obvious emotional power of the moment overwhelmed almost everyone there and skewed their vision of the declaration of war.[21]

That said, there can be no doubt that a great many patriotic demonstrations occurred throughout the country. Throughout the realm, provincial officials arranged for patriotic demonstrations to be held as men marched off to war, and these seem to have been fairly well attended. Again Kuchernigo best described the scene that occurred in many local towns where reservists congregated:

What crowds of people! It was hard to get through the streets. They were carrying portraits of the emperor decorated with flags. The noise was such that it was hard to understand anything. Some sang "God Save the Tsar," others yelled "Long Live the Tsar and the People [*narod*]," and others

---

19. Khristina D. Semina, *Tragediia russkoi armii pervoi velikoi voiny 1914–1918 gg.: Zapiski sestry miloserdiia kavkazskogo fronta* (New Mexico, 1963), 1:11.

20. Anna Akhmatova, "Iiul' 1914," in *Primite etot dar . . . : Stikhotvoreniia* (Moscow, 1995), 171.

21. In addition to Buchanan, see Paleologue, *An Ambassador's Memoirs*, 46–52; Pares, *Fall of the Russian Monarchy*, 187–89; M. V. Rodzianko, *Krushenie imperii i Gosudarstvennaia Duma i fevral'skaia 1917 goda revoliutsiia* (Valley Cottage, N.Y., 1986), 100–107.

yelled "Down with the Germans, death, death to the Germans!" "Long live the Invincible Russian Army! Hoorah! Hoorah! Hoorah!"[22]

Mariia Bochkareva, living in Siberia at the time, remembered the days of mobilization as an "elevating, glorious, unforgettable moment," a feeling that many Russians who joined in the patriotic demonstrations must have experienced as well.[23] It was an intoxicating experience to participate in the life and activities of a large community, and that feeling of transcendence was eagerly sought around the empire.

These demonstrations did not, however, necessarily mean that there was support for the war itself. Most Russians harbored few illusions that they would gain any particular benefit from a military victory. War had always meant sacrifice and loss, and there was no reason to believe that this one would turn out any differently. As we will see below, there was a significant outpouring of distaste for the war itself from the very beginning in the form of riots, but other forms of resistance were also present from the outset. In Riga, alongside the portraits of the tsar, workers and reservists flew banners proclaiming "down with the war!"[24] Less showy resistance began in earnest as well. At one district office during the first week of mobilization, of the approximately 2,000 men who had initially shown up, over 200 promptly disappeared.[25]

Even given these caveats, there can be no doubt that there was a significant minority of the population that was enthusiastic about the war in 1914. Part of this enthusiasm was expressed by young men who rushed to district military offices to volunteer after the war broke out, despite the fact that volunteering for service was an option available only to those men who were neither in active forces, nor the reserves, nor the first tier militia.[26] This was an occurrence that completely took state and military men by surprise. Indeed, as General Vladimir Sukhomlinov, the war minister, admitted a few days after mobilization began, they had simply not foreseen the possibility of men volunteering during wartime.[27] It was not until 23 July that the rules governing the induction of volunteers were approved by the tsar and not until 28 July that they were distributed.[28] By that time, the confusion surrounding volunteering was already apparent. Angry telegrams decrying the inactivity of district military commanders, patriotic telegrams

22. "Zapisi starshego unter-ofitsera kom. 253 pekhotnogo Cherekopnogo polka Ivan Vasil'evich Kuchernigo," GARF, f. 6281, op. 1, d. 178, l. 4–4ob.

23. Maria Botchkareva [Mariia Bochkareva], *Yashka: My Life as Peasant, Officer and Exile*, as set down by Isaac Don Levine (New York, 1919), 64.

24. A. Pireiko, *V tylu i na fronte imperialisticheskoi voiny: Vospominaniia riadovogo* (Leningrad, 1926), 9.

25. GARF, f. 1745, op. 1, d. 58, ll. 370–421 (daily reports of Plotsk district military commander, 17 July through 26 July 1914).

26. Rossiiskii gosudarstvennyi voenno-istoricheskii arkhiv (RGVIA), f. 2000, op. 3, d. 2647, l. 1 (letter from Nikolai Ianushkevich to chief of the Main Staff, 18 July 1914).

27. RGVIA, f. 400, op. 19, d. 86, l. 8 (Sukhomlinov report, 22 July 1914).

28. "Pravila o prieme v voennoe vremia okhotnikov na sluzhbu v sukhoputnye voiska." Approved by the tsar, signed by Sukhomlinov, ibid., l. 10; distributed as "Prikaz po voennomu vedomstvu no. 454," 28 July 1914, ibid., ll. 34–35.

offering services, and frustrated notes from local officials asking for guidance flowed into central military offices.²⁹

The rules finally sent out initially forbade enlisting men younger than 18 or older than 43 (rules that were soon bent or broken), and since all men already obligated to serve were not allowed to volunteer, the pool of possible volunteers was quite restricted. The majority came from men in the second tier militia, men with student deferrals, or men of ethnicities not yet drafted. Unfortunately, no statistics about the number of men enrolled as volunteers appear to be available, but the "significant influx" was great enough to cause logistical difficulties only in the Caucasus, where the Muslim population paid a tax in lieu of military service.³⁰ Though the volunteer rush was therefore probably fairly small in numerical terms, and we cannot assume in any case that all volunteers were inspired by "hurrah-patriotic" motives, it is clear that there were people scattered throughout the empire who genuinely responded in a patriotic way and thirsted to fight in the war, from Siberian women like Mariia Bochkareva, to underage Jewish boys, to the sons of prominent politicians like Mikhail Rodzianko and Aleksandr Krivoshein.³¹

The final response to the declaration of war is one that has had far less coverage than it deserves. This was active public opposition. Throughout Russia, the declaration of war sparked off draft riots, some of them enormous and serious. These riots, as I noted above, do not fit well with the existing historical paradigm of 1914. Compare Buchanan's claim that the "only act of mob violence" throughout Russia was targeted at the German Embassy with the following telegram sent from Tomsk during the mobilization period:

> Reservists are producing disorder almost everywhere in Tomsk province: in Novonikolaevsk [present-day Novosibirsk] a mob of reservists sacked stores and began to sack the bazaar, the disorders were stopped with the assistance of [army troops].... The mobs threw stones at them, one rifleman was wounded with bullets, as a result of which the troops opened fire ... two were killed, two were seriously wounded. In light of these disorders the horse requisition committee stopped its work. Reservists smashed liquor stores in the villages of Iudikh, Tiumentsev, and Klochki in Barnaul district, reservists demanded provisions from county authori-

---

29. See, for instance, RGVIA, f. 2000, op. 3, d. 2647, l. 16 (telegram from "volunteers under the leadership of P. Shaposhnikov" to Sukhomlinov, 23 July 1917); ibid., l. 30 (letter from N. Bogomolov to the Mobilization Department, 22 July 1914); ibid., l. 15 (telegram from chairman of the Kostroma draft board to the war minister, 22 July 1914); RGVIA, f. 400, op. 19, d. 86, l. 38 (telegram from General Ebelov [Odessa] to chief of Main Staff, 27 July 1914).

30. RGVIA, f. 2000, op. 3, d. 1159, l. 6 (letter from Pension and Service Department of the Main Staff to the Mobilization Department of the General Staff, 15 August 1914).

31. Botchkareva [Bochkareva], *Yashka*, 64; RGVIA, f. 2003, op. 2, d. 28, l. 53 (petition to the tsar from 11-year-old Vulf Iankel'son of Riga, n.d.); for Rodzianko's request to enlist his son despite the fact that he had failed his medical exam (and approval of request), see RGVIA, f. 2000, op. 3, d. 2608, l. 85 (report from Sukhomlinov to the tsar, 21 July 1914); for Krivoshein children, see ibid., l. 88.

ties in Iudikh, they deserted in Tiumentsev and drove away the police chief in Iudikh.[32]

As we can see from this account and the accounts below, Knox's belief that "all the wine shops were closed and there was no drunkenness" was simply false. Instead, extant sources show that one of the most popular activities of the rioters was to loot liquor stores.[33] Military officials, desperately wishing to preserve their heady vision of popular support for the war as hostilities began, quickly latched onto the liquor factor as the sole reason that the "disorders" occurred. "Liquor," one official bravely declared after the 1914 riots had cooled, "was the source of all misfortune."[34]

The rampages for liquor were understandable, perhaps even predictable. Induction into the active forces had long been an occasion for drunkenness on the part of young Russian men and was a cultural ritual in many places across the empire. Some villages even upheld a tradition of paying for the vodka that young conscripts consumed.[35] Needless to say, this ritual was frowned upon by military officials seeking a quick and efficient mobilization, and they successfully argued that liquor sales should be cut off during the mobilization period. The obvious solution from the perspective of reservists was simply to break open the closed stores, and in locations where local officials neglected to heed the warnings of the Ministry of Internal Affairs and failed to provide police protection for the stores, it was a solution that was carried out. In the city of Lugansk, riots began with an attack on liquor stores; the crowd then proceeded to loot food and clothing stores before breaking windows in private residences "with shouts of 'hurrah!'"[36]

But the closing of liquor stores and the effects of drunkenness after the stores were looted cannot be taken as the sole explanation for these widespread riots. As we saw in the telegram from Tomsk, far more was occurring than simple raids for vodka. Reservists were also protesting the lack of provisions, the requisitioning of their horses, and the war itself. This multiplicity of factors was in evidence around the empire. In Ekaterinoslav, the riot was sparked, not by a run on the liquor store, but by the un-

32. Telegram from Tomsk province included in "O bezporiadkakh na sbornykh punktakh vo vremia mobilizatsii," report from department of police to the MVD Conscription Administration, 1914, Rossiiskii gosudarstvennyi istoricheskii arkhiv, St. Petersburg (RGIA), f. 1292, op. 1, d. 1729, l. 26.

33. For an analysis of the July riots in the context of liquor disturbances, see William Arthur McKee, "Taming the Green Serpent: Alcoholism, Autocracy, and Russian Society, 1881–1914" (Ph.D. diss., University of California, Berkeley, 1997), esp. 525–32.

34. RGVIA, f. 2000, op. 3, d. 1196, l. 93 (telegram of the governor-general of the Steppe district to Sukhomlinov, 18 August 1914). All liquor stores were required by law to remain closed during the mobilization period, a law that generally appears to have been enforced. See also Golovin, *Russian Army*, 204, for a similar interpretation of the riots.

35. RGVIA, f. 2000, op. 3, d. 18, l. 6–6ob. (report of commander of Kazan' military district to the war minister, 8 January 1910).

36. RGVIA, f. 2000, op. 3, d. 1154, ll. 242–43 (report of the chief of the Lugansk garrison to the war minister, 24 July 1914).

furling of a patriotic flag and an attempt to start a prowar demonstration by members of the Black Hundreds, at which point reservists set upon the man who had produced the flag while others threw bricks at policemen, touching off a brawl that ended only when police fired into the crowd, killing one and wounding seven. In the Belebeevskii district of Ufa province, the riots began with the looting of bread stores and finished with an attack on liquor stores. In the city of Birsk (again in Ufa province), liquor played no part in the riot. Reservists "dispersed the police and destroyed the induction center, thanks to which the medical examinations and formation of units to send to the front had to stop."[37]

In most places, rioters included an attack on liquor stores in the context of other activities. In Barnaul, rioters seized control of the city for a time, torching houses, stores, and a liquor warehouse, prompting a full-scale flight by local residents. More than one hundred men would die in battles between reservists and police before order was restored.[38] The battle in Barnaul was the largest of its kind, but there were gunfights and numerous episodes of stone throwing throughout the empire, activities that should have given pause to officials who blamed everything on the booze. Many of the rioters were deadly serious, willing to die even before the liquor started flowing. In all, people were wounded and killed in draft rioting in the provinces of Astrakhan', Vitebsk, Vologda, Viatka, Ekaterinoslav, Novgorod, Penza, Perm', Podol'sk, Samara, Saratov, Simbirsk, Tambov, Tobol'sk, Tomsk, Ufa, and the Region of the Don Host. These riots left 51 state officials wounded and 9 dead, while 136 rioters were wounded and 216 killed.[39]

The only satisfactory model for explaining most of these riots, therefore, is to recognize that though the word *mob* is a singular noun in Russian (*tolpa*) as well as English, in fact a riot is a set of activities, not a single one. Once the balance of power is tipped and the forces of traditional authority are visibly inferior, it opens a space for all kinds of activities. Some men attack the police, others steal bread, others get drunk, and many take part in all of the above.

Using this framework, we can usefully indicate the several factors behind the draft riots of 1914. One, to be sure, was a desire to get drunk. Another was to demand sufficient provisions for themselves and obtain the goods promised to their families. Yet another reason, clearly, was to show displeasure with the war and do everything possible to delay or derail the process of being sent to the front. Military officials preferred to explain the riots purely in terms of the first factor, but this explanation became less and less plausible as the war went on. When the second tier of the militia was called up in September 1915 and riots exploded again, the fiction

---

37. RGVIA, f. 2000, op. 3, d. 1154, ll. 238–41 (report of commander of Kazan' military district to war minister, 24 July 1914).

38. Accounts of these events are collected in RGIA, f. 1292, op. 1, d. 1729.

39. "Svedeniia o chisle lits, postradavshikh vo vremia byvshikh v iiule mobilizatsiiu 1914 g. bezporiadkov v nekotorykh mestnostiakh imperii," RGIA, f. 1292, op. 1, d. 1729, ll. 129–30.

that rioting reservists wanted nothing more than booze proved impossible to maintain.[40]

Just as explanations that "Russia" responded monolithically to the war are unconvincing, so are attempts to understand the response by using broad social categories like "worker," "peasant," or "elite." Within each of these groups, there was noticeable differentiation. For, at the same time that many young elites with legal deferrals and exemptions flocked to conscription offices to volunteer for service, a significant portion of their compatriots who were due to appear spent July pulling strings to obtain a reprieve. Sergei Dobrorol'skii, the head of the mobilization department, read "all kinds of requests and petitions" from young men from "our cultured society and from the midst of the bourgeoisie." "They pressed every possible button," and, he resignedly admitted, for the most part succeeded in their attempts.[41]

The divergence of opinion within social groups extended all the way down the social ladder. At the same time that some workers in Riga and St. Petersburg were raising banners stating "down with the war," workers in Tula were actively chasing down Tolstoians posting antiwar leaflets around town and threatening them with mob justice.[42] Meanwhile, in villages and small towns across the empire, proud patriotic citizens were turning in their neighbors for avoiding the draft and deserting the army. The volume of these denunciations had reached such "enormous" proportions by 1915 that A. A. Polivanov, the war minister, began to suspect that the Ministry of Internal Affairs was being insufficiently attentive to the problem of draft evasion and wrote the minister of internal affairs to protest.[43]

These civilian complaints were broadly framed and were often sent to specific central state institutions. They were not the parochial spasms of ignorant peasants. Nor were they only targeted at specific individuals; they were often critical of state policy as well. One group of rural dwellers wrote to the Duma urging that policemen be drafted before only sons were. "The peasantry," they claimed, "sees that the motherland groans under the burdens of war. And the peasantry is ready to bear . . . the horrible sacrifice of war, but it appeals to the . . . State Duma and requests that fairness be seen in everything. . . . It is necessary that everyone, regardless of class or property qualifications, defend the motherland. With that fairness, victory over the enemy will be guaranteed."[44] These anonymous authors claimed to speak for the whole peasantry. One other rural dweller wrote in even

---

40. For a summary of the 1915 riots, see "Perechen' 'besporiadkov,' uchinennykh ratnikami 2-go razriada prizyva 5 sentiabria 1915 g., sostavlennyi v departamente politsii," secret, 2 November 1915, RGIA, f. 1292, op. 1, d. 1729, ll. 131–81.

41. Cited in Golovin, *Voennye usiliia*, 2:121.

42. See account of the conflict between workers and Tolstoians in Tula in the court proceedings against the Tolstoians in Gosudarstvennyi muzei istorii religii (GMIR), f. 13, op. 1, d. 376.

43. RGVIA, f. 2000, op. 3, d. 1196, l. 91 (letter from Polivanov to Shcherbatov, 5 August 1915).

44. RGIA, f. 1278, op. 5, d. 1193, l. 106–106ob. (letter from "The peasantry" to the State Duma, 5 August 1915).

more grandiose terms that he knew that the "*whole people* is terribly unhappy with conscription policy because it is unequally applied and not everyone has to serve."[45] The authors of these letters were using a new political framework by demanding equality for all citizens and by making political claims on the basis of representing "the people." That framework, as we will see below, was national in form and in content.

The Question of the Russian Nation

The argument outlined above has been "deconstructive." I have argued that the common assumptions about the behavior of Russians upon the outbreak of war in 1914 are problematic, if not untenable. "Peasants," "workers," and "elite" did not act monolithically. Neither, of course, did "Russia." But deconstruction is not enough, for the evidence supports a more "constructive" analysis of political community and political behavior in Russia in 1914. More specifically, the reaction of reservists and their families to the outbreak of the war allows us to ask rather different questions about the formation of the Russian nation than were possible to ask within the old historical paradigm.

The first question to ask is one most recently addressed by David Moon: did peasants become Russian citizens in the waning years of Romanov rule?[46] Both the question and Moon's analysis deserve a detailed response. Moon says that peasants did not become citizens prior to 1917, claiming that since the Russian state "had not (yet) devoured its peasants ... these peasants had not become Russian citizens."[47] The basis of Moon's argument is an extensive and erudite comparison between the situation in "constitutional Russia" (ca. 1905–1917) and that of the French Third Republic described by Eugen Weber in his celebrated book *Peasants into Frenchmen: The Modernization of Rural France, 1870–1914*.[48] The crux of the problem of nationhood for Moon is not whether peasants were *aware* of events of national significance (they had been aware of these, as Moon points out, for quite some time) but whether they would *act* as "members of a wider, national society with which they felt they shared more common interests than they had sources of conflict."[49]

Moon is quite right, I think, to insist that action is as important to consider as "awareness" or "consciousness." Nations *do* preside over the site where thought and behavior, culture and politics, intersect. Unfortunately, I think that he errs when he attempts to define national belonging in terms of unity. Segments of the population do not need to "devour" each

---

45. RGVIA, f. 400, op. 19, d. 147, l. 5 (letter from "a peasant" to the war minister, 20 January 1915). Emphasis added.
46. David Moon, "Peasants into Russian Citizens? A Comparative Perspective," *Revolutionary Russia* 9, no. 1 (June 1996): 43–81.
47. Ibid., 76.
48. Eugen Weber, *Peasants into Frenchmen: The Modernization of Rural France, 1870–1914* (Stanford, 1976).
49. Moon, "Peasants into Russian Citizens?" 44.

other to be co-national; neither do they have to "share more common interests" than they have sources of conflict. Unity is a national desire, not a precondition for the nation itself. This is an error commonly made not only by nation-builders themselves, who idealize the nation precisely because it promises unanimity, but by critics of nationalism as well. Marxists in particular viewed nationalism as an ideology that "masked" dissent by painting a veneer of national unity over "real" class divisions. It was the great (and, for Marxists, exasperating) success of nationalism that it created a "false consciousness" in the masses.

This focus on "consciousness" when analyzing nationalism is still a common one. As Prasenjit Duara has pointed out, the big guns of recent theorizing on the nation like Ernest Gellner and Benedict Anderson also focus on national identity as a "distinctive mode of consciousness: the nation as a whole imagining itself to be the unified subjectivity." In Duara's view, though, the nation is not the unified product of collective imagination but is a site of significant, indeed often heated, contestation about identity and power. The problem with most earlier theories about nationalism, he claims, is the "general postulate of a cohesive subjectivity."[50] I fully agree with Duara's move away from Anderson and Gellner and with Rogers Brubaker's similar call to focus more upon the nation as a "category of practice"[51] than upon states of consciousness or properties of collectivities.

The nation, like all political fields, is an arena where multiple subjectivities and multiple behaviors interact within certain parameters. They play according to a short list of rules, a set of governing ideals. Among these is the idea that central "national" institutions ought to supersede local power structures, the belief that no members of the nation should possess special rights and privileges that other members do not possess, and the notion that a historical, territorialized community is the legitimizing political force in the country. Finally, as Moon suggests, there lies the idea that citizens must be political *actors*.

To get to the heart of questions relating to the nation, therefore, we must answer the question of how political action is framed. It is here that Moon's argument is weakest in regard to Russian behavior during World War I. He argues that the simultaneous mutinies of the French and Russian armies in 1917 were fundamentally dissimilar, citing Leonard Smith's conclusion that the French mutiny was primarily a political contest between "citizen-soldiers" and their commanders while the disintegration of the Russian army was precipitated by peasant-mutineers and deserters who were "primarily concerned with their own interests as peasants" and "had only a very weakly developed sense of national consciousness."[52] He derives this conclusion from Allan Wildman's magisterial study of the army in 1917, but I read Wildman much differently than Moon does. Wildman

50. Prasenjit Duara, "Historicizing National Identity, or Who Imagines What and When," in Geoff Eley and Ronald Grigor Suny, eds., *Becoming National: A Reader* (Oxford, 1996), 152–53.
51. Rogers Brubaker, *Nationalism Reframed: Nationhood and the National Question in the New Europe* (Cambridge, Eng., 1996), 21.
52. Moon, "Peasants into Russian Citizens?" 45, 47.

argued that Rodzianko elicited cheers from soldiers in 1917 when he appealed to a "new Mother Russia," that peasant soldiers in 1917 "keenly sensed their own power to impose changes," and that their breaches of discipline were connected almost wholly with suspicions that their officers were violating the popular will. "This Revolution," Wildman concludes, "should be regarded as the conquest by the masses of undivided Soviet power, the realization of their vision of direct democracy without compromises with the propertied elements, and the immediate execution of the agenda of the Revolution on land, peace, and workers' control of industry."[53] These conclusions hardly seem to fit with the picture of parochial, prepolitical peasant-soldiers.[54]

Moon wisely did not press his argument that soldiers acted parochially as peasants but moved on to assert that it was the peasants left at home who were most important in 1917 and therefore deserve primary attention. Here again, though, he is on shaky ground. He acknowledges that during the war there "were cases of peasants lynching landowners with German surnames, claiming that they were traitors, and seizing idle land in order to increase food production for the war effort," but he claims that these "justifications" were self-serving: "The notions of going without to support the nation's war effort or 'digging for victory' would not have met with much resonance in the Russian countryside during the First World War, unless peasants could see some advantage for themselves."[55]

In the first place, it hardly matters whether the "justifications" were self-serving or not. If we disqualify all nations whose "rules" have been manipulated by self-interested actors, then a great many scholars of the nation will go hungry. Indeed, we might argue that manipulation *proves* both the ubiquity of the nation as a political field and the need to appeal to it to make political claims. The power of ideology, national ideology included, lies not in inspiring belief but in structuring action. As Václav Havel once noted about a somewhat different ideo-political structure, "individuals need not believe in all these [ideological] mystifications, but they must behave as though they did. . . . It is enough for them to have accepted their life with it and in it. For by this very fact, individuals confirm the system, fulfill the system, make the system, *are* the system."[56]

In the second place, Moon adduces no evidence to support his claim that the "notion of going without to support the nation's war effort" would have been alien to rural Russians. For good reason, too, since Lars Lih, in the most extensive study of rural attitudes toward production and con-

53. Wildman, *End of the Russian Imperial Army*, 195–96, 375, 379, 380.
54. Moon conscientiously acknowledges here that his interpretation "conflicts with some recent work on the evolution of Russian national identity among peasants," citing the work of A. V. Buganov on collective memory and Jeffrey Brooks on popular literature in particular. He deals with the former by agreeing with David Ransel's criticism that Buganov had a weak conceptualization of national consciousness and with the latter by claiming that Brooks inadequately dealt with "the critical analytical problem of recreating the attitudes of the readers rather than the content of what they read." Moon, "Peasants into Russian Citizens?" 47.
55. Ibid., 49.
56. Václav Havel, *Open Letters: Selected Writings, 1965–1990* (New York, 1992), 136.

sumption during World War I, claims that "in line with the view of the state as essentially a protector, the peasant producers made a sharp distinction between grain deliveries for the army and deliveries for the town. The peasants understood the necessity of supplying the army by giving up his grain without compensation, but they saw no such necessity to supply the town."[57]

Lih's addendum to this claim highlights the essential difference between my analysis and Moon's: "This attitude exasperated food-supply officials, who obviously felt the peasants were too backward to grasp that supplying the cities was a civic duty on a par with supplying the army."[58] The progressive, patriotic food-supply officials, just like the progressive, patriotic military reformers who blamed peasant parochialism for the loss of the war, assumed that because many rural Russians did not *agree* with their vision of the nation, they did not *have* a vision of the nation. The Russian reformers, Moon, and indeed Weber himself all presumed that since the nation requires unity, the precondition for the rise of the nation is urbanity. Anything else is "backward" or "pre-political."

Even more problematically, these nationalists and theorists all assumed that national unity also implied loyalty to the government. But the national political form does not require agreement or loyalty, either between segments of the population or between citizens and the regime. Indeed, the nation by definition opens up this space of contestation: if the political community is separate from the regime, then there must always be the possibility that members of that community, individually or collectively, will make the claim that other political actors do not represent the "true" political will of the community. What is important is not a "unified subjectivity" but the framework of political action.

To understand that framework in regard to 1914, we need to understand the relationship between mass mobilization and the emergence of a nation. Brubaker provides a clue with his argument that we should regard "nationness" as "an event . . . something that suddenly crystallizes rather than gradually develops, as a contingent, conjuncturally fluctuating, and precarious frame of vision and basis for individual and collective action, rather than as a relatively stable product of deep developmental trends in economy, polity, or culture."[59] This is Brubaker's most original contribution to the literature on the nation, and it is implicitly critical of earlier approaches (like Gellner's and Weber's) that treated the nation as one of the many by-products of industrialization and "modernization."

I prefer a physical rather than a chemical metaphor. Nationness is an event, but it is a kinetic event that requires the building up of potential energy beforehand. Nationness is *both* an event that suddenly crystallizes *and* one that is the product of deep developmental trends. It is not, therefore, that Anderson, Gellner, and Weber are wrong to point to the importance of print-capitalism, industrialization, railroad building, and military conscription as factors in nation formation, but that they do not exhaust

57. Lars Lih, *Bread and Authority in Russia, 1914–1921* (Berkeley, 1990), 71.
58. Ibid.
59. Brubaker, *Nationalism Reframed*, 19.

that analysis. The compression and homogenization of space and time, the increase in literacy rates and awareness of the outside world, the economic integration with other communities, and the construction of a national literature are all factors that built tremendous potential national energy throughout Europe and the Americas in the nineteenth century. But these processes in themselves did not "build" nations. They built up the potential for mass national politics. The nation would not emerge until that potential for mass national political action was mobilized, made kinetic.

Those processes that built up national potential happened in Russia as they did in western Europe, though a bit later and not quite as comprehensively. Moon, indeed, spends the second half of his article proving just this point. He outlines with great subtlety and knowledge the muted way in which the great "nation-building" institutions formed and developed in Russia after the Great Reforms. Railways and rural-urban migration had an "undeniable impact on at least sections of the peasantry," but peasant society and culture proved resilient, and as a result only "a very small proportion of peasant-migrants assimilated to urban culture." Primary schools and literacy courses came to the village, but those schools "failed to achieve the state's objective of 'civilising' peasant children and giving them a 'heavy dose of patriotism' . . . in spite of their education and literacy, they remained peasants." Universal military conscription was introduced, but only a minority of possible conscripts were actually drafted. Citing John Bushnell, he claims that because even those men drafted spent much of their active duty working according to peasant cycles within the regimental economy it was "scarcely credible that military service could have done much to reshape peasant mentality." In short, he claims that "in Russia the rural population 'peasantised' the very factors that, in Weber's argument, served as the 'agencies of change' which acted as conduits for the transmission of national culture to the French peasantry."[60]

But why should "peasantization" preclude the building up of potential national energy? The answer, as I suggested above, is that Moon and Weber both implicitly assumed that nationness is essentially urban. Moon acknowledged that Weber took a great deal of criticism on precisely this issue from scholars like James Lehning, who stressed that peasants were not passive recipients of change and argued that the institutions identified by Weber were not so much sites of one-way peasant assimilation as they were sites of "cultural contact."[61] But Moon does not follow through on the implication of this revision, namely that in other contexts peasant culture might prove stronger and more influential than it had in France and that the question of whether these institutions were predominantly urban or rural is far less important than the fact that a site of cultural negotiation had been opened up. Though institutions may have been 'peasantized' in Russia, this does not imply that they were thereby rendered nonnational.

Moon is on much firmer ground, though, in his concluding section. He argues there, on the basis of works by Scott Seregny, Francis Wcislo, and

60. Moon, "Peasants into Russian Citizens?" 55–67.
61. James R. Lehning, *Peasant and French: Cultural Contact in Rural France during the Nineteenth Century* (Cambridge, Eng., 1995).

David Macey, that it was not the peasantry that impeded the formation of the Russian nation, but state officials. Part of the blame lay with well-meaning reformist officials who wanted to integrate rural Russians into political life but failed to articulate their vision to the "masses." The real barriers to nation-formation, though, were the conservative state officials who feared an active populace and scuttled plans for formal incorporation of peasants into national political structures whenever they could. "It was not," Moon concludes, "that peasants were unaware of national politics in the years of the constitutional experiment; they were excluded from participating in them in any meaningful way."[62]

The potential national energy, in other words, had been built up, but since most rural Russians could not *act* nationally, that energy had not been made kinetic. More precisely, that energy had not been made kinetic on a mass scale. The politically mobilizing events familiar in other historical circumstances, most notably voting, but also participation in so-called civil society or in trade unions, never occurred on a mass scale in Russia prior to 1914. Several partially mobilizing events had occurred in the late imperial period, most notably in 1904–05, but the nine partial military mobilizations during the Russo-Japanese War replicated the jerky, discontinuous, and befuddled social and political mobilizations over the same period.

Part of the reason for the "failures" of these mobilizations, perhaps the largest part, was ideological. No shift of political frames occurs painlessly or smoothly, and Russia in 1905 was no exception. Part of the reason for the disjointed nature of the events in 1905 was uncertainty regarding the most effective or most appealing frame for political action. As General A. N. Kuropatkin, the minister of war and commander of Russian forces during the first half of the Russo-Japanese War, worriedly noted: "belief in God, devotion to the Tsar, [and] love of the Fatherland" were the factors that had previously made the "uneducated peasantry . . . fearless and obedient, but these principles have latterly been much shaken amongst the people."[63] Likewise, Father Gapon's anguished cry on Bloody Sunday that "there is no tsar" signaled not so much the end of a naive monarchist consciousness as the incapacitation of the monarchist political framework, the failure of which was felt even at (perhaps especially at) the highest level of the political elite.[64] With the old framework crippled, the contest was on between 1905 and 1914 for one to replace it.

In the military, that contest was gradually being won by young military reformers convinced that the looming war would be a massive total war. Modern war, they argued, could only be won by soldiers imbued with a civic spirit, with a sense of initiative, independence, and with a strong dose of masculine vigor. They turned immediately to the citizen-soldiers of western Europe as their model. Even more important, they recognized

62. Moon, "Peasants into Russian Citizens?" 68–73.
63. General [A. N.] Kuropatkin, *The Russian Army and the Japanese War*, trans. A. B. Lindsay, 2 vols. (London, 1909), 1:296.
64. The definitive work on the ideological crisis among Russian elites in this period is Andrew M. Verner, *The Crisis of Russian Autocracy: Nicholas II and the 1905 Revolution* (Princeton, 1990).

The Mobilization of 1914 and the Question of the Russian Nation

that the coming war would be won on the home front as surely as it would be on the battlefield. In the words of one of these reformers, "preparation for war must come *from all corners, with the effort of everyone, and with all the moral and material strengths of the state* . . . we must prepare for war, not only in the *purely military* sense, but also from the point of view of *society*, from the point of view of *politics*, and finally, in the *broad economic sense*."[65] These vibrant reformers articulated their vision of the militarized nation to other influential social and political actors, most notably Aleksandr Guchkov, the leader of the Octobrist Party, who spoke often in the Duma about the need for army and society to become national in nature.[66]

As a result of this broader shift in Russian politics, the outbreak of war in 1914 was marked by intensive and extensive mobilization. The military mobilization in July was the first general mobilization of reserve armed forces in Russian history, and it was followed by mobilization in nearly all realms of social life, from medical care to economic production to sports activities. From the start, this mobilization was political, massive, and contentious. Patriotic rallies and draft riots took place in the same small towns across the empire in late July, sometimes on consecutive days.[67] The mobilization was therefore multidirectional, but people were politically active.

They acted, moreover, within the same political framework, because the war itself provided the context for all the mobilization activity. As we saw in the passage from Kuchernigo, the war was understood not as a fight between indeterminate enemies and parochial *Viatskie* but within the framework of a broad community, as a fight between Russians and Germans. This was so not simply because of a general awareness on the part of rural Russians about possible international conflicts, but more specifically because of the stridently national military training that the vast majority of reservists had received during the ascendancy of young reformers in the military establishment in the years between 1905 and 1914. That reserve base was comprised of young men, and it was a good deal more literate than the population as a whole. Only 36.7 percent of the young men inducted in 1909 were illiterate, and that number was dropping by more than 1 percent a year. In 1912, 32.6 percent could neither read nor write, a number high by late twentieth-century standards, but quite in line with early twentieth-century standards.[68] When the United States conducted a draft of its young men in 1917, for instance, 24.9 percent were illiterate.[69]

---

65. Col. A. G. Elchaninov, *Vedenie sovremennykh voiny i boia (lektsiia)* (St. Petersburg, 1909), 12, 13. Emphasis in the original.

66. See A. I. Guchkov, *K voprosu o gosudarstvennoi oborone: Rechi v Gosudarstvennoi dume tret'iago sozyva 1908–1912 gg.* (Petrograd, 1915).

67. See the 1 August 1914 report from Nizhegorod included in "O bezporiadkakh na sbornykh punktakh vo vremia mobilizatsii," report from Department of Police to the MVD Conscription Administration, 1914, RGIA, f. 1292, op. 1, d. 1729, ll. 106–7.

68. These statistics in Joshua A. Sanborn, "Drafting the Nation: Military Conscription and the Formation of a Modern Polity in Tsarist and Soviet Russia, 1905–1925" (Ph.D. diss., University of Chicago, 1998), 541. These are literacy rates at the time of induction. Reading classes in the army itself meant that by the time a soldier left the army he was still less likely to be illiterate.

69. Meirion and Susie Harries, *The Last Days of Innocence: America at War, 1917–1918* (New York, 1997), 137.

Furthermore, military trainers were given a new set of texts that stressed the importance of initiative and independence for soldiers and placed the interest of the "nation" at least on a par with the interest of the tsar. Young junior officers and noncommissioned officers imbibed this new ethos eagerly. Many spent a large amount of time with new recruits, training them in the ways of the soldier with fraternal affection rather than patriarchal disdain.[70] Increasingly, they began to disparage their older colleagues, who looked upon military study as a waste of time and upon their soldiers as their chattel.[71] Even those soldiers who had old-style officers were not insulated from the influence of nationalist training, for they were targeted directly through special publications for soldiers saturated with references to the national community.[72]

It should be noted that this community was not primarily ethnically defined in 1914. Instead, members of many different ethnic groups talked of their inclusion in a multiethnic Russian (*rossiiskii*) brotherhood. A mullah in the city of Ural'sk prayed with his flock for "all troop commanders and soldiers" to "defeat the Germans, those open enemies of *our* motherland who initiated this war against us."[73] In Riazan' province, the governor noted that the Muslim population responded to the crisis of war with "a complete consciousness of the importance and seriousness of the moment" and that there was "no difference between reservist Russians [*russkie*] and Muslims."[74] For these Muslims and their ethnically Russian Orthodox neighbors, involvement in the common business of the war overrode ethnic difference, and the war was articulated as a fight conducted by the "people" for their "motherland," quite a different type of wartime ideology from those traditionally used in autocratic states, in which war is the business of the ruler for the ruler.[75]

Even among the populations that had the least reason to be concerned with the events unfolding in Galicia and Poland, like nomads in Turkestan

70. Recent studies of the competence of junior officers and soldiers more broadly have emphasized the relative success of their training in the years before World War I. For the judgment of the preeminent American historian of the tsarist army to this effect, see Bruce Menning, *Bayonets before Bullets: The Imperial Russian Army, 1861–1914* (Bloomington, 1992), 273; see also Jacob Kipp, "Mass, Mobility, and the Origins of Soviet Operational Art, 1918–1936," in Carl W. Reddel, ed., *Transformation in Russian and Soviet Military History* (Washington, D.C., 1990), 94. Despite the dates in the title of Kipp's article, he spends the first pages of his article discussing the tsarist era.

71. See the comments made by one such junior officer to Sir Alfred Knox. Knox, *With the Russian Army*, 2:452–53. See also the dislike and scorn for old-style officers among the junior officers in Fedor Stepun's artillery unit evident throughout his wartime letters. F. Stepun, *Iz pisem praporshchika artillerista* (Prague, n.d.).

72. The most prolific private publisher for soldiers was the publishing house of V. A. Berezovskii, which had published more than 3,000 books and several periodicals for soldiers by 1910. See S. V. Belov, "Izdatel'stvo V. A. Berezovskogo (Iz istorii izdaniia voennoi literatury v Rossii)," *Voenno-istoricheskii zhurnal*, 1989, no. 11:85–90.

73. RGIA, f. 821, op. 133, d. 603, l. 64ob. (translated prayer from a mullah in Ural'sk). Emphasis added.

74. RGIA, f. 821, op. 133, d. 603, l. 26ob. (letter from the governor of Riazan' province to E. V. Menkin [chief of the Ministry of Internal Affairs' Department of Spiritual Affairs] 16 September 1914).

75. Peter Paret, *Understanding War: Essays on Clausewitz and the History of Military Power* (Princeton, 1992), 41, 44.

who were still exempt from the draft in 1914, officials noted that "everyone is interested in the war."[76] Another official dealing with draft-exempt nomads added that although the Kirgiz were "barely cultured . . . and almost completely uninterested in questions of state life," even they did not remain "indifferent" to the "moment of extreme flowering of patriotic feeling that Russia is experiencing."[77]

As in all the belligerent countries of the Great War, mobilized participation in general affairs went well beyond men in uniform. In Russia, as well as in the rest of Europe, the mobilization was especially noteworthy among women, who had had far fewer opportunities to transform their potential energy into kinetic energy.[78] Over the course of the war, both civilian men and women actively worked in charity organizations, in the Red Cross, in Zemgor, and in the War-Industrial Committees, and they became political actors through their economic production, which was explicitly linked to the war effort.[79] The war mobilized and framed nearly all political action. Not all political frameworks marked by mass mobilization are national in their particularities (that is, not all posit a territorialized cultural community that confers legitimacy upon a ruling regime and in which all community members are formally equal in status), but most have been.

Russian political practice during the war was certainly national in its particularities, a fact most clearly seen in mobilizational material. Here a significant change had occurred in the years between the Russo-Japanese War and the outbreak of World War I. The official army catechism during the Russo-Japanese War, as Kuropatkin attested, had been that soldiers served for "Faith, Tsar, and Fatherland," but the mobilizational literature during the Great War paid far more attention to the people (*narod*) and the motherland. Here is just one example of many:

> The type of people determines the type of army. Let our enemies say what they want about us, but in difficult times for the motherland, the Russian narod is always able to prove that it is a great narod, that a blazing flame burns in the Russian spirit with all that is good, blessed, and excellent, and that there is something there that is strong. . . . In order to feel and to act this way, one must be a hero in spirit and not only fear nothing, but also have a heart that beats with a hot love for the motherland, for one's comrades in arms, and for people in general.[80]

---

76. RGIA, f. 821, op. 133, d. 603, l. 77 (letter from Saltykov [military veterinarian] to the governor-general of Turkestan, secret, 1 November 1914).

77. RGIA, f. 821, op. 133, d. 603, l. 102 (letter from the director of the Chancellery of the Steppe Region to E. V. Menkin, 28 November 1914).

78. The literature on women's mobilization and World War I is large and growing. See, for instance, Margaret Randolph Higonnet et al., eds., *Behind the Lines: Gender and the Two World Wars* (New Haven, 1987); Angela Woollacott, *On Her Their Lives Depend: Munitions Workers in the Great War* (Berkeley, 1994).

79. See here especially Lih, *Bread and Authority in Russia*, Semina, *Tragediia russkoi armii*, and Lewis H. Siegelbaum, *The Politics of Industrial Mobilization in Russia, 1914–17: A Study of the War-Industries Committees* (New York, 1983).

80. "Nasha slava," publication of *Sel'skii vestnik*, included in RGIA, f. 821, op. 133, d. 603, ll. 40, 43.

Nor was this simply the way that propagandists framed questions of political action and political loyalty. Regardless of ethnicity, soldiers spoke of fighting together within a multiethnic brotherhood. Even when complaints were voiced in private letters, recruits usually framed their anger in terms of disappointed promise, as one Muslim soldier's intercepted letter revealed:

> the Russians have clergymen in war who administer the sacraments to their soldiers, but for us Muslims there is nothing. They don't assign mullahs to us, not withstanding the fact that more than half the soldiers [in the unit] are Muslim, who die without mullahs, and who are buried together with Russians in a single grave. I think we should bring this to the attention of the government.[81]

Again, the idea that questions of ethnic relations and cultural respect should be mediated by the central government is a crucial one, for it reflects the fact that even those Russian citizens who were traditionally classed as outsiders and were the victims of discrimination within imperial society often considered themselves part of a single political community with all the many ethnic groups that were ruled by the imperial state.

I have intentionally used evidence gathered from the periphery of the country in the last few paragraphs to show that the idea of a multiethnic nation flourished even in areas that were not ethnically Russian, where the project of propagating a national idea was hardest, and where the presence of a discriminatory imperial ideology among ethnic Russians was stronger than it was in the center of the country. The evidence from central locales is quite similar.

As we saw earlier in this essay, the theme of fairness dominated the popular response to mobilization and the war, as regular reservists and civilians alike articulated their feeling that every Russian citizen should bear an equal burden and that the tsar and government had to serve the army rather than the other way round. Both the theme of the equality of citizens and the idea that states were the servants of territorialized cultural communities were national ones, and both were ubiquitous in public discourse throughout the war.[82] From throughout the empire, the complaints were the same and echoed this one:

> Your Excellency. Throughout Kiev province, and maybe throughout Russia, there is at present a mass of people evading their duty before Throne and Fatherland by any possible means.... At present anyone who doesn't want to serve in the troops serves on the railroad. On the railroads, guards are freed (I don't know what they're guarding), porters are freed (I don't know who they're opening doors for at present), guards for railroad gardens, gardeners, assistants, and others (I don't know who can think about gardens at a time like this, and anyway the garden wouldn't die if the gardener left it for a half year or a year). And anyway the "necessary" Rus-

---

81. RGIA, f. 821, op. 133, d. 603, l. 89 (letter from Kazan' governor to E. V. Menkin, 10 November 1914).

82. For a more detailed exploration of this topic, see Josh Sanborn, "Conscription, Correspondence, and Politics in Late Imperial Russia," *Russian History/Histoire Russe* 24, nos. 1–2 (Spring–Summer 1997): 27–40.

sian public is living in clover, and even allows itself to reproach those who went to the war . . . I cannot in my heart blame government circles for this, but I want just to tell you this, Your Excellency.

The "wives of reservists" who authored this letter wrote in conclusion that they relied on "His Excellency's fairness, as all Russian people do. The whole Russian narod will stand in the ranks of the army, not even excluding cripples, to defend against the enemy, but only when fairness is seen in everything."[83] It bears noting as an aside that the ideal of national equality was expressed partially in a class key in this letter. These women articulated their anger at the "necessary" public that was better able to avoid induction into the army, but could not yet, in 1915, "blame government circles" for the chicanery of wealthy citizens. That hesitancy would disappear over the next two years.

In sum, the extant evidence related to social response to the 1914 mobilization supports rather different conclusions than those that have heretofore dominated the historical literature. "Russia" did not go off to war patriotically, nor was there unanimity within sociologically defined groups about the wisdom of the war effort. Patriots and protesters were present in all walks of Russian life in 1914.

The fact of dissent, however, does not imply that the other major pillar of the dominant paradigm, the lack of a sense of national identity on the part of Russian peasants, holds firm. In fact, quite the opposite is the case, for when we look at how that dissent was expressed by rural Russians, we find that it was framed in "national" terms, not local ones. Country dwellers turned to central state institutions with complaints, constantly referred to the need to protect the "interests of state" in their denunciations of their shirking neighbors, articulated an ideal of civic equality, and appealed to a historical, territorialized community as the legitimizing political force in the country. That relatively new sense of the nation as the dominant framework of political practice in the land grew stronger during the war, and the antinational autocracy weakened correspondingly. The final fall of the monarchy in 1917 and the withdrawal of the soldiers from a war that had been unpopular from its inception were therefore signs of the tangible presence of the Russian nation, not of its absence.

83. RGIA, f. 1292, op. 7, d. 298, l. 125 (letter from "wives of reservists" Tat'iana Iaremenko, Sinklatia Bozheiko, and Serafima Totskaia [from Radomysl'] to minister of internal affairs, 8 October 1915).

[4]

"The East Gives Nothing Back": The Great War and the German Army in Russia

DENNIS E. SHOWALTER

"THE EAST GIVES NOTHING BACK," mused Chief of Staff Erich von Falkenhayn, considering resource allocations for the campaign of 1915. His observation seemed surprisingly arbitrary in the aftermath of the stunning German victory of Tannenberg, the subsequent triumph in the head-down fighting of the Masurian Lakes, and a brilliant redeployment into Poland that shored up a collapsing Austrian army and then culminated in the incredible escape of a German corps from annihilation.

Contemporaries tended to interpret the Chief of Staff's pessimism as the reflection of his personal dislike for the eastern command team of Paul von Hindenburg and Erich Ludendorff.[1] Yet, for the balance of the Great War, the Russian Front never quite repaid the efforts of the Second Reich. Even the Treaty of Brest-Litovsk proved the work of Faust's Lemures, who helped to dig Germany's grave while its leaders dreamed of fresh resources and eastern empires.

Today, however, historians increasingly contend that the East did give something back–to the German army as an institution, and to the Germans who spent all or part of their war in that theater.

Recent research into the nature of Nazi administration in Eastern Europe during World War II reveals "a motley assemblage of career officials, individuals recruited for [emergency service], incompetent employees of the Reich administration, and, not infrequently, freelance soldiers of fortune."[2] Few had ever read *Mein Kampf*. Their villainy was more frequently appetitive than principled. What, then, provided the matrices for the everyday behavior of this mixed bag of losers?

In the context of the Wehrmacht's chronic personnel shortages, German officers and officials from the former Habsburg Empire and those who had gained occupation experience during the Great War were often sent to the east for no better reason than that they were assumed to have a particular ability to "handle" Slavs, much as the United States Army during World War II regularly assigned Southern-born officers to segregated Black units.[3] An increasing body of literature correspondingly argues that the German army's experiences in the east front from 1914 to 1918 provided structures and attitudes for the specifically Nazi aspects of the second, exponentially more ferocious and avowedly genocidal round.[4] Most recently, Omer Bartov has demonstrated the motivating power of Nazi principles in military contexts.[5] National Socialism, however, was at best an incomplete ideological system, whose essential nihilism depended heavily on its capacity to insert itself into other traditions and experiences. This interpretive strategy currently shapes a general process among historians to re-contextualize racial and ethnic relationships, rendering them foci of historical causation and analyzing them in twentieth century contexts. Recent writing on Nazi Germany stresses public and institutional acceptance of the Reich's racist ideology and complicity in even the worst of its genocidal crimes.[6] Scholars of the Second Empire use church sermons and slander trials to argue that public attention focused constantly and negatively on the "Jewish Question" and that seemingly

THE EAST GIVES NOTHING BACK

minor anti-Semitic manifestations could have significantly wider repercussions.[7]

The insights provided by this interpretation at times obscure the risk of writing history backwards. Roots may be found for any present-day perspective, if one searches for them zealously enough. The meaning of events and ideas, however, depends heavily on context. During the second half of the nineteenth century, the Prussian/German image of Russia as a civilization and a military power began to change. An earlier respect that approached deference gave way to Otto von Bismarck's increasing concern for Russia's dynamism, which he saw as the crucial challenge to the post-1871 European order emerging from St. Petersburg.[8] A liberalism critical of Russian absolutism, and a Socialism strongly influenced by Marx's contempt for Russian "character," gradually eroded conservative admiration for Russia's stability. Freelance intellectuals like Paul de Lagarde and university academics like Theodor Schiemann increasingly described Russians as degenerate primitives, whose women lacked the emotional resources to be successful call girls and whose men could not manage to use modern plumbing correctly.[9]

These concepts spread into a German army that was increasingly defining itself in ethnic terms. Although Junker aristocrats did not account for overwhelming numbers in the officer corps, East Elbian influences figured disproportionately, and East Elbian attitudes were widely copied. The growing importance of seasonal gang labor in rural eastern Germany, where the population was declining, only reinforced the anti-Polish nationalism fostered by Bismarck and the ethnic patrioteers of the HKT Society. The Poles and Russians who brought in the harvests were nameless and faceless.[10] So, increasingly, were Polish conscripts, whose language, as well as cultural and religious differences, often made them easy scapegoats for superiors and comrades alike. The "Polack" with dull wits and two left feet became a stock figure of German army humor. Suicide rates in the corps recruited from Posen and Silesia, which held large Polish populations, regularly stood high in the army's list.[11]

When the German army, an institution organized to manage and control violence, looked eastward, it confronted an intimidating paradox. On one hand, Germany could neither match nor counter Russia's increasing military power. On the other hand, Russia's force was more basic—indeed, more primitive—than the gentlemanly cabinet war of 1866 and the embryonic people's war of 1870–71.[12] In August 1914, the Cossacks provoked the greatest fear among Germans, soldiers or civilians. The cry, "Kosaken kommen!" could send villagers onto the roads and drive soldiers to heedless flight. It did not seem to matter that the Russian army's Cossacks were, on the whole, thoroughly domesticated and often no more than farm boys mounted on plow horses, led by officers who wore glasses and sported paunches.[13] Yet the image of Cossacks as savages who raped, killed, and plundered at will, which dated back to the Wars of Liberation, remained so strong that even officers groveled for their lives when they fell into Cossack hands.

Initial losses of German life and property in the 1914 campaign were relatively limited—and more often the result of accident than policy. Things changed in the aftermath of the Masurian Lakes operation. The retreating Russians took over 10,000 men of military age with them, along with numerous women and children. Both stragglers and organized units looted and burned the towns, and they slaughtered or drove off the livestock. Official historians calculated the losses with Teutonic precision: over 1600 civilians dead, 200,000 cows, a quarter million pigs. The exact figures are open to debate, but the impression permitted no doubt. Matters were even worse further south. In Austrian Galicia, Russian occupying authorities sought to Russify the province by an early form of ethnic cleansing. Germans, Ukrainians, and Jews were murdered, imprisoned, or driven into Russia by hundreds and thousands. Retreating Russians scorched the earth in a pattern that continued as the

THE EAST GIVES NOTHING BACK

campaign moved to Russian territory—where, again, German "settlers" were expelled eastward and their property destroyed, confiscated, or simply allowed to fall into ruin.[14]

Military experience shaped attitudes as well. From Tannenberg in 1914 to Riga in 1917, the Russian soldier acquired an image of being easy to defeat, but hard to kill. The battle of Gorlice-Tarnow in 1915 typified the Eastern Front. A handful of German divisions, using a comprehensive plan to pit high-tech, heavy artillery, and chlorine gas against large numbers of inert troops, tore open the front on a thirty-kilometer sector, captured more than 300,000 prisoners, and absorbed Russia's available resources, from anesthetics to ammunition. Somehow, nevertheless, the Russians retreated faster than the Germans could chase them.

In one sense, Gorlice-Tarnow and its aftermath merely confirmed the prewar General Staff conclusion that the possibilities of decisive military action against Russia were too limited to pursue. German forces always faced another day's march with more Russians at the end of it in their earth-colored uniforms with their incomprehensible ways and behaviors. Russians might surrender in masses, white rags raised on the points of bayonets, and form themselves into POW columns. Or they might fight to the end, with single machine gunners holding up whole battalions and men without rifles turning to rocks and fists.[15] Even in battle they were aliens, "not-like" Germans in a way different from French or British troops, with whom one might exchange family snapshots or play football during an occasional truce.

Rear security in the narrow sense was seldom a problem in 1914–15. The Russians themselves had evacuated potential partisans; most of the peasants who remained were determined to mind their own affairs. The German army paid for most of what it took. Its soldiers, still civilians in uniform with few case-hardened freebooters of the Ernst Juenger model in their ranks, usually behaved well even when intoxicated—a sharp contrast to many civilians' experiences with

THE JOURNAL

Russian troops, whose NCOs seldom tested their limited authority against a mass of drunks.[16] But ad hoc policies could not endure. At minimum, the German army needed to secure its communications and supply lines and, according to international law, protect the welfare of enemy civilians under their control. The military High Command East exercised direct control of the territories further east—the Baltic Region and White Russia—and the Germans organized Russian Poland as a "General Government" under a general officer who reported directly to Berlin. The foreign linguistic and cultural patterns of the occupied Eastern territories complicated the normal difficulties of occupation, which were worsened by the Russian policy of evacuating civilians when the army retreated. The Germans often had to form administrations entirely from scratch, without even the structure of minor officials, postmen, firemen, and clerks that their counterparts had to work with in Belgium and northern France.[17]

The German army had nothing that resembled a civil affairs department. They expected a short war, so the army front-loaded its organization and focused its rear echelons on the conduct of operations rather than on administration. As the German army tried to cope with the problems of occupation, it drew on its heritage of paternalism, the consequence of its self-assumed position as "the school of the nation." In peacetime, NCOs supervised the individual hygiene and collective order of their troops to keep the barracks habitable. Since messing was a unit affair, everyone was involved. Even officers, whose caste honor theoretically forbade them from dealing with tradesmen except at arm's length, boasted in their professional journals of saving a few pfennigs per ton of potatoes by buying wholesale, or of improving the Spartan government rations by cultivating battalion gardens.[18]

These domestic skills found ample scope in Russia. Germans of all ranks were frequently, perhaps even universally, shocked by their first visual and olfactory encounters with Poles, Russians, and

THE EAST GIVES NOTHING BACK

Jews—perhaps, above all, Jews, whose poverty lacked even the limited romanticism associated with the gentile countryside. Although Yiddish had moved far enough from its German roots that it was no longer a cognate language, many Jews could make themselves understood in German. Some of them regarded the relatively affluent, relatively free-spending *Landser* as ideal customers, but the best elements of a community rarely cluster around occupying armies. German reactions to the *Ostjuden* differed. Probably the most common reaction prefigured that of United States troops in Vietnam, with "kike" instead of "gook" as the contemptuous epithet reserved for people who sounded funny, smelled strange, and seemed ready to haggle over anything. Some German Jewish soldiers—and some non-Jews as well—came to admire the "authenticity" of a Jewish life lived by Jews who neither questioned nor apologized for their identity. Arnold Zweig emerged from his experiences in Russia as a Zionist. Victor Klemperer, on the other hand, found his identity as a German when he visited a Talmud school in Vilna. What he called "the "repellent fanaticism" of that environment convinced Klemperer, "...I did not belong to these people even if one proved my blood relation to them a hundred times over...I thanked my creator that I was a German."[19]

First impressions of any kind did not always endure. Officers and enlisted men often modified their prejudices when they fell in love. And fall in love, they did, with girls of every ethnic identity, from respectable "higher daughters" to whores with the proverbial hearts of gold.[20] Men learned to communicate in local languages, and invitations to dinner or for an evening of music in middle-class homes reminded some Germans of earlier and happier days. The perceived attractions of the rear eventually inspired the army to introduce an elaborate structure of "Soldiers' Homes," theaters, movies, and other officially sanctioned attractions designed, not merely to keep men on pass out of trouble, but to provide them with the best German culture had to offer, such as dramas like Schiller's

THE JOURNAL

Wallenstein's Camp, with its presumed appeal to soldiers cut off from home.[21]

As the front stabilized, the German army initiated what amounted to a civilizing campaign behind its lines. This progress of that campaign distanced the occupiers from a strangeness they found disorienting, and it imposed order on a cultural mixture as frightening as it was exotic. The campaign's vision of civilization reflected an arguably distinctive German work ethic, as well as a belief common in most armies that planned activity is inherently good.[22] But abstract justifications seemed unnecessary when, for example, a clean-up crew in Vilna discovered cobbled pavement under the many layers of debris in one of the city's main streets.[23] A similar project in Grodno unearthed a human skeleton. Since before the Thirty Years War, European armies had paid increasing attention to cleanliness, latrine discipline, and other forms of what might be called preventive sanitation. One officer put the matter bluntly: It was, he said, a question of "Soap. Only when the population has learned to wash themselves can we think of political measures."[24]

Wherever the Germans went, they scoured. Much of the anecdotal material focuses on the clean-up of the ghettoes, and it stemmed less from anti-Semitism than from the realities of ghetto life: the ghettoes offered concentrations of buildings and people, and therefore allowed some economy of effort on the part of German forces. Usually, however, the cleanups began in Gentile districts and focused on public spaces, markets, and *Bahnhofsplaetze*. Work details—increasingly German-supervised crews of local workers, for whom the jobs replaced those lost in the war—branched out from these locations to clean streets, disinfect schools and bathhouses, and establish public toilets. First school children, then whole communities, were deloused and bathed in mass events that were more effective than polite.[25]

German behavior is easy to dismiss as a bourgeois/Freudian obsession with cleanliness, or as symbolically prefiguring other kinds

The East Gives Nothing Back

of "cleansing."[26] Both characterizations invite exaggeration. At best German authorities took little account, for example, of the strong nudity taboos of eastern Jewish communities, or of historically conditioned concern for the safety of women in the immediate hands of any conqueror. But German health officials faced varying degrees of indifference and antagonism from individuals and communities for whom generations of Tsarist rule had made a bad joke of the concept "I'm from the government. I'm here to help you."

There was more to German hygiene than a principled uplifting of the natives. The Russian defeats and retreats of early 1915 resulted in a near-breakdown of public welfare and utility systems that had been barely adequate from the start. The deliberate evacuation of civilians from the fighting zones only worsened the situation. An already-overworked Tsarist administration could not manage these mass movements of people, and as a consequence, masses of the dispossessed wandered behind both front lines. Some refugees tried to return home, and others drifted into towns and cities where, cold and hungry, they stole food and fuel. Refugees with no access to toilet facilities polluted the water, and refugees with no opportunity to wash became lousy. With lice came disease. By 1915 typhoid and cholera were endemic in the Eastern Theater of war, and they soon were joined by a typhus epidemic almost medieval in its scope.

According to common cliché, World War I was the first conflict in which deaths in battle exceeded those from disease. In the east, however, the German army suffered almost four times as many sick as wounded.[27] German doctors, most of them from established communities in the Fatherland, were not prepared emotionally or professionally for the conditions they found in Russia. The common methods on which they relied to cope with typhoid, typhus, and their relatives were—and remain—the no-nonsense public health measures that fit the German army's institutional framework. They collected and deloused refugees, disinfected or burned their possessions, and confined their persons in

THE JOURNAL

abandoned buildings or open-air camps. Sanitary and hygiene regulations were at times enforced with persuasion, at others with fines and jail terms, and frequently with the application of boots, fists, and rifle butts, seasoned with barrack-room insults. Although such methods may offend, and typhus and related dirt-and-hunger diseases never disappeared from German zones of occupation, they at least remained manageable and did not explode into pandemics.[28]

The connections of this behavior to World War II policies that described Jewish ghettos as quarantine areas, and the propaganda that equated lice with death, requires little elaboration. These connections are complicated, however, by the widespread conviction among German medical and administrative personnel, who enacted the anti-typhus campaign of World War I and similar efforts, that they were doing good—albeit good *de haut en bas*—for people who were unable to care appropriately for themselves. Only among a few centers of advanced social consciousness, notably the army newspapers published in the larger cities, did a debate emerge over Germany's ultimate responsibility for the situation by invading Russia in the first place.[29] Overwhelmingly, Russians were cast as simpleminded, good-hearted primitives. One of the best examples of this kind of characterization emerged from the POW camps. A married prisoner who has been working for two years on a Russian farm returns to camp white-faced with worry. Her husband is coming home, and the family has grown a bit in his absence. When POW and muzhik meet, however, the Russian is effusive: "How can I thank you for all you have done? The fields are planted, the cows are giving milk—and the baby is a prize boy!"[30]

Most POW humor is compensatory; it highlights the stupidity of "goons" and "ferrets" to make up for the humorist's position behind barbed wire.[31] This anecdote reflects a deeper form of "colonial" discourse—a "colonialism" often reinforced by Germany's Habsburg allies. A photo in the Nuremberg City Archive shows an Austrian lieutenant smiling broadly, with a girl in local costume

The East Gives Nothing Back

perched on each knee. The accompanying letter, by a German officer, indignantly describes a Jewish merchant who offered his daughters to sweeten negotiations on a supply contract. The high-minded German refused; the Austrian eagerly accepted. The literal truth of the incident is open to question—although common sense suggests that Austrians, with their greater linguistic fluency and their more open manners, had certain personal advantages in what might be called "social" situations in the occupied East. The unexpected element is that the German officer denounces, not the greedy and degenerate Jew, but the Austrian, who is dead to honor and noblesse oblige when he agrees to accept the father's offer.[32]

Yaffa Eliach's "Tower of Life," an exhibit in the Holocaust Museum in Washington, D.C., that describes the shtetl of Eishyshok near Vilna, describes the Germans as caring for victims of hunger and disease, painting houses, constructing sidewalks, planting trees—even introducing the villagers to new crops like tomatoes and strawberries. The German occupiers receive credit for the inauguration of a cultural renaissance by supporting and participating in local art and theater groups. Eliach—who, it hardly needs to be said, is anything but Teutonophilic—praises the German army for their introduction of a cosmopolitan atmosphere into the previously isolated townlet, but even more for the level of "civil order and well-being" the army sustained.[33] Such encomiums were by no means unusual—and hardly calculated to reduce a sense of cultural superiority that was enhanced every time an occupier brushed his teeth.

German generals and politicians increasingly began to play with the East in a manner that invited comparison with Charlie Chaplin's "Great Dictator" and his balloon. It began soberly enough, when the High Command sought to develop and exploit the occupied zone's resources in order to make the Eastern Theater self-sufficient in routine contexts. Exploitation in the form of taxes and confiscations rapidly took precedent over the forming of infrastructure—not least because the military command included many more bureaucrats than economists, agronomists, or anyone capable of building rather than administering. Efforts to produce loyal German clients through education similarly unraveled as compulsion replaced resources. As plans failed and goals went unmet, "native" fecklessness and inferiority made handy scapegoats for imported German paper-shufflers.[34]

A Central European customs union, new thrones in the Baltic states and Poland, German colonization of lands vacated by wartime migrations—these and similar grandiose projects became, as time passed, the stuff of memoranda and working papers at the highest levels of the German command. At the Crown Council held in February 1918, William II discussed Russia's partition into four lesser empires. Hindenburg asserted that he needed the Baltic States to maneuver his left wing in the next war. Ludendorff suggested annexations that extended as far away as the Caspian Sea. Appropriately, the meeting took place at a sanitarium: The dialogue at Bad Homburg matched for absurd abstractions anything held on Thomas Mann's *Magic Mountain*. The discourse, nonetheless, reflected a developed understanding of the East as a source of power—perhaps, indeed, the mythic successor to the United States as a "land of limitless possibilities."[35]

The Russians themselves had indicated what might, for example, be done with population transfers. Their failure was to be expected, since the state system could not cope even with the prisoners of war its armies captured. But the Russians had broken down the "cakes of custom" that restricted the behavior of governments toward peoples. As the Russian revolution progressed, "spatial mobility"—e.g., refugee status—became a common experience.[36] German think-tanks between the wars, in particular the *Institut fuer Ostforschung*, would address in more or less abstract contexts the possibilities for managing population transfers, in contrast to the Great War's more random processes. The repeated deportation of Jews under the Third Reich was only part—indeed, merely a preliminary—to the

THE EAST GIVES NOTHING BACK

comprehensive resettlement of the east: a mixture of ethnic cleansing and ethnic domination.[37]

The dreams of generals, politicians, and professors foundered on ordinary Germans' reactions to the Russian revolutions of 1916–1917. The collapse of the Tsar's empire was accompanied by enough scenes of large-scale, bestial ferocity to enhance the sense of growing isolation felt by those Germans who had escaped repeated recruitment efforts for the Western Front. Russia seemed an enormous place, and, especially to men who, prior to 1914, had seldom been beyond the sound of their church bells or factory whistles, a forbidding one. In German forests the trees seemed to stand to attention. Russian forests, the uncultivated tangles of old trees that seemed impervious to human influence, suggested to German romantics that "forest" meant something quite different east of the Vistula.[38] Even in Russian towns, one felt a sense of open horizons.[39] Lieutenant Ernst Rosenhainer, a front-line soldier, described the terrain, the climate, and the distances as almost overshadowing the experiences of combat:

> I proceeded with the (third platoon) through the dense forest. Then there were more swampy meadows. With every step we sank deeper into the morass.... After that, the forest once again closed on us. In the end we lost contact..., and there I was, all alone with a handful of men. Our shouting and whistling was of no use—no response. Then all of a sudden nerve-wracking rifle fire...[40]

Perhaps the cultural activities Germans introduced to places like Eishyshok were successors to the fires made by primitive man to provide a focus against the dangers of the night. Russia was dangerous as well—both psychologically and physically. Edwin Erich Dwinger was captured as a junior officer and subsequently fought with the Whites. His "fiction-memoir" trilogy became a best seller in Weimar Germany, and it highlighted the obscene brutalities committed by both sides in the Civil War. Dwinger simultaneously sympathized with what he called the "real" Russia, and left a strong impression that what that Russia most needed was a strong hand in the service of order and justice.[41]

Dwinger, however, told only half of the story. Another, arguably deeper, set of German emotions found expression in the increasingly widespread myth of *Flintenweiber*. These were "Eastern" women, Russians and Jews, who carried guns and used their sexuality to trap unwary Germans in a variety of bizarre scenarios that say more about the psychology of their authors than any realities of irregular warfare in post-Tsarist Russia. The importance of the myth, carried back to Germany proper to become an important element of the *Freikorps* psychology, has been described as "woman as castrator."[42] A more developed examination of the myth might suggest "woman as transgressor"—or, rather, woman as a symbol of transgressive behavior in a land in which the very stones and trees seemed hostile. Apocryphal though she may be, the *Flintenweib*, like the woman sniper in the Vietnam War film *Full Metal Jacket*, embodies the fear of facing the alien and unnatural that finally overwhelmed German efforts to "civilize" the East with band concerts and delousing stations supported by bayonets.

In post-war Germany as well, Easterners played a direct role as symbols of entropy. Prisoner exchange was a major stumbling block in the 1918 negotiations at Brest-Litovsk. The Germans held almost a million and a half Russians, but only about a tenth of that number of Germans were in Russian captivity. The Bolsheviks insisted on a general exchange, but the Germans demanded one for one—the Russian prisoners had proved too valuable a labor source for the Fatherland's farms and estates to be released without a second thought. The result was an irregular process of release and exchange that even before November 1918 left increasing numbers of Russians and other undocumented eastern aliens to wander aimlessly across a Second Reich that had no resources to spare for them.[43] But it did have

THE EAST GIVES NOTHING BACK

prewar laws and regulations designed to control the peripatetic and the itinerant, in part to prevent the in-migration of foreign gypsies.[44] Individual German states, responsible historically for alien policies in Germany's federal system, responded to the new challenge with increasingly stringent deportation regulations and then with internment camps for foreigners whose expulsion was not immediately possible. Most research emphasizes the anti-Semitic, counterrevolutionary aspects of detention and expulsion and links these practices to a general hatred of Jews from Eastern Europe, who, according to right-wing mythology, had used the war to bring their radical politics and their dishonest commercial practices to the Fatherland.

It is not necessary to deny this perspective to suggest another dimension. Even today, international law recognizes the right of countries to control their own frontiers. Wartime experience in Russia had shown the compound risks of allowing the Brownian movement of peoples. A bankrupt and defeated Germany was not likely to allow foreigners to wander its roads and streets at random. But the consequences of restriction and repression should not be exaggerated. The Bavarian camp at Ingolstadt, probably the toughest of the detention centers, provided clean clothes and bathing and delousing facilities as a matter of policy for inmates whose percentage of Jews steadily declined in favor of Russians and so-called *Landstreicher*—the latter principally German.[45]

Historians increasingly depict the Great War as opening a door to the barbarization of Europe. That war, however, only unleashed the murderous potential—millions of senseless deaths, political instability, cultural collapse—which was latent in modernity itself. In so doing, it established a pattern of "industrial killing" still alive and well into the new century.[46] German actions and experiences in Russia thus invite interpretation as a precursor to the worst of Nazi atrocities in the East only a quarter-century later. Theweleit describes attitudes from the pages of Krafft-Ebing. Weindling speaks of a "German medical obsession" with the East. Aschheim describes a particular reinforcement of anti-Semitic stereotypes. There is merit in each position, but all suffer from overstatement. In *Epidemics and Genocide*, for example, Weindling comes close to denying the reality of epidemic disease by focusing disproportionately on the attitudes held by the Germans who combated it. Considered in context, two characteristics of the German army's experience in Russia stand out. First, the army's attitudes to the "Ostvoelker" developed within existing matrices and paradigms, rather than generating new ones. Those broad-spectrum attitudes incorporated indifference, amusement, and contempt, as well as fear and hostility. Primarily, they reflected a basic sense of cultural superiority, comprehensively reinforced by the way Germans in the East processed everyday events that lost any "charm of difference" with the passage of time.

A process of racializing the mind-set of alienated superiority clearly surfaced as the German occupation continued. Its consequences, however, were checked by the second characteristic of the occupation: It overwhelmingly involved involuntary participants. Whether killing Russian soldiers, shaving Jewish heads, or having sex with Polish women, the *Ostritter* of World War I were conscripted conquerors. If they were racists, they were, above all, homesick racists. They saw nothing in the East that was not exponentially better in Germany—and certainly nothing worth the effort of ruling over the natives for the long term. The concept of an eastern imperium may have attracted generals and politicians, but almost everyone else was marking time until he could board the freedom train back home. To the extent that racialization influenced thinking, it propounded a negative: to keep these aliens, their folkways, and their lice, as far away from Germany as possible.

The compound produced by the German army's experience in the East was unpalatable but not toxic. It would require reification by *voelkisch* scholars and Nazi ideologues before it became the stuff of genocide. More reasonable comparisons might be to the United States military's reaction to Vietnam—or, indeed, to the American

The East Gives Nothing Back

Expeditionary Force's near-contemporary processing of its collective exposure to Western Europe.[47] In each case, events suggest that mass armies of conscripts may be less than ideal goodwill ambassadors—but they are not always potential mass murderers.

NOTES

1. Cf. Holger Afflerbach, *Falkenhayn: Politisches Denken und Handeln im Kaiserreich* (Munich, 1994), pp. 211 ff.; and Ekkehard P. Guth, "Der Gegensatz zwischen dem Oberbefehlshaber Ost und dem Chef des Generalstabes des Feldheeres 1914/15," *Militaergeschichtliche Mitteilungen* 35 (1984), 75–111.
2. Dieter Pohl, "The Murder of Jews in the General Government," in *National Socialist Extermination Policies: Contemporary German Perspectives and Controversies*, ed. U. Herbert (New York, 2000), p. 91.
3. Walter Manoschek, "The Extermination of the Jews in Serbia," ibid., 164–165.
4. The best and most familiar examples are Vejas Gabriel Liulevicius, *War Land on the Eastern Front: Culture, National Identity, and German Occupation in World War I* (Cambridge, 2000); and Paul Julian Weindling, *Epidemics and Genocide in Eastern Europe, 1890–1945* (Oxford, 2000).
5. Omer Bartov, *Hitler's Army: Soldiers, Nazis, and War in the Third Reich* (New York, 1991).
6. Cf., among many possible examples, *Die Wehrmacht: Mythos und Realitaet*, ed. R-D Mueller, H-E Volkmann (Munich, 1999); and Michael Burleigh, *The Third Reich: A New History* (New York, 2000).
7. Barnet Peretz Hartston, "Judaism on Trial: Antisemitism in the German Courtroom (1870–1895)," Dissertation, University of California, San Diego, 1999.
8. Detailed and stressing Bismarck's Russophobia is Heinz Wolter, *Bismarcks Aussenpolitik 1871–1881* (East Berlin, 1983). Cf. as well Andreas Hillgruber, *Bismarcks Aussenpolitik* (Freiburg, 1972).
9. The images are from Viktor Hehn, *De Moribus Ruthenorum. Zur Charakteristik der russischen Volksseele*, ed. Theodor Schiemann, reprint ed. (Osnabrueck, 1966).
10. William W. Hagen, *Germans, Poles, and Jews: The Nationality Conflict in the Prussian East, 1772–1914* (Chicago, 1980).
11. In 1895, for example, V Corps was second at 8.87 per thousand, VI Corps stood sixth of sixteen at 8.17. "Zur Selbstmordsterblichkeit in der Preussischen Armee," *Militaerwochenblatt* 9, 1896.
12. This position is developed in the author's *Tannenberg: Clash of Empires* (Hamden, CT, 1991), pp. 58 ff.
13. See the vignette in A. M. Knox, *With the Russian Army*, Vol. I (London, 1921), p. 123.
14. Cf. Daniel Graf, "The Reign of the Generals: Military Government in Western Russia, 1914–1915," Dissertation, University of Nebraska, 1972; and Peter Gatrell, *A Whole Empire Walking: Refugees in Russia during World War I* (Bloomington, Ind., 1999), pp. 16–23. The statistics are from *Der Weltkrieg 1914–1918*, Vol. 2, *Die Befreiung Ostpreussens*, ed. Reichsarchiv (Berlin, 1925), pp. 325 ff.
15. These images are taken almost at random from Oskar Tile von Kalm, *Gorlice* (Oldenburg, 1930), pp. 48–85, an account of the first day's fighting.
16. John Bushnell, "Peasants in Uniform: The Tsarist Army as a Peasant Society," *Journal of Social History* 13 (1980), 565–576, establishes the limits of NCOs'

real authority—a fact that does much to explain Russian soldiers' behavior under stress during World War I.
17. Richard Cobb, *French and Germans: Germans and French: A Personal Interpretation of France under Two Occupations, 1914–1918/ 1940–1944* (Hanover, NH. 1983), pp. 4–32, is welcome for its common sense approach to the subject.
18. Dennis E. Showalter, "Army and Society in Imperial Germany: The Perils of Modernization," *Journal of Contemporary History* 18 (1983), 583–618.
19. Arnold Zweig, *Das ostjuedische Antlitz* (Berlin, 1920); Victor Klemperer, *Curriculum Vitae. Erinnerungen, 1881–1918,* Vol. II (Berlin, 1996), p. 684, 687. The best general treatment of this subject is Steven E. Aschheim, *Brothers and Strangers: The East European Jew in German and German Jewish Consciousness, 1800–1923* (Madison, Wis., 1982), pp. 143 ff.
20. The latter was the experience of that most unwilling of fighters for the Fatherland, the Alsatian Dominik Richert. He abandons his usual cynicism to tell the story in *Beste Gelegenheit zum Sterben. Meine Erlebnisse im Kriege 1914–1918,* ed. A. Tramitz and B. Ulrich (Munich, 1989), pp. 279–282.
21. Liulevicius, 139–144. At the risk of cynicism, it seems appropriate to note that for all the highminded enlightenment, VD rates in the occupation forces were consistently high. See *Sittengeschichte des Weltkrieges,* ed. M. Hirschfeld, 2 vols (Leipzig, 1930), I. 346–357.
22. Joan Campbell, *Joy in Work, German Work: A National Debate* (Princeton, NJ, 1989).
23. Liulevicius, 44.
24. Aschheim, 148.
25. Paul Julian Weindling, *Epidemics and Genocide in Eastern Europe, 1890–1945* (Oxford, 2000), pp. 90 ff.
26. See for example Theo Schwarzmutter, *Zwischen Kaiser und "Fuehrer:" Generalfeldmarschall August von Mackensen,* 2nd ed. rev. (Paderborn, 1996), pp. 111–113; and Weindling, essentially passim. The widely accepted argument (Cf. Aschheim, 178–182) that Jews were systematically treated worse than either Russians or Poles because of the occupiers' anti-Semitism depends heavily on respective perceptions of abuse.
27. Liulevicius, 22. It must be emphasized that this particular use of physical force was part of an escalating pattern of violence by Germans, especially officers, against "eastern peoples." Liulevicius, 107, sees this ideologically, as part of a larger program of control built on violence. Another possible paradigm is the pragmatism of the drill instructor, the straw boss, or the schoolmaster: A blow is a teaching device that makes an example and saves time.
28. R. Otto, "Fleckfieber (Typhus exanthematicus)," in *Handbuch der aerztlichen Erfahrungen im ersten Weltkrieg,* ed. W. Hoffmann (Leipzig, 1922), pp. 403–460; Alfred Cornebise, *Typhus and Doughboys: The American Polish Typhus Relief Expedition, 1919–1921* (Newark, NJ, 1982), shows there no significant differences between authoritarian German and democratic American approaches to the disease.
29. Even there ethnic solidarity with Slavs of any type was at generally low levels. Dennis E. Showalter, "The Homesick Revolutionaries: Soldiers' Councils and Newspaper Propaganda in German-Occupied Eastern Europe, 1918–1919," *Canadian Journal of History,* 9 (1976), 69–88.
30. This particular version is modified slightly from the one in Alon Rachamimov, "Marginalized Subjects: Austro-Hungarian POWs in Russia, 1914–1918," Dissertation, Columbia, 2000, p. 119.
31. Cf. Stuart I. Rochester and Frederick Kiley, *Honor Bound: American Prisoners of War in Southeast Asia, 1961–1973* (Annapolis, Md., 1999), pp. 416–417.

The East Gives Nothing Back

32. Notes taken by the author—albeit without noting the photo's specific location in the archive.
33. Yaffa Eliach, *There Was Once a World. A 900-Year Chronicle of the Shtetl of Eishyshok* (Boston, 1998), p. 57.
34. Cf. Aba Strazhas, *Deutsche Ostpolitik im Ersten Weltkrieg: Der Fall Ober Ost, 1915-1917* (Wiesbaden, 1993); and Liulevicius, 54 *passim*.
35. Cf. Holger H. Herwig, "Tunes of Glory at the Twilight Stage: The Bad Homburg Crown Council and the Evolution of German Statecraft, 1917/18," *German Studies Review,* 6 (1983); 53–63; and Winfried Baumgart, *Deutsche Ostpolitik 1918* (Vienna and Munich, 1966).
36. Gatrell, 196.
37. Michael Burleigh, *Germany Turns Eastwards. A Study of "Ostforschung" in the Third Reich* (Cambridge, 1988).
38. Liulevicius, 27–28.
39. Klemperer, 462.
40. Ernst Rosenhainer, *Forward, March! Memoirs of a German Officer*, tr. and ed. by I. Hance (Shippensburg, Pa., 2000), p. 20.
41. See especially *Between White and Red*, tr. M. Saunders (New York, 1932).
42. Klaus Theweleit, *Male Fantasies*, tr. S. Conway *et. al.* (Minneapolis, 1987), pp. 70 ff.
43. Gerald H. Davis, "The Life of Prisoners of War in Russia, 1914–1921," in *Essays on World War I: Origins and Prisoners of War*, ed. S. Williamson, P. Pastor (New York, 1983), pp. 162–196.
44. Guenter Lewy, *The Nazi Persecution of the Gypsies* (New York, 2000), pp. 4–5 makes the point that racial considerations played a minor role in legislation aimed less at an ethnic group than at a lifestyle perceived to be threatening and antisocial.
45. See most recently Dirk Walter, *Antisemitische Kriminalitaet und Gewalt: Judenfeindschaft in der Weimarer Republik* (Bonn, 1999), pp. 52 ff.
46. Omer Bartov, *Murder in Our Midst: The Holocaust, Industrial Killing, and Representation* (New York, 1996).
47. Mark Meigs, *Optimism at Armageddon: Voices of American Participation in the First World War* (New York, 1997), particularly focuses on the American experience as "tourists of war."

[5]
Rumania and the Belligerents 1914–1916

Glenn E. Torrey

As the intention of Austria–Hungary to utilize the assassination of Archduke Franz Ferdinand for a reckoning with Serbia became increasingly evident during July 1914, the Rumanian government manifested corresponding concern. It was widely believed in Bucarest, and not without reason, that an Austro-Serbian conflict would lead to the aggrandizement of Bulgaria, thereby threatening Rumania's aspirations in the Balkans and her security as well. Even more disquieting was the possibility that the Austrian action would touch off a general European war in which Rumania might become merely a battleground for the great powers. But for King Carol I, a prince of the South German branch of the Hohenzollern family, an Austro-Russian conflict was especially unwelcome. His personal inclinations and a secret alliance of more than thirty years standing linked him to the Central Powers. Until recent years at least, Rumania's isolation and traditional Russophobia gave reasonable justification to Carol's association with the Triple Alliance. But in the decade before 1914 the memory of Russia's past iniquities and even the indignation over the treatment accorded the Rumanian minority in Bessarabia had been eclipsed in Bucarest by resentment over Austria's support of Bulgaria during the Balkan Wars, and especially by anger over the plight of the larger Rumanian minority 'languishing under the Magyar yoke' in Transylvania. The latter, together with the Austrian province of Bukovina, now became the prime object of Rumanian irredentism. The role of Vienna in championing Bulgaria's cause at the Peace of Bucarest (1913) unleashed an outburst of Austrophobia which was still re-echoing in the Rumanian press the following summer and which prompted the first steps towards a rapprochement with Russia.

Carol became acutely conscious of this contradiction between his personal inclinations and the interests of his adopted land when he realized, even before the delivery of the Austrian ultimatum, that Russia would probably intervene. His first response, completely justified by the circumstances, was to resist the application of the *casus foederis* in his alliance with Austria. Yet as the war became a reality, repeated appeals from his fellow monarchs in Vienna and Berlin persuaded him to advocate a declaration of war on Russia at the famous Rumanian crown council convened in his summer palace at Sinaia on the afternoon of 3 August. With only one exception, this assemblage of cabinet ministers, elder statesmen, parliamentary officers, and party leaders spoke out for neutrality, arguing that the aggressive and unilateral nature of Austria's action relieved Rumania of any obligation. Carol accepted this consensus with surprisingly little resistance.

One cannot avoid the conclusion that Carol welcomed this opportunity to shift the responsibility for Rumanian policy to other shoulders. In explaining his action to the German and Austrian ministers, he insisted that he was 'true to the alliance through and through', but that it was impossible for him to 'draw the sword' against the will of his people. Prime Minister Ion Bratianu, fearing censure and possible retaliation, likewise stressed his loyalty to the Central Powers and implied the intention to bring Rumania into the war as soon as public opinion and military preparations permitted. He sought to sweeten the bitterness in Berlin and Vienna over the decision of the crown council by renouncing any intention of impeding a Bulgarian attack on Serbia. In conversation with the Russian Minister S. A. Poklevsky, however, Bratianu spoke in a different strain. Although he declined the Minister's offer of Transylvania as an inducement for an immediate attack on Austria–Hungary, he said that Rumania's eventual co-operation with the Entente was not excluded and asked that the proposition be kept open. Thus, from the very beginning, Bratianu began to practise the diplomatic dissimulation for which he became justly famous. His duplicity should not be exaggerated, however. The German and Austrian diplomatic correspondence reveals that as a rule it was the Central Powers who were victims of his deception. His negotiations with the Entente, though cautious and guided exclusively by Rumanian interests, were relatively straightforward.

While Bratianu was quick to see the opportunity as well as the danger for Rumania in the Austro-Russian conflict, he avoided committing himself during the first month of the war, awaiting the

RUMANIA AND THE BELLIGERENTS 1914–16

outcome of the great battles then under way on both the eastern and western fronts.

By early September the initial results were in. In the east, the Russian army had smashed a precipitate Austrian offensive and was in the process of overrunning Galicia and Bukovina. Simultaneously in the west the myth of German invincibility was being demolished at the Marne. The victories of Hindenburg in East Prussia went hardly noticed.

The military success of the Entente, especially the Russian invasion of Austria–Hungary, had an electrifying effect on Rumanian irredentism. Whereas a month earlier a Rumanian attack on Austria–Hungary seemed remote, if not unthinkable, the Russian capture of the Galician capital of Lemberg on 3 September marked the emergence of a strong interventionist movement. A number of former Russophobes, including Constantin Mille, editor of the important Bucarest daily, *Adevarul*, now joined in the increasingly loud and insistent call to action. Mille, who only a few days previously had declared 'Not with Russia! Not with Austria!', utilized the 'moment of Lemberg' to demand an attack on Austria–Hungary, 'Now ... Now ...!' These sentiments were echoed in the other major Bucarest daily, *Universul*, and in a host of less important newspapers. Virtually drowned out by the clamour of the warmongers were the voices advocating neutrality. Professor Nicolae Iorga's *Neamul Romanesc*, the socialist *Lupta*, the government press, and those few newspapers oriented towards the Central Powers.

The universities, the popular cafés, and especially the streets provided settings for other manifestations of Rumanian chauvinism. More than forty professors at Bucarest university, sharing the opinion of the historian A.D. Xenopol that 'Rumania has had no greater enemy in one thousand years than Hungary', sent a manifesto to the king demanding the immediate invasion of Transylvania. Self-appointed experts, mostly reserve officers, held forth in prominent meeting places, explaining with maps and charts the daily progress of the French and Russian armies. Street demonstrations, many of them organized by professional agitators, were the order of the day. Not a few ended with a march on the German and Austrian legations, where windows were broken and the occupants insulted. The government was obliged to provide these buildings with continuous protection, giving them the appearance of be-

173

RUMANIA AND THE BELLIGERENTS 1914-16

sieged fortresses; the Austrian minister even felt constrained to distribute revolvers among his staff. The activity of a number of emigrés from 'across the mountains', among them the talented poet and future Iron Guardist, Octavian Goga, lent authenticity to the irredentist cause.

The interventionist current flowed across party lines, opening a schism in the ranks of the Conservatives and disturbing the unity of Bratianu's ruling Liberal Party. Nicolae Filipescu, a leading Conservative and former war minister, embraced interventionism with a fervour which can only be described as fanatical, and sought to persuade his party to utilize this issue to overturn Bratianu. Party chief Alexandru Marghiloman succeeded in keeping the Conservatives committed to neutrality, although Filipescu kept the party in an uproar by continuing to advocate an attack on Austria–Hungary. Together with Take Ionescu, the head of the splinter group of Conservative Democrats, he assumed the titular leadership of the warmongers. The Liberal Party, on the other hand, experienced less serious internal tension. Finance Minister Emil Costinescu, whose partisan use of official powers quickly earned him the title of 'Minister for the Entente', maintained close contact with Filipescu and Ionescu. On the other extreme of the Liberal spectrum stood the party theoretician and highly respected rector of the university at Iasi, Constantin Stere, an implacable Russophobe. (A Bessarabian, he had suffered deportation to Siberia before emigrating to Rumania.)

The extent to which the Rumanian people as a whole sympathized with the interventionist movement is impossible to determine. At least eighty per cent of them were illiterate, unfranchised peasants preoccupied with a bitter struggle for existence. No assessment of their feelings can be found in Rumanian newspapers, which were almost without exception either personal and party organs or irresponsible scandal sheets, all notoriously susceptible to bribery. Like so much in Rumanian public life, they were controlled by a relatively small number of intellectuals, large landowners, business leaders, and professional politicians. The leaders of the irredentist movement formed only a minority of this elite, albeit an extremely vocal one. But because they represented honest Rumanian nationalism (as well as sordid personal opportunism) their potential strength exceeded their formal support; but they would have needed the co-operation of the police and the army to

CONTEMPORARY HISTORY

enable them to force their will upon the government. Despite the fears of many, including the king, conclusive evidence of serious disloyalty in either arm of the security forces is lacking.

The role King Carol was forced to play in the interventionist crisis was a tragic one. Fatally ill, under continuous pressure from his family and peers in Germany to join them in the war against Russia, he was thrown into panic by the increasingly articulate demand to sanction war against the Central Powers. Early in September he let Berlin know indirectly that the hostile attitude of his people might be reversed if Austria–Hungary would offer a 'boundary rectification' in Bukovina and internal reforms in Transylvania. Later in the month, as the agitation reached its peak, he conceived of a foreign threat as a means of dampening the spirit of the warmongers and asked Berlin to 'stir up' Bulgaria. Deeply pessimistic, he confided to the German minister that he might be forced to countenance a 'preventive occupation' of Transylvania. Finally, he prepared an abdication manifesto to be used as his ultimate weapon against the interventionists or, if that proved ineffective, as an escape from his dilemma. While there is evidence that rumours of the king's intention to leave the country, possibly with the crown prince as well, sobered some of the moderate Austrophobes, his threat had little effect on the radicals. They took heart from a report that Crown Princess Marie had vowed to remain and carry on the fight should Carol depart, even if her husband went with him.

Carol's suggestion that Austro-Hungarian concessions might reverse the unfavourable trend in Bucarest, though totally divorced from reality, found a sympathetic reception in Berlin, and the German government sent a sharply-worded request to Austria–Hungary to make the requisite sacrifices. Initially the Habsburg leaders flatly refused 'to enter into Rumania's blackmail', pointing out quite correctly that appeasement would simply exacerbate Rumanian chauvinism. But after extremely heavy pressure from their German allies and a plea from the hard-pressed Austrian military, the Habsburg government agreed to make an offer if Rumania agreed in return to 'march against Russia with all its power'. Bratianu received the offer cordially but insisted that it would be insufficient to reverse the trend of public opinion. However, he held out the prospect of co-operation later and snggested that the same concessions be offered for neutrality alone.

The German leaders, depressed by their reverse at the Marne, now demanded in no uncertain terms that Austria–Hungary placate Rumania, at whatever cost was necessary, arguing that an attack from the latter would mean the 'end of both imperial monarchies'. Furthermore, the Germans advised their ally, in the event of an attempted invasion of Transylvania, to 'be satisfied with a protest and let Rumania enter without opposition'. The Austro-Hungarian leaders, possessing a superior insight into the situation in Bucarest, refused to accede to the German demands. Count Stephen Tisza, the Hungarian premier, did agree to introduce minor reforms relative to the status of the Transylvanian Rumanians, but these were not announced publicly at that time because, as the Austrian minister in Bucarest, Count Ottokar Czernin, aptly commented, they would sound like a 'bad joke' and would be as ineffectual as attempting 'to extinguish a burning house with a garden sprinkler'. The Austro-Hungarian government instead stiffened its attitude toward Bucarest. Bratianu and Carol were reminded that any attempt to enter Transylvania would mean war. Czernin visited Filipescu, Ionescu, and Princess Marie, threatening the complete destruction and partition of Rumania if it attacked the Dual Monarchy, and was supported by the German minister, Baron Hilmar von dem Bussche. Bulgaria and Turkey both assumed menacing attitudes. Rumours that German troops were already being sent to aid Austria were allowed to circulate because, as Czernin remarked, 'if General Hindenburg were only suspected [of being] in Transylvania with one company. no Rumanian would step over the boundary'.

Bratianu, too, was embarrassed by the interventionists and took energetic steps to keep them from getting out of hand. On 25 August he ordered his cabinet to see that anti-Austrian demonstrations were 'dispersed with all strictness', and through the Liberal Party press he issued warnings against intemperate action. His neutralism was not motivated by Germanophile sentiments or indecision. On the contrary, the available evidence indicates that after the battle of the Marne, if not before, he came to the conclusion that the Entente would ultimately be victorious. Determined to use their victory for the completion of Rumanian national unity, he did not waver from this purpose even at times when the war

RUMANIA AND THE BELLIGERENTS 1914-16

favoured the Central Powers. He showed no interest in their repeated offers of Bessarabia and at no time did he enter into serious negotiations to share in their possible victory. Bratianu's diplomacy becomes comprehensible only when understood, not as an attempt to play off the belligerents until the course of military operations indicated on which side Rumania should range herself, but as a cautious, steady preparation for joining in the partition of Austria-Hungary. The premier's aims, therefore, were identical with those of Filipescu and Ionescu, except that he realized, as they did not, the necessity of careful military and diplomatic preparation. Rumania was certainly in no condition for war. The army, as its French adviser found even two years later, was 'admirably disorganized'; ammunition was in short supply and the country produced none of its own; the only war plan possessed by the general staff, drawn up in accordance with the commitment to the Triple Alliance, called for an attack on Russia. Bratianu also realized that it would be equally foolish to enter into action without proper diplomatic preparation. Like most Rumanians he was haunted by the memory of Russia's treatment of Rumania in 1877-78 (when his father had been premier) and he was determined not to commit Rumania to action again without far-reaching guarantees.

While avoiding military action in the fall of 1914, Bratianu did not hesitate to press ahead with the diplomatic groundwork for such action, whenever it might come. His first step was to give formal shape to Rumania's community of interest with Italy. Mutual reluctance to take the initiative had prevented a written accord during the first month of the war, but in mid-September Rome responded favourably to Bratianu's suggestion that 'it would be best for Italy and Rumania to proceed in agreement to the liquidation of Austria-Hungary in their favour (if liquidation there must be)'. An agreement providing for consultation and, if necessary, joint action was signed in Bucarest on 23 September. Bratianu hoped to make close co-operation with Italy an integral feature of his foreign policy, thereby enhancing Rumania's bargaining power with the Entente and obtaining assistance in resisting Russian influence in the Balkans after the war.

Simultaneously, Bratianu dropped his reserve in negotiations with Russia. He refused to be seduced into the war by an invitation from the Foreign Minister, Sazonov, on 16 September to act jointly with the Russian army and 'occupy without delay the Southern Bukovina and Transylvania'. Instead he demanded the same compensation in return for a Rumanian promise of continued neutrality. What advantage there would be to Russia from such an agreement is difficult to discover. Rumania's attitude would be determined exclusively by self-interest and this dictated the destruction of Austria–Hungary. If the tide of war turned irrevocably against Russia, a written promise to remain neutral would no more determine Rumania's policy than the alliance with Austria did now, in the moment of Russia's victory. Nevertheless, Poklevsky, who seems to have overestimated the strength of the Germanophile element in Rumania, succeeded in persuading Sazonov to accede to Bratianu's wish. In an agreement signed in St Petersburg on 2 October, Rumania pledged herself to remain neutral towards Russia until the end of the war and received in return a guarantee of territorial integrity, the recognition of her right to annex those provinces of Austria–Hungary inhabited by a Rumanian majority, and the right to choose the moment to occupy these areas.

This was a major triumph for Bratianu. Active intervention later was of course still necessary; no one believed that the Entente would actually reward Rumania without a substantial military effort on her part. But the agreement did mark an important step towards recognition of Rumania's claims. It outlined a minimal price for Rumanian intervention, one at which Russia would be forced to begin the bidding at a later date. Furthermore, the agreement of 2 October, like the Italo-Rumanian accord, took some of the urgency out of Rumania's decision and gave her time to prepare. Bratianu did not hesitate to use this argument with the warmongers, and to good effect. On the other hand, it would be going too far to argue, as has been done, that if Sazonov had stood firm in his demand for active intervention and publicized the offer of 16 September, he might have 'stampeded Rumania into war'. As a matter of fact, the Russian offer was widely rumoured in the Rumanian press and known in detail by those few Rumanians who wielded political influence. Bratianu, the king, the vast majority of Liberals, and a good many Conservatives were opposed to immediate intervention. It is more than questionable that their resistance could have been overcome by a Russian attempt to 'make diplomacy in the streets'. Furthermore, the Austro-Hungarian army, assisted by German reinforcements, began to stabilize the Galician

RUMANIA AND THE BELLIGERENTS 1914-16

front before the end of September. Even Filipescu and Ionescu soon agreed that neutrality was now necessary.

The approach of winter meant that Rumania would remain quiet for several months. All observers in Bucharest agreed, however, that after this time of preparation she intended to enter into action in the spring, almost certainly in association with Italy. This view was correct. In October, Bratianu dispatched an ordnance officer to western Europe to purchase munitions; in January, he ordered the Rumanian general staff to prepare 'an offensive against Austria–Hungary in Transylvania ...'; in February, he took the initiative in negotiating a more comprehensive agreement with Italy. All the while, in his contacts with the Central Powers, Bratianu assumed the role of loyal ally, impeded only by public opinion from placing Rumania alongside the Central Powers. While Czernin was not taken in, Bussche continued to insist that the premier's 'heart is on our side'.

Bratianu's position was eased by the death on 10 October of King Carol, who had acquiesced in the neutrality agreement with Russia but would hardly have been a party to a declaration of war on the Central Powers. His nephew and successor Ferdinand promised at his accession to be 'a good Rumanian', and, as he told a Russian diplomat, he intended to disregard his German background and act 'exclusively according to his duty and the interest of Rumania'. Lacking experience and indecisive by nature, Ferdinand appears to have welcomed the opportunity to turn over the direction of foreign affairs to Bratianu, whose policy had an influential advocate at court in the person of Queen Marie. Popular, spirited, clever – everything her husband was not – Marie emerged during the dark days of 1916–18 as the heart and soul of the regime. While her contribution to the determination of Rumanian policy during the period of neutrality is more difficult to document, it can hardly have been inconsiderable. The daughter of the Duke of Edinburgh, Marie was unwaveringly dedicated to the Entente cause, and urged her views on her husband and her lover, Prince Barbu Stirbey (Bratianu's brother-in-law and a close adviser to Ferdinand). Stirbey was used by the German legation as its secret liaison with the King. More than anything else it was his deliberately misleading reports which gave Bussche and, in turn, Berlin, such an inaccurate view of Ferdinand's intentions.

CONTEMPORARY HISTORY

Convinced that 'if Italy remains neutral Rumania is hardly to be feared', the Central Powers concentrated their diplomatic efforts in Rome during the winter and spring of 1915. In Bucarest they concentrated upon propaganda and bribery, attempting to create an atmosphere favourable to a change in Rumanian policy. The Balkan tradition of bribery, one of the most unfortunate legacies of Turkish rule, encouraged them to think that anything could be accomplished with money. An official though incomplete audit made late in the war reveals that in the years 1914–16 the Wilhelmstrasse spent over 40 million marks in Rumania. This was more than the amount utilized to foment revolution in Russia and dwarfed the allocations for all other countries. The chief recipients of this largesse were newspapers and political figures, although at the time it seemed as if almost every important public figure, and many unimportant ones, were profiting in one way or another.

Ludwig Roselius, a Bremen importer and reputed inventor of caffeine-free coffee, who had extensive business experience in the Balkans, was sent to Bucarest at the beginning of the war to take charge of the German operation. He had virtually unlimited funds at his disposal and quickly built up an extensive organization with the aid of the directors and staff of large German corporations such as the Disconto-Gesellschaft and Deutsche Bank, men with years of business experience in Bucarest and well-versed in the art of dispensing *baksheesh*.

Attempts to bribe Filipescu, Costinescu, and Ionescu directly proved unsuccessful. The first two were millionaires and beyond reach. Ionescu, on the other hand, had a tarnished reputation and was more approachable. Early in 1915 he negotiated with the Austrian legation through a middleman for a bribe of 30 million but backed out before the deal was consummated. A more successful practice was to offer subsidies for political purposes, thus lessening the stigma of personal corruption. According to German sources, Bratianu accepted a gift 'for the next election'; Marghiloman received money for political and propaganda activity; Carp was given money to found a newspaper to campaign for a war against Russia. Newspapers founded or purchased with Austro-German money included *Ziua, Moldova, Minerva, Seara*. However, public knowledge of the source of their support made these newspapers the target of popular scorn and even physical violence; their value to the Central Powers appears to have been questionable. A more successful approach was to subsidize individual journalists and editors to publish stories favourable to the Central Powers, or simply to headline Austro-German victories in larger type. Even *Adevarul*, the mouthpiece of the interventionist movement, was influenced in this manner occasionally. At the same time Roselius and his organization worked to impede the publication of pro-Entente newspapers by cutting off supplies of newsprint, ink, and even by smashing press equipment. In general, however, Rumanian publishing establishments profited immensely. One Bucarest firm printed both the irredentist scandal sheet *Epoca*, and *Ziua*, the organ of the German and Austrian legations. A wide variety of other outlets for Austro-German propaganda activity were found. A well-organized team regularly staged antiRussian street demonstrations. Not infrequently they came to blows with counter-demonstrations run by partisans of the Entente. The formation of a special wire service, the publication of a popular Sunday 'illustrated', the purchase of movie houses and the distribution of propaganda films, are but a few of the other methods by which Berlin and Vienna attempted to mould opinion in Bucarest.

But this indiscriminate use of money in fact damaged the already tarnished image of the Central Powers. The pro-Entente press took delight in exposing scandals involving Austro-German agents. In one *cause célèbre* late in 1915, one Rumanian and two Hungarians recruited by German military intelligence to destroy bridges in Russia, decided to use a portion of their explosives to blow up the homes of Filipescu and Ionescu. One of their number, quite possibly recruited by the Entente as a double agent, made a detailed confession to the police which created a major diplomatic incident. Roselius himself became so notorious that he was forced to return to Germany. Despite some accomplishments, his organization served rather as a happy hunting grounds for criminals, swindlers, and opportunists of all varieties. The Wilhelmstrasse was besieged by cranks like the one who argued that Rumania could be won for the Central Powers by sending 200 German *Koketten* to Bucarest. The authorities in Berlin commissioned too many of these adventurers, and Bussche warned his Berlin superiors against them. When their visits continued to proliferate despite his warnings, he threatened to resign.

It is not possible to document the propaganda activity of the Entente in such detail. Nevertheless, scattered evidence indicates that it was extensive though not, of course, on such a grand scale as that of the Central Powers. But in the final analysis one cannot avoid the conclusion that, despite the expenditure of enormous sums, neither side appears to have exercised a decisive influence on Rumanian policy.

Another attempt to influence policy by bribery concerned the Rumanian refusal to permit the transit of munitions intended for Turkey. The closure of this vital rail route between Berlin and Constantinople followed the Russo-Rumanian agreement of 2 October 1914, and indeed seems to have been the major benefit accruing to the Entente from this accord. The Russians applied continual pressure on Bucarest to keep it closed and Finance Minister Costinescu served as their watchdog. Bratianu answered every Austro-German démarche on the subject with the argument that acquiescence in the transit of munitions would provoke a Russian declaration of war. While this was an overstatement, abrogation of the transit ban would certainly have seriously estranged the Entente.

The Germans were able initially to smuggle through a small quantity of munitions after a liberal distribution of *baksheesh* among Rumanian railroad and customs officials. For each freight car successfully passed, the Germans paid 10,000 lei, but only 170 if the shipment was betrayed. This ceased when the Entente ministers assigned special agents to check all trains and Costinescu gave plenipotentiary power to an agent of the French legation for the specific purpose of monitoring the conduct of customs officials. After the struggle at Gallipoli began and the Turkish need for munitions became critical, German ingenuity increased. Munitions were encased in asphalt and concrete or buried in shipments of lime. False bottoms were installed in freight cars and munitions hidden in the lower compartments. All these methods failed, as did a novel attempt to ship explosives in beer kegs. Not infrequently the captured arms were put on exhibition, much to the embarrassment of the Austrian and German legations. No substantial amount of war material passed through Rumania until the defeat of Serbia opened an alternative route and reduced the transit issue to unimportance.

The Treaty of London (26 April) like the 'moment of Lemberg' some months previously, was widely interpreted in Bucarest as ushering in a new and decisive stage in the war. *Adevarul*, taking

RUMANIA AND THE BELLIGERENTS 1914–16

note of Italy's obvious intention to intervene, proclaimed on 28 April that the 'twelfth hour' for Rumanian action had come. A familiar pattern of agitation appeared: mass meetings, street demonstrations, and hysterical journalism. Filipescu and his followers made their long-expected break with the Germanophile wing of the Conservative Party and, if we can believe newspaper reports, the schism was accompanied by fisticuffs and revolver shots. Troops and police once again went into action to disperse unruly demonstrators, and the cartoonists pictured Bratianu as receiving his orders at the German legation.

Bratianu was, of course, not indifferent to Italy's example, having done everything to co-ordinate his policy with Rome. But despite two written agreements, the Italian leaders had never really taken the Rumanian government into their confidence. They proceded to work out their own deal with the Entente without consulting Bucarest. Ignored by Rome, Bratianu pressed ahead on his own and on 3 May presented Rumania's demands in St Petersburg. The price he demanded for an attack on Austria–Hungary was high: Transylvania, Bukovina to the Prut, the entire Banat, and parts of Hungarian counties along the river Tisza. The Russians were angered at the extravagance of these claims, regarded as irreconcilable with their own interests in Bukovina and those of Serbia in the Banat. This resistance was short-lived. On the same day as Bratianu's démarche, an Austro-German offensive in Galicia pierced the Russian lines at Gorlice, throwing the Tsar's armies into a catastrophic retreat. As they continued to give ground, Sazonov's resistance to Rumania's claims gradually diminished. Finally, in late July, he agreed to accept them in full, provided Rumania agreed to enter the war within five weeks.

Despite the Russian retreat, Bratianu had been determined to intervene in mid-June. On the 19th he ordered his chief of staff, General Iliescu, to prepare mobilization plans in anticipation of Russia's acceptance of his demands. But a month later, with virtually all of Galicia and Poland in the hands of the Central Powers, the premier began to have second thoughts. On 23 July he reaffirmed his willingness to sign a political agreement but now pleaded that he could set no date for actual intervention. The continued deterioration of the Russian position, highlighted by the fall of Warsaw on 4 August, soon made Bratianu unwilling to sign even the political accord. However, he promised to consider the un-

183

signed agreement as being in effect and reaffirmed his determination to prevent the transit of munitions for Turkey.

Although the negotiations of 1915 produced no written document, they mark what was perhaps the most crucial stage in Rumania's rapprochement with the Entente. St Petersburg's willingness to concede Bratianu's full territorial demands meant that any reasonable improvement in the Russian military position would make Rumanian intervention virtually inevitable.

The Central Powers also tried to draw Bratianu into an agreement in the summer of 1915. The German government, preoccupied with the threat posed by Italy's entry into the war and the munitions shortage at Gallipoli, thought it imperative to placate Rumania with Austro-Hungarian concessions. The Habsburg leaders considered appeasement dangerous as well as useless. The Foreign Minister, Count Burian, insisted that in view of the Gorlice breakthrough 'the jackal in them' would soon cause the Rumanian leaders to embrace the Central Powers. If not, he boasted to a German visitor, he planned to 'grab Rumania by the throat'. Bratianu was well aware of the danger in estranging Germany and Austria–Hungary at a moment when the Entente was impotent to aid him, and attempted to breathe new life into his well-worn role as a loyal partisan of the Central Powers. With complete composure he admitted his negotiations with Russia, but explained that the whole affair was a ruse to satisfy the 'war party'. The Austro-Hungarian leaders were not inclined to negotiate further with Bratianu, but the German government, bombarded with frantic pleas from Constantinople for the opening of a supply route, insisted that its ally seek to purchase Bratianu's acquiescence in the transit of munitions. Lobbyists were sent to Vienna and Budapest to mobilize support for an offer of concessions to Rumania. Chancellor Bethmann Hollweg invited Tisza to Berlin and gained his backing for a boundary cession in Bukovina and additional reforms in Transylvania. Burian, however, remained adamant and rejected the concessions approved by Tisza. Upon learning of this, Bethmann Hollweg decided to visit Vienna immediately. During three days of conferences, he exerted every form of pressure at his command to force concessions on Burian, but without success. The latter argued that a territorial cession was too high a price to pay for a promise of benevolent neutrality and pointed out, quite correctly, that Bratianu was unlikely to

RUMANIA AND THE BELLIGERENTS 1914–16

permit transit in any case, a view confirmed by Bratianu's continuing evasion of all attempts to draw him into negotiations. Finally, in response to a direct request that he name his price for transit, the Rumanian premier replied on 26 June that he saw 'no chance for an agreement now'. This episode marks the last attempt made by the Central Powers to deal with Bratianu on the basis of appeasement. Military developments soon permitted them to use a more peremptory tone.

The second half of 1915 saw the military initiative in Eastern Europe pass to Germany and Austria-Hungary. Their armies were deep in Russia and still advancing; the Entente admitted failure at Gallipoli and withdrew; Bulgaria joined the Central Powers in crushing Serbia. In these circumstances Bratianu wisely remained quiet. The Bulgarian mobilization, of course, touched off a demand by Filipescu and Ionescu that Rumania take counter-action, but the premier refused to heed their plea. It would be better, he told a few close advisers on 23 September, to delay action until the Entente was in a position to take up a general offensive, probably in the spring. Bratianu's inactivity earned him the censure of the interventionists, but they were still unable to mount a serious challenge to his direction of Rumanian policy. In response to repeated interpellations by Ionescu during the December session of parliament, the premier accepted full responsibility for his action but refused to discuss it, pleading *raison d'état*. With his party holding 80 per cent of the seats in the Chamber and 70 per cent in the Senate, Bratianu could afford to ignore his critics. On the other hand he was obviously worried lest the Central Powers, their triumph over Serbia nearly completed, now turn their armies against Rumania. This anxiety was heightened by the fact that the Bulgars made no secret of their desire to march into Dobrudja to settle old accounts, and by a chance remark of the Kaiser during an inspection tour of prostrate Serbia early in January, that 'Ruschuck is only sixty kilometers from Bucarest'. The words stirred a small panic in the Rumanian capital. Bratianu had no intention of submitting to intimidation but, on the other hand, he did everything possible to avoid provoking the Central Powers. When Octavian Goga and Father Vasile Lucaciu, like the former a Transylvanian emigré, stood as candidates for the Chamber of Deputies, he felt their election would be an incitement to Austria-Hungary and

CONTEMPORARY HISTORY

forced their withdrawal. But undoubtedly his most significant act of accommodation towards the Central Powers was to lift restrictions on the export of grain and oil.

From the fall of 1914 to the beginning of 1916 Rumania exported only negligible quantities of grain. Initially, restrictions had been imposed to insure domestic supplies, but they had been extended and tightened under Russian pressure and the influence of Costinescu. In August and September 1914, before the intentions of the Rumanian government were fully known, a German grain importer working with German diplomatic officials succeeded in buying up 750,000 tons of cereals. Only a small amount reached Germany before the imposition of restrictions; the remainder went into storage. This purchase temporarily eliminated an important means of applying economic pressure on Rumania and was generally viewed in Berlin as a colossal blunder. But the approach of the 1915 harvest restored this economic weapon to the Central Powers' arsenal. The Rumanian landowners, eager to profit from inflated wartime prices and lacking adequate storage facilities, demanded that the government permit free export, whereupon the Central Powers commissioned a special agent to harness this discontent for their own purposes, hoping that it might lead to the overthrow of the Bratianu government. During the summer and fall of 1915, Bussche and Czernin utilized this opening to promote the formation of a coalition government under the Conservative elder statesman Titu Maiorescu, which would initiate a policy of benevolent neutrality, permitting the transit of munitions, as a prelude to a declaration of war on Russia. The hope was a vain one; the Conservatives were discredited and the king gave full support to Bratianu and his policy of alignment with the Entente.

However, the agitation of the agriculturists and the military success of the Central Powers convinced the Bratianu government that it was expedient to sell grain. On 6 June Costinescu expressed willingness to do business and on 1 August the ban was lifted. But a high duty payable in gold was imposed on grain exports, which both moderated the effect of foreign sales on the domestic market and at the same time boosted Rumania's gold reserves. The Central Powers were far from happy about the higher prices and the outflow of gold, but their need for food made Rumanian imports imperative. On 27 December a contract for 500,000 tons of cereals was signed in Bucarest. The same agreement guaranteed

RUMANIA AND THE BELLIGERENTS 1914–16

export for the German-owned cereals stored since 1914. News of the Austro-German purchase touched off an attempt by the British government to forestall additional sales by pre-empting the entire remaining supply. Bratianu appears to have believed that it would be dangerous to provoke the Central Powers by agreeing to this, but he did allow the sale of 820,000 tons to reassure the Entente of his continued loyalty.

The German government was not mollified; the English sale was 'an unfriendly act from which Germany will draw the consequences'. Bussche, then on leave in Berlin, was sent back immediately with instructions to press for the dismissal of Bratianu. Despite an ominous warning that the prime minister's policy had brought Rumania's relations with the Central Powers 'near the breaking point', Ferdinand refused to sacrifice Bratianu. He had neither the desire nor the power to repudiate him. Although no ultimatum as such was actually delivered, the German démarche was interpreted in many quarters as a threat of war and Bratianu was worried enough to query St Petersburg about possible assistance. The German 'threat' was nothing more than a bluff. General Falkenhayn was firmly committed to the attack at Verdun and this meant that German troops would no longer be available for action against Rumania. German economic officials likewise opposed a hard line in Bucharest, insisting that early Rumanian grain imports were absolutely imperative for the army as well as the populace. A promise by Ferdinand that his government would end all 'chicanery' in meeting this demand for grain helped to melt German anger.

Thereafter, Rumanian trade with the Central Powers expanded rapidly. On 16 March, arrangements were completed for the purchase of an additional 1,400,000 tons of grain, and on 1 April a general trade agreement was signed for the exchange of goods other than war materials. Now it was Russia's turn to fulminate. Bratianu's reply to St Petersburg stressed the danger to his regime from agricultural discontent and insisted, less plausibly, that the grain sales would deceive the Central Powers about his true intentions.

To move the Austro-German purchases, totalling more than two and a half million tons, to the beleaguered populations of Central Europe was a colossal task, but it was accomplished in the few months of peace that remained, primarily via the Danube, but also on the famous 'cereal trains' organized by the German military railroad genius, Colonel Groener. The arrival of Rumanian grain gave a powerful lift to the hunger-conscious Central Powers. The production and export of Rumanian petroleum followed approximately the same pattern as for grain, although a shortage of railroad tank cars severely restricted its shipment to Germany and Austria–Hungary. Only 15 per cent of Rumania's oil production was exported in 1915–16, as compared to 65 per cent in 1913–14.

Bratianu had decided upon intervention, in principle, in 1914; he gained acceptance of his political demands in 1915; military arrangements, therefore, were all that remained in 1916. In regard to these, the allied attack at the Somme and the spectacular Russian offensive under General Brusilov went a long way towards fulfilling his basic precondition, a general offensive on all fronts. But he still refused to set a date for Rumania's intervention until two additional points were settled: an adequate supply of munitions and 'unconditional security' against Bulgarian attack. It was around these two issues that the final negotiations revolved. The Allies found it relatively easy to satisfy Bratianu on the first. Previously purchased munitions already en route were to be expedited through Russia, and in addition the Entente promised to supply 300 tons of war material per day to the end of the war. This promise was given and accepted without any real understanding of the difficulties involved in its fulfilment, as Rumania was soon to learn.

To immobilize Bulgaria, Bratianu and his military advisers had previously insisted on the assistance of a Russian force of 200,000 in the Dobrudja, supported by an Allied force of 500,000 taking the offensive from Salonika. When told in 1916 that the requirements of the Brusilov offensive would cut Russia's contribution to 50,000, Bratianu shifted his search for security to Salonika. The resolution of this issue, which lay at the heart of the negotiations over a military convention, delayed Rumania's entry into the war by several weeks. Meanwhile, the Brusilov offensive sputtered and stalled, so that when Rumania finally did intervene she contributed little to the Russian effort and suffered a military disaster herself. The Central Powers, who had intercepted a large number of Italian diplomatic radiograms concerning the Russo-Rumanian negotiations, made good use of this additional time for defensive

RUMANIA AND THE BELLIGERENTS 1914-16

preparations. The blame for this unfortunate delay has usually been placed at Bratianu's doorstep. True, he negotiated stubbornly and raised new demands at the last minute. But, as a recent Soviet study based on unpublished material demonstrates, the Allies were also responsible for the failure to reach early agreement. Unprepared themselves at Salonika, the British and French insisted that Rumania support their attack on Bulgaria with an offensive south from Dobrudja. This clashed with the Russo-Rumanian plan to remain on the defensive there while concentrating Rumania's power against Transylvania. The Allies eventually dropped their demand but irrecoverable time had been lost. As it turned out, their effort at Salonika was far from what Rumania expected.

The military convention and the political agreement were finally signed on 17 August 1916 in Bucharest. The most important terms of the first have been mentioned. Of prime importance in the second was article 4, which outlined Rumania's territorial gains, now slightly enlarged since the 1915 negotiations: Transylvania, Bukovina to the Prut, the entire Banat, and additional Hungarian counties bounded on two sides by the Tisza River and on the third by a line running just to the east of Szeged and Debreczen. Only one additional point merits attention. Article 6 incorporated Bratianu's insistence that Rumania be granted equal rights with the great powers in all peace negotiations. The emphasis which Bratianu placed upon this demand mystifies many commentators but seems entirely understandable when it is remembered that Rumania was excluded from the Congress of Berlin. The premier felt that a full voice at the peace conference was essential for the coming struggle to convert the treaty's promises into reality. Bratianu waited until 26 August, one day before the stipulated date for declaring war, before presenting the treaty to a crown council. And then it was to announce a *fait accompli*, not to seek approval. On 27 August, as scheduled, the Rumanian minister in Vienna visited the Ballplatz with a declaration of war.

Rumanian intervention was the logical and, by August 1916, inevitable climax of a policy Bratianu had pursued with great constancy since the autumn of 1914. He did not overvalue the Brusilov offensive and blunder into war, as has been often claimed. In fact, the immediate military situation seems to have played a secondary role in his decision. What seems to have been the case is

CONTEMPORARY HISTORY

that Bratianu became convinced that the last hour for intervention had arrived. To delay any longer would jeopardize the achievement of Rumania's war aims. He knew full well that he had exhausted the patience of the Entente with his repeated postponements and uncompromising insistence upon Rumania's full territorial claims. He believed that he had gone beyond the point of no return. There was no Russian ultimatum, as some believe, but Bratianu did recognize that Marshal Joffre's earlier warning of 'now or never' accurately represented the temper of the Entente.

Perhaps equally important in underlining the urgency of intervention was the widespread talk of peace. War weariness and the prospect of a third winter of conflict, had greatly increased the desire in all countries to end the bloodshed. The Austro-Hungarian empire was torn by internal dissensions, aggravated by defeat, hunger, and minority discontent. The government in Vienna was known to be dispirited and Hungarian negotiations for a separate peace were widely rumoured. German peace-feelers proliferated in 1916. Bratianu was certainly aware of the growing eagerness among the Central Powers for a negotiated settlement; there is some evidence that Czernin's secret memorandum of mid-July, conceding that the war was lost and calling for peace, even a costly peace, may have fallen into Rumanian hands. Disquieting signs were also emanating from France and especially from Russia, where Sazonov's replacement in July by Stürmer was widely interpreted as an indication that peace could thus be more easily achieved. Bratianu had good reason to wonder how long an Austro-Russian accord, which would be fatal to Rumania's aspirations, might be delayed. As he explained to his son a week before the crown council: 'The moment before us is decisive. If peace is concluded without us, we will be crushed between a great Hungary and a great Bulgaria. The world must be forced to see what we want....'

This last phrase suggests that Bratianu conceived of Rumania's intervention, in part at least, as a way of dramatizing her demands. With a premonition of what lay ahead, he argued in the crown council that even a military reversal would advance this aim. As in the case of Italy at Novara, he pointed out, there are defeats which are steps to victory. 'The majority of Europe sanctions our historic claims ... whatever the outcome of the war, the claims established

RUMANIA AND THE BELLIGERENTS 1914-16

will remain.' It was indeed through defeat, not victory, that Rumania authenticated her national claims.

Rumania's intervention, so decisive for her own national destiny, also had an important bearing on the fate of the Central Powers. The fact that it committed the Entente irrevocably to the partition of Austria-Hungary, thereby sealing the doom of the Dual Monarchy, is widely recognized. Not sufficiently appreciated, however, is the influence the Rumanian action exercised upon Germany's destiny. As Professor Ritter has recently pointed out so clearly, Rumania's declaration of war was the catalyst in a decision which proved momentous for German history. Bratianu's long record of indecision had led the German high command, especially General Falkenhayn, to believe, in spite of the revelations contained in the Italian radiograms, that Rumania's intervention would come somewhat later. Consequently, when the Austrians forwarded the news it fell like a bomb at German supreme headquarters. The Kaiser, who had just rejected a bid by Hindenburg and Ludendorff to unseat the Chief of Staff, was completely unnerved and now surrendered to the demand from Falkenhayn's critics that the war effort be turned over to the heroes from the east. The consequences of this event need no elaboration. Rumania's belligerency also seems to have deprived Bethmann Hollweg of a powerful argument against unrestricted submarine warfare and thus, it would appear, contributed indirectly to his capitulation on this issue. A full consideration of the influence of Rumania's intervention, and of her quick defeat, upon the peace negotiations of 1916-17, lies beyond the scope of this study but should prove equally interesting.

(*This article represents some tentative results of a longer study of Rumanian diplomacy 1914-18, which is being supported in part by grants from the American Council of Learned Societies and the American Philosophical Society. Detailed reference to the extensive archival material upon which it is based has not been attempted.*)

[6]

TURKEY'S ENTRY INTO WORLD WAR I: AN ASSESSMENT OF RESPONSIBILITIES

ULRICH TRUMPENER

ON October 29, 1914 the cruisers "Goeben" ("Jawus Sultan Selim"), "Breslau" ("Midilli"), and other ships of the Ottoman fleet under the command of the German admiral Wilhelm Souchon[1] launched a surprise attack on the Russian Black Sea coast. Four days later the tsarist government declared war on the Ottoman Empire, and the other Entente powers followed suit shortly thereafter. Turkey's participation in the war, long demanded by Berlin on the basis of the secret German-Turkish alliance of August 2, 1914,[2] thus became an irrevocable fact.

While the body of literature dealing with Turkey's intervention has been growing steadily, the historical record on this subject has remained controversial and confused. Lack of reliable documentary evidence and an array of conflicting testimony have made it exceedingly difficult to arrive at a balanced view of the situation. While some historians, notably in Germany, have depicted Turkey's intervention as a rather natural consequence of her alliance with the Reich,[3] others have emphasized that the

[1] Upon their arrival at the Straits on August 10, 1914 the German cruisers "Goeben" and "Breslau" had been officially incorporated into the sultan's navy by a bogus sale, and Souchon had been appointed commander of the Ottoman fleet. Although the two cruisers were given Turkish names, they retained their status as ships of the German imperial navy and will, therefore, be referred to as "Goeben" and "Breslau" in this article. For the background story, see especially Hermann Lorey, *Der Krieg in den türkischen Gewässern*, issued by the Marine-Archiv and the Kriegswissenschaftliche Abteilung der Marine (2 vols.; Berlin, 1928–38), I, 1–32; Wangenheim to foreign office (hereafter cited as "FO"), Aug. 11, 1914, No. 473; Jagow to Wangenheim, Aug. 11, No. 366; Wangenheim to FO, Aug. 12, No. 485; Zimmermann to Wangenheim, Aug. 13, No. 384; and Wangenheim to FO, Aug. 14, No. 499, German foreign ministry archives, National Archives, Washington, D. C., microfilm collection, ser. 3834, 3866, 3884 (hereafter cited as NA), frames 849127–29, 849133, 849283–84, 849471–72.

[2] On the conclusion of the alliance, which obliged the Ottoman Empire to intervene against Russia, see especially Carl Mühlmann, *Deutschland und die Türkei 1913–1914* (Berlin, 1929), pp. 28–43, 92–96.

[3] Cf. *ibid.*, pp. 49–80; Kurt Ziemke, *Die neue Türkei* (Berlin, 1930), pp. 9–38; Bernadotte E. Schmitt, *The coming of the war 1914* (2 vols.; New York, 1930), II, 431–40; Ernst Schüle, "Der Eintritt der Türkei in den Weltkrieg," *Berliner Monatshefte*, XIII (March 1935), 211–31; Carl Mühlmann, *Das deutsch-türkische Waffenbündnis im Weltkriege 1914–1918* (Leipzig, 1940), pp. 9–23, 241–54; Gotthard Jäschke, "Der Turanismus der Jungtürken," *Die Welt des Islams*, XXIII (1941), 9–12; and Pierre Renouvin, *Les crises du XX⁰ siècle; I. De 1914 à 1929* ("Histoire des relations internationales," ed. P. Renouvin, Vol. VII [Paris, 1957]), p. 40. See also G. Jäschke, "Beiträge zur Geschichte des Kampfes der Türkei um ihre

Ottoman Empire was pushed into the war by German intrigue. Authors holding the latter view have charged that even though some Turkish leaders may have co-operated with the Germans, the Porte was not really free in its decisions, owing to the ever present threat of German guns.[4] Some historians have gone even further in this direction by asserting that Admiral Souchon's attack on Russia was launched entirely without Turkish knowledge and consent.[5]

The availability of the German foreign ministry archives and other material now makes it possible to re-evaluate this question. The picture that emerges shows quite clearly that the thesis of Turkish subservience to the dictates of the Reich is no longer tenable, and that the Ottoman Empire was not "the toy" of a German admiral who "dragged" it into war by "a *fait accompli*."[6] Despite their subsequent denials, many Turkish leaders were fully aware of Souchon's plans, and it was through their machinations—rather than through the threat of German guns—that the break with Russia was completed.

From the very first days of the war, Germany's political and military leaders had manifested their desire for prompt Turkish intervention.[7] However, because of the rise of neutralist feelings within the Porte, Turkey's obvious lack of military preparedness, and her failure to secure an effective alliance with Bulgaria and Rumania,[8] Berlin was forced

---

Unabhängigkeit," *Die Welt des Islams*, n.s., V (1957), 1–2.

[4] See, e.g., Harry N. Howard, *The partition of Turkey* (Norman, Okla., 1931), pp. 110–15; A. F. Miller, "Vstupleniie Turtsii v pervuiu mirovuiu voinu" [Turkey's entry into the first world war], *Izvestiia Akademii Nauk SSSR*, ser. "History and Philosophy," III:4 (1946), 321–40; A. F. Miller, *Ocherki noveishei istorii Turtsii* [Outline of the recent history of Turkey] (Moscow, 1948), pp. 28–45; W. W. Gottlieb, *Studies in secret diplomacy during the First World War* (London, 1957), pp. 30–62; and Altemur Kilic, *Turkey and the world* (Washington, 1959), pp. 24–30.

[5] Cf. Ahmed Emin, *Turkey in the World War* (New Haven, Conn., 1930), p. 75; A. J. P. Taylor, *The struggle for mastery in Europe, 1848–1918* (Oxford, 1957), p. 534; René Albrecht-Carrié, *A diplomatic history of Europe since the Congress of Vienna* (New York, 1958), p. 335; and the more cautious statement of the same thesis in L. S. Stavrianos, *The Balkans since 1453* (New York, 1958), p. 558. See also Luigi Albertini, *The origins of the War of 1914* (3 vols.; London, 1952–57), III, 617.

[6] This charge was formally made in 1926 by the Angora Tribunal of Independence. See Emin, p. 75; and Kilic, p. 30.

[7] See Mühlmann, *Deutschland und die Türkei*, pp. 57–60; Moltke to FO, Aug. 5, 1914; Jagow to Wangenheim, Aug. 7, No. 328, NA, frames 848526–27, 848707–9; Bethmann-Hollweg to Wangenheim, Aug. 10, No. 350, German foreign ministry archives, 1867–1920, University of California, Berkeley, microfilm collection, ser. II (hereafter cited as "UC-II"), reel 12, frame 249; Zimmermann to Wangenheim, Aug. 19, No. 433, NA, frame 849851; and Bethmann-Hollweg to FO, Aug. 28, No. 26, German foreign ministry archives, 1867–1920, University of California, Berkeley, microfilm collection, ser. I (hereafter cited as "UC-I"), reel 13, frame 372. Cf. Gottlieb, pp. 57–58, for the assertion that German interest in Turkey's belligerency became pronounced only in mid-September, when "the beer-cellar dreams of another Sedan dissolved in blood and mire on the Marne."

[8] See Mühlmann, *Deutschland und die Türkei*, pp. 49–71 *passim*. While a defensive Turko-Bulgarian alliance was signed in Sofia on August 19, 1914 (August 6 according to the Julian calendar), the Porte remained uncertain of Bulgaria's future attitude. Rumania, in turn, remained cool to alliance proposals from both Turkey and Bulgaria. Cf. F. I. Notovich, *Diplomaticheskaia borba v godi pervoi mirovoi voini* [The diplomatic struggle during the years of the first world war], I (Moscow, 1947), 209–65; Wangenheim to FO, Aug. 7, 1914, No. 447; Aug. 13, No. 490; Aug. 15, No. 505; Michahelles to FO, Aug. 18, No. 83; Aug. 20, No. 84; Aug. 21, No. 86; Austro-Hungarian embassy, Berlin, to FO, Aug. 22; Waldthausen to FO, Aug. 30, No. 211; Michahelles to FO, Sept. 15, No. 140, UC-II, reel 12, frames 234, 306, 318–20, 335, 342, 346, 353, 408, 453; and Wangenheim to FO, Sept. 8, No. 752, UC-I, reel 13, frames 405–7. See also the explanatory comments in Wangenheim to FO, Dec. 17, No. 1644; Michahelles to Bethmann-Hollweg, Jan. 3, 1915, No. 3; and Wangenheim to same,

to accept the postponement of overt Turkish participation in the war.

Throughout the month of August, the military preparations for Turkey's intervention were pushed vigorously. By mid-September, several shipments of German military personnel and matériel had arrived in Constantinople, and German officers had been assigned to key positions in the Ottoman army and navy.[9] However, in spite of repeated German representations, the Porte continued its policy of procrastination. While the powerful war minister, Enver Pasha, was willing to fulfill the alliance obligations through prompt action, the grand vizier, Prince Said Halim, and most of the other cabinet members clung to the position that the time for such a step had not yet come.[10]

The issue came to a head when Enver authorized Admiral Souchon to conduct fleet maneuvers in the Black Sea.[11] In a cabinet meeting on September 16, the grand vizier protested that such action would lead to war and threatened to resign if the war minister insisted on going through with it. Since most of the other cabinet members sided with the grand vizier, Talaat Bey, the minister of interior and a leading member of the Committee of Union and Progress,[12] urged Enver to reconsider. Upon Talaat's assurance that "no minister would any longer oppose the departure of the fleet" once Turkey could be sure of Bulgaria's military support, Enver finally agreed to countermand his orders to Souchon.[13]

In view of Berlin's increasing demands for the opening of hostilities in the Black Sea, Souchon decided to call on Enver and the grand vizier in person. After telling the Turks that he had not come to Constantinople "to play the comedian," the admiral demanded that the fleet be

---

Jan. 24, 1915, No. 48, German foreign ministry archives, 1885–1920, St. Anthony's College, Oxford, microfilm collection (hereafter cited as "SA"), reel 72.

[9] See Lorey, II, 1–19; Mühlmann, *Das deutsch-türkische Waffenbündnis*, pp. 19–20; and Ulrich Trumpener, "German military aid to Turkey in 1914: an historical re-evaluation," *Journal of modern history*, XXXII (June 1960), 145–48.

[10] Although Said Halim had personally signed the alliance with Germany, he steadfastly refused to involve Turkey in the war "prematurely." His policy of procrastination was supported above all by the finance minister, Djavid Bey. On the division of opinion in the Turkish cabinet, see Wangenheim to FO, Aug. 6, 1914, No. 438, UC-I, reel 13, frames 325–26; same to same, Aug. 9, No. 463, *ibid*., reel 17, frame 139; same to same Aug. 11, No. 473, NA, frames 849127–29; same to same, Aug. 14, No. 499, *ibid*., frames 849471–72; same to same, Aug. 15, No. 505, UC-II, reel 12, frames 318–20; same to same, Aug. 22, No. 575, UC-I, reel 13, frame 362; same to same, Aug. 26, No. 609, *ibid*., frames 366–67; same to same, Aug. 30, No. 645, NA, frames 850596–97; Austro-Hungarian embassy, Berlin, to FO, Aug. 31, *ibid*., frame 850746; Wangenheim to FO, Sept. 3, No. 690, UC-I, reel 17, frame 205; and same to same, Sept. 8, No. 752, *ibid*., reel 13, frames 405–7.

[11] According to the plan agreed upon by Enver and Souchon, the Ottoman fleet was to demonstrate off the Bulgarian and Rumanian coasts and attack all Russian men-of-war it "might encounter." Wangenheim to FO, Sept. 13, 1914, No. 795, UC-I, reel 13, frame 418; and same to same, Sept. 19, No. 834, *ibid*., frame 438.

[12] In 1914, the committee included about forty leaders of the Party of Union and Progress, among them several cabinet ministers. The exact relationship between this body and the official organs of the government is rather obscure, but there is some evidence that the decisions of the Porte tended to reflect the majority opinion in the committee. Cf. below, pp. 375–80; and the conflicting interpretations in Mühlmann, *Deutschland und die Türkei*, pp. 51–52; Emin, pp. 96–102; Gottlieb, pp. 24–25; A. F. Miller, "Turtsia pod gnetom germanskovo imperializma v godi pervoi mirovoi voini" [Turkey under the oppression of German imperialism in the years of the first world war], *Istoricheskii journal*, No. 12 (1942), 12–16; and Gotthard Jäschke, "Auf dem Wege zur Türkischen Republik," *Die Welt des Islams*, n.s., V (1958), 206.

[13] Cf. Wangenheim to FO, Sept. 19, 1914, No. 836, UC-I, reel 13, frame 440; and "Anlage zur Besprechung mit Enver Pascha am 20.9.1914," papers of Ernst Jäckh, Yale University Library, Historical Manuscripts Collection, drawer 69 (hereafter cited as "Jäckh papers"), No. 9.

allowed to enter the Black Sea for "training purposes" and intimated that he might depart even without orders.[14] This statement promptly provoked another cabinet crisis. After short deliberation, the council of ministers reiterated its previous decision, but allowed, at least, the departure of two torpedo boats for the Black Sea.[15]

On September 20, Lt. Com. Hans Humann, a personal friend of Enver and a key member of the German ambassadorial staff,[16] called on the war minister to discuss the situation. He told Enver that Admiral Souchon did not consider himself bound by the decisions of the Porte, since his official incorporation into the Turkish naval service was only a fiction designed to mislead the Entente powers. As a German naval commander he was primarily responsible to the kaiser, although he would, of course, try to act in accordance with the wishes of the Porte. Since the Turks had hitherto failed to honor their alliance obligations and were even allowing Entente shipping to pass through the Straits, it was unlikely that the German naval personnel in Turkey would accept their passive role much longer.[17]

Meanwhile Souchon had sent the small cruiser "Breslau" into the Black Sea. As the German ambassador, Hans von Wangenheim, explained to the grand vizier a few hours later, the "Goeben" and "Breslau" had come to the Straits to serve the interests of both Germany and her Ottoman ally. Even though they were now flying the Turkish flag, the two cruisers had not relinquished their German character. The "Breslau" had departed for the Black Sea because it was contrary to "the spirit prevailing on German ships to be afraid of imaginary dangers." It was "outright shameful" that the Turkish fleet should hide from the Russians in the Straits, especially since the latter had given no indication of hostile intentions.[18]

Said Halim remained unconvinced and repeated his suspicion that Souchon was eager to provoke a clash with Russia. Wangenheim countered with the ingenious argument that the admiral would do nothing without the approval of the Turkish military high command—that is, Enver. However, the Turks should realize that continued procrastination would deprive them of any claim to preferential treatment after the war. Germany had the right to expect prompt fulfillment of the treaty obligations incurred by the Porte on August 2. The least the Turks could do was to demonstrate their "superiority vis-à-vis Russia through naval operations in the Black Sea," to promote the "Islamic movement," and to keep their army fully mobilized.[19]

Confronted with these demands, the Porte decided to make some concessions. On September 21, Enver notified Wangenheim that his colleagues recognized Souchon's right to "maintain German

---

[14] Wangenheim's dispatch No. 834, *loc. cit.*; Lorey, I, 43–44.

[15] See Mühlmann, *Deutschland und die Türkei*, p. 72; Wangenheim's dispatch No. 834, *loc. cit.*; and "Besprechung mit Enver Pascha am 20.9. 1914," Jäckh papers, No. 9.

[16] Humann, who had been commandant of the German stationary in Constantinople and liason officer between Wangenheim and the chief of the German Mediterranean Squadron (Mittelmeer-Division) prior to the war, became Wangenheim's unofficial naval attaché in August 1914. See Humann to Jäckh, n.d., UC-I, reel 345, frames 614–18; and Ernest Jackh (Ernst Jäckh), *The rising crescent* (New York, 1944), pp. 118–20.

[17] Besprechung mit Enver Pascha am 20.9. 1914," Jäckh papers, No. 9.

[18] Wangenheim to FO, Sept. 20, 1914, No. 848, UC-I, reel 13, frames 442–43.

[19] *Ibid*. Wangenheim's insistence on continued full mobilization was a direct reaction to Djavid Bey's efforts to bring about drastic reductions in the strength of the army. Cf. "Vertrauliche Mitteilungen vom 23.9. früh," Jäckh papers, No. 9; and Jäckh to Zimmermann, Sept. 26, UC-I, reel 13, frames 451–57.

TURKEY'S ENTRY INTO WORLD WAR I

interests, even if these collide with Turkish interests." However, any future operations in the Black Sea would have to be restricted to the "Goeben" and the "Breslau." If they became involved in an incident with Russia, Turkey would point out that she was "not identical with her ally." Enver added, however, that the Porte was willing to permit the entire fleet to depart provided that Souchon accepted command of a German naval mission yet to be created. Then, if an "incident should occur," the Porte would declare that Souchon had "overstepped his authority, that he had been forbidden to do anything against Russia."[20]

It is difficult to believe that the grand vizier and the other anti-interventionists in the cabinet were fully aware of the implications inherent in this proposal. Whatever their motives may have been,[21] we know that two days later the Turkish ambassador in Berlin, Moukhtar Pasha, duly communicated to the Wilhelmstrasse a request from the Porte that Souchon be made the chief of a German naval mission. As Moukhtar explained to Undersecretary of State Arthur Zimmermann, his government wished to formalize Souchon's *de facto* command of the Turkish fleet and to entrust him with the supervision of general naval reforms to be carried out by a group of German officers and technicians.[22]

The kaiser immediately approved the plan, and on September 24 Wangenheim was notified that Souchon's official appointment as a Turkish vice-admiral would be acceptable as long as his status as a regular officer of the German navy remained unaffected thereby.[23] Shortly thereafter, Souchon and Humann called on the Turkish navy minister, Djemal Pasha. The latter demanded to know whether the admiral had any intention of deploying Turkish ships without specific orders from Turkish headquarters. In their reply the German officers assured the minister that the Turkish ships would never be used without proper authorization.[24]

On September 26, British ships patrolling the vicinity of the Dardanelles stopped a Turkish torpedo boat and informed the German officer aboard that henceforth all Turkish vessels leaving the Straits would be treated as enemy forces. When this British policy was confirmed by the English ambassador, Sir Louis Mallet, Enver ordered the immediate closure of the Dardanelles to all foreign ships.[25] Several new mine fields were laid across the Dardanelles to secure them against both surface vessels and submarines.[26]

---

[20] Wangenheim to FO, Sept. 21, 1914, No. 847, UC-I, reel 13, frame 445.

[21] According to confidential information obtained by Humann about two weeks later, the council of ministers had decided that it would be easier to control Souchon if he became a full-fledged member of the Ottoman navy: if Turkey left her fleet at the disposal of a German admiral, she might be charged with "a violation of [her] neutrality," while as a Turkish admiral Souchon could be disavowed by the Porte as an insubordinate officer. See "Vertrauliche Mitteilungen vom 5. Oktober 1914," Jäckh papers, No. 10.

[22] Zimmermann to Jagow, Sept. 23, 1914, No. 533, SA, reel 77.

[23] See Jagow to FO, Sept. 24, 1914, Nos. 191, 193, UC-I, reel 13, frames 448–49.

[24] "Besprechung mit Djemal Pascha," Sept. 24, 1914, SA, reel 77.

[25] Wangenheim to FO, Sept. 27, 1914, No. 906; Sept. 28, No. 915, UC-I, reel 13, frames 461, 464. Cf. Lorey, II, 20, and Maurice Bompard, "L'entrée en guerre de la Turquie," *Revue de Paris*, XXVIII (July 1921), 277–78, who attribute the initial order to close the Dardanelles to the German admiral Merten and to the German general Weber, respectively.

[26] Wangenheim to FO, Sept. 29, 1914, No. 931, UC-I, reel 13, frame 469; Lorey, II, 21. A suggestion by the German shipping magnate Albert Ballin to block the Straits by sinking several large ships in the navigation channels was indignantly rejected by Adm. Guido von Usedom, who was in charge of all Turkish coastal instal-

Toward the end of September the financial problems of the Porte became increasingly apparent. Whereas previously the Turks had limited their requests for German financial aid to specific operations, such as the build-up of an expeditionary corps in Palestine (for an attack against Egypt) and the delivery of German war matériel,[27] they now began to ask for large-scale loans.

The opening request was made by the Turkish ambassador in Berlin. On September 30 he told Zimmermann that his government would like to borrow 5 million Turkish pounds (T£) in gold from German banks. Zimmermann pointed out that such a loan could be arranged "as soon as the Porte had actively intervened" on Germany's side. Moukhtar countered that a down payment, about half a million T£, should be made before the outbreak of hostilities in order to "strengthen the advocates of an active Turkish policy" and to prove to their opponents that the Reich was willing and able to support Turkey's future war effort.[28]

In his report to State Secretary Gottlieb von Jagow, Zimmermann pointed out that the directors of the Deutsche Bank were in favor of aiding the Porte financially. However, since negotiations between the bank and the Turkish government would necessarily involve Finance Minister Djavid Bey, well known for his sympathies with the Entente, Zimmerman suggested that the loan be advanced directly by the German treasury. To avoid excessive risks, most of the money, 4 million T£, was to be paid in monthly instalments *after* Turkey's intervention.[29]

Zimmermann's proposal was quickly approved by the German chancellor, Theobald von Bethmann-Hollweg, and the treasury (Reichsschatzamt) was ordered to make a quarter of a million T£ available for shipment to Turkey.[30] Wangenheim, who seems to have aroused Zimmermann's ire by several highly pessimistic telegrams concerning the situation in Constantinople, did not receive any notification of the loan approval for several days.[31] Instead, he was instructed on October 4 to explain to Berlin "as soon as possible" why Souchon had not yet been given a chance to attack the Russians. As Zimmermann wrote, conditions seemed to be "suitable for an offensive even without the explicit approval of the Porte"; in fact, it appeared that the "Porte *wants* to be forced into a decision."[32] To impress the ambassador with the need for bold action, Zimmermann dispatched a second telegram shortly thereafter, warning Wangenheim that the Turks seemed to be slipping away from Germany.[33]

Wangenheim, who had never shown much enthusiasm for Turkey's immediate entry into the war,[34] reacted rather

---

lations. See Zimmermann to Wangenheim, Sept. 28, No. 819; and Wangenheim to FO, Sept. 29, No. 924, NA, frames 852664, 852753.

[27] See Wangenheim to FO, Sept. 11, 1914, No. 785; Jagow to FO, Sept. 13, No. 140, UC-I, reel 13, frames 414, 423; and Trumpener, pp. 145–47.

[28] Zimmermann to Jagow, Sept. 30, 1914, No. 613, SA, reel 46.

[29] Ibid.

[30] Bethmann-Hollweg to FO, Oct. 1, 1914, No. 65, SA, reel 46.

[31] See Wangenheim to FO, Oct. 4, 1914, No. 965, ibid.; and "Vertrauliche Mitteilungen vom 5. Oktober 1914," Jäckh papers, No. 10.

[32] Zimmermann to Wangenheim, Oct. 4, 1914, No. 862, UC-I, reel 13, frame 476.

[33] Same to same, Oct. 4, 1914, No. 872, ibid., frame 477.

[34] There is considerable evidence that Wangenheim had grave misgivings concerning the value of the German-Turkish alliance. His efforts to involve the Ottoman Empire in the war were half-hearted, and he was by no means the reckless and brutal gambler depicted in Henry Morgenthau, *Ambassador Morgenthau's story* (New York, 1918), pp. 4–10. See, e.g., *Die deutschen*

sharply to these admonitions. He advised his impatient superior[35] that he considered the benevolent neutrality of the Turks "a great advantage" for Germany, while "the premature involvement of Turkey in the war would be a risky undertaking."[36] According to Wangenheim, the Turks were not yet strong enough militarily to face the Entente with any great chance of success. On the other hand, he was convinced that he could keep the Turks in the German camp[37]—unless it became apparent that the Central Powers were going to lose the war. In conclusion, the ambassador assured his superior that Souchon would strike as soon as the Central Powers had won a decisive battle "in Russia or France."[38]

During the following week, Enver intensified his efforts to strengthen his position in the cabinet. As he told Wangenheim on October 9, Talaat and the president of the chamber, Halil Bey, agreed with him that they would need the unqualified support of Djemal in order to involve Turkey in the war. According to Enver, Djemal had hitherto been rather faint-hearted in the cabinet while playing "the role of an enterprising soldier" in the Committee of Union and Progress. Enver proposed, therefore, to force the navy minister to take an unequivocal stand at a meeting of ministers and committee members scheduled for the following evening. In the event that Djemal failed to side with the interventionists, Enver and Talaat would provoke a cabinet crisis by demanding the immediate opening of hostilities against Russia. Should the grand vizier persist in his refusal to sanction such action, both ministers would resign. They were sure that "the larger part of the cabinet" would follow their example, especially since the "overwhelming majority" of the committee was on their side.[39]

As Enver explained to Wangenheim, a new cabinet would then be formed, composed of men willing to strike within the next few days. The war minister was confident that the empire was militarily ready to intervene. In fact, the only difficulty was the lack of money; he had to be sure of Germany's financial support once the Turks had started marching. Enver hastened to add that the German embassy could "keep the cash in storage until after the first battles."[40]

Wangenheim's reaction to these proposals indicated once more that he was far less eager for Turkey's intervention than his superiors in Germany. He wrote to Berlin:

My reservations concerning the premature intervention of Turkey still apply. I also do not believe that belligerent acts by Turkey in the Black Sea will suffice to provoke

---

Dokumente zum Kriegsausbruch, ed. Karl Kautsky *et al.* (Berlin, 1919), I, No. 117; Wangenheim to FO, Aug. 9, 1914, No. 463, UC-I, reel 17, frame 139; same to same, Aug. 15, No. 505, UC-II, reel 12, frames 318-20; same to Jagow, Sept. 24, No. 3, UC-I, reel 13, frames 528-29; and below, pp. 375-78.

[35] Zimmermann was completely unaware of Wangenheim's lukewarm attitude, since he knew nothing of the ambassador's special report No. 3 of September 24, cited above. In this report, which had been dispatched directly to German imperial headquarters, Wangenheim had sharply criticized the chief of the German Military Mission, General Otto Liman von Sanders, for his impatience with the Turks and had warned Jagow that it was inadvisable to bring about "a premature Turkish declaration of war."

[36] Wangenheim to FO, Oct. 6, 1914, No. 985, UC-I, reel 13, frames 486-87.

[37] According to Wangenheim, Turkey's continued collaboration with the Central Powers was ensured by the fact that the Porte could "do nothing against public opinion and especially against Enver Pasha, the man of the army" (*ibid.*).

[38] *Ibid.*

[39] Wangenheim to FO, Oct. 9, 1914, No. 1010, UC-I, reel 13, frame 499.

[40] *Ibid.*

uprisings in India, Persia, Egypt, etc. It should be considered also that transit through Rumania is blocked, perhaps for money shipments, too. On the other hand, I cannot guarantee that if we do not exploit the war sentiments of the Turks now, we may not later, after a possible German setback, be altogether unable to induce Turkey to strike.[41]

In his reply, Bethmann-Hollweg advised Wangenheim that he should "effect immediate intervention."[42] The following day, 1 million T£ in gold sovereigns was dispatched from Berlin. The railroad car containing the shipment was attached to a train carrying Prince Karl von Wedel, an aide-de-camp of the kaiser, and the Rumanian ambassador in Berlin, Alexander Beldiman, for a visit to Bucharest—Beldiman having offered to facilitate the entry of the gold into his own country.[43]

In Constantinople, Enver had meanwhile "forced Djemal Pasha to make a decision and the latter [had] completely moved over to the side of the action party," i.e., the interventionists. As a result, Enver, Talaat, Halil, and Djemal announced to Wangenheim on October 11 that Souchon would receive orders to attack the Russian fleet as soon as the ambassador could prove to them that he had 2 million T£ in cash or ingot at his disposal. The Turkish statesmen pointed out that payment could wait until after war had broken out, but that they had to have absolute assurance, "in view of Rumania's attitude, that the cash assets required for the conduct of a lengthy war would be available" in Constantinople.[44]

Once the 2 million T£ had arrived, the action party would confront the grand vizier with the alternative of collaboration or retirement. Said Halim "would probably give in; if not, a new cabinet would be formed the very same hour." Until such time, the plan was to be kept secret from both the grand vizier and Moukhtar.[45]

As a result of this discussion, Wangenheim notified Jagow on October 14 that an additional million T£ should be sent to Constantinople immediately.[46] Although the Reichsschatzamt was rather reluctant to agree to a further depletion of German gold reserves, a shipment of 900,000 sovereigns was dispatched from Berlin on October 17. Like the preceding transport, it was routed by rail through Rumania and Bulgaria.[47]

Unlike most of the German matériel shipments to Turkey in the preceding two months, both gold transports passed through Rumania without any delays and reached Constantinople in record time, the first shipment arriving on October 16, the second on October 21.[48] Although the

[41] *Ibid.* Wangenheim's reference to Rumanian transit restrictions was based on the fact that the Bucharest government had closed the borders to all German war matériel shipments on October 2. See Trumpener, p. 149.

[42] See Jagow to FO, Oct. 11, 1914, No. 254, UC-I, reel 13, frame 511.

[43] See Zimmermann to Wangenheim, Oct. 11, 1914, No. 924; Oct. 12, No. 931; and same to Bussche, Oct. 12, No. 528, SA, reel 46.

[44] See Wangenheim to FO, Oct. 11, 1914, No. 1022, UC-I, reel 13, frame 511; and the "Bericht über die Beratung beim Botschafter am 11.10. 1914," Jäckh papers, No. 10. According to the latter report, "these ministers *and their group in the Committee* [were] resolved to start the war" (italics added). Cf. the vague account given by Djemal Pasha, *memories of a Turkish statesman, 1913–1919* (London, n.d.), p. 129.

[45] Wangenheim's dispatch No. 1022, *loc. cit.* It is obvious from other dispatches that the interventionists did not fully trust the Turkish ambassador in Berlin. See, e.g., Wangenheim to FO, Sept. 21, 1914, No. 847, UC-I, reel 13, frame 445.

[46] Wangenheim to FO, Oct. 14, No. 1031, SA, reel 46.

[47] See Zimmermann to Jagow, Oct. 14, 1914, No. 742; same to Tschirschky, Oct. 17, No. 814; Kühn to FO, Oct. 18; and same to Reichshauptkasse, Oct. 18, *ibid.*

[48] Wangenheim to FO, Oct. 17, 1914, No. 1051; Oct. 22, No. 1076, *ibid.*

Russians had gained considerable information on the nature and purpose of the gold shipments, they were unable to prevent their transit through Rumania.[49] The successful completion of "this most tricky" operation provoked great jubilation in the Wilhelmstrasse, while the Russian foreign minister, Serge Sazonov, felt compelled to warn the commander of the Russian Black Sea fleet that a Turkish attack might occur "within the next few days."[50]

Sazonov's suspicions were well founded. One day after the second gold shipment had arrived in Constantinople, Enver submitted his war plan to the German imperial headquarters. As had been planned for a long time, the opening blow was to be delivered by a surprise attack on the Russian fleet. An order to this effect had already been drawn up and was to be delivered to Admiral Souchon within the following forty-eight hours. In addition, instructions to all Turkish naval commanders were being prepared to make sure that they would obey Souchon, "designated chief of the fleet by His Majesty the Sultan, in war and peace and at all times."[51] Furthermore, Enver's plan provided for defensive land operations in Transcaucasia and the advance of an expeditionary corps against Egypt, while the bulk of the Ottoman army was to stand by for action against Russia's southern flank.[52]

In Berlin, Zimmerman noted that in view of Enver's personal vanity and in order to strengthen his position vis-à-vis the other members of the Porte, the plan should be accepted without reservations.[53] His opinion was shared by the chief of the general staff, General Erich von Falkenhayn, who had the following message dispatched to Constantinople:

German Supreme Army Command agrees with Enver Pasha's operational plan in all points. Immediate naval action in the Black Sea and speedy execution of the operation against Egypt are still of the greatest interest [to Germany].[54]

Falkenhayn's message crossed with a dispatch from Wangenheim in which the latter gave warning that the Turkish situation had once again deteriorated. Faced with a message from Rome that Italy would be placed in a "difficult position" if Turkey abandoned her neutrality, Talaat and Halil had told the Austro-Hungarian ambassador, Johann von Pallavicini, that a postponement of Ottoman intervention seemed advisable. In addition, the Austro-Hungarian military attaché in Constantinople, Gen. Joseph Pomiankowski, had protested that a "premature intervention" of the Turks might easily induce Italy to attack the Dual Monarchy.[55]

Wangenheim himself was quite impressed by these problems. In fact, his lengthy report on the arguments against

---

[49] See *Die Internationalen Beziehungen im Zeitalter des Imperialismus; Dokumente aus den Archiven der Zarischen . . . Regierung . . .*, German edition by Otto Hoetzsch, ser. 2, VI:1 (Berlin, 1934) (hereafter cited as "*IB*"), 320-21.

[50] See the marginal comments on Wangenheim's dispatch No. 1076, *loc. cit.;* and *IB*, p. 320.

[51] See Wangenheim to FO, Oct. 22, 1914, No. 1087, UC-I, reel 13, frames 540-41. Cf. Gotthard Jäschke, "Mitteilungen: Zum Eintritt der Türkei in den Ersten Weltkrieg," *Die Welt des Islams*, n.s., IV (1955), 51, for the final version of the order directing the Turkish naval commanders to obey Souchon, issued under Djemal's signature on Oct. 25, 1914.

[52] Wangenheim's dispatch No. 1087, *loc. cit.;* and Mühlmann, *Deutschland und die Türkei*, pp. 101-2. Enver emphasized, however, that immediate Ottoman troop movements through the Balkans or across the Black Sea were not feasible under the prevailing diplomatic and military conditions.

[53] See Zimmermann's marginal comments on Wangenheim's dispatch No. 1087, *loc. cit.*

[54] See Jagow to FO, Oct. 24, 1914, No. 305, UC-I, reel 13, frame 544.

[55] Cf. Wangenheim to FO, Oct. 24, 1914, No. 1094, *ibid.*, frames 545-46; and *IB*, pp. 329-30.

Turkish intervention advanced by his Italian and Bulgarian colleagues seems to indicate that he considered a closer scrutiny of the whole question by the Wilhelmstrasse advisable. Even though Enver and Djemal had already worked out an elaborate plan for Souchon's attack on Russia,[56] the ambassador summarized the situation in the following cautionary remarks:

I have the impression that Enver Pasha himself doubts that the attack by Souchon with the Turkish fleet . . . will have any effect on Islam unless the advance against Egypt and the Caucasus is made simultaneously— which is impossible at the moment—but [I believe] that he wants to fulfill under all circumstances the treaty concluded with us and the promise given to us.[57]

If these remarks were meant to stimulate further thought in Germany concerning the opportuneness of Turkey's intervention, they were in vain. On October 25, Jagow wired the ambassador that "we are reckoning firmly on immediate action by Enver in accordance with the plan approved by our Army Command."[58]

Meanwhile Enver had succeeded in regaining Talaat's unqualified support for prompt action. Halil, on the other hand, insisted on going to Berlin, where he hoped to prove to the German government that Ottoman intervention would "do more harm than good" to the Central Powers. Enver, Talaat, and Djemal did not "want to refuse Halil's wish [to go to Berlin]," but they were sure that Halil would support intervention if Germany insisted on it.[59]

On the morning of October 25, Souchon received written instructions from Enver to conduct maneuvers with "the entire fleet" and to attack the Russians if he found "a suitable opportunity." As Wangenheim pointed out to his superiors in Berlin, he had "insisted upon a clear, written order from Enver to Souchon so that later on it will be impossible to charge us with having pulled Turkey by guile into a war she did not want."[60]

Two days later, on October 27, the Ottoman fleet steamed out of the Bosporus. At 3:45 P.M., Souchon informed his senior officers that he intended to open hostilities against Russia. The Turkish commanders were reminded that by order of the Ottoman navy minister they owed complete obedience to Souchon, and each ship was dispatched to a specific target area along the Russian coast.[61]

In general, the raid was carried out as planned. In the early morning hours of October 29, Odessa and other Russian ports were shelled and several Russian vessels were sunk at sea.[62] When the news of Souchon's raid reached the Porte, Said Halim and Djavid demanded the immediate cessation of hostilities. According to plan,[63] Enver obliged by sending not only an order to that effect, but also a "hint" directing Souchon to disregard the same.[64]

---

[56] As Enver explained to Wangenheim, the fleet was to depart for the Black Sea "as soon as possible." Careful arrangements had been made to allow Souchon freedom of action even if some members of the Porte tried to stop the raid. In that case, the admiral would receive wireless instructions not to open Enver's sealed order of attack, but this would be merely a formality. See Wangenheim's dispatch No. 1094, *loc. cit.*

[57] *Ibid.* Cf. Humann to Busse, Oct. 25, 1914, Jäckh papers, No. 12.

[58] See Jagow to FO, Oct. 25, 1914, No. 312, UC-I, reel 13, frame 549.

[59] Wangenheim to FO, Oct. 25, 1914, No. 1107, *ibid.*, frame 548; and Enver to Humann, Oct. 24, Jäckh papers, No. 11.

[60] Wangenheim's dispatch No. 1107, *loc. cit.* For another copy of Enver's order, dated Oct. 24, 1914, see Jäckh papers, No. 11.

[61] Lorey, I, 45–50.

[62] *Ibid.*, pp. 50–56.

[63] See above, n. 56.

[64] Wangenheim to FO, Oct. 30, 1914, No. 1160, UC-I, reel 13, frame 554.

TURKEY'S ENTRY INTO WORLD WAR I

On October 29, Enver and his adherents informed Wangenheim that they were giving the grand vizier and Djavid one more day to reconsider their position. If they persisted in their opposition to intervention, they would "be induced to resign," and Enver or Talaat would take over as grand vizier.[65] To create a more favorable atmosphere in the cabinet and the committee, the ambassador thereupon requested Berlin's permission to pay the Porte 1 million T£ immediately.[66]

Meanwhile the Russian ambassador in Constantinople, M. N. Giers, had called on the grand vizier to demand his passport, but the latter was unable to receive him because of "ill health."[67] "Toward noon," he, Djavid, and three other ministers announced their resignation from the cabinet. The Committee of Union and Progress, which had previously voted 17 to 10 in favor of military action,[68] was thereupon called back into session. Djemal informed the members that Souchon's operation had averted great danger from Turkey. He argued, in particular, that the Russian "Pruth," sunk by the "Goeben" off Sevastopol, had intended to lay 700 mines at the Bosporus.[69]

The committee then decided to send a delegation to Said Halim to urge that it was his patriotic duty to remain at his post. As a result, the grand vizier and the other four ministers withdrew their resignations.[70]

The following evening, Enver told Humann that the unity of the cabinet had been re-established. However, as a sop to Said Halim, the action party had agreed to the dispatch of a conciliatory note to St. Petersburg—a gesture that they were sure would have "no real effect." Humann protested that this maneuver was both dangerous and contrary to prior agreements. He intimated, furthermore, that a disavowal of the alliance by the Porte might force Germany to make a deal with Russia at Turkey's expense, but Enver insisted that his hands were tied.[71]

On November 1, the Turkish note was duly delievered to Sazonov. While conciliatory in tone, its effect was offset by the assertion that the clash in the Black Sea had been provoked by the Russian fleet. Sazonov replied that the time for negotiations had all but run out, though an arrangement might still be possible if Turkey expelled all German military personnel at once.[72]

In the meantime, the action party in Constantinople was working hard to keep Said Halim from resigning once again.

---

[65] *Ibid.*

[66] Wangenheim to FO, Oct. 30, 1914, No. 1168, SA, reel 46.

[67] *IB,* pp. 337–38.

[68] See "Vertrauliche Mitteilungen vom 31. Oktober 1914," Jäckh papers, No. 12; and Wangenheim to FO, Nov. 1, No. 1183, NA, frames 854856–59.

[69] *Ibid.* Djemal's assertion concerning the "Pruth" was apparently based on reports from Souchon and his chief of staff, Wilhelm Busse. Judging from all available evidence, these reports were false. Cf. Wangenheim to FO, Oct. 30, 1914, No. 1163, UC-I, reel 13, frame 555; same to same, Oct. 31, No. 1174, NA, frame 854747; same to same, Oct. 31, No. 1176, UC-I, reel 13, frame 568; and the protocols concerning the interrogation of the captured crew members of the "Pruth," signed on Oct. 29, 1914 by the German navy doctor Willrich, Jäckh papers, No. 12. The official German naval history (Lorey, I, 51) records that the "Pruth" was heading for Sevastopol.

[70] See Wangenheim's dispatch No. 1183, *loc. cit.* Many historians have asserted that the deliberations of the Turkish cabinet were deeply affected by the threat of German guns. However, the only artillery wholly at the disposal of the Germans were the guns of the "Goeben" and the "Breslau," and they did not return to Constantinople until October 31 and November 1, respectively. See Lorey, I, 52, 56.

[71] "Vertrauliche Mitteilungen vom 31. Oktober 1914," Jäckh papers, No. 12.

[72] *IB,* pp. 355–56.

As Enver, Talaat, and Halil explained to Wangenheim on November 1, it was essential to keep the grand vizier in office in order to prevent a possible split in the committee and unfavorable impressions both at home and abroad.[73]

The solution to this problem was achieved the very same night in a meeting of cabinet and committee members. According to a report given by Halil to the German embassy, Talaat told the grand vizier "in the name of the Party" that since Said Halim himself had signed the alliance with Germany, he "would have to assume responsibility for all the consequences" arising therefrom and that the majority of the cabinet would resign if he failed his "country and its allies." As Halil put it, Said Halim had thereupon agreed to stay in office,[74] but there is some evidence that he did not have much choice anyway.[75]

With the bombardment of the Dardanelles by an Anglo-French task force on November 3 and the outbreak of hostilities on the eastern and southern borders of the Ottoman Empire, Turkey's involvement in the war was established beyond any doubt. After three months of prodding, Berlin had finally achieved the desired result. In this development, the presence of German military and naval personnel in Turkey was certainly an important factor, but it is now clear that the Germans would not have succeeded without the willing co-operation of the Turkish action party. Enver, Talaat, Djemal, Halil, and their supporters in the Committee of Union and Progress can no longer be considered the unsuspecting or helpless tools of the Reich. Souchon's attack on Russia was not an independent coup, but planned in close collaboration with several members of the Porte and executed upon explicit orders from the Ottoman war minister.

STATE UNIVERSITY OF IOWA

---

[73] Wangenheim to FO, Nov. 2, 1914, No. 1205, UC-I, reel 13, frames 571–72. Judging from this dispatch, Djavid was still a member of the cabinet at this time. Although he and three other ministers resigned from their posts shortly thereafter, it should be pointed out that Djavid's influence on Turkish governmental policies continued virtually unabated. Concerning his activities during the following months, see the vast documentation in SA, reels 46, 47; and Gottlieb, pp. 110–12. See also the Constantinople paper *Le Moniteur Oriental*, Nov. 3 and 4, 1914, for the brief announcements regarding the personnel changes in the cabinet.

[74] See Wangenheim's dispatch No. 1205, *loc. cit.* Cf. Djemal, pp. 131–33, for his version of what took place in the cabinet "the day Russia, France, and England announced to the Ottoman Government the opening of hostilities."

[75] According to the "confidential" information received by Humann on Nov. 3, the committee ordered Said Halim "very categorically" to stay at his post, and "the grand visier obeyed this order for fear of his life." See "Vertrauliche Mitteilungen vom 3. November 1914," Jäckh papers, No. 13.

Part II
Home Fronts

[7]

SHARING SCARCITY: BREAD RATIONING AND THE FIRST WORLD WAR IN BERLIN, 1914–1923

By Keith Allen   American University

The destruction of local bread rationing center #46 made a lasting impression on its daytime inhabitants. Those first to arrive at the scene on the drizzling October morning found splinters strewn across the sidewalk and a gaping hole where the door had been. The interior of the normally meticulously-arranged office looked even worse. Using a crowbar to pry open doors, desks, and cabinets, the burglar had demolished almost everything in the office. All that was left was a tattered trail of expired rationing coupons.[1]

As the immediacy of the intrusion faded, thoughts turned to the individual behind the act. The burglar had struck sometime in the late afternoon and had not even bothered to draw the curtains. Cigarette butts left next to the office manager's desk indicated that the scoundrel had felt comfortable at the scene of the crime. The circumstantial evidence pointed to an inside job, a suspicion the office manager felt confirmed by a third clue, the perpetrator's unforced entry to the building.

The office manager could raise the specter of foul play without fearing retribution. Acting on orders from above, local #46's bread boss had taken the next week's bread ration-cards home with him after work.[2] The beleaguered chief knew that Berlin's bread commission offices were often burglarized, particularly during the uncommonly harsh winter of 1916/17. As the crime wave took on new dimensions, metropolitan officials not only sent cards home with the boss. They also raised fines, lengthened jail sentences, and requested that subordinates carry coupons to the local police precinct. Steglitz's bread boss boasted to his superiors that he had the problem well in hand: his ration-card cases were forged of iron, tripled-locked, and bolted to the floor.[3]

The break-ins at Berlin's local rationing centers demonstrate one, though by no means the most important, consequence of wartime scarcity: hard times engendered conflict. Burglary and triple-locked iron cases were just the beginning. The inability of the government to provide citizens with an acceptable quantity of foodstuffs at reasonable prices fueled the growth of black markets (though rarely in breadstuffs) and exacerbated urban-rural tensions.[4] Wartime shortages tore other holes in the social fabric, straining relations between bureaucracy, on the one hand, and labor, commerce, women's groups, and the consuming public, on the other.

These social tensions have led historians to judge Germany's food supply system a failure, and the bureaucrats who managed it inept.[5] According to Gerald Feldman, the inability of provincial and national authorities to cope with the problems of modern war not only hurt ordinary citizens. "Slow moving, ponderous and bureaucratic," the German wartime governments' "absence of adequate leadership" also contributed to illiberalism's postwar ascendancy.[6]

First articulated over thirty years ago, Feldman's account of German food policy during the First World War remains the standard interpretation. Most recently, Thierry Bonzon and Belinda Davis have argued that " ... [from late 1915 on] authorities [in Berlin] seemed to have breached the pact between society and state, a social contract of loyalty and sacrifice in return for adequate and fairly apportioned food supplies. The rupture of this informal but palpable understanding undermined the authority and legitimacy of the state."[7] "Problems of food supply and distribution," Bonzon and Davis conclude, "clearly played a decisive role in the unraveling of the German war effort in the last two years of the war."[8] Bonzon, Davis, Feldman, and Jürgen Kocka all agree that the ensuing sharpening of class tensions—and the marked unwillingness of wartime authorities to embrace compensatory reforms—was a primary determining factor in the collapse of state authority in 1918.[9]

In fact, the line of conflict first drawn by Feldman between army, industry and labor on the one side, and an isolated, inept bureaucracy on the other, never characterized the wartime provision of the most important foodstuff in urban Germany. Rather, a coalition of particular interests—local bureaucrats, trade union leaders, women's groups, and favored consumers—laid the groundwork for the nation's remarkable social cohesion in the face of total war. Despite setbacks, municipal rationing authorities nonetheless diffused tensions produced by the First World War. As evidence from the nation's capital suggests, when faced with the choice to support the central authority or to look out for themselves, Berliners favored cooperation over conflict.[10]

Rationing of bread was introduced in Berlin in January, 1915 and extended to the rest of the country six months later. Rationing worked in the capital because city fathers persuaded citizens to accept their burden-sharing scheme. While Germany's soldiers were losing the war on the battlefield, the nation's bureaucrats were winning the home front with a subtle combination of patriotic appeal, collective bargaining agreements, voluntary assistance, and material concessions. Policies that demanded great sacrifices were never popular, and, as the story of the break-in at local bread rationing office #46 illustrates, they were challenged. When war broke out in the summer of 1914, Britain could call upon its command of the seas, the empires of Russia and Austro-Hungary, their vast surpluses of agricultural resources.[11] Germany's participation in total war, however, required unity of authority and leadership: a sense of common purpose forged in efforts to provision households with a steady supply of bread, the main element of every German meal.

The First World War began in German cities with unprecedented demonstrations of social harmony. The surge of patriotic fervor made possible the most important piece of wartime social policy: the regulation of the food supply. In Berlin, in December's last days a hastily summoned municipal war commission, including representatives from the city's upper-and lower-chambers of government, consumer cooperativists, captains of local industry, and leaders of the local bakers' federation, sanctioned the decision of the municipal government to create a Bread Supply Office.[12] Staffed by ten city councilors and five representatives from the Mayor's office, the "Mixed Deputation for the Supply of Berlin with Foodstuffs" acted largely independently of the government that created it.[13] Three prominent figures at City Hall ran the Department as their own private fiefdom: Georg Simonsohn, architect of the city's bread rationing scheme and manager of the Bread Supply Office until 1920; Adolf Wermuth, former imperial

SHARING SCARCITY

secretary of the treasury and lord mayor of Berlin; and Erich Simm, Simonsohn's closest confident and a senior administrator in Berlin's municipal government. In an unparalleled attempt to shore up the home meal, German civil authorities assumed direct responsibility for the price, quantity, and quality of grain stores.

Twelve civil servants and sixty-five assistants staffed the office that sought to meet the basic dietary needs of the capital's 3.6 million inhabitants.[14] Large enough to generate the steady stream of narrow paper strips that provided Berliners with food, the structure proved far too small to contain the coupons once they completed their migration through the city's tenement-house apartments and its bustling bakeries. The scale of the problem necessitated a larger staff and more space. In the next few years, town fathers would acquire real estate in the city's expensive administrative quarter and employ a battery of high-priced assistants. By the end of the war, twenty-two high-ranking civil servants, over eighteen hundred administrative assistants, and two hundred and forty five volunteers checked the weight of flour sacks, distributed cards, and inspected the purity of bread. The customer service section alone, one of the Bread Office's many concessions to consumer goodwill, employed over two hundred people.[15]

Every city in Germany had a somewhat different ration, depending on such considerations as its size, proximity to rural areas, municipal competence, and location within the region. In Berlin, acting on guidelines established by imperial authorities, the city's Bread Supply Office initially gave people over the age of eighteen coupons that permitted them to buy 1950 grams of bread, or the equivalent amount of flour, each week. The Office distributed ration cards on a weekly basis, usually on the Thursday before the start of the next rationing week. Beginning on the following Monday, consumers could exchange coupons at bakery and pastry shops, paying 80 pfennig for either a ration of bread or an equivalent amount of flour. Most preferred bread to flour. Even before the war, the vast majority of Berlin housewives had ceased to bake bread on a regular basis, preferring instead to purchase their loaves, cakes, and sweets at the corner bakery. These purchases constituted a substantial portion of most Berliners' incomes. An average German household in 1914 (with its two adults, three children, and combined annual income of one thousand marks) spent nearly 12% of its income on bread.[16]

To the bakers fell most of the responsibility, if little of the glory, for making the new commercial regime work. Bakers were required to submit new ration coupons weekly, along with an itemized flour inventory book, to their local bread commission office. While the bread maker anxiously watched, an official weighed his bloated burlap coupon sacks. If the scale confirmed that he had commerced virtuously, the baker received another ration of raw materials for the coming week. Restaurateurs had it easier, at least at first. Much to the chagrin of pastry makers, the owners of the city's restaurants, cafés, and hotels could serve customers without the bother of cards. Proprietors were merely required to record the purchases of bread. By October 1916, however, even most purveyors of prepared foods had to meet the strict codes of commercial conduct.[17]

Despite all of the new adjustments required, the first weeks of rationing worked surprisingly well. Bakers accustomed themselves to the changes, and consumers set aside skepticism to do their part for the boys at the front. At the prompting of city officials, Berlin women not only agreed to get by with roughly a third less bread per week, but also voluntarily gave up bread made from imported white flour in favor of home-grown rye. Convincing Berliners to bake with rye flour was no mean feat, for as those who did not already know soon found out, the coarse grain could only be used to bake bread.[18]

The enthusiasm that characterized the first months of the controlled economy, however, slowly gave way to the more melancholy mood of fall and winter. Few people had predicted a long war, and virtually no one had expected the hardship the war entailed to last an entire year, much less two, three, and four. No plan existed to replace the intricate network of shops, warehouses, and processing facilities that had delivered bread to the peacetime masses, and there was little room in the city or in the largely urbanized surrounding area to produce grain. The new rationing measures exacerbated relations between city and countryside, as farmers, despite their best efforts, were unable to compensate for the nation's basic dependency on foreign foodstuffs. When farmers hid stores, refused to slaughter animals, or sold grain on the black market, urban bureaucrats had to adjust.[19]

Much like their counterparts on the general staff, the officials of the city's bread commissions were forced to learn by doing, with predictable results. After a reasonably harmonious first twelve months, the second year brought attempts to prescribe the sizes, shapes, weights, and ingredients of pastries and other bread stuffs. The Bread Office issued stern instructions not to mix foreign with domestic flours. In cases where the grains had nonetheless been combined, pastry makers were instructed to place a sign in the window warning customers that the proprietor offered "baked goods made from foreign flour."[20]

The year's most notable fiasco followed the attempt of city authorities to replace the long-cherished white-bread breakfast roll with a standard loaf, produced from equal portions of wheat and rye. Bruno Haase, a private citizen from the wealthy district of Charlottenburg, expressed the popular response: "The intention of the city government to do away with the white bread rolls horrifies me. For health reasons, I have been a white-bread eater all of the 53 years of my life. If the city goes ahead with its plans for the introduction of a 'standard loaf,' there is no way I will ever be able to satisfy my hunger pangs again."[21]

Contrary to Mr. Haase's impression, rationing authorities did not intend to be hard-hearted. The nation's sudden shortage of farm hands, the disruption of trade networks, the insatiable needs of the army, merchants' speculation, unreliable shipments from the neutrals, and British authorities' decision to impose a "hunger embargo" drove metropolitan authorities to contemplate depriving him of his favorite breakfast rolls.[22] After a storm of consumer protest, Berlin's city planners reversed their decision. They let their hungry citizens keep their breakfast favorites, provided they continued to keep the home fires burning.[23]

Rationing's direst days came during the harsh winter of 1916/17, in Germany as elsewhere in wartime Europe. The harvest of 1916 was a poor one worldwide. In Paris, food riots led by women workers forced the municipal government to introduce a comprehensive series of food controls. Even in London, where food rationing (with the important exception of bread) did not begin until February 1918, TheTimes reported long lines in front of East End food shops.[24] In Berlin, matters were far worse, as potato flour initially replaced flour made from grain, and the weekly bread ration dipped to an all-time low of 1600g. From the first

SHARING SCARCITY

week of February to the beginning of April, the lord of the city's granaries searched his delivery list each morning for a train car of potatoes. In its place, he found turnips. As it became clear that the bloodless beet had assumed a place of prominence in the unholy trinity of wartime hunger, townspeople took to the streets.

Bonzon and Davis correctly insist that "bureaucratic foul-ups were inevitable given the structure of civil administration in Berlin."[25] Still, it is worth noting that when Berlin's hunger victims converged on the citadel of city power, the *Rathaus*, Wermuth emerged to listen.[26] After hearing their demands, the former Imperial trade commissioner to the United States invited representatives to join him in a frank discussion of the city's food supply. The next morning, the elected officials joined Wermuth, Georg Michaelis, the Prussian Food Commissar, and Adolf von Tortilowicz Batocki, President of the Imperial War Nutrition Office, in the *Rathaus* ballroom.[27] During the next three and a half years, Wermuth continued to meet with labor leaders each Saturday morning. The atmosphere was not always cordial, and many a patrician's heart beat faster to hear her lord mayor "scolded like a mere schoolboy."[28] Still, the long sessions paid dividends, for city officials and labor alike. An initial concession was a decision to compensate for the harshest winter in centuries by doubling summer meat rations. In return, Wermuth solidified the city's claim to represent the urban laboring classes before the Prussian provincial government, the empire, and the army.[29] As Feldman demonstrated in his landmark study, under the pressure of the wartime embargo Germany's bureaucrats proved remarkably adept at forging compromises with the reformist left.

In the subsequent years, Wermuth and labor leaders would illustrate that Germany's local councilors were anything but "impotent" in the face of the capital's food problems.[30] True, the first frost of autumn 1917 provoked further signs of civil unrest. In September alone, the city's two hundred and forty-six offices witnessed seventeen burglaries, though in only two cases did bandits make off with a substantial booty of rationing cards. Most of the thefts, and, for that matter, other indirect effects of the blockade such as black market activity and urban-rural strains between the capital and other parts of the country, did not occur during the war, but after its unsuccessful conclusion.[31] The availability of food actually increased slightly in the last year of the worldwide conflict, though prices had slowly begun to rise. These changes, however, meant little to most Berliners. Their diets, like those of their grandparents, now moved in lock step with the seasons. Things did not really improve until the mid 1920s.

In retrospect, the city government's attempts to provision bread stuffs seemed doomed to failure. In contrast to the Austro-Hungarian and Russian monarchies, each of which in peacetime produced more than enough food to feed their populations, before the war Germans imported almost six million tons of fodder, mostly grain, yearly. In fact, the shortfall was larger still, since much of the rye cultivated on German farms was used as fodder, while bread was baked from three million tons of imported wheat. The British embargo ensured that during the war years comparable amounts of rye were diverted from animals to breadmaking.[32] Although Britain imported still more wheat, with about four-fifths of its total bread grains coming from abroad, the Royal Navy ensured that Manitoba's wheat continued to reach Manchester's masses.[33] Almost immediately, German citizens like Haase demanded that foreign grains return to German kitchens. As the Entente's hunger blockage began to bite, Berlin's bakers rushed to fill the orders of their customers, proving that old habits died hard for producers and consumers alike.

Although they were absolutely crucial to the war effort, the towns, particularly the larger ones, stood at the end of the nation's food supply line. In light of this fact, Simonsohn and his associates in Germany's fifty or so *Großstädte*, towns of 100,000 or more inhabitants, grasped that if they were to win on the home front, they would have to ally themselves with both consumers and bakers; no laissez-faire policy as in England would suffice. In Berlin, the greatest fear was that townspeople would revolt against controls. For this reason, city spokesmen rushed to establish their populist credentials. In a rare address to "Berlin's Citizens and Housewives," Simonsohn, a newly-elected member to the city's upper house, complained that bakers were producing "incredibly tiny" breakfast rolls even as grain prices fell. "This lust for profit," he concluded, "must be condemned in the strongest possible terms."[34] The government's generous dispersal of blame knew no bounds. In the coming years, Simonsohn and his colleagues hurled abuse at pastry makers: "They bake more pastries than allowed, they sell adulterated flour. They insist on baking more white bread than rye, and many provide favored customers with bread advances." Bakers were accused of falsifying ration cards, honoring cards they knew were imitations, and purposely over-valuing the coupons of favored customers.[35]

The pastry makers had good reason to resent these charges. For most of the war and the subsequent five hard years of peace, bakers had no control over the type or quality of flour they received. It is hardly any wonder that a nearly decade-long dependence on the city government for flour, coal, wood, and gas bred animosity. With flour making up more than half of the cost of production, and electricity and coal an additional fifteen percent, each baker's survival hinged upon the municipality's timely delivery of raw materials and energy each week.[36] When the city government failed to live up to its end of the bargain, artisans accused City Hall of purposely misreading entries in the flour log books and favoring larger competitors over smaller ones.

Harsh words were common currency in this command economy, and yet hard times encouraged everyone, bakers included, to moderate their demands. Recognition of their dependence on City Hall, and perhaps a desire to win the hearts of their clientele, led bakers to voice their grievances in the idiomatic phrases of patriotic duty. Take, for example, a letter to municipal rationing authorities penned by a baker near the city's Lehrter train station.

> A lot of soldiers come by here on their way to the Front to buy bread. Well, they don't have bread coupons, but I give them bread anyway. I know I am not supposed to do this, but the soldiers reproach me, and, well, to put in their words: 'We're fighting for the Fatherland and we can't even get anything here to eat.' I feel morally compelled, in the interest of the Fatherland, to give them bread without asking for a bread ration card. I am convinced this is the right thing to do, and I know many of my colleagues do the same thing.[37]

City rationing authorities certainly had their hands full. As if keeping citizens, soldiers, and bakers happy was not enough, they also had to answer to their superiors in provincial and imperial ministries. Beginning on 1 February 1915,

SHARING SCARCITY

the Bread Department of Berlin, and its counterparts elsewhere in Germany, received shipments of wheat, barley, oats, and rye exclusively from an imperial allocation office. Berlin's authorities welcomed this decision, for it ended precautionary hoarding, price fluctuations, and the speculation of the first weeks of the war. The new order returned metropolitans to a more familiar form of town rivalry, as local civilian and military authorities honed their skills at portraying the nutritional state of their charges in the direst terms.[38] Arbitrary seizures never disappeared completely. Military interference after 1916 took on a new guise, when the army pushed provincial and imperial authorities to allow it to supply factories directly. In the meantime, however, the new regulatory system limited the involvement of the army long enough to halt the ruinous intramunicipal competition that threatened to devour city treasuries.

The subjection of bread distribution and processing to a single system of supply controls provided the municipalities with a basis for regulating demand. Throughout the war, local authorities made effective use of their limited autonomy. In Ulm, for example, shortly after the outbreak of war city fathers planted potatoes on city properties. Their prescient efforts yielded enough tubers to provision nearly the entire population throughout the war. Stuttgart's administrators showed similar ingenuity. When, in August 1916, food ran short at three municipal welfare institutions, rationing authorities purchased—and farmed—740 acres of land. To feed pigs kept on the land, officials organized a kitchen waste recycling program. During the difficult winter of 1916/17, they sold the pigs at a handsome profit. Proceeds from the sale of the animals were used to feed 7500 of the city's schoolchildren.[39] For the constituents they served, the improvisations of local bureaucrats ameliorated the worst effects of the siege economy. They also, as few historians have acknowledged, sustained the long war effort.

Unfortunately for city officials, those who made the rules which governed food distribution also broke them. The more desperate military leaders became, the greater was their willingness to tinker with the home front's local food markets. Imperial and provincial authorities could not prevent General Erich Ludendorff, quartermaster-general of the army and second in command to Field Marshal von Hindenburg, from seizing precious grain resources.

Like the bakers they sought to control, municipal authorities were caught in a double bind. Both pastry cooks and policymakers had to accept the flour given to them and appear thankful to receive it. Both groups were forced to adjust to a constant stream of regulations and had to explain to customers why some grains were available while others were not. Like the provincial and imperial ministers, each existed ultimately to serve the burgeoning needs of the military. All three groups faced citizens' complaints about bread of poor quality. Public outrage against producers, rationing authorities, wholesalers and farmers could, and sometimes did, lead to violence in the streets.

It is no surprise that civil servants and bakers from time to time threw up their hands in despair. Nor is it any wonder, in light of the unprecedented hardships they were asked to bear, that consumers came to insist upon having their favorite foods at supper. The plight of bureaucrats and business people paled in comparison to that of most Berliners, the majority of whom belonged to working-class families that had been stripped of their wage-earning male members. The hard years of sacrifice led Regine Eller, "a very busy housewife," to reflect on the injustice of it all. No doubt many Berliners felt, as she did, that "the well-paid gentlemen at City Hall have everything they need. With their warm stoves and attentive staff, they suffer no privation. What's more, their private stashes of milk, meat, and flour enable them to gorge themselves whenever they feel like it."[40]

The long, daily wait for life's necessities that began early each morning and often extended well until the evening gave Frau Eller plenty of time to reflect upon the miserable state of her affairs. The growing number of Berlin women engaged in paid labor fared even worse. Between 1913 and 1918, the percentage of German women who worked at factories increased by 46%.[41] Holding down a job while raising a family was hard enough before 1914. The war made it virtually impossible. The dangerous and often poorly-paid hours at the factory, followed by the endless wait at countless shops, plagued many Berlin women. The fear that the wait would end, as so many had, with an empty-handed walk home to hungry dependents was unbearable.

Popular resentment of privilege focused on City Hall, though it also had class dimensions. As Carl Timm, physician from the district of Prenzlauer Berg noted,

> housewives (let's be honest, their servants) in the city's western suburbs merely display their rationing coupons and receive their goods without any hassle. That's a lot different from how things are in the city's northern and eastern districts, where municipal authorities really throw up obstacles. First, they pronounce with full fanfare how much of each good, at what weight, each citizen shall receive. Next, citizens exchange their wait number for a ration card. At this point, the nonsense truly gets underway. In vain, our women here in the North and East try to find out just what exactly they can expect to receive in exchange for their 'coupons.' And so it goes, day in, day out, until finally the commissioners have gotten rid of consumers and shopkeepers alike.[42]

Rationing in Berlin was never popular, as these letters from Herr Timm, Frau Eller, and others indicate. Nonetheless, at the local level the camaraderie that characterized the first war months never dissipated completely. The success of local government in sustaining the war effort rested upon broad public participation in its bread rationing program. In order to fulfill their day-to-day obligations to customers, the city government called upon the assistance of able bureaucrats, loyal bakers, members of organized labor, and representatives of the women's movement.

Berlin's rationing system created conflicts among consumers, planners, and merchants, but it also contained mechanisms to ensure that tempers did not reach a boiling point. Harsh words and hurt feelings notwithstanding, the bakers and bureaucrats worked together in a court of appeals to adjudicate bread producers' grievances. The new body represented both master artisans and senior civil servants. Members of the pastry makers' federation and civil servants also sat together in a special division of the Bread Office that was established to catch falsifiers and to eliminate black-market activity. When Berlin's government leveled charges of unfair trading practices against bakers, it did so with the approval of at least three of the city's master bakers.

Relations among civil rationing authorities were often tense. Still, here too mechanisms existed to ensure cooler heads prevailed. In both provincial and imperial ministries, the municipal government was far from isolated. Berliners, particularly city officials, were overrepresented in the agencies charged with the national and provincial distribution of meat, fruits and vegetables, potatoes, and bread. Moreover, the lord mayor, formerly a member of the imperial civil service, was on close terms with a number of well-placed government officials, including the emperor, Prime Minister Bethmann-Hollweg, General Ludendorff, and General Kessel. When Simonsohn disobeyed orders, he did so with the full concurrence of the lord mayor, who then turned to his superiors and proclaimed his ignorance, all the while shielding the Bread Office's day-to-day operations from provincial and imperial intervention. In contrast to the state of affairs in Petrograd, where even a suggestion of introducing a rationing system for bread provoked bitter disputes among the workers' representatives, the city administration, and the Imperial bureaucracy, cooperation among German food supply officials guaranteed a daily norm, however low, of flour and bread to all inhabitants.

German wartime rationing succeeded because a wide range of consumers supported it. Gestures of conciliation did not have to be large to be meaningful. Simonsohn knew that the bread scheme worked only when communal authorities took the time to respond promptly and politely to customers' seemingly endless questions. He understood that the art of civil service lies in the ability to refuse without offending. While anxious to keep the peace within his expanding department, Simonsohn nonetheless refused to tolerate rudeness from communal rationing authorities. The local bread commissioners certainly did their best, but sometimes their best simply was not enough. Responding to press complaints that citizens were not being treated with the proper respect, Simonsohn instructed local managers that "office staffers must meet all public requests with politeness."[43] The bread chief helped ensure that professionalism with a personal touch won over the city's skeptical consuming classes.

The Bread Office's gestures of goodwill involved still other, more substantial, concessions to the public. In response to consumer requests, Simonsohn and Simm extended local commissions' hours, from 5 to 8 p.m. on weekdays and added another two hours on Saturday. They also allowed the city's few vegetarians to substitute meat rations for extra barley, semolina, rolled oats, and pasta, as well as providing Jewish citizens with matzos for Passover. They sought to eliminate distinctions between downtown and the suburbs, making where one worked, and, by implication, where one ate, the guiding principle of card distribution. These persistent and ultimately successful efforts to integrate the city's outer districts not only made commuters' lives easier. They also acknowledged the city's real economic boundaries, and thereby laid the groundwork for the provincial entity of Greater Berlin that emerged in 1920.

Enlightened self-interest guided the bread lords' decisions. Keeping managers at their desks well into the evening helped prevent break-ins; providing vegetarians with alternatives ensured that more meat was available to the rest of the population; and allowing commuters to draw on the inner city's reserves meant that they too had a stake in the system's successful operation.

Other gestures to the city's hungry poor are not easily explained in terms of narrow-minded self-interest. The provisions established for the city's Jewish population fall in this category, as did the municipal government's efforts to ensure that domestic servants received their full rations. In a dramatic break with precedent, the Bread Office instructed local newspapers to impress upon heads of households that domestics had a right to receive bread ration-cards. Those who failed to meet their obligations to their servants, Simonsohn warned, faced the possibility of fines or imprisonment. True to its word, the city government tried three cases within the first three months of rationing.

What about the bottom line? While the price of most commodities rose appreciably during the war, the price of bread did not. On the contrary, Berliners paid less during the hard winter of 1916/1917 for a standard loaf than they did during the summer of 1915. The price for a standard loaf of bread was only one pfennig higher than it had been three years earlier. In Berlin, in real terms, the price of bread during the war fell dramatically. Not until the postwar years was inflation in breadstuffs felt in Berlin.

Low prices certainly do not connote high quality, of course. The imperial government's War Wheat Corporation was notorious for mixing and matching cereals. Shortly before the lean months of winter 1916/17, the imperial authorities asked Berliners to ingest breadstuffs made from seven different grains. No one will ever know how often Berliners' wartime foodstuffs were adulterated, though it is clear that the problem greatly concerned the inner circle of the Bread Supply Office.[44] While Simonsohn and his associates could do little to control quality, they spared citizens the indignity of putting more and more good money into bad bread. Compared to other big German cities, Berlin's authorities did reasonably well. The average price of bread per kilo in Berlin during the war (38.4 marks) was lower than in Cologne (40.8) and Munich (41.9), though higher than in the nation's leading trade city, Hamburg (32.9).[45]

Scholars of food rationing in Germany acknowledge that the German population, unlike the British, suffered from serious food shortages during the First World War. My essay supports this contention, insofar as it points to significant level of wartime of deprivation among a broad range of Berlin citizens. Importantly, however, this essay demonstrates that the sense of domestic catastrophe one gains from most accounts of food rationing in Germany is exaggerated. On the most important point of all—the physical suffering induced by malnutrition—new evidence suggests that the efforts of Germany's local bureaucrats paid dividends. From February 1917 onwards, two professors in Leipzig began a systematic survey of nutrition in their city. Their sample of fifty-nine families spanned the classes, from independent businessmen to manual laborers, with an emphasis on skilled labor and the lower middle class. Their findings show that, "except for the period of the 'turnip winter' and for the summer of 1918, the levels of civilian food consumption in Germany (taking weight loss into account) approximated to prewar norms."[46] Postwar testimony from Germany's wartime enemies offer further evidence of the success of local rationing authorities. In Hamburg in February 1919, a British officer noted that "the adult population does not, to the lay eye, show very obvious signs of under-nutrition," while in Berlin, as another member of a military mission observed, "people in the streets looked well-nourished."[47] Four months later, an American visitor echoed these sentiments, reporting that "the most striking external feature of Germany at the present moment is the apparently almost complete normality of the life of the population."[48] Observations made in

SHARING SCARCITY

early May, 1919 led the Cambridge economist, C.W. Guillebaud, to a similar conclusion.

> I was surprised by the good external appearance of the vast majority of the persons whom I met about the streets. There are very few fat people in Berlin to-day, but equally there is no obvious expression of hunger and exhaustion on the faces of the people. The bulk of the middle and upper classes looked in quite normal health, and their faces did not appear sunken or pinched. The poor certainly showed the influence of privation to a greater extent, but although lack of food and the depressing influence of defeat have taken the desire and the capacity to work hard from the majority of people, the bulk of adults are, in appearance at least, a long way from actual starvation. The food of the poor is monotonous and unpalatable to a high degree, but it is at least sufficient to maintain life for the healthy adult who is neither old nor constitutionally liable to disease.[49]

Personal contacts, decent service, enlightened self-interest, and patriotism were among the most important elements of Berlin's rationing program. A less obvious, though no less important, source of social consensus, was general agreement on whose hunger pangs should be eased first. The ultimate justification for the people's sacrifices was the widely-shared sentiment that those at the front should receive the best food available. If Edwin Schuster, member of Bavarian Engineering Company Number 8 is to believed, the common foot soldier had considerably more food, in particular, bread, than he needed.

> No difference is more glaring than the paucity of foodstuffs at home and their *waste here in the battle field*. The squandering begins immediately. During the transport, men receive a number of warm meals, and upon arrival at the Front, each soldier obtains four pounds of bread, sausages, and an additional pound and a half of red meat. These provisions are fully superfluous, for *virtually every man receives in care packages from home enough foodstuffs to keep himself stuffed* . We have no idea what to do with all the bread we receive, the Home Front's most important foodstuff. As soon as we arrived at the battle field, we also get an entire week's ration of bread. Many throw the rock-hard loaves away. Others feed them to the horses.[50]

Schuster's testimony illustrates that wartime rationing was based upon widely-accepted notions of civilian sacrifice and military reward. This common priority underpinned a wartime policy that held army rations above the availability of foodstuffs to civilians. When authorities felt least assured of popular support, they voiced sacrifice in terms of military exigency. By and large, civilians agreed to pay the price. The irony was, as Schuster noted, packages from home not only endangered the lives of loved ones, they also added to the front's abominable rat plague.

Civilian willingness to keep a stiff upper-lip also rested upon their belief, sometimes shaken but often confirmed, that their leaders were doing their best to help civilians who sacrificed the most. The first group to receive the recognition of the authorities were workers whose jobs involved unusual physical strain. Acting on instructions from the War Wheat Commission, Berlin's city government moved in the spring of 1915 to provide supplemental bread rations to workers over twenty-one years of age who were engaged in heavy labor. Soon thereafter, qualified laborers received an extra 450 grams of bread per week.[51]

Simonsohn, Simm, and Wermuth pushed imperial authorities to cover many more people than their plan originally envisioned. Simm instructed local commissioners that they should not, as the food administrators from the War Wheat Commission prescribed, ask workers to submit a letter of approval from their employers. "It is self-evident," Simonsohn added, that "the applicant's entire economic status must be considered, above all the number of children in his household."[52]

In the ensuing months, Simonsohn, Simm, and their subordinates ensured that every Berlin household received an application for a supplemental bread card. By the end of 1915, the city had issued over 625,000 cards, and by the end of 1916, the number of supplemental cards distributed weekly had reached 600,000. During the winter of 1916/17, at the insistence of Prussian and imperial authorities, the city government trimmed the number of cards to 400,000 per week. The cuts, which coincided with a reduction of the supplemental ration from 450 to 350 grams, were extremely ill-timed, and Berlin's municipal authorities protested to their superiors.

The city government nonetheless supplied a wide spectrum of workers with supplemental bread coupons throughout the war. Many of these occupations were essential to the war effort. This was true of workers on Berlin's rail and waterways, as well as munitions workers. The labor of other Berliners, such as nightshift workers, textile workers, street cleaners, or construction workers was, however, probably not essential to waging total war.[53] The Office's commitment to the laboring classes earned it the grudging praise of critics. As an otherwise disgruntled anonymous "member of the majority party" (the German Social Democratic Party) acknowledged to trade union bosses, "if work is demanded, than you all [trade union leaders and municipal rationing authorities] step in and make sure laborers receive an adequate diet."[54]

The bread card supplement acknowledged the special importance of skilled labor, the rank-and-file members of the country's potentially revolutionary majority party. In Berlin as elsewhere, the war brought a dramatic change in policy toward the country's Social Democratic Party and the party-affiliated Free Trade Unions. Beginning in early 1915, the former pariahs of German society were regularly consulted on the division of the country's meager grain reserves among the laboring classes. After the April uprising of 1917, cooperation between the bureaucracy and organized labor in Berlin took on special importance. During the difficult year of 1917, Adolf Cohen, head of the metalworker union of Greater Berlin, and Alvin Körsten, a Social Democratic delegate in the Reichstag, attended numerous meetings, private and public, with Simonsohn and Simm. Labor's demand was simple. Handbills pasted to the walls of an armaments' factory in Wedding during that winter by "politically indifferent" workers summarized laborers' demand: "Equal food and equal pay, and soon we'll have seen the war's last day!"[55] Acting on their constituents' wishes, Cohen and Körsten asked that supplemental cards be distributed to any worker who held sickness insurance, that is, to virtually everyone who worked outside of the home. Simonsohn and Wermuth agreed. Labor leaders rewarded this goodwill gesture on the part of city government by joining municipal authorities in the renunciation of Prussian government demands to raise the weekly supplemental bread ration to its previous level of 500g. Supplemental bread cards certainly helped ease the hunger pangs of laborers. They also signified social worth. The provision of extra food to men waging war, or to those who produced the material necessary

SHARING SCARCITY

to supply the front, not only reflected planners' priorities, but also elicited the support of the city's laboring classes.

The war brought about dramatic changes in the nature of production, as Berlin's workers left the light-manufacturing sectors of the economy to accept employment in heavy industry. Labor mobility had always been high in Berlin. In the years leading up to the war, for every 200,000 workers who came to the capital each year, another 100,000 returned to the surrounding countryside or to Prussia's eastern provinces. Higher rates of migration, coupled with mass conscription, ensured that the city's laboring classes in the postwar era would be younger, less skilled, and include more women.[56]

Berlin's Social Democratic leaders could not help but notice these changes. While acknowledging the wishes of provincial and imperial authorities to favor workers in armaments industries, Cohen and Körsten nonetheless aligned themselves with policies that profited all workers, regardless of age, sex, or skill level. In this decision, labor found an important but unlikely ally in the Office for Bread Supply.

On 1 October 1915, Simonsohn proposed that a supplemental bread ration card be distributed to young people between the ages of nine and twenty-one. In his view, this supplemental bread ration would recognize the contribution of youth to the war effort, though he emphasized that it was more than merely another reward to hungry laborers. All youth, he insisted, regardless of economic class, were to be included in the program.

The Prussian and imperial authorities at first agreed to make young people's diets a priority, though they successfully lobbied to limit supplements to those between the ages of twelve to seventeen. By the summer of 1917, however, Prussian authorities sought to reverse their decision, arguing that the desperate military situation justified eliminating the measure in favor of increasing rations to metalworkers. Simonsohn, Simm, Cohen, and Körsten refused.[57] Since laborers in armaments factories were already receiving higher wages and working longer hours than their comrades who produced foodstuffs and textiles, Cohen and Körsten argued against further benefits to workers engaged in wartime production. Shoring up Social Democracy's shrinking ranks, not promoting further divisions within an increasingly diverse range of workers, remained the guiding principle of socialist leaders.[58] Unlike workers in industrial centers such as Chemnitz and Mannheim, Berlin's bureaucrats and labor leaders together faced the opprobrium of their superiors. Batocki and Michaelis attacked the Office for Bread Supply in the imperial and provincial parliaments, and Berlin's civilian leaders and their Social Democratic allies responded in kind in the city assembly and in the national organization of cities, the *Städtetag*. The Berliners refused to budge. In the last months of the war, provincial and imperial authorities tried again to bring the capital's administrators to heel, decreeing that the de facto reward system for youth go instead to pregnant women.[59] Only the end of the war cut short the renewal of further hostilities.

Friendly service, reasonable prices, and the cooperation of organized labor help explain the success of Berlin's bread rationing program. Yet in order to fulfill their day-to-day obligations to customers, the city government needed shock troops. It found them in the Berlin branch of the Women's National Service, or *Nationaler Frauendienst*, the umbrella organization for women's associations during the war.

On 1 August 1914, Hedwig Heyl, later head of Berlin's municipally-sponsored network of take-out restaurants, and Gertrud Bäumer, the writer and feminist thinker, had presented the Prussian Interior Ministry with the plan for this distinctly German service organization intended to replace the Red Cross. At the Berlin branches, tens of thousands of women handed out bread rations, cooked and delivered meals to school children, delivered lectures on domestic science, offered traveling cooking courses, and distributed bread rations to wounded soldiers at city train stations. Without their energy and ingenuity, Berlin's rationing scheme would not have survived the first difficult months, much less the break-ins, the Turnip Winter, and the confusion that followed demobilization.

The success of the local rationing schemes hinged upon the participation of women's charitable organizations. One of the central problems for Simonsohn and his staff was keeping tabs on the city's bakers, and to this end women's groups rendered invaluable services. Responding immediately to the government's request for help with "the confidential supervision of the bakeries," Josephine Levy-Rathenau, recent founder of Berlin's women's employment bureau, instructed her charges to "present yourselves as consumers at bakeries during their busiest hours and record whether merchants observe the city's regulations."[60]

By keeping bakers honest, citizens satisfied, and bureaucrats vigilant, the new guardians of shortage helped the work of rationing. Women's efforts as overseers were so indispensable that they came to work not only for Simonsohn's department, but also for his Prussian and imperial counterparts. Herein lay the roots of conflict. Initially charged with helping Berlin's municipal authorities spy on the bakers, the women's organizations ended up caught between the bureaucratic fronts. Frau Ilse Müller-Oestreich, member of Women's Advisory Food Council, established by the Reichstag in January 1916 to oversee the War Nutrition Department's efforts, repeatedly chastised Berlin's city government for its handling of investigations initiated by evidence her zealous volunteers had gathered. In a 1918 letter to Simonsohn's superiors, Müller-Oestreich explained that in many cases "it is hardly worth the effort of submitting a report."[61] After outlining two cases where the city government had failed to follow up on two leads, Müller-Oestreich turned the ethos of civil service to her own advantage. "You will understand that my time is too precious to waste on reports no one reads. I will assume that you do not intend to call my credibility into question. The effect, however, is the same." Müller-Oestreich threatened to direct "future observations to other authorities," a thinly-veiled reference to Simonsohn's foes in the Imperial government.[62] Careful not to provide his many opponents with an excuse to eliminate his office, Simonsohn responded cautiously, stating his willingness "to continue the work we began together" while nonetheless pinning the blame for the sorry state of relations "solely" on the advisory council's "method of communicating individual cases" instead of, as the food director insisted, "establishing common principles for meaningful, long-term cooperation."[63]

Simonsohn's expressed desire to "establish common principles" with the women's organization was cynical enough to be mistaken for irony. In the course of gathering information about the availability of foodstuffs and their price, leaders of the women's movement came to entertain hopes that their service to the nation would pay postwar dividends. At each opportunity, Berlin's bread com-

SHARING SCARCITY

missioners blocked their progress. As early as 1916, Levy-Rathenau, Bäumer, and other leaders of the women's movement asserted their claim to participate in the formation of municipal bread policy. In each instance, the commissioners defended their decision-making prerogative tooth-and-nail, arguing that "the inclusion of women in planners' decision-making bodies would destroy their character as administrative organs of the state." For this reason, they insisted, women's participation at the highest levels of governance "cannot be justified."[64] Even with the ostensible support of the Prussian State Commissioner for Public Nutrition, volunteers were unable to leverage their devotion to the Fatherland into formal political participation.

In early October 1918, the German Army High Command unexpectedly but insistently urged stunned civilian leaders to request an armistice based on the American President Wilson's famous "fourteen points" of January 1918. In later years, many Germans—and historians—would come to share General Erich Ludendorff's view that the Home Front had stabbed the army in the back. In truth, as C. Paul Vincent has put it, "the general [and many later commentators] overlooked the fact that the army had fashioned the knife."[65] The shattering news of defeat on the battlefield made the sacrifice of all German citizens appear tragically wasted; suffering, as many civilians bitterly concluded, had lost its point.

The news of defeat on the battlefield did lead to a collapse of internal order in the capital, though not, importantly, as early or as completely as many historians have assumed. "In Berlin," Bonzon and Davis insist, "the authorities' inability to gain a hold on the [food] situation was an essential element in the erosion of the authority of the state."[66] In fact, the war's revolutionary finale did not end the municipal rationing coalition. Instead, the wartime liberal-socialist alliance, with its tested policy of conciliation among the local political class and active exclusion of radical left-wing elements, prevailed. Just as they had done during the long war years, labor representatives continued to join Lord Mayor Wermuth every Saturday morning to discuss food policy. Under the stern gaze of the lord mayor, the revolutionary council for the provision of foodstuffs eliminated the supplement to "hard working" and "hardest working" industrial laborers and raised the overall bread ration to 2350 grams per citizen per week.[67]

Wermuth's presence at the council's meeting demonstrated that the end of hostilities did not end cooperation between local bureaucrats and organized labor. Even in the heady days of Berlin's revolutionary November, the soldiers' and workers' councils acceded to Simonsohn's wishes, agreeing to deny soldiers' efforts to obtain bread by merely presenting an identity card.[68] Simonsohn showed his gratitude by lobbying for the national elimination of the supplements which Berlin's revolutionary government had already declared null and void. When it came to the defense of the city's autonomy, local bureaucrats were more comfortable dealing with leaders of November revolution than were their provincial and national counterparts.[69] At the local level, the unity of the political class transcended many ideological allegiances. The transfer of control over Berlin's food supply to elected authorities, a concession denied to Petrograd's municipal officials by state agricultural officials, laid the foundation for consensus among Berlin's Majority Socialists[70] and the bourgeois democratic bloc through both war and revolution.

Price controls that the Office of Bread Supply had created during the lean years of war remained in place during the equally lean years of peace. With few changes in personnel, bread bosses like local commissioner #46 continued to fulfill local government's first responsibility: to ensure all citizens got something to eat.[71] Ties to labor, firm since the April uprising, were strengthened, as city food authorities enlisted representatives of Social Democracy, liberal unions, and Christian workers' organizations in the struggle against black market activity. Women's organizations, the backbone of the Department's surveillance efforts, remained an integral part of the postwar supervision of bakeries. When, in fall 1919, the city needed help in storing winter potatoes, public advertisements brought out hundreds of female volunteers.

The city government of socialist ministers eliminated supplemental bread cards, though they continued to play favorites with the old groups in new ways. Precious little changed in the management of the city's bread resources, save a thick, black pencil line on the stationary masthead through the words, "Royal Residence." Wermuth remained in office until the end of 1920. It was not the socialists, the left-wing independents, or the centrist majority who left the lord mayor in the lurch, but his former monarchist allies instead. Neither the First World War's deprivations nor the postwar uprising of Spartacist radicals (who had hoped that hunger would pave the way for a coup) brought about a reconstitution of social relations in Berlin. In the immediate postwar era, the continued Allied blockade promoted further collaboration between the forces of parliamentary democracy and repression against opponents on the right and left.

The inflation, not the war or revolution, terminated wartime rationing in Germany.[72] Despite all the deprivations they suffered during the war, citizens reported that really hard times for most of them set in after the armistice and continued until 1923, when postwar inflation ended. The mounting insolvency of Germany's municipalities took many faces; among the first signs of deterioration was a dramatic rise in the number of break-ins. Burglaries were so common in March of 1919 that the entire batch of cards had to be declared invalid. As the troubles worsened in the ensuing months, bakers in the city's north and east closed on Friday and Saturdays, leaving customers with empty stomachs and a lot of time on their hands to consider their predicament.[73] In spring 1920, hundreds of women led protest marches on the now-socialist City Hall with banners reading: "Down with the Food Profiteers" and "Give us Cheap Bread."[74] Mass plundering of bakeries ensued, led neither by socialists nor communists, nor by armed para-military bands, but instead by the city's women and young men.[75] Rising prices and the explosion of the black market made impossible what had always been a Herculean task: promoting relative equity in the distribution of basic foodstuffs among citizens of dramatically unequal incomes.

The economic crisis of the early twenties destroyed the Bread Supply Office, though it did little to solve the problem that had hamstrung rationing efforts throughout the period: the quiet tyranny of consumer taste. The problem of getting Berliners the kind of bread they wanted worsened in the 1920s, as efforts by Berlin and other municipalities to raise rye consumption fell flat. What city governments could not accomplish seemed like an opportunity for the Reichstag.

SHARING SCARCITY

In 1930, the national parliament passed tariff legislation that sought to discourage working-class consumption of imported wheat grain in favor of home-grown rye.[76] After 1933, a new generation of politicians would offer a racially-inspired response to the country's perceived agricultural inadequacy.

The huddled heads at Berlin's City Hall could not solve the riddle of consumer desire, though it seems unfair to expect that they could achieve what few since have even attempted. Faced with the unprecedented supply challenges of total war, Simonsohn and his staff created alliances with labor, offering enticements to the family's most threatened, and used female volunteers to supervise bread shops. In this sense, Berlin's bureaucrats defied the place in history assigned to them by later historians.

Four years of scarcity had pitted bakers against planners, city against countryside, and consumers against rationing officials. Nonetheless, growing dissatisfaction did not lead to social upheaval until well after the war. Hardship neither brought to a boil prewar social tensions nor unraveled the nation's social and moral fabric. On the contrary, the most ambitious program in the field of wartime social policy fostered goodwill among thousands of traders and millions of working families. The success of local government in war, not its failure, is the main lesson of Berlin's rationing experience. The willingness of Berliners to make do with less bread for so long suggests that Germany's twentieth-century history, so often written with expressions of conflict as its master narrative, must also be examined in terms of cohesion and stabilization.

Department of History
Washington, DC 20016

ENDNOTES

For their helpful comments on this essay I would like to thank Deborah Cohen, Wendy Goldman, Donna Harsch, Hanco Jürgens, Mary Lindemann, Sun Lixin, Ulrike Thoms, Jonathan Wiesen, Christine Worobec, and Tetsuya Yamane, and the anonymous reviewers of the *Journal*.

1. Landesarchiv Berlin, Aussenstelle. (Hereafter referred to as LA Berlin), Kubath, An sämtliche Brotkommissionen, 7 October, 1916, Rep. 13–01 Deputation für das Ernährungswesen, 15109 Rundschreiben an Brotkommissionen.

2. LA Berlin, Kubath, An sämtliche Brotkommissionen, 7 October 1916, Rep. 13-01 Deputation für das Ernährungswesen, 15109 Rundschreiben an Brotkommissionen. See also, Simonsohn, 14 March 1916, Rep. 13-01 Deputation für das Ernährungswesen, 657 Geschäftsverfahren der Brotkommission.

3. LA Berlin, Simonsohn, An Herrn Dezernenten Magistratsassessor Dr. Simm, 11 October 1916, Rep. 13-01 Deputation für das Ernährungswesen, 657 Geschäftsverfahren der Brotkommission.

4. By 1918 Germans bought between 1/7 to 1/8th of all of their bread, flour, and potatoes from the black market. Milk, butter, and cheese were more frequently purchased from illegal sources. I would emphasize that the black market *supplemented*, not *supplanted*, the control system on such basic foodstuffs as bread.

5. See, for examples, Gerald Feldman, *Army, Industry, Labor in Germany 1914–1918* (Princeton, 1966); Jürgen Kocka, *Facing Total War: German Society, 1914–1918* (Cambridge, 1984); Anne Roerkohl, *Hungerblockade und Heimatfront: Die kommunale Lebensmittelversorgung in Westfalen während des ersten Weltkrieges* (Stuttgart, 1987). In the 1920s, the Carnegie Endowment for International Peace commissioned several studies of the food situation in wartime Germany. The most important of these was August Skalweit's *Die deutsche Kriegsernährungswirtschaft* (New Haven, 1927). The picture of bureaucratic ineptitude which emerges in present-day historical accounts was already formed in the 1920s, when the blockade was still in force and commentators sought to extract concessions from the victorious Allies.

6. Feldman, *Army, Industry and Labor in Germany*, 503. See also pages 3–27; 97–135; 283–91.

7. Thierry Bonzon and Belinda Davis, "Feeding the Cities," in *Capital Cities at War. Paris, London, Berlin 1914–1919* edited by Jay Winter and Jean-Louis Robert (New York, 1997), 339.

8. Bonzon and Davis, "Feeding the Cities," 308.

9. Kocka, *Facing Total War*, 44, 159.

10. The analogy is borrowed from Lars T. Lih. His excellent book on grain procurement in Russia during the wars and revolutions of 1914–21 is *Bread and Authority in Russia, 1914–1921* (Berkeley, 1990), see 231–3; 246, 247.

11. The fundamental basis of the UK's fortunate wartime food shortage situation was the maintenance of imported supplies. Jay Winter, "Paris, London, Berlin 1914–1919: Capital Cities at War," in *Capital Cities at War*, 23. Winter correctly notes that "after 1915 the Allied capitals rarely faced critical material constraints. When they did, as in the case of coal, administrators on national and inter-Allied levels reacted, and the national and international reserves of the Allies were brought into the equation. In this framework, we can see on the local level what such imperial abundance meant for the well-being of civilians in London and in Paris, and what the absence of such reserves meant for Berliners."

12. For examples, see *Vossiche Zeitung*, no. 351, 19 July 1914; *Berliner Morgenpost*, no. 33, 3 February 1914; *Gemeinde Blatt*, no. 32, August 9, 1914.

13. The municipal government of Berlin, like that of many other German cities, was formally divided into two parts. One was a representative assembly, or *Stadtverordnetenversammlung*. Its members were elected by all citizens, albeit in accordance with (prior to 1918) the highly undemocratic Prussian three-class voting system. The members, in turn, elected the members of the other part of the city government, the magistrate. The latter consisted of the lord mayor and the city councilors (*Stadträte*). Had Berlin's elections been held according to proportional representation, Social Democrats would have controlled city government by the 1890s. As it was, socialists learned to exercise their influence indirectly.

14. Roughly 6 percent of all Germans lived in the capital.

15. LA Berlin, Niederschrift über die Sitzung des Ausschusses für die allgemeine Lebensmittelversorgung am Montag, den 21 Februar 1921, Rep. 13-01 Deputation für das Ernährungswesen, 13620 Brotkommission Groß-Berlin.

16. See, Silbergleit, "Brotpreise," in *Handwörterbuch der Staatswissenschaften*, 4th ed., vol. 3, ed. Ludwig Elster, Adolf Weber, and Friedrich Wieser (Jena, 1927), 28.

SHARING SCARCITY

17. At industrial canteens, hospitals, clinics, and other charitable institutions, overwrought bureaucrats agreed to trade flour against mere receipts. The Bread Commission nonetheless reserved the right to make surprise inspections.

18. See Eduard David, *Das Kriegstagebuch des Reichstagsabgeordneten Eduard David 1914–1918*, edited by Erich Matthias and Susanne Miller (Düsseldorf, 1986), 107. As the Social Democratic Reichstag deputy wrote at the end of February, "Die Brotkarten [in Berlin] sind eingeführt. Das hätte man vor Jahresfrist gar nicht ausdenken können. Und die Organisation ist einfach und funktioniert jetzt glatt."

19. In 1917/18, Germany produced roughly half as many cereals as in 1912/13; production figures for meat were even lower. For information on this subject, see Frank M. Surface and Raymond L. Bland, *American Food in the World War and the Reconstruction Period. Operations of the Organizations Under the Direction of Herbert Hoover 1914 to 1924* (Stanford, 1931), 189, 91.

20. LA Berlin, Simonsohn, "Auslandsmehl!," June 3, 1916, Rep. 13-01 *Deputation für das Ernährungswesen*, 15263 Verordnungen.

21. LA Berlin, Bruno Haase, 26 January 1917, Rep. 13-01 Deputation für das Ernährungswesen, 8544 Das Einheitsbrot.

22. Hostility to soya, potato, and other cereal flours was by no means limited to Germany. For similar objections to the "war loaves" in Britain, see James P. Johnston, *A Hundred Years of Eating. Food, Drink, and the Daily Diet in Britain Since the Late Nineteenth Century* (Bristol, 1977), 20–8.

23. White-bread rolls, available today in the smallest hamlet, were at this time an almost exclusively urban phenomenon. See, Erwin Topf, *Der Menschheit täglich Brot* (Jena, 1926).

24. Bonzon and Davis, "Feeding the Cities," 330.

25. Bonzon and Davis, "Feeding the Cities," 341. Oddly, however, the authors fail to discuss any of the individuals directly involved in the municipal distribution network in Berlin.

26. According to Kocka, some 200,000 workers, particularly munitions workers, took part in the April strikes. See Kocka, *Facing Total War*, 49, 61. The number of strikes increased in each war year except, importantly, the last; strikes during the war were, compared to the prewar period, relatively rare. Wartime statistics offer the following tally: in 1915, 137, in 1916, 240, in 1917, 561, in 1918, 531. In 1912 and 1913, the numbers had been roughly 2,500 and 2,100 respectively.

27. Adolf Wermuth, *Ein Beamtenleben* (Berlin, 1922), 373–8. Wermuth was elected Lord Mayor of Berlin on the 15th of May 1912, against the votes of the lower-house's Social Democratic faction. On the Saturday morning meetings generally, see the account of wartime rationing in George Yaney, *The World of the Manager. Food Administration in Berlin during World War I* (New York, 1994), 134–41.

28. Hedwig Heyl, *Aus meinem Leben* (Berlin, 1925), 155. The observation, and perhaps also the reaction, were Heyl's.

29. Kaeber, "Die Oberbürgermeister Berlins seit der steinischen Städteverordnung," 94.

30. Bonzon and Davis insist that the success of Allied food efforts—and the failure of German attempts to control the food supply— stemmed from the ability of French and British officials to transfer responsibility away from local authorities and to higher

levels. Bonzon and Davis, "Feeding the Cities," 30. On the contrary, Germany's long participation in total war was a direct result of the municipalities' influence over food policy throughout the war.

31. Even the most vocal critics of Berlin's wartime rationing program concede this point. Bonzon and Davis, "Feeding the Cities," 317. Resources such as fertilizer and fodder were also in very short supply.

32. Avner Offer, *The First World War: An Agrarian Interpretation* (New York, 1989), 63. Shortages of coal, locomotives, rolling stock, repair parts, and labor further curtailed Germany's ability to deliver grains to the cities. See Feldman, *Army, Industry, Labor*, 254–9. Although eastern Europe was the most important source of German grain imports, the shipments arrived by sea through western seaports. Germany's railways did not have sufficient capacity to carry grain from the east to offset the grain imported by sea. Offer, *The First World War*, 341.

33. Dewey, "Nutrition and Living Standards in Wartime Britain," 201. Food rationing was not introduced in London until Februrary 1918. In Paris, government controls on foodstuffs were not begun until the middle of the war. As Offer notes, "by drawing on the staggered harvests of its different suppliers, on the American, Indian and Russian winter- and spring-wheat harvests in one half of the year, and on Australian and Argentinian harvests during the second half, Britain simply kept much of her stocks on the grainfields themselves (thus eliminating the thorny problems of stockpiling)." Offer, The *First World War*, 346.

34. LA Berlin, An Berliner Bürger und Hausfrauen, Simonsohn, 15 August 1914, Rep. 13-01 Deputation für das Ernährungswesen, 13611 Generelle Abmachungen mit Wohltätigkeitsanstalten und Krankenhäuser.

35. See, for examples, Preußisches Geheimes Staatsarchiv (hereafter referred to PrGStA), Rep. 197A Preußischer Staatskommissar für Volksernährung, It Volksernährung, Liste 48 Generalia A. Oberste Behörden, I. Staatskommissariat für Volksernährung, 1 Einrichtung des Staatskommissariats für Volksernährung.

36. Calculations are based on figures provided by Silbergleit, "Brotpreise," *Handwörterbuch der Staatswissenschaften*, 29.

37. LA Berlin, W. Trenn, An den Magistrat, Abteilung für Brotversorgung, 19 June 1915, Rep. 13-01 Deputation für das Ernährungswesen, 14862 Geschäftsverfahren der Abteilung Brotversorgung.

38. For this reason, local authorities' assessments (particularly those made by home-based regional military commanders) of citizens' nutritional needs were often exaggerated. Accounts, such as Jürgen Kocka's, which rely heavily on such reports should be met with a certain degree of skepticism. Kocka, *Facing Total War*, 41.

39. Günther Mai, *Kriegswirtschaft und Arbeiterbewegung in Württemberg 1914–1918* (Gerlingen, 1983), 414–5.

40. Regine Eller, *Berliner Tageblatt*, no. 274, 14 August 1919.

41. Factory is defined here as a production facility with ten or more workers. The overall percentage of female factory workers in Germany increased during the War from 22% to 34%; Kocka, *Facing Total War*, 36.

42. LA Berlin, Carl Timm, Abschrift! 10 April 1917, Rep. 13-01 Deputation für das Ernährungswesen, 9066 Die Zuteilung von Milch an Kranke, 133.

SHARING SCARCITY

43. LA Berlin, Simonsohn, An sämtliche Brotkommissionen, 12 December 1916, Rep. 13-01 Deputation für das Ernährungswesen, 15109 Rundschreiben an die Brotkommissionen.

44. See, for the prewar period, Karl-Peter Ellerbock, "Lebensmittelqualität vor dem ersten Weltkrieg: Industrielle Produktion und staatliche Gesundheitspolitik," in *Durchbruch zum modernen Massenkonsum. Lebensmittelmärkte und Lebensmittelqualität im Städtewachstum des Industriezeitalters*, edited by Hans Jürgen Teuteberg, (Münster, 1987), 127–89.

45. This calculation is my own, based on figures provided by Silbergleit, "Brotpreise," in *Handwörterbuch der Staatswissenschaften*, ed. Ludwig Elster, Adolf Weber, and Friedrich Wieser 4th ed. vol. 3 (Jena, 1927), 31, 32.

46. Offer, *The First World War*, 48. The basis of the authors' inquiry, that food requirements decline in relation to body weight, family size, and work performed, was unique among wartime studies. Even though basic energy needs were met, as Offer rightly insists, the decline of cheap fats such as margarine and lard, as well as meat, certainly left many feeling extremely hungry.

47. Offer, *The First World War*, 389. See also Gerald Feldman's detailed description of the three British officers' impressions in *The Great Disorder. Politics, Economics, and Society in the German Inflation, 1914–1924* (New York, 1993), 99–103.

48. Offer, *The First World War*, 389.

49. C.W.Guillebaud, "Report of a Visit to Berlin, May 2nd to May 8th, 1919" cited in Offer, *The First World War*, 389–90.

50. PrGStA, Abschrift V 9611. An das Ministerium des Innern (Zentralstelle der Lebensmittelversorgung), Betreffend: Verbot von Lebensmittelsendungen ins Feld, Priv. Doz. Pionier i. d. Bayer. Pion. Park-Komp. Nr. 8, Im Felde, 7 April 1916, Rep. 197 A Preuß. Staatskommissar für Volksernährung, Io Ausschreitungen, Ausstände.

51. LA Berlin, Wermuth, "Verordnung über Zusatzbrotkarten," 15 June 1915, Rep. 13-01 Deputation für das Ernährungswesen, 14065 Verordnungen des Magistrats.

52. LA Berlin, Simonsohn, 7 July 1916, Rep. 13-01 Deputation für das Ernährungswesen, 15109 Rundschreiben an Brotkommissionen.

53. LA Berlin, Unsigned, 29 November 1916, Rep. 13-01 Deputation für das Ernährungswesen, 11842 Verordnungen und Verfügungen betr. Zusatzkarten.

54. LA Berlin, An den Gewerkschaften Berlin, 25 January 1917, Rep. 13-01 Deputation für das Ernährungswesen, 8544 Das Einheitsbrot.

55. "Gleicher Lohn und gleiches Fressen, dann wäre der Krieg schon längst vergessen!" Cited in Klaus Retlaw, *Spartakus. Aufstieg und Niedergang eines Parteiarbeiters* (Frankfurt a.M., 1971), 51.

56. Kocka, *Facing Total War*, 17–9, 48–9; Ute Daniel, *Arbeiterfrauen in der Kriegsgesellschaft: Beruf, Familie und Politik im Ersten Weltkrieg* (Göttingen, 1989), 98.

57. Brandenburgisches Landeshauptarchiv, Potsdam (Hereafter referred to as BLHA), Allgemeine Angelegenheiten der Abteilung I Lebensmittel, Rep. 1A, Staatliche Verteilungsstelle für Groß-Berlin, No. 29.

58. Primarily because of conscription, SPD membership rolls declined dramatically during the War. Nationwide there were 1,086,000 party members in 1914; 586,000 in 1915; 433,000 in 1916; and 243,000 in 1917. Kocka, *Facing Total War*, 52.

59. LA Berlin, Unsigned, An das Preußisches Landes-Getreide Amt. Betrifft: Verbrauchsregelung im Erntejahre 1918, Rep. 13-01 Deputation für das Ernährungswesen, 12631 Die Versorgung der Jugendlichen alten Leute, Schwangeren, und Wöcherinnen.

60. LA Berlin, Josephine Levy-Rathenau, An Herrn Stadtrat Simonsohn, Rep. 13-01 Deputation für Ernährungswesen, 1201 Einrichtung der Brotkommission.

61. LA Berlin, Frau Ilse Müller- Öestreich, Sekretariat des Frauenbeirats des Reichs-Ernährungs-Ministeriums, An Lehmann, 5 June 1919, Rep. 22-02 Lebensmittelverband Groß-Berlin, 2381 Schleich- und Kettenhandel.

62. LA Berlin, Frau Ilse Müller- Öestreich, Sekretariat des Frauenbeirats des Reichs-Ernährungs-Ministeriums, An Lehmann, 5 June 1919, Rep. 22-02 Lebensmittelverband Groß-Berlin, 2381 Schleich- und Kettenhandel.

63. LA Berlin, Simonsohn, 11 July 1919, Rep. 22-02 Lebensmittelverband Groß-Berlin, 2381 Schleich- und Kettenhandel.

64. LA Berlin, Simonsohn, Runge, Lehmann, Gordon, Henshel, Simm, Kamnitzer, Fischer, 22 October 1918, Niederschrift über die Sitzung des Lebensmittelausschusses, Rep. 13-01 Deputation für das Ernährungswesen, 13208 Verordnungen und Bekanntmachungen der Abteilung für Brotversorgung.

65. C. Paul Vincent, *The Politics of Hunger. The Allied Blockade of Germany, 1915–1919* (Athens, OH), 23.

66. Bonzon and Davis, "Feeding the Cities," 341.

67. LA Berlin, Verordnung über Brotmenge sowie den Fortfall der Zusatzbrotkarten, Wermuth, 27 November 1918, Rep. 13-01 Deputation für das Ernährungswesen, 16149 Verordnungen und Bekanntmachungen der Abteilung für Brotversorgung. On Wermuth's postwar cooperation with labor, Annemarie Lange, *Berlin in der Weimarer Republik* (Bonn, 1987), 68, 9.

68. LA Berlin, Simonsohn, An sämtliche Brotkommissionen, 13 November 1918, Rep. 13-01 Deputation für das Ernährungswesen, 15132 Rundschreiben an die Brotkommissionen.

69. See, BLHA, Pr. Br. 1A: Staatliche Verteilungsstelle von Groß-Berlin. No. 7 Die Veränderungen in der Geschäftsführung nach Beginn der Revolution (1918).

70. By the outbreak of the Revolution roughly 100,000 laborers had defected from the SPD to a new, left-wing Independent Socialist Party, or USPD.

71. LA Berlin, Simonsohn, An sämtliche Brotkommissionen, 13 November 1918, Rep. 13-01 Deputation für das Ernährungswesen, 15132 Rundschreiben an die Brotkommissionen.

72. Feldman, *The Great Disorder*, 409; 561–4; 622, 637–8; 701–2; 705–7; 768.

73. LA Berlin, Müller, Obermeister, Bäcker-Zwangsinnung in Berlin, An den Magistrat Berlin, Rep. 13-01 Deputation für das Ernährungswesen, 10175 Brotknappheit in den Bäckereien.

SHARING SCARCITY 393

74. *Vorwärts*, no. 323, 28 June 1920; *Vossische Zeitung*, no. 322, 29 June 1920.

75. *Rote Fahne*, no. 533, 29 November 1921; *Berliner-Lokal-Anzeiger*, no. 530, 16 November 1921; *Vossische Zeitung*, no. 549, 20 November 1921.

76. Sächisches Hauptstaatsarchiv, Dresden, *Dresdner Anzeiger*, no. 343, 24 July 1930, Nachrichtenstelle der Staatskanzlei. Zeitungsausschnittsammlung, no. 1004.

[8]
MILITARY RECRUITING AND THE BRITISH LABOUR FORCE DURING THE FIRST WORLD WAR

P. E. DEWEY
Royal Holloway College, University of London

I

During the First World War, Britain was obliged for the first time for over a century to raise a mass army. Initially, this seemed to raise no insuperable problem; by the end of 1914, slightly over one million men had enlisted. Thereafter, however, civilian enthusiasm waned, and the government had to employ other means to stimulate the flow of recruits – alteration of the military service age limits and, later, the introduction of compulsory military service. Taken together, voluntary recruiting and conscription permitted the raising and maintenance of a mass army. By the time of the armistice on 11 November 1918, almost five million men had entered the army, and a further half million had entered the two other services.[1]

The loss of this large amount of labour (about one-third of the pre-war male labour force) had important implications for the working of the British economy. In particular, it made it difficult to equip the resulting large armies; a process clearly brought out in the 'shell scandal' of early 1915. Thus the attention of historians has been drawn naturally to the problems of labour supply in wartime industry (particularly in industries producing goods directly for military use), and to the ways in which these problems were overcome by drawing in fresh, unskilled labour (chiefly female).[2]

There are, however, two other, more fundamental questions, which have not been posed so far, and which have implications both for the economic and the military history of the war; from what sections of the economy were these men drawn, and what were the main factors influencing the process of recruitment? In so far as these questions have previously been considered, the tendency has been to assume that the dominant force at work was patriotic feeling (at least, until the introduction of conscription), and that, since this was a universal and uniform phenomenon, each sector of the economy yielded up the same proportion of its male labour to the armed forces (chiefly the army). Writing shortly after the end of the war, the historian of wartime labour supply commented, à propos of the rush of recruits to the army in the first few months

[1] War Office, *Statistics of the military effort of the British empire during the Great War 1914–20* (1922), p. 363.
[2] E.g. H. Wolfe, *Labour supply and regulation* (Oxford, 1923).

of the war; 'all classes, and...all types of industry gave equally'.³ More recently, Correlli Barnett has described the influences behind this initial wave of enlistment in the following terms:

> Moved by patriotism, by desire for a bit of adventure, by a desire to escape from poverty and unemployment, the crowds queued outside the recruiting offices.⁴

In the same work he refers to the new, mass army of 1915 as 'a cross-section of the nation'.⁵

The emphasis placed so far upon generalized psychological factors such as patriotism, with the accompanying implication that recruitment impinged equally upon all sectors of the economy, is somewhat unsatisfactory. In the first place, such concepts are subjective, and therefore explanations relying on them tend to be imprecise. In the second place, the idea that recruiting tended to have a uniform impact upon different industrial or occupational groups is suspect; to take an obvious, if neglected point, different occupations may well have had differing proportions of their male labour force within the military age limits. To take a further example, certain industries had a low level of activity during the war, others a much higher one. It might therefore be expected that in certain industries the tendency for labour to leave (either for other occupations or for the forces) would differ from that in others. Whatever the workings of patriotic and other feelings, it seems improbable that recruiting impinged equally upon different sectors of the economy, even in the period of voluntary recruiting, and still less after the introduction of conscription, when certain industries received greater protection from military service than others.

II

There are, therefore, two theses presented here. The first is that recruiting, both before and after the introduction of conscription, differed widely in its impact upon different industries. The second is that the most important factors affecting recruitment were not only generalized ones such as patriotism, but also more specific ones – economic, demographic, medical and institutional. The next step is to test the first of these theses. At first this seems to present some difficulties, since there appears not to exist any direct information on the actual losses of labour suffered by each industry as a result of military recruiting. The government itself did not keep a tally of such losses as they occurred.⁶ Nor would it be feasible to look for the answer in the papers of the recruiting authorities themselves; even if the latter had made an accurate note of the former occupations of their recruits, the research effort involved would be prohibitive. There remains, however, one major source which may be used

---

³ Wolfe, *Labour supply*, p. 12.
⁴ C. Barnett, *Britain and her army 1509–1970; a military, political and social survey* (1970), p. 377.
⁵ Barnett, *Britain and her army*, p. 379.
⁶ A fact admitted by Lord Derby (Director-General of recruiting) *à propos* of agriculture (Parl. debates, house of lords, 5th series, XXIV, 325–6, 28 Feb. 1917).

MILITARY RECRUITING

to test this thesis. Whilst not actually counting losses of labour from each industry as they occurred, the government did the next best thing; it conducted a continuous sample survey on the matter throughout the war. This was organized by the Board of Trade; from October 1914, and at least quarterly thereafter, the board's statistical branch conducted a survey of employers, with a view to obtaining information on levels of enlistment and employment in various industries in the U.K. The board proceeded by sending a questionnaire to a large number of employers, asking for information as to the numbers of employees who had enlisted, the numbers currently employed, and other matters from time to time. The first of the ensuing reports was issued in respect of the situation at the end of October 1914, and the last in respect of the end of April 1919, being concerned with the post-war position. In all, 20 reports were issued, of which 18 referred to the war period. Of these, 17 have survived.[7]

Whilst this source is of interest in itself, and relevant to our purpose, it should be stressed that it is derived for the most part from samples of employers, and thus is not the same as an actual counting of the number of enlistments or of the number of men employed in the industries concerned. This point needs emphasizing, if only because it has become common practice, when quoting the results of these surveys, to treat them as if they were obtained by actually counting heads. With certain exceptions (i.e. government agencies, or industries coming under government control during the war), this is not the case.[8]

Having obtained information from employers on the number of men who had enlisted from their particular firms since the beginning of the war, the information was processed by the board in what appears to have been the following manner (although the procedure followed is not specifically described in the reports); the figures of enlistments from all employers in each industry were added up, and then expressed as a percentage of the pre-war labour force of those employers. This percentage was then applied to the whole of the industry in question, and converted back into numbers of men. A hypothetical example will make this clear:

Enlistment from industry X

Pre-war labour force of employers answering questionnaire	100,000 (a)	
Number of enlistments	20,000 (b)	
Enlistment percentage	20% (c)	$[(b) \div (a) \%]$
Pre-war labour force of the industry	500,000 (d)	
No. of men enlisted from the industry	100,000 (e)	$[(c) \times (d)]$

[7] Board of Trade, *Report on the state of employment in the United Kingdom in...* (various dates). This is the main series, of which the first three reports were issued as parliamentary papers (Cd. 7703; Cd. 7755; Cd. 7850). The methodology of these surveys is discussed in Appendix 1.

[8] Thus, eg., Wolfe, *Labour supply*, p. 12; S. Pollard, *The development of the British economy 1914–1950* (London, 1962), p. 78; A. J. P. Taylor, *English history 1914–1945* (London, 1965), p. 38. It should be said in fairness to these authors that they are all following authorities who had made the same assumption. The source of this error seems to have been A. W. Kirkaldy, in his *Industry and finance* (1917; 2nd edn 1920). The second edition contains a large tabulation of wartime employment in various industries (pp. 96–7), which seems to have been drawn directly from the Board of Trade surveys, and does not mention that the basis of the figures was a sample survey.

The reliability of these surveys clearly depends upon several factors; the representativeness of the sample of employers; the proportion of the national labour force sampled; the proportion of the national labour force in respect of which replies were actually received. About the first there is unfortunately no information, although it seems likely that the board sampled the larger employer for preference. The sample of employees, however, was large; the initial surveys covered about four million employees in manufacturing and agriculture. The third report (February 1915) extended the survey to include some commercial firms in London, but this did not materially affect the size of the sample. The January 1916 report, however, shows a very large increase in the sample, which now rises to 10·6 million employees, that is, the great bulk of the male labour force (which before the war was about 15 millions).[9] From then on, the surveys cover most manufacturing, service and transport industries in the U.K., as well as British agriculture. The only major occupational groups excluded (apart from employers themselves) were the self-employed, domestic servants, the merchant marine, and Irish agriculture.

The proportion of the national labour force actually represented in the replies to the board's questionnaires is also impressive. Of the initial sample of about 4 millions, replies were received in respect of about 1.7 million men. Of the post-1915 sample of 10·6 millions, replies were received in respect of at least 4 millions, and at most 5 millions, depending on the survey in question. It should be noted, however, that the response to the survey varied considerably between different industries. The lowest rate of response was consistently that of agriculture, which was about 7 per cent throughout the war, whilst central government, mining and metals showed rates which by the end of the war approached 100 per cent, since they were either government agencies *ab initio*, or became controlled by the government during the war. Between these extremes lay the bulk of manufacturing industry, which began the war with response rates of about 40 per cent and finished with about 65 per cent.

What we are presented with, therefore, is a sample survey which indirectly gives information based on a sample of some 1·7 million men until January 1916, when the sample rises to between 4 and 5 million men. These amount to about 11 per cent of the national labour force before 1916, and to between 26 and 32 per cent thereafter. These are very large samples by any standards, but sheer size is not necessarily a guarantee of reliability, and in the absence of any information on how the sample was drawn, it is not possible to apply statistical tests to the survey results to see how reliable they are. All that can be done is to find some external criterion against which to judge the success of the surveys. The most useful test here is obviously the official enlistment

[9] Fifteen millions is in fact an excessive estimate. The 1911 census of population recorded 12.9 million occupied and 2·5 unoccupied males in Britain – B. R. Mitchell and P. Deane, *Abstract of British historical statistics* (Cambridge, 1971), p. 60. However, the 'unoccupied' group seems to have included some occupied persons. The total labour force was thus between 12·9 and 15·4 millions. In so far as the true figure was nearer to 12·9, the scope of the board's surveys becomes even more impressive.

Table 1. *Enlistment, 1914–18*

	Board of trade enlistment estimate to November 1918		Official enlistment totals to 11 November 1918
A. Reported in board's surveys	4,981,000	Army	4,970,000
B. Additional estimate for unsurveyed industries and employers	797,000	Navy	407,000
		R.A.F.	293,000
Totals	5,778,000		5,670,000

figures themselves. When these are compared to the survey results, the correspondence is very close (Table 1).[10]

The correspondence is indeed so striking as to raise the question as to whether it is genuine. However, the actual survey results seem to be quite genuine; they are consistent throughout the war, and there is no sudden break or change of direction in the enlistment rates recorded. If there is a dubious element here, it is estimate B, which seems to be largely guesswork on the board's part, and brings the total estimate up to the official total a shade too neatly. However, even ignoring estimate B, the Board managed to record about 88 per cent of the actual enlistment which occurred. It seems, therefore, that the board's surveys may be accepted as a reliable guide to wartime enlistment rates in different industries. These rates may now be presented (Table 2).[11]

Differences in enlistment rates appeared early on in the war. By July 1915, rates in the twelve industries surveyed at that time (eleven manufacturing industries and British agriculture) range from 13 per cent (government establishments) to 24 per cent (food, drink and tobacco). Even if one ignores government establishments as atypical,[12] rates still vary considerably, from 15 per cent (agriculture) to 24 per cent. By July 1916 one can consider a much wider range of industries, and the differences are even more marked, not only between individual industries, but between different sectors of the economy. By the end of the war, both these types of difference showed large variations. Amongst individual industries, rates varied from 23 per cent (canals) to 69 per cent (government establishments). These were small industries before the war, and so perhaps unrepresentative, but large industries also show wide variations; in July 1918 they ranged from 28 per cent (railways) to 64 per cent

---

[10] Board of Trade, *Report on the state of employment... on November 11th 1918 and January 31st 1919*; War Office, *Statistics*, p. 363.
[11] Board of Trade, *Report on the state of employment* (1914–18). In order to obtain a clearer picture of trends in enlistment during the war, July figures only have been used here.
[12] See Appendix 1.

Table 2. *Enlistment in the United Kingdom, 1914–1918*

	Male labour force July 1914 ('000)	Enlistment since July 1914 as % of July 1914 labour force				Enlistment to July 1918 ('000)
		July 1915	July 1916	July 1917	July 1918	
1. Manufacturing						
Building	920	19	33	43	47	430
Mining	1,266	21	24	28	35	448
Metals	1,634	19	25	33	42	681
Chemicals	159	23	34	46	53	85
Textiles	625	16	31	42	47	292
Clothing	287	18	37	52	59	170
Food, drink and tobacco	360	24	40	54	61	221
Paper and printing	261	20	35	47	52	135
Wood	258	21	36	48	53	136
Government establishments	76	13	26	54	69	53
Other trades	393	21	32	41	46	180
Totals	6,239					2,831
Average enlistment rates		20	30	39	45	
2. Agriculture (permanent labour: Great Britain only)						
	800	15	22	30	35	281
3. Transport						
Railways	656	n.a.	18	25	28	184
Docks	100	n.a.	16	26	31	31
Trams (private)	15	n.a.	40	43	51	8
Trams (local government)	57	n.a.	37	46	50	28
Omnibus	20	n.a.	47	60	63	12
Cab	33	n.a.	40	54	56	18
Road	273	n.a.	33	50	57	156
Canal	20	n.a.	n.a.	19	23	5
Totals	1,174					442
Average enlistment rates		n.a.	23	33	38	
4. Commerce, finance, services						
Commerce (wholesale and retail)	1,225	n.a.	41	57	64	784
Banking and finance	176	n.a.	41	52	56	99
'Professions'*	143	n.a.	43	57	63	90
Entertainment	185	n.a.	44	65	65	115
Totals	1,729					1,088
Average enlistment rates		n.a.	41	57	63	

Table 2. *Enlistment in the United Kingdom, 1914–1918 (cont.)*

	Male labour force July 1914 ('000)	Enlistment since July 1914 as % of July 1914 labour force				Enlistment to July 1918 ('000)
		July 1915	July 1916	July 1917	July 1918	
5. Public services						
Central government	52	n.a.	25	39	54	28
Local government	323	n.a.	24	31	34	110
Post Office	188	n.a.	33	40	43	81
Gas, water, electricity	62	n.a.	24	32	35	22
Teaching	54	n.a.	34	39	42	23
Totals	679					264
Average enlistment rates		n.a.	27	35	39	
Grand totals (1–5)	10,621					4,906
Average enlistment rates		n.a.	30	40	46	

* Chiefly clerks in professional firms such as solicitors.   n.a. = not available.

Table 3. *Average sector enlistment rates, July 1916 and July 1918 (per cent)*

July 1916		July 1918	
Commerce	41	Commerce	63
Manufacturing	30	Manufacturing	45
Public services	27	Public services	39
Transport	23	Transport	38
Agriculture	22	Agriculture	35

(commerce). It is also noticeable that there are wide variations within broad economic sectors; in manufacturing, for example, from 35 per cent (mining) to 61 per cent (food, drink and tobacco), and in transport from 28 per cent (railways) to 63 per cent (omnibus). The differences between sectors become apparent from the beginning of the war, and continue throughout it, the ranking of the sectors being unchanged (Table 3).

III

It is clear that substantial differences existed in the propensity of different industries to supply men to the forces, and that these differences persisted throughout the war. Further, these differences antedate the introduction of conscription (first effective in March 1916),[13] being apparent for maufacturing industries in 1915, and for a much wider range of industries at the time of their first inclusion in the survey (January 1916).[14] Thus the observed differences in enlistment rates cannot be attributed to conscription.

To what, therefore, can these differences be attributed? In order to attempt a solution of this problem, it was decided to examine four possible explanations which seemed, *a priori*, to be worth attention. These explanations are economic, demographic, medical and institutional. The economic explanation hinges on the questions of wages and industrial activity levels. As far as wages were concerned, it is clear that for all except the lowest-paid, joining the forces involved a financial sacrifice. Even with the separation allowances which were paid to men's dependants, and the compulsory deductions from pay which were passed on to their dependants, the resulting family income was only slightly above that of the ordinary English agricultural labourer, who on the eve of the war was one of the worst-paid of all manual workers.[15] It may therefore be thought that the desire to enlist would be less in high-wage industries than in low-wage ones. Also, since wages during the war rose much faster in some industries than in others, it may be the case that a similar disincentive existed in the high wage-*rise* industries; men in such industries who enlisted would be giving up a relative improvement in their wages (both actual and prospective) by doing so. Finally, it is also clear that the levels of activity varied between different industries in wartime; some expanded greatly and some contracted. While it was usually the case that high activity levels were accompanied by high rates of wage increase, and low activity levels by low rates of wage increase, so that the incentive to enlist would be weaker in high activity industries than in low activity ones, it may also be suggested that activity levels had an effect on the perceived prospects of unemployment. A high activity rate meant little prospect of unemployment as long as one remained in that

---

[13] Although conscription, in the form of the Military Service Act, passed into law on 27 January 1916, it only came into effect from 2 March, and then only by stages. Full conscription did not appear until the second M.S.A. of 1916, which did not take effect until 24 June – N. B. Dearle, *An economic chronicle of the Great War for Great Britain and Ireland* (Oxford, 1929), entries for 27 Jan.–25 May 1916.

[14] Board of Trade, *Report on the state of employment... January 1916*.

[15] Separation allowances were first paid by the army from 1 October 1914; for the families of corporals and privates they ranged from 12s. 6d. for a childless wife to 22s. for one with four children; these figures include the deduction from pay made by the army. These rates were raised from 1 March 1915 to a range of between 12s. 6d. and 25s.; *Allowances and pensions in respect of seamen, marines and soldiers and their wives, widows and dependants* (P.P. 1914–16, XL, Cd. 7662); War Office, *Regulations for the issue of army separation allowance allotments of pay and family allowances during the present war* (1916), pp. 5–6. These rates may be compared with the earnings figures on p. 208 below.

particular industry, and might well serve to attract labour into that industry from elsewhere. Thus high activity industries would be liable to show low enlistment rates on the grounds of job security; conversely, industries with low activity rates carried with them a greater prospect of unemployment. Since, as ever, a simple and quick way to avoid this was to join the forces, low activity levels may also have served to stimulate enlistment from the industries concerned, quite apart from questions of wages.[16]

The demographic explanation is simply that of the relative differences in age-structure encountered in different industries. Clearly, the existence of a high proportion of males of military age in an industry would tend to permit high levels of enlistment; a low proportion would inhibit enlistment. This rather obvious point has been neglected so far.

The medical explanation is that standards of health and physical fitness may have varied amongst industrial groups widely enough to cause enlistment rates to differ appreciably.

The institutional explanation is that of protection from enlistment. This is normally considered as effective only during the conscription period. However, some degree of protection may be found in certain industries at an early stage in the war; later on, such protection was reinforced in some industries and denied to others. Thus protection has an obvious bearing on the differential enlistment tendency which has been observed.

The question of wages and their influence on enlistment rates may be examined first. Data on pre-war earnings are available for seven major industries, and are presented in Table 4.[17]

The impression from Table 4 is that the hypothesis of an inverse correlation between earnings and enlistment is unjustified. It is certainly not borne out in the case of the lowest-wage industry of all (agriculture), and the highest-wage industry (building) has a high enlistment rate. The same seems to be true of printing (although compositors' wages may not be a very good proxy for those in paper and printing as a whole). Whilst the case of textiles might seem to support the original hypothesis, the data relate to all employees, of whom a large number were women and young persons, who were paid less than men, so that male textile workers were higher up the scale than the table indicates. Railways have a low enlistment rate, but do not really seem to qualify as a high-wage industry. Only in the cases of engineering ('metals' in the surveys) and mining might there be grounds for thinking that high wages provided some degree of disincentive to enlistment.

The impression that wages played only a minor role in determining enlistment variations is supported by considering the *rate* at which they changed in different industries (Table 5).[18]

---

[16] Barnett, *Britain and her army*, caption to plate facing p. 428.
[17] A. L. Bowley, *Prices and wages in the United Kingdom, 1914–1920* (Oxford, 1921), pp. 113, 127, 149, 159, 163, 172, 179, 183.
[18] Ibid. p. 105.

Table 4. *Industrial earnings and enlistment rates*

Industry	Occupation	Pre-war weekly earnings s. d.		Enlistment rate (July 1916)
Building	Bricklayers (8 cities)	42	10	33
Engineering	Turners (Sheffield)	41	0	25 (metals)*
Mining	All employees	39	0	24
Printing	Compositors (London)	39	0	35 (paper and printing)*
Railways	All employees	26	6	18
Textiles	All employees (cotton and wool)	18	7	31
Agriculture	Ordinary labourers (England and Wales	16	10	22

* Parent group in Board of Trade surveys.

Here, the only support for the thesis that high rates of wage increase tended to inhibit enlistment comes from docks, coal mining, and perhaps also railways. In the case of the other industries, the link is less clear; thus textiles show a rate of enlistment which is about average for manufacturing, but is split between a high-rise section (woollens) and a low-rise one (cottons). But it is noticeable that the enlistment rate in the Yorkshire textile industry (i.e. woollens) was particularly low, so perhaps the thesis applies in this case.[19] It might be the case that a low rate of increase in printing tended to stimulate enlistment, but the drawback to citing compositors' wages in this context has already been pointed out.

The only example of a major industry which contracted during the voluntary recruiting period, and which thus might be expected to show a high enlistment rate, is building. Here the main problem was the wartime decline in housebuilding. The average number of houses built each year in Britain between 1909 and 1913 was 72,000. On the outbreak of war, the level of housebuilding activity fell immediately, and in 1916 (the last war year for which figures are available) only 17,000 were built.[20] Nor was this decline made good by government contracts for barracks, airfields, etc. Raymond Postgate was of the opinion that the decline in activity was the major factor in encouraging building workers to join the forces.

[19] See below, p. 217.   [20] Mitchell and Deane, *Abstract*, p. 239.

Table 5. *Wage-rate increases and enlistment rates*

Industry	Wage-rates July 1916 (July 1914 = 100)	Enlistment rate July 1916 (%)
Docks (labourers)	130	16
Coal mining	129	24
Woollens and worsteds	126	31 (textiles)*
Railways	120	18
Bricklayers' labourers	115	33 (building)*
Engineering artisans	111	25 (metals)*
Bricklayers	108	33 (building)*
Cotton operatives	107	31 (textiles)*
Compositors	105	35 (paper & printing)*

* Parent group in Board of Trade surveys.

Unemployment increased with the cessation of private building. Building trade workers poured into the army, and their history from 1914 to 1918 is the history of the British army in Flanders.[21]

This is clearly an exaggerated view; the enlistment rate in building at July 1916 was above the average for manufacturing, but only slightly (33 per cent as compared with 30 per cent). Still, in view of the peculiar problems of building, which were not shared by any other major industry, it may be that a low level of activity did make some contribution to raising the rate of enlistment.

On the whole, therefore, it does not seem that considerations of wages and activity levels go very far to explain enlistment rate differentials except in a few cases; it may be that high wages discouraged enlistment from metals and mining, that high wage-rises discouraged enlistment from docks, railways and coal mining, and that a low rate of activity in building stimulated a slightly higher than average enlistment rate. But for the economy as a whole, the evidence is that such economic factors played a subordinate role in determining enlistment rates.

The second explanatory variable to be considered is the age-structure of the industries concerned. The hypothesis here is simply that industries with a high proportion of their labour force within the military age-limits would be likely to show a high enlistment rate, and those with a low proportion a low enlistment rate; a hypothesis which may seem merely otiose, but which has the distinction of being unexplored so far. In order to test this hypothesis, the relationship between enlistment rates and age (from the 1911 census of

[21] R. Postgate, *The builders' history* (n.d., ? 1923), p. 423.

Table 6. *Industrial age-structure and enlistment rates*

Industry	Percentage of labour force aged 20–34 (England and Wales)	Percentage of labour force aged 20–44 (Great Britain)	Enlistment rate (%) July 1915	Enlistment rate (%) July 1916
Omnibus	44	74	n.a.	47
Other road transport	42	64	n.a.	33
Hotels, etc.	41	61	n.a.	44
Post Office	40	69	n.a.	33
Chemicals	40	62	23	34
Metals	40	60	19	25
Food, drink, tobacco	39	59	24	40
Mining	39	59	21	24
Paper and printing	38	58	20	35
Commerce	38	57	n.a.	41
Woodworking	37	56	21	36
Building	36	57	19	33
Clothing	35	54	18	37
Textiles	34	51	16	31
Docks	34	61	n.a.	16
Agriculture	34	50	15	22
Railways	31	50	n.a.	18

n.a. = not available

population) was examined. The census age-groups selected as most usefully approximating to the military age-limits were 20–34 years (England and Wales) and 20–44 years (Great Britain); Ireland was excluded from consideration. The proportion of each industry's male labour force falling within these age-limits in 1911 was calculated in respect of seventeen industries. The results are presented in Table 6, in conjunction with enlistment rates for July 1915 and July 1916.

Clearly, the proportions of recruitable labour in each industry varied quite widely, and a cursory glance at this comparison does suggest that, at least in certain cases, there did exist a significant relationship between these age-groups and the rate of enlistment. It was decided to see if this presumed relationship was statistically significant by applying Spearman's formula for rank correlation. The results were as shown in Table 7.[22]

Generally, the implication of this analysis is that age was the largest single

[22] See Appendix II.

Table 7. *Rank order correlation coefficient (r) of age-groups and enlistment rates*

	20–34 group (England and Wales)		20–44 group (Great Britain)
July 1915	r = 0·81	July 1915	r = 0·78
July 1916	r = 0·58	July 1916	r = 0·37
July 1917	r = 0·56	July 1917	r = 0·23
July 1918	r = 0·56	July 1918	r = 0·25

Table 8. *Percentage of male employees aged 18–40 enlisting*

	April 1915	October 1915	February 1916
Average rate (10 industries)	32	40	46
Highest rate	35	48	58
Lowest rate	27	36	40

determinant of enlistment variations during the first year of the war; thereafter, and especially after the introduction of conscription, age was only a minor factor in determining enlistment variations, although by no means negligible. Thus age correlates quite well with enlistment rates for both age-groups in 1915; there is a moderately strong correlation between the 20–34 age-group and enlistment for the rest of the war, but only a weak correlation between the 20–44 age-group and enlistment after 1915. However, these conclusions are subject to the qualifications expressed in Appendix II.

These remarks are confirmed by the available information on the proportion of young males enlisting from the various industries. This consists of an analysis by the Board of Trade of the proportions of male employees aged 18–40 enlisting at various dates (Table 8).[23]

It seems clear that, in the early months of the war, the tendency for young men to enlist was almost uniform between different industries, and thus there is a strong presumption, to put it no higher, that age was the main determinant of enlistment rate variations. But by February 1916 this correlation seems to be weaker, since the enlistment rates clearly vary more widely than before.

The third explanation to be examined is the medical one. Here, the thesis is that standards of fitness and general health may have varied so much between different industries or occupational groups that enlistment rates may have been materially affected.

[23] P.R.O., RECO I/832, Board of Trade, *Enlistment from the industrial classes and the state of employment on government and other work in mid-February 1916*, pp. 8–9.

In order to test this thesis, what is required is an analysis of the medical categories achieved by recruits throughout the war, and in particular details of those rejected for service, in relation to the occupations or industrial provenance of intending recruits. Unfortunately, no such information exists. The nearest substitute is a report prepared by the ministry of national service on the results of some two-and-a-half million medical examinations in the year November 1917–October 1918.[24] While this might seem to be a sample of respectable size, there are certain problems in using the report to test the above thesis. The most obvious defect of the report for this purpose is that it comes late in the war, when presumably the physical condition of recruits was very different from what it was earlier. Also, there is no adequate overall analysis of the results in the report; although it abounds in figures, these are compiled on non-comparable bases, and are of a fragmentary nature. Finally, many of the comments to be found in the general introduction can be either contradicted, or are not substantiated, in the regional reports which make up the bulk of the volume. However, for certain types of labour – i.e. miners, metal workers and agricultural workers – it is possible to extract some general conclusions on the relationship between health and recruitability.[25]

As far as miners were concerned, there is general agreement amongst the doctors who contributed to the report that they formed the fittest type of recruit everywhere, with the least percentage of rejections. A comment from the Glamorgan area may stand as typical:

As compared with other industries in Wales, mining, apart from certain disabilities peculiar to the calling of a collier, produced an excellent type of recruit.[26]

In the case of metal workers, opinions were more mixed and, on the whole, unfavourable. In Sheffield, it was pointed out that the iron and steel trades required men of strong physique, the implication being that they were very suitable recruits. But in Wales it was stated that the physique of men drawn from the local metal industries was 'not of a high standard, and in no way approaches that of the miners'. In the West Midlands, adverse comments were passed on the condition of men from the brass trades, and the 'Birmingham trades' generally.[27]

As for the agricultural worker, he does not emerge as the healthy peasant of popular fiction. While the Cambridge reporter did refer to the healthy nature of farming life, the Norwich reporter spoke of 22 per cent of agriculturalists

---

[24] Ministry of national service, *Report upon the physical examination of men of military age by national service medical boards from November 1st, 1917–October 31st, 1918* (P.P. 1919, XXVI, Cmd. 504).

[25] In spite of the deficiencies of the above report, it probably provides a better guide to the relationship between work and military fitness than earlier records; the medical examinations in the first few months of the war were chaotic, and allowed thousands to pass into the army 'without any medical examination worth the name'. P.R.O., NATS 1/14/20, *Report upon the medical department of the ministry of national service*, p. 13.

[26] Ministry of national service, *Report upon the physical examination*, p. 147.

[27] Ibid. pp. 71, 107, 148.

being rejected due to 'deformities, epilepsy, defective intelligence and tuberculosis'. In the Hertford and Watford districts:

> The younger agriculturalists are of good physique, but they fall off rapidly after 35. Varicose veins and distorted toes are common...A large percentage have cardiac murmurs.

These defects were not confined to eastern England. In Wales, the farm worker was considered generally a good type of recruit, but it was noted that those from arable and dairying districts tended to suffer to a great extent from bad feet and rheumatism.[28]

Whether these general impressions from a late stage of the war were reflected in enlistment rates throughout it is another matter. In the case of mining, which had a fairly high proportion of young men, yet an average to low enlistment rate (especially after 1915), it seems unlikely that the alleged fitness of miners did much to increase the rate of recruitment above what it would otherwise have been. More paradoxically, the metal industries, which had a similar proportion of young men to that of mining, yet were supposed to produce a less healthy recruit, show a higher enlistment rate than that in mining (at least after 1915). Again, it seems unlikely that occupational health considerations had much to do with enlistment rates. In the case of agriculture, other considerations seem to have been overshadowed by the strikingly low proportion of men of recruitable age; it can only be surmised that the mixed picture of the agriculturalist's health presented in the above report did not influence recruiting much either way.

The final explanatory variable to be considered is that of protection from enlistment. In this context, it is perhaps natural to think of the moves made in 1915 to protect essential munitions labour, culminating in the work of the newly formed ministry of munitions. However, some degree of protection came much earlier for some industries; thus on 4 September 1914 the body that controlled the railways of Britain, the Railway Executive Committee, stated that men who wished to enlist could only do so if the company that employed them certified that they could be released for military service. This decision, which also applied to canals controlled by the railway companies (about one-third of the canal mileage in the U.K.) was confirmed by the War Office in a subsequent notice to recruiting officers.[29] The next organization that acted to protect its labour was the Admiralty, which began to protect its production workers 'in the later months of 1914'. This process culminated in December 1914 in the issuing, for the first time, of badges to denote that the wearer was an essential worker who should not be asked to enlist. This precedent was followed in March 1915 by the War Office, which began issuing badges to its own workers in Royal Factories, and also to those in private firms engaged on War Office work. Badges were issued in large quantities, especially by the

---

[28] Ibid. pp. 117, 120, 149.
[29] E. A. Pratt, *British railways and the Great War* (2 vols., London, 1921), I, 349.

Admiralty, which had issued (perhaps over-issued) some 400,000 by July 1915; the War Office was responsible for the more modest total of 80,000. In May 1915 recruiting officers had been told by the War Office that certain skilled munitions workers were not to be enlisted (although it was up to the employer to decide whether a man was skilled or not). Finally, in July of the same year, the newly created ministry of munitions became the sole badging authority for the munitions industry, although the actual issuing of badges was still the responsibility of the employer. In effect, the latter could retain whom he wished; the ministry did little to check the process.[30]

There seems no doubt that by the end of 1915 a large number of men of military age were effectively exempt from military service, chiefly those in the munitions industry. Indeed, by early 1916 the large number of badges already issued had become a subject of concern to the government. In an endeavour to find more men for the forces, a process of 'debadging' was initiated, via the cabinet committee on exemptions.[31] The attempt to debadge was unsuccessful, since the advice tendered by the committee to the ministry of munitions went largely unheeded. By the end of August 1916, reports had been received by the ministry on the cases of some 850,000 badged men (there were in all some 1·1 million),[32] but only about 40,000 badges had actually been withdrawn. As the historian of the munitions labour supply aptly commented: 'Mountains had been in labour, but from the recruiting point of view, 40,000 was a ridiculous mouse.'[33]

The introduction of conscription did not reduce the amount of protection enjoyed by the British labour force. Indeed, it tended to increase it somewhat, and to make it subsequently more difficult to reduce. The reason for this was that, parallel with the introduction of conscription went the realization that such a scheme would have to be accompanied by some form of systematic exemption, since otherwise conscription would render it impossible to produce the necessary goods for civilian and military use. This realization began as early as August 1915, with the passage of the National Registration Act, which aimed to produce a comprehensive listing of the occupations of all civilians of working age. Subsequently, 'reserved' lists were drawn up which included coal mining, steel production, iron mining, skilled farm work and certain occupations on the railways. In October this work was taken over and continued by the newly created reserved occupations committee, which began to draw up a comprehensive list of occupations that would be exempt from military service. In January 1916 the committee issued its first list of certified occupations, detailing those which should be considered as exempt when the Military Service Act (i.e. conscription) should become law (it did so on 27 January 1916).[34]

Before the introduction of conscription, protection had been chiefly confined to munitions, via the system of badging. Now it was extended to cover a variety

---

[30] Wolfe, *Labour supply*, pp. 19–28. [31] Ibid. p. 40.
[32] Ibid. p. 38. [33] Ibid. p. 40.
[34] Ibid. pp. 29–33; Dearle, *An economic chronicle*, entry for 27 January 1916.

MILITARY RECRUITING

of other industries in manufacturing, transport, agriculture and the public services. Thus, as well as metals (largely synonymous with munitions, and thus well protected already), substantial protection was now given to mining, textiles, footwear, transport (in the form of railways, canals and docks), agriculture, cement and brick production, chemicals, leather, flour milling and baking, public utilities and local government. The omissions from the list are employers themselves, office workers, the retail trades, most wholesale trades, the bulk of the building industry, 'light' (i.e. non-military) clothing, road transport and central government administration.[35]

The system of exemption was completed by the introduction of tribunals to decide upon particular exemptions. The main function of these was to decide the cases of men who were not in exempt occupations, but claimed exemption either on the ground of being indispensable to a particular trade or enterprise, or on more personal grounds such as medical incapacity or the existence of dependent relatives. However, tribunals could also consider cases in which the military authorities challenged the exemption of a man who was, in fact, in an exempt occupation; theoretically this did not constitute absolute protection, and each case could be considered on its merits. In practice, however, these were difficult cases to challenge, and if a man's occupation was exempt he was more or less immune from military service.[36]

The evolution of the exemption system led to a steady rise in the numbers of men protected from conscription. At the end of October 1916 about 1·4 million men were in possession of badges;[37] by the end of April 1917 about 2 million were in protected occupations,[38] and by the end of October 1918 the figure had risen to 2·3 million. To these should be added tribunal exemptions, which fluctuated at about the three-quarter million mark for the last two years of the war.[39] Various attempts were made by the government during these years to reduce the number of exemptions. Thus the list of certified occupations was revised four times in 1916–17 (usually by raising the age at which exemption commenced), and was completely recast in February 1918 (now appearing as the 'schedule of protected occupations'). Finally, in April 1918, whole classes of exemptions were cancelled by royal proclamation, to meet the increased demand for soldiers consequent upon the German offensive. However, the figures above indicate that none of these expedients succeeded in reducing the number of exemptions.[40]

[35] P.R.O., NATS I/53, *List of certified occupations* of 4 April 1916 (R. 74); 7 July 1916 (R. 94); 20 Nov. 1916 (R. 105).

[36] Ibid.; the coal mining industry had its own system of tribunals, the colliery recruiting courts, which were established shortly before the passage of the first Military Service Act – G. D. H. Cole, *Labour in the coal-mining industry (1914–1921)* (Oxford, 1923), p. 39.

[37] P.R.O., NATS I/53, memorandum dated 25 October 1916 addressed to the War Committee. However, only 1,050,000 of these were of military age.

[38] *General annual reports of the British army (including the territorial force from the date of embodiment) for the period from 1st October 1913 to 30th September 1919, prepared by command of the Army Council* (P.P. 1921, xx, Cmd. 1193), pp. 10–11. [39] Ibid. p. 10.

[40] Dearle, *An economic chronicle*, entries for 1 Jan. 1916; 7 July 1916; 17 Nov. 1916; 20 June 1917; 1 Jan. 1918; 20 April 1918.

Table 9. *Sectoral enlistment rates, July 1918*

Sector	Degree of protection	Enlistment rate (%)
Agriculture	High	35
Transport	High	38
Public services	High	39
Manufacturing	High/moderate	45
Commerce, etc.	Very low	63

Table 10. *Regional enlistment rates (%), July 1915 (10 industries)*

London	21	Yorkshire	17
South East	22	North West	20
South West	22	North	22
West Midlands	20	Scotland	24
East Midlands	17	Wales	20
	Average	20	

The exemption system goes far to explain the differences in enlistment rates between different sectors and industries after the introduction of conscription. The industries which received the greatest protection were metals, mining, agriculture and the railways (with the minor additions of docks and canals). These all show notably low enlistment rates by the end of the war. There is in fact only one case of a highly protected industry showing a high enlistment rate – the chemical industry. The moderately protected ones such as the remainder of the manufacturing sector show moderate enlistment rates; the unprotected ones show high rates. In the case of the commercial sector, which was almost completely unprotected, the rates are all very high, and much higher than those for any other sector of the economy. The sectoral differences are brought out most clearly when the degree of protection is contrasted with the enlistment rate towards the end of the war (Table 9).

In attempting to provide some explanations for enlistment rate differences, it may finally be suggested that there is some evidence to show that all the explanatory variables considered so far – economic, demographic, medical and institutional – were subject to regional influences. The evidence for this is limited to July 1915 (Table 10).[41]

Clearly there are noticeable regional variations, which reflect the different influences affecting the same industry in different regions, as well as the differences in industrial structure between regions. The regions whose enlistment rates differ most from the average are the East Midlands, Yorkshire and Scotland. The East Midlands figure is kept down by low rates for building (15

[41] Board of Trade, *Report on the state of employment... July 1915*, pp. 7–9.

per cent) and clothing and textiles (17 per cent); its biggest industry, mining, has also a lower than average rate (18 per cent). The Yorkshire figure is kept down by its largest industry (metals: 16 per cent) and also by an astonishingly low 12 per cent recorded by textiles (the third biggest industry in the region). The Scottish experience is that rates are higher than average for every industry, and although its biggest industry (metals) did not show a recruitment rate much above the British average (21 as opposed to 19 per cent), the Scottish average was raised sharply by the very high rate recorded in the building industry (30 per cent), compared with a British average of only 19 per cent. As far as differences in industrial structure are concerned, the usual rule was that the more unbalanced a region's industrial structure, the more did enlistment rates follow those of the dominant industries. Thus in Wales, 60 per cent of the industrial workforce was in mining, which had an enlistment rate of 20 per cent, so it is hardly surprising that Wales as a whole also recorded 20 per cent enlistment. In the West Midlands the dominant industry was metals, with a 19 per cent enlistment rate, so the regional rate followed this closely. But the dominant industry did not provide the whole explanation; in Scotland, 34 per cent of the workforce was in metals, which had a 21 per cent rate, but the regional average was raised above this by a 24 per cent enlistment rate in mining, and the 30 per cent in building already mentioned. Clearly, the analysis so far made at the national level could be repeated at the regional level, and there is scope for much further work here.

IV

Certain conclusions may now be drawn from this study. The first concerns the tendency of different industries to supply men to the forces. It is clear that this varied considerably. This differential tendency is apparent, as far as our information goes, from the earliest months of the war. Thus by July 1915 enlistment rates amongst the larger industries surveyed by the Board of Trade vary from a low of 15 per cent (agriculture) to a high of 24 per cent (food, drink and tobacco). These early differences did not diminish thereafter; indeed they became greater, both absolutely and relatively, as time went on. By July 1918 the extreme rates were those of canals (23 per cent) and government establishments (69 per cent). These cases may be misleading, since both were small industries before the war, but more reliable examples from larger industries still show marked differences – e.g. railways (28 per cent) and commerce (64 per cent).

The second conclusion is that the immediate factors affecting enlistment rates differed from, and were more complex, than those which have usually been cited. As already mentioned, it is common to assume that patriotic feeling played the dominant part in stimulating enlistment, at least during the pre-conscription period. However, even if this were the case, patriotism had to work within certain constraints, the chief of which was the age-structure of the industry concerned. This could sometimes vary considerably. At the 1911 census the proportion of men aged 20–44 averaged 59 per cent in the seventeen industries studied above (p. 210); this average concealed variations amongst the larger industries from 50 per cent (agriculture) to 64 per cent (road transport). These variations could make a great difference to the capacity of an industry to yield men to the forces. For example, pre-war agriculture and building were not too dissimilar in size, yet agriculture, by reason of its more aged workforce, was much less vulnerable to the forces than was building.

	Agriculture	Building
Percentage of workforce aged 20–44 (1911)	49·8	57·3
Number of men aged 20–44 (1911)	398,000	527,000

Even if both had been exactly the same size before the war, there would still have been a large disparity in the numbers of recruitable men; building would have had some 69,000 more men in this age-group than would agriculture.

It is also noticeable that there are only three major industries in which the proportion of enlistable men is much below the average; textiles, agriculture and the railways. The latter two are notable for a very low rate of enlistment throughout the war, and it seems likely that this was largely due to their having comparatively elderly populations; in the case of textiles, this may have assisted to keep enlistment low in 1915, but may have been outweighed by other factors thereafter.

Generally, age-structure differences seem to constitute the largest single factor affecting enlistment rates in the pre-conscription period. To this may be added two subsidiary factors, which may have had some influence in certain cases; activity levels and wages. Thus, for example, it may be that enlistment from the building industry was stimulated somewhat by lack of employment or employment prospects; it may also be that enlistment was retarded by high wages in metals and mining, and by high wage increases in docks, coalmining, railways and the woollen industry. But for the economy as a whole, neither activity levels nor wages serve to explain enlistment differences to any great extent.

After the introduction of conscription, with its accompanying lists of exempt occupations, it seems clear that the largest single influence on enlistment rates was the degree of protection in particular industries. To a great extent, the new forms of protection reinforced existing differences in enlistment rates. Thus the industries receiving the most protection were four - mining, metals, railways (including docks and canals) and agriculture.[42] In all these, enlistment

---

[42] Thus in October 1918 there existed the following number of exemptions: coal mining, 502,000; metals, 1,032,181; railways, 401,641; agriculture, 340,506. In the case of coal mining and agriculture, these amount approximately to three-quarters of the pre-war male labour force

MILITARY RECRUITING

Table 11.

		Proportion of national male labour force (July 1914) (%)	Enlistment proportion, July 1918 (%)
1	Manufacturing	58·7	57·7
	of which: mining	(11·9)	(9·1)
	metals	(15·4)	(13·9)
2	Agriculture (Great Britain)	7·5	5·7
3	Transport	11·0	9·0
	of which: railways	(6·2)	(3·7)
4	Commerce, etc.	16·2	22·2
5	Public services	6·4	5·4
		99·8*	100·0

* Rounding error.

rates were already on the low side, especially in agriculture and (probably) railways, docks and canals. The introduction of systematic exemption ensured that their enlistment rates continued to be low. On the other hand, certain industries which remained virtually unprotected after 1916 already had high enlistment rates; commerce, road transport and certain manufacturing industries such as food, drink and tobacco.

The final conclusion is concerned with the implications of differential enlistment rates for the composition and history of the forces themselves. In so far as the previous occupations of First World War recruits have received any attention, there has been a tendency to assume that the Forces (i.e. chiefly the army) were a cross-section of the nation.[43] Conversely, there is an occasional tendency to assume that the heavy industries such as coal mining contributed disproportionately highly to the creation of the armed forces.[44] Neither of these suppositions is supported by the present evidence. The Forces were clearly not a cross-section of the nation, and the heavy industries played a rather smaller role in the expansion of the Forces than might have been expected from a consideration of their importance in the pre-war economy. This may be seen by analysing the pre-war sizes of the industries in the Board of Trade surveys, and comparing these to the proportion of total enlistment emanating from each sector of the economy (Table 11).[45]

of military age (taken here as 20–44). Classification problems prevent similar calculations being undertaken for metals and the railways. *Census of population*, 1911; *General annual reports of the British army*, p. 11.

[43] Barnett, *Britain and her army*, p. 379.
[44] (Sir) R. A. S. Redmayne, *The British coal-mining industry during the war* (Oxford, 1923), p. 12.
[45] Board of Trade, *Report on the state of employment...July 1918*.

It can be seen that the contribution of manufacturing as a whole was almost identical with its importance in the pre-war economy. This, however, conceals important distinctions within the sector. The two largest pre-war industries, metals and mining, made a rather smaller contribution than did other industries. Since these two were by far the largest manufacturing industries, other made a much higher contribution to the Forces than their size might seem to warrant. Had metals and mining made a contribution commensurate with their pre-war size, their enlistment figures by July 1918 should have been higher by 74,000 and 135,000 respectively.

However, enlistment rates for manufacturing as a whole are much higher than those in agriculture and the railways. As a result, both the latter industries made a disproportionately low contribution to the Forces; about two-thirds of what it would have been if commensurate with the pre-war importance of these industries. In both these cases, one can see the influence of two factors – a low proportion of males of military age in the labour force, and a high degree of protection from military service, especially after the introduction of conscription.

Conversely, there were industries which made a disproportionately high contribution to the Forces. Such were those manufacturing industries which received only partial protection from conscription such as food, drink and tobacco, paper and printing, wood and clothing. But the highest contributions relative to size were not made by manufacturing industries at all, but by those appearing here as 'commerce, etc.', that is, wholesale and retail trade, banking and finance, 'professions' (mainly clerks in professional firms such as solicitors) and entertainment (hotels, public houses, music halls, cinemas, etc.). The enlistment rate for this commercial sector is by far the highest of all. Workers in this sector were not regarded as essential for the prosecution of the war, and thus received no protection from military service, either before or after the introduction of conscription.[46] Nor did they work in occupations which were particularly active and well rewarded, such as munitions, and so did not even have the lure of high wages to keep them in civilian life in the pre-conscription period. Nor for the most part were employers disposed to put obstacles in the way of their workers' enlistment.[47] In addition, there was a ready supply of cheap alternative labour available, in the form of women. The latter could be inducted into the procedures of office and shop with far less difficulty than into those of munitions or other manufacturing industry; it is no accident that after the war the commercial sector was the only one to retain female labour on a

[46] P.R.O., NATS I/53, *List of certified occupations*; it was noted by a former official of the shop assistants' union that shopkeeping became an unprotected occupation during the war. P. C. Hoffman, *They also serve, the story of the shop worker* (London, 1949), p. 245.

[47] Thus some white-collar employees were protected from financial loss on joining the forces; Scottish bank employees who enlisted had their incomes made up to the level of their previous salary by the banks, and the Royal Exchange Insurance Co. gave those enlisting leave on full pay, with a guarantee of their jobs back on their return, at pro rata increases in salary. S. G. Checkland, *Scottish banking; a history, 1695–1973* (London, 1975), p. 563; B. Supple, *The Royal Exchange Assurance; a history of British Insurance 1720–1970* (Cambridge, 1970), p. 423.

permanent basis to any appreciable extent.[48] The result was to lay the commercial sector wide open to the pressures making for voluntary enlistment before 1916 and conscription thereafter. The soldiers of the First World War were as likely to have been clerks or shop assistants in civilian life as to have been miners or engineers.

APPENDIX I

The Board of Trade employment surveys, 1914–1918

These surveys were conducted by the Board of Trade industrial (war enquiries) branch between October 1914 and April 1919. This branch was sometimes referred to as the 'Z 8' branch, and thus the surveys are sometimes referred to as the 'Z 8' surveys. Survey results are available in respect of the following months:

1914	1915	1916	1917	1918	1919
Oct.	Feb.	Jan.	Jan.	Jan.	Jan.
Dec.	Apr.	Apr.	Apr.	Apr.	Apr.
	July	July	July	July	
	Oct.	Oct.	Oct.	Nov.	

Prior to 1918, results for manufacturing, government establishments, docks and (occasionally) railways are for the mid-month; for other industries, the end of the month. Thereafter, all results are for the end of the month. The results for November 1918 are for Armistice Day (the 11th). A report for July 1917 was undoubtedly written, but has not survived; the July 1917 results have been drawn from subsequent reports.

Sampling

References in the reports to sampling procedures are rare. It seems likely that the method adopted was simply to concentrate on the employers with the largest numbers of employees; thus in December 1914 the entire sample was described as consisting mainly of 'large firms', and in April 1915 the Scottish agricultural sample was described as one of 'large farmers'. In the case of English and Welsh agriculture, the average size of farms in the sample was about 340 acres, which was very substantial.

Bases

Originally, the 1911 census of population was used in the reports in order to estimate the size of the pre-war labour force of each industry. This was found to be unsatisfactory, and in October 1915 these bases, upon which the enlistment and employment totals were calculated, were altered. The principle followed was not specified, but the operation was described as being intended 'to substitute for the Census figures estimates of the populations to which the percentages in the tables may be safely applied'. (October 1915 report, p. 1.)

---

[48] In 1911 there were 157,000 females in commercial occupations in Britain; in 1921 the number had risen to 587,000; Mitchell and Deane, *Abstract*, p. 60.

Geographical scope

Although designed to cover the whole of the United Kingdom, the surveys had one large omission, that of Irish agriculture. Since this was by far the most important occupation in Ireland, the surveys are for all practical purposes restricted to Great Britain alone.

Presentation of results

The way in which the results are presented (above, pp. 204–5) may be misleading in two minor respects.

The table does not show that about half the recruiting losses of the economy were made good by new entrants to the labour force, who would themselves become liable in many cases for enlistment. This fact is of most importance in the case of the industries which showed the greatest rate of expansion during the war; in these cases, the rate of enlistment shown on pp. 204–5 is in reality lower than appears. However, this problem probably only renders the enlistment rates meaningless in the case of government establishments, which were of negligible size before the war, and expanded several times over during the war.

The numbers of men enlisted by July 1918 are shown *gross*; they do not take account of men returning from the forces to civilian life – some 775,000 by July 1918, of whom the bulk probably went into manufacturing industry; N. B. Dearle, *The labour cost of the war to Britain* (London, 1940), p. 16.

APPENDIX II

The correlation of enlistment rates with age-groups

The correlation coefficients derived here suffer from certain sources of error, of which the most important are the following.

1. The enlistment rates are derived from the Board of Trade surveys, which are on the whole reliable, but not perfect.

2. The population census includes employers in the industrial totals, but the Board of Trade surveys exclude employers.

3. The census age-groups are not consistent as between England and Wales, and Scotland, and do not fit in with the military age-limits particularly neatly; the latter were in any case changing during the war.

Census age-groups		Military age-limits*	
England and Wales	Scotland		
15–19	18–19	August 1914	19–30
20–24	20–24	May 1915	19–40
25–34	25–44	May 1916	18–41
35–44	45–64	May 1917	18–50
45–54		Apr. 1918	18–51

* Dearle, *An economic chronicle*.

On the whole, it was felt that the most useful comparisons would be with the 20–34 age group (England and Wales) and the 20–44 age group (Great Britain). If there is one particularly unsatisfactory aspect of this selection, it is not being able to

MILITARY RECRUITING

incorporate the 18- to 19-year-olds, who probably provided a high number of recruits.

4. It is possible that emigration in the years 1911–14 changed the relative size of the various industries so as to vitiate the use of the census as a guide to industrial age-structure. The available statistics show that 573,816 U.K. citizens migrated to non-European countries in 1912–14 (intra-European emigration being negligible); N. H. Carrier and J. R. Jeffrey, *External migration, a study of the available statistics* (London, 1953), p. 91. While this seems a large number, it amounts to only some 3·6 per cent of the British population aged 20–44 in 1911 (Mitchell and Deane, *Abstract*, pp. 12–14). Even taking into account the imbalance in the occupations of emigrants (e.g. a large proportion of agriculturalists) it seems unlikely to have substantially affected the industrial structure of Britain, and the statistics of migrants' sex and occupation are in any case imperfect (Carrier and Jeffrey, pp. 103, 124).

[9]

Improvising the British War Effort: Eric Geddes and Lloyd George, 1915–18

Keith Grieves

At the end of the First World War much effort was put into identifying the key contributors to the victorious war effort. In Britain Asquith chose Hankey and Cowans. F.S. Oliver selected Lloyd George, Lord Milner, Henry Wilson and Hankey.[1] Lord Beaverbrook regarded Lloyd George's role as outstanding and the Prime Minister no doubt agreed.[2] Had immense pressure been placed on Lloyd George to consider a second name, albeit of lesser significance than himself, he might have referred to his 'best find from the business world'—the general manager designate of the North Eastern Railway—Eric Campbell Geddes.

In a valedictory note to Geddes in 1922 Lloyd George wrote, 'To me you have been one of the luckiest "discoveries" in life. When I think of the quaffly [sic] places on the road you with your strength and resource helped to lift the cart out of'.[3] Lloyd George's discovery of Geddes was largely fictional on two grounds. First, the Secretary of State for War, Lord Kitchener, was well aware of his potential value to the war effort. Second, Geddes was clearly recommended by the Board of the North Eastern Railway to the government 'for his drive and organising faculty'.[4] However recruited for organising work, Geddes was appropriated by Lloyd George. He became the embodiment of the men of 'push and go' and, subsequently, the pre-eminent troubleshooter of the British war effort.

Geddes personified Lloyd George's method, as described by Lord Esher, 'of placing reliance upon personal responsibility by bestowing extended powers upon individuals selected for their capacity, vigour and courage'.[5] These men operated on specific tasks, on the direct authority of Lloyd George. Each challenge grew in scale as Lloyd George's career advanced, until having to emerge out of the shadows the men of 'push and go' had to respond to the full glare of public interest and parliamentary scrutiny.

On Geddes' death in 1937 Lloyd George noted:

> His energy, his drive, coupled with his mastery of details made of him an administrator who had few equals and no superiors on either side in that terrible struggle. The work he accomplished in

connection with munitions and transport contributed largely to the Allied victory.⁶

In the light of this statement it is the purpose of this article to consider a remarkable wartime career. Initially, it will discuss the absence of historical interest in businessmen or, more accurately, managers at war (for Geddes was not an owner of capital), and then examine aspects of his work at the Ministry of Munitions, GHQ and the War Office and at the Admiralty so that light can be shed on the nature of his working relationship with Lloyd George.

Three major factors are pertinent to the historiography of businessmen, and particularly Geddes, at war. First, despite the valuable material at the Public Record Office and in the Lloyd George papers, no major collection of papers has survived. While his brother's study of the family provides some insight, *The Forging of a Family* is more noteworthy as evidence of the substantial impact of eugenic thought on Edwardian society.⁷ Second, Geddes' wartime career was at the juncture of civil/military relations, bridging the gulf between spheres of responsibility which was certainly inappropriate if a more integrated total war effort was to be pursued. It is only within the framework of war studies, as developed during the last twenty years, that the discussion of hybrid organisers such as Geddes has taken place. Hitherto, the dysfunction of politics and administration, of military and civilian spheres was constantly underlined by separate histories which focussed on the compartments of front or factory, personalities or policy. Third, an organiser such as Geddes offended existing hierarchies because he operated in such an apparently unfettered way, providing relief in the emergency conditions which resulted from breakdowns in the war effort. This role was hardly one which the victors' historiography wished to highlight and its neglect was compounded by Lloyd George's decline. Geddes' work either detracted from the celebration of the Prime Minister as the architect of victory in the general election of 1918, or it constituted a relationship so indistinguishable from Lloyd George's sweep of influence that such a wartime role was subsumed by the post-war reputation of the Coalition government. It is, therefore, the further aim of this article to locate the specific contribution which Geddes made to the development of the total war effort.

On the eve of war the North Eastern Railway (NER) was one of the largest private enterprises in Britain. On the assumption of government control of the railways there was little for the Deputy Manager to do, except what most controllers of industrial manpower did early in the war. The NER raised and equipped two Pioneer battalions of the Northumberland Fusiliers.⁸ Like most 'raisers', Geddes asserted the local identity of these units in correspondence with the War Office. In particular, he urged that men should not be used from these battalions as drafts for other formations, which diluted the separateness of locally raised units of Kitchener's 'New Armies'. The task of organising NER endorsed battalions was largely complete in December 1914. Thereafter Geddes awaited the instruction to go to the Vickers Company to manage one of their production sites or to France to look at military railways, but in the *mêlée* of tasks requiring his attention, Kitchener was unable to organise the deployment of businessmen to mobilise the nation's *matériel* resources.

It was only in the creation of a separate departmental sphere for munitions in May 1915 that 'leading hustlers' were secured from industry on any scale. As Geddes later reflected to A.J. Sylvester in 1932, managers were hired for the Ministry of Munitions in a manner similar to that of labour at the dockyard gates.[9] In the recruitment of businessmen Lloyd George drew a distinction between two categories of industrial leadership. He avoided cautious men who had built their business gradually through total mastery of the minutiæ of their trade. Instead, he sought 'great improvisers' who thrived in emergency conditions and could draw on 'gifts of intuition, rapid decision and force'.[10] The ability to initiate change was crucial for the rapid development of the Ministry of Munitions as a 'battery of dynamic energy'[11] and on that basis Eric Geddes became a central figure of this hastily collected group of men. He was appointed Deputy Director of Munitions Supply and, as a member of the senior management team at Armament Buildings, he was immediately handed responsibility for the production levels of machine-guns, rifles, small arms ammunition, transport vehicles and optical instruments.[12]

Throughout the early life of the Ministry of Munitions one of the less than beneficial aspects of 'improvisation'—a term used so constantly in 1915—was the necessary unravelling of one responsibility from another, of one instruction from another, usually in the daily meetings of the Deputy-Directors of Munitions Supply.[13] Geddes formed the astute habit of writing down a directive from Lloyd George and securing his signature before acting on the agreed contents. While being pressured to pursue 'hastening action', to secure improvements in supply flow, the senior officials did not have frequent access to the minister. Geddes was aware of the limitations of his position, particularly as a manager without technical expertise. Nowhere were the pressures more intense and the problems more fraught than in the machine-guns versus rifles debate which erupted in the summer months of 1915.

For the purpose of clarification, Geddes described the problem as similar to the form in which currency is obtained from a bank.[14] Thirteen rifles can be produced for each machine-gun but which were most needed? Kitchener indicated that as many of both as could be produced were wanted. This response was marginally more helpful than Lloyd George's celebrated statement. He urged Geddes to take Kitchener's figures on machine-guns per battalion 'square it; multiply that result by two; and when you are in sight of that, double it again for good luck'.[15] This perverse instruction recommended 64 machine-guns per battalion in comparison with the pre-war figure of two. Even on a target of eight Lewis machine-guns per battalion in mid-1915, Geddes was forced to reduce rifle output by 10,000 per month.[16] Only in 1916 did GHQ in France demand 16 machine-guns per battalion, but the unrelenting pressure to increase production focussed Geddes' attention on the supply of the second million rifles required after March 1916.[17] British industrial output covered equipment wastage levels, but Geddes realised, earlier than most, that if a 70 division force was the political objective large scale orders would have to be placed in the United States and Canada. He urged that these contracts be supervised and Russian orders in North America monitored to avoid the postponement of early deliveries to Britain.

This problem was much debated by munition officials. Contrary to the celebratory tones of the *History of the Ministry of Munitions* and the Parliamentary Secretary, Christopher Addison's published work, *Politics from Within, 1911–18*, the Ministry was a far from harmonious organisation.[18] In his diary Addison frequently complained about the 'big businessmen' who found it 'difficult among themselves to subordinate their departments one to the other and generally to play the game'.[19] This comment was representative of Addison's frustration with what he regarded as egotistical, quarrelsome organisers, as was the reference to the 'dozen Geddeses in the office'.[20] In fact, these comments were prompted by Addison's fear that the ministry would disintegrate if Lloyd George ever departed and the bonding he provided was lost. Dr Christopher Wrigley has highlighted the problem of securing managerial control over the whole organisation,[21] and from the correspondence between Geddes and Lloyd George it was clear that the Minister of Munitions neither trusted his subordinates nor knew exactly what they were doing.

In December 1915 Geddes became head of the Filling Factories and Component Distribution organisation. Arthur Lee, Joint Parliamentary Secretary, described the construction of the National Filling Factories as a 'race against time' to produce munitions for the summer offensive in 1916.[22] In this dramatic context, Geddes adopted a pessimistic view of new shell-filling capacity. However, most of the first ten Filling Factories were in production within three months of the commencement of their construction.[23] As a direct result of new productive capacity and the reorganisation of Woolwich and other Ordnance Factories, the amount of explosive filled into high explosive shell rose from a weekly average of 258 tons in January 1916 to 760 tons by 20 May and 1322 tons by 1 July.[24]

As a complete round of 4.5 ammunition required 57 components, this improved production level was evidence of an efficient flow of material between different sites, resulting from more effective overall organisation. Until this point was reached relations between Lloyd George and Geddes were uneasy. Until Geddes was appointed to secure an improved shell-filling programme, deficiencies in supply had not been scrutinised despite the origins of the Ministry, which lay partially in the well-publicised shell crisis in France. In the preparations for the summer offensive in 1916 pressure remained intense, as the weekly reports revealed, and it was not until May that Lloyd George wrote, 'I shall be delighted to break bread with your merry men. The best menu will be your Weekly Reports, and the returns of the last few weeks will provide the most sparkling champagne'.[25] From this point Lloyd George never lost confidence in his work, and one month later Geddes announced that shell-filling in Britain would meet all probable demands.[26]

Geddes' newly-won confidence in the flow of munitions supply arose out of the successful implementation of a production review procedure. He developed a weekly schedule based on a knowledge of available capacity and the accurate forecasting of assembly levels at individual factories. Each week a realistic order was placed with every factory and on Wednesday the scale of work completed was compared with the allocation target and previous performances. On Thursday and Friday the deficient areas of production were checked and each Saturday at 12 noon the outcome was discussed so that the following week's targets were adjusted in relation to recent experience. For example, the impact of specific problems such as air raids, late snowfall, holidays and accidents were quantified and the variables of production thereby monitored. Consequently, shortfalls in supply became more explicable and remedial action was pursued more vigorously, where possible. Geddes was responsible for this stringent review mechanism and several months after it was introduced, the system was explained to Lloyd George.[27] This innovation arose from an appreciation of information flow, rather than from ministerial intervention, and Geddes was therefore responsible for introducing the notion of statistical control as an adjunct to munitions work.

The supervision of independently operating units of production was based on trunk, or cumulative, statistics which arose from branch statistics. The section which collected this information was headed by J. George Beharrell, whom Geddes had known at the NER since 1904. Overall, the heads of sections in Geddes' department represented a meshing of managerial, statistical and technical expertise, comprising military and civilian personnel. He secured the services of NER staff, including S.T. Burgoyne, his private secretary, mechanical engineers from Teeside, artillery officers and Professor A.L. Bowley from the London School of Economics.

Lloyd George's departure from the Ministry of Munitions in July 1916 to become Secretary of State for War, on Kitchener's death, had an immediate impact on many men of 'push and go'. Their authority was dependent on their proximity to Lloyd George as unpaid quasi-civil servants. In munitions work their power had developed through delivering data, assigning priorities and establishing production schedules for the minister. Lloyd George took many managers with him to the War Office and in so doing he highlighted the explicit link between his ministerial ambition and the avoidance of existing administrative practices. The new Secretary of State for War secured personnel who would prove invaluable in surveying aspects of the military sphere which required reform, not least of whom was Geddes.

Throughout the autumn months of 1916 the new Minister of Munitions, Edwin Montagu, was distraught. He drew a parallel between his ministry and the condition of Fricourt after a British bombardment. He observed that Lloyd George's story of the Ministry originally comprising a table and some chairs and little else was a condition which would shortly be restored. His complaints, however, concerned personnel. On 11 October Montagu informed Lloyd George:

> When Geddes left this ministry, he took with him Nash and Beharrell, and since then I can hardly bear to look at War Office correspondence, for almost every day, if you will excuse a slight exaggeration, I receive a request for the services of some new men to be sent somewhere or other, sometimes China, sometimes France. By a curious coincidence they are nearly always NER men, and it looks as though we shall be left without a railway man anywhere about.[28]

By the time this letter was written Geddes had visited France at Lloyd George's instigation to survey the congestion on the rearward military lines.

Geddes went to France in late August 1916 with a proven record and an appropriate background. As an expert in railway administration he was required to consider how filled shell could best be transported to the front. In September 1916 Geddes was appointed Director General of Military Railways at the War Office and, concurrently, at Haig's invitation, Director General of Transportation on the staff of GHQ. The dual appointment caused friction, particularly in France where the establishment of a separate transport base, soon known as Geddesburg,[29] caused a 'fluttering of military dovecotes'. Colonel Le Roy-Lewis George, military attaché at the British Embassy in Paris, informed Lloyd George:

You can never get over military prejudices. The appointment of anybody who does not belong to the Military Trade Union is as welcome to soldiers as the appointment of a bishop drawn from the ranks of stockbrokers would be to the clergy.[30]

Geddes was greeted with hostility by whispering careerist staff officers, which was channelled through Lord Esher and found expression in *The Times*.

In London Lloyd George ignored the opposition which was clearly expressed by the Military Members of the Army Council by appointing Geddes as an honorary Major-General and placing him on the Army Council. Having had a transforming impact on munitions supply prior to the Somme offensive, Geddes was similarly expected to resolve *la crise de transportation* in time for the beginning of offensive activity in 1917, so that ammunition was available for the initial bombardment in all necessary sectors. In this work, as in munitions, Geddes' work provides evidence of the merging of separate military and civilian spheres of the war effort. Ironically, the crucial ingredient which made Geddes' adventurous role viable was the support of Haig. He appreciated more quickly than his staff that a civilian with wide relevant experience might make possible the grand military schemes of 1917. Geddes possessed the authority to secure steel allocation from the Ministry of Munitions and the appropriate manpower to build the light railways which were so urgently needed.[31] The rapport between them impressed Lloyd George whose relations with Haig grew increasingly embittered. In November 1917 Lloyd George reflected 'I do not know two men who ever worked in more thorough harmony than Sir Douglas Haig and Sir Eric Geddes'.[32] The partnership was one of the most striking of the war. In particular, it revealed Haig's readiness to utilise expertise otherwise unavailable at GHQ.

In November 1916, 490 locomotives and at least 3000 wagons were required within three months in France[33] and many more, if the transport nightmare became reality and British forces advanced into eastern Belgium. Future plans were again built on statistical data, collated by Beharrell. This included the amount of *matériel* ports could receive, the priority of requirements in France and the capacity of existing rolling stock. The solution to the problem lay in reorganisation and the supply of additional rolling stock. Geddes' role was notable for two reasons. First, he managed the extension of Britain's contribution well beyond the pre-war railway agreement towards a new definition of its obligations, but short of French expectations. Second, he demanded a levy of facilities from British railway companies and private wagon owners, which led in 1917 to the ruthless pruning of passenger traffic, the brewery trade and the closure of lines and stations. Through Geddes' intervention, the integrated war effort became clearly apparent in the organisation of transport facilities. The deficiencies of the military railways in France were surveyed and recommendations were sent by the expert to the Railway Executive Committee. The War Cabinet endorsed the removal of resources from Britain to meet the clearly stated railway needs behind the Allied lines in France. Similarly, railway managers were sent to Salonika and Egypt to review railway provision,[34] but this process was not far advanced when the Inspector General of Transportation in all theatres of war (as from March 1917) was assigned to new and bewilderingly complex duties, laden with political significance and heavy with menace.

In May 1917 'Sir Hindenburg Geddes', the 'Napoleon of Transport', became Controller of the Navy, while briefly retaining some responsibilities for military transport. Thus, to the glee of cartoonists he was Vice-Admiral, Major-General Geddes. The post of Controller was more obviously untenable than any previous task undertaken at the behest of Lloyd George. His initial work at the Admiralty was to supervise ship-building resources, both manpower and *matériel*, thereby freeing Jellicoe, First Sea Lord, from this onerous responsibility. Although the question of labour supply in the dockyards was unfamiliar to Geddes, there was logic in appointing an organiser to carry out for the Admiralty the functions which the Ministry of Munitions had long operated for the army. However, Geddes was unwelcome as a civilian Controller, despite his uniform, and as the general manpower problem was at its most chaotic in the first half of 1917, this task was of immense proportions. Transport might have been Geddes' religion, but he loathed the move because he became immersed in a political conflict which was far advanced on his arrival.

The history of the Admiralty in 1917–18 was the struggle for an executive board which would avoid administrative detail and advocate broad lines of strategy. The gulf between the Grand Fleet and the Admiralty arose out of the board's failure to evolve naval policy appropriate to changing conditions. Lloyd George's appointment of Geddes as Controller represented an initial intervention which was much resented, particularly as he introduced managerial methods which were alien to the badly co-ordinated existing administrative practices which so inhibited innovation. Admiral Sir Henry Oliver, later Deputy Chief of Naval Staff, wrote of Geddes:

> To get peace and to keep him away and occupy him and his staff, my staff used to make up data mixed with weather conditions and phases of the moon which kept them occupied. In a few months wonderful graphs arrived but you cannot run war like a railway; you must look ahead not back.[35]

Oliver was exasperated by the quest for tabulated data and personified an ethos which refused to make sense of the possibilities of the future in the light of a quantitative knowledge of past experience. Geddes' arrival brought Lieutenant-Colonel Beharrell as Director of Statistics, which enabled the deterioration of ship construction in relation to losses to be admitted with a degree of clarity. Consequently, Geddes' period as Controller established the vital priority for the construction of anti-submarine craft.

In July 1917 Geddes' appointment as First Lord of the Admiralty was greeted with some ambivalence, expressed in terms that lacked enthusiasm but were respectful. Rear-Admiral Evan Thomas' note was typical:

> We have made the great Enrico Geddes now First Lord of the Admiralty—the other day assistant manager of a Railway—a bullet-headed sort of a cove who anyway looks you straight in the face which is more than those confounded Politicians will do. So perhaps he will suit us quite well.[36]

Despite gaining rapidly a considerable amount of naval expertise, if not on strategic issues, it was as First Lord of the Admiralty that Geddes became vulnerable. At sub-ministerial level the managers had happily improvised. They were deferential to political power and implemented policy away from the scrutiny of Parliament and the press. Hustlers had succeeded in well-defined areas of the war effort within departments, but in becoming First Lord of the Admiralty, Geddes became politicised.

He was required to become accountable and cooperate with politicians who were not reconciled to Lloyd George's innovatory approach to government and the appointment of 'new ministers'. The acquisition of the label Unionist was no guarantee of political support and the idea of a parliamentary constituency was an onerous irrelevance. Furthermore, in the vying for scarce resources, Geddes enjoyed no greater access to the Prime Minister than other ministers. Indeed, during the manpower crisis of March-April 1918 the Admiralty was a beleaguered department defending its dockyard labour from the blandishments of the Ministry of Munitions and its contingents of Royal Marines afloat from the War Office.[37]

Geddes did not seek political office and feared the Prime Minister's 'sacrificial lamb' technique.[38] For Lloyd George the advantage of the appointment was transparently clear. Who better to inaugurate a post-Fisher era of naval administration and overcome entrenched resistance from the Sea Lords to the prospect of transcending co-ordination? Through sheer 'driving power' Geddes proceeded to transform the casual arrangements. He secured agendas, minutes, votes and the classification and circulation of information. New directorates were established, particularly for mercantile movements, to ensure the more effective co-ordination of convoy, escort and route planning. The decentralisation of work and search for offensive schemes were persistently opposed by the First Sea Lord and the Geddes-Jellicoe battle for supremacy, which culminated in the events of December 1917, was a bruising and unhappy one.

The suggestion by Professor Marder that the handling of Jellicoe was not entirely tactful was fair. However, much mitigation lay in the fact that Jellicoe's dismissal was complicated by a press attack, in which Geddes had no part, and worsened still by the collective manoeuvrings of the Sea Lords. Captain Roskill's presentation of this controversy neglected the vital longer perspective. His selection of letters encompassed the events of late December 1917 only and he suggested that the reader should judge whether 'Geddes' method of making the change was judicious, and whether he was justified in claiming the political support for his action which he did claim'.[39] However, the dismissal of Jellicoe should be viewed in relation to his obstruction of policy changes, for example in failing to pursue with greater vigour the control of the Dover Straits. The logic of Jellicoe's caution was increasing executive inactivity and his departure arose from the failure to employ Britain's diminishing naval supremacy as a more definite offensive weapon.

Geddes firmly intended to avoid the *dénouement* of the struggle with Jellicoe. His wish to leave the Admiralty was clear in the correspondence in 1917 between Lloyd George and the Secretary of State for War, Lord Derby. In late November Derby wrote 'I was absolutely flabbergasted when Geddes came to my room and told me of his suggestion that he should give up his present appointment and return to France'.[40] He added '[t]he French are quite hopeless at running their own railways and we must get the whole management into our hands'.[41] On several occasions Geddes attempted to take up the question of inter-allied transportation as a result of the promise of wide-ranging consultation held out by the establishment of the Supreme War Council.

Somewhat prematurely, Geddes looked forward to full involvement in the expected review of the inter-allied war effort. During December Geddes asked Arthur Lee if he would be Deputy First Lord in the event of being called away for a long period.[42] Undoubtedly, linkage in the planning of maritime and railway traffic was important if American resources and the Anglo-French support of the Italian war effort were to be managed effectively rather than wastefully compartmentalised. Derby argued that Geddes was the only British figure who stood the remote chance of being accepted in France for co-ordination work. Nonetheless, Lloyd George understood more fully the limitations of inter-allied co-operation before the imperative of the German spring offensive in March 1918. The Prime Minister remained firm in his resolve to retain Geddes as First Lord to complete the administrative reforms introduced in 1917.

In political terms, Geddes fended off Churchill's persistent attempts to interfere and had good relations with Beatty which led to closer co-operation between Whitehall, the Harwick Force and the Grand Fleet. He kept at bay the former First Sea Lord, Fisher, whose lobbying notes included the message 'I may <u>be old!</u> but <u>my arteries are all right!!!</u>'.[43]

More importantly, Geddes accepted that the lower deck was 'one great combustible mass'[44] of discontent and he instituted a naval pay review. In 1918 there was the reappearance of a trouble-shooting role for Geddes away from both Parliament and the Admiralty. In the last year of the war he cultivated the role of scrutinising problems and proposing recommendations which were then taken to the War Cabinet. He therefore partially recaptured the freedom of action which he had enjoyed during his period on the staff of GHQ. Geddes thereby avoided the monotony of daily participation in committees and other bureaucratic structures which were so alien to him.

In February 1918 he went to Rome to attempt a more intelligible liaison of allied activity in the Mediterranean and proposed that Jellicoe be appointed Admiralissimo. The failure to secure closer co-operation reflected the problem of Italy's role in the war. In June Geddes travelled to Murmansk to review the naval situation and the 'comic opera' on land. Like many British observers he underestimated Bolshevik military power in north Russia—'only a few scattered ragamuffins'—as well as the obstacles to foreign intervention. In Washington in September-October 1918 Geddes' mission gained access to the President in pursuit of fuller naval co-operation in the organisation of American troop convoys. The availability of transport ships and the respective spheres of operations were contentious issues throughout the months of trans-Atlantic troop movement, but in the autumn months of 1918 the Allied perceptions of the British war effort were proving to be of greater concern to Geddes. In frequently challenging their misconceptions he truly represented Admiralty opinion.

Geddes pursued a more constructive relationship with the British press than previous wartime First Lords, to ensure that the allies were aware of Britain's role as the most substantial shipbuilder, ship repairer and naval power. During the course of the war since the Battle of Jutland it was possible to forget these factors, so vital to the sustenance of the land war. Geddes feared that the importance of naval power was being actively denied by Britain's allies as the end of the war approached. In conversation with Lord Riddell on 25 October the newspaper proprietor recorded that Geddes was

> anxious that the newspaper should comment upon the part taken by the Navy in the war, so that our people, the Americans, our Allies and the enemy may understand what we have done.[45]

Early in November 1918 he lobbied Balfour and Bonar Law for stiff naval terms at the armistice, which infuriated Lloyd George. Like Balfour three years before, Geddes was forced to remind the allies that the contribution of the British Empire should not be solely judged in terms of the number of men in uniform on the western front.

Geddes relished the search for solutions to supply deficiencies and, ultimately, strategic choices. The Admiralty was an exception to the themes of mismanaged initiatives and dispersed political control which was characteristic of much departmental organisation in the wartime Coalition government.[46] In contrast, the political climate of the general election in December 1918 proved utterly unnerving. An early speech was criticised for its dispassionate comments and Geddes responded to public clamour in no uncertain way in stating that 'we will squeeze the German lemon until the pips squeak'.[47] The current of public opinion initially eluded him and was then too forcefully expressed by this businessman in a context perilously close to politics. Geddes left the Admiralty which in peacetime he regarded as a political office and therefore best avoided. Ministerial office would continue beyond 1918 because grand post-war schemes existed, which assumed the continuation of wartime controls. The development of an integrated transport system was regarded as a potential central stimulus to the regeneration of the British economy. As Minister of Transport Geddes continued to serve Lloyd George. The portfolio had a specific purpose which was as crucial in peace as his three roles were in war.

Sir Eric Geddes made a central and largely under-rated contribution to the British war effort as the quintessential 'man for the job'. In December 1915 and August 1916 he focussed on problems whose unravelling was vital if the efficiency of the war effort was to be sustained. His organisational ability, powers of improvisation and industrial experience were particularly appropriate to the questions of production and transport which emerged with such force and scale in 1915–16. Lord Riddell remarked:

> Geddes is a clear headed, forcible man—one of the best of the Ministers. He is a business man with drive, knowledge of organisation and no prejudices in favour of existing methods.[48]

Shell-filling, the congestion of Woolwich Arsenal and the building of military railways in France were facets of the industrial organisation which rendered the war effort more total than in previous conflicts. As a result of the mobilisation of *matériel* and the widening process of participation, relevant expertise did not reside solely in the military domain. On the scale on which problems arose there was no reason to think that the Board of Ordnance was any more capable of providing solutions than managers from private enterprise. In the emergency conditions which arose in 1915 a 'business-man organisation' was founded at the Ministry of Munitions. It was a forcing ground where independently-minded, astute, administratively efficient improvisers survived, especially those without political ambition. Although initially without a technical knowledge of munitions work, Geddes was a Chief Goods Manager at the NER in the pre-war period and he possessed a commercial appreciation of supply questions.

Geddes resisted the sanctity of existing methods but in offending bureaucratic conventions, however irrelevant, opposition arose as the hustling tasks became more visible, for two reasons. First, his proximity to Lloyd George led Esher, Haig and Derby to underestimate his actual independence of action until they met him.[49] Lloyd George's patronage provided a diminishing return and was not expressed in the content of surveys and solutions prepared by Geddes and other leading hustlers such as Sir Hardman Lever, Sir Glynn West, Sir Charles Ellis, Sir Henry Fowler, Sir Arthur Duckman, George Booth, James Stevenson and Lord Weir.[50]

Indeed, ministerial intervention rarely arose from a detailed insight into a particular problem. In this respect Lloyd George's *War Memoirs* misleadingly convey powers of omniscience. Instead, at the Ministry of Munitions and, to a lesser extent, the War Office, Lloyd George received informed advice from organisers who enjoyed considerable autonomy within *ad hoc* sub-sections of the munitions organisation and Army Council. Such freedom of inquiry was not available at the Admiralty. In 1917 the Prime Minister was worried about his long-term political prospects and vulnerability to attack from Asquith. He could not maintain the protective relationship which was available in 1915 to the managers on government war work. Three months after Jellicoe's dismissal, Geddes noted that the questions which continued to be raised required fuller Prime Ministerial support for the position which he had to sustain. Geddes commented to Lloyd George 'You, I know, realise that I am feeling my position personally infinitely more than probably would be the case had I gone through the hardening process of some years in Politics'.[51]

The second reason for the opposition which arose to men of 'push and go' lay in the affront they posed to high politics by working as unpaid organisers beyond existing hierarchical forms of control. They remained outsiders in Whitehall because they embodied the strongest critique of existing methods. Geddes' appointment as First Lord of the Admiralty shocked the political establishment[52] and, despite the hopes of senior naval officers, he did not regard it as a sustainable position after November 1918. While Geddes was from a large private enterprise and loaned for the duration of the war, he was never consciously a representative of the business community. He remained available for further tasks at the war's end but in no sense was he aware of contributing to a wider corporate process of decision-making. For three and a half years from May 1915 he became incorporated loosely within the different tiers of government while modifying pre-war assumptions with regard to civil/military relations. His work and successive posts became evidence of a more total war effort, yet the survival of the departmental framework co-ordinated by the War Cabinet upheld the political process in wartime despite the party truce. Organisers from business responded to successive impediments to the effective prosecution of the war within military, naval and political contexts which they never made their own. Consequently, Geddes' contribution to the war effort was illustrative of the opportunities for innovation which arose and the constraints which impinged on the wartime decision-making process. The eventual retreat of Geddes and other surviving businessmen from the political arena in the post-war years was the logical outcome of the terms on which they had accepted a role in government. Their involvement was temporary but, from an examination of Geddes's work, their participation proved efficacious.

Notes

I am very grateful for the support I have received from Mr A.J. Robertson, Lecturer in Economic History, University of Manchester, in this area of study. An earlier version was read to the Seminar on Military History at the Institute of Historical Research, University of London, which was chaired by Dr David French. A research award from the Leverhulme Trust has enabled me to undertake further work in this area and I am appreciative of the Trust's financial support. Permission to quote from material in their copyright has been obtained from the Beaverbrook Foundation, the House of Lords Record Office and Mr Milton Gendel.

1. Stephen Roskill, *Hankey. Man of Secrets* I (London 1970), 631.
2. Lord Beaverbrook, *Men and Power 1917-18* (London 1959), 345.
3. Lloyd George to Geddes, 24 February 1922, House of Lords Record Office (HLRO), Lloyd George MSS, F/18/4/36.
4. A.K. Butterworth (General Manager, NER) to Lloyd George, 26 June 1915, HLRO, Lloyd George MSS, D/1/2/1.
5. Lord Esher to Lord Murray of Elibank, 28 November 1916, HLRO, Lloyd George MSS, F/41/5/2.
6. Tribute, Sir Eric Geddes, 23 June 1937, unsigned, HLRO, Lloyd George MSS G/8/7/21.
7. Lord Geddes, *The Forging of a Family* (London 1952). P.K. Cline briefly examined some wartime aspects in 'Eric Geddes and the "Experiment" with Businessmen in Government, 1915-22', in Kenneth D. Brown (ed.), *Essays in Anti-Labour History* (London 1974), 75-87.
8. *The Forging of a Family*, 222.
9. Colin Cross (ed.), *Life with Lloyd George: The Diary of A.J. Sylvester* (London 1975), 84.
10. Lloyd George, *War Memoirs*, I (London 1938), 149.

11. C. Addison, diary entry, 28 May 1915, Bodleian Library, Oxford (BLO), Addison MSS, Box 97.
12. Lloyd George to Girouard, Draft letter, 12 June 1915, BLO, Addison MSS, Box 15.
13. Duncan Crow, *A Man of Push and Go. The Life of G.M. Booth*, (London 1965), 117 and 125.
14. *The Forging of a Family*, 224.
15. *War Memoirs*, I, 360.
16. Lloyd George to Geddes, 15 November 1915, HLRO, Lloyd George MSS, D/3/2/20.
17. Geddes, Confidential memorandum for Girouard of Rifles, 17 June 1915, HLRO, Lloyd George MSS, D/3/3/10.
18. *History of the Ministry of Munitions*, 8 vols, (London 1921-2); C. Addison, *Politics from Within 1911-18*, 2 vols, (London 1924).
19. C. Addison, diary entry, 8 July 1915, BLO, Addison MSS, Box 97.
20. C. Addison, diary entry, 6 July 1915, BLO, Addison MSS, Box 97.
21. C. J. Wrigley 'The Ministry of Munitions: an Innovatory Department' in Kathleen Burk (ed.), *War and the State* (London 1982), 41.
22. A. Lee to Lloyd George, Minute, 17 January 1916, HLRO, Lloyd George MSS, D/4/1/4.
23. Geddes to Lloyd George, 1 April 1916, HLRO, Lloyd George MSS, D/3/1/7.
24. Geddes, Memoranda on Filling, 26 May 1916 and 7 July 1916, HLRO, Lloyd George MSS, D/5/1/10 and D/5/2/12.
25. Quoted in *The Forging of a Family*, 230.
26. Geddes, Memorandum on Filling, 17 June 1916, HLRO, Lloyd George MSS, D/5/2/3.
27. Geddes to Lloyd George, 15 March 1916, HLRO, Lloyd George MSS D/3/1/6.
28. Montagu to Lloyd George, 11 October 1916, HLRO, Lloyd George MSS, E/2/19/8.
29. *The Forging of a Family*, 237.
30. Colonel Le Roy-Lewis to Lloyd George, 8 November 1916, HLRO, Lloyd George MSS, E/3/14/26.
31. T. Jones, *Lloyd George*, (London 1951), 74.
32. Draft question and answer, unsigned, 29 November 1917, HLRO, Lloyd George MSS, F/14/4/82.
33. E. Geddes, W. Granet, Transportation. Critical position regarding French rolling stock, 24 November 1916, HLRO, Lloyd George MSS, E/6/1/1.
34. E. Geddes, Memorandum on Transport Facilities in the various theatres of war, 28 October 1916, HLRO, Lloyd George MSS, E/6/1/1.
35. Quoted in A. J. Marder, *From the Dreadnought to Scapa Flow, IV, 1917: Year of Crisis* (London 1969), 176.
36. Ibid., IV, 214.
37. Stephen Roskill, *Hankey. Man of Secrets*, I, 531-2.
38. *The Forging of a Family*, 228.
39. Stephen Roskill, 'The dismissal of Admiral Jellicoe', *Journal of Contemporary History*, I(4) (1966), 72.

40. Lord Derby to Lloyd George, 24 November 1917, HLRO, Lloyd George MSS, F/14/4/78.
41. Ibid.
42. A. Lee, diary entry, 3 December 1917, in Alan Clark (ed.), 'A Good Innings': The Private Papers of Viscount Lee of Fareham (London 1974), 173-4.
43. Fisher to Captain Crease (for Geddes), 12 January 1918, Churchill College Archives Centre, Fisher MSS, FISR 1/25.
44. Lionel Yexley, Editor of *The Fleet*, undated memorandum (seen by Geddes), HLRO, Lloyd George MSS, F/18/2/17.
45. Lord Riddell, *War Diary 1914-1918* (London 1933), 375.
46. For example, on the National Service Department, see K. Grieves, *The politics of manpower, 1914-18* (Manchester 1988), 90-148.
47. See his letter to *The Times*, 15 December 1933.
48. *War Diary 1914-1918*, 341.
49. Lord Esher to Lloyd George, 13 August 1916, HLRO, Lloyd George MSS, E/2/11/2.
50. *War Memoirs*, I, 150-1.
51. Geddes to Lloyd George, Copy, 8 March 1918, British Library London, Balfour MSS, Add. Ms. 49709.
52. See the leader in *The Times*, 18 July 1917, and M. Cole (ed.), *Beatrice Webb's Diaries 1912-24* (London 1952), diary entry for 18 July 1917, 91.

[10]

White Feathers and Wounded Men: Female Patriotism and the Memory of the Great War

Nicoletta F. Gullace

On August 30, 1914, Admiral Charles Penrose Fitzgerald, an inveterate conscriptionist and disciple of Lord Roberts, deputized thirty women in Folkstone to hand out white feathers to men not in uniform. The purpose of this gesture was to shame "every young 'slacker' found loafing about the Leas" and to remind those "deaf or indifferent to their country's need" that "British soldiers are fighting and dying across the channel."[1] Fitzgerald's estimation of the power of these women was enormous. He warned the men of Folkstone that "there is a danger awaiting them far more terrible than anything they can meet in battle," for if they were found "idling and loafing to-morrow" they would be publicly humiliated by a lady with a white feather.[2]

The idea of a paramilitary band of women known as "The Order of the White Feather" or "The White Feather Brigade" captured the imagination of numerous observers and even enjoyed a moment of semi-official sanction at the beginning of the war. According to the *Chatham News* an "amusing, novel, and forceful method of obtaining recruits for Lord Kitchener's Army was demonstrated at Deal on Tuesday" when the town crier paraded the streets and "crying with the dignity of his ancient calling, gave forth the startling announcement: 'Oyez! Oyez!!

NICOLETTA GULLACE is an assistant professor of history at the University of New Hampshire. The author would like to thank Tom Laqueur, Eliga Gould, Sue Grayzel, and Susan Kent for advice and encouragement on drafts of this paper. She would also like to acknowledge the staff of the Imperial War Museum for their abundant help in conducting the research. The research and writing of this article were supported by the Fulbright Hays Commission, the Institute on Global Conflict and Cooperation at the University of California, San Diego, and the John M. Olin Foundation in conjunction with the International Security Program at Yale University.

[1] "Women's War: White Feathers for 'Slackers,'" *Daily Mail* (August 31, 1914), p. 3.
[2] Ibid.

Oyez!!! The White Feather Brigade! Ladies wanted to present the young men of Deal and Walmer . . . the Order of the White Feather for shirking their duty in not coming forward to uphold the Union Jack of Old England! God save the King.' "[3] Numerous women responded to the cry and began to comb the city placing white feathers in the lapels and hat bands of men wearing civilian clothes.[4] The practice was widely imitated by women all over the country and continued long after conscription was instated in 1916, creating one of the most persistent memories of the home front during the war.[5] Dr. M. Yearsley is one of many diarists who recalled that "young girls of all ages and styles of beauty, but particularly those of the type called 'Flappers,' were parading the streets offering white feathers to young men in mufti, with a fine disregard of discrimination. . . . [I]t is an established fact," Yearsley insisted, that "one of these inconsequent children offered her emblem of cowardice to a young man on leave who had just been awarded the V.C."[6]

Despite such vivid recollections, the white feather campaign has generally received only passing attention from historians of the war. Feminist scholars in Britain and America, influenced in the early eighties by the women's peace encampment at Greenham Common, have focused almost exclusively on the much celebrated history of feminist pacifism.[7] Responding to the work of Arthur Marwick, David Mitchell, and others,[8]

---

[3] " 'White Feathers' a Novel Method of Making Young Men Enlist," *Chatham News* (September 5, 1914), p. 8.

[4] Ibid.

[5] Although white feathers were given out in many parts of the country, the practice was most common in London and in port towns where the long history of impressment may have created a culture favorable to such coercive practices. For a sense of the geographical range of white feather incidents, see Imperial War Museum staff, "Great War Index to Letters of Interest," n.d., Imperial War Museum, London (henceforth IWM). According to one contemporary, the "idea spread like a virulent disease." It is unclear exactly how the practice caught on, but it is probable that rumor, newspaper reports, and the depiction of the practice in popular theater and fiction helped spread the idea. See Francis Almond to the British Broadcasting Corporation (BBC), May 25, 1964, IWM, BBC Great War Series [hereafter BBC/GW], vol. ALL-ANT, fol. 339.

[6] M. Yearsley, "Memoirs," IWM, Documents, DS/Misc/ 17, p. 19.

[7] See, e.g., Claire M. Tylee, *The Great War and Women's Consciousness: Images of Militarism and Womanhood in Women's Writings, 1914–64* (Iowa City, 1990); Catherine Foster, *Women for All Seasons: The Story of the Women's International League for Peace and Freedom* (Athens, Ga., 1989); Jill Liddington, *The Road to Greenham Common: Feminism and Anti-militarism since 1820* (Syracuse, N.Y., 1989); Margaret Kamester and Jo Vellacott, eds., *Militarism versus Feminism: Writings on Women and War* (London, 1987); Jo Vellacott, "Feminist Consciousness and the First World War," *History Workshop* 23 (Spring 1987): 81–101; Joan Montgomery Byles, "Women's Experience of World War One: Suffragists, Pacifists and Poets," *Women's Studies International Forum* 8, no. 5 (1985): 473–87; Anne Wiltsher, *Most Dangerous Women: Feminist Peace Campaigners of the Great War* (London, 1985).

[8] Arthur Marwick, *Woman at War, 1914–1918* (London, 1977), pp. 35–36; David Mitchell, *Women on the Warpath: The Story of the Women of the First World War* (Lon-

who recounted graphic tales of female war enthusiasm, the Greenham Common school tended to dismiss the white feather campaign as primarily misogynistic propaganda meant to discredit women and hide the more significant achievements of feminist pacifists.[9] Although recent work in women's history has shifted attention away from the exclusive focus on pacifism,[10] feminist scholarship has nevertheless failed to produce any detailed study of the very issue so painfully emphasized in the older historiography: that of women's participation in the recruiting campaign, particularly their wielding of the language of sexual shame to coerce young men into military service.[11]

The general exclusion of white feather giving from the feminist historiography, I would argue, is more the result of the shameful meaning this practice acquired after the war than of any absence of convincing sources testifying to its contemporary prevalence. Although Virginia Woolf may have been one of the first to suggest that the white feather campaign was more a product of male hysteria than of actual female practice, she has by no means been the last, and the continued skepticism surrounding this practice necessitates some discussion of historical sources.[12] The contemporary evidence consists primarily of local and na-

---

don, 1966). This tradition has also been passed down by word of mouth, in the form of anecdotal evidence that is often repeated but has not inspired much detailed investigation.

[9] See, e.g., Claire M. Tylee, " 'Maleness Run Riot'—the Great War and Women's Resistance to Militarism," *Women's Studies International Forum* 11, no. 3 (1988): 199–210; and Anne Wiltsher, p. 1.

[10] Several excellent studies of women's involvement in various aspects of the war have recently appeared, showing the growing breadth of interest in the diversity of women's experience. See, e.g., Susan Kingsley Kent, *Making Peace: The Reconstruction of Gender in Interwar Britain* (Princeton, N.J., 1994); Angela Woollacott, *On Her Their Lives Depend: Munitions Workers in the Great War* (Berkeley, 1994); Philippa Levine, " 'Walking the Streets in a Way No Decent Woman Should': Women Police in World War I," *Journal of Modern History* 66, no. 1 (March 1994): 34–78.

[11] Most feminist work that has dealt with this aspect of female militancy has been in the fields of literary criticism and political science and has focused on images of women in literary culture. See, e.g., Sandra M. Gilbert, "Soldier's Heart: Literary Men, Literary Women, and the Great War," in *Behind the Lines: Gender and the Two World Wars*, ed. Margaret Higonnet et al. (New Haven, Conn., 1987), p. 208; Helen M. Cooper et al., eds., *Arms and the Woman: War, Gender, and Literary Representation* (Chapel Hill, N.C., 1989), pp. xiii–24; Sharon Ouditt, *Fighting Forces, Writing Women: Identity and Ideology in the First World War* (London, 1994), pp. 89–129; Jean Bethke Elshtain, *Women and War* (New York, 1987), pp. 163–79.

[12] Commenting on the psychological basis of bestowing white feathers and its seemingly disproportionate historical legacy in the memory of those men who witnessed, experienced, or heard about these acts, Virginia Woolf noted that "external observation would suggest that a man still feels it a peculiar insult to be taunted with cowardice by a woman in much the same way that a woman feels it a peculiar insult to be taunted with unchastity by a man." Woolf rightly argues that the number of women who "stuck feathers in coats must have been infinitesimal compared with those who did nothing of the kind" but goes on to blame what she calls "the manhood emotion" for the exaggerated psychological

tional newspaper reports, literary sources (such as plays and stories), and admonitions to women decrying the practice and imploring ladies not to give out white feathers.[13] By far the most abundant evidence, however, comes from postwar memoirs, diaries allegedly written during the war, but published after, and a collection of remarkable letters sent to the BBC by old soldiers forty-five years after the armistice, describing this painful experience to researchers compiling an anniversary special on the history of the Great War.[14]

---

effect of perhaps "fifty or sixty feathers." See Virginia Woolf, *Three Guineas* (New York, 1966), p. 182. Although Woolf's psychological insights are profound, receiving a white feather was a much more common experience than she allows. In the BBC Great War Oral History Series at the Imperial War Museum scores of men and women wrote in telling of their experiences as receivers or witnesses of the white feather. In my sampling of this source I have found over 200 accounts of white feather giving. Considering that many of the recipients would have been killed or died of natural causes between the time of receiving a feather and 1964 when the survey was advertised, and that some recipients may not have seen the advertisement or chosen to write, Woolf's estimation of "fifty or sixty feathers" seems very short of the mark. I have also found numerous accounts of white feather giving in sources unrelated to the BBC Great War Series. For a fuller account of the BBC source, see n. 14 below.

[13] It also includes the occasional question in Parliament and one or two official reports pointing to the practice as an embarrassing nuisance in need of suppression. For some contemporary references to white feather giving, see *The Vote* (June 18, 1915), p. 648; *Clarion* (September 4, 1914), p. 12; *Daily Mail* (August 31, 1914), p. 3; *Chatham News* (September 5, 1914), p. 8; *John Bull* (April 3, 1915), p. 11; *Hole's Illustrated Review* (June 12, 1915), cover; *The Times* (September 1, 1914), p. 1; Lechmere Worall and J. E. Harold Terry, *The Man Who Stayed at Home* (London, 1916); Helen Hamilton, "Jingo Woman," n.d., quoted in Catherine Reilly, ed., *Scars upon My Heart: Women's Poetry and Verse of the First World War* (London, 1981), pp. 47–48; E. A. Mackintosh, "I'll Make a Man Out of You," n.d., quoted in Peter Parker, *The Old Lie: The Great War and the Public School Ethos* (London, 1987), p. 181; T. W. H. Crosland, "The White Feather Legion," n.d., quoted in E. S. Turner, *Dear Old Blighty* (London, 1989), p. 69; A. M. B. Meakin, *Enlistment or Conscription* (London, 1915), pp. 10–11; Annie Swan, *The Woman's Part* (London, [1916]), p. 170; Coulson Kernahan, *The Experiences of a Recruiting Officer* (London, 1915), p. 69; *House of Commons Parliamentary Debates*, March 1, 1915, col. 548, September 15, 1915, col. 91, November 16, 1915, col. 1708; "The Northcliffe Press and Foreign Opinion," Cabinet Document 1184, November 1, 1915, p. 3: Public Record Office (PRO), INF 4/1B.

[14] In May 1964, Gordon Watkins, the producer of a BBC series celebrating the fiftieth anniversary of the Great War, issued an advertisement soliciting responses from white feather women and the men they had shamed. In the ad, Mr. Watkins tauntingly suggested that "I doubt if any of these women will be brazen enough to admit it now," and given the wording he used, it is not wholly surprising that his prophecy came true. The BBC was inundated with responses from men who had received white feathers, but the reply from women to an advertisement that proclaimed its intention to "deal with the lunatic fringe which existed at home during part of the war" was so low that I have found only two letters in the collection from women who claim to have bestowed white feathers. Responses from men who received white feathers and from women who saw them given, however, should not be dismissed out of hand because of the reticence of the givers or the recipients' temporal distance from the war. As Mr. Watkins' tone suggests—and many of the letters corroborate—claiming to have given a white feather during the 1914–18 war was by the 1960s a highly embarrassing and shameful admission. Mrs. Thyra Mitch-

Although postwar sources no doubt reflect the complicated mediation of time, what changed in the intervening years was not the description of white feather giving itself but the ominous frequency with which this practice came to be remembered and commented on by survivors of the war.[15] My contention is that the practice occurred, much as described in both contemporary and postwar accounts, but that its meaning, seriousness, and symbolic load were greatly enhanced as the war drew to a close and people began to count the dead. Though always more acceptable rhetorically than in actual practice, the wartime context of white feather giving endowed this feminine affront with enough patriotic, romantic, and civic legitimacy to entice some bold and impudent women to brave disapproval and bestow a white feather. As the larger cultural landscape encompassing the white feather campaign gradually receded, however, the practice itself came to be remembered as an emblematic act of feminine betrayal, easily disembodied from the social context in which it had originally thrived. This essay thus examines one of the most contentious gestures of the war in order to look at the way the language of patriotism implicated women in the raising of armies while subsequently providing veterans with a concise rhetorical trope with which to remember gendered patriotism during the Great War.

"Women of Britain Say—'GO!'"

The white feather campaign originated within a system of voluntary recruiting that vociferously called on women to send their men to war. Until the institution of conscription in 1916, recruiting propaganda relied heavily on a patriotic appeal that welded masculinity to military service and branded the unenlisted civilian as a coward beneath contempt.

---

ell, one of the two women who did write in, found herself in the *Daily Mirror* hailed as a self-proclaimed "chump," and although the tone of the article was more one of astonishment over the admission than hostility for Mrs. Mitchell, such notoriety is not necessarily of the sort many women would have wished for. See "BBC Seeking White Feather Women," *Daily Telegraph* (May 15, 1964), in IWM, BBC/GW, vol. APL-AYR, fol. 242; *Daily Mirror* (May 29, 1964), p. 7. The BBC advertisement was published in a variety of other newspapers, though not all of them even solicited letters from women.

[15] Undoubtedly these letters, like oral history interviews, reflect the intervention of time and a new historical context, yet they offer insight into a set of practices as interpreted by a class of respondent that is too important to be ignored. Letters from the 1960s match closely accounts written in the 1930s as well as contemporary anecdotes and advice to women proffered during the war, implying that the commemoration of this gesture was not as mutable we might expect. I wish to make sense of this practice by situating it within the cultural context of the war and then to examine white feather narratives themselves as a literary form with historiographical and political implications. For an excellent discussion of the use of oral history evidence, see Woollacott, *On Her Their Lives Depend*, pp. 206–9.

Women not only functioned in this campaign as the direct voice of conscience but appeared more subtly as the objects soldiers fought to defend, the rewards only heroes dared to desire, and as the specter of what a man might become were he to "show the white feather" and fail in his duty. Gendered conceptions of patriotism thus implicated women in defining the parameters of male citizenship, while endowing women's traditional domestic, maternal, and sexual roles with an openly expressed importance to the military state.[16] As John Oxenham reminded the women of the Women's League of Honour in a war poem composed for that group:

> O maids, and mothers of the race,
> And of the race that is to be
> To you is given in these dark days
> A vast responsibility. . . .
> Remember!—as you bear you now,
> So Britain's future shall be great
> —Or small. To your true hearts is
> given a sovereign duty to the state.[17]

While Oxenham's poem, and much of the literature of the League of Honour, referred explicitly to the beneficial influence on men and the nation of women's physical purity, during the war "women's influence" took on a specifically military function as it became central to the language of recruiting.

As early as August 1914 personal advertisements appearing in *The Times* accused unenlisted men of cowardice and effeminacy in the name of presumed female acquaintances.[18] We have no idea whether these

---

[16] For provocative discussion of gender, masculinity, and civic obligation, see Robert Westbrook, " 'I Want to Marry a Girl Just Like the Girl Who Married Harry James': American Women and the Problem of Political Obligation in World War II," *American Quarterly* 42 (December 1990): 587–614; and Nicoletta F. Gullace, "Women and the Ideology of War: Recruitment, Propaganda, and the Mobilization of Public Opinion in Britain, 1914–1918" (Ph.D. diss., University of California, Berkeley, 1994), pp. 62–109. An influential interpretation of the multivalent use of women in the promotion of war is found in Elshtain, pp. x–xiv, 106–20.

[17] John Oxenham, "The League of Honour War Memorial" (London: League of Honour, [1914]), in IWM, Women at Work Collection (hereafter WW), BO6/2/7.

[18] One personal advertisement tauntingly announced: "Englishwoman undertakes to Form and Equip a Regiment of Women for the Firing Line if lawn tennis and cricketing young men will agree to act as Red Cross nurses in such a Regiment." See *The Times* (August 31, 1914), p. 1. Another advertisement asked for "Petticoats for all able-bodied youth in this country who have not yet joined the army." See *The Times* (August 27, 1914), p. 1. Dr. M. Yearsley describes this appeal in his memoirs and associates it with the feminine practice of giving white feathers. See M. Yearsley (n. 6 above), p. 19. The Germans apparently made much of a personal advertisement where a woman named "Ethel M." informed her lover, "Jack F.G." that "if you are not in khaki by the 20th

taunts were actually written by women, though contemporaries generally supposed they were,[19] and even those advertisements that clearly were not—such as the productions of the Parliamentary Recruiting Committee—nevertheless implicated women in a recruiting rhetoric that hinged on a masculinized sexual identity policed by women and the humiliating threat of appearing unmanly. "It will not be very long before every woman in the country will be looking 'coward' at every man she sees at home," *The Times* forbodingly warned. For the writer "has talked with six women, varying in station from servant-maid to marchioness, all of whom have asked why so many young and active men are seen around who do not appear to be doing anything about going to war."[20]

Recruiters, legally barred from resorting to conscription until the enactment of National Service in 1916, put much thought into the motivation of young men, appealing both to threatened masculinity and to sexual desire as means of persuasion. In this way, Henry Arthur Jones was using commonplace logic when he declared that "the English girl who will not know the man—lover, brother, or friend—that cannot show an overwhelming reason for not taking up arms—that girl will do her duty and will give good help to her country."[21]

The incitement to such tactics was by no means unusual, especially during the first two years of the war. One recruiting leaflet addressed to "MOTHERS!" and "SWEETHEARTS" reminded mothers of Belgian atrocities and warned sweethearts that, "If you cannot persuade him to answer his Country's Call and protect you now *Discharge him* as unfit!"[22] A poster designed for the lord mayor of London put the same message even more bluntly. Addressing "The Young Women of London," the mayor asked: "Is your 'Best Boy' wearing Khaki? ... If not don't *YOU THINK* he should be? If he does not think that you and your country are worth fighting for—do you think he is *worthy* of you? Don't

---

I shall cut you dead." The Germans, according to British sources, translated this as something closer to "hack you to death." See *Times* (July 8, 1915), quoted in Turner, p. 70.

[19] In *The Experiences of a Recruiting Officer,* for example, Coulson Kernahan launches into a philippic against "folk who inform me that this or that man 'ought to go.'" This practice he attributes primarily to malicious and jealous women. Quoting a letter that is both anonymous and addressless, Kernahan assumes that it is from a lady and even paints an imaginary picture of her as someone who "was living in ease and comfort, if not in luxury, the preservance of which, and her own personal safety, she was more anxious to assure and to insure by sending other people's menfolk to fight for her." See Kernahan, pp. 54–55.

[20] "Public Opinion and the Laggards, Unpatriotic or Afraid," *The Times* (August 28, 1914), p. 6.

[21] Henry Arthur Jones to *The Times* (August 29, 1914), p. 9.

[22] Duke of Bedford, "Recruiting Pamphlets and Leaflets, 1914–1915," IWM, 325.1 NP K. 44699.

pity the girl who is alone—her young man is probably a soldier—fighting for her and her country—and for *You*. If your young man neglects his duty to his King and Country, the time may come when he will *Neglect You*. Think it over—then ask him to JOIN THE ARMY *TO DAY!*"[23]

In this way, while "Women of Britain" were told to "Say 'Go!'"[24] something as private as female sexuality took on a military significance at the expense of all those unenlisted men who appeared reluctant to defend its sanctity. While this poster and others like it were criticized in Parliament and in the feminist press for their blatant manipulation of gender, the state had nevertheless assumed the guise of a woman for the purpose of recruiting.[25]

This propagandistic turn implicated women's most intimate domestic and sexual relationships in the raising of the new armies. According to *The Times:* "Many correspondents point out that lectures are not the best means of reaching the workingman and that all-important recruiting agency, his sister or sweetheart."[26] Instead, one such correspondent suggested in a metaphor that melded women and recruiting posters: "Show their eyes." In this way propaganda, both in the deployment of gendered images and in its ability to instigate female behavior, turned women themselves into a form of propaganda. Ideal-typical notions of masculinity and femininity were key to this process since they represented both

---

[23] "To the Young Women of London," IWM 4903, reproduced in Maurice Rickards, *Posters of the First World War* (New York, 1968), no. 23. This appeal further conflates the virtues of citizenship with the virtues of a responsible lover.

[24] E. V. Kealey, "Women of Britain Say—'GO!'" Parliamentary Recruiting Committee no. 75, IWM 0313, reproduced in Libby Chenault, ed., *Battlelines: World War I Posters from the Bowman Gray Collection, the Rare Book Collection Wilson Library, the University of North Carolina at Chapel Hill* (Chapel Hill, N.C., 1988), p. 122; anonymous, "To the Women of Britain," in *Keep the Home Fires Burning: Propaganda in the First World War*, by Cate Haste (London, 1978), p. 54.

[25] Angelsey's Ellis John Griffith, M.P., protested in August 1915 that "the walls of our country and the pages of our newspapers are defaced by official jibes and taunts at our manhood, some of these actually being addressed to women." See *Manchester Guardian* (August 6, 1915). He was not alone in opposing tactics which called on women to do the dirty work of the state. *The Vote* denounced "an insolent advertisement that has been published in the daily papers putting 'four questions to the women of England,' and accusing men of having to be *sent* by them to 'join our glorious army.'" *The Vote* (January 22, 1915), p. 472. And the Ministry of Information feared the influence such advertisements might have on foreign opinion, lamenting that "The *Times* writes that recruiting is deteriorating, that intimidation and flattery are employed alternately, resulting in scandals. The inciting to enlist through young girls, the presentation of white feathers (a symbol of cowardice in England) by excited women, are only surface signs of the national degeneration." See "The Northcliffe Press and Foreign Opinion," Cabinet Document 1184, November 1, 1915, p. 3: PRO, INF 4/1B.

[26] "A Fight to the Finish: Work of National Enlightenment," *The Times* (August 31, 1914), p. 4.

the traditional values that the British were apparently fighting to defend and the modes of gendered behavior that seemed necessary to wage war successfully.[27] What came as more of a shock to many observers, however, was that many women, in turn, donned the aspect of the state as they used their own physical and rhetorical power in the service of the crown.

Although propagandists like Admiral Fitzgerald, Lord Esher, and Arthur Conan Doyle urged women to shun men out of uniform, to show contempt for the unenlisted, and even to hand out white feathers to men wearing mufti, the authorities showed almost universal horror when women actually practiced what many publicists themselves had preached. In the same lecture in which he exhorted the girls of the Women's League of Honour to send their men to war, Major Leonard Darwin made clear that he was "very far from admiring those women who go up to young men in the street . . . and abuse them for not enlisting, a proceeding which requires no courage on the woman's part, but merely a complete absence of modesty."[28] And the recruiting sergeant Coulson Kernahan, ordinarily a vigorous advocate of female recruiting, warned women that "the sending or offering of white feathers, so far from witnessing to your patriotism, witnesses only to the fact that you are unpardonably ignorant, vulgar, and impertinent. The woman (I do not recall a case of one of the other sex doing anything of the sort) who offers a man a white feather exposes herself, and not undeservedly, to rudeness and to insult. If she do worse than offer the feather personally and send it anonymously by post, she thereby classes herself . . . as what in the other sex would be called a 'cad.' "[29]

Clearly, a rhetorical taunt and the threat of an emblem like the white feather were ideally meant to obviate the need of actually handing one out; indeed, that women heeded these calls was not necessarily the intention of those propagandists who made double edged appeals to such unlikely groups as "The Young Women of London." For Kernahan, actual demonstrations of the type of female behavior advocated in much propaganda appeared "unnatural" and mortifying when endorsed or performed by women themselves. "One meets, of course, a number of women who lie and lie shamelessly in begging off a son or brother who has already enlisted," Kernahan thus observed. "For these women and their racking anxiety one is sufficiently sorry to find it easy to forgive, but the woman I cannot forgive is the one who would turn even her

[27] See Kent (n. 10 above), pp. 12–30; and Gullace (n. 16 above), pp. 62–92.
[28] Major Leonard Darwin, "On the Meaning of Honour," a lecture delivered to the Women's League of Honour, 1915. IWM, WW, BO6/3/2/8, p. 6.
[29] Kernahan (n. 13 above), p. 69.

country's emergency into an opportunity to vent her vengeance or her spite either upon another woman, of whom she is jealous, or upon some man, who has perhaps shown himself indifferent to her charms. These are the women who remind one of Frances Willard's saying that 'the worst of some women is that they can never be gentlemen.' "[30]

Although Kernahan was able to forgive those women who attempted to shield their men, he could not forgive those whose recruiting activities he suspected of being undertaken for ulterior and self-serving ends. His distinction between women with "racking anxiety" for the safety of their men and those who used the country's emergency to wreak revenge on men "indifferent" to their "charms" reveals a deep suspicion about female patriotism.

The discrepancy between the behavior of women apparently necessitated by the war and a sense of womanliness that transcended necessity propelled contradictory observations on women's role in recruiting and placed white feather giving outside the boundaries of acceptability, as a sort of emblem of all that was wrong with female patriotism. *The Times* correspondent Michael MacDonagh was thus horrified when going home in a tramcar one night he witnessed the presentation of white feathers. "The victims were two young men who were rudely disturbed from their reading of the evening paper by the attack of three young women. . . . 'Why don't you fellows enlist? Your King and Country want you. We don't.' One of the girls was a pretty wench. She dishonoured one of the young men, as she thought, by sticking a white feather in his buttonhole, and a look of contempt spoiled for a moment her lovely face."[31]

Although MacDonagh worked for a journal complicitous in prompting women to acts of patriotic disdain, he was nevertheless deeply troubled as he witnessed a practice entirely in keeping with the sentiments endorsed by such respected authorities as the lord mayor of London. As they parodied the rhetoric of propaganda posters, the actions of these young women turned a ubiquitous call to arms into a monstrous distortion of femininity. Spoiling her pretty face with a look of contempt, the girl became emblematic of an act that marred that which should be lovely as it perverted the sentiments of both courtship and war.

MacDonagh's reservations were shared by a wide variety of observers, particularly when the victim was already enlisted. J. P. Cope remembered the fury of his wife when a similar incident took place while he took her to tea at the Mikado Cafe on Long Row. Mrs. Cope had been

[30] Ibid., p. 40.
[31] Michael MacDonagh, *In London during the Great War* (London, 1935), pp. 79–80.

disinfecting her husband's uniform and thus he was wearing civilian clothes when "3 young ladies passed me and placed 3 white feathers in my hand." According to Mr. Cope, "I said to her look what them girls gave me as I did not know what they was for." His wife then accosted them and "they told her I ought to be in khaki out in France and she told them they ought to be in a Munitions Factory making Ammunition for the Soldiers to defend themselves."[32]

Ordering the girls to return to Long Row the next day, Mrs. Cope turned their misguided accusations into an embarrassing retort:

> The next day we went down I had my khaki on then with all my Decorations ... we met them ... and stopped them and told them to give me the feathers back but they was too ashamed to do so we left them and went in the cafe and sat down they followed us and told my wife they would pay for our teas my wife told them that my Husband would pay for us as it would be an Insult to take their money they little knew what I had gone through in the first year of war always wet through from frost snow rain wounded at Neuve Chappel and how many battles I had been in I was wounded 2 and gassed 2.[33]

Mrs. Cope's display of her husband in full regimental attire and her challenge to the women to give back the white feathers became the means by which she cast aspersions on the wielders of shame. Like women who refused to take seats offered by men out of uniform, Mrs. Cope spurned the offer of tea from the insightless women who "little knew" what her husband "had gone through in the first year of war."

Given the disapproval of observers ranging from Coulson Kernahan to Mrs. Cope, why did women persist in giving out white feathers, and what did it mean in the context of the war? To decipher the significance of white feather giving for those who literally or rhetorically wielded this remarkable taunt, we must turn to the romantic popular culture offered to patriotic men and women seeking entertainment on the home front.

Sexual Selection and Imperial Order

The inspiration for the use of the white feather, and its significance in the construction of masculine honor and feminine disdain, were borrowed from *The Four Feathers,* a popular imperial adventure by A. E. W.

---

[32] J. P. Cope to BBC, May 1964, IWM, BBC/GW, vol. COC-COY, fol. 141.
[33] Ibid.

Mason first published in 1902.³⁴ The white feather of cowardice referred to the white feather in a game bird's tail widely regarded as a mark of inferior breeding.³⁵ In popular parlance to "mount" or "show" the white feather was to display signs of cowardice, since a properly bred fighting cock would demonstrate the aggression and tenacity valued in the ring. The symbol of the white feather thus bound together issues of sexual selection, bravery, and cowardice—a confluence highlighted in the novel, which had gone into four editions by 1918.

In the novel Harry Feversham, a young military officer who cannot stand the thought of battle, resigns his commission on learning that he is to be sent to the Sudan on active duty.³⁶ Suspecting the cowardly motives behind his resignation, three of Harry's comrades send him white feathers forcing him to confront the devastating truth of his own martial inadequacy. The emotional climax of the novel comes when Harry must offer an explanation of the incident to his fiancée Ethne. As the narrator dramatically explains, "[T]he dreadful thing for so many years dreadfully anticipated had at last befallen him. He was known for a coward. ... It was the girl who denied, as she still kneeled on the floor. 'I do not believe that it is true,' she said. 'You could not look me in the face so steadily were it true. ... Three little white feathers,' she said slowly and with a sob in her throat, 'three little white feathers and the world's at an end.' "³⁷

After returning her engagement ring, Ethne breaks a white ostrich feather from her ornamental fan and returns it to Feversham along with the three original feathers. As the narrator explains: "The thing which she had done was cruel no doubt, but she wished to put an end—a complete, irrevocable end; ... She was tortured with humiliation and pain. ... Their lips had touched ... she recalled with horror."³⁸

This final act of humiliation at the hands of the woman he loves spurs Harry to redeem himself—a redemption possible only in the spilling of blood. On leaving Ethne, Harry embarks on a trek to the Sudan to save his former friends from rebellious Dervishes who have refused to submit to colonial rule. In Africa, his symbolic passage to manhood occurs when Harry sinks his untried dagger into the body of an Arab, infusing his sanguinary quest for personal courage with visceral phallic

---

³⁴ Francis Almond to the BBC, May 25, 1964, IWM, BBC/GW, vol. ALL-ANT, fol. 339.

³⁵ *The Oxford English Dictionary,* 2d ed., s.v. "feather."

³⁶ His mission is significantly to "avenge the death of General Gordon" by accompanying Kitchener's forces on the reconquest of Khartoum.

³⁷ A. E. W. Mason, *The Four Feathers* (London, 1902), p. 35.

³⁸ Ibid., pp. 41–42.

imagery. "A brown clotted rust dulled the whole length of the blade, and often . . . he had taken the knife from his breast and stared at it with incredulous eyes and clutched it close to him like a thing of comfort. . . . He ran his fingers over the rough rust upon the blade, and the weapon spoke to him and bade him take heart."[39] As Harry caresses the dried blood of his victim—a testimony and proof of manhood encrusted on the very blade of his knife—the novel's juxtaposition of sex and empire begins to emerge, vividly highlighting a number of cultural assumptions that underlay the bestowal of the white feather of cowardice.

In the novel imperialism and sexuality are intimately related since the masculine traits needed to satisfy the woman are the same as those required in the conquest of empire. After rescuing his comrades from the clutches of Dervishes, proving his willingness to kill and his indifference to danger and death, Harry's redemption is complete and he is able to return the feathers and reclaim his bride. On Harry's heroic return, Ethne treasures his redeemed white feather "because it was no longer a symbol of cowardice but a symbol of cowardice atoned."[40] The mock order of the white feather becomes instead the true badge of courage, as Harry's atonement allows for the rehabilitation of his name and his reintegration into the society of his friends, his family, and the woman he loves.

As both the symbol of Harry's humiliation and the instrument of his redemption, the white feather endows womanly scorn with rich creative possibilities. For wartime enthusiasts, the objective of giving a white feather was thus not only to shame a man but to change him as well, and as numerous men later testified, it could be wielded with a certain amount of patriotic self-righteousness by those would-be Ethnes who regarded a slacker as an affront to the ideal of manhood itself.[41] A. M. Woodward perfectly summed up this attitude when she wrote to *The Times* to remind women that "there is a wider duty than making garments. . . . Young men must be persuaded to think what this war really means. . . . So I am commencing a little missionary work. To-morrow I mean to give a leaflet to every man who is apparently a possible recruit. I shall watch for them on the tram, in the street, at cricket and tennis grounds, at the theater, at the restaurant; and I hope that the little single

---

[39] Ibid., p. 147.
[40] Ibid., p. 210.
[41] Alfred Allen, a young munitions worker, and his friend Christopher Crow were attacked by an indignant white feather woman in 1915. Although the incident left Allen "too shocked to move," his workmate "roared like a wanton bull as she took hold of his lapel." The woman was led away "shouting at the top of her voice 'If the cap fits wear it!' " See Alfred Allen to BBC, May 31, 1964, IWM, BBC/GW, vol. ALL-ANT, fol. 263.

appeal 'from the women of England' will at least rouse their thought and will possibly help them to act.''[42]

While leaflets, rather than feathers, were Woodward's symbolic medium, her faith in the creative power of womanly censure is abundantly clear. If Woodward compared herself to a missionary, however, such evangelism often had decidedly sexual overtones as well. In a sort of inversion of "khaki fever," scorning a coward can be read as the other side of loving a hero—a potentially transformative demonstration of that female patriotism so seductively displayed by Mason's heroine.[43]

Indeed, the imperial/sexual assumptions evident in *The Four Feathers* pervaded both the language of patriotic femininity and the ideal of romantic love during the war. If courage was the key to both sexual selection and the conquest of empire, every woman's imperial/eugenic task was to love a soldier and scorn a coward.[44] As the *Girl's Own Paper* solemnly explained, "Women will forgive almost anything in a man except cowardice and treason." For "not only is this feeling instinctive, but it comes to her through long years of human evolution. . . . With hearts full but tranquil souls, women can send forth their sons, their husbands, their sweethearts, their protectors, to danger or to death—to anything saving halting and dishonour. A great Admiral put it neatly when he said 'victory was won by the woman behind the man behind the gun.' ''[45]

In the suggestion that both women and war demanded the same qualities out of a man, female sexuality became central to contemporary understanding of the forging of martial identity. "The soul's armour is never well set to the heart unless a woman's hand has braced it," the Mother's Union warned, "and it is only when she braces it loosely that the honour of manhood fails.''[46]

During the war, female journalists, music hall entertainers, and an array of patriotic publicists of both sexes popularized these sentiments by articulating women's military purpose in terms of their sexual and moral power over men. Indeed, if the act of bestowing a white feather

---

[42] *The Times* (August 28, 1914), p. 11.

[43] The dynamics and implications of "khaki fever" are well addressed in Angela Woollacott, " 'Khaki Fever' and Its Control: Gender, Class, Age and Sexual Morality on the British Homefront in the First World War," *Journal of Contemporary History* 29, no. 2 (April 1994): 325–47.

[44] For an interesting discussion of the idea of sexual selection in Victorian culture, see Gillian Beer, *Darwin's Plots: Evolutionary Narrative in Darwin, George Eliot and Nineteenth-Century Fiction* (London, 1983), pp. 210–35; and Greta Jones, *Social Darwinism and English Thought: The Interaction between Biological and Social Theory* (Sussex, 1980), pp. 99–120.

[45] "Women and Patriotism," *Girl's Own Paper*, vol. 1914–1915, p. 36.

[46] The Mother's Union, *To British Mothers: How They Can Help Enlistment, by One of Them* (London, n.d.), p. 1.

required no words to be understood, it may have been because contemporary discourse about women's influence gave unmistakable meaning to a gesture that invested feminine discrimination with explicit military utility. When the Baroness Orczy, author of *The Scarlet Pimpernel,* called for the "First Hundred Thousand" female recruiters to join her "Active Service League" in 1914, she made explicit the logic latent in such patriotic acts of feminine disdain.[47] "Women and Girls of England—Your hour has come!," the Baroness declared. "The great hour when to the question . . . 'what can I do?' your country has at last given an answer: 'Women and girls of England' she says, 'I want your men, your sweethearts, your brothers, your sons, your friends. . . . Will you use your influence that they should respond one and all?' . . . Women and girls of England, you cannot shoulder a rifle, but you *can* actually serve her in the way she needs most. Give her the men whom she wants . . . use all the influence you possess to urge him to serve his country."[48]

The baroness posed the influencing of men as literally a form of "active service" for women and offered a military style badge and a place on the League's "Roll of Honour" to any woman or girl who pledged to "persuade every man I know to offer his service . . . and never to be seen in public with any man who being in every way fit and free . . . has refused to respond to his country's call."[49] The baroness succeeded in enrolling 20,000 women and for her efforts received a letter of commendation from the king.[50] Yet Orczy was merely one of a multitude of commentators and patriots who bade women to persuade their men to enlist and to scorn those who refused.

To Orczy, the withdrawing of the feminine body—in the refusal to be seen in public with a man out of uniform—worked in conjunction with moral coercion to isolate the man who refused to enlist. Her assumption seems to have been that what persuasion and female patriotism could not achieve, sexual desire and public shame could. If the presence of women were contingent on the wearing of a uniform, the purpose of the League was to assure that the signs of military and sexual prowess would be worn together or not at all.

As patriotic women's groups posed the raising of recruits as a form of military service for women—a patriotic duty comparable, according

---

[47] The Baroness Orczy, "To the Women of England, the Answer to 'What Can I Do?' . . . ," *Daily Mail* (September 4, 1914).

[48] Ibid.

[49] Ibid.

[50] The Baroness Orczy to Miss Conway of the Imperial War Museum, [1918], in IWM, WW, BO/6/6/2i. The Baroness's League was reputed to have raised 600,000 men for the king's army.

to the Baroness Orczy, to "shouldering a rifle"—popular singers, writers, and artists represented the soldier hero as a romantic ideal worthy of a woman's love and hopeful of her body. Highlighting the distinction between the sexually attractive recruit and the contemptible slacker,[51] female music hall stars such as Vesta Tilly and Clara Butt became famous for their sexualized recruiting songs and their erotic impact on enlistment.[52] At venues ranging from local music halls to the carnivalesque recruiting rallies of Horatio Bottomley, the alleged contingency of love on war dominated the period of voluntary recruiting, turning military service itself into a sort of national aphrodisiac.[53] In the most famous recruiting song of the war, women explained that, "Now your country calls you to play your part in war / and no matter what befalls you we shall love you all the more. . . . Oh, we don't want to lose you / But we think you ought to go, . . . / We shall want you and miss you / But with all our might and main / We shall cheer you, thank you, kiss you / when you come back again."[54]

In the song, women offer their love and kisses as mens' reward for going to war, yet in many music hall songs the sexual implications of soldiering were even more explicit. In "I'll Make a Man Out of You," popularized by Gwendoline Brogden in "The Passing Show," the artiste enthusiastically proclaimed to the audience her "perfect dream of a recruiting scheme": "If only all the girls would do as I do / I believe that we could manage it alone, / For I turn all suitors from me but the sailor and the Tommy, / I've an army of my own. . . . [O]n Saturday I'm willing, if you'll only take the shilling / To make a man out of you. . . . / I teach the tenderfoot to face the powder, That gives an added lustre to my skin. . . . / It makes me almost proud to be a woman, when you make a strapping soldier of a kid. / And he says 'You put me through it and I didn't want to do it / But you went and made me love you so I did.' "[55]

The use of double entendres—in this instance comparing making a man face gunpowder to a woman applying face powder—played with the idea of the eroticism of war and its stimulating effect on female sexu-

---

[51] For a pictorial version of this motif, see anonymous, "He, She, and It," popular postcard reproduced in Parker (n. 13 above), pp. 192–93.

[52] *John Bull* (March 6, 1915), p. 1.

[53] Ibid. According to Francis Almond, "Songs like: 'We Don't Want of Lose You, but We Think You Ought to Go. . .' and 'On Monday I Walk out with a Soldier. . .' were rendered by women vocalists throughout the land." See Mr. Francis Almond to the BBC, May 1964, vol. ALL-ANT, fol. 339. See also Woollacott, "Khaki Fever," pp. 325–27.

[54] Tony Howarth, ed., *Joe Soap's Army Song Book,* IWM Great War Series (London, 1976), p. 2.

[55] Ibid.

ality. In making a soldier the woman makes a man and in making a man she conversely creates a soldier; this transformative power in itself becomes a source of erotic pleasure as the singer flaunts her ability to counter a man's volition by stimulating his desire. As the song's reluctant recruit puts it: " 'You put me through it and I didn't want to do it / But you went and made me love you so I did.' "

Female entertainers themselves frequently tried to recruit men from the audience in the highly patriotic atmosphere of the music hall.[56] Major D. K. Patterson, an "Old Contemptible" home on leave in 1915, went to the Royal Hippodrome in Belfast where a comedienne sang "We Don't Want to Lose You" directly to him. The mirth of the company surprised the vocalist who, much to Major Patterson's satisfaction, burst into tears on being told that he was already in the army.[57]

The longing to transform men into soldiers and the virtual identification of erotic masculinity and martial prowess was as evident in popular women's fiction as in bawdy music hall lyrics. In September of 1914, for example, *Women's World* began a serial called "A Soldier's Wife," which ran with the sensational advertisement: "Amy Had Married the Only Coward in France." Through a mistake, Amy believes that she was saved from a fire by Jules and marries him instead of the true hero Jack. After marrying Jules, Amy discovers her mistake. To the humiliation of Amy and Jules's mother, "a gallant old lady who loved her son to the point of adoration [but] loved her country and her son's honour better,"[58] Jules tries to desert even before joining the French army. The concerted effort of the two women, however, finally gets Jules to the front where he shows his bravery and saves his marriage in the single act of performing well as a soldier.

Similar motifs appeared in popular women's literature even after the institution of conscription in 1916. In August 1917, for example, *Women at Home* magazine published a romantic story by M. McD. Bodkin, K.C., called "The White Feather." In the story, Molly Burton, "a

---

[56] For a discussion of the patriotic and conservative nature of the music hall, see Gareth Stedman Jones, "Working-Class Culture and Working-Class Politics in London, 1870–1900: Notes on the Remaking of a Working Class," in his *Languages of Class: Studies in English Working Class History, 1832–1982* (Cambridge, 1983), pp. 179–238; and Chris Waters, "Manchester Morality and London Capital: The Battle over the Palace of Varieties," in *Music Hall: The Business of Pleasure*, ed. Peter Bailey (Milton Keynes, 1986), p. 158.

[57] Major D. K. Patterson to the BBC, [May 1964], IWM, BBC/GW, vol. LIN-LYO, fol. 328.

[58] Norah Kinnaird, "A Soldier's Wife," *Woman's World* (September 19, 1914), p. 262. Jules's mother was even commended by female readers in "Heart to Heart Chats." See "Auntie Jean" to the "Editoress," "Britain's Brave Women," *Women's World* (November 28, 1914), p. 559.

bright, pretty, warm hearted little girl and as brave as another" accidentally gives a white feather to a recipient of the Victoria Cross.[59] Molly is intensely drawn to posters "urging young men to join their comrades in the trenches, to fight for England and liberty against the ravishers and murderers in Flanders. Shirkers and slackers awakened her utmost scorn. . . . 'If I were a man' she said, 'I would go at first call. I would not have other men out fighting for me while I skulked at home amongst the women.' "[60]

Molly is troubled by the presence in the neighborhood of "a splendid figure of a man" who was not at the Front. Molly could not bear the sight of "the handsome young lounger" for "here was indeed a slacker *in excelcis* for whom no excuse was possible to linger ingloriously at home while his compeers were facing the horror of war."[61] Molly's contempt grows daily as she sees the handsome coward "lazing around Brighton, while England, through the medium of many-coloured and illustrated posters, proclaimed that every man was needed at the Front."[62] Finally, able to stand it no longer, she gives him a white feather snipped from her favorite hat.

The culmination of the story and the fruition of its sexual/military motif, comes when Molly is invited to a grand ball "for a military angel . . . Robert Courtney, most illustrious of Victoria Cross heroes [who] has been residing anonymously at Brighton for nearly a fortnight."[63] Predictably, "the hero of the Victoria Cross was her slacker, still wearing the White Feather." The revelation of his bravery solves the puzzle of how Molly could have found herself "in danger of loving this self confessed slacker" and culminates in the conflation of romantic and martial masculinity in the person of the hero. As the narrator explains, Captain Courtney "valsed [sic] as he fought, superbly." In the final passage of the story he "caught her close in his arms, half resisting, wholly yielding, and kissed her on the lips. When she emerged panting and blushing from the close embrace without a word more spoken on either side, they were engaged."[64] As the narrator reminds us, "Captain Courtney was no slacker in love or war!"

Sex, romantic love, heroism, and cowardice are all entwined in this story of misidentification. The girl's patriotism and bravery win her the

---

[59] M. McD. Bodkin, K.C., "The White Feather," *Women at Home* (August 1917), pp. 153–60.
[60] Ibid., pp. 153–54.
[61] Ibid., p. 154.
[62] Ibid., p. 155.
[63] Ibid., p. 159.
[64] Ibid., p. 160.

attention and admiration of the man of her dreams, whose prowess in war is paralleled and mirrored by his prowess in love, just as his white feather foils his Victoria Cross. Though "The White Feather" is unusual in presenting a positive view of the practice of handing out white feathers relatively late in the war, it may offer some insight into the way women envisioned this practice themselves.

The story was published in a popular woman's magazine and is adamant in its depiction of Molly as a brave, enticing, and patriotic girl whose nationalistic gesture sets her on the path of adventure and romance. In doing something for her country Molly reaps rewards for herself, as an impertinence justified by the exigencies of a national emergency leads to her own engagement to one of the greatest heroes of the war. In the linking of patriotism and romantic imagination, the story offers some insight into why the categories of courage and cowardice, which became the foundation of women's romantic war literature, seemed to have inspired patriotic action in an assortment of women during the war.

In a context where waging war was regarded as the single most important civic task, the paradigm of courage and cowardice made it possible for women to envision national service in sexual terms. In turning women's romantic fantasies into supreme public duty, a variety of stories, songs, and patriotic appeals promised women a vicarious attachment to the front through the honor of the men they inspired, while elevating such amusements as the selection of beaux into tasks of national and imperial importance. This aspect of white feather giving comes across with remarkable vividness in a variety of accounts written by men who received white feathers during the war. Bill Lawrence, writing from an old peoples' home in Warwickshire many years later, remembered being upbraided by a lady milliner on a train for not offering his seat to a wounded soldier. "I got up straight away . . . and took my trousers down so far, I had a thick pad of cotton wool and a bandage I had had a *very* severe wound in the back . . . it was a bit smaller than a wallnut and all jagged edged and poisoned." Mr. Lawrence then warned the woman that if he'd "been a nasty tempered man she may have got what they call a smack in the gab," but quickly notes that "she was a very good friend afterward" when she took him to her shop. Leaving the girl to manage the store, the woman took Mr. Lawrence to her room, "put a bottle of whiskey [at] the side of the bed took [off] all clothes and got in bed and said do as you like you earned it."[65]

Although Lawrence's tale of patriotic female sexuality is seen

---

[65] Bill Lawrence to BBC, [May 1964], IWM. BBC/GW, vol. LAB-LAZ, fol. 275.

through the eyes of a man (and at a distance from the war that endows it with the complications of postwar oral history), he is not unique among those who remember a decidedly erotic dimension to female recruiting. About a year after the war had begun, Mr. H. Symonds was listening to a ginger-haired girl giving a recruiting speech at Hyde Park Corner. He was seventeen at the time but eager to go "so when ginger gently tucked a white duck feather into my button-hole I went off to the recruiting office and, putting two years on my age, joined up." Although Symonds saw nothing unusual in this incident, he did believe that the experience was unique in one respect: "I believe I am the only recipient of a feather, who had it taken back by the giver and was given a kiss in return! ... When, some three or four days later in uniform I again stood in Hyde Park and listened to 'Ginger' she recognized me and in front of the crowd round her stand she came up to me and asked for the return of her feather. Amidst mixed cheering and booing I handed it to her. She had tears in her eyes as she kissed me and said 'God Bless.' "[66]

Symonds's account of the receipt of his white feather is quite rare. His ability to exchange the white feather for the kiss of a lovely woman turns what men generally regarded as a hostile taunt into an erotic event that won the bestower admiration and inspired the recipient to enlist willingly. As Symonds explains, "Few people realize that those women who gave feathers were not just flighty empty-heads, but had a far deeper insight into *mysterious man* than is generally supposed. I was wounded twice but never regretted the quietly given push from a girl that sent me to the recruiting station."[67]

Ginger's insight into "mysterious man" and Symonds's starry-eyed response to her red-headed beauty and tearful patriotism offer a rare moment of insight into the cultural configuration of female recruiting in its most erotic form. On the one hand, the event turned Ginger's beauty to political use as she imitated the public call to arms now frequently on the lips of actresses, music hall stars, and other popular women who "coaxed thousands to the colours"; on the other, she drew on and, through her success, legitimated a romantic tradition of female patriotism initiated well before the war.

Although white feather giving is generally remembered as an event that excited enormous hostility, it is thus possible that at the time women like Ginger received a certain amount of now forgotten encouragement. Not only did both the official and the unofficial productions of the volun-

---

[66] H. Symonds to BBC, 18 May 1964, IWM. BBC/GW, vol. SNE-SYM, fols. 427–28.
[67] Ibid.

tary recruiting movement brandish female sexuality as a means of shaming men into uniform, but popular fiction, musical theater, and advice literature frequently asserted the military efficacy of sexual desire even after conscription made such incentives redundant. Those few women who have since commented on their recruiting activities remember feeling an anger toward men who appeared to be shirking their duty entirely in keeping with the sentiments expressed in vast sections of the press as well as by scores of patriotic Britons. As Mrs. Thyra Mitchell recalled years later, she gave a white feather to her acquaintance Jack Mills, because she "was very angry" and "felt he should be doing his bit."[68] Within a social context where people displayed the most extreme hostility toward conscientious objectors, shirkers, and those regarded as cowards, and where few propagandists shied away from employing women to make these points, the white feather campaign should not come as an entire surprise, despite the criticism it intermittently provoked.[69]

White Feathers and Wounded Men

In spite of the extravagant promotion of gendered patriotism in wartime popular culture, historical understanding of the white feather campaign has been shaped less by the domestic situation in which it occurred than by the manner in which those who survived the war perceived and committed to memory these civilian acts.[70] While receiving a white feather must have been deeply mortifying even in the heady days of "war fever," an encounter that might have been dismissed as foolish, trivial, or vulgar in 1914 became part of a more ominous symbolic shorthand in the years that followed, particularly as increasing numbers of men were wounded in the war. Although men did not "invent" white feather stories, returning soldiers increasingly endowed them with ironic significance, especially when women's insulting gestures seemed to suggest feminine oblivion to their own masculine pain.[71]

---

[68] Mrs. Thyra Mitchell to the BBC, April 16, 1964, IWM, BBC/GW, vol. MIL-MIT, fol. 479; and Nicholas Wall, "Notes on Telephone Interview with Mrs Thyra Mitchell," May 26, 1964, IWM, BBC/GW, vol. MIL-MIT, fols. 477–78. For a fuller account of this episode, see Mrs. Mitchell's interview with the *Daily Mirror* (May 29, 1964), p. 7.

[69] Vivid accounts of the treatment of these men can be found in memoirs and oral history interviews with conscientious objectors. See, e.g., IWM, Department of Sound Records, Oral History Recordings, "The Anti-war Movement, 1914–1918."

[70] The cultural history of memory has become increasingly important to the history of the Great War since the publication of Paul Fussell's seminal work *The Great War and Modern Memory* (1975; 2d ed., Oxford, 1978). For an excellent essay on the historiography of memory, see Adrian Gregory, *The Silence of Memory: Armistice Day, 1919–1946* (Oxford, 1994), pp. 1–6.

[71] Paul Fussell and Eric Leed have both commented on the alienation soldiers began to feel toward those at home who seemed unable to comprehend their suffering. See

As we have seen, women's reading of the signs of manhood relied on that external emblem of courage—the military uniform. Though exemption badges, medical certificates, and armbands were meant to protect exempted civilians from feminine taunts,[72] men frequently complained that these signs of goodwill were invisible to those patriotic women whose only measure of a man was the fabric of his clothes.[73] Not only did women sometimes mistake "starred" men for "shirkers," but, in incidents that caused still more outrage, they inadvertently bestowed their tokens of shame on wounded men recuperating in civilian dress—a mistake that may have occurred as late as 1918.[74]

For men resentful of the paradigm of courage and cowardice manifested in the marked distinction between the man in uniform and the supposed coward in mufti, masculinity was more than a series of external symbols but part of the essence of a man who had served or been willing to serve as a soldier or officer at the front. The ironic contrast between the authentic bravery of men who fought and women's sartorial reading of male courage thus fills narrative accounts of the white feather cam-

---

Fussell, pp. 79–113; and Eric Leed, *No Man's Land: Combat Identity in World War I* (Cambridge, 1979), pp. 44–48. For a brilliant discussion of the gender dimension of this problem, see Gilbert (n. 11 above), pp. 197–226.

[72] According to Reuben W. Farrow, a conscientious objector imprisoned for "prejudicing recruitment," during the war: "Railway employees had been given certificates of 'indispensability' temporarily. This resulted in a number of youngish men having their 'call-up' delayed. This resulted in certain women accosting them and scornfully demanding 'why haven't *you* gone to the front?' So [a scheme] was instituted whereby a man could 'attest,' that is, signify his willingness to enlist, and he was given an armband to wear, thus silencing the scornful ones!" See R. W. Farrow, "Recollections of a Conscientious Objector," IWM, Documents, 75/111/1, fol. 289.

[73] Mr. B. Upton remembered an incident where his arm-band failed to deter the scornful admonitions of women. According to his grandson, "My grandfather . . . was standing with a friend, both on war work, in the Strand; when a young woman rushed up and gave them both 'feathers.' He still has his original 'war work' badge, which the young lady, in her excitement, failed to notice." See Mr. B. Upton to BBC, May 15, 1964, IWM, BBC/GW, vol. UDA-VOS, fol. 38. Apparently women's enthusiasm for khaki was equally great when it came to choosing their own fashions. For a fascinating discussion of women's relationship to military fashion, see Susan Rachel Grayzel, "Women's Identities at War: The Cultural Politics of Gender in Britain and France, 1914–1919" (Ph.D. diss., University of California, Berkeley, 1994), pp. 316–46.

[74] While the majority of those who received white feathers seem to have gotten them in 1915 (the gesture perhaps having caught on after its inception in 1914), the practice was still quite common in 1916 and 1917 and, though less frequent, was not unheard of in 1918. For this information I am grateful to the Imperial War Museum staff member who painstakingly recorded the dates of white feather incidents included in letters to the BBC. Although this evidence is fragmentary, excluding anyone who predeceased the BBC appeal, did not wish to write in, or failed to include the date of his feather story, it nevertheless refutes the idea that the practice was confined to 1914 and 1915 or that it ended with conscription. See Imperial War Museum staff, "Great War Index to Letters of Interest," n.d., IWM.

paign, endowing this descriptive medium with rich retributive possibilities.

Michael MacDonagh's "well authenticated" version of the most famous of white feather stories vividly illustrates the way women's patriotic actions could in retrospect become their own revenge. According to his diary, "A gallant young officer was recently decorated with the V.C. by the King at Buckingham Palace. Later on the same day he changed into mufti and was sitting smoking a cigarette in Hyde Park when girls came up to him and jeeringly handed him a white feather. ... He accepted the feather without a word and, as a curiosity, put it with his V.C. It is said he remarked to a friend that he was probably the only man who ever received on the same day the two outstanding emblems of bravery and cowardice—the V.C. and the white feather. Within a week he had returned to the front and made the Great Sacrifice."[75]

In stories like MacDonagh's, women recruiters not only miss the signs of a masculine willingness to brave death—an exemption badge, a stump, or a wound—but in the most famous emblem of their wrongheaded activities they are unable even to distinguish courage from cowardice, the very feminine discrimination on which the eugenic health of the nation was supposed to depend. The official symbol of courage is bestowed by the king at the palace, the feminine symbol of cowardice is bestowed by a group of girls in the park; they are both orders, and the presentation of one mocks the bestowal of the other. The recounting of the tale thus avenges the gesture as the shame cast on the soldier is thrown back on the women who are narratively and morally hoist on their own petard.

As women used the uniform to identify the soldierly spirit and manly will inherent in every British Tommy, soldiers, military rejects, and conscientious objectors all began instead to assert personal suffering as the locus of true manhood. The language of the khaki uniform thus became highly ironic, especially in retrospect. As women, intoxicated with that enthusiasm for soldiers known as "khaki fever," saw in the glamour of the uniform the mark of a true soldier, men home from the front regarded this superficial remnant as only a vulgar symbol of the signs of manhood written on the body. P.C.S. Vince of Surrey remembered the vast discrepancy between the external emblems of military duty and the hidden wounds of battle to which civilians, particularly women, seemed almost incomprehensibly blind. Vince was wounded on

---

[75] MacDonagh (n. 31 above), p. 80. MacDonagh's book is a published version of the diary he kept during the war. I have not compared the published version with the original and do not know if it still exists. Such a comparison would be useful in determining the distance between postwar memory and more immediate wartime perceptions.

WHITE FEATHERS AND WOUNDED MEN

April 24, 1917, and was waiting to be admitted to Roehampton Hospital to be fitted for an artificial leg. He used to go to Victoria Station to await troop trains coming from France, and he went in his civilian clothes. On one occasion, however, his experience was different. A woman, who boarded the tram at Brixton, failed to notice his crutches and handed him a white feather. Vince reacted swiftly: "Having on my overcoat and my stump covered up, I did no more but stand up on my good leg and put my stump right into her face, and her reaction was awful and she did no more than flew off the tram."[76]

As women read manhood in terms of the wearing of a uniform, accounts like Vince's continually spoke of brave soldiers, wounded men, and recipients of the Victoria Cross whom women mistakenly branded as cowards because they were out of uniform. Yet as men noted, if a uniform could be taken off the wounds of battle could not. These hidden scars—clothed and covered in the romance of a uniform or the ignominious attire of civilian clothes—were the indelible marks of manhood etched deeply into the bodies and consciousness of those who fought. Mr. J. Jones was thus furious when on returning home after being wounded in France he was presented with a white feather. "In those days there was a part of Clarence Pier call the 'Bull Ring' and we used to go there to try and get a girl," Mr. Jones recalled. "I saw a girl I liked and tried to get talking to her but she didn't seem interested and then I saw her talking to another soldier. So next time she passed, . . . I said 'you spoke to him why can't you speak to me?' She replied 'I don't speak to toy soldiers only those with guts, so you'd better have this' and gave me a white feather."[77]

Jones promptly slapped her in the face whereupon her friend, a local dock worker, challenged him to a fight. "I opened my tunic and pulled up my shirt and showed my wound and told them I had only just come out of hospital after having been to France and done my bit. The bloke apologized . . . and the girl just ran off."[78]

Although he wore a newly issued uniform, the girl rejected Jones as a suitor because the pristine condition of his clothes led her to believe he had not yet been to the front—an apparent deficiency that rendered him an undesirable object of love, unworthy even of address. The tale

---

[76] P.C.S. Vince to BBC, May 18, 1964, IWM, BBC/GW, vol. UDA-VOS, fol. 199. This is a very common trope. C. Ashworth was given a white feather while riding a train with shrapnel in his kidney, and both Reuben Farrow and Mrs. Ruth Brown tell of witnessing the bestowal of the white feather to amputees. See C. Ashworth to the BBC, May 18, 1964, BBC/GW, vol. ALP-AYR.

[77] Mr. J. Jones to the BBC, May 29, 1964, IWM, BBC/GW, fols. 285–86.

[78] Ibid., fol. 286.

is one of many that is about women's inability to read men, their attention to superficial detail, and their failure to tell a hero from a coward, even if this distinction should literally "hit them in the face."

In stories like these the uniform becomes to the body what language is to meaning—an inadequate approximation of a vast complex of suffering that women, irretrievably fixated with surfaces, fabrics, and colors, could never comprehend. Emblematic of the civilian lack of understanding for what lay beneath the khaki uniform, the actions of women became a narrative medium with which eloquently to display men's hidden suffering. As Reuben W. Farrow recalled of an almost metaphoric event: "a woman scornfully asked a young man in a tram car 'why are *you* shirking your duty?' . . . He quietly withdrew from his pocket a handless stump and showed it to her! In confusion she tried to apologize—and quickly left the car."[79]

In this incident and others like it,[80] the silent response of the Tommy hints at the idea that the scarred body itself was simply a physical sign of the even deeper scars that could only be understood by those who understood the horrors of the front. If a man's clothes seemed to hide the meaning of battle written on his body, the body itself could show only an approximation of what he had been through as a soldier.

For those men who remembered the white feather campaign, however, hidden wounds were not just soldiers' wounds, but included also the psychological scars receiving a white feather left on many men who did not wish to fight. The advent of the white feather women thus appeared to MacDonagh to be "almost as terrible to the young male who has no stomach for fighting as an enemy army with banners—and guns. At the sight of them he is glad of the chance of being able to hide anyhow his diminished head."[81] In this rhetorical turn, the emotional wounds inflicted by women at home mimic the physical wounds inflicted by the enemy in battle. Although MacDonagh is speaking figuratively, such metaphorical usage of the language of combat took a quite literal form in the recollections of many men who survived the war.

[79] R. W. Farrow, "Recollections," p. 290. Ironically, amputees and humpbacks were not to be issued armbands because it was imagined that their reason for being out of uniform was already graphically written on their bodies. See Lord Derby to Headley Le Bas, November 22, 1915, British Library, Add. MS 62170, fol. 182.

[80] Mrs. Ruth L. Brown vividly recalls the way such a moment of misrepresentation impressed her, though just a schoolgirl of ten years old: "A young man was sitting on a seat by the bus stop near Kent gardens, Ealing, . . . when a lady came up to him, said something, and passed him a small white feather. The young man took it, turning it about in his hand for some time, then, very quietly, moved his leg from under the seat and showed her his empty foot!" See Mrs. Ruth L. Brown to BBC, May 16, 1964, IWM, BBC/GW, vol. BRO-BRY, fol. 261.

[81] MacDonagh, p. 79.

G. Backhaus tells the story of two friends of his who received white feathers, claiming that "unfortunately both the men I know who suffered that terrible [fate] died because of it."[82] Relating the story of how his underaged cousin had enlisted as a result of female taunts and was "blew to pieces" and how an overaged friend of his "died of madness" as a direct consequence of these insults, Backhaus makes it clear that women, rather than the enemy, were responsible for these tragic deaths. As Backhaus concludes, in rhetoric reminiscent of that used to describe death in the trenches, "the look in his eye has haunted me ever since. ... The cruelty of that white feather business needs exposing."[83]

Backhaus's impression is not exceptional. Earnest Barnby also believed that such a gesture resulted in the premature loss of his brother who, in spite of his Derby armband, "was presented with a white feather by some scatty female and as a result was seized by a depression which developed into tuberculosis which killed him."[84] And Granville Bradshaw bitterly claimed that his friend Basil Hallam, who was famous for his song "Gilbert the Filbert the Colonel of the Nuts," was de facto killed by white feather women. According to Bradshaw, the two men were walking down Shaftsbury Avenue after Hallam's show when "we were both surrounded by young, stupid, and screaming girls who stuck white feathers into the lapels of our coats. . . . When we extricated ourselves Basil said, 'I shall go and join-up immediately'—he did. . . . I heard a few weeks later that my friend Basil Hallam had joined the paratroops and in his first descent with a parachute it failed to open. He was killed and he died during the afternoon."[85]

In these accounts, the emasculating attacks of women on the domestic front are comparable to the eviscerating assault of the enemy in battle. Insofar as the fear of one prompted men to brave the other, women and the enemy in some sense became one.

As the cultural landscape encompassing the white feather campaign was gradually overshadowed by the seriousness of the war, public officials, returning soldiers, and a variety of other responsible citizens increasingly saw this feminine affront as an outrageous disruption of public order rather than as an even marginally legitimate means of coaxing or cajoling men to the colors. In 1915 Cathcart Wason warned the home secretary, Reginald McKenna, that state employees were being "subjected to insolence and provocation at the hands of some advertising

---

[82] G. Backhaus to BBC, May 15, 1964, IWM, BBC/GW, vol. BAB-BAP, fol. 18.
[83] Ibid., fol. 19.
[84] Ernest Barnby to BBC, May 19, 1964, IWM, BBC/GW, vol. Bar, fol. 393.
[85] Granville Bradshaw to BBC, May 15, 1964, IWM, BBC/GW, vol. BRA-BRI, fol. 54.

young women presenting them with white feathers" and inquired whether he would authorize the arrest of "such persons" for "acting in a manner likely to create a breach of the peace."⁸⁶ While the home secretary dismissed this extravagant request, its lavish rhetoric suggests a sense of outrage that would only continue to grow as the war progressed.

By 1916 changes in recruiting had distanced white feather giving from what rationale it once possessed. Not only did passage of the National Service Bill end official recruiting appeals, but rising casualties and the induction of large numbers of men into the army meant that women who continued to upbraid men out of uniform did so without official sanction and at increasing risk of making mistakes. While formal recruiting appeals ended with conscription, however, it is important to remember that public hostility toward unenlisted men in no way subsided. The press singled out conscientious objectors and "shirkers" for especial attack, while the practice of white feather giving continued intermittently into 1918, nourished by an increasingly bitter atmosphere of suspicion toward those apparently unwilling to "do their bit."⁸⁷

In this conflicted environment, women's patriotic disdain became the source of particular resentment, despite the fact that they were by no means alone in harassing young men. It was Parliament, after all, not women, who disenfranchised conscientious objectors for five years after the war, and it was conscription, not white feather giving, that was responsible for sending thousands of hesitant youths to the front.⁸⁸ Why then were women singled out for especial reproach, particularly when only a small, if persistent, minority of them could have participated in this insulting act?

As quintessential noncombatants and as the conflict's apparent political and economic beneficiaries, women, as feminist historians have noted, became an object of particular hostility in the aftermath of the war.⁸⁹ During the period of voluntary recruiting, white feather women

---

⁸⁶ House of Commons Parliamentary Debates, March 1, 1915, col. 548.

⁸⁷ John W. Graham, *Conscription and Conscience: A History, 1916–1919* (London, 1922), passim.

⁸⁸ J. Renwick Seager, J.P., *The Reform Act of 1918* (London, 1918), pp. 46–49; Arthur Marwick, *The Deluge: British Society and the First World War* (London, 1979), pp. 76–85.

⁸⁹ The debate over the "gender backlash" began with the feminist contention that women lost many of the economic gains they had made during the war in the postwar period. See, e.g., Gail Braybon, *Women Workers in the First World War* (London, 1981). Recently the debate has been expanded to encompass the psychological and psychoanalytic dimensions of the backlash and the impact of the war on the "demise" of feminism. See Kent (n. 10 above), pp. 97–139; and Michelle Perrot, "The New Eve and the Old Adam: French Women's Condition at the Turn of the Century," in Higonnet et al., eds. (n. 11 above), pp. 51–60.

had crossed the boundary of acceptable female behavior in their enthusiasm to enforce what they and the majority of their contemporaries regarded as appropriate male behavior; yet the cultural environment in which they displayed these sentiments was gradually losing its legitimacy, particularly among those with some knowledge of the war. In an atmosphere of growing male resentment, white feather giving became the guilty emblem of women's complicity and a vivid medium through which men could remember and moralize on the meretricious relationship of the home front to those who served. Since strident female patriotism contrasted so dramatically with women's nurturing roles, white feather giving became the ironic symbol of a world gone awry—a world where husbands, sons, and fathers were sacrificed by the women back home.[90]

White feather stories are thus both a description of what actually occurred and an aggressive articulation of masculinity that claimed for those who suffered exclusive custody over the interpretation of the war. In white feather narratives, male suffering becomes an alternative propagandist motif, drawn from experience, to be sure, but wielded in highly strategic ways to reassert an essentially masculine patriotism sacramentally distinct from the discredited female patriotism that once flourished at home.[91] The spirit of the Somme, in this way, superseded the levity of the music hall, endowing bitter meaning on a gesture that, in retrospect, would dishonor the giver far more than the recipient.

In the process of remembering, the larger cultural context that explained women's actions receded as returning soldiers claimed the authority to interpret the war, its stories, and its evasive moral for themselves and their communities.[92] Caroline Rennles, a young munitions

---

[90] Sandra Gilbert has observed that the efforts of women recruiters "reinforced male sexual anger by implying that women were eager to implore men to make mortal sacrifices by which they themselves would ultimately profit." See Gilbert (n. 11 above), p. 208. For a vivid account of the development and implications of these sentiments, see Kent, pp. 31–50, 90–91.

[91] The wielding of these tales was not isolated to veterans, however, but could also be used by men and women close to a victim or by former pacifists who wished to vindicate their wartime stance. Perhaps the most strategic use of white feather stories was by the pacifist Sylvia Pankhurst who credited members of the Women's Social and Political Union (WSPU) with handing out white feathers during the war. The WSPU was of course run by her prowar nemeses and blood kin, Emmeline and Christabel Pankhurst. According to Miss Pankhurst, "Mrs. Pankhurst toured the country making recruiting speeches. Her supporters handed out white feathers to every young man they encountered wearing civilian dress, and bobbed up at Hyde Park meetings with placards [reading] 'Intern Them All.'" See Sylvia Pankhurst, *The Suffrage Movement: An Intimate Account of Persons and Ideals* (London, 1931), p. 594.

[92] For an excellent discussion of this theme, see Margaret R. Higonnet, "Not So Quiet in No-Woman's Land," in *Gendering War Talk*, ed. Miriam Cooke and Angela Woollacott (Princeton, N.J., 1993), pp. 205–26. In spite of the new "ironic" tone that

worker during the war, recalled that, being "very patriotic during the First War," if she "saw a chap out in the street" she'd say, " 'Why aren't you in the army?' " Indeed, she would taunt her unenlisted male colleagues at Woolwich Arsenal because the sight of them used to drive her mad. "I used to call them all white-livered whatsonames I could lay my tongue to." By the Second World War, however, Rennles shunned such tactics and would not "have told anybody to go."[93] While Rennles attributes her changed attitude to maturity, it was also the result of a new way of looking at war and male suffering that turned the risqué high jinks of the voluntary recruiting movement into the focus of embittered memory in years to come.

Fussell notes coming out of the war, writers like Robert Graves nevertheless preserve a number of martial conventions even as they criticize the romanticization of the war. See, e.g., Robert Graves's treatment of his regiment, the Royal Welch Fusiliers: Robert Graves, *Good-Bye to All That* (1929; new rev. ed., New York, 1957), pp. 82–105.

[93] Caroline Rennles, IWM, Department of Sound Records, 000566/07, p. 10, quoted in Woollacott, *On Her Their Lives Depend* (n. 10 above), pp. 197–98.

[11]

The outbreak of war and the urban economy: Paris, Berlin, and London in 1914[1]

By JON LAWRENCE, MARTIN DEAN,
and JEAN-LOUIS ROBERT

When war broke out in August 1914 most observers agreed that it was certain to be a short war; they also agreed that it would be a war with dire social and economic consequences.[2] These were not contradictory expectations. One of the main assumptions behind 'the short war illusion' was economic rather than military. It was believed that the financial and commercial interdependence of modern states meant that any war between them would inevitably produce such colossal economic dislocation that all sides would soon be suing for peace. It is clear that Angell's arguments about the irrationality of modern warfare were widely held to have been vindicated by the pacific role of Europe's financial communities during the Moroccan war scare of 1911.[3] Judging by his additions to the 1912 edition of *The great illusion* this was certainly the lesson that Angell himself drew from the Moroccan episode; and it appears to have been a lesson with which most bankers and financiers were happy to concur until swept along by the events of July and August 1914.[4]

Expectations of economic collapse and an early peace proved groundless. True, the outbreak of war brought a sharp fall in economic activity and employment in all combatant countries, but these were only transitory phenomena. By mid 1915 the economies of Britain, France, and Germany were rapidly adapting to the demands of total war; production was already straining capacity in many sectors and labour shortages were widespread.

In this study we propose to examine the initial impact of the outbreak of

---

[1] This essay forms part of a larger project on the social and demographic history of Paris, London, and Berlin during the decade of the Great War, directed by J. M. Winter and Jean-Louis Robert, in collaboration with Thierry Bonzon, Joshua Cole, Jonathan Manning, and Armin Triebel. It is funded by the Economic and Social Research Council, the Centre National de la Recherche Scientifique, and the Fritz Thyssen Stiftung.

[2] See Clarke, *Voices prophesying war*, pp. 126-34, and Morris, *Radicalism against war*, esp. pp. 413-5. Morris quotes Ramsay MacDonald's claim on 2 August 1914 that 'In three months there will be bread riots and we shall come in'. However, a few commentators had a more prescient view of the nature of the coming war; see Howard, 'Men against fire', pp. 41-5; and Clarke, *Liberals and social democrats*, p. 165 on Wallas's fear of a 30 years' war.

[3] Angell, *The great illusion*; for a discussion of Angell see Weinroth, 'Norman Angell and *The great illusion*'. By 1914 Angell's book had been translated into at least 17 languages including French, German, Italian, Japanese, and Russian: *The great illusion* (April 1913 ed.). See also de Bloch, *Is war now impossible?*, discussed in Howard, 'Men against fire'.

[4] Angell, *The great illusion* (1912 ed.), p. v and ch. IX, esp. pp. 138 and 149-53. For reactions to Angell's thesis in the wake of Agadir see *J. Inst. Bankers*, XXXII (Dec. 1911), pp. 485 and 517-20, and *Bankers' Magazine*, XCIII (Jan. 1912), pp. 236-51. See also Offer, 'The working classes', esp. pp. 221-6.

war on the urban economies of Paris, Berlin, and London between August and December 1914. Because of the nature of the sources available, special attention will be paid to the state of employment and unemployment in the three cities, although the labour market cannot, of course, be taken as a wholly reliable indicator of the state of the underlying economy. Where available, statistics on short time and overtime working will be used to give a more complete picture of economic activity, while use will also be made of more general indicators of social distress.

The central concern of the analysis will be to explain why the radically different economies of Berlin and London adapted well to the demands of war (albeit after an initial period of severe dislocation), whereas Paris underwent an economic and social crisis which strongly resembled the visions of the more apocalyptic prewar commentators. Was the crisis of the Parisian economy purely the product of wartime (and hence contingent) factors: its proximity to the front, the 'flight of the bourgeoisie', and the loss of its industrial hinterland to the north? Or were there more long term factors which inhibited the adaptation of the Parisian economy but were absent in the cases of Berlin and London? In other words, was the key variable the differential impact of military conflict on the three cities, or underlying differences in their social and economic structure?

The socio-economic characteristics of the three cities must be the point of departure. Table 1 presents summary statistics on various aspects of the prewar social and economic structure of Paris, Berlin, and London. On the eve of the 1914-8 war, London was considerably larger than either Paris or Berlin, whether judged by the population of municipal areas or of the larger conurbations (rows A and B). The population of greater Berlin accounted for only 6 per cent of the population of Germany before the war, compared with figures of 16 per cent and 10 per cent respectively for greater London and greater Paris (row C). But then Berlin had only been the capital of a united Germany for a little over 40 years, whereas both London and Paris had functioned as the political, social, and commercial heart of large, relatively centralized nation states for many centuries.

This contrasting historical development is also reflected in the greater significance of administrative, financial, service, and transport employment in London and Paris, compared with Berlin (rows F and G). Employment in Berlin was biased more towards the manufacturing sector (row E), and particularly towards the manufacture of semi-finished and capital goods (engineering and machines: row H), although consumer goods such as clothing and textiles were also important, especially for the female workforce. In greater Berlin nearly 60 per cent of male industrial workers in firms with more than 25 employees worked in either metals or machines.[5]

A much higher proportion of adult women had paid employment in Paris than in either Berlin or London (row D, columns 2, 5, and 8). Although statistics on female paid employment are notoriously unreliable because of the tendency to underestimate women's paid work within the home, the difference here is too large to be ascribed to errors of compilation, and

---

[5] *Monatsberichte Gross-Berlin* (1913), pp. v and vi.

Table 1. A summary of the prewar economic and social structure of Berlin, London, and Paris

		Berlin			London			Paris		
		Male	Female	M&F	Male	Female	M&F	Male	Female	M&F
A	Population of city ('000)[a]	994	1,077	2,071	2,135	2,405	4,521	1,331	1,512	2,843
B	Population of metropolitan conurbation ('000)[b]	1,730	1,897	3,626	3,406	3,845	7,251	1,936	2,154	4,090
C	Population of conurbation as % of national population			6			16			10
D	Adults (aged 15+) engaged in workforce (%)[c]	87	38	67	93	43	66	92	58	74
E	Workers engaged in productive sector (%)[d]	59	61	59	42	34	39	40	48	43
F	Workers engaged in service sector (%)[d]	35	39	37	41	66	50	48	52	50
G	Workers engaged in transport and communications (%)[d]	6	0.4	4	18	0.6	12	12	0.5	7
H	Workers engaged in engineering and metals (%)	20	7	16	9	2	6	10	1	6
I	Industrial workers in firms with fewer than 100 staff (%)[e]			61			63			83
J	Industrial firms with fewer than 20 employees (%)[e]			94			66			94

K Age structure: % aged				
under 20 years	33	31	38	25
20–59 years	60	33	54	66
60 years +	7		8	8
L Birth rates: average births per 1,000 population (1909–13)	20.9		25.1	17.1
M Population born outside the city (%)[f]	60	61	32	62
N Average annual unemployment, 1910–4 (%)[g]	4.8	—	6.0	—
O Unemployed July 1914 (%)[h]	6.5	—	4.6	—

Notes: [a] Berlin 1910, London, 1911, Paris 1911

[b] Area covered by extended Berlin limits of 1921; area covered by the Metropolitan Police District (plus the City of London); the city of Paris and the *département de la Seine*.

[c] The Berlin statistics are taken from the 1907 trade census, and corrected to allow for government employees excluded from the census. This census probably underestimates total employment because many homeworkers and casual workers were excluded.

[d] The Berlin statistics are for 1913. They refer only to firms employing more than 25 workers and exclude the professions and domestic service. They therefore overestimate employment in other sectors.

[e] Berlin and London statistics refer to separate firms, Paris statistics to individual workplaces. The Berlin data on firms with fewer than 20 employees refer only to the central districts.

[f] Berlin and London statistics refer to those born outside the city, Paris statistics to those born outside the *région de la Seine*.

[g] Berlin figures represent weighted trade union returns from six trades (metals, wood, transport, textiles, factories, and office work). London returns are for 1910–3, and represent weighted trade union returns from six trades covering the London region (carpentry, plumbing, engineering, shipbuilding, printing, and bookbinding).

[h] By 1914 there were also separate returns for London covering the trades included under the National Insurance Act, 1911. In these trades, which included the highly casualized building industry, unemployment in July 1914 was 7.1 per cent.

Sources: *Statistiche Jahrbuch der Stadt Berlin*, 32–4; *Monatsberichte Gross-Berlin*, 1913–4; *Statistisches Taschenbücher Berlins*; *Population census of England and Wales*, 1911; Registrar General's annual returns for England and Wales, 1909–14; London Intelligence Committee Papers, I–IX; Board of Trade, *Labour Gazette*; London County Council, *London Statistcs*, 1900–14; Bowley, 'Survival of small firms', pp. 113–5; *Résultats statistiques de renencsement général de la population effectué le 5 mars 1911*, II and III; and *Population présène par départements*.

reflects the comparatively high rates of female labour force participation within the French economy as a whole.⁶

On average, Parisian firms were much smaller than those of either Berlin or London. Nearly 94 per cent of industrial workshops in Paris employed fewer than 20 workers (row J); the figure was even higher in the service sector at 97 per cent. The London figures are not directly comparable because they refer to firms rather than places of work, but they do suggest that the small firm was less dominant than in Paris. The Berlin statistics present other problems in that they refer only to the central districts, where the artisanal trades were concentrated, and not to the outlying industrial suburbs with their massive engineering and metalworking plants. This explains why such a high proportion of firms (94 per cent, as in Paris) had fewer than 20 workers. It should be noted, however, that even central Berlin had a higher proportion of its industrial workforce employed in large factories than either Paris or London (row I). There was probably some convergence in the size of firms in the three cities between the Paris census of 1906 and the outbreak of war, but not sufficient to transform the essentially artisanal character of Parisian industry, especially in the central districts.⁷

Berlin can reasonably be characterized as a predominantly manufacturing city in which export orientated heavy industry played a prominent part, whereas both Paris and London had large service sectors and consumer orientated industries concerned primarily with the satisfaction of home, and specifically metropolitan, demand. Berlin can also be characterized as demographically a more dynamic city than either Paris or London. Its birth rate was significantly higher than that of Paris (though not of London),⁸ while it also continued to see high levels of permanent immigration from rural districts (rows L and M). In contrast permanent migration to London had slowed noticeably by the eve of the Great War, so that by 1911 more than two-thirds of all Londoners had been born in the city. The comparable figure for Paris and Berlin was approximately 40 per cent.

Finally, it can be seen that prewar male unemployment levels were generally somewhat lower in Berlin than in London, although this was not true in 1914 (rows N and O; unfortunately there are no reliable figures for Paris). These figures should, however, be treated with considerable caution since they refer overwhelmingly to the employment experience of skilled male workers in trade unions. This is a particular problem in London where only a small proportion of the labour force belonged to a trade union, and casual employment was common in most trades. When employment by the day, or even by the hour was so prevalent, it is clear that 'the reserve army

---

⁶ See Alexander, 'Women's work'; Roberts, *Women's work, 1840-1940*; Tilly and Scott, 'Women's work'; Guécaud-Léridon, *Le travail des femmes*.

⁷ On French economic growth in this period see Carré, Dubois, and Malinvaud, *French economic growth*; Kemp, *The French economy*; Kindleberger, *Economic growth in France*; Kuisel, *Capitalism and the state*, pp. 26-30; Asselain, *Histoire économique*; Verley, *Nouvelle histoire économique*; Beltran and Griset, *La croissance économique*.

⁸ As with the question of female participation in the labour market, the differences here were not so much metropolitan as national.

of labour' must have been much larger than the available statistics would indicate.⁹

The casual labour market represented a rational response by employers to the peculiar conditions facing industry in the British capital. These were a chronic oversupply of labour (caused by the decline of many traditional industries such as shipbuilding and textiles), high production costs (especially due to rising rental values in the central industrial districts), and sharp fluctuations in the volume and nature of consumer demand. These factors encouraged employers to concentrate on highly flexible labour intensive production techniques rather than to invest capital in fixed plant and machinery, since this meant that both the number of employees and the finished product could be varied at short notice and little cost. Moreover, the chronic oversupply of labour in declining trades such as shoemaking, tailoring, and cabinet making, or in unskilled occupations like carting and dock work, meant that employers could further reduce costs by extensive use of outworking and low paid casual workers.¹⁰

In Paris casualization was much less important. Relatively low wage rates for manual workers meant that employers had little incentive to hire casual labour, especially since labour was in any case less plentiful than in London as a result of the low birth rate.¹¹ The Parisian labour market was still highly fluid, but its instability owed more to the rapid turnover of workers moving from job to job than to the arbitrary power of the employer to hire and fire.¹² In Berlin, casualization was even less widespread, not least because production costs remained low and so capital goods industries could continue to prosper alongside consumer industries and the service sector.¹³

In many respects, therefore, Paris and London can be said to have possessed broadly similar economic structures before the Great War, while Berlin retained many of the characteristic features of a major provincial manufacturing and commercial centre. And yet, as we have noted, by December 1914, both Berlin and London were adjusting relatively smoothly to total war, while Paris experienced a crisis from which it had not fully emerged by the end of 1915. Can this contrasting experience be understood in terms of prewar factors, or must we acknowledge that the key variable was the war itself, and its disproportionate impact on life in the French capital?

To answer this question we turn predominantly to two types of source material: unemployment statistics and surveys of employment. Although these were never compiled in precisely the same way for the three cities, they do provide the basis for a comparison of economic trends during the first months of the conflict. Unemployment statistics are most comprehensive

---

⁹ Dearle, *Problems of unemployment*; Jones, *Outcast London*, pt. 1. Also Booth, ed., *Life and labour*, esp. IV, *passim* and IX, pp. 197-213 and 326-61.
¹⁰ Jones, *Outcast London*, esp. ch. 1.
¹¹ Cottereau, 'Problèmes de conceptualisation'. See also Calixte, 'Le travail à domicile'.
¹² Charle, *Histoire sociale*.
¹³ See *Dokumente aus geheimen Archiven*, Bd. IV (1914-8), p. xiii. However, on the eve of the Great War there were signs of economic crisis in Berlin caused in part by rising food prices and rents. Berlin's rapid expansion between 1870 and 1914 had begun to erode many of the advantages that it had previously enjoyed over great capitals like London and Paris.

for Paris, because of the introduction of a universal scheme of unemployment benefits in August 1914. However, these statistics only begin in October 1914 and therefore tell us little about the initial impact of war on Parisian employment. Moreover, it was not until January 1915 that they were available on a trade-by-trade basis, and even then they detailed only the total number of people unemployed in each trade, not the percentage unemployed. This can be estimated, though only approximately since the only base figures of employment available are those from the 1911 census, which, besides being three years out of date, were also based on a slightly different system of classifying occupations. Moreover, although an allowance can be made for the number of men called up from the prewar workforce of each trade, it is not possible to estimate how many workers transferred from one trade to another. Since the transition to war was a period of unusually high mobility of labour, this inevitably introduces a second source of error into the figures reproduced in table 7. In Berlin and London unemployment statistics refer to a much smaller proportion of the workforce. The Berlin figures refer solely to trade unionists (perhaps one-third of the city's total workforce), while those for London are a composite based on trade union returns from the printing and book trade, and government returns for all workers in trades covered by the National Insurance Act of 1911: building, engineering, shipbuilding, and vehicle building. Neither series can therefore be considered truly representative; they indicate, not absolute levels of unemployment, but the broad trends in the unemployment experience of the two cities. In addition, it should be noted that the London data refer to the metropolitan area as a whole, rather than just to the administrative county of London.

If the unemployment statistics for London are relatively weak, the employment surveys for the city are remarkably comprehensive. Between 22 August 1914 and 31 July 1915, the London Intelligence Committee of the Local Government Board produced eight statistical surveys of employment in the capital.[14] They were undertaken in cooperation with the Board of Trade, and relied on the voluntary returns of selected employers to provide a representative sample of the experience of all firms. From the beginning the sample used was a large one, covering approximately 65 per cent of employees in large firms (those with more than 100 employees) and 10 per cent of employees in small firms by early September.[15] The importance (and difficulty) of securing accurate returns from small firms was fully recognized. The Committee used Home Office lists of London workshops and factories to ensure the representativeness of its sample, which by mid September had been increased to cover nearly 18 per cent of the workforce in small firms.[16]

[14] Local Government Board, London Intelligence Committee Papers, 9 vols., Aug. 1914-July 1915 (hereafter L.I.C.), unpublished, but held at the British Library of Political and Economic Science, London (hereafter B.L.P.E.S.).
[15] L.I.C., II ('Statistical survey of employment in each trade and industry in London, week ending September 5th 1914'), pp. 11-2.
[16] L.I.C., I ('Statistical return of employment'), p. 112, and *idem*, II ('Statistical survey of employment for mid-September'), p. 240. See also Dewey, 'Military recruiting', pp. 201-2 and 221-2, which discusses the Board of Trade's national surveys of employment. See Board of Trade, 'Reports on the state of employment in the United Kingdom', April 1915-April 1919, held at the B.L.P.E.S., and the three published 'Reports on the state of employment'.

Although it seems likely that in the first months of the war the sample method may have led the authorities to underestimate the number of firms which had ceased trading (since they could be mistaken for companies failing to reply to the Committee's circulars),[17] these surveys remain a valuable guide to changing patterns of employment for which there is no equivalent in either Paris or Berlin.

For Paris all that we have are occasional estimates from the *Inspecteur du Travail* concerning the number of workshops still open and the total numbers of workers still employed. These estimates are essentially impressionistic, and cannot be used to provide a series from which to calculate trends in employment. The Berlin data, produced monthly in the *Gross-Berlin Monatsberichte*, are stronger, but they are still inferior to the London statistics, because they refer only to firms with more than 25 employees (a serious problem, since we know from the London data that there was a significant transfer of workers from small to large firms during the first months of the war). More comprehensive data exist for parts of Berlin, but their value is limited because they do not form part of a continuous series, and because their representativeness remains open to question.[18]

The differences in the sources available for the three cities are thus considerable, but, as long as these differences are kept in mind, they do not preclude a comparative analysis of the impact of war on the urban economies of Paris, London, and Berlin. This is the purpose of the remainder of this essay. Section I examines the immediate impact of war in August 1914, and demonstrates that, while all three cities faced severe dislocation, the situation was worse in Paris and Berlin because of the much greater impact of immediate military mobilization in France and Germany. Section II examines political responses to the immediate crisis, and shows that in Paris dislocation was particularly severe because it was exacerbated by the government's financial policies which gave absolute priority to military needs. Section III focuses on the prolonged economic crisis in Paris between September and December 1914, and highlights the extent to which this crisis was the direct result of the proximity of the war to the French capital. Finally, section IV contrasts the extended crisis in Paris with the slow, but uninterrupted, economic recovery which occurred in Berlin and London during the autumn of 1914.

I

The outbreak of war in August 1914 brought economic dislocation and increased unemployment to the capital cities of all the major combatant countries. In Berlin unemployment among male trade unionists rose from 6 to 19 per cent in the first two weeks of the conflict and was probably even

---

[17] Certainly the Board of Trade felt that this was a weakness of its early surveys of national employment; see Board of Trade, 'Report on the state of employment in the United Kingdom in April 1918' (unpub., held at the B.L.P.E.S., London), pp. 6-7.

[18] See esp. State Archive, Potsdam, Province Brandenburg Rep. 30, Tit. 35, no. 1465, Berlin SO, 10 Oct. 1914.

more severe among unorganized workers.¹⁹ The rise in London was more modest, with unemployment rates among workers covered by the National Insurance Act increasing from 7 to 10 per cent during August.²⁰

Although Parisian unemployment statistics are not available before October 1914, it is clear from other sources that dislocation was even more severe in the French capital. Estimates produced by the *Inspecteur du Travail* during August 1914 suggest that employment levels in Paris had fallen by a remarkable 70 per cent since the beginning of the war, and that 68 per cent of workshops in the Paris region had closed altogether.²¹ Unofficial estimates of unemployment in the capital suggest that up to 600,000 Parisians were without work a few weeks after the outbreak of war.²² The official returns on workplace accidents tend to support this picture. They show that only 4,961 accidents occurred in the Paris region during August and September 1914, compared with 27,106 in the same period during 1913 (a fall of 82 per cent).²³

The contraction of employment was not as severe in either Berlin or London. Indeed in London, overall industrial employment appears to have contracted by less than 10 per cent by mid August, and by only 13 per cent at its low point in mid September (see table 2).²⁴

Table 2. *The contraction of industrial employment (male and female) in Paris, London, and Berlin at the outbreak of war in 1914 (July 1914 = 100)*

Date	Paris	London	Berlin
mid-Aug. 1914	—	91	—
late Aug./early Sept. 1914	29	—	76ᵃ
mid-Sept. 1914	—	87	—

Note: ᵃ refers only to firms with more than 25 employees (see text)
Sources: *Bulletin du Ministère du Travail*, 1914-20; London Intelligence Committee Papers, I and II; *Monatsberichte Gross-Berlin*, 1914-5.

Although the Berlin statistics are much less comprehensive than those for London, the monthly survey of employment published in the *Gross-Berlin Monatsberichte* shows that by early September industrial employment in the greater Berlin area had fallen by approximately 24 per cent (table 2). However, because the survey covered only firms with more than 25 workers, this may understate the aggregate fall in employment. When the Factory Inspectorate for north Berlin carried out a survey of local firms in early September 1914, it found that most of the firms that had closed down were

---

¹⁹ *Monatsberichte Gross-Berlin*, 1914. The figures refer to six employment categories: metals, wood, transport, textiles, factories, and office work. The proportion of workers in trade unions was high in Berlin, embracing perhaps one-third of the total workforce, but even so these figures should be read as indicative of trends rather than of absolute levels of unemployment.
²⁰ Board of Trade, *Labour Gazette*, Aug. and Sept. 1914. The figures refer to building workers, engineers, shipbuilders, and vehicle builders in the London *region*. They are not therefore directly comparable with the Berlin statistics.
²¹ The figures have been constructed from series which appeared in the *Bulletin du Ministère du Travail*; see Robert, 'Ouvriers et mouvements', ch. 2.
²² See Fontaine, *French industry*, p. 22.
²³ *Bulletin du Ministère du Travail*, May-June 1915.
²⁴ L.I.C., I, pp. 112-24 and II, pp. 240-55.

small businesses.²⁵ Similarly, the only source presently available that gives details of the changing pattern of employment across firms of all sizes shows a much more substantial contraction than that revealed in the *Gross-Berlin Monatsberichte*. This survey of industrial employment in south-east Berlin found an overall contraction of employment of more than 39 per cent in mid October, compared with a figure of only 22.5 per cent in the *Monatsberichte* for October (table 3). It may be that south-east Berlin was peculiarly severely hit by the outbreak of war, but in any case this more detailed survey confirms the war's greater impact on small firms.²⁶

Table 3. *Industrial employment in south-east Berlin, 10 October 1914 (July 1914 = 100)*

Industry	Employed in Oct. 1914
Leather	141
Clothing	88
Textiles	87
Food	87
Machines	52
Wood	51
Metalwork	44
Printing	35
Paper	23
All trades surveyed	61

Source: State Archive, Potsdam Province, Brandenburg Rep. 30, Tit. 35, no. 1465, Berlin SO, 10 Oct. 1914.

Even when small firms are included, however, it is clear that the contraction of employment was much less severe in Berlin than in Paris. Thus, whereas the Parisian inspectorate reported that at least 68 per cent of firms in the Paris region had closed in the first month of the war, the local report for north Berlin found that only 18.5 per cent of the district's firms had closed *in the previous 12 months*.²⁷ Even so, it found few firms unaffected by the outbreak of war, with nearly 85 per cent of the firms still open working some form of short time.²⁸

The contraction of employment in Berlin was markedly uneven between trades (table 3). In part this reflected the composition of each trade's prewar workforce by sex and age, since one major cause of the contraction of employment was the mass mobilization of young male workers into the armed forces. But it also reflected the very uneven impact of the war on different trades. Thus, although the leather industry, the printing trade, and

---

²⁵ State Archive, Potsdam Province, Brandenburg Rep. 30, Tit. 35, no. 1465, Gewerbeinspektion N, 12 Sept. 1914. The report also noted that many firms in the fashion and luxury goods trades had been forced to close.

²⁶ Ibid., Berlin SO, 10 Oct. 1914.

²⁷ Ibid., Gewerbeinspektion N, 12 Sept. 1914. A year later the Paris factory inspectorate found that 38 per cent of firms were still closed.

²⁸ Ibid. Of the firms still open the report found 33.6 per cent to be working between 2 and 4.5 fewer hours per day, 14.8 per cent working only 1 or 2 days per week, 11.8 per cent working normally, and 3.9 per cent working overtime. The remaining 35.9 per cent of firms were not explicitly accounted for, but were presumably also working short time.

the paper industry employed roughly equal numbers of men and women, their experience of the transition to war was very different.[29] In the leather trade the sudden demand for military accoutrement work led to a rapid expansion of employment, while in printing and paper the interruption of raw material supplies and the curtailment of civilian demand appear to have led to a massive collapse.

Although the first Parisian statistics to be broken down by trade date from January 1915, it is noticeable that they too suggest considerable variation by trade. Only 11.1 per cent of workers in commerce and banking are recorded as unemployed compared with 46.5 per cent of those in fine metal work and 45.2 per cent of those in printing.[30] The story is similar for London, although no trade suffered as severely as the paper industry in south-east Berlin or fine metal work in Paris. Worst hit during August 1914 was the cycle and motor trade where 46 per cent of men in small firms had lost their jobs (fewer than one-sixth of them had joined the forces).[31] In contrast large engineering firms had already seen an 11.5 per cent *net increase* in employment by the end of August (after allowing for the enlistment of 4.5 per cent of the prewar workforce).[32]

It should already be clear that the initial impact of war was far less severe in London than in either Berlin or Paris. Undoubtedly the major reason for this was simply that mobilization was on a much more modest scale in Britain than in either France or Germany. By late September approximately 300,000 Parisian males had been drafted into the armed forces; roughly 30 per cent of the total male workforce. In Berlin the comparable figure was approximately 28 per cent by early September,[33] but in London perhaps 6 per cent of the male workforce enlisted during August, and only 8.2 per cent had done so by mid September. It was not until July 1915 that enlistment in London exceeded 20 per cent of the prewar male workforce, by which time it stood at more than 40 per cent in both Paris and Berlin.[34]

Mass mobilization by state decree placed an incalculably greater burden on the urban economies of Berlin and Paris during the first month of war than did the voluntary scheme embraced in Britain to supplement the British Expeditionary Force.[35] The enlistment of so many workers was itself guaranteed to cause a significant contraction of employment in both Paris

---

[29] See *Monatsberichte Gross-Berlin*, 1913, pp. v and vi.

[30] See below, tab. 7. For a discussion of how these unemployment rates were calculated see below, section III.

[31] L.I.C., I, pp. 115-6. Among large firms only 9 per cent of cycle and motor workers had been laid off. All the L.I.C. statistics are disaggregated by sex and size of company during this period. It should be noted that the survey did not cover the government arsenal at Woolwich which was taking on large numbers of skilled workers during this period; see L.I.C., II, p. 259 and P.R.O., SUPP5/1051, 'Statement of employees in O.F. Woolwich from week ending 1.8.1914 to week ending 5.2.1916'.

[32] L.I.C., I, pp. 115-6. Among small firms there had been a net fall in employment of 6.5 per cent (after allowing for the enlistment of 7.5 per cent of the prewar workforce).

[33] *Correspondenzblatt der Gewerkschaften*, 1914, p. 562, which shows that 27.7 per cent of Germany's unionized workers had been called up by early September.

[34] L.I.C., IX, p. 229 and *Jahresberichte der Gewerbeaufsicthen*, 1914-8, p. 75. For Paris the estimates were calculated from the statistics for French male age groups serving, and the mobilization orders by age. On this question see Maurin, *Armée, guerre, société*.

[35] A significant proportion of Londoners joining the armed forces in August would have been Territorials and men on the Reserve rather than civilian volunteers.

and Berlin during August 1914. Unfortunately it is difficult to gauge precisely what proportion of the fall in employment in the two cities can be attributed directly to mobilization, because in neither case are employment statistics disaggregated by sex. In Paris the overall fall in employment, at approximately 70 per cent, was clearly far too great to be attributed solely to mobilization, but even in Berlin the threefold increase in male unemployment would suggest that the contraction of employment cannot be attributed solely to the direct effects of mass mobilization.

Mobilization, however, had an indirect as well as a direct impact on the overall level of employment in the three cities. The men who enlisted in the respective armed forces were overwhelmingly young and probably included a high proportion of the most productive workers in many industries. In France the 16 *classes* of 1896-1910 and 1914 were all mobilized by the government during the first month of the war (the *classes* of 1911-3 were already under arms).[36] Moreover, within each *classe* the rate of mobilization varied between 80 and 85 per cent; clearly the Parisian economy had been almost wholly denuded of young male workers by the end of August 1914. Not surprisingly, many firms found that they had lost so many key workers that it was impossible, at least in the short term, to maintain production. Worse still, in both Paris and Berlin many of those who enlisted were small employers who were consequently forced to close their workshops and lay off their hands.[37]

These difficulties were further compounded by the fact that, in both France and Germany, the transport network was placed largely at the disposal of the military authorities to carry men and materials to the front. In addition municipal transport, including the Métro, virtually ceased to operate in Paris during the crisis. As a result many firms found themselves effectively cut off both from their sources of supply and from non-local markets. Inevitably the problem was most acute for export orientated industries such as the Berlin piano trade, where employment fell from 600 to 50 at the outbreak of war, or Siemens, which lost foreign orders for 5.8 million light bulbs.[38]

Significantly, when the London Intelligence Committee held an inquiry into the causes of the dislocation of trade in early September 1914, few firms pointed to mobilization as a factor in their difficulties (table 4). Instead the inquiry concluded that the primary cause of the depression in trade was the disruption of peace-time markets, as a result either of diminished demand or of specific wartime conditions (for instance the loss of enemy markets and the closure of the Baltic ports).[39] To a lesser extent war conditions also had a direct impact on many trades through shortages of raw material, lack of inland or overseas transport, and the restriction of credit facilities. As in Paris and Berlin, mobilization played its part in transport difficulties, and also to some extent in the collapse of normal patterns of demand, but its overall importance was much less than in the other capitals. Indeed, it

---

[36] For a discussion of the impact of mobilization on French industry see Fontaine, *French industry*, pp. 22-39.
[37] See ibid., p. 22 and *Jahresberichte der Preussischen Gewerberaete*, p. 69.
[38] *Jahresberichte der Gewerbeaufsichten*, p. 224 and Siemens, *Der Weg*.
[39] L.I.C., II ('Report on the causes of depression in various trades'), pp. 25-39.

should already be clear that at this stage the war as a whole impinged much less directly on civilian life in Britain than it did on life in France, Germany, or for that matter Russia and Austria-Hungary.

Table 4. *Percentage of all London firms identifying certain causes of trade depression, early September 1914*

Cause of depression	Large firms[a]	Small firms
Lack of orders	60	61
Lack of material	36	24
Stoppage of exports	36	16
Lack of inland transport	25	7
Financial difficulties		32
Shipping difficulties	17	8
Other difficulties		6
No complaint to make	12	13
No answer given	1	4

Notes: the column percentages total to more than 100 because many firms referred to two or more causes of depression.
[a] more than 100 employees
Source: London Intelligence Committee Papers, II ('Report on the causes of depression'), p. 26.

Table 5. *The course of employment in industrial firms in London, August–September 1914 (percentages)*

	Male workers							
	Large firms				Small firms			
	on short time (A1)	fall in employment (B1)	joined forces (C1)	net change in employment (D1)	on short time (A2)	fall in employment (B2)	joined forces (C2)	net change in employment (D2)
Aug. 1914	18.5	4.0	6.0	+2.0	18.0	10.0	6.0	−4.0
Sept. 1914	12.5	6.5	10.0	+3.5	16.5	17.0	10.5	−6.5
	Female workers							
	Large firms				Small firms			
	on short time (A1)		fall in employment (B1)		on short time (A2)		fall in employment (B2)	
Aug. 1914	41.0		6.0		24.0		8.5	
Sept. 1914	31.0		7.0		29.0		12.0	

Note: all figures are percentages of workers employed in July 1914.
Source: London Intelligence Committee Papers, II, p. 245.

In London almost one-third of all small firms (those with fewer than 100 employees) reported that their trade was suffering because of a shortage of credit (table 4). Indeed it would appear that many small London firms were unable to weather the initial period of dislocation because they could not obtain sufficient credit either to produce for stock, or to invest in the new productive capacity which would allow them to tap new wartime patterns of demand. As a result, it was small rather than large firms that were most severely hit during the first months of the war in London (table 5).

Remarkably, as early as mid August, at the height of the initial crisis, there had already been a 2 per cent net increase in male employment in large firms, after allowing for enlistment, compared with a net contraction of 4 per cent in small firms (table 5, D1 and D2). By mid September this had become a 3.5 per cent net increase for large firms and a 6.5 per cent net contraction for small ones. Hence there are strong grounds for believing that London experienced a significant transfer of workers from small to large firms during the first six weeks of war. One factor in this transfer of labour may well have been the greater propensity of small firms to lay workers off rather than to put them on short time (table 5, A1-B1 and A2-B2).

There are no comparable statistics for Paris or Berlin, but, since we know that there small firms also suffered significantly more than large, it seems likely that a similar transfer of labour occurred, though perhaps not as quickly, given the greater disruption caused by mobilization for war.

II

Having looked briefly at the nature of the immediate crisis in the three cities, we will now examine how government authorities, local and national, responded to the challenge of financial crisis and economic dislocation in the first months of the war. This section therefore will explore two main areas of government policy during the immediate crisis: financial affairs and social welfare.

Ironically an examination of government responses to the war suggests that intervention occurred in inverse relationship to the seriousness of the social crisis in the three cities. In London, where the crisis was least severe, government agencies were most active in the pursuit of the twin objectives of alleviating distress and returning economic life to its normal channels. In Paris, where the crisis was most severe, relief work was underfunded (although unemployment and separation allowances *were* paid), and measures to stabilize the economy were sacrificed to the immediate goal of national defence.

This ordering of priorities was not, however, as perverse as may at first appear. For France the military crisis was so extreme that not only did it overshadow all other considerations, but it guaranteed that the military would have an absolute call on all resources whether human, material, or financial. In many respects German government circles were dominated by a similar outlook, although since the military crisis there was less desperate, there was a less single-minded devotion to military interests over all others. In Britain the greater remoteness of the conflict, encapsulated in the semi-official slogan of 'business as usual', meant that government at all levels felt better able to devote attention to the social and economic consequences of war.

In Paris, as in Berlin and London, the period of ultimatum and counter-ultimatum which led up to the outbreak of war was one of extreme financial uncertainty. Prices on the Paris Bourse fell sharply during the last week of July, while public uncertainty was reflected in a general movement to withdraw funds from the banks.[40] The period of economic crisis therefore preceded the formal outbreak of war, especially in France where the fear of invasion was perhaps greatest. On 31 July the government introduced a series of bold measures to halt the mounting crisis. Settlement day on the Bourse was deferred to avert the failure of many firms unable to meet their obligations. At the same time the government announced a moratorium on bills of exchange, and declared that bank deposits would be limited to withdrawals of 250 francs and 5 per cent of the total balance.[41] At this time the Banque de France still possessed considerable financial assets in both cash and bills, but, unlike the Bank of England or the Reichsbank, it was not free to use its reserves to restore economic confidence because of a secret agreement which pledged the bank to help finance general mobilization.[42] Under this agreement the bank was obliged to find the massive sum of 2,900 million francs, and thus had virtually no funds available to maintain liquidity within the domestic economy. National defence was given absolute priority over the needs of civilian life. In many respects it is this choice which lies behind the unparalleled collapse of industrial employment in Paris during the first weeks of war.[43] The government's financial restrictions were so severe that not only did credit become virtually unavailable, but cash itself became scarce. The result was that many firms faced such a severe liquidity crisis that they were simply forced to close down.

Although both Britain and Germany also faced a period of considerable financial uncertainty during the immediate prewar period, neither country's political leaders were forced to make similarly stark choices between civilian and military requirements. On Friday 31 July both the London and Berlin stock markets ceased trading in response to the mounting sense of crisis throughout Europe. London, as the centre of the world's money and commodity trading markets, was affected particularly severely by the near total collapse of international commerce.[44] Between 28 July and 1 August the Bank of England had raised its base (or re-discount) rate from 3 per cent to 10 per cent in an attempt to halt cash withdrawals. On Sunday 2 August the Chancellor of the Exchequer, Lloyd George, met representatives of the Bank of England and the main joint stock banks to develop a concerted strategy for avoiding prolonged financial crisis in the event of war. The result was a series of measures designed both to defuse the immediate crisis (including the closure of all banks until 7 August, and a moratorium on all debts and obligations exceeding £5), and to restabilize the economy (including a reduction of interest rates to 6 per cent, the classification of government

---

[40] Poëte, 'La physionomie de Paris', pp. 69-87.
[41] See Bonnefous, *La Grande Guerre*, pp. 70-2.
[42] This agreement between bank and state dated back to 11 November 1911, that is to the post-Agadir period when many European governments began to re-examine their preparedness for war. See Marion, *Histoire financière*.
[43] By late August employment in Paris had fallen to 29 per cent of its July level, while in France as a whole it had fallen to 34 per cent (see below tab. 6).
[44] According to the *Bankers' Magazine*, XCVIII (Sept. 1914), p. 323, by 1 August 1914 the London money markets were in total chaos as a result of the 'complete breakdown in the matter of foreign remittances'. The French declaration of a moratorium on bills was said to have proved particularly destabilizing.

£1 and 10s. notes and postal orders as legal tender, and the coining of additional silver).[45]

In contrast to the French case, the British government's policies were designed to control the financial crisis without plunging the economy into a severe liquidity crisis.[46] The reserves of the Bank of England were used, not to underwrite mobilization, but to cover the cash liabilities of the great joint stock banks. As a result the Bank's reserves fell by £17 million during the week 29 July to 5 August, or from 51 per cent of total liabilities to just 14.5 per cent.

The financial crisis was less severe in Germany, perhaps partly because, as a net debtor nation, Germany was less affected by the near-suspension of international commercial transactions. Even so, the last week of July placed severe pressure on German banking reserves, and culminated, on 31 July, in the decision to suspend convertibility in an attempt to preserve the large gold reserves which had been built up over the preceding five or six years.[47] On 1 August the Reichsbank raised the discount rate from 5 to 6 per cent, but there was no move to introduce a moratorium on debt.[48] On the contrary, the government implemented a series of policies designed specifically to restore liquidity to the economy. Since at least 1909, the German authorities had been trying to increase the use of paper money within the economy. They had also drawn up plans for easing the financial and economic crisis likely to be caused by a European war. Whereas French plans involved exacerbating the liquidity crisis by withdrawing large sums from the economy to help finance mobilization, the German plans involved greatly increasing the quantity of small denomination banknotes in circulation, and releasing 550 million marks to help small businesses hit by the crisis.[49] This money was distributed through a network of local lending institutions, and was intended to help firms overcome the short-term cash-flow problems caused by the sudden collapse of normal patterns of supply and demand.[50] Similar institutions were called for in Britain to ease the plight of firms starved of credit, but no legislation was introduced. As has been suggested, this was almost certainly one of the factors behind the disproportionate fall in employment in London's small firms during August and September 1914.[51]

Thus the contrasting responses of national governments to the financial crisis which accompanied the outbreak of war had an important influence on the pattern of economic dislocation identified for each of the capital cities. Government decisions also played a vital part in determining the extent and duration of the social crisis in Paris, Berlin, and London. In all three

---

[45] 'The great crisis', *Bankers' Magazine*, XCVIII (Sept. 1914), pp. 317-38.

[46] On 13 August 1914 the government announced a second series of bold measures to tackle the continuing liquidity crisis on London's discount and money markets. (ibid., pp. 333-4).

[47] For a discussion of the background to the financial crisis in Germany see Zilch, *Die Reichsbank*. The authors would like to thank Dr Nial Ferguson of Peterhouse, Cambridge for this reference, and for his valuable advice on the crisis period in Germany.

[48] *Berliner Börsen-Courier*, 1 Aug. 1914.

[49] Zilch, *Die Reichsbank*.

[50] *Berliner Börsen-Courier*, 20 Aug. and 31 Dec. 1914.

[51] L.I.C., II ('Report on the causes of depression'), pp. 25-39. Small firms producing for a wholesale merchant or factor, rather than directly for the market, were particularly dependent on short-term credit.

countries politicians were quick to recognize that existing, predominantly charitable, mechanisms for social provision could not cope with distress on the scale that the war would bring. Indeed in France and Germany many private charities ceased to function because of the disruption brought by war. Within days of the outbreak of war, however, Britain, France, and Germany had each introduced an ad hoc system of social payments to provide for the families of men mobilized into the armed forces, and to relieve the distress caused by war-related unemployment. These new schemes were broadly similar in the three countries: each relied on local government and charitable agencies to deliver relief to those in need, and each assumed that benefits should be 'uncovenanted' and should offer no more than the bare minimum necessary for survival.

Although the genesis and purpose of the governments' welfare schemes may have been similar, they had very different results in the three capitals. In Berlin and London welfare provision appears to have operated relatively smoothly, albeit after an initial period of administrative confusion, but in Paris government attempts to relieve distress had largely collapsed by late August. As the war came to the outskirts of the French capital, both local and national government began to disintegrate, and so too did the machinery for relieving distress. Paris itself was effectively under martial law during this period, and the main authorities such as the *Conseil Général de la Seine* did not meet between 14 August and late December 1914.[52] In addition the *Commission de Travail*, set up by the central government in August 1914 specifically to deal with the capital's severe economic crisis, was suspended a month later during the confusion which accompanied the withdrawal of the government to Bordeaux.[53] The Parisian population was thrown largely onto its own resources as it battled to survive the near-total collapse of social and economic life in the city.[54]

In Berlin and London, welfare agencies were not placed under comparable pressure. Local government, in particular, continued to play an active part in the relief of distress. Indeed, in Berlin the municipal authorities introduced their own welfare measures including, in late August, a supplement to the basic state unemployment and dependants' benefits, which was intended to compensate for the high cost of living in the capital, and in October a scheme of rent support for war families.[55] In London the 28 borough councils formed Local Representative Committees under the direction of the government's Committee for the Prevention and Relief of Distress. These local committees had a broad membership including councillors, employers, administrators, charity workers, and trade unionists, and were charged with distributing grants from the centrally organized National Relief Fund,

---

[52] See Bonzon, 'La politique sociale'.

[53] On the *Commission de Travail* see Picard, *Le mouvement syndical*. On the reticence of the *Préfecture de la Seine* to continue public works see the declaration of Léon Jouhaux to the congress of the CGT in July 1918, in *Compte-rendu du travaux de CGT*, p. 226.

[54] Robert, 'Ouvriers et mouvements', esp. chs. 2-5.

[55] See *Gemeinde Blatt Berlin*, 1914, p. 375; *Berliner Morgenpost*, 28 Aug. 1914; Kaeber, *Berlin im ersten Weltkrieg*, pp. 49-50; and State Archive, Berlin, Rep. 00-02/2 316, 'Stadtverordnetenversammlung Vorlagen', 1914, p. 837 (13 Oct. 1914).

inaugurated by the Prince of Wales as a special war charity.[56] Thus welfare in London was a mixture both of national and local, and of public and private effort. It was far from perfect: many committees appear to have been remarkably complacent about local distress (especially among women workers),[57] but, like the efforts of the Berlin municipal authorities, their work remains impressive when compared with the meagre system of social support that existed in Paris.

III

If the French government's decision to give the military absolute priority over financial resources all but guaranteed that France would suffer more severe economic dislocation than the other nations during the first weeks of the conflict, the rapid success of the subsequent German offensive through Belgium and northern France made it equally certain that there would be no speedy recovery of economic fortunes during the autumn. By October 1914, after the German offensive had been halted at the Battle of the Marne, the first official unemployment returns revealed that more than 300,000 Parisians were without work. The real total was probably even higher since these returns excluded anyone in receipt of a refugee's or soldier's dependant's allowance.[58] Three months later, in January 1915, there were still 230,000 officially out of work despite the continued mobilization of male workers into the armed forces. These figures represent a level of unemployment not witnessed in either Berlin or London.

Table 6. *The course of employment in the Paris region and in France, July 1914 to October 1915 (July 1914 = 100)*

	July 1914	Aug. 1914	Oct. 1914	Jan. 1915	April 1915	July 1915	Oct. 1915
Paris	100	29	33	50	57	63	73
France	100	34	44	56	63	67	74

Source: constructed from a series in *Bulletin du Ministère du Travail*, 1914-5; see Robert, 'Ouvriers et mouvements', ch. 2.

By early 1915 the Parisian experience of employment was already beginning to converge towards that of France as a whole (table 6). The period of profound divergence was between August and October 1914, when employment rose by nearly one-third nationally, but hardly improved in Paris. To understand this divergence of experience we must look, not to the structural weaknesses of the Parisian economy, but to contingent factors arising directly out of the war itself. Above all, we must again stress the importance of the proximity of Paris to the front, and hence to the effects of the German offensive. At

---

[56] See *Memorandum on the steps taken for the prevention and relief of distress due to the war* (P.P. 1914, LXXI), p. 877; *Report on the special work of the Local Government Board arising out of the war up to 31st December 1914* (P.P. 1914-6, XXV), pp. 300, 305-6.

[57] See *Woman's Dreadnought*, 31 Oct., 7 Nov., and 12 Dec. 1914. For a different perspective see *Toynbee Record*, XXVII, 1 (Nov. 1914), pp. 10-2, 'The Borough of Stepney and the relief of distress', and pp. 15-23, 'Unemployment amongst women in Stepney'.

[58] Fonvieille, 'Étude critique'.

the height of the military crisis in August and September 1914, Paris seemed in imminent danger of falling to the advancing German armies. The city suffered its first aerial bombardment on 30 August 1914 and on 2 September almost the entire administrative machinery of government departed for Bordeaux to protect it from the advancing enemy, staying there until 9 December 1914 (by which time the front had been stabilized north of the capital). The government of Paris was effectively placed in the hands of the military, who proceeded to redirect the entire life of the city towards one end: the defence of the nation in its moment of crisis. From the taxi-cabs used to ferry soldiers and munitions to and from the Marne, to the navvies working on the city's fortifications, all Paris was part of the battle to stem the German advance.[59] Inevitably this total concentration of the capital's resources on the war and on the city's defence occurred at the expense of the economic restructuring that would have been necessary to overcome the dislocation of the immediate crisis.

The Parisian economy was also affected badly by the loss of Belgium and large parts of northern France to the invading German armies. Suddenly the capital's major source of raw materials and semi-processed goods was gone, along with one of the most important markets for its skilled finishing trades. On the eve of the war the area directly affected by invasion accounted for approximately two-thirds of French iron and steel production, three-quarters of coal and coke production, four-fifths of pig-iron and woollen production, and over 90 per cent of the output of linen goods and copper.[60] The French economy as a whole was seriously weakened by the loss of this vital productive capacity, much of it in the key war industries, but Paris was particularly badly hit because of its proximity to, and consequently high level of economic integration with, the northern industrial region.[61]

Another factor retarding recovery during this period was the massive exodus from the capital during the military crisis. An analysis of the results of a census carried out during September 1914 suggests that only 1.8 million people were still resident in Paris at this time; more than 1 million fewer than on the eve of the war.[62] Assuming that approximately 300,000 of these had been mobilized, that still leaves more than 700,000 civilians who had fled the capital. From the census it appears that approximately 220,000 of these were children under 15 years old, while the remainder was made up of 310,000 women and 200,000 men. Moreover, these figures almost certainly underestimate the exodus because large numbers of refugees from northern France and Belgium were flooding into Paris at the time this census was taken.

This voluntary evacuation was particularly heavy among the Parisian bourgeoisie, and resulted in the depopulation of many of the wealthiest districts such as the sixteenth *arrondissement* and Neuilly-sur-Seine.[63] Indeed

---

[59] See Becker, *Août 1914*.
[60] Fontaine, *French industry*, pp. 16-7. These figures refer not just to the area invaded, but also to adjacent areas under fire or seriously disorganized by military action.
[61] See Centre de Documentation d'Histoire des Techniques, *Evolution de la géographie*.
[62] *Annuaire statistique de la ville de Paris et du département de la Seine*, 1914, pp. 652-4.
[63] See Robert, 'Ouvriers et mouvements', map 5, p. 1311.

Table 7. *An estimate of unemployment by trade in Paris, January 1915*[a]

Trade	Male workers		Female workers		Men & women
	Unemployed (no.) (1)	Unemployed (%) (2)	Unemployed (no.) (3)	Unemployed (%) (4)	Total unemployed as % of July 1914 workforce (5)
Food[b]	4,504	31	5,129	57	41.3
Building	17,262	45	7	—	40.9
Clothing[c]	8,840	35	43,827	17	19.0
Crafts	5,784	65	5,361	36	46.5
Printing	5,316	29	7,459	75	45.2
Wood	10,202	32	3,875	67	36.9
Chemicals	2,815	26	2,149	83	37.0
Leather	3,217	15	2,525	13	14.4
Engineering[d]	9,288	15	2,579	35	17.3
Commerce	15,377	9	15,364	14	11.1
Professions	4,263	10	5,757	15	12.6
Service[e]	7,281	37	32,428	19	21.1
Total	94,149	20	126,460	20	20.0

Notes: [a] col. 2, col. 4, and col. 5 represent the number unemployed as a percentage of the *estimated* number employed in July 1914 (after allowance for enlistment into the armed forces). This calculation therefore makes no allowance for movement between trades after July 1914 (see text).
[b] Food may include the food service industries as well as manufacture
[c] Clothing and textiles sector
[d] Engineering, electrical, and metal trades
[e] Domestic service
Source: Bulletin du Ministère du Travail, Jan.-March 1915.

most of the capital's great commercial banks and its 'quality' newspapers such as *Le Figaro* and *Le Temps* followed the government to Bordeaux during September. As a consequence Paris became effectively a workers' city during the worst months of the crisis. The cost of this social transformation was, however, very high, since the flight of the bourgeoisie meant the flight of bourgeois capital. This retarded recovery in two main ways. First, it hit the already depressed finished goods and service industries by removing many of their most affluent customers. Second, many of the small businessmen who fled the city during the autumn closed their workshops before leaving, despite appeals from the *Inspecteur du Travail* to keep them open.[64]

In the absence of direct information about the impact of economic dislocation on different trades during the autumn of 1914, we must again turn to the unemployment returns of January 1915. These figures are worth examining in some detail, since they illustrate the uneven impact of the employment crisis in Paris.[65] (It will be recalled that the unemployment percentages in table 7 are only rough estimates because the exact size of the wartime labour force of each trade is unknown.)

In marked contrast to the situation in London and Berlin, there was little difference in the pattern of employment of men and women in January 1915.

---

[64] See *Bulletin du Ministère du Travail*, Jan.-Mar. 1915.
[65] *Bulletin du Ministère du Travail*, Jan. 1915.

In a few trades female unemployment appears to have been exceptionally high (in chemicals 83 per cent, in printing 75 per cent), but overall the rates for men and women were almost identical. Much more marked was the difference between the situation of manual and non-manual workers. In the service sector unemployment rates appear to have ranged between 10 and 20 per cent, but in the industrial sector they were generally around 30 per cent, rising to between 40 and 50 per cent in trades such as building, printing, and the luxury craft trades. It may be that unemployment rates among non-manual workers were deflated by the after-effects of the September exodus (though most Parisians returned once the immediate crisis had passed), but nevertheless it seems clear that unemployment was overwhelmingly an experience of manual workers.

The crisis was most severe in the city's consumer orientated trades, affected by the flight of the bourgeoisie and by the collapse of working-class purchasing power through enlistment and unemployment.[66] The apparent exception of the clothing trade could be the result of underestimation caused by the informal employment structures of the sector, which tended to obscure unemployment (especially among outworkers) from the official gaze. On the other hand, it may be that, like the leather trade, clothing could transfer relatively easily from civilian to military production. Certainly in Berlin and London sections of the clothing industry such as tailoring were among the first trades to enjoy boom conditions during the autumn of 1914.

Thus, as Angell and his followers would have predicted, the outbreak of war threw the manual workers of Paris into a period of prolonged social crisis. The severity of this crisis was probably most acute in industries catering predominantly for the civilian population, such as printing and food. There is, however, some uncertainty about the definition of the food industry used in the Parisian statistics. At the national level food production was the industry least affected by the contraction of employment during August 1914, and by January 1915 employment stood at 68 per cent of its prewar level, despite heavy male enlistment into the armed forces.[67] The food industry was also relatively little affected by the outbreak of war in Berlin and London. Indeed, by mid December 1914 employment in the London food industry had declined by only 7.6 per cent, compared with perhaps 40 per cent in Paris a month later.[68] Significantly, statistics for industrial accidents in the food industry of the Paris region do not show a decline from prewar levels commensurate with the contraction of employment suggested in table 7. In the first quarter of 1915 industrial accidents were only 24 per cent below their level for the same period in 1914, by far the lowest fall for any industry in the Paris region.[69] One explanation for this discrepancy may be that the Parisian unemployment figures for the food industry included workers in the food service industries, or even domestic cooks, as well as those employed in the manufacture of food and drink.

---

[66] The collapse of working-class purchasing power was partially mitigated by the introduction during August of the basic unemployment and separation allowances discussed in section II.
[67] *Bulletin du Ministère du Travail*, Jan.-Mar. 1915.
[68] L.I.C., VI, pp. 9–28.
[69] *Bulletin du Ministère du Travail*, May-June 1915.

To recapitulate, therefore, the severe and prolonged employment crisis in Paris during the autumn of 1914 must be understood in terms, not of structural weakness, but of immediate and overwhelming war-related factors of which the proximity of the front was undoubtedly the greatest. When combined with the destabilizing impact that mass mobilization and financial collapse had had in August, this explains why the economic crisis associated with the transition to war was so much greater, and so much more protracted, in Paris than in either London or Berlin. Structural factors may have played a secondary role, especially in prolonging the crisis after the immediate threat to Paris had passed, but they did not determine the nature of the Parisian crisis of 1914.[70] It could be argued, however, that the massive exodus from Paris had its roots in structural factors since it reflected the long-established tradition of people not born in the city returning to the provinces in times of crisis. Had fewer Parisians been born outside the city, the exodus might well have been less extreme.

IV

Whatever indices one chooses, it is clear that neither London nor Berlin experienced such severe dislocation as Paris during the autumn of 1914. For instance, trade union returns for Berlin show that unemployment peaked in early September, falling sharply thereafter, so that by January 1915 male unemployment was already below prewar levels (table 8). Female unemployment rates took much longer to return to prewar levels, although again they fell continuously from October 1914 (these figures may be unrepresentative because so few women were members of trade unions at this time). The story was broadly similar in London, although there unemployment never rose as sharply, and by December 1914 was already below prewar levels among insured workers (table 8).[71]

On the basis of its statistical surveys, the Local Government Board's London Intelligence Committee concluded, with hindsight, that the low point of the recession was reached by 22 August, the date of its first comprehensive employment survey.[72] At first sight this may seem a classic example of official optimism. As we have seen, male unemployment continued to rise until mid September, while other indices of social distress peaked even later. For instance, in London boroughs as diverse as Shoreditch and Stoke Newington, the numbers of children receiving free school meals because of poverty continued to rise until early October.[73] However, the committee's statement was concerned neither with unemployment nor with social distress, but with economic activity as measured by aggregate employment levels. Its optimism was therefore based on the substantial

---

[70] Robert, 'Ouvriers et mouvements', I, *passim*.

[71] This was despite the fact that in London nearly two-thirds of insured workers were employed in the building sector, which was particularly badly affected both by the war itself and by seasonal unemployment during the winter months.

[72] L.I.C., I (22 Aug. 1914), p. 28; ibid., II (5 Sept. 1914), pp. 11-24, and (12 Sept. 1914), pp. 133-6.

[73] Ibid., I, II, and III: 'reports on the highest number of necessitous children fed, by borough, for each week between August and October' (App. C of the main reports).

Table 8. *Unemployment rates in Berlin and London, July 1914-April 1915*

	Greater Berlin[a]		London[b]
	male trade unionists unemployed (%)	female trade unionists unemployed (%)	insured workers unemployed (%)
July 1914	6.3	2.4	7.1
Aug. 1914	19.2	12.4	9.6
Sept. 1914	19.9	18.8	10.0
Oct. 1914	14.5	17.9	8.2
Nov. 1914	10.5	13.6	7.7
Dec. 1914	7.2	10.7	5.9
Jan. 1915	5.5	9.8	4.7
Feb. 1915	3.6	7.0	3.9
April 1915	1.5	4.7	1.8

Notes: [a] trade unions in six sectors: metal, wood, transport, textiles, factories, and office work
[b] building workers, engineers, shipbuilders, and vehicle builders in the London region covered by National Insurance
Sources: *Monatsberichte Gross-Berlin*, 1914-5; Board of Trade, *Labour Gazette*, Aug. 1914-May 1915.

reduction in the number of workers on short time between the August and September surveys. In mid August 1914 45 per cent of women and 16 per cent of men were either on short time or had been laid off. By September the figure for women had fallen to 36 per cent, although there had been a slight increase among men to 16.5 per cent.[74] Thereafter the improvement was rapid so that by mid October only 21 per cent of the prewar female workforce was either on short time or unemployed, and the corresponding figure for the male workforce was only 9.5 per cent (thanks largely to enlistment which accounted for another 11.5 per cent of the prewar male workforce).[75]

There are no comparable statistics for aggregate employment in Berlin, but it seems unlikely that the recovery set in as early, mainly because of the greater impact of mobilization. However, there is no doubt that by the spring of 1915, Berlin (like London) was suffering, not from the problems of unemployment and social distress, but from acute labour shortages in all sectors of the economy. This is borne out by the Berlin Factory Inspectors' reports which by March 1915 had ceased to mention problems of unemployment, and were focusing instead on the complaints of employers about the high wages demanded by scarce skilled workers.[76] It also finds corroboration, not only in the low unemployment rates seen in table 8, but also in the employment survey of April 1915 conducted by the Berlin city factory inspectorate. The results of this survey are summarized in tables 9 and 10. Similar data for London are included for comparative purposes, although it should be noted that the Berlin statistics

---

[74] Ibid., II ('Statistical survey of employment in each trade and industry in London: based on employers' returns for mid-September'), pp. 240-1. The figures refer to manual and non-manual workers, but exclude the building trade, the railways, dock work, the professions, government employees, and domestic service.

[75] Ibid., III ('Statistical survey for mid-October'), p. 260.

[76] See State Archive, Potsdam, Province Brandenburg Rep. 30, Tit. 35 no. 1466, reports from factory inspectorates in north-west, east, and south-east Berlin, as well as Neuköln (March 1915).

concern only employees of large firms, whereas the London statistics are comprehensive for the sectors covered (hence the much greater numbers involved in the London data).

By April 1915 Berlin had seen a major shift of both male and female workers into large industrial firms (tables 9 and 10), with female employment increasing by 50 per cent since July 1914, and male employment by 36 per cent in net terms. However, only a few trades such as chemicals, metalwork, machines, and leather seem to have benefited from this movement of labour. In most Berlin trades employment in large firms either remained static or fell during the first nine months of war. Clearly the dynamic trades were those boosted by massive war contracts, while largely civilian trades such as printing, paper, laundries, and even clothing all lost workers.[77]

Table 9. *The fluctuation of female industrial employment in Berlin and London, July 1914-April 1915*

Trade group	Berlin		London	
	Est. of no. employed, July 1914 (large firms)[a]	Change over period to 1 April 1915 (%)	Est. of no. employed, July 1914[b]	Change over period to 16 April 1915 (%)
Mining & quarrying	1,238	−26	—	—
Metalwork	2,031	+95	7,700	+12
Machines & instruments	14,325	+92	7,500	+10
Chemicals	1,576	+292	6,500	+4
Textiles	5,568	−13	—	—
Clothing	1,992	−17	153,300	−5
Leather	898	+8	12,000	−21
Paper	569	−34	18,300	−9
Printing	1,187	−44	17,800	−5
Wood	176	+58	7,500	+2
Food & drink	2,984	+33	20,000	0
Laundries	943	−15	36,500	−13
Total	34,845	+50	289,100	−4

Notes: [a] Berlin figures refer only to women over 16 in firms employing 50 or more persons.
[b] London figures refer to all female workers in each trade group.
Sources: *Jahresberichte der Gewerbeaufsichten*, 1914-8, pp. 76-7; London Intelligence Committee Papers, VIII (April 1915).

As tables 9 and 10 indicate, the basic pattern of labour force mobility was similar in London, although the aggregate shifts in employment appear to have been considerably lower. Partly, this reflects the fact that the London data cover firms of all sizes, and so are not boosted by the transference of workers from small to large firms. However, even in large firms, defined as those with over 100 employees in the London data, the increase in employment was much less than that revealed in the Berlin returns (2.5 per cent for women, and 6.4 per cent for men in April 1915 in the industrial and commercial sectors combined).[78] A number of factors may explain this

[77] A survey of firms in south-east Berlin in October 1914 found that military contracts were most common among firms in the leather trades, metalwork, textiles, machines, and wood working (in that order); State Archive, Potsdam, Province Brandenburg, Rep. 30 Tit. 35 no. 1465, Berlin SO, 10 Oct. 1914.

[78] L.I.C., VIII ('Statistical survey for April 16th 1915'), p. 3.

Table 10. *The fluctuation of male industrial employment in Berlin and London, July 1914-April 1915*

Trade group	Berlin				London			
	(1) Est. of no. employed in July 1914 (large firms)[a]	(2) Percentage of col. 1 total employed on 1 April 1915	(3) Percentage of col. 1 total called up	(4) Net change in employment since July 1914 (%)	(5) Est. of no. employed in July 1914 (large firms)[a]	(6) Percentage of col. 1 total employed on 1 April 1915	(7) Percentage of col. 1 total called up	(8) Net change in employment since July 1914 (%)
Mining & quarrying	5,693	35	40	−24	—	—	—	—
Metalwork	12,587	127	45	+72	27,800	91	17	+8
Machines & instruments	64,445	97	41	+38	98,300	91	17	+8
Chemicals	7,331	149	41	+90	17,600	93	18	+11
Textiles	3,133	78	21	−1	—	—	—	—
Clothing	1,621	69	22	−9	67,100	87	14	+1
Leather	1,358	93	40	+33	18,200	102	17	+19
Paper	788	64	17	−18	8,400	81	19	0
Printing	1,549	54	27	−19	61,300	84	14	−2
Wood	3,328	55	25	−20	51,300	79	17	−5
Food & drink	3,971	91	38	+29	41,700	90	18	+8
Building	1,930	54	34	−12	117,000	85	14	−1
Laundries	880	63	18	−18	5,100	86	30	+15
Total	108,614	97	39	+36	513,800	87	16	+3

Notes: [a] Berlin figures refer only to men over 16 in firms employing 25 or more.
[b] London figures refer to all male workers in each trade group.
Sources: Jahresberichte der Gewerbeaufsichten, 1914-8, p. 75; London Intelligence Committee Papers, VIII (April 1915).

contrast, including the spur to labour mobility provided by greater dislocation in Berlin during the immediate crisis, the prewar strength of Berlin's metal and machine industries, and the more rapid emergence of a war economy in Germany than in Britain, where the real turning point came only with the so-called shells crisis of May 1915.[79]

The stabilization of the Berlin and London economies during the autumn of 1914 cannot, therefore, be attributed to the same social and economic processes. In Berlin the powerful metal-working and machine-making industries led the recovery—once they had been able to re-organize production, both to offset the impact of mobilization, and to meet the new pattern of war-related demand. In London the essential war industries (metals, machines, and chemicals) were all much weaker than in Berlin. Indeed, in mid February, government war contracts had created more jobs in London, in aggregate terms, in clothing and related trades than in all the essential war industries combined.[80] As a result of this relative weakness in metals and engineering, government contracts provided work for only one-fifth of male industrial workers in London compared with one-third in Britain as a whole.[81] This may help to explain why male unemployment fell more slowly in London than either in Berlin (table 8), or in Britain as a whole.[82]

However, the London economy had advantages as well as disadvantages when compared with Berlin, and these help to explain why it was relatively successful in negotiating the transition to war. London benefited from the stabilizing influence of its large service and transport sectors, since both proved far less vulnerable to dislocation than manufacturing. In September 1914 only 65 per cent of male workers and 57 per cent of female workers in the industrial sector were still employed full time (compared with July 1914). The equivalent figures for the commercial and service sectors were 84 per cent and 88 per cent respectively. By December 1914 male industrial employment was already showing a net increase, but among women there was still a net contraction of 5.5 per cent, compared with a contraction of only 1.5 per cent in the commercial sector.[83] There are no precise figures for employment in transport, government service, or the Post Office, but two reports on labour mobility during the transition to war suggest that

---

[79] See Feldman, *Army, industry and labor*; Trebilcock, 'War and industrial mobilisation, 1899 and 1914'; French, 'Business as usual'; Turner, *British politics*, pp. 4, 55-61.

[80] See L.I.C., VII ('Statistical survey for 12th February 1915'), p. 19. From this it can be calculated that in the metal, machine, and chemical industries the equivalent of 45,644 people were employed full time on government work, compared with 47,987 in clothing, leather, and fur.

[81] Ibid., p. 4; ibid., VIII ('Statistical survey for April 16th 1915'), p. 4; Board of Trade, 'Supplementary report on the state of employment in February [1915]', p. 6 (unpub., B.L.P.E.S., London). The two sources differ with regard to the percentage of female workers on government contracts, but it was probably 17 per cent in London compared with 21 per cent nationally. The difference is much lower because of war work in the London clothing trade. In all cases the figures refer to the number of full-time equivalent workers on government work.

[82] If one takes a weighted average of trade union and National Insurance returns, unemployment nationwide fell from 6.6 per cent in August 1914 to 1.8 per cent in February 1915, whereas in London it fell from 10.2 per cent to 3.5 per cent over the same period. (Board of Trade, *Labour Gazette*, Sept. 1914-March 1915).

[83] L.I.C., V ('Statistical survey for December 11th 1914'), pp. 11-2.

these sectors were all actively recruiting labour, especially male labour, during this period.⁸⁴

There is also evidence that many of the peculiar features of London—its emphasis on labour-intensive production processes, its experience of rapid product change to meet shifting consumer tastes, and the relatively high occupational, if not geographical, mobility of labour within the casualized trades—all helped to facilitate the process of adaptation necessary to meet the altered demand patterns of a wartime economy. This argument is hard to verify, but it is clear that in tailoring, boot making, leather working, and other consumer trades, London manufacturers were very quick to adapt their production processes in anticipation of government contracts.⁸⁵

V

It is clear that we must look primarily to contingent, war-related factors, rather than to structural factors, as the key determinants of dislocation and recovery in the urban economies of Paris, Berlin, and London in 1914. This is most evident in the case of Paris, where normal civilian life was all but destroyed in 1914 by two successive crises of war: first, by the colossal effort to mobilize all resources, human, material, and financial, for the anticipated 'short war' with Germany, and then by the dire consequences of military action which brought war to the gates of the city. Within the course of two months Paris had lost one-third of its male workforce through mobilization, and a further 40 per cent of its population through flight, and had seen the near collapse of both credit and the cash economy. Moreover, those who remained in the capital were living effectively in an armed camp in which the defence of the nation took absolute priority over all other concerns.

This unparalleled crisis cannot be explained by reference solely to the prewar structure of the Parisian economy. There are some reasons for believing that the effects of mobilization and financial collapse were exacerbated by the relative small scale of industry in Paris (many small workshops never reopened after the crisis). But the German occupation of Belgium and northern France, the traditional industrial hinterland of Paris, was probably a more important factor in prolonging the crisis during 1915.

The limitation of structural explanations is underlined by the strong similarities in the experience of Berlin and London during the first months of the war, despite the fact that their economies were radically different. Both cities experienced an initial period of severe dislocation (worse in Berlin because of heavier mobilization), followed by a sustained recovery which had brought acute labour shortages by spring 1915. Contrary to the prewar expectations of Angell and his followers, the transition to war in Berlin and London would appear to demonstrate that, when war itself did not impinge directly on urban life, adaptation could prove remarkably smooth, whatever the prewar economic structure.

Structural factors are not, however, irrelevant, and account for many

---

⁸⁴ Ibid., VII ('Report on transference of trade based on trade returns relating to February 12th, 1915'), pp. 158-75, and Board of Trade, 'Supplementary report February [1915]', pp. 6-9.
⁸⁵ See ibid., and Board of Trade, 'Report on the course of employment in the United Kingdom from July 1914 to July 1915' (unpub., B.L.P.E.S., London).

essential features, not of the crisis period, but of the subsequent recovery. The fact that the process of recovery was radically different in Berlin and London can only be understood adequately by reference to the prewar economic structure of the two cities. Thus in Berlin, recovery was led by the rapid expansion of the city's prewar base in heavy industries like metalworking, machines, and chemicals. In contrast London's recovery was largely the result of the rapid adaptation of its traditional consumer industries to war production, and the buoyancy of employment in the large public service and transport sectors.

The process of adaptation and recovery was far from complete by early 1915, even in Berlin and London. In both cities female employment was still below its prewar level, especially in the manufacturing sector, and the war industries which came to dominate economic life were as yet in their infancy. Neither city had developed a fully fledged war economy by early 1915; nor had there been any significant dilution of the predominantly male labour force. Paris was, of course, even further from developing a war economy at this point. There were still 230,000 officially unemployed in January 1915, a figure that was to fall only slowly over the following 12 months. Indeed it was only in the latter half of 1916 that the rapid growth of new war industries, largely in the suburbs, finally began to absorb the slack in the Parisian labour market.

The comparative urban history of war remains in its infancy, but this paper has shown that, as long as due recognition is paid to the influence of exogenous factors such as the decisions of national governments and the course of the war itself, it can provide valuable insights into the divergent local consequences of war. In particular, the contrast between London and Paris highlights, perhaps in a particularly extreme manner, the uneven nature of the Allied war economy during 1914-5. Or again, the analysis of developments in Berlin demonstrates that in this period there were few signs of the economic and social problems that would ultimately undermine the German war effort. Further research on other, non-metropolitan, manufacturing centres would probably reinforce this picture of diversity at the local level, and might also provide a clearer understanding of the processes behind economic recovery—how important were economic variables such as place in the trade cycle and traditional patterns of seasonality?[86] However, it should already be clear that comparative urban history offers the historian the chance to abandon over-arching models of the emergence of war economies, in favour of an approach which recognizes both the uneven chronologies of change and the very different processes of change visible at the local level.

Faculty of History, University of Cambridge
University of Paris, I

---

[86] But see Beveridge's discussion of the longer-term cycles that can influence urban economies in Smith, ed., *New survey of London life*, I, pp. 341-60 ('Unemployment and its treatment'). Beveridge identifies three distinct economic phases for London between 1890 and 1930 excluding the war years: 1890-1902, when trade union unemployment in London was significantly below the national average; 1902-14, when it was significantly higher—largely as a result of the long-term depression in building; and finally post-1918, when London again fared much better than the rest of Britain.

Footnote references

Official publications
Annuaire statistique de la ville de Paris et du département de la Seine, 1914.
Board of Trade, *Labour Gazette*, 1910-5.
Board of Trade, 'Reports on the state of employment in the United Kingdom', P.P. 1914-6, XXI (Oct. 1914); P.P. 1914-6, XXI (Dec. 1914); P.P. 1914-6, XXI (Feb. 1915).
Bulletin du Ministère du Travail, 1914-5.
Compte-rendu du travaux de CGT, 1919.
Dokumente aus Geheimen Archiven, Bd. IV (1914-8).
Jahresberichte der Gewerbeaufsichten, 1914-8 (Regierungsbezirk, Potsdam).
Jahresberichte der Preussischen Gewerberaete (Berlin, 1919).
London County Council, *London statistics*, 1900-14.
Memorandum on the steps taken for the prevention and relief of distress due to the war (P.P. 1914, LXXI).
Monatsberichte Gross-Berlin, 1913-4.
Population census of England and Wales, I, 'Administrative areas', P.P. 1912-3, CXI; VII, 'Age and conjugal conditions', P.P. 1912-3, CXIII; IX, 'Birthplaces', P.P. 1913, LXXVIII; X, 'Occupations', P.P. 1913, LXXVIII and LXXIX.
Population présénte par départements (Paris, 1913-4).
Registrar General's annual returns for England and Wales, 1909-14: P.P. 1911, X (1909); P.P. 1911, XI (1910); P.P. 1912-3, XIII (1911); P.P. 1913, XVII (1912); P.P. 1914-6, IX (1913); P.P. 1916, V (1914).
Report on the special work of the Local Government Board arising out of the war up to 31st December 1914 (P.P. 1914-6, XXV).
Résultats statistiques de rencensement général de la population effectué le 5 mars 1911, II and III.
Statisches Taschnebücher Berlins.
Statistiche Jahrbuch der Stadt Berlin, 32-4.

Secondary sources
Alexander, S., 'Women's work in nineteenth-century London: a study of the years 1820-1850', in J. Mitchell and A. Oakley, eds., *The rights and wrongs of women* (1976), pp. 59-111.
Angell, N., *The great illusion: a study of the relation of military power in nations to their economic and social advantage* (1910).
Asselain, J. C., *Histoire économique de la France du XVIIIème siècle à nos jours* (Paris, 1984).
Becker, J. J., *Août 1914: comme les Français sont entrées dans la guerre* (Paris, 1977).
Beltran, A. and Griset, P., *La croissance économique de la France, 1815-1914* (Paris, 1988).
Bonnefous, G., *La Grande Guerre* (Paris, 1957).
Bonzon, T., 'La politique sociale du Conseil Municipal de Paris et du Conseil Général de la Seine pendant la Grande Guerre' (unpub. D.E.A. thesis, Univ. of Paris I, 1990).
Booth, C., ed., *Life and labour of the people in London*, 9 vols. (1892-7).
Bowley, A. L., 'The survival of small firms', *Economica*, I (1921), pp. 113-5.
Calixte, B., 'Le travail à domicile au début de XXème siècle' (unpub. M.A. thesis, Univ. of Paris I, 1989).
Carré, J. J., Dubois, P., and Malinvaud, E., *French economic growth* (Stanford, Cal., 1976).
Centre de Documentation d'Histoire des Techniques, *Evolution de la géographie industrielle de Paris et la proche banlieu au XIXème siècle* (Paris, 1976).
Charle, C., *Histoire sociale de la France au XIXème siècle* (Paris, 1991).
Clarke, I. F., *Voices prophesying war, 1763-1984* (1966).
Clarke, P. F., *Liberals and social democrats* (Cambridge, 1978).
Cottereau, A., 'Problèmes de conceptualisation comparative de l'industrialisation: l'exemple des ouvriers de la chaussure en France et en Grande-Bretagne' in S. Magri and C. Topalov, eds., *Villes ouvrières, 1900-1950* (Paris, 1989), pp. 41-82.
De Bloch, J., *Is war now impossible? The future of war in its technical, economic and political relations* (1899).
Dearle, N. B., *Problems of unemployment in the London building trade* (1908).
Dewey, P. E., 'Military recruiting and the British labour force during the First World War', *Hist. J.* 27 (1984), pp. 199-223.
Feldman, G., *Army, industry and labor in Germany, 1914-1918* (Princeton, 1966).
Fontaine, A., *French industry during the war* (New Haven, 1926).
Fonvieille, A., 'Étude critique du régime des allocations aux familles des militaires soutiens indispensables' (unpub. Ph.D. thesis in Law, Univ. of Montpellier, 1919).
French, D., 'The rise and fall of "business as usual"', in K. Burk, ed., *War and the state: the transformation of British government, 1914-1919* (1982), pp. 7-31.
Guécaud-Léridon, F., *Le travail des femmes en France* (Travaux et Documents de l'Institut National d'Études Démographiques, no. 42) (Paris, 1964).

Howard, M., 'Men against fire: expectations of war in 1914', *Int. Security*, 9 (1984), pp. 41-57.
Jones, G. S., *Outcast London: a study in the relationship between classes in Victorian society* (Oxford, 1971).
Kaeber, E., *Berlin im ersten Weltkrieg* (Berlin, 1920).
Kemp, T., *The French economy, 1913-1939: the history of a decline* (1972).
Kindleberger, C. P., *Economic growth in France and Great Britain, 1851-1950* (Oxford, 1964).
Kuisel, R. F., *Capitalism and the state in modern France: renovation and economic management in the twentieth century* (Cambridge, 1981).
Marion, M., *Histoire financière de la France depuis 1715*, 6 vols. (Paris, 1927-31).
Maurin, J., *Armée, guerre, société: soldats Languedoçiens, 1889-1919* (Paris, 1982).
Morris, A. J. A., *Radicalism against war, 1906-1914: the advocacy of peace and retrenchment* (1972).
Offer, A., 'The working classes, British naval plans and the coming of the Great War', *P. & P.*, 107 (1985), pp. 204-26.
Picard, R., *Le mouvement syndical pendant la guerre* (Paris, 1927).
Poëte, M., 'La physionomie de Paris pendant la guerre', in H. Sellier and A. Bruggeman, eds., *Paris pendant la guerre* (Paris, 1926), pp. 68-87.
Robert, J. L., 'Ouvriers et mouvements ouvriers Parisiens pendant la Grande Guerre et l'immédiat après guerre: histoire et anthropologie' (unpub. higher doctoral thesis, Univ. of Paris I, 1989).
Roberts, E., *Women's work, 1840-1940* (Basingstoke, 1988).
Siemens, G., *Der Weg der Elektrotechnik* (Munich, 1961).
Smith, H. L., ed., *New survey of London life and labour*, 9 vols. (1930-5).
Tilly, L. and Scott, J., 'Women's work and the family in nineteenth-century Europe', *Comp. Stud. Soc. & Hist.*, XVII (1975), pp. 36-64.
Turner, J., *British politics and the Great War* (1992).
Verley, P., *Nouvelle histoire économique de la France contemporaine: l'industrialisation, 1830-1914* (Paris, 1989).
Trebilcock, C., 'War and the failure of industrial mobilization, 1889 and 1914', in J. Winter, ed., *War and economic development: essays in memory of David Joslin* (Cambridge, 1975), pp. 139-64.
Weinroth, H., 'Norman Angell and *The great illusion*: an episode in pre-1914 pacifism', *Hist. J.*, XVII (1974), pp. 551-74.
Zilch, R., *Die Reichsbank und die finanzielle Kriegsvorbereitung, 1907 bis 1914* (Berlin, 1987).

[12]

The Color Line behind the Lines: Racial Violence in France during the Great War

TYLER STOVALL

THE GREAT WAR WAS A TURNING POINT FOR FRANCE in many respects. It produced issues that would dominate the life of the nation during the twentieth century. Most important, it signaled the decline of church-state conflicts and the birth of the French Communist Party, gave new impetus to the public role of women and demands for gender equality, further reinforced the role of the centralized state in French life, and created a dynamic new intelligentsia that sharply questioned the nineteenth-century faith in positivism.[1] However, one critical development that has received relatively little attention from historians is racial difference and the presence of people of color on French soil. Nonwhites[2] have lived in France for many centuries, but after 1914 they became a widespread and integral part of French life.[3] During World War I, several hundred thousand people came from China and various parts of the French Empire in Africa and Asia to serve the French war effort as either soldiers or workers. While many received a warm reception from the French people, others encountered suspicion and hostility. During the latter years of the war, conflicts between the French and these nonwhite newcomers escalated into a wave of racial violence, ranging from numerous small-scale incidents to a few major riots. Although World War I would give a powerful boost to the myth of French racial egalitarianism, especially among African Americans, it would also produce conflicts contradicting that myth.[4]

Funding for this article was provided by the Academic Senate of the University of California, Santa Cruz, and the Center for German and European Studies of the University of California, Berkeley. I would like to thank George Cotkin, Laura Lee Downs, Lynn Hudson, and Earl Lewis for their helpful comments and suggestions.

[1] The historical literature on France and World War I is of course voluminous. For a good overview, see in particular Jean-Baptiste Duroselle, *La France et les Français, 1914–1920* (Paris, 1972). On the home front, see Jean-Jacques Becker, *1914: Comment les français sont entrés dans la guerre* (Paris, 1977); Becker, *The Great War and the French People*, Arnold Pomerans, trans. (Leamington Spa, 1985); and Patrick Fridenson, ed., *The French Home Front, 1914–1918* (Providence, R.I., 1992). Useful memoirs include Remy Cazals, ed., *Les carnets de guerre de Louis Barthas, tonnelier 1914–1918* (Paris, 1978); Louise Delétang, *Journal d'une ouvrière Parisienne pendant la guerre* (Paris, 1936); and H. Pearl Adam, *Paris Sees It Through* (London, 1919).

[2] Although the term "nonwhites" is more than a little problematic, I choose to use it here because it expresses precisely the kind of reductionist view of peoples from outside Europe that arose in wartime France. In particular, the term here refers to North Africans, black Africans, Indochinese, and Chinese.

[3] On the presence of nonwhites in France before the twentieth century, see William B. Cohen, *The French Encounter with Africans: White Response to Blacks, 1530–1880* (Bloomington, Ind., 1980); Shelby McCloy, *The Negro in France* (Lexington, Ky., 1961); Michel Fabre, *La rive noire* (Paris, 1985).

[4] On the perception of France as a color-blind society, see Fabre, *La rive noire*; McCloy, *Negro in*

I define race riots, as opposed to incidents of racial violence, as conflicts involving sustained fighting over at least several hours by large numbers of participants on both sides of the battle. In contrast to much of the literature on collective violence, however, I would argue that the difference between small incidents and large riots is more one of scale than degree, suggesting a fundamental unity between acts of racial violence in wartime France. In analyzing this subject, the historian is able to draw on a rich literature offering varied approaches. Students of collective violence have succeeded in giving nuanced, complex portraits of the ostensibly anonymous crowd, providing information about riot patterns, the sociological backgrounds of rioters, and the value systems that motivated their actions. Scholars such as George Rudé and E. P. Thompson have called into question traditional views of "the mob" as an irrational, emotional maelstrom, instead demonstrating that rioters were motivated by specific agendas and goals.[5] Studies of race riots in the United States during World War I constitute another important body of inquiry. Historians of America's "Red Summer" have written incisive case studies of individual incidents, using them to explore the dynamics of American race relations. This approach combined detailed chronological accounts of the riots with portraits of the white and black communities involved to argue that these riots were not isolated incidents but significant benchmarks of American life at the end of the war.[6] More recently, historians of racial violence have turned toward theories of difference grounded in postmodern and cultural studies approaches.[7] This new perspective on racial conflict considers the phenomenon as both providing a glimpse into the cultural markers that construct racial difference and as an integral part of that process of

---

France; Phyllis Rose, *Jazz Cleopatra: Josephine Baker in Her Time* (New York, 1989); Léon-François Hoffman, *Le Nègre romantique* (Paris, 1973); Roi Ottley, *No Green Pastures* (New York, 1951); James Weldon Johnson, *Along This Way* (New York, 1933); Tyler Stovall, *Paris Noir: African Americans in the City of Light* (Boston, 1996).

[5] Major historical studies of collective violence include George Rudé, *The Crowd in the French Revolution* (Oxford, 1959); Rudé, *The Crowd in History: A Study of Popular Disturbances in France and England, 1730–1848* (New York, 1964); E. J. Hobsbawm, *Primitive Rebels: Studies in Archaic Forms of Social Movement* (New York, 1963); Albert Soboul, *The Sans-Culottes: The Popular Movement and Revolutionary Government 1793–1794* (Garden City, N.Y., 1972); Georges Lefebvre, *The Great Fear of 1789: Rural Panic in Revolutionary France* (New York, 1973); E. P. Thompson, "The Moral Economy of the English Crowd in the Eighteenth Century," *Past and Present* 50 (February 1971): 76–136; Charles Tilly, *The Contentious French* (Cambridge, Mass., 1986).

[6] Elliott M. Rudwick, *Race Riot at East St. Louis, July 2, 1917* (Carbondale, Ill., 1964); William M. Tuttle, Jr., *Race Riot: Chicago in the Red Summer of 1919* (New York, 1970); Robert V. Haynes, *A Night of Violence: The Houston Riot of 1917* (Baton Rouge, La., 1976).

[7] Some of the most important works taking a cultural studies approach to questions of race include Henry Louis Gates, Jr., ed., *"Race," Writing, and Difference* (Chicago, 1986); bell hooks, *Yearning: Race, Gender, and Cultural Politics* (Boston, 1990); Paul Gilroy, *The Black Atlantic: Modernity and Double Consciousness* (Cambridge, Mass., 1993); Patricia Hill Collins, *Black Feminist Thought: Knowledge, Consciousness, and the Politics of Empowerment* (Boston, 1990); Cornel West, "Black Culture and Postmodernism," in Barbara Kruger and Phil Mariani, eds., *Remaking History* (Seattle, Wash., 1989); Abdul JanMohamed and David Lloyd, *The Nature and Context of Minority Discourse* (New York, 1990); Thomas C. Holt, "Marking: Race, Race-making, and the Writing of History," *AHR* 100 (February 1995): 1–20. Also important in this regard are the recent studies of "whiteness" as a type of identity formation based in racial conflict. See David Roediger, *The Wages of Whiteness: Race and the Making of the American Working Class* (London, 1991); Roediger, *Towards the Abolition of Whiteness: Essays on Race, Politics, and Working Class History* (London, 1994); Alexander Saxton, *The Rise and Fall of the White Republic: Class Politics and Mass Culture in Nineteenth Century America* (London, 1990); Toni Morrison, *Playing in the Dark: Whiteness and the Literary Imagination* (Cambridge, Mass., 1992).

identity formation. In a recent article, for example, J. William Harris argues that lynching in early twentieth-century Mississippi was a symbolic act that created not just the boundary between blacks and whites but their very existence as separate groups.[8] The stress on the subjective, culturally driven character of race and racial violence has not remained unchallenged, however, as some scholars have reemphasized the important, if not exclusive, role of material conditions in generating racial conflict.[9]

In my discussion of race riots in wartime France, I wish to emphasize that culture and material life are not separate, distinct aspects of the human condition but are constantly interacting and mutually reinforcing one another. While culture shapes material life, the reverse is also true. Historical studies of racial conflict should abjure both material and cultural determinisms, instead analyzing the ways in which these clashes have revealed the interaction of thought and action, the conditions of daily life and the representation of those conditions. In discussing French racial violence during World War I, therefore, I stress its specific historical conjuncture, arguing that material as well as cultural factors were mediated by the time and place of its occurrence.[10] This violence formed one important way in which racial categories were defined in wartime France, both expressing old concepts of race and creating new ones. Race thus appears as a discourse in which material and cultural considerations were interwoven and transformed.[11]

Accordingly, I contend that one must view French racial conflict in conjunction with the crisis of wartime morale that overtook the nation in 1917 and 1918. For a variety of reasons, in certain contexts, people of color came to symbolize both the war in general and its deleterious impact on the French working class in particular, and some members of the latter targeted colonial laborers[12] as an outlet for

[8] J. William Harris, "Etiquette, Lynching, and Racial Boundaries in Southern History: A Mississippi Example," *AHR* 100 (April 1995): 387–410; see also W. Fitzhugh Brundage, *Lynching in the New South: Georgia and Virginia, 1880–1930* (Urbana, Ill., 1993); George C. Wright, *Racial Violence in Kentucky, 1865–1940: Lynchings, Mob Rule, and "Legal Lynchings"* (Baton Rouge, La., 1990); Michael Keith, *Race, Riots and Policing: Lore and Disorder in a Multi-Racist Society* (London, 1993); Herbert Shapiro, *White Violence and Black Response: From Reconstruction to Montgomery* (Amherst, Mass., 1988). Some very interesting contributions to this subject have been made by writers studying the intersections of race, sex, and violence in colonial history. See Hazel Carby, "'On the Threshold of Woman's Era': Lynching, Empire, and Sexuality in Black Feminist Theory," in Gates, *"Race," Writing, and Difference*; Pamela Scully, "Rape, Race, and Colonial Culture: The Sexual Politics of Identity in the Nineteenth-Century Cape Colony, South Africa," *AHR* 100 (April 1995): 335–59.

[9] Barbara J. Fields, "Slavery, Race and Ideology in the United States of America," *New Left Review* 181 (1990): 95–116; Robert Miles, *Racism* (London, 1989); Nell Irvin Painter, "French Theories in American Settings: Some Thoughts on Transferability," *Journal of Women's History* 1 (Spring 1989): 92–95; Steve Vieux, "In the Shadow of Neo-liberal Racism," *Race and Class* 36 (July–September 1994): 23. Of particular interest in this regard is Laura Tabili, *"We Ask for British Justice": Workers and Racial Difference in Late Imperial Britain* (Ithaca, N.Y., 1994).

[10] As Stuart Hall has argued, "One must start, then, from the concrete historical 'work' which racism accomplishes under specific historical conditions—as a set of economic, political and ideological practices, of a distinctive kind, concretely articulated with other practices in a social formation." Hall, "Race, Articulation, and Societies Structured in Dominance," in *Sociological Theories: Race and Colonialism* (Paris, 1980), 338.

[11] I draw here on the ideas of Michael Omi and Howard Winant, who have shown how discourses on race have been key to recent American history, emphasizing race as a social and political construct. Omi and Winant, *Racial Formation in the United States: From the 1960s to the 1980s* (New York, 1986).

[12] The phrase "colonial workers" (or "exotic workers") applied to people of color in general, including Chinese contract laborers, in wartime France. It contrasted with the use of the term "immigrant workers" for non-French Europeans and thus served to construct the identity of both

frustrations about the ongoing conflict. The negative identification of nonwhite workers with the war did not come automatically in France but resulted from conscious and specific initiatives undertaken by French unions, employers, and above all by the French state. In this perspective, racial violence appears not just as a reaction to unprecedented diversity, it also casts new light on the escalating clash between French capital and labor at the end of the war. Yet race did not simply appear as an epiphenomenon of class in France; the French distinguished sharply between white and nonwhite foreign workers, so that race determined, rather than reflected, wartime class identity. More broadly, a consideration of French racial violence leads one to look at wartime labor history, especially renewed labor militancy and the rise of a radical movement against President Raymond Poincaré's notion of the *union sacrée* (united government), in a somewhat different light. This violence, and the racist attitudes it expressed, shows that dissatisfaction with the war was more complex and diverse than the movement led by major antiwar union activists. During World War I, concepts of racial difference based on skin color became a significant factor in French working-class life for the first time, establishing a discourse of conflict and intolerance that remains powerful today.[13]

INTER-ETHNIC VIOLENCE has a long history in France. Natalie Zemon Davis has analyzed the bloody riots between French Catholics and Protestants that occurred in the sixteenth century.[14] During the more recent past, such conflict has often taken the form of attacks by French workers on foreign immigrants. In 1775, for example, coopers in Sète assaulted foreign workers after demanding their expulsion from the city. During the 1840s and 1850s, French workers in the Nord frequently attacked Belgians for what they saw as unfair competition. By the late nineteenth

---

groups along racial lines. In order to conform to French practices at the time, in this article I have followed the practice of including the Chinese in the category of colonial workers.

[13] An important and rapidly growing body of literature currently exists on race and immigration in contemporary France. While much of the literature views immigration as primarily not a racial issue, other works highlight racial distinctions. For examples of the former, see Gérard Noiriel, *The French Melting Pot: Immigration, Citizenship, and National Identity*, Geoffrey de Laforcade, trans. (Minneapolis, 1996); Noiriel, *Population, immigration et identité nationale en France: XIXe–XXe siècle* (Paris, 1992); Yves Lequin, *La mosaïque France: Histoire des étrangers et de l'immigration* (Paris, 1988); Patrick Weil, *La France et ses étrangers: L'aventure d'une politique de l'immigration, 1938–1991* (Paris, 1991); for the latter, see Maxim Silverman, ed., *Race, Discourse, and Power in France* (Aldershot, 1991); Silverman, *Deconstructing the Nation: Immigration, Racism, and Citizenship in Modern France* (London, 1992); G. Kepel, *Les banlieues d'Islam: Naissance d'une religion en France* (Paris, 1991); Cathie Lloyd and Hazel Waters, "France: One Culture, One People?" *Race and Class* 32, no. 3 (1991): 49–66; Pierre-André Tagguieff, "The New Cultural Racism in France," *Telos* (Spring 1990): 109–22; William Safran, "The French and Ethnic Pluralism," *Ethnic and Racial Studies* (October 1984): 447–61. Interesting case studies on racism in contemporary France include Françoise Gaspard, *A Small City in France*, Arthur Goldhammer, trans. (Cambridge, Mass., 1995); Eric Roussel, *Le cas Le Pen: Les nouvelles droites en France* (Paris, 1985); Martin Schain, "The National Front in France and the Construction of Political Legitimacy," *West European Politics* 10 (April 1987): 229–52.

[14] Natalie Zemon Davis, "Rites of Violence," in *Society and Culture in Early Modern France: Eight Essays* (Stanford, Calif., 1965). The link between religious and ethnic hatred certainly did not disappear in the twentieth century, as demonstrated by the anti-Semitism of the 1930s and 1940s, as well as the hostility to Islam so prevalent in contemporary France. In spite of the unprecedented presence of Muslims on French soil, however, religion does not seem to have played a role in the racial violence of World War I.

century, Italians seem to have borne the brunt of this working-class xenophobia, and the worst violence was directed against them. A fight between French and Italian salt miners in the southern town of Aigues-Mortes degenerated into full-scale carnage in 1893, resulting in the deaths of eight people.[15] These attacks occurred in the context of increasing immigration; from 1881 on, French census takers counted over a million resident aliens in France, mostly workers from the neighboring countries of Belgium, Italy, and Germany. Those hostile to foreigners at times used the size of this population, especially prominent in Paris and frontier regions of the country, to make it a scapegoat for French working-class discontent. Attacks on immigrant workers during the *fin de siècle* thus fit neatly into longstanding traditions of violence against outsiders in order to protect one's own community. Like Italians in the 1890s, colonial workers during World War I came to be seen as outsiders to the national community, a perception that underlay the attacks directed against them.[16]

A clear parallel exists between attacks on foreign workers in nineteenth-century France and the violence directed against colonial laborers during World War I, but it is by no means straightforward. The physical and cultural distinctiveness of this new population and the peculiar circumstances of its introduction into French life combined to transform xenophobia into racial violence. By 1914, France possessed the second largest colonial empire in the world and did not hesitate to draw on the human resources of its overseas possessions in its struggle against Germany. The nation's greatest need was for soldiers, and hundreds of thousands from West Africa, North Africa, and Indochina fought and died on French battlefields during the war.[17] But the exigencies of industrial warfare also created a shortage of labor in France's war industries and on its farms, forcing the French to import workers as well as soldiers. During World War I, over half a million foreigners came to labor in French fields and factories. The majority of these, some 330,000, came from within Europe, primarily Spain. However, roughly another 300,000 individuals journeyed from overseas. Official statistics recorded the entry of 78,556 Algerians, 48,995 Indochinese, 36,941 Chinese, 35,506 Moroccans, 18,249 Tunisians, and 4,546

---

[15] Tilly, *Contentious French*, 194, 269; Noiriel, *French Melting Pot*, 258–62; Eugen Weber, *France, Fin de Siècle* (Cambridge, Mass., 1986), 134–35; Michelle Perrot, "Les rapports entre ouvriers français et étrangers (1871–1893)," *Bulletin de la Société d'histoire moderne* (1966); Anne-Marie Faidutti-Rudolph, *L'immigration italienne dans le Sud-Ouest de la France* (Gap, 1964); Paul Gemähling, *Travailleurs au rabais: La lutte syndicale contre les sous-concurrences ouvrières* (Paris, 1910); Yves Lefebvre, *L'ouvrier étranger et la protection du travail national* (Paris, 1901).

[16] Henri Bunle, *Mouvements migratoires entre la France et l'étranger: Etudes et documents* (Paris, 1943), 67. On immigrant labor in France during the early twentieth century, see Gary S. Cross, *Immigrant Workers in Industrial France: The Making of a New Laboring Class* (Philadelphia, 1983); Juliette Minces, *Les travailleurs étrangers en France* (Paris, 1973); Serge Bonnet, "Italian Immigration in Lorraine," *Journal of Social History* 2 (Winter 1968): 123–55; Georges Mauco, *Les étrangers en France* (Paris, 1932); Bernard Granotier, *Les travailleurs immigrés en France* (Paris, 1970); Nancy L. Green, *The Pletzl of Paris: Jewish Immigrant Workers in the Belle Epoque* (New York, 1986); Andre Kaspi, *Le Paris des étrangers* (Paris, 1989); Laurent Azzano, *Mes joyeuses anneés au faubourg* (Paris, 1985).

[17] On French colonial soldiers in World War I, see Marc Michel, *L'appel à l'Afrique: Contributions et réactions à l'effort de guerre en A.O.F. (1914–1919)* (Paris, 1982); Charles John Balesi, *From Adversaries to Comrades-in-Arms: West Africans and the French Military, 1885–1918* (Waltham, Mass., 1979); Agustin Bernard, *L'Afrique du nord pendant la guerre* (Paris, 1926); Charles Agéron, *Les Algériens musulmans et la France (1871–1919)*, 2 vols. (Paris, 1968); Joe Harris Lunn, "Kande Kamara Speaks: An Oral History of the West African Experience in France 1914–18," in Melvin E. Page, ed., *Africa and the First World War* (London, 1987).

Malagasy, for a total of 222,793 colonial workers.[18] The balance was made up by workers employed directly by the French army, those already present in France in 1914, and those who migrated on their own.[19] The war thus brought a large non-European, racially distinct population to France for the first time in the nation's modern history.[20]

The history of racial categorization in France is both lengthy and very complex. The concept of "race" has always been notoriously difficult to define and has varied tremendously according to time and place; only in the twentieth century has it come to be widely associated with differences in skin color. In early modern France, for example, those writing about race generally emphasized the distinction between Franks and Gauls as the nation's most important historical instance of racial difference. In 1932, Jacques Barzun, in a survey of such racial thinking in France before the revolution, argued that "the very roots of French history since the sixteenth century have been buried deep under and around the issue of race."[21] The concept of race was also often used to distinguish between aristocrats and commoners. By the nineteenth century, in contrast, the Enlightenment and the French Revolution had combined to produce a racialized view of the nation as an independent biological entity. As historians of racism have been at pains to point out, racism and nationalism together helped usher in the modern era.[22]

The numerous interconnections between concepts of race and class are important not just for the subject of this essay but for the history of race in general. Not only have class and race identities and conflicts frequently intersected, but the very articulations of these concepts are inextricably intertwined. While Marxist scholars in particular have emphasized this interrelationship, many others have also analyzed the ties between these two types of social fissures. Historians of nineteenth-century Europe have shown how bourgeois representations of the lower classes were often racialized.[23] In his seminal *Essai sur l'inégalité des races humaines*

---

[18] Bertrand Nogaro and Lucien Weil, *La main-d'oeuvre étrangère et colonial pendant la guerre* (Paris, 1926), 25.

[19] See Gilbert Meynier, "La France coloniale de 1914 à 1931," in Jacques Thobie, Gilbert Meynier, Catherine Coquery-Vidrovitch, and Charles-Robert Agéron, *Histoire de la France coloniale*, Vol. 2, *1914–1990* (Paris, 1990), 78. Meynier mentions one French officer who argued that the number of colonial workers was as high as 310,000 during World War I.

[20] On foreign labor in France during World War I, see Nogaro and Weil, *La main-d'oeuvre étrangère*; John Horne, "Immigrant Workers in France during World War I," *French Historical Studies* 24, no. 1 (1985): 57–88; Jean Vidalenc, "La main d'oeuvre étrangère en France et la première guerre mondiale (1901–1926)," *Francia* 2 (1974): 524–50; Mireille Favre, "Un milieu porteur de modernisation: Travailleurs et tirailleurs vietnamiens en France pendant la première guerre mondiale," 2 vols. (Doctoral thesis, Ecole Nationale des Chartres, Paris, 1986); Tyler Stovall, "Colour-blind France? Colonial Workers during the First World War," *Race and Class* 35, no. 2 (1993): 33–55.

[21] Jacques Barzun, *The French Race* (New York, 1932), 251.

[22] On the historical evolution of race as a category, see Michael Banton, *Racial Theories* (Cambridge, 1987); Etienne Balibar and Immanuel Wallerstein, *Race, Nation, Class: Ambiguous Identities*, Chris Turner, trans. (London, 1991); Colette Guillaumin, "The Idea of Race and Its Elevation to Autonomous Scientific and Legal Status," in *Sociological Theories*. Also very interesting in this regard is Ann Laura Stoler's recent discussion of Michel Foucault's ideas on colonialism and race, *Race and the Education of Desire: Foucault's History of Sexuality and the Colonial Order of Things* (Durham, N.C., 1995).

[23] This has been remarked on in particular by historians of British-Irish relations: see, for example, Richard Ned Lebow, *White Britain and Black Ireland: The Influence of Stereotype on Colonial Policy* (Philadelphia, 1976); Lynn Hollen Lees, *Exiles of Erin: Irish Migrants in Victorian London* (Ithaca, N.Y., 1979). For France, see in particular Louis Chevalier, *Laboring Classes and Dangerous Classes in Paris*

(1853–55), Arthur de Gobineau portrayed blacks as an insurgent mob threatening white civilization, very much along the lines of the French Revolution's sans-culottes. Social Darwinism was merely the most prominent current of thought to conflate racial and class conflict at the turn of the century, and George Mosse has demonstrated how the rise of racial ideology at the end of the nineteenth century at times took the form of workers' movements, setting the precedent for the idea of national socialism.[24] The complex interaction of race and class dynamics that characterized the history of colonial workers in France during the Great War thus closely conformed to the broader evolution of these concepts in modern times. In assessing this relationship, the point is not to argue that race or class was more important but rather to examine how each reinforced and contradicted the other.

In the case of France, the development of racial categorization that emphasized differences in skin color, and the contrast between Europeans and non-Europeans, has been intimately associated with the nation's colonial history. As William B. Cohen has demonstrated, negative French perceptions of nonwhites go back well before the beginnings of French overseas expansion in the seventeenth century, yet the colonial experience combined with intellectual changes in Europe to produce a view of whites and nonwhites as biologically distinct. In particular, such categorizations often centered on the question of labor. One of the first official French documents to elaborate this concept of race, the Code Noir of 1685 effectively defined blackness in conjunction with the exigencies of racially based slavery in the French Caribbean.[25] By the late nineteenth century, French stereotypes of North Africans, Indochinese, black Africans, and other imperial subjects frequently targeted their perceived inadequacies as workers. As Albert Memmi later argued, "Nothing could better justify the colonizer's privileged position than his industry, and nothing could better justify the colonized's destitution than his indolence. The mythical portrait of the colonized therefore includes an unbelievable laziness, and that of the colonizer, a virtuous taste for action."[26] The numerous objections to colonial workers expressed by French administrators, employers, and workers during the war—laziness, lack of skill or intelligence, physical weakness, and moral corruption—had all previously appeared in discussions of native labor within the empire.[27] Therefore, both the broader racialization of differences in skin color and the more specific view of nonwhite workers as distinct and inferior had a prominent colonial heritage.

Yet the legacy of the French Empire alone does not explain the largely negative reception of colonial workers in wartime France. By the early twentieth century, French consciousness of racial difference had been influenced by global patterns of

---

during the First Half of the Nineteenth Century, Frank Jellinek, trans. (Princeton, N.J., 1973); Eugen Weber, *Peasants into Frenchmen: The Modernization of Rural France, 1870–1914* (Stanford, Calif., 1976).

[24] George L. Mosse, *Toward the Final Solution: A History of European Racism* (1978; rpt. edn., Madison, Wis., 1985).

[25] Cohen, *French Encounter with Africans*; Louis Sala-Molins, *Le Code Noir* (Paris, 1987).

[26] Albert Memmi, *The Colonizer and the Colonized*, Howard Greenfeld, trans. (1965; rpt. edn., Boston, 1965), 79.

[27] See, for example, Jules Ninine, *La main-d'oeuvre indigène dans les colonies françaises* (Paris, 1934).

domination and subordination. Michelle Perrot has demonstrated, for example, that antagonism to Chinese "coolie" labor was widespread among French workers in the late nineteenth century, based on a belief that French employers hoped to import them in order to lower wages and worsen working conditions. In 1882, Socialist leader Jules Guesde wrote an article congratulating the workers of California on their struggle for anti-Chinese exclusionary legislation.[28] The role of this American example is highly significant, for if the empire provided one model of race relations, the United States furnished another. The experience of nonwhite workers in France resembled aspects of both: although they mostly came from the French Empire and were treated as colonial subjects in France, they also constituted a non-indigenous racial minority in a predominantly white nation, like blacks and other peoples of color in America.[29] Consequently, the reaction of French authorities and workers to wartime colonial laborers both expressed colonial traditions and at the same time set forth new postcolonial patterns for race relations in France.[30]

Colonial workers occupied a singular, highly differentiated position in France's wartime labor force. Most notably, they worked and lived in conditions distinct not only from French workers but also from non-French European immigrants. As part of a broader effort to rationalize labor supplies, the French government sought to impose greater controls on foreign labor in general. Although in theory, these policies did not distinguish between Europeans and colonials, in practice Spaniards, Greeks, and other white foreigners often successfully evaded such attempts at regulation.[31] Nonwhite workers, by contrast, were recruited directly at their point of origin by the French government, frequently by force.[32] Once in France, they were not permitted to fend for themselves but were closely regimented by the War Ministry's Colonial Labor Organization Service (SOTC). The SOTC grouped these workers by nationality into labor battalions, assigned them to their employers, and made all arrangements for their transportation, housing, and food. Colonial laborers worked and lived in isolation from their French counterparts, in conditions more reminiscent of war prisoners or even slaves than independent workers. Such segregation was in effect an attempt to transplant colonial conditions to French soil,

[28] Jules Guesde, "La vraie solidarité," *Le citoyen* (May 7, 1882), cited in Michelle Perrot, *Les ouvriers en grève: France 1871–1890* (Paris, 1974), 1: 178.

[29] During World War I, 200,000 African Americans served the U.S. Army in France, most being employed as laborers rather than soldiers. Their presence in France, not to mention the role of the war in spurring black migration from the South to the North, underlines the parallel between African-American and French colonial workers. See Arthur E. Barbeau and Florette Henri, *The Unknown Soldiers: Black American Troops in World War I* (Philadelphia, 1974).

[30] Following the lead of Anne McClintock, I would argue here that colonialism and postcolonialism are not necessarily sequentially arranged along a linear time line but represent different aspects of racial and global history that can occur at the same time. The experience of colonial labor in wartime France thus represents an instance of these two phenomena overlapping. McClintock, *Imperial Leather: Race, Gender, and Sexuality in the Colonial Conquest* (New York, 1995).

[31] This was especially true of the Spaniards, roughly 70 percent of all European immigrant workers in France during the war. Many of them entered France clandestinely and, once in the country, successfully resisted attempts to prevent them from changing jobs in search of higher wages. See Horne, "Immigrant Workers," 64–67.

[32] In theory, enlistment in the French colonies for work duty in France was voluntary, but an examination of recruitment procedures in North Africa, Indochina, and Madagascar makes clear that more than a little pressure was brought to bear on potential workers. See Stovall, "Colour-blind France?"; also Favre, "Un milieu porteur," 1: 241–47.

enabling the French war economy to benefit from colonial labor without threatening the dichotomy between empire and metropole. While couched in "separate but equal" terminology, it essentially reproduced racial hierarchies found in the colonies.[33]

French authorities justified this system, known as regimentation (*encadrement*), with numerous arguments, citing the nation's need to derive the maximum possible return from imported labor, the problem of providing interpreters for people who spoke no French, and a paternalistic desire to prevent the "corruption" of its colonial subjects by the temptations of French society.[34] In particular, they often argued that separating workers of color from the French people was necessary in order to prevent racial conflict. A July 1917 report on the use of North Africans in the mines of the Pas-de-Calais recommended isolation as a means of ensuring social peace.

> One can now furnish the mines with North African workers by applying the following rules: choosing workers who have already worked in the mines of France or Algeria, strict regimentation of these workers, housing them in special barracks in order to avoid contact with the local population ... [The Pas-de-Calais mines] show little interest in hiring North Africans, objecting especially on the basis of incidents that could occur because of the opposition of the local population.[35]

Another report, on the use of Chinese labor, recommended regimentation as a way of forestalling the kinds of racial conflict that had greeted Chinese workers in America.[36]

Such hostility toward colonial laborers certainly existed, yet a good deal of evidence suggests that the regimentation system worked to promote rather than hinder the development of racial antagonisms. Concentrating non-European workers together in large numbers, it underlined both their "exoticism" and their possible threat to the employment of French workers. More concretely, the system's stricture of preventing colonial workers from changing jobs kept them poorly paid, thus reinforcing the already entrenched idea that people of color, like women, would lower wage levels for all. Although the contracts signed by colonial laborers upon recruitment guaranteed them fixed wage rates equal to those of the French, such rates soon became obsolete under the pressure of wartime inflation and the ability of both native French and European immigrant workers to raise their wages by seeking out higher paid jobs. The contrasting lack of mobility among colonial workers soon made them the poorest paid laborers in France. A February 1918

---

[33] Created on January 1, 1916, the SOTC worked in coordination with other government agencies, especially the Ministry of Labor. Nogaro and Weil, *La main-d'oeuvre étrangère*, 18. On the administration of colonial workers, see the numerous documents in the following cartons at the French National Archives (hereafter, AN): F 14 11331, F 14 11332, F 14 11334, 94 AP 135, 94 AP 140.

[34] The files of CIMO, the Interministerial Labor Committee, contain numerous discussions of this issue. See AN F 14 11331: letter of September 21, 1917; AN F 14 11334, report of March 10, 1917, report of April 14, 1917, report of June 9, 1917. See also AN 94 AP 135, report of December 10, 1915, report of December 17, 1915, report of August 16, 1916; Société Historique de l'Armée de Terre (hereafter, SH): 7 N 144, letter of February 20, 1916; SH 6 N 149: "Rapport sur le fonctionnement du Bureau Annexe des Affaires Indigènes au Havre pendant le 2ème semestre 1917"; letter of June 17, 1918, letter of April 16, 1918.

[35] AN F 14 11334, report of July 7, 1917.

[36] AN 94 AP 135, report of August 16, 1916.

report from a camp of Chinese workers in Brest noted, "In spite of the formal protests of the War Minister the colonial workers do not receive anywhere near the same wages as French workers of the same category working in the same shipyards."[37] Such "protests" notwithstanding, there are some indications that French authorities saw colonial labor as a means of keeping wage demands low. In March 1918, for example, an administrator of the port of Bordeaux requested one hundred colonial workers as a way of regulating the price of local labor.[38] The regimentation of colonial labor thus worked to create a split labor force in wartime France.[39]

Finally, while hoping to avoid conflict between nonwhite and French workers, the officials of the SOTC had other reasons for keeping contacts between the two groups to a minimum. They feared that colonial laborers would learn bad habits from French colleagues; not only might they gain a taste for strong drink and white women, but exposure to local workers might give them experience with strikes and unions.[40] Such "contamination" would limit their utility for the French war effort but, above all, would risk upsetting established hierarchies in the empire itself by returning to the colonies a seasoned body of revolutionaries. A May 1916 report from the Marseilles postal censor's office noted this danger, citing as evidence the observations of a French *colon* in Tonkin:

At this moment they are recruiting Annamite volunteers. 50,000 more are needed. I do not know where they will find them, nor what will result from this . . . certainly nothing good, without a doubt; this will eventually create malcontents and revolutionaries, as well as the upsetting of our beautiful colony. They will no longer feel like planting rice in their fields after they have seen in France a number of things that one must not let them see or hear. This will be terrible, and this is not only my humble opinion, but that of all who know their race well.[41]

The differences between French and colonial workers were not natural but arose to a significant extent from specific actions by the French state. Public authorities in France must consequently bear responsibility for the conflicts that pitted the two groups against one another in the latter years of the war.

Gender concerns played a key role in prompting French authorities to segregate colonial workers. France's use of colonial labor took place in a context of gender

[37] AN F 14 11331, report of February 16, 1918. The report went on to note the hostility of local dockworkers to the Chinese. See also the March 5, 1916, report on Indochinese workers in the Tarbes arsenal, AN 94 AP 135. There are several reports in AN cartons F 14 11331 and F 14 11334 about the high wages of French workers relative to those of their colonial colleagues.

[38] AN F 14 11331, letter of March 21, 1918.

[39] On the theory of split labor markets, see above all the works of Edna Bonacich, such as "A Theory of Ethnic Antagonism: The Split Labor Market," *American Sociological Review* 37 (1972): 547–59; and "Advanced Capitalism and Black/White Relations in the United States: A Split Labor Market Interpretation," *American Sociological Review* 41 (1976): 34–51.

[40] For example, in August 1916, an inspector visiting a camp of Indochinese workers in the Dordogne observed with alarm colonial and French workers drinking together in local cafés. His concern reflected not just fears of alcoholism but also a desire to prevent the integration of the Indochinese into French working-class culture. Archives Nationales, Section Outre-Mer (hereafter, ANSOM), SLOTFOM 10, carton 2, report of August 27, 1916.

[41] SH 7 N 993, report of May 15, 1916. As the postwar histories of anticolonial activists Ho Chi Minh and Messali Hadj demonstrated, this was no idle fear. See Claude Liauzu, *Aux origines des tiers-mondismes: Colonisés et anticolonialistes en France (1919–1939)* (Paris, 1982).

relations unusual in two major respects. First, the drafting of millions of French men radically feminized wartime civilian life: whole villages lost their adult male populations, except for the elderly. Second, French authorities only recruited nonwhite men from the empire, leaving women of color behind. The use of colonial women never seems to have been considered; at a time when occupational restrictions on French women were being suspended, separate spheres of work for nonwhite men and women remained in force. The reluctant use of French women in war industries plus the refusal to bring in women from the empire reversed the traditional colonial relations of race and gender, bringing together large numbers of white women and men of color in the absence of white men and nonwhite women. As the quotation above suggests, government authorities thus managed to create the colonialist's worst nightmare on French soil.

Even more than foreign and colonial laborers, French women were central to the mobilization of the nation's industry during the war.[42] Women and colonial workers in wartime France had much in common. Both groups came as neophytes to the world of heavy industry, were paid less than French men, and were often assigned the least skilled and desirable tasks to perform. As a result, women and nonwhite men often worked side by side in the war industry. Nothing in France came as a greater shock to colonial workers than the sight of women working in the factories: one Malagasy worker stationed in Toulouse wrote a friend, "Would you believe that white women, who at home love to have us serve them, here work as much as men. They are very numerous in the workshops and labor with the same ardor as men."[43] In such a situation, sexual relations between non-European men and French women were not surprising and seem to have occurred frequently.[44] As Mahmoud ben Arrar noted in a letter to friends in Tunisia, "the city where we are stationed [Montereau] is full of women, and here fornication is as abundant as grains of sand."[45] Although French censors and labor inspectors tended to portray the mistresses of colonial workers as women of easy virtue, many were doubtless factory workers who had met their lovers on the job. The threat, and the reality, of miscegenation thus spurred French authorities to isolate nonwhite workers, in an

---

[42] On French women in the war industries, see Laura Lee Downs, "Women's Strikes and the Politics of Popular Egalitarianism in France, 1916–1918," in Lenard R. Berlanstein, ed., *Rethinking Labor History* (Urbana, Ill., 1993); James F. McMillan, *Housewife or Harlot? The Place of Women in French Society, 1870–1940* (New York, 1981); Françoise Thébaud, *La femme au temps de la guerre de 14* (Paris, 1986); Mathilde Dubesset, Françoise Thébaud, and Catherine Vincent, "The Female Munitions Workers of the Seine," in Fridenson, *French Home Front*; Annie Fourcaut, *Femmes à l'usine* (Paris, 1982); Jean-Louis Robert, "Women and Work in France during the First World War," in Richard Wall and Jay Winter, eds., *The Upheaval of War: Family, Work, and Welfare in Europe, 1914–1918* (Cambridge, 1988).

[43] SH 7 N 997, "Rapport Mensuel," July–August 1917, letter from Landriamanalina.

[44] The question of relations between French women and male colonial workers was crucial for French administrators. By 1918, they had become a major source of concern for the censors who supervised colonial correspondence, leading them to keep monthly reports on instances of such liaisons. SH 7 N 1001, report of June 1917; Favre, "Un milieu porteur," 2: 527–45; Horne, "Immigrant Workers," 80–81; Tyler Stovall, "Love, Labor, and Race: Colonial Men and White Women in France during the Great War," unpublished paper, "(Im)migrant Identities," 12th annual conference of the Critical Theory Program, University of California, Davis, October 1996.

[45] He went on to claim that he had four girlfriends himself, and that he was "au comble de la volupté." SH 7 N 1001, "Rapport sur les operations de la commission militaire de contrôle postal de Tunis," April 1917.

attempt to reestablish the colonial hierarchies that their own policies had undermined.

The attitude of French unions also justified the decision of public authorities to isolate colonial workers. Labor organizations remained generally hostile to the massive infusion of non-European workers during the war. Before 1914, French unions paid virtually no attention to the dramatic growth of the overseas empire, judging it irrelevant to the direct concerns of French workers. During thirty-two national meetings held between 1886 and 1914, only two resolutions were passed dealing with the colonies, both merely demanding that national labor legislation be applied to the workers of the empire.[46] The Socialist Party paid more attention to colonial affairs, frequently criticizing government exploitation of indigenous populations. Yet the majority of French Socialists before the war, notably Jean Jaurès, stopped short of demanding independence for the colonies, recommending instead more humane forms of tutelage that would gradually prepare the natives for self-government.[47] As several historians have pointed out, French workers in the late nineteenth century were by no means immune to pro-colonial propaganda, which usually included an emphasis on white racial superiority. In spite of a theoretical commitment to working-class internationalism, therefore, the French labor movement's lack of concern with workers in the nation's colonies comes as no surprise.[48]

During the war, French unions reluctantly accepted the importation of foreign laborers for the needs of the national effort yet closely supervised the process in order to preserve the interests of union members.[49] The Confédération Générale du Travail (CGT) insisted that foreign workers be as few as possible, that they be paid the same as French laborers to prevent them from lowering wages, and that the CGT take part in (or at least be consulted about) setting immigrant labor policies.[50]

---

[46] These resolutions were passed by the Fédération des Bourses du Travail, at its meetings of 1901 in Nice and 1902 in Algiers. The CGT never addressed the issue. François Bédarida, "Perspectives sur le mouvement ouvrier et l'impérialisme en France au temps de la conquête coloniale," *Le mouvement social* 86 (January–March 1974): 25–43.

[47] Bédarida, "Perspectives sur le mouvement ouvrier"; see on this point the work of Charles-Robert Ageron, especially *L'anticolonialisme en France de 1871 à 1914* (Paris, 1973); *France coloniale ou parti colonial?* (Paris, 1978); "Jaurès et les socialistes français devant la question algérienne (de 1895 à 1914)," *Le mouvement social* 42 (January–March 1963): 1–29. The major French Socialist writer on imperialism was Paul Louis; see his *Le colonialisme* (Paris, 1905).

[48] Bédarida, "Perspectives sur le mouvement ouvrier"; Cohen, *French Encounter with Africans*; Jacques Ozouf and Mona Ozouf, "Le thème du patriotisme dans les manuels primaires," *Le mouvement social* 49 (October–December 1964): 5–31; William Schneider, *An Empire for the Masses: the French Popular Image of Africa, 1870–1900* (Westport, Conn., 1982); Thomas August, *The Selling of the Empire: British and French Imperialist Propaganda, 1890–1940* (Westport, 1985).

[49] Concerns about foreign labor paralleled union fears about the use of women in heavy industry during the war. While most unions and male workers accepted the national need for women to work in the war plants, many still expressed misgivings. Some feared that working women would be used to free men to be drafted and sent to the front lines. Another concern was the belief that employers would use women to lower wages for male workers and to promote Taylorist means of workplace organization that would devalue the talents of skilled workers and weaken workplace control. Some union leaders believed that, since women had lower rates of union membership than men, employers would use women workers to weaken the union movement. Finally, many male workers shared the natalist concern that work in heavy industry would weaken women's fertility and thus intensify the nation's crisis of reproduction. See Jean-Louis Robert, "La CGT et la famille ouvrière, 1914–1918," *Le mouvement social* 116 (July–September 1981): 47–66; Downs, "Women's Strikes."

[50] On the CGT's attitude to foreign labor during the war, see especially Jean-Louis Robert,

In September 1916, Léon Jouhaux, head of the CGT, wrote the labor minister to express his concerns about the use of Chinese workers.

> I must in the name of the C.G.T. ... protest against the introduction into our labor market of 20,000 new Chinese. After an earlier interview with you, we agreed that the introduction of Chinese workers would be limited to 5,000, solely for the needs of the arsenals and state [armaments] factories ... we judge it necessary that the use of Chinese coolies be limited once and for all to the circumstances that motivated it, and that everywhere upon demobilization French workers should be able to find, in the factories, the workshops, the stores and the yards the jobs they held before they left for military service.[51]

As part of its new acceptance of European labor, the union did move to counter xenophobia against European immigrants during the war. A number of articles appeared in *La bataille syndicaliste* discussing the conditions of workers from Spain, Italy, and Belgium. Often written by immigrants or their national representatives, they argued that immigrants were not taking French jobs and instead emphasized solidarity between French and foreign workers.[52] By contrast, union attitudes toward colonial workers from the empire remained unenthusiastic at best. An article on the labor shortage in French mines at the end of 1916 commented on the possible use of nonwhites by saying, "Kabyle, Chinese, Annamite labor? ... Hmph! ... inept and mediocre."[53] In a major 1916 editorial on Chinese labor, Jouhaux reemphasized the theme of equality for all workers, French and foreign, arguing that, "no matter their color or their language, we cannot accept that the worker be brought among us as a slave, and be treated as a pariah." However, he then went on to say:

> This land must not become a cosmopolitan boulevard where all races may meet each other, with the sole exception of the French, because they have disappeared. It is imperative that all, in spite of the necessities of the present hour, concern themselves with the problem of the survival of the race. This will be the most important means to ensure "that the French people do not lose the benefit of national prosperity, acquired at such cost."[54]

"Ouvriers et mouvement ouvrier parisiens pendant la grande guerre et l'immédiat après-guerre," 9 vols. (Thèse doctorat d'Etat, Université de Paris-1, 1989), 2: chap. 9; John Horne, *Labour at War: France and Britain, 1914–1918* (Oxford, 1991), 107–13. CGT immigration policy was largely based on a report drawn up by Léon Jouhaux early in 1916 that emphasized union control of immigrants over their exclusion. See Jouhaux in *La bataille syndicaliste* (September 22, 1916): 1.

[51] AN 94 AP 135, letter of September 23, 1916. On the attitude of the CGT to the question of foreign labor during the war, see Cross, *Immigrant Workers*, chap. 1; Horne, "Immigrant Workers," 83–84. In July 1917, partly to allay the concerns of French unions about immigrant workers, the French government created the CIMO, the Interministerial Conference on Labor, to bring together government, employer, and union representatives in discussions of concerns about labor policies; see the documents in AN F 14 11334.

[52] *La bataille syndicaliste* (May 3, 1916): 1; (April 29, 1917): 1; (August 5, 1917): 1; (August 15, 1917): 1; (September 1, 1917): 2; (September 26, 1917): 2; (November 19, 1917): 3; (November 22, 1917): 2; (November 24, 1917): 1; (January 13, 1918): 1. The Belgians, frequent targets of pre-war hostility, were now portrayed as refugees from German oppression who deserved the support of French patriots.

[53] *La bataille syndicaliste* (December 22, 1916): 1.

[54] Léon Jouhaux, "L'emploi de la main-d'oeuvre étrangère: A propos des travailleurs chinois," *La bataille syndicaliste* (November 18, 1916): 1. Such fears of the disappearance of the French race as a result of the war once more linked discussions about colonial workers to questions of natalism. See Ruth Harris, "The Child of the Barbarian: Rape, Race and Nationalism in France during the First World War," *Past and Present* 141 (November 1993): 170–207. On the broader issue of natalism in

In the article, Jouhaux played on France's wartime peril to racialize the discussion of Chinese labor. He also used the presence of an alien people to set forth the concept of the French as a race, treating the Chinese as the classic Other on whom the construction of whiteness depended. Colonial workers thus linked hands with the Germans as a threat to France. Far from contributing to the struggle against Germany, they represented another way of achieving its objectives.

Given this kind of perspective, it is not surprising that the CGT's rank and file felt little inclination to welcome colonial workers into their midst. Delegates to union meetings frequently and loudly voiced anger against foreign and colonial workers during the war.[55] Opposition to European immigrants did not disappear; for example, in 1917, the Paris café workers' union engaged in a series of protests against the use of Spanish labor.[56] In spite of the arguments of union leaders, however, nonwhite laborers bore the brunt of this hostility; I have come across no records of physical attacks on European immigrants by French workers during the war. Whereas French workers sometimes took part in strikes along with European immigrants, especially Italians, colonial workers were left to their own devices. French unions made no appreciable attempts to broaden their conception of the working class to include these strangers from a distant shore. When the widespread hostility against colonial laborers degenerated into violence in 1917, their refusal to deal with the issue helped contribute to an explosive situation.

THE FRENCH GOVERNMENT BEGAN TO IMPORT large numbers of non-European workers early in 1916, but serious conflicts between them and the local population did not occur until a year later. The spring of 1917, a time of crises and the low point of the French war effort, ushered in a series of racial incidents, ranging from brawls between individuals to riots involving hundreds of people. These continued through the summer months, declining in number after September but surfacing again at times in 1918. One report on Parisian attitudes toward foreign workers clearly noted the change of mood in the early months of 1917.

During the month of March no problems have come to my attention. The population observes the native workers with a kind, even benevolent, gaze.

During April one observes a change in mood, due perhaps to certain newspaper articles.[57] The crowd loses little by little its benevolent disposition; jeers become numerous and sometimes bitter.

Rumors circulate among the population of the working-class neighborhoods; in certain circles it is said that the North Africans are really soldiers stationed in Paris primarily to suppress any insurrectional movements that might erupt.

---

wartime and postwar France, see Mary Louise Roberts, *Civilization without Sexes: Reconstructing Gender in Postwar France, 1917–1927* (Chicago, 1994).

[55] Favre, "Un milieu porteur," 2: 508–23; Robert, "Ouvriers," 2: 390–419; Vidalenc, "La main d'oeuvre étrangère," 540; AN F 14 11334, report of July 7, 1917; SH 6 N 149, letter of January 29, 1918.

[56] *Humanité* (July 19, 1917): 4.

[57] For example, on March 16, 1917, the right-wing newspaper *Le figaro* printed an article entitled "L'action kabyle," which lampooned Kabyle street sweepers for lounging around gawking at the sights of Paris rather than doing their jobs. Interestingly, on the very next page (p. 3) of the same issue, an article appeared praising the courage of Moroccan soldiers on the French front lines.

Finally violent incidents start to appear from the beginning of May on.⁵⁸

Racial violence constituted an extreme expression of much more widely held prejudices against colonial workers. The public officials and employers who worked with them frequently portrayed colonials as inefficient, unskilled workers who also suffered from laziness and a propensity to the vices of gambling and drink. More significantly, many French civilians viewed them with suspicion. Louise Delétang, a Parisian seamstress, recorded in her diary an encounter with a Moroccan in the street. Delétang noted his "rough" appearance and the fact that he was accompanied by French street toughs; she gave thanks that an upright French policeman was there to save her from him.⁵⁹ In a January 1918 report subtitled "Kabyle Manners," a Parisian police spy noted,

> These people are the terror of the neighborhood where they are housed. They provoke fights with the French and do not hesitate to resort to knives. Last week, several women working the night shift at CITROEN, quai de Javel, were attacked around 9 PM by Kabyles. A petition will be circulated in the factory to demand action against these attacks. It would be better if the Kabyles did not live in the Paris area and were housed in barracks. Their own manners and actions would justify such a measure.⁶⁰

For some French soldiers, the colonial worker symbolized the ability of foreigners to enjoy the fruits of civilian life while the French risked their lives for France, in spite of the fact that colonials also served in the army and died at the front. Even though colonial subjects were almost always victims, not perpetrators, of racial violence, many in France considered them unsavory foreigners who caused trouble for innocent French men and especially innocent French women.

Most of the racial violence during the spring and summer of 1917 was brief and small in scale, usually conflicts between a few individuals. Reports of such violence are scattered and incomplete, often incidents alluded to in letters written by colonial workers and soldiers or mentioned in official reports.⁶¹ Attacks on

---

⁵⁸ ANSOM, DSM, carton 5, report of June 19, 1917.

⁵⁹ Delétang, *Journal d'une ouvrière Parisienne pendant la guerre*, 50. The Moroccan never spoke to her or threatened her in any way.

⁶⁰ Archives de la Préfecture de Police de Paris, B/a 1587, "Physiognomie de Paris: Kabyle Manners," report of January 8, 1918, p. 9.

⁶¹ Thanks to the wartime practice of censorship and the desire to monitor the feelings of this new labor force, French archives contain detailed reports on the letters written by colonial workers to friends and relatives, including hundreds of copies of the letters themselves. These letters constitute an extremely valuable source, a rare example of testimony by people at the bottom of French society. Yet they are by no means the direct, unmediated voice of these individuals, and thus must be approached carefully. The censors had their own agendas, often choosing to emphasize examples of defeatist speech or sexual relations with French women, and their selection of specific letters for reproduction reflects both these perspectives as well as a real effort to understand colonial workers' state of mind. Many of the authors of these letters were illiterate, and the scribes who wrote their missives certainly must have altered their contents at times. Finally, the authors were aware that French authorities read their mail, and composed their messages with this in mind. One censor noted that letters written by Tunisian workers in French expressed contentment, whereas those written in Arabic were full of complaints. SH 7 N 1001, report of May 1917. Rather than dismissing the importance of these letters for such reasons, however, I would argue that the historian can use them as a way of analyzing relations of knowledge and power between colonial workers, the foremen who often served as scribes, French authorities, and the French public in general. On the history of the military censorship commissions, see the documents in SH 7 N 949, 7 N 995; G. Liens, "La Commission de censure et la Commission de contrôle postal à Marseilles, pendant la première guerre mondiale," *Revue d'histoire moderne et contemporaine* (October–December 1971): 649–67.

non-Europeans by French men, both soldiers on leave and civilians, constituted the general pattern.[62] At times, a provocative gesture of some sort would trigger an attack, but more often than not incidents of racial assault were unprovoked by the victim. The level of violence ranged from verbal insults to beatings to, all too often, mortal wounds with knives and guns. While reliable statistics do not exist, it seems clear that racial violence claimed the lives of at least twenty individuals, both foreign and French, during the third year of the war.[63]

A typical incident occurred in the Norman town of Dives-sur-Mer. On the evening of June 22, 1917, two Moroccans were returning home from work when they were suddenly attacked from behind by four French construction workers. The assailants knocked one of the Moroccans to the ground, kicked him in the shoulder and the chest, then struck the other in the face with a bottle. Hearing the noise of the fight, about thirty Moroccans from the same work regiment came running up, and only quick intervention by their French commander forestalled the outbreak of a pitched battle. As the commander commented in his report, "All the observers of the incident affirmed that the attack committed by the French workers against the Moroccan workers of my group had profoundly revolted them, since the aggressors had in no way been provoked."[64] A similar but more tragic series of attacks took place the same month in Versailles. On June 3, two French soldiers on leave and one civilian, all of whom had a history of racial assaults, attacked Moroccan workers in three separate incidents.[65] After unsuccessfully chasing one individual who refused to buy them wine, the group accosted Hamidi ben Allal ben Omar in a restaurant, and one of the soldiers stabbed him in the forehead. Brandishing the bloody knife above his head, the enraged soldier then shouted, "this is how we will cut their throats!" The three attackers lost no time in making good on this promise. Later that evening, they attacked another Moroccan, Allal ben Hossaine ben Mohamed, beating him and stabbing him to death.[66] As these incidents indicate,

[62] Conflicts between French and nonwhite individuals did not constitute the only kind of racial violence to take place in France during the Great War. There were also several incidents of fighting between different groups of nonwhite workers and soldiers. For example, a battle between Senegalese soldiers and Indochinese workers in Saint-Médard resulted in the death of one of the latter, as well as wounding several on both sides. ANSOM, DSM, carton 5, report of Agent Massebeuf to the Minister of War, Saint-Médard, July 26, 1917. Also see AN F 14 11334, report of June 9, 1917; SH 6 N 19, letter from Minister of War to Minister of Foreign Affairs (n.d.); SH 7 N 997, reports of July–August, August, and November 1917. A very different series of conflicts involved fights between white American military personnel and nonwhites, usually French colonial soldiers. In contrast to the racial violence discussed in this article, in these incidents French civilians at times intervened against the Americans in favor of French nonwhites. See Barbeau and Henri, *Unknown Soldiers*; Addie W. Hunton and Kathryn M. Johnson, *Two Colored Women with the American Expeditionary Forces* (New York, 1920); Louis Chevalier, *Montmartre du plaisir et du crime* (Paris, 1980), 323. Whereas conflict between colonial workers seems to have followed the general chronological pattern of French/colonial violence, fights with Americans took place mostly at the end of the war and during 1919.

[63] A good overview of this racial violence is provided by Minister of the Interior to Minister of Colonies, July 10, 1917, ANSOM, DSM, carton 5.

[64] ANSOM, DSM, carton 5, report of June 23, 1917, noting that the four Frenchmen had committed a similar assault on Moroccan workers a few weeks previously.

[65] ANSOM, DSM, carton 5, report of June 5, 1917. One of the two soldiers had lost a leg in the war and was equipped with a wooden leg and crutches, which he used to beat his victims that night.

[66] See reports on similar incidents in Le Mans (report of June 24, 1917), Bourg (report of May 3, 1918), and Rochefort (undated telegram). The latter document described the incident as "provoked by civilian workers and one soldier in a state of drunkenness. They wounded three Moroccans, one seriously, with bottles ... the Moroccans in no way provoked this incident."

racial violence was often the work of a few individuals, and in fact many if not most French citizens strongly disapproved of their actions. Yet the violence took place in an overall context of hostility to colonial workers and, as such, represented the most extreme example of the reaction against them.

In a report to the War Ministry, the commander of North African workers in Paris recorded fourteen cases of racial assault in the French capital over six weeks during May and June 1917.[67] Most involved attacks by French soldiers and/or civilians on North Africans working in the streets of the city. The most significant example of the presence of colonial workers in Paris was the municipality's use of North Africans, especially Kabyles from Algeria, to clean its streets. The figure of the Arab street sweeper that would symbolize immigration in France after 1945 thus appeared for the first time during World War I and in 1917 became a convenient target for public hostility.[68] On May 31, Mena Brahim ben Sliman was peacefully cleaning the boulevard Macdonald in the city's 19th arrondissement when a French soldier suddenly stabbed him, fortunately only tearing his coat. On May 5, Rabah ben Ali Charbi was returning to his barracks from the movies when a dozen individuals surrounded him, robbing him, stabbing and beating him to the ground. Although these assaults took place primarily in working-class neighborhoods like the 19th and 15th arrondissements, they also occurred in more central areas, including the Palais Royal and the Latin Quarter. Seven were perpetrated by soldiers, seven by civilians.[69]

North Africans accounted for roughly 60 percent of the non-European workers in France, and they seem to have been the most frequent targets of racial violence in 1917 and 1918. However, other groups were not immune. In an August 1917 letter, an Indochinese worker named Cang Xuong described two separate conflicts with the French.

> The other day, on returning from Renée's, I met a gang of French hoodlums who attacked me. I submitted to their blows and afterwards continued on my way.
>
> Last Saturday, sergeants Sung and ... [unknown] got into a fight with the French in the Café de la Fouguette. After receiving a few light blows, our sergeants took to their heels ...
>
> Here, relations between the French civilians and the Annamites are very poor.[70]

During the spring and summer of 1917, the large gunpowder factory at Saint-Médard near Toulouse, which employed roughly 5,000 Indochinese workers out of

---

[67] In addition to these, a report from the Ministry of War to the Ministry of Colonies alludes to a riot in the Parisian neighborhood of La Villette between North African workers and French soldiers and civilians. ANSOM, DSM, carton 5, June 24, 1917. Another report, July 2, 1917, suggests that anti–North African violence in Paris may have resulted in a few deaths but gives no details.

[68] The presence of these workers provoked several discussions in the Paris City Council, frequently hostile. One such debate not only included a resolution from the Street Cleaners Union attacking North African labor but also used the derogatory term for Arab, "sidi"; on this occasion, the council drafted an appeal to the prefect of the Seine to recruit more French workers as street cleaners. *Conseil Municipal de Paris—Procès-verbaux, 1917,* November 30, 1917, no. 55.

[69] ANSOM, DSM, carton 5, report of June 19, 1917. A report from the Ministry of Colonies to the Ministry of War noted that, given popular hostility to North Africans, "it seems that it would make sense to utilize elsewhere, if possible, the Kabyle workers employed in the streets of Paris, whose presence in the capital has given rise on several occasions to regrettable incidents that could have had the gravest consequences." ANSOM, DSM, carton 5, July 26, 1917.

[70] SH 7 N 997, "Extraits de lettres adressées en Indochine," August 1917.

a total labor force of 16,000, witnessed numerous racial conflicts.[71] Several occurred between French and Malagasy workers in Toulouse at the end of January 1918. A fight on the 27th of that month seems to have assumed the proportions of a street battle: "gunshots were fired by the Europeans while the Malagasy defended themselves with sticks or attacked by throwing stones. There were several wounded, men and women, and perhaps even some dead. A bar next to the [Malagasy] encampment was literally torn apart."[72] A telegram of September 1918 noted that one Chinese worker had been killed and several injured in a riot near Troyes, and other reports noted the poor relations between the Chinese and French soldiers and civilians.[73]

Although assaults by the French on non-Europeans were the dominant pattern of racial violence in wartime France, exceptions to this general rule did occur. Sometimes, colonial workers fought back or even initiated the conflicts. In August 1918, several Vietnamese workers lay siege to the house of a French man who had beaten one of their fellow workers. The Indochinese completely destroyed the house, killing or critically wounding at least three of its inhabitants, while four of their number were wounded by gunfire from the French defenders.[74] In January 1918, a disagreement between a Chinese dockworker and his French superior in Rouen erupted into a full-scale battle between Chinese and French longshoremen. At one point, about seventy Chinese stormed the police station, where the unfortunate French officer had taken refuge, and were about to throw him into the Seine when police intervened to restore order. In commenting on the incident, the commander of the Chinese work battalion noted that his charges had been provoked by "the shouts of the civilians, mostly dockworkers, people of uncertain reputation whose opinions of Chinese workers are well known. They are convinced that the Chinese have come to France to take their jobs, thereby preventing them from earning a living."[75]

As these two examples demonstrate, individual instances of racial conflict could and sometimes did escalate into collective violence. Although much fewer in number, several race riots occurred during 1917. One broke out in the Breton port of Brest on the night of August 4, 1917. The Brest barracks for colonial workers, primarily Kabyles and Arabs, were located next to a large flea market, a haunt for French hoodlums and prostitutes, much frequented by the workers housed next door.[76] At 11:15 PM, about twenty colonial workers were attacked in the flea

---

[71] ANSOM, SLOTFOM 10, carton 2, reports of July 31, August 1, August 10, August 25, and September 4, 1917; SH 7 N 997, report of August 1917. On the Indochinese workers at Saint-Médard, see Favre, "Un milieu porteur," vol. 2. The largest concentration of Indochinese workers was located at the huge state arsenal in Toulouse, where they numbered over 9,000 out of a total number of 32,000 people employed there.

[72] ANSOM, SLOTFOM 1, carton 8: "Contrôle Postal Malgache," report of February, 1918.

[73] SH 17 N 156, telegram of September 9, 1918; letter of May 12, 1918; letter of October 20, 1918; AN F 14 11331, reports of February 1, 1918, March 1, 1918, December 11, 1918, April 24, 1919; AN 94 AP 135, report of August 16, 1916; AN F 7 13619, report of November 20, 1918.

[74] ANSOM, SLOTFOM 1, carton 8: "Contrôle Postal Indochinois," August 1918. In response, French authorities confined the Indochinese who took part in the attack to their barracks for three months.

[75] AN F 14 11331, "Rapport de l'ingénieur," Rouen, January 25, 1918; see also the letter from the Ministry of Public Works, February 8, 1918.

[76] French reports on colonial workers are full of warnings about the danger of allowing them to

market by a large number of French civilians, who forced them to flee and in the process destroyed many of the local merchants' stalls. As the fighting moved toward the workers' barracks, many of those inside poured out to join the battle, demolishing a wooden wall to arm themselves with planks. The local police, finding themselves quickly overwhelmed, telephoned for reinforcements, which soon arrived in the shape of two detachments of soldiers. Led by a sergeant one report described as "in an obviously inebriated state," the soldiers invaded the barracks, bayoneting and firing randomly on the remaining workers there. Unarmed and caught by surprise, the colonials inside had no chance to fight back. As a result, three were killed outright and thirty-four wounded, two of them fatally. In Brest, therefore, a riot between colonial workers and French civilians, initiated by the latter, was transformed into a bloodbath by French soldiers. Investigators of the incident blamed the nervousness and poor leadership of the troops, but their tragic errors in judgment resulted from a more general perspective that assumed nonwhite workers, not those who attacked them, to be the source of trouble.[77]

Although less bloody, the riot that broke out in Dijon on June 19, 1917, involved more people. The violence began in a paradoxically peaceful scene. That evening, five Moroccans were strolling through town listening to the sounds of a mandolin played by one of their number. The music prompted a drunken French sergeant in a nearby café to yell at him to shut up. Not understanding French, the young man continued to play, at which point the officer threw himself upon him, grabbed the mandolin, and stabbed its owner several times. The friends of both men intervened, and soon a large number of French civilians joined in the fighting. After the Moroccans fled, the crowd turned its fury on any others they could find, chasing them through the streets and beating those they caught. At one point, the crowd, estimated at 500 to 1,500 people, surrounded the workers' barracks, threatening to knock down the gates and massacre all the Moroccans inside. The rioters controlled the streets around the barracks for much of the night, only dispersing the next morning. Several Moroccans trapped between the crowd and their barracks took shelter for the night in a military infirmary, where the wounded were also brought for care. No one was killed, although several individuals suffered serious wounds. As one of the colonial workers' commanders commented, "it is intolerable that drunken fanatics can publicly and with impunity attack peaceful workers, solely for playing a mandolin."[78]

The most serious race riot in wartime France took place during the same week of June in Le Havre. The French made widespread use of nonwhite workers in port

---

associate with less respectable elements in the society surrounding them. Judging from this and other observations, however, it seems likely that any French person, especially a French woman, who associated with nonwhites was considered amoral and criminal, or at least not respectable. See also ANSOM, SLOTFOM 10, carton 2, report of July 31, 1917. Laura Tabili has recently made a similar observation with regard to interracial settlements in interwar Britain. See *"We Ask for British Justice,"* 135–60.

[77] AN 94 AP 140, Rennes, telegram of August 6, 1917; ANSOM, DSM, carton 5, Brest, report of August 5, 1917.

[78] ANSOM, DSM, carton 5, Dijon, June 20, 1917, reports by Temsil, Benaich; telegram of June 19, 1917. Benaich's report suggests that troubles arose after a drunken French soldier tried to pluck a boutonniere from the jacket of a Moroccan worker.

cities, with large contingents living in Marseilles, Bordeaux, Rouen, Nantes, Cherbourg, and Dunkirk.[79] By the spring of 1917, 1,300 Moroccans were employed on the docks of Le Havre. Unlike in other areas, they had not been regimented but were left to their own devices to find lodgings, usually in the poorest areas of town.[80] The conflict between French and colonial workers for jobs was thus reinforced by competition for scarce wartime housing.[81] On June 17, an exchange of insults between a Moroccan and a Frenchman quickly degenerated into an all-out brawl in the streets, as other French soldiers, civilians, and Moroccans intervened. By the time military and police authorities could stop the fighting, an estimated fifteen people had been killed and many more wounded. In order to protect the Moroccans from the enraged local population, authorities shut two to three hundred of them in a fort for the next three days. Immediately after the riot, the commanders of colonial workers in the area proposed sending the Moroccans back home, but local employers complained that this would leave them without sufficient labor resources. Ultimately, the tragedy led to the imposition of regimentation on colonial workers in the area; as the report on the riot noted, "our Arab colonial subjects are men and deserve to be treated as such ... It is impossible, however ... to leave them without benevolent but firm surveillance, both for their safety and our own."[82]

The official reaction to conflicts between colonial workers and the French varied but in general emphasized reestablishing control and preventing further clashes rather than bringing the perpetrators to justice. Military authorities invariably undertook investigations of racial violence, which usually concluded that the colonial workers were the victims of French aggression and often recommended their isolation from the surrounding population. Yet they made few arrests, none at all in the cases of the Brest, Dijon, and Le Havre riots, and no records exist of any judicial proceedings against the rioters. The objects of these attacks knew little of the French legal system and generally had no recourse beyond appealing to their commanders. Given a desire to avoid or downplay any indications of lack of discipline among their subjects, or conflict and disunity among the French population as a whole, the military authorities in charge of colonial labor seem to

---

[79] This was also true of both the United States and Britain. During the war, French ports were full of men of color from throughout the world unloading Allied ships full of war material. On the British, see Tabili, *"We Ask for British Justice,"* 15–29; Albert Grundlingh, *Fighting Their Own War: South African Blacks and the First World War* (Johannesburg, 1987); P. Wou, *Les travailleurs chinois et la grande guerre* (Paris, 1939). On the employment of African-American laborers on French docks, see Barbeau and Henri, *Unknown Soldiers*; Hunton and Johnson, *Two Colored Women*; Emmett J. Scott, *The American Negro in the World War* (Chicago, 1919); Isaac Marcosson, *S.O.S.: America's Miracle in France* (New York, 1919).

[80] The report on the riot emphasizes the exploitation of Moroccan workers by both French landlords and fellow Moroccans, painting a lurid portrait of a naïve population sunk in the iniquities of gambling and prostitution.

[81] On the housing of colonial workers during the war, see AN F 14 11331, reports of September 21, 1917, July 18, 1918; AN 94 AP 135, reports of March 18, March 21, 1916. On the French housing crisis during World War I, see Susanna Magri, *La politique du logement* (Paris, 1972); Anthony Sutcliffe, *The Autumn of Central Paris: The Defeat of Town Planning, 1850–1970* (Montreal, 1971); Henri Sellier, et al., *Paris pendant la guerre* (Paris, 1926); Tyler Stovall, *"Sous les toits de Paris*: The Working Class and the Paris Housing Crisis, 1914–1924," *Proceedings of the Western Society for French History* 14 (1987): 265–72.

[82] SH 6 N 149, "Rapport sur le fonctionnement du Bureau Annexe des Affaires Indigènes au Havre pendant le 2ème semestre 1917"; AN 94 AP 135, message of June 19, 1917; AN F 14 11334, letter of July 2, 1917; Vidalenc, "La main d'oeuvre étrangère," 536.

have done little to punish the instigators of racial violence. This failure to administer justice certainly sent a message to those most hostile to the presence of colonial workers in France that such attacks would be tolerated, or even sanctioned, by public authorities. Moreover, dealing with the problem by segregating colonial workers not only punished the victims of this violence but made them a more convenient and visible target for future assaults.[83]

If the authorities most directly concerned devoted little attention to racial violence, this was much more true of the civilian public sphere. One searches the French press at the time in vain for any mention of such incidents. Even the labor press remained largely silent about the issue and, for that matter, about colonial workers in general. *Humanité*, the official organ of the French Socialist Party, published only a few articles about them in 1917 and none at all in 1918.[84] Only one article actually dealt with racial violence; in an editorial condemning attacks personally observed against Kabyle workers in Paris during June 1917, Pierre Renaudel wrote:

This is all the more difficult to understand given that one cannot say about the Kabyles what has been rumored about the Annamites. The Kabyles are not armed, they are only employed as laborers, their presence should not give rise to any concern. If they are molested, the only excuse is a general hatred "of the foreigner" ... The result of all this could be that these men, who have come from foreign lands *at the request of France*, let us not forget, since we brought them here for their labor, can report overseas how badly treated they have been by us. We could only lose from such a situation.[85]

Far more eloquent than Renaudel's denunciation of these attacks, however, was its singular quality. French labor, and the French public in general, manifested much more concern about the potential threat posed to France by colonial workers than about the very real attacks on them.[86]

In these incidents of racial violence in France during the war, a few patterns emerge.[87] Virtually all the violence consisted of attacks by French men on male colonial workers. They thus both fit into longstanding traditions of male violence and at the same time represented something new, racial assaults on people of color. French soldiers on leave played a notable role in many of these incidents. For many of these individuals, the presence of numerous exotic foreigners must have symbolized both changes on the home front and the hated *embusqués*, those lazy workers who stayed behind enjoying high wages while the French risked their lives

[83] This could also reflect a certain lack of concern with nonwhites in general. It is interesting to note that, of the few cases in which assailants were arrested, one involved the injured Moroccans themselves rounding up the culprits, whereas the other concerned the arrest of six Moroccans accused of attacking French civilians. ANSOM, DSM, carton 5, reports of June 5, 1917, June 24, 1917.

[84] *Humanité*, May 13, 1917, August 19, 1917, September 17, 1917. *La bataille syndicaliste*, official organ of the CGT, only devoted a little more attention to the issue: April 17, 1916, April 21, 1916, August 27, 1916, November 18, 1916, December 22, 1916, July 14, 1918, November 25, 1918.

[85] *Humanité* (June 23, 1917): 1.

[86] This lack of attention to racial violence undoubtedly reflects the isolation of colonial workers, their control by the military, and the broader impact of wartime censorship.

[87] All reports agree that violence between nonwhites and the French was almost always the fault of the latter. As a report noted in July 1917, "It has been established, almost every time, that the North African or colonial workers had been provoked by the military or civilian French population." ANSOM, DSM, carton 5, report of July 10, 1917.

in the trenches.⁸⁸ The soldiers' conviction that importing colonial labor enabled the government to draft more French men for service at the front lines, so that these foreigners were able to enjoy the pleasures of wartime France while they had to return to the slaughter of the trenches, fueled racist attacks. As Mary Louise Roberts has argued, the war represented a crisis of French masculinity, and attacks on nonwhite laborers represented one dimension of that crisis.⁸⁹

In general, the segregation of colonial workers did not prevent them from suffering racial attacks. The Le Havre riot did provide an example of trouble breaking out when French and nonwhites mixed freely, but in Brest the concentration of North Africans in a military barracks enabled French soldiers to shoot them like fish in a barrel. Only a policy that hermetically sealed off colonial workers and reduced their contact with the local population to zero could have made a difference, and such a policy was simply not feasible.⁹⁰ Finally, although both the Dijon and Le Havre riots, as well as several smaller incidents, involved Moroccans, racial assault victimized all groups of colonial workers in wartime France: Indochinese, Chinese, Algerians, Tunisians, and Malagasy.

It is difficult to explain why the Moroccans seem to have been so singularly unlucky. Complaints from civilians against colonial workers did not mention them more than any other group. In fact, more than one report commented on them positively. For example, in 1916, authorities noted, "The workers from Morocco have given full satisfaction . . . [The Moroccan] is robust, sober, hardworking, and thrifty; placed in a good moral environment, directed firmly but without brutality, he will maintain his racial qualities."⁹¹ Although it is possible that they were blamed for anti-French agitation and revolts in North Africa during the war, Morocco was in fact relatively free of armed resistance to colonial rule. In contrast, a major anti-French insurrection broke out in northeastern Algeria in 1916, while smaller revolts occurred in Tunisia in 1915 and 1916. Yet neither Algerians nor Tunisians suffered the level of violence experienced by Moroccans in France.⁹²

---

⁸⁸ On the hatred of French soldiers for shirkers, see Jean Norton Cru, *War Books: A Study in Historical Criticism*, Stanley J. Pincetl, Jr., ed. (San Diego, Calif., 1988); Stéphane Audoin-Rouzeau, *Men at War, 1914–1918: National Sentiment and Trench Journalism during the First World War*, Helen McPhail, trans. (Providence, R.I., 1992); André Ducasse, et al., *Vie et mort des Français, 1914–1918* (1959; rpt. edn., Paris, 1969); Jacques Meyer, *La vie quotidienne des soldats pendant la grande guerre* (Paris, 1966). For a classic statement of the confusion experienced by a French soldier on leave, see the memoir by Louis Barthas: Cazals, *Les carnets*, especially 536–39.

⁸⁹ Roberts, *Civilization without Sexes*. Such reasoning could, of course, lead a soldier on leave to attack civilians in general, but there is no indication of any significant number of such assaults. I would argue that colonial workers were more likely targets because civilians seemed to hate them as well (many attacks involved soldiers and civilians working together), and because French soldiers rarely if ever had the kind of kinship or affective ties to colonial workers that bound them to French civilians. The soldier's duty was to fight for France, but this idea of "France" did not necessarily include colonial workers.

⁹⁰ For one thing, it would have required a level of investment in colonial workers' encampments that the French were simply not prepared to undertake during the war.

⁹¹ AN 94 AP 135, report of August 16, 1916. If any group of nonwhite workers had a notably bad reputation in France, it was certainly the Chinese. French authorities often considered them lazy, obstreperous, and particularly prone to violence. See, for example, AN F 14 11331, report of February 8, 1918; SH 17 N 156, letter of May 12, 1918.

⁹² Gilbert Meynier, *L'Algérie révélée: La guerre de 1914–1918 et le premier quart du XXe siècle* (Geneva, 1981), 565–98; Mohamed-Salah Lejri, *L'histoire du mouvement national*, Vol. 1: *Evolution du mouvement national, des origines à la deuxième guerre mondiale* (Tunis, 1974), 157–63.

The Color Line behind the Lines

A more likely reason for the assaults on Moroccans has to do with the history of Morocco and its role in the French imagination just before 1914. From 1900 to 1912, the gradual French takeover of Morocco produced two international diplomatic crises, making that nation a symbol of Franco-German rivalry and fueling bellicose French nationalism. In 1911, the French took advantage of an uprising against the sultan of Morocco to launch a full-scale military invasion of that country, capturing the capital city of Fez and declaring a protectorate the next year. This colonial war continued until the end of 1914, giving the French control of much of the country, until the demands of war in Europe led France to suspend operations there. The war, widely covered in the French popular press, gave Moroccans the image of warlike savages fighting the French, rather than loyal colonial subjects, and may have contributed to attacks against them during World War I. Moreover, the issue of loyalty to the Ottoman Empire, German ally and nominal suzerain of Morocco before the French conquest, also may have contributed to attacks on Moroccan workers.[93]

By far, the dominant pattern of racial violence lay in its timing. Most of these incidents took place in the summer of 1917, with further examples in the rest of the year and in 1918. It thus closely corresponded to the crisis of morale and the rise of war weariness in France. Moreover, most of these incidents involved French workers, a group whose patience with France's war effort was clearly being strained by the spring of 1917. It is therefore impossible to analyze the wave of racial assaults in France without placing it in the context of the working-class insurgency that shattered the wartime *union sacrée* and unleashed a wave of radicalism culminating in the general strike of 1920 and the foundation of the French Communist Party.[94] Thus the final section of this article will focus on the ways in which working-class militancy during World War I helped shape the climate of racial conflict.

THE INITIAL REACTIONS OF FRENCH WORKING PEOPLE to the new nonwhite population in their midst were not necessarily hostile. French authorities concerned with

---

[93] John P. Halstead, *Rebirth of a Nation: The Origins and Rise of Moroccan Nationalism, 1912–1944* (Cambridge, Mass., 1967), 3–40; Douglas Porch, *The Conquest of Morocco* (New York, 1982). During the war, German agents actively spread pro-Islamic and Ottoman propaganda throughout colonial North Africa, depicting Germany as the ally of the Arab world against the infidel French. In 1916, Germany created a Committee for the Independence of North Africa, based in Berlin, and also supported the anti-French propaganda of the Young Tunisians in Switzerland. Meynier, "La France coloniale de 1914 à 1931," 86.

[94] On the history of French labor during World War I, see above all Robert, "Ouvriers." See also Robert, "La CGT et la famille ouvrière, 1914–1918"; Fridenson, *French Home Front*; Patrick Fridenson, "The Impact of the First World War on French Workers," in Wall and Winter, *Upheaval of War*; Max Gallo, "Quelques aspects de la mentalité et du comportement ouvriers dans les usines de guerre, 1914–1918," *Le mouvement social* 56 (July–September 1966): 3–33; Horne, *Labour at War*; Albert Rosmer, *Le mouvement ouvrier pendant la première guerre mondiale*, 2 vols. (Paris, 1936, 1959); Annie Kriegel, *Aux origines du communisme français*, 2 vols. (Paris, 1964); Kriegel and Jean-Jacques Becker, *1914: La guerre et le mouvement ouvrier français* (Paris, 1964); Gilbert Hatry, *Renault usine de guerre 1914–1918* (Paris, 1978). For a more general view of working-class radicalism at the end of the war, see Charles Bernard, ed., *Situations revolutionnaires en Europe, 1917–1922 = Revolutionary Situations in Europe, 1917–1922* (Montreal, 1977); James E. Cronin, "Labor Insurgency and Class Formation: Comparative Perspectives on the Crisis of 1917–1920 in Europe," in Cronin and Carmen Sirianni, eds., *Work, Community and Power: The Experience of Labor in Europe and America, 1900–1915* (Philadelphia, 1983).

colonial labor generally noted acceptance or indifference to their charges in 1916.[95] A September 1916 article in *Humanité* on war industries in Bourges commented on "the foreign and colonial invasion" of the city in favorable terms:

> One encounters, on their way to the factory, numerous stocky Serbs, Kabyles, Moroccans wearing strange clothing and religiously carrying their *chechias*. Italians follow a group of Annamites, small but well built. If blacks are not yet employed here, one sees on the other hand solid Portuguese workers. I imagine that, were Caesar to return to *Avaricum*, he would have trouble recognizing his legions in this new Babylon.
> But what does the native population think of this veritable foreign and colonial invasion? I have asked many people and must say that the population is only grateful for these cosmopolitan workers.[96]

In April 1917, just as attitudes toward colonial workers were beginning to harden, a Tunisian stationed in Paris named Ahmed ben Haya wrote, "The people here honor foreigners; we do not encounter injustice in this land but only justice and freedom. These people love us more than our own parents."[97]

Yet such relatively positive observations paled in comparison with the flood of indications of racial hostility and violence, by both French officials and colonial workers themselves, beginning in the spring of 1917. The early months of that year represented the low point of French morale during the war. Not only did mutinies break out in the French army,[98] but a series of strikes erupted in factories across the country, renewing the tradition of labor militancy in France that had abruptly ceased at the start of the war. The strike wave started among women dressmakers in Paris during April and May of 1917, spreading from the capital to munitions plants throughout the country. After dying down somewhat, but not completely, during the fall and winter, strikes returned, larger and more militant than ever in the spring of 1918, involving hundreds of thousands of workers. To a large extent spurred by inflation and the consequent decline in real wages, strikes in France during World War I gradually took on a certain antiwar, even revolutionary, dimension, especially those of May 1918. The crises of industrial discipline spilled over into French politics as well, as the French Socialists came out formally against the war at their July 1918 national congress. After long years of supporting the war effort, by the summer of its final year many French workers had clearly begun to tire of government policies that seemed to place the burden of the conflict disproportionately on working-class shoulders while enriching munitions makers and war profiteers.[99]

Attacks on colonial workers in France took place in this context; archival and newspaper sources do not indicate a single instance of wartime racial violence

---

[95] AN 94 AP 135, report of August 16, 1916; ANSOM, SLOTFOM 10, carton 2, report of August 27, 1916.

[96] *Humanité* (September 4, 1916): 1.

[97] SH 7 N 1001, letter from Ahmed ben Haya, April 1917. See also ANSOM, SLOTFOM 10, carton 2, report of May 28, 1917; and ANSOM, SLOTFOM, carton 8, report of February 1918, for instances of cooperation between French and colonial workers in 1917 and 1918.

[98] Guy Pedroncini, *Les mutineries de 1917* (Paris, 1967); Leonard V. Smith, *Between Mutiny and Obedience: The Case of the French Fifth Infantry Division during World War I* (Princeton, N.J., 1994).

[99] On the strike wave of 1917–1918, see, in addition to works cited above, Kathryn E. Amdur, *Syndicalist Legacy: Trade Unions and Politics in Two French Cities in the Era of World War I* (Urbana, Ill., 1986), 56–107; Downs, "Women's Strikes."

before the spring of 1917. Nonwhites had only come to France with the outbreak of war and thus constituted a highly visible symbol of the conflict. French workers did not attack their colonial counterparts simply because they hated war, however. In explaining the reasons for outbursts of racial violence, historians have frequently pointed to fears of economic and sexual competition, and both kinds of tension certainly played a role in France during 1917 and 1918. Racial antagonisms were frequently expressed in terms of the belief that colonial workers had come to France to take French jobs. Dockworkers in particular often argued that foreign and especially nonwhite labor threatened their economic survival. The same month the riot broke out in Le Havre, for example, the local dockworkers' union noted that it had been complaining about the "excessive" use of Belgian and Moroccan labor in the port since 1915, and claimed that 1,400 French dockworkers lacked jobs.[100] In general, fears of displacement, rather than actual job shortages, helped motivate hostility to colonial labor. It is interesting to note that complaints about colonial workers by French labor emphasized these concerns about job loss much more than the problem of the lowering of wage levels, for example, even though there was far more evidence for the latter than the former. In part, the idea of foreign labor, especially nonwhite foreign labor, threatening French jobs was already well established before the war, and wartime hostility was simply grafted onto previous stereotypes. At the same time, most people in France recognized that the war was temporary; they feared that even if there was enough work for all while it lasted, this would not be true once the soldiers came home. Such anxieties about economic competition appeared frequently in government reports on relations between French and non-European workers.[101]

Sexual competition also lay behind racial violence. Colonial workers who went out in public in the company of French women sometimes found themselves attacked by French men, both soldiers and civilians. In commenting on the January 1918 riot in Toulouse, a Malagasy worker named Emmanuel Rasafimanjary described how he and a friend beat up three Frenchmen who called them "dirty niggers" after seeing them walking with French women; Rasafimanjary added that "such incidents are frequent, French men being very jealous of the favors women show the Malagasy."[102] A report from Saint-Médard concerning assaults on Indochinese laborers by French soldiers noted, "Jealousy concerning women is usually the cause of these aggressions."[103] In contrast to the myths that portrayed France as a land where love recognized no boundaries, both French officials and

---

[100] AN F 14 11334, Senator Henry Berenger to the Minister of Labor, July 2, 1917. See also a similar protest by the docker's union of Dunkirk, letter of June 3, 1917.

[101] For example, "the opposition of French workers to the employment of [foreign and colonial] labor arises from two motives: wage differences between citizens and immigrants, and racial prejudice. The Interministerial Conference has always, in the contracts it has provided for immigrant workers, provided for equal wages with French workers, thus eliminating this first reason for opposition." AN F 14 11334, report of June 9, 1917. As I have tried to demonstrate, this was certainly not true. See also AN F 14 11334, report of July 7, 1917; AN F 14 11332, letter of December 5, 1919; AN F 7 13619, reports of August 25, 1918, November 20, 1918; SH 6 N 149, letter of January 29, 1918. In February 1918, a censor in Bourges noted that several letters accused foreign workers of contributing to wartime inflation in France by their large numbers. ANSOM, SLOTFOM 1, carton 8, "Contrôle Postal Indochinois," report of February 1918.

[102] ANSOM, SLOTFOM 1, carton 8: "Contrôle Postal Malgache," report of February 1918, p. 4.

[103] ANSOM, SLOTFOM 10, carton 2, report of May 28, 1917.

ordinary French men frequently made their dislike of interracial relationships clear during the war years. French authorities strongly disapproved of these interracial love affairs and pressured colonial workers to abstain from them, threatening them with prison terms; there was in fact a legal ban on marriages between French women and Chinese men. Of particular concern to the authorities was the interest displayed by many nonwhites in pornographic postcards featuring nude French women: censors prepared detailed statistical analyses of the flow of such materials to North Africa and Indochina. The postcards were especially disturbing because they threatened to undermine established racial and sexual hierarchies in the empire, giving its inhabitants a radically new image of white women. As one censor observed about Indochinese workers, "their private conduct, such that we would prefer in order to leave the prestige of the European woman in Indochina intact, leaves more and more to be desired."[104]

Whereas such tensions existed before the spring of 1917, they only produced racial violence in the last year and a half of the war. Colonial labor's role in the great strikes of 1917 and 1918 reinforced its position as a symbol of war in the eyes of many French workers, thus prompting violence against them. One key issue was the numerous rumors about colonial troops, especially Senegalese and Indochinese, firing on striking French workers. In June 1917, for example, one such rumor claimed that Vietnamese soldiers had shot women strikers in Paris after French soldiers had refused to.[105] Though never proven, the report was accepted by many and helped lead to new assaults against Indochinese workers in Bourges, Saint-Médard, and Toulouse.[106] Another rumor alleged that African soldiers had killed thirty demonstrators during a demonstration in Saint-Etienne. The revival of working-class activism in 1917 revived memories of the time a decade earlier when the French government had used troops to break strikes, memories reinforced by the return of Georges "Strikebreaker" Clemençeau to power in November. As a June 1917 report noted, "People interested in sowing trouble in our ranks have been saying that the Annamites were sent to France in order to shoot upon 'the People,' and that in Paris strikes have been suppressed by Annamite contingents."[107]

The belief that colonial workers worked as strikebreakers had perhaps more importance and certainly more validity. Indochinese laborers were used to break strikes at war plants in Angoulême, Bergerac, and Saint-Médard in June 1917. Colonial workers came from nations without functioning unions and had virtually

[104] See the October 1917 report "Moralité, liaisons, projets de mariage," SH 7 N 997.

[105] This image of men of color shooting white women, while white men refused, fits into colonialist stereotypes of colonized men as both unmanly and as brutish violators of women. On constructions of masculinity in the colonial context, see Mrinalini Sinha, *Colonial Masculinity: The "Manly Englishman" and the "Effeminate Bengali" in the Late Nineteenth Century* (Manchester, 1995).

[106] Favre, "Un milieu porteur," 2: 508–23. It is interesting that such rumors provoked attacks against colonial *workers*, not *soldiers*. The fact that soldiers were frequently armed and therefore a formidable target is of course one possibility. More significantly, whereas the general impression of colonial soldiers was positive, seen as defenders of France against the Germans, that of colonial workers was overwhelmingly negative; rumors of the former shooting strikers did not undo this basic dichotomy.

[107] ANSOM, SLOTFOM 10, carton 2, reports of June 20, 1917, June 14, 1917; ANSOM, DSM, carton 5, reports of June 19, 1917, July 10, 1917. In an article on the subject, a Paul Adam commented that "soldiers are writing in their letters that the Annamites are massacring their women and children in Paris." Cited in *Humanité*, September 17, 1917.

no experience with labor solidarity. Their isolation from French workers (language barriers at times preventing even the most elementary communication) meant that they knew little of French unions or the reasons for the dissatisfaction of French workers. Consequently, when French workers struck, their colonial colleagues simply went to work as usual. Yet colonial workers frequently staged their own strikes about work conditions, food, and other issues. The Chinese were particularly noted for this. During July 1917, for example, 1,100 Chinese workers went on strike at a factory in Unieux and were immediately fired and deported.[108] The greater level of repression faced by colonial workers, who found themselves in a foreign country and closely controlled by the military, must be considered in explaining their willingness to work during French strikes when ordered to.

In this case as in so many others, therefore, the policy of isolating colonial workers served to transplant another key characteristic of colonial life, the absence of established labor unions and interracial working-class coalitions, to the metropole. A report from Saint-Médard praised Indochinese workers at the munitions factory for their "ardor for work" and their "resolute attitude" in face of a strike that ostensibly did not concern them at all.[109] As another report from Saint-Médard noted a month later, "French workers, a large number of whom have just left for other destinations, hate the Annamites, and one has felt this hatred, which has made cooperation impossible, since the strike, when the demonstrators wanted the natives to make demands like themselves."[110] The refusal of colonial workers to go on strike with French unions confirmed for many French laborers the idea that their presence in France lowered wages and in general weakened the position of French workers on the job.[111]

In addition, many French workers suspected that the government used colonial labor to free up more French men for military service. In July 1917, the Ministry of the Interior remarked, "the wives of mobilized men believe that if the colonials had not come to France, their husbands would be working in the factories." This conviction was powerfully reinforced by the Mourier law of August 1917, which sought to provide more (desperately needed) military manpower by drafting skilled workers from the war plants. The law not only deepened the hostility of striking workers to the *union sacrée* but also further underscored the distinction between them and colonial labor. Having been hired under contract to serve in farms and factories, colonial workers were exempt from conscription in spite of their status as French subjects (except for the Chinese). For many French workers, therefore, they came to symbolize the hated *embusqué*, the shirker who stayed behind in the safety

---

[108] Favre, "Un milieu porteur," 2: 520–23; AN 94 AP 140, reports of July 5, 1917, July 17, 1917, September 5, 1917; SH 17 N 157, letter of March 2, 1918.

[109] ANSOM, SLOTFOM 10, carton 2, report of July 1, 1917. This report raises the intriguing possibility that the refusal of colonial workers to go on strike may have bolstered their reputation among French soldiers, who often viewed the strikes with deep hostility. However, at the same time, it notes that attacks on Indochinese workers by French soldiers seemed to be continuing.

[110] ANSOM, SLOTFOM 10, carton 2, report of August 25, 1917.

[111] The idea of a dominant sector of the working class viewing a subordinate one as unfair and cheap competition is one of the key themes of split labor market theory. See Bonacich, "Advanced Capitalism."

of the war plants taking the jobs of those forced to risk their lives in battle.[112] Colonial workers were well aware of this attitude; in a July 1917 letter, a Mr. Lestang, a worker from Tonkin t the munitions factory in Tarbes, noted, "The animosity manifested against the Annamites arises especially . . . from the fact that many French soldiers have been replaced in the factories by colonial workers."[113]

The relationship between women and colonial workers in wartime France further emphasizes the close connection between labor militancy and racial violence. While the two groups had much in common, the strikes of 1917 and 1918 graphically revealed the differences between them. Striking women often appealed to colonial workers in their factories to join their protests but almost always failed to win them over.[114] In consequence, like French men, some women workers came to view nonwhites primarily as strikebreakers and enemies of the people, and they reacted accordingly. Several of the attacks on North Africans in Paris during the spring of 1917 involved women strikers. One gardener watering a lawn found himself accosted by several women who asked him to stop work and join them; when he refused, they called him a "dirty Sidi come to France to eat the bread of French workers," and struck him in the face. He escaped by turning his hose on them, holding them at bay until two policemen came to his rescue. In another incident, a group of North Africans was surrounded by women strikers who called them "weaklings" and "shirkers."[115] Generally, racial violence in wartime France was almost exclusively a male affair; no one was killed or seriously injured in the encounters described above, and the attacks of most French women on colonial workers remained restricted to verbal aggression. It is nonetheless significant that the only instances of female participation in racial assault involved women strikers. The fact that only women directly participating in France's crisis of civilian morale became involved in racial violence underscores the link between the two phenomena. For women on strike, attacks on colonial workers represented another aspect of their commitment to militant activism.

While certainly not supporting racial violence, French unions did little to

[112] ANSOM, DSM, carton 5, Paris, July 10, 1917. One of the ironies of this viewpoint is that many in French society, especially on the right and in the army, tended to look at *all* men working in the war industries as idle, overpaid *embusqués* whose militant strikes represented the height of arrogance if not actual treason. On the Mourier law, see the writings of John Horne: "Immigrant workers," 85; "L'Impôt du Sang: Republican Rhetoric and Industrial Warfare in France, 1914–1918," *Social History* 14 (May 1989): 201–24.

[113] ANSOM, SLOTFOM 1, carton 8, "Rapport du Contrôle Postal," July 1917; "Contrôle Postal Indochinois," August 1917; ANSOM, DSM, carton 5, letter of July 10, 1917.

[114] The July 1, 1917, report from Saint-Médard notes, "The working women who tried to hinder them [Indochinese workers] from going to work were forced tò cede before their resolute attitude." See also ANSOM, SLOTFOM 1, carton 8, "Contrôle Postal Indochinois," August 1917.

[115] ANSOM, DSM, carton 5, report of June 19, 1917. One of the more interesting phenomena here is the prospect of women in a traditionally male role (workers in heavy industry) insulting colonial workers by in effect calling them women. On one occasion, for example, a Moroccan sweeping the Boulevard Saint-Michel was accused of performing "women's work" by a group of French men and women. Such incidents are related to a broader wartime discourse that characterized colonial workers as feminine. Such gender-bending stereotypes were most frequently applied to the Indochinese. One report called them "mild and submissive," while another emphasized their aptitude for work requiring dexterity rather than physical force. At the same time, some Frenchmen argued that the use of colonial labor was necessary precisely in order to avoid having to use women in the factories. AN 7 N 144, report of February 20, 1916; AN 94 AP 135, report of August 16, 1916; Pierre Hamp, *La France, pays ouvrier* (Paris, 1916).

condemn or restrain workers who took part in them. It is important to note that the attacks on nonwhites in 1917 and 1918, and the strike wave of those years, occurred independently of the CGT leadership and, in fact, represented a challenge to its support of the war effort. Yet both the embattled majority and the surging leftist minority in the CGT took a generally negative view of colonial workers. The perspective of antiwar union activists on colonial labor was especially complex and contradictory.[116] Most rejected xenophobia and believed strongly in working-class internationalism. At the same time, they recognized the strength of French feeling against non-European workers and spoke out against their use as another example of the evils of war and its negative impact on the French working class. In March 1916, for example, leading *minoritaire* Gabriel Péricat decried "the superpatriots who import Kabyles, Moroccans, and Chinese who will work for them without complaint."[117] Supporters and ostensible leaders of the labor insurgencies of 1917 and 1918, they did nothing to restrain the racial attacks that accompanied them.[118] Itself ill-disposed toward the presence of colonial workers in France, the French labor movement was therefore unwilling and unable to prevent racism and racial violence from becoming one type of working-class anti-establishment discourse at the end of the Great War.

RACIAL VIOLENCE, AND NONWHITE WORKERS IN GENERAL, received relatively little attention from French society during World War I. Yet the phenomenon is significant for several reasons. The wave of racial attacks in 1917 and 1918 casts a new light on the history of working-class insurgency. The war itself brought about a temporary lessening of tensions between French and European immigrant workers. The pre-war violence against Italians was not repeated: the two groups worked together at times in strikes, and French unions commented favorably, or at least neutrally, on their presence in France. However, this was motivated in large part by the arrival of a new group, colonial workers, who assumed the previous position of European immigrants at the bottom of the nation's socioeconomic hierarchy. As a result, during the war, xenophobia became racialized, and hostile comments about nonwhite workers spoke not just of their economic or sexual threats to French labor but also of racial differences and inferiority.[119] The rise of racial violence as a part of the movement against the *union sacrée* also suggests that a straightforward view of working-class activism in 1917 and 1918 as the revival of progressive politics in France is incomplete. French workers could and did reject national-defense policies for reasons and in ways that had little to do with the perspectives of the antiwar leadership. The anti-colonial subtheme suggests another

---

[116] On the antiwar and revolutionary minority in the CGT, in addition to works already cited see Maurice Labi, *La grande division des travailleurs, 1914–1921* (Paris, 1964); Nicolas Papayanis, "Collaboration and Pacifism in France during World War I," *Francia* 5 (1977): 425–51; Roger Picard, *Le mouvement syndical durant la guerre* (Paris, 1927); Colette Chambelland and Jean Maitron, eds., *Syndicalisme révolutionnaire et communisme: Les archives de Pierre Monatte, 1914–1924* (Paris, 1968).

[117] Cited in Robert, "Ouvriers," 2: 417–18.

[118] Favre, "Un milieu porteur," 1: 81–85; Robert, "Ouvriers," 2: 412–19.

[119] For example, in January 1918, the metalworkers union in Bourges complained about its members having to train Indochinese workers, "labor of an inferior race." SH 6 N 149, letter of January 29, 1918.

perspective, one that sees war weariness as in part racially derived and dedicated to the preservation of white privilege. In this sense, violence against colonial workers strongly resembles the New York draft riots of 1863 in its combination of white working-class protest, opposition to war, and racial hostility.[120]

The widespread antagonism toward colonial workers contrasts sharply with the reception accorded colonial soldiers. Roughly 600,000 soldiers from the empire fought in France during the war. Like colonial workers, they were generally segregated from French civilians and sent home as soon after the war as possible. Yet the reaction of civilians to them was much more positive. In her memoir *Des inconnus chez moi*, the French woman Lucie Cousturier describes how the initial trepidation of her neighbors in a village where black African troops were stationed soon turned to a warm spirit of welcome.[121] (African-American soldiers serving in the U.S. Army reported similar treatment, in contrast to the bigoted attitudes of their own white officers.[122]) Many colonial soldiers viewed their encounters with the French favorably. Kande Kamera, from maritime Guinea in French West Africa, commented on the fair treatment he received in the French army, especially France's willingness to give black officers power over white soldiers.[123] The twenty African war veterans interviewed by Charles John Balesi all insisted on French racial egalitarianism: said one, "Blacks were highly esteemed there; there was no question of race."[124]

The striking difference between attitudes to colonial workers and colonial soldiers underscores the contextual nature of racism, and especially racial violence, in wartime France. In the years before 1914, a debate had raged in France over whether or not the nation, with its revolutionary tradition of a citizen army, should use colonial subjects as soldiers. The forces in favor, led by General Mangin, had carried the day, and the war itself was largely seen as proof that they had been right.[125] The use of colonial soldiers was highly popular in wartime France; they were seen as a way of counterbalancing Germany's larger population and, in fact, as a primary justification for the empire in general. Given France's loss of over a million soldiers by 1917, *anyone* who came to fight the Germans would most likely have been very welcome. Colonial workers, in contrast, were seen not only as competitors for French jobs and French women but also as a substitute labor force that permitted the government to send more French men to battle. Indeed, one of the most common complaints addressed against all foreigners, both European and

---

[120] See Iver Bernstein, *The New York City Draft Riots: Their Significance in American Society and Politics in the Age of the Civil War* (New York, 1990); Adrian Cook, *The Armies of the Streets: The New York City Draft Riots of 1863* (Lexington, Ky., 1974); James McCague, *The Second Rebellion: The Story of the New York City Draft Riots of 1863* (New York, 1968).

[121] Lucie Cousturier, *Des inconnus chez moi* (Paris, 1920).

[122] As one black soldier commented in a letter to his mother, "These French people don't bother with no color line business. They treat us so good that the only time I ever know I'm colored is when I look in the glass"; cited in W. Allison Sweeney, *History of the American Negro in the Great World War* (Chicago, 1919), 195. Such reports helped foster the myth of color-blind France after the war.

[123] Lunn, "Kande Kamara Speaks," 44–45.

[124] Cited in Balesi, *From Adversaries to Comrades-in-Arms*, 117. As Gilbert Meynier has argued, "The French had, it seems, a rather favorable image of North African soldiers. The image of black Africans evolved: from bad savages, they became good savages." Meynier, "La France colonial de 1914 à 1931," 105.

[125] Charles Mangin, *La force noire* (Paris, 1910).

colonial, was that they were lounging around safe behind the lines in France while French soldiers risked their lives at the front.[126] Whereas the colonial soldier became a positive symbol of the international effort to free France from German aggression, the colonial worker became a negative symbol of all, especially shirkers, who profited at the expense of the average French person. Racial violence in wartime France was not directed indiscriminately against all nonwhites, therefore, only against those seen as a threat to French interests.

While the assaults and riots that took place in France during the war were very much tied to a specific time and place, they also offer insights into the more general history of race, class, and racial violence. In important ways, they correspond to analyses of whiteness and intraclass racial conflict proffered by David Roediger and Alexander Saxton, but with some significant twists.[127] French racial violence did represent a successful attempt to redefine the working class by excluding people of color, and to a certain extent, as in the United States, this process involved merging people of different European backgrounds into a common white identity. Yet the greater marginality and temporary presence of nonwhite labor in France brought about the triumph of a discourse of class over *any* conscious racial identity; unlike Americans, the French succeeded in so totally excluding people of a different race that the very concept of race disappeared from working-class life in metropolitan France, relegated back to the colonies where it belonged. Few French workers thought of themselves as white *workers* during the interwar years.[128] Many undoubtedly did participate in the French fascination with "exotic" and colonial cultures during the interwar years, listening to jazz and the biguine or visiting the 1931 Colonial Exposition in Paris. But they did so as undifferentiated members of a broader French public, rather than as workers. One indication of the absence of nonwhites was the reassertion of prejudices against European foreigners in the interwar years, culminating in the harsh and ultimately murderous anti-Semitism directed against foreign Jews during the Depression and the Vichy era. The French experience thus suggests that the ultimate goal of strategies of racial exclusion may not be integration into a racial upper stratum but rather the consolidation of racial hierarchy through a denial of its existence.[129]

Yet France's spate of violence against colonial workers also demonstrates that working-class racial conflict cannot be separated from class conflict in general. Many French workers held racial stereotypes for a variety of reasons, but they

---

[126] For example, see Archives de la Préfecture de Police de Paris, "Physiognomie de Paris," police report of January 3, 1918, p. 8; January 12, 1918, p. 8.

[127] Roediger, *Wages of Whiteness*; *Towards the Abolition of Whiteness*; Saxton, *Rise and Fall of the White Republic*.

[128] For example, none of the memoirs of interwar working-class life that I have examined mention whiteness or racial identity. See, among others, Fernand Grenier, *Ce bonheur-là* (Paris, 1974); René Michaud, *J'avais vingt ans* (Paris, 1967); Jeanne Bouvier, *Mes mémoires, ou 59 années d'activité industrielle, sociale et intellectuelle* (Paris, 1983); Laurent Azzano, *Mes joyeuses années au faubourg* (Paris, 1985); Mrs. Robert Henrey, *The Little Madeleine* (London, 1951). See also the works of Jacques Valdour, especially *Ouvriers parisiens d'après-guerre* (Paris, 1921); and *Ateliers et taudis de la banlieue de Paris* (Paris, 1923).

[129] Feminist historians of working-class life have for years demonstrated the ways in which appeals to class solidarity can conceal gender hierarchies. A particularly good example of this is Beatrix Campbell's rereading of George Orwell's classic *The Road to Wigan Pier*, in *Wigan Pier Revisited: Poverty and Politics in the Eighties* (London, 1984).

resorted to racial *violence* in a specific context of heightened tensions between labor and capital, as part of a strategy to bolster the position of labor. In investigating the dynamics of race and class as far as violence is concerned, historians should consider less who is to blame for racist behavior and more the ways in which the interests and strategies of all the parties to class conflict interact to create or reinforce racial hierarchies.[130] During the Great War, it took the willingness of employers and the French state to employ nonwhites against the interests of French workers as well as the refusal of French labor to reach out to these newcomers from overseas to produce an explosive situation.

In addition, racial violence in France must be considered in the broader context of total war. The tendency of twentieth-century race riots to erupt during wartime is well known and has generally been explained by historians as the result of the large-scale movement of racial groups to new areas. This is of course undeniable, but another way of looking at this conjuncture should be considered. Wartime intercommunal violence represents an implicit rejection of the war effort: it subverts the attempts of nation-states to create a climate of internal unity and refocus violence exclusively against the external enemy, instead reintroducing domestic conflict and calling into question the solidity of the national community. Racial violence, which throws into conflict physically and culturally distinct communities, not only undermines national unity but symbolically reproduces the war between nations on the home front. French attacks on colonial workers were also attacks on the spirit of the *union sacrée*, and those hostile to nonwhites at times represented them as enemies behind the lines. Racial conflict in this context thus shows how total war can not only suppress internal social divisions but accentuate and provide a model for them as well.

The introduction of 300,000 non-European workers into France during the war constituted a massive new demographic event, one that clearly would require some adjustment on the part of the local population. Yet the racial hostility that led to violence in 1917 did not develop naturally but arose from conscious policies undertaken by different groups in French society. Employers paid colonial workers the lowest wages in France and were happy to use them to break strikes when the opportunity arose. Unions fostered the idea that colonial labor would lower wages and take jobs from the French, but they made little effort to ensure equality of salaries for colonial workers or organize them to defend themselves. Above all, the French state, with its policy of regimentation, created a climate that effectively defined colonial workers as the Other, in both concrete and symbolic terms. Ostensibly set up to prevent racial clashes, regimentation also had the goal of preventing the integration of nonwhites into working-class militant culture and traditions. It achieved the latter goal but only at the cost of subverting the former. Racial violence in wartime France thus played a role in the strategies of both organized labor and the French state.

Racial violence during World War I represented France's introduction to an issue

[130] Some of the historical literature on whiteness tends to attack white workers for racism without sufficiently demonstrating how such groups could be both dominant and subordinate at the same time in the broader context of race and class relations. See, for example, Noel Ignatiev, *How the Irish Became White* (New York, 1995).

that would become a major preoccupation during the second half of the twentieth century. It demonstrates that race did not simply appear as an issue for the first time after 1945, it has played a role in French working-class life for most of the century. After 1918, the French government sent colonial workers home as quickly as possible, judging that France was not ready to become a multi-racial society. The massive immigration of the 1920s focused almost entirely on European immigrants.[131] Yet the interwar years represented not the disappearance of the racial question from French working-class life but rather its forced suppression; racial conflict thus became an artificially constructed silence during the 1920s and 1930s. Nonetheless, the wave of violence against colonial workers during the Great War both anticipated and prepared the ground for difficulties France would face in confronting new populations of color on its soil in the late twentieth century. French authorities may have wished to re-create a monochromatic image of French identity after the armistice, but, as with so many other changes unleashed by World War I, this was much easier said than done.

[131] A January 1920 article in the *Bulletin du Ministère du travail* justified importing European as opposed to colonial workers after the war in order to avoid bringing an "ethnographically distinct" population onto French soil. Cited in Robert, "Ouvriers," 2: 395.

Tyler Stovall is a professor of the history of modern France at the University of California, Santa Cruz. He is the author of *The Rise of the Paris Red Belt* (1990) and *Paris Noir: African Americans in the City of Light* (1996). His current research interests include labor and urban history, as well as colonial and postcolonial France. Stovall is working on two projects at present: working-class protest and consumerism in Paris at the end of World War I, and migration from the Caribbean to France in the nineteenth and twentieth centuries.

Part III
Western Front

[13]

To the Last Limits of Their Strength
The French Army and the Logistics of Attrition at the Battle of Verdun
21 February – 18 December 1916

By Robert B. Bruce

During the First World War, near the fortress city of Verdun, the French Army endured the largest battle of attrition the world had yet seen. Verdun epitomized the massive contests of attrition which were the hallmark of that war, leading one historian of the First World War to observe "that in the total war, the battle of Verdun was [the] total battle."[1] The purpose of the German offensive at Verdun was not to achieve the chimerical "breakthrough" which would burst the contestants out of the gridlock of trench warfare. Instead the German objective at Verdun was to drag the French into a battle of attrition in an area where the Germans held local superiority and could slowly bleed the French Army to death, inflicting such punishment that neither the French Army nor the French nation would survive Verdun. Yet while the French would indeed suffer frightful losses in the coming battle, they would perform such incredible feats of logistics that they would be able to muster and maintain a mighty army in front of Verdun which would not only halt the advance of the Germans but also inflict grievous losses on them.

More than any other man it was General Henri Philippe Pétain,[2] commander of the French Second Army and later France's Central Army Group during the battle of Verdun, who was responsible for the French victory. Pétain's triumph was made possible by his exceptional ability to master the logistics of attrition, which enabled him to implement a new tactical doctrine of overwhelming firepower to inflict massive losses on the Germans while conserving his own forces. This enabled the French to emerge victorious from one of most grueling battles the world has ever seen—the battle of Verdun.

On Christmas Day 1915 the chief of the German General Staff, General Erich von Falkenhayn, wrote a report to Kaiser Wilhelm II regarding Germany's overall strategic situation in the First World War after the battles of that year. Falkenhayn was extremely optimistic about Germany's prospects for 1916, but at the same time he cautioned the kaiser that Germany's advantage in the war was a fleeting one. Falkenhayn wrote, "Our enemies [France, Britain, Russia, and Italy], thanks to their superiority in men and material, are increasing their resources much more than we are. If that process continues a moment must come when the balance of numbers itself will deprive Germany of all remaining hope."[3]

Therefore Falkenhayn decided to take advantage of Germany's then favorable situation to strike a blow in early 1916 that would resolve matters once and for all in the sector which he deemed the most important, the Western Front. By 1916 the Western Front was a solid line of trenches and barbed wire from the English Channel to the Swiss Alps, where gains were measured in yards and casualties in tens of thousands. Yet it was here that Germany faced the two adversaries whom Falkenhayn deemed the most dangerous, France and Britain, and thus this was where he felt the only decisive result could be obtained. Of these two Allies, Falkenhayn believed the French to be the more vulnerable as they had "been weakened almost to the limits of endurance, both in a military and economic sense."[4] Falkenhayn believed that

The strain on France has almost reached the breaking point—though it is certainly borne with the most remarkable devotion. If we succeeded in opening the eyes of her people to the fact that in a military sense they have nothing more to hope for, that breaking point would be reached. . . . To achieve that object the uncertain method of a mass breakthrough, in any case beyond our means, is unnecessary. . . . Within our reach behind the French sector of the Western Front there are objectives for the retention of which the French General Staff would be compelled to throw in every man they have. If they do so the forces of France will bleed to death. . . . If they do not do so, and we reach our objectives, the moral effect on France will be enormous.

The objectives of which I am speaking now are Belfort and Verdun.

[Of these] the preference must be given to Verdun.[5]

Falkenhayn's plan involved the largest concentration of artillery yet seen on the battlefield, which he proceeded to position around the Verdun salient. Falkenhayn would commit the German Fifth Army to an attack which would either seize Verdun or threaten to take it and then assume strong defensive positions, backed by massive amounts of artillery fire that would shred the expected French counterattacks and turn Verdun into a slaughter-pen for the French Army. Falkenhayn's plan, dubbed Operation *GERICHT* (place of execution), relied for success upon both the national character of the French and the aggressive doctrine of their army, which reflected this character.

France had entered the First World War still haunted by the ghosts of its defeat in the Franco-Prussian War of 1870–71, when its mighty army had been destroyed by the unified German states. It was a humiliation with which France, a nation that considered itself to be "the premier warrior race of Europe," struggled for decades to cope and which caused its army not only to deeply analyze the reasons for its defeat but also to begin a search for a new doctrine which would assure that a similar disaster never again befell the French nation.[6]

Inspired in the years before the Great War by such military thinkers as Georges Gilbert, Ferdinand Foch, and Louis Loyzeau de Grandmaison, the French came to the conclusion that their defeat in the Franco-Prussian War was a result of being too passive at all levels of command and relying excessively on defensive firepower, in lieu of pursuing direct offensive action to stop the enemy at the tactical level. These French thinkers developed a school of thought that came to be known as the "cult of the offensive," which maintained that the principal weapon of a French infantryman was his bayonet and that success on the battlefield relied on an attacker's *élan* and his ability to establish moral superiority, which would overcome any amount of firepower the defender might put up. In the opinion of these offensive theorists, the French soldier was in his element while on the attack where his *élan* would be coupled with his natural *furia française* (a term coined by Gilbert) to make him an irresistible force on the battlefield. The new doctrine was referred to as the *offensive à outrance* (attack to the death) and became codified when General Joseph Jacques Césaire Joffre, an ardent follower of Grandmaison, became chief of the General Staff in 1911.[7] While trying not to repeat their mistakes of the last war, the French committed new errors for a new war.[8]

The French Army's baptism of fire in the Great War was horrific, as French infantry stormed forward in dense formations, bayonets fixed, pitting *élan* and cold steel against machine guns and rapid-fire artillery. The result was catastrophic. In a series of indecisive battles and outright defeats, France lost an estimated 301,000 men killed in action during 1914 and a further 349,000 men killed in 1915—annual totals which each exceeded the death toll the United States would experience in the entire Second World War. A further 2 million French soldiers were listed as wounded or missing in action during this same time period, bringing France's total casualties for the first two years of the Great War to almost 3 million men.[9]

As casualties mounted, the French Army's belief in its doctrine of the *offensive à outrance* began to waver, and the military leaders of France sought a different answer to the deadlock in which they found themselves on the Western Front. Gradually, the French began to embrace a new doctrine, which was best described by its leading proponent, General Henri Philippe Pétain, by the phrase "firepower kills." Although Pétain is perhaps best remembered today for his leadership of the Vichy regime during the dark years of 1940–44, this is unfortunate because Pétain was a gifted military commander who long before the First World War had argued that firepower, and not *élan* and *l'arme blanche*, or bravery and cold steel, as the Grandmaisonites believed, would dominate the modern battlefield. As a consequence of this "heresy" Pétain was passed over for promotion on numerous occasions and, in spite of his obvious abilities, found himself a 58-year-old colonel, just one year away from mandatory retirement, in temporary command of a brigade when the war began in 1914. The bloody French defeats of 1914–15, however, made Pétain seem more the prophet than the heretic, and he began a meteoric rise in France's military hierarchy. In June 1915 Joffre placed Pétain in command of the French Second Army.[10]

The French Army's shift toward the emphasis on firepower espoused by Pétain was a difficult one, for at first the French lacked large quantities of guns and munitions that were required to implement the new doctrine. In particular the French suffered from a severe shortage of heavy artillery. The French Army had gone to war in 1914 with its field artillery batteries equipped with the famous 75-mm. gun, but it possessed virtually no medium or heavy artillery except that used to arm the numerous fortresses dotting France's eastern frontier. This choice of light artillery to the exclusion of heavier pieces was influenced by the doctrine of *offensive à outrance*, which emphasized speed of maneuver and bayonet charges over firepower. The light 75-mm. gun was a remarkably accurate, flat-trajectory weapon with a tremendous rate of fire—a formidable weapon in the war of maneuver and open-field battles that French prewar planners had anticipated.[11]

However by mid-1915, the French Army was slowly realizing that in this new war its 75-mm. gun simply lacked the power to cut through belts of barbed wire or to smash in bunkers or trenches. The major armaments manufacturers of France geared up to produce guns with calibers of 90-mm. and larger, but this process took time. So the French commander-in-chief, General Joffre, decided to meet the pressing need for heavy artillery on the battlefield by removing heavy guns from numerous French fortresses, including the forts in and around Verdun. Increased industrial output, combined with Joffre's draconian measures, resulted in a significant increase in heavy artillery for French field armies between January 1915 and January 1916, especially with regard to "super" heavy pieces of 220-mm. and larger. (*Table 1*)[12]

Finding enough ammunition for this sudden influx of new guns was a logistical challenge which rivaled the acquisition of the guns themselves. Prior to 1914 the French Army, like all other belligerents, had grievously underestimated the ammunition needs of its artillery. The French Army entered the Great War with a stockpile of approximately 5 million 75-mm. shells. Its prewar plans estimated a consumption rate of 100,000 rounds of artillery monthly. This estimate proved to be grossly in error as early as 1914, when the French fired an average of 900,000 rounds per month.[13]

French industry rose to meet the new need for

Table 1

Number of Heavy Artillery Pieces in Service With the French Army[14]

Caliber	1 January 1915	1 January 1916
90-mm.	600	1,230
95-mm.	270	650
120-mm. (long)	300	900
120-mm. (short)	60	120
155-mm. (long)	190	470
155-mm. (short)	110	320
220-mm. howitzer	17	180
270-mm. howitzer	0	30
280-mm. howitzer	0	6
370-mm. howitzer	0	10
TOTALS	1,547	3,916

artillery ammunition with a massive increase in its monthly production of shell. The French military released experienced munitions workers from their service obligations so they could return to their factories, and the French munitions industry made Herculean efforts to meet the demand for shells. In December 1914 French factories churned out an average of 34,322 rounds of 75-mm. ammunition and 3,000 rounds of heavy artillery ammunition per day. By December 1915 daily production had risen to 84,460 75-mm. shells and approximately 52,000 rounds of heavy artillery ammunition, with plans to increase shell production even further in 1916.[15]

Thus the year 1916 dawned on a French Army in a state of transition from an antiquated doctrine of bayonet charges to one of modern firepower delivered in unprecedented amounts, perpetually resupplied by a massive industrial base. This new doctrine was about to be put to the test in the largest and longest battle of attrition the world had yet seen, the battle of Verdun.

The French high command (*Grand Quartier Général* or G.Q.G.) was slow to realize that the Germans were planning to strike at Verdun. Although Joffre and his staff had reports as early as December 1915 that the Germans were planning a large offensive against the Fortified Region of Verdun (*Région Fortifiée de Verdun* or R.F.V.), they were more concerned about preparations for the forthcoming Anglo-French offensive along the Somme planned for later that year.

Joffre's indifference to the threat to Verdun became a scandal when Lt. Col. Emile Driant, a member of the Chamber of Deputies who commanded two battalions of elite chasseurs in the center of the French front line in the R.F.V., sent a letter to the president of the Chamber of Deputies complaining about the lack of defensive preparations in the region. In response, the Chamber of Deputies and the Ministry of War sent out a joint inspection team, which, much to the anger and consternation of Joffre, decided that Driant was correct.[16]

The commission found that the French trench system at Verdun was poorly constructed and lacked any secondary or tertiary lines of resistance and that the front line was not connected to the rear by communication trenches. The mighty fortresses of the R.F.V. had been stripped by Joffre of virtually all of their artillery and their garrisons had been reduced to half-strength. A furious Joffre decried the commission's statements about the state of the R.F.V.'s defenses and angrily wrote to the minister of war that the report could not be justified. Joffre and his staff at the G.Q.G. did little to implement the commission's recommendations and quickly refocused their attention on the preparations for the Somme offensive, never concerning themselves with the possibility that the Germans might not sit idly by while the British and French made ready for their attack.[17]

On 21 February 1916, Operation *GERICHT* exploded across the front of the *Région Fortifiée de Verdun* with the largest artillery barrage yet seen in the Great War. The poorly constructed French trench system of the R.F.V. collapsed under the hail of German shells. Specially trained German storm troops followed behind the barrage, heavily laden with grenades and armed with a new device employed for the first time on the battlefield: the *flammenwerfer* (flamethrower). In spite of the massive firepower directed upon them, isolated pockets of French forces fought back with near suicidal courage in a desperate attempt to stem the German advance, as urgent messages requesting reinforcements were rushed to the G.Q.G.[18]

By 25 February the French had been pushed completely out of their frontline positions east of the Meuse, and it seemed as if the entire R.F.V. east of the river, with its numerous forts, would have to be abandoned. When Fort Douaumont, the largest and most powerful fort in the Verdun system, fell due to a combination of German daring and French blundering, General Fréderic Georges Herr, commanding the R.F.V., ordered that the forts still in French hands be rigged for demolition so as to deny their use to the enemy if the French were forced to retreat and abandon them. The withdrawals executed by Herr in the face of near overwhelming pressure from the Germans began to concern the G.Q.G., and so General Joffre dispatched to Verdun his second-in-command, General Noel Joseph de Castelnau, to assess the situation and recommend a course of action.

On 25 February de Castelnau issued the following order to the R.F.V.: "The Meuse must be held on the right [east] bank. There can be no question of any other course than of checking the enemy, cost what it may, on that bank."[19] This order affirmed that the French Army would stand and fight for Verdun. On that same day, Joffre met with Pétain, briefed him on the situation at Verdun, and ordered him to move his Second Army into the R.F.V. and to go immediately to Bar-le-Duc, where he would receive specific instructions from de Castelnau.[20]

Pétain and his staff set out in an automobile, "and to be as quick as possible" they went via Souilly, a town midway between Bar-le-Duc and Verdun that would become Pétain's headquarters during the battle. Driving through a heavy snowstorm, Pétain arrived at Souilly on the evening of the 25th. Pétain was concerned at the chaos he found along the main road connecting Bar-le-Duc to Verdun: "I passed the procession of supply trains, making their way towards Verdun, columns of soldiers blocking all the roads, ambulance sections moving southward [away from Verdun], and above all, most distressing of sights, the wretched horde of inhabitants seeking refuge outside of the devastated region."[21]

One item, however, caught Pétain's attention more than any other, and that was the precarious supply situation of the French forces at Verdun. There were two major rail lines to Verdun, but they were both useless because one "passed through the enemy's lines at Saint-Mihiel" and the second "was often shelled . . . and over which nothing could be carried except some of the engineers' material." This narrowed Pétain's options for a supply route to a light, narrow-gauge railway and a seven-yard-wide, dirt road that ran seventy-five kilometers from the nearest railhead at Bar-le-Duc to Verdun. Through these tenuous arteries the lifeblood of France was to be poured into the cauldron of Verdun.[22]

Pétain used the narrow-gauge railway—dubbed *le Meusien*—to transport food and fodder for the men and supply animals of the Second Army, but all of its reinforcements, replacements, and munitions had to be transported by truck up the departmental road from Bar-le-Duc. To accomplish this, Pétain employed the infant *Service Automobile dans l'Armée Française* in the largest use of motor vehicles for logistical purposes seen in warfare to that time.

The *Service Automobile* had been officially founded in 1914, but it traced its origins to the Military Commission of Automobiles which the French Army had formed in 1896 to study the possible military use of motorized vehicles. This commission was fortunate in having several forward-thinking junior officers placed in charge of its development. These young men included Brevet Capt. L.-J. Dubost, who in 1902 authored a study that stated that automobiles would prove instrumental in the next war by permitting the rapid movement of troops. This would allow a numerically inferior force to compensate for its lack of numbers with maneuverability. In his study, Dubost argued that a corps of motorists should be formed to implement this new technology. Dubost's ideas found some acceptance among the French high command, and as a consequence the French Army maneuvers in the autumn of 1910 tested the use of heavy vehicles operating in convoy systems to supply the units taking part in the exercise.[23]

At the first battle of the Marne, General Joseph Simon Galliéni had utilized the *Service Automobile*, as well as some taxis and buses dragooned from the streets of Paris, to move the French 7th Infantry Division into position on the right flank of the German First Army, in preparation for a French counterattack that would turn aside the German drive on Paris in September 1914. The *Service Automobile* had also seen limited action in the French offensives of 1915, when it was utilized to move reserves up to the front lines, but Verdun would prove to be both its greatest trial and its greatest accomplishment.[24]

Pétain's efforts at organizing this motorized supply system were ably assisted by Major Richard, an engineer officer who was in charge of motorized transport for the R.F.V. In the days immediately after the German offensive began and prior to Pétain's arrival in Verdun, Richard had recognized the critical need for motor vehicles to supply any large commitment of force by the G.Q.G. to the R.F.V. and had thus assembled a fleet of over 700 trucks, buses, and assorted motorized vehicles for the express purpose of supplying the needs of the French forces at Verdun.[25]

Pétain quickly set about organizing this motor fleet into an efficient force. The road from Bar-le-Duc to Verdun "was divided into six sections, each in charge of an officer who was responsible for the movements over it, with the Military Police to assist him." The motorized supply convoys were administered by the *Service Automobile* and the specially created Traffic Commission of Bar-le-Duc, which together would eventually number 300 officers, 8,500 men, and 3,900 vehicles organized into 175 automobile units.[26]

This force was responsible not only for moving reinforcements to the R.F.V., but also for evacuating wounded and supplying the ammunition needs for an army that eventually numbered over 500,000 officers and men. The road from Bar-le-Duc to Verdun became the French Army's lifeline during the battle, and writer Maurice Barrès best described its importance to the cause of France when he dubbed it *La Voie Sacrée*, the Sacred Way.[27]

Before Pétain had time to effectively organize his novel supply system, disaster struck when, beginning on 28 February, the bitter cold that had dominated the first days of the battle unexpectedly broke and a thaw set in. The *Voie Sacrée* soon became a river of mud that was completely impassable to the motorized French supply columns. Although provisions could still be brought in along the narrow-gauge railway, the supply of ammunition and replacements and the evacuation of wounded soldiers relied on the trucks of the *Service Automobile*. If these vital logistical needs could not be met, the French position at Verdun would soon become completely untenable. Pétain, realizing the gravity of the situation, reacted quickly to confront the danger and rectify the situation.[28]

Pétain dragooned the local populace who lived along the route of the *Voie Sacrée* into opening a large number of rock quarries, and he set up relay teams to move the gravel they produced from the quarries to sites along the road. Colonial troops from France's holdings in West and North Africa were brought in to serve as work crews for a round-the-clock effort to shovel gravel onto the roadbed to firm up the road. Soon trucks were once more rolling toward Verdun, and their weight smashed the gravel flat. Through this incredible effort the road was solidified and the greatest threat to the French logistical effort at Verdun overcome.[29]

Yet within weeks the solution to the softening road caused another set of problems to emerge. The sharp gravel began to gouge holes in the tires of the trucks and the bumpier ride caused by rocks in the road, along with the strain on the trucks resulting from their constant use, added an increased number of mechanical breakdowns to the incessant problem of flat tires, and thus once again France's vital supply artery to Verdun was threatened. Lieutenant Colonel Girard, the head of the *Service Automobile*, rose to the occasion by setting up repair shops along the length of the *Voie Sacrée*. The shops included hydraulic presses that worked twenty-four hours a day stamping out new tires for the motorized vehicles.[30]

In spite of the numerous problems encountered by the French motorized supply columns, the performance of the *Service Automobile* in the critical opening stages of the battle of Verdun was absolutely outstanding. From 22 February to 8 March 1916, French trucks carried 190,000 men; 22,500 tons of munitions; and 2,500 tons of various other materials up the *Voie Sacrée* to Verdun. Given the ferocity and suddenness of the German attack, the trying weather conditions, and the primitive vehicles then in use, it was an amazing logistical achievement.[31]

Those loads of men and munitions were needed in ever increasing numbers by the French forces as 1916 wore on and the battle of Verdun settled into the grueling contest of attrition which would become its hallmark. Of all the numbers involved in analyzing the logistics of the French Army at Verdun, certainly the most shocking is the casualty rate. The exact number of men lost by France during the battle of Verdun remains a matter of some speculation. The French Army's official history of the Great War states that, during the course of the ten months of battle at Verdun, France lost 162,440 men killed or missing and 216,337 wounded, for a total of 378,777 casualties. These are very conservative casualty figures. Some historians have estimated that France suffered over 500,000 casualties at Verdun, including perhaps as many as 250,000 killed.[32]

These losses are even more frightful when one considers that France had already suffered well over 2 million casualties during the Great War before the battle at Verdun began. In addition, by January 1916 France had mobilized 87 percent of the total manpower it would muster during the war and had reached the end of its manpower reserves even before the battle began, thus making every soldier lost at Verdun literally irreplaceable. This shortage of manpower also meant that there would be no relief for the men already in the trenches as there was no one with whom to replace them. As a consequence, the French Army that fought at Verdun would be virtually the same one that France would have for the remainder of the war.[33]

The lack of fresh replacements did not bode well for the future of France's war effort as overexposure to the rigors of fighting on the Western Front in the Great War often led to severe psychological disorders. The industrialized nature of warfare in the trenches produced an environment where the individual soldier was helpless before artillery and machine guns which impassively killed hero and coward alike from great distances, and against which a soldier had very limited means to strike back. The incredible firepower and range of modern weaponry transformed the soldier from a fighter to a helpless victim, and a whole host of psychological disorders, commonly lumped together under the generic term of "shell shock," began to appear in soldiers of all armies in the Great War.[34]

At first, military commanders and physicians interpreted such disorders as merely a morale problem and commonly treated psychological casualties as ordinary malingerers. They were commonly referred to as "moral invalids," whose only real problem was a lack of courage and fortitude which could best be restored by severe discipline and physical punishment. As the science of psychiatry advanced during the war, psychological casualties began to be distinguished from shirkers, but treatments for their neurological maladies were often barbaric. "Disciplinary therapists" favored the extensive use of electric shock in treating war neuroses, in spite of the poor results obtained. Although more humane, and more effective, treatments such as psychoanalysis began to be used later in the war, during the battle of Verdun disciplinary therapy was the standard practice for handling psychological casualties in both the Allied and German armies.[35]

One of Pétain's major qualities as a commander, which separated him from virtually every other high-ranking officer of the First World War, was his sincere concern for the psychological well-being of his men. Pétain wrote that:

Indeed my heart bled when I saw our young twenty-year-old men going under fire at Verdun, knowing as I did that with the impressionability of their age they would quickly lose the enthusiasm aroused by their first battle and sink into the apathy of suffering, perhaps even into discouragement, in the face of such a task as was theirs. . . . I singled them out for my most affectionate consideration as they moved up into the line with their units. . . . I loved the confident glance with which they saluted me. But the discouragement with which they returned! . . . Their eyes stared into space as if transfixed by a vision of terror. . . . Horrible memories made them quail. When I questioned them, they scarcely answered, and the jeering tones of the old poilus awakened no spark of response in them. [36]

Pétain understood what a tremendous sacrifice was being asked of the soldiers in each division that he sent into the line at Verdun and also realized that he simply could not allow them to be destroyed physically or emotionally in the fighting, or France would have no army left.

Pétain therefore instituted a rotational system whereby after approximately three days in the line a division would be withdrawn from Verdun for a week or so to a quiet area where it would be allowed to rest and recover from the fighting. The division would then be moved into a somewhat more active sector, before finally being sent once more into battle at Verdun, where the whole process would begin anew. Pétain's system thus allowed for fresh, full-strength units to be placed in the front line as opposed to depleted and morally shattered units that had fought themselves to

General Pétain at Baccarat, France, in September 1918 (Signal Corps photograph)

pieces in the inferno of Verdun. Pétain wrote

> Our system of rapid and frequent reliefs necessitated our keeping within the territory occupied by the army twice the number of units actually concerned in the fighting. The turning of the mill-wheel had already [1 May 1916] swept through Verdun forty divisions, by which I do not mean that all these had been used up. As a matter of fact, most of these divisions had been withdrawn before they were exhausted, and transferred for a time to quiet sectors, then again shortly afterwards into sectors where fighting was in progress.[37]

What made this rotation system possible was the *Service Automobile*, which moved soldiers quickly and efficiently from Verdun to reserve area billets and then back again to the front.

Erich Ludendorff, who became Germany's First Quartermaster-General in August 1916, was very much impressed with the French use of motorized vehicles to rotate their divisions at Verdun. Ludendorff wrote that

> The enemy, backed by his enormous industries, found it easier and easier, not merely to move his reserves quickly in lorries [trucks], but also to use them on an increasing scale for bringing troops up from billets to the line and taking them back again, thus achieving an important economy of physical and moral strength. We had to be content if we could find [trucks] enough for troop movements in cases of the greatest urgency.[38]

In spite of Ludendorff's ringing endorsement, Pétain's rotation system was heavily criticized at the time by his own commander-in-chief, General Joffre, and the staff at the G.Q.G., who, even at the height of the battle of Verdun, pushed forward that summer with plans to join the British in a powerful attack along the Somme.

At a conference in December 1915, Joffre had promised the British that he would provide forty divisions for the forthcoming Somme offensive, but the manpower needs imposed on the French Army by the battle of Verdun and Pétain's generous use of reserve divisions through his rotational system quickly consumed most of the planned French contribution. In the end, France would be able to provide only nine divisions to the British effort along the Somme, but considering the strain that Verdun placed upon the French Army it was a logistical miracle in its own right that the French were able to provide any support at all to the British offensive.[39]

These conflicting manpower needs produced considerable friction between Pétain and Joffre, and each accused the other of failing to understand how to defeat the Germans. Joffre's argument was that you should never allow the enemy to dictate your actions but should always remain free to strike at him rather than merely react to his assaults. Joffre argued that the best way to halt the German attack on Verdun was for the French and their British allies to launch their own offensive in a different sector. Joffre increasingly began to feel that Verdun was consuming Pétain and that he had become so obsessed by the battle that he was losing proper perspective on the event.[40]

Pétain, on the other hand, was exceedingly frustrated by a high command that did not recognize that the climactic battle of the war had arrived for France, and he believed that neither the French Army nor the French nation would be able to survive the moral blow that the fall of Verdun would inflict. To Pétain there was more than France's honor at stake at Verdun. The very life of France itself was at risk, and Pétain would act accordingly. Pétain steadfastly refused to cancel his rotation system, and he continued to demand more men, guns, and ammunition for the battle, never hesitating to threaten to take the matter out of military channels and to appeal to the political leadership of the nation, if necessary, to meet his requirements.[41]

Joffre responded to Pétain's intransigence in April 1916 by "kicking him upstairs" to the command of France's Central Army Group, composed of Pétain's old Second Army as well as the French Third, Fourth, and Fifth Armies. Although this promotion in theory relieved Pétain of his responsibilities at Verdun, which was only one sector of his new command, he nevertheless continued to direct French strategy at that battle, keeping his successor at Second Army, General Robert Nivelle, on a very short leash.[42]

Although he exasperated Joffre, the French commander-in-chief had great respect for Pétain and later wrote that

> [Pétain] was endowed with very great qualities and these, during the course of the war, and especially at the beginning of the battle of Verdun, have brought him a

justly earned reputation. What saved Verdun was his highly developed tactical sense, his continual perfecting of the methods of defence, and the constant improvement he effected in the organization of the command of the higher units. General Pétain was the heart and soul of the action. Moreover, it should never be forgotten that it was his accurate and unceasing study of the enemy's fighting methods that brought about in our own army the greatest tactical improvement seen in it at any time during the war.[43]

The "tactical improvement" to which Joffre referred was Pétain's implementation of the French Army's new doctrine of firepower, for it was at Verdun that Pétain first obtained the weapons and materiel necessary to fully implement his theory of warfare, best expressed by his slogan "firepower kills."

From the moment of his arrival at Verdun, Pétain had made the establishment of French artillery supremacy on the battlefield his number one priority. Pétain wrote, "I unremittingly urged the activity of the artillery. When the liaison officers of the various army corps, meeting at Souilly for their daily report, began to explain to me in detail the course of fighting on their several fronts, I never failed to interrupt them with the question: 'What have your batteries been doing? We will discuss other points later.'"[44]

On 19 March 1916, Pétain issued a directive to the Second Army that specified that artillery fires should be concentrated and ordered artillery observers to utilize a new report form which would detail the type and objectives of each barrage, the types of projectiles used, the enemy batteries spotted that were vulnerable to counterbattery fire, and other general observations on the effect of the fire. Pétain used these daily reports to direct and coordinate the fire of every battery in the French Second Army, a truly monumental task given the incredible number and variety of artillery pieces that Pétain had at his disposal.[45]

Pétain used his guns to lay down enormous amounts of fire on the Germans. (*Table 2*) The artillery consumption rate in the R.F.V. during Pétain's tenure as the commanding general of the Second Army was truly astounding, especially when one considers that virtually every shell fired had been brought into Verdun by truck via the *Voie Sacrée*. Thanks in part to Pétain's lavish use of firepower, the overall artillery ammunition consumption rate for the entire French Army climbed in 1916 to a monthly average of 4.5 million rounds.[47]

Table 2
Artillery Shells Fired by the French Army in the R.F.V., 21 February – 15 April 1916[46]

Caliber	Rounds Fired
75-mm.	3,818,935
80-mm.	45,040
90-mm.	115,730
95-mm.	168,825
105-mm.	168,070
120-mm.	484,970
155-mm.	372,585
220-mm.	9,665
240-mm.	602
305-mm.	74
TOTAL	5,184,496

Falkenhayn's plan had relied on the French to counterattack his German forces under their old doctrine of the *offensive à outrance*, but instead his soldiers faced a "storm of steel" from Pétain's artillery which caused the Germans to suffer grievous losses, thus making the battlefield of Verdun as much a "place of execution" for the Germans as for the French.

By May 1916 Pétain felt comfortable enough with the overall situation at Verdun to launch a counterattack aimed at retaking Fort Douaumont. Pétain placed artillery Col. Jacques Estienne in charge of the artillery support for the attack. Estienne explained, "The operation consists in directing on the position and in firing so as to get the greatest possible effectiveness out of our artillery, a thousand tons of shell a day for six or seven days, so as to dominate the enemy's artillery, to destroy his means of defense, and to break down his morale within the area of a hundred and fifty acres which is to be occupied."[48]

Dropping 2 million pounds of shell a day, for seven days, on an area of 150 acres would seem to be an amazing concentration of firepower, but when the French assault failed after three days of bloody combat Pétain concluded that "The lesson to be learned from this fighting was that, when we should renew the attempt, we must see that greater pressure [will be] applied by our artillery."[49]

The reason that the Germans were able to withstand the French shelling was, in part, due to the protection offered them by Fort Douaumont. The Germans had captured Douaumont virtually without a fight on 25 February, just prior to Pétain's arrival, when General Herr redeployed two corps and each corps commander thought that the other one would take responsibility for Douaumont. As a result neither corps commander had provided a garrison, and a German infantry company wandered in and occupied the abandoned fort. The tragic irony of Douaumont was that its mighty walls sheltered the German army rather than the French, which lost tens of thousands of men in a series of futile attempts to retake the fortress in the spring and summer of 1916.

Douaumont was the most modern fortress in the R.F.V., and its concrete walls withstood an incredible pounding from the artillery of both sides during the course of the battle. Pétain wrote, "At the lowest estimate, 120,000 shells fell on Douaumont. At least two thousand of these were of 270[-mm.] caliber or larger. The southern face of the casemates, of masonry construction [as opposed to concrete], was demolished by our artillery, but was the only part of the work to be destroyed."[50]

An examination of aerial photos taken of Fort Douaumont after the battle reveal that Pétain grievously underestimated the damage suffered by the fortress during the fighting, although it is true that the underground portions of Douaumont did indeed survive virtually intact, in spite of being hit by artillery shells far larger and more powerful than anything imagined by the engineers who had designed the fortress. Even the older fortresses in the R.F.V. proved capable of withstanding an incredible pounding, and the French sheltered wounded men and reserves as well as stockpiles of supplies in the many forts of the R.F.V.

The only other fort besides Douaumont which the French lost to the Germans during the battle was Fort Vaux, and the incredible defense put up by the French defenders of this humble fortification, approximately one-quarter the size of Douaumont, revealed the tremendous defensive benefits offered by the forts. Maj. Sylvain-Eugène Raynal and approximately 600 men, including many wounded soldiers who had sought shelter in the fort during the battle, defended Vaux. Fort Vaux was pounded daily by massive German railway guns and heavy howitzers of 150-mm. and larger and then attacked by an entire German corps, led by special assault teams armed with flamethrowers. Yet for almost an entire week Raynal and his gallant force turned aside the German assaults, until they were overcome by the one weakness of Fort Vaux, its lack of an internal water supply.[51]

Fort Vaux's water was stored in large cisterns that were refilled periodically once the water level declined to a certain depth. The German attack on Vaux fell at a time when the fort's cisterns were already low, and the Germans quickly surrounded the fort cutting off any attempt to move supplies there. Soon after the German attack struck, Raynal discovered that the gauges used for measuring the water in the cisterns were faulty and that his supply of water, which he already knew to be low, was in fact about half what he thought it was. Though there were many barrels of salted meat for food, the water shortage for the overcrowded garrison quickly reached crisis proportion until finally, after going two full days without water, Raynal was left with no other choice than to surrender his beleaguered force to the Germans.[52]

The heroic French defense of Vaux proved that, as was so often the case at Verdun, it was logistics that was the final arbiter. Vaux's stout walls had resisted incessant German shelling, and the gallant garrison had withstood the full fury of an entire German corps for almost a week. Yet in the end, the inability of the French to supply their garrison with water caused the fort to fall.

The beginning of the battle of the Somme on 1 July 1916 marked the end of Falkenhayn's offensive at Verdun, as the Germans were forced to shift large numbers of men and guns out of the Verdun sector and rush them north and west to halt the Anglo-French assault. The French contribution to the Somme offensive had been seriously reduced by the massive logistical pressures at Verdun, but the French Ninth Army, under the command of General Foch, did participate and, unlike the massive repulse the British suffered on the first day at the Somme, the French overran the German front line and secured virtually all of their objectives on the first day of the battle. In spite of its initial success, however, the Ninth Army's assault soon bogged down due to the failure of the British attack and inability of the French reserves to exploit their gains.[53]

Some staff officers at the G.Q.G. argued that had Pétain's rotation system not drained the French reserves, the decisive "breakthrough" so long sought after in the First World War would have occurred in the French sector at the Somme. This is certainly a debatable contention. Indeed it could equally be argued that without Pétain's rotation system the physical and moral strength of the French Army would have been so worn down by the struggle at Verdun that it would have been incapable of taking part at all in the Allied offensive along the Somme.[54]

Pétain launched limited offensives against the Germans in the R.F.V. during the summer of 1916, but he realized that if he was ever going to retake Douaumont he would need more artillery, especially "super-heavy" guns of 370-mm. or larger. The G.Q.G. promised Pétain that more artillery would be sent to Verdun and that two brand new 400-mm. mortars in particular would arrive by autumn. So he decided to bide his time until then, and the fighting at Verdun died down during the months of August and September. Meanwhile Pétain, Second Army commander General Nivelle, and the French tactical "genius" at Verdun, General de Brigade Charles Mangin, formulated their plans for an offensive aimed at retaking both Forts Douaumont and Vaux in October.[55]

While Pétain organized his counteroffensive, Kaiser Wilhelm II grew so restless over the failure of GERICHT to destroy the French that he dismissed Falkenhayn on 20 August 1916, replaced him as chief of the General Staff with Field Marshal Paul von Hindenburg, and named Hindenburg's brilliant associate, Erich Ludendorff, as First Quartermaster General. Neither Hindenburg nor Ludendorff was pleased with the German situation at Verdun. Hindenburg later wrote his assessment of the German situation there in August 1916:

Verdun had not fallen into our hands, and the hope of wearing down the French army in the mighty arc of fire which we had drawn round the northern and northeastern fronts of the fortress had not been realized. The battles there exhausted our troops like an open wound. The battlefield was a regular hell and regarded as such by the troops. When I look back now, I do not hesitate to say that on purely military grounds it would have been far better for us to have improved our situation at Verdun by the voluntary evacuation of the ground we had captured. In August 1916, however, I considered I could not adopt that course. To a large extent the flower of our best fighting troops had been sacrificed in the enterprise. The public at home still anticipated a glorious issue to the offensive. It would be only too easy to produce the impression that all these sacrifices had been incurred in vain.[56]

Hindenburg's statement reveals that the Germans themselves had become obsessed with Verdun, and that there could thus be no easy end to this contest. It would be a fight to the finish for both sides, no matter what the cost.

The French offensive planned over the summer began on 24 October 1916. It was supported by the fire of 300 pieces of heavy artillery (155-mm. and larger), including the new "super-heavy" 400-mm. guns which directed their crushing fire against the massive walls of Fort Douaumont and the less impressive, but equally sturdy, defenses of Fort Vaux. The French employed a novel form of artillery support in this offensive. They abandoned the former practice of conducting days, or even weeks, of preparatory bombardment, which cost them the element of surprise, in favor of one massive all-out barrage lasting only a few hours. This "drumfire barrage" was followed by a new artillery tactic developed by the French at Verdun called the "creeping barrage," which coordinated artillery fires with the attacking infantry so as to drop a curtain of steel in front of the advancing troops as they slowly moved forward. The attacking French forces met a badly demoralized and exhausted group of German defenders, who gave way under the massive impetus of the French offensive. The French retook Fort Douaumont on the first day of the offensive after a brief, hard fight, and Fort Vaux was retaken one week later.[57]

The recapture of Fort Douaumont by the French marked the beginning of the end for the Germans at Verdun. French historian Jacques Meyer, himself a veteran of Verdun, later wrote that "They [the Germans] crumbled as we regained our feet. As the loss of Douaumont, through confusion and surprise, had long demoralized the French, its recapture in the autumn of 1916 sealed the reverse of the Germans and definitely destroyed their hopes. . . . They would not take

Verdun; they would not yet finish a war which might never end."[58]

The battle of Verdun would sputter on until 15 December 1916, when the French launched a final offensive that, after three days of hard fighting, forced the Germans back almost entirely to the positions they had originally occupied when the battle had begun in February.

The French Army's magnificent stand at Verdun was a logistical feat of monumental proportions. For the first time in warfare, motorized supply columns had supported an entire army of over 500,000 men in the field almost exclusively. While credit for this success goes to many men, certainly General Pétain should be granted the lion's share.

Pétain implemented his doctrine of firepower at Verdun first to halt the German offensive and then to literally blast the Germans back to their original positions. Pétain's ceaseless activity in organizing and running the massive effort which was required to build and maintain a large force at Verdun and then defeat the Germans in a battle of attrition, in spite of the R.F.V.'s poor lines of communication and supply, certainly represented a logistical achievement of the first order. Yet though he was most assuredly the savior of Verdun, Pétain himself gave credit to all the soldiers who, whether on the front lines or in a support capacity, contributed to the French victory. Addressing a gathering of French veterans at the 1927 dedication ceremony for the *Ossuaire* in which the remains of many of those who had fallen at Verdun would be interred, Pétain stated that

Every man of you should be mentioned by name, soldiers of Verdun, soldiers in the line and soldiers in the rear. For if I give the place of honor, as is meet, to those who fell in the front of the battle, still I know that their courage would have availed nothing without the patient toil, continued day and night, to the last limit of their strength, on the part of the men to whose efforts were due the regular arrival of the reinforcements, of munitions, and of food, and the evacuation of wounded: the truck drivers along the Sacred Way, the railroad engineers, the ambulance force.[59]

Verdun had held, and, though the French Army had paid a dear price for its victory, it had saved its nation's cause for one more year and had brought Imperial Germany one step closer to its demise.

Robert E. Bruce is a Ph.D. candidate in history at Kansas State University.

NOTES

1. Professor Stéphane Audoin-Rouzeau, interviewed in the video series *The Great War and the Shaping of the 20th Century* (New York, 1996).
2. General Pétain's French rank was *général de division*, as was the rank of every other French general mentioned in this article with the exception of the French Army's commander, General Joseph Jacques Césaire Joffre.
3. Erich von Falkenhayn, *General Headquarters, 1914–1916, and Its Critical Decisions* (London, 1919), pp. 210–11.
4. Ibid., p. 209.
5. Ibid., pp. 217–18.
6. Charles W. Sanders, Jr., "No Other Law: The French Army and the Doctrine of the Offensive," Rand Paper P–7331 (Santa Monica, Calif., 1987), pp. 2–3.
7. Joffre was named vice-president of the *Conseil Supérieur de la Guerre*, with the minister of war (a civilian) serving as president. In time of war, the vice president of this body was designated to become commander-in-chief of the French Army, while in time of peace his title was chief of the General Staff. See Joseph Joffre, *The Personal Memoirs of Joffre*, trans. T. Bentley Mott, 2 vols. (New York, 1932), 2: 3–13.
8. Ferdinand Foch, *De la conduite de la guerre: la manoeuvre pour la bataille*, 5th ed. (Paris, 1919); Douglas Porch, *The March to the Marne: The French Army 1871–1914* (New York, 1981); and Ronald H. Cole, "'Forward With the Bayonet': The French Army Prepares for Offensive War, 1911–1914," University of Maryland Ph.D. dissertation, 1975.
9. Jean-Jacques Becker, "Mourir à Verdun," *Histoire* 76 (April 1985): 24, and "Pertes des Armées Françaises (Nord-Est et Orient) Reparties Par Periodes," Journal Officiel, Documents parliamentaires, Session extraordinaire 1920, Annexe 633, Séance du 29 Mars 1920, proposition de résolution Marin. Reprinted in Winston S. Churchill, *The World Crisis*, 5 vols. (London, 1923–31), 3 (pt. 1): 290.

10. Richard M. Watt, *Dare Call It Treason* (New York, 1963), pp. 101–05. Pétain would be named to the position of commander-in-chief of the French Army in 1917 and be promoted to the rank of Marshal of France shortly after the war's end. For more information on Pétain before and during the Great War, see: Guy Pedroncini, *Pétain*, vol. 1: *Le soldat et la gloire, 1856–1918* (Paris, 1989); Bernard Serrigny, *Trente ans avec Pétain* (Paris, 1959); and Stephen Ryan, *Pétain the Soldier* (New York, 1969).
11. Joffre, *Memoirs*, 2: 588–89.
12. Ibid., 2: 597.
13. Ibid., 2: 599, and David T. Zabecki, *Steel Wind: Colonel Georg Bruchmüller and the Birth of Modern Artillery* (Westport, Conn., 1994), p. 8.
14. Joffre, *Memoirs*, 2: 597.
15. Ibid., 2: 600–601.
16. Ibid., 2: 438–40; Alistair Horne, *The Price of Glory* (New York, 1962), pp. 52–53.
17. Joffre, *Memoirs*, 2: 440.
18. Horne, *The Price of Glory*, pp. 70–82.
19. Henri Philippe Pétain, *Verdun*, trans Margaret MacVeagh (New York, 1930), p. 70.
20. Ibid., pp. 71–72.
21. Ibid.
22. Ibid., p. 95.
23. Ministère des Armées, "L'action du service automobile dans les grands batailles de 1914–1918," *Revue historique des armées* 5 (September 1978): 85.
24. Ibid., pp. 89–92.
25. Horne, *The Price of Glory*, pp.146–47.
26. Pétain, *Verdun*, pp. 95–99, with the quotation on pp. 95–96; France, Armée, Etat-major, Service Historique, *Les Armées Françaises Dans la Grand Guerre*, 11 tomes (Paris, 1922-37), Tome IV: *Verdun et la Somme*, vol. 1 (henceforth *LAF*), annex 1232.
27. Horne, *The Price of Glory*, pp.147–48.
28. Pétain, *Verdun*, p. 96.
29. Ibid.
30. Ibid., pp. 96–99.
31. *LAF*, annex 1261.
32. France, Armée, Etat-major, Service Historique, *Les Armées Françaises dans la Grande Guerre*, Tome IV, vol. 3, p. 509. Also see "Pertes des Armées Françaises (Nord-Est et Orient)"; Holger Herwig, *The First World War: Germany and Austria–Hungary 1914–1918* (New York, 1997) p. 184, and Horne, *The Price of Glory*, pp. 327–28.
33. Leonard V. Smith, *Between Mutiny and Obedience: The Case of the French Fifth Infantry Division during World War I* (Princeton, N.J., 1994), pp. 126–27.
34. Eric J. Leed, *No Man's Land: Combat & Identity in World War I* (Cambridge, England, 1979), pp. 170–74; Great Britain, War Office, *Report of the War Office Committee of Enquiry into "Shell-shock"* (London, 1922).
35. Leed, *No Man's Land*, pp. 176–80.
36. Pétain, *Verdun*, pp. 122–23.
37. Ibid., pp. 117–18 and 133–34, with the quotation on pp. 133–34.
38. Erich Ludendorff, *Ludendorff's Own Story, August 1914 – November 1918*, reprint ed., 2 vols. (Freeport, N.Y., 1971) 1: 401–02.
39. Jean de Pierrefeu, *French Headquarters, 1915–1918*, trans. C. J. C. Street (London, 1924), p. 73.
40. Joffre, *Memoirs*, 2: 449–50.
41. Pétain *Verdun*, pp. 121–22; Pierrefeu, *French Headquarters*, p. 73.
42. Pétain, *Verdun*, pp. 127–28: Joffre, *Memoirs*, 2: 451.
43. Joffre, *Memoirs*, 2: 450.
44. Pétain, *Verdun*, pp. 93.
45. *LAF*, annex 1346.
46. Ibid., annex 2105.
47. Zabecki, *Steel Wind*, p. 8.
48. Pétain, *Verdun*, pp. 149.
49. Ibid., p. 158.
50. Ibid., p. 228.
51. Sylvain-Eugène Raynal, *Le Drame du Fort Vaux* (Paris, 1919); Pétain, *Verdun*, pp. 164–71.
52. Raynal, *Le Drame du Fort Vaux*; Horne, *The Price of Glory*, pp.252–66.
53. Joffre, *Memoirs*, 2: 461–88.
54. Pierrefeu, *French Headquarters*, pp. 73–74.
55. Pétain, *Verdun*, p. 194.
56. Paul von Hindenburg, *Out of My Life* (New York, 1921), pp. 201, 262.
57. Alain Derizot, "Verdun, Novembre 1916: Victoire en enfer," *Historama*, no. 33 (November 1986): 10–21.
58. Jacques Meyer, "Verdun, 1916" in George A. Panichas, ed., *Promise of Greatness: The War of 1914–1918* (London, 1968), p. 64.
59. Pétain, *Verdun*, pp. 210–13.

[14]
The Meaning of Attrition, 1914–1916

THE phrase 'the strategy of attrition' has now become a pejorative term used to describe British war policy between 1916 and 1918. Lord Hankey, the secretary of the various Cabinet committees responsible for the conduct of the war, argued in his memoirs that the Asquith coalition government adopted the policy of attrition at the beginning of 1916. The evacuation of Gallipoli made it apparent that there would be no rapid end to the war and ministers felt they had no option other than to accept the recommendations of the Chantilly conference of 6–8 December 1915 that the British should concentrate their army in France to take part in a grand co-ordinated allied offensive in 1916.[1] Two of Sir Douglas Haig's earliest post-war apologists, G. A. B. Dewar and J. H. Boraston, argued that for the British the battle of the Somme marked the start of 'the real war of attrition...',[2] a contention which has been followed by others not always so sympathetic to Haig.[3]

The exponents of attrition have been censured on the grounds that their policy involved an enormous waste of life and treasure for little apparent gain and that a modicum of imagination would have shown that there were easier and certainly less costly ways of waging the war. In February 1916 the Labour MP and future Chancellor of the Exchequer, Phillip Snowden, warned the House of Commons that 'War by attrition will be long and costly and it will leave everyone of the belligerent nations financially and commercially ruined...'.[4] In 1923 Winston Churchill wrote in *The World Crisis* that during the battle of the Somme 'The flower of that generous manhood which quitted civilian life in every kind of workaday occupation, which came at the call of Britain, and as we may still hope, at the call of humanity, and came from the most remote parts of her Empire, was shorn away for ever in 1916.'[5] And in his *Great Contemporaries* he returned to the charge, characterizing Sir Douglas Haig as being 'unconscious of any theatre but the Western Front. There were the Germans in their trenches. Here he stood at the head of an army corps, then of an army, and finally of a group of mighty armies. Hurl them on and keep slogging at it in the best possible way – that was war.'[6] Churchill's friend and political ally J. E. B. Seely, a former Secretary of State for War in Asquith's pre-war Liberal administration and a brigade commander in France during the war, wrote bitterly in his memoirs that

---

1. Lord Hankey, *The Supreme Command 1914–1918* (London, 1961), ii. 466–67.
2. G. A. B. Dewar and Lt Col J. H. Boraston, *Sir Douglas Haig's Command, December 19th, 1915 to November 11, 1918* (London, 1922), i. 87.
3. See, for example, B. H. Liddell Hart, *Reputations* (London, 1928), p. 100.
4. 80 HC. Deb. 5s., col. 718.
5. W. S. Churchill, *The World Crisis 1911–1918* (London, 1931–68), p. 750.
6. W. S. Churchill, *Great Contemporaries* (London, 1939), p. 230.

THE MEANING OF ATTRITION, 1914–1916

'Some foolish people on the allied side thought that the war would be ended on the Western Front by killing off the Germans. Of course this method could only succeed if we killed a great many more of them than we lost ourselves.'[1]

But the most sustained and passionate condemnation of the strategy of attrition flowed from the pen of David Lloyd George, the Prime Minister who presided over Britain's victory in 1918. In his *War Memoirs* he insisted that allied strategy, especially in the first two years of the war, had been fatally mistaken. Instead of exploiting the immense superiority in manpower which the Entente powers of Russia, France, the British Empire, Serbia, Italy, Roumania and Belgium possessed and instead of attacking the Central Powers where they were weakest, on the eastern and Balkan fronts, the British government heeded the advice of Lord Kitchener and threw their weight into the war on the western front. 'We hammered at the breastplate of Achilles and neglected his heel. And we called it sometimes "striking at the vital parts" and sometimes "attrition".'[2] This article will attempt to demonstrate that attrition was in fact first adopted by the British in early 1915, not early 1916 and that it was originally designed to minimise British casualties and not, as it must have seemed to its critics in 1916, to maximize them.

In 1914 Asquith's Liberal government had three objectives. They sought to hold together for the duration of the war the Entente Alliance, which was created by the Pact of London of 5 September 1914; they wished to defeat the Central Powers; and they wanted to ensure that when the time came for the belligerents to make peace that Britain was the strongest of them all and therefore was in a position to impose her peace terms on both her enemies and her allies. They confidently expected to be able to achieve these ends at comparatively little cost to themselves. In August 1914, after some hesitation, the Cabinet despatched a small expeditionary force to northern France as a token of their determination to stand by France and Russia. But they intended that Britain's main war effort would revolve around her navy and her economy. The navy began to impose a blockade on the Central Powers and enabled Britain and her dominions to gobble up Germany's overseas colonies at leisure. The Cabinet hoped that they could be used as bargaining counters at the eventual peace conference. And by September 1914 British bankers and manufacturers were beginning to supply the allies, at a price, with the money and munitions they needed to defeat the German and Austrian armies. This was the strategy of 'business as usual'.[3]

---

1. J. E. B. Seeley, *Adventure* (London, 1930), pp. 229–30.
2. D. Lloyd George, *War Memoirs* (London, 1933), pp. 618–19.
3. D. French, *British Economic and Strategic Planning, 1905–1915* (London, 1982), pp. 98–123.

THE MEANING OF ATTRITION, 1914–1916

In the meantime Lord Kitchener had begun to raise his New Armies. Why he did so deserves some explanation because it throws important light on the origins of attrition and because in 1916 they provided the military wherewithal which allowed Haig and Robertson to pursue their own variant of it. But it is a question to which there is no easy answer. Kitchener was an autocratic centralizer who was loath to work through elaborate committee and council systems and equally loath to commit his thoughts to paper if he could avoid it. As a result he never wrote a full account of his reasons for raising the Kitchener armies. The historian therefore has to turn to remarks he made in the comparatively few state papers he did write or to incidental comments he made which were written down by colleagues and friends. Lord Esher recorded in his diary two private conversations with Kitchener in which he gave some glimpses of the notions behind his plans. On 13 August Esher recorded that Sir Archibald Murray, the chief of staff of the British Expeditionary Force, believed that financial and economic exhaustion would mean that the war would not last longer than eight months. He then added that 'I had two hours with Lord Kitchener yesterday, and this is not his opinion. He thinks that if things go wrong, the war might last two or three years at least.'[1] Kitchener's own experience in Egypt and the Sudan had demonstrated, at least to his own satisfaction, that it was possible to wage war on a financial shoestring. His private secretary at the War Office, Sir George Arthur, recorded in his biography of his dead chief that Lord Cromer once wrote of him that 'He did not think that extravagance was the necessary handmaid of efficiency. On the contrary he was a rigid economist and, whilst making adequate provision for all essential and necessary expenditure, suppressed with a firm hand any tendency towards waste and extravagance.'[2] Kitchener explained why he believed that German resistance would be so prolonged in his second conversation with Esher on 9 October. He reminded Esher that in the American Civil War, even though the Confederate States only began to organize themselves for war after it had broken out they were still able to fight for four years. This was despite the fact that they could place only one and a half million men in the field compared to the three million men mustered by the North. The German economy in 1914 was in a much stronger position than the Confederacy had been at the outbreak of the Civil War. Germany's domestic food supply was probably well organized for war. The Entente's blockade was not water-tight as she could still purchase food from the Baltic states. Like the Southern States the Germans were determined to fight the war to the bitter end. 'No financial pressure has ever yet stopped a war in progress', he concluded. 'At the end of the American War, there were a million lads of under

1. Esher diary, 13 August 1914, Esher MSS 2/13.
2. Sir George Arthur, *Life of Lord Kitchener* (London, 1920), i. 70–1.

388 THE MEANING OF ATTRITION, 1914–1916 April

17 in arms for the North; and in the Armies of the South, boys of fourteen and fifteen were fighting in large numbers. It should be assumed that before Germany relinquishes the struggle, she will have exhausted every possible supply of men and material'.[1]

It therefore followed that it was worthwhile to raise large numbers of new troops because the war would not be over quickly. Kitchener explained the role he hoped they would play in an interview he gave a few days after entering the War Office to Lt Col Charles a Court Repington, the military correspondent of *The Times*. 'He allowed', Repington later recorded, 'that we had stout Allies, but said that France was throwing the whole of her manhood into the field, leaving little behind except the successive annual contingents of recruits, while Russia, with all her immense capacity for defence, had untried and unproved offensive powers. He thought, in these circumstances, that the war would last very long, and that it was his duty so to prepare our land forces that by their steadily expanding numbers and constantly increasing efficiency they should enable us to play a part worthy of England, and at the peace to impose terms in consonance with our interests. ... There must, he declared, be no question of peace except in our terms...'.[2] The troops of the Kitchener armies were enlisted for three years, or the duration of the war, because Kitchener wished to ensure, as he told the Financial Secretary of the War Office, that 'our Army should reach its full strength at the beginning of the third year of the War, just when France is getting into rather low water and Germany is beginning to feel the pinch.'[3]

He gave some indication of why he was so determined that Britain should be the dominant military power at the peace conference in two Cabinet memoranda he wrote in the spring of 1915. The first was written on 16 March as part of the Cabinet's discussions of Britain's desiderata in the Middle East in the aftermath of the signing of the Constantinople agreement, and the second on 21 April in reply to a suggestion by Lord Haldane that the Cabinet should give serious consideration to the establishment of a post-war League of Nations charged with the settlement of international disputes. Kitchener had spent most of his career defending the frontiers of the empire against France and Russia. He did not believe that the mere fact that Britain was now allied to them meant that the war had extinguished their pre-war rivalries and he was afraid that in the post-war world they would reassert themselves. Consequently he was anxious to secure a peace settlement which would increase Britain's security not just against her current enemies, the Central Powers, but against her current allies, France and Russia, as well. If at the end of the war Russia acquired

---

1. Esher diary, 9 October 1914, Esher MSS 2/13.
2. Lt Col C. a Court Repington, *The First World War 1914–1918* (London, 1920), i. 21–2.
3. Arthur, *Life of Lord Kitchener*, iii. 244.

THE MEANING OF ATTRITION, 1914-1916

Constantinople and France acquired Syria, they would both be able to menace Egypt. He therefore wanted to maintain a Turkish buffer state stretching from Anatolia to the Persian frontier to ensure that Britain and Russia did not have a common land frontier and he wanted Britain herself to acquire Mesopotamia together with the port of Alexandretta as its Mediterranean outlet. The alternative was that the Russians would be free to occupy the country and menace the Persian Gulf and British India.[1]

This evidence suggests that when Kitchener was raising the New Armies he did not intend that they should be prematurely committed to a series of costly wearing-out battles on the western front. In 1914, like his Liberal colleagues, he was for the time being content to pursue 'business as usual' and to allow the main burden of the land fighting to fall upon the French and Russian armies. In the meantime he intended to prepare his own troops so that by the begining of the third year of the war, when the French, Russian, German and Austro-Hungarian armies had fought each other to a standstill and were running short of men, Britain's reserves of military manpower would still be intact. She would then be able to dominate the councils of the Entente, her armies would inflict the coup de grace upon the Central Powers, and she would be able to dictate her own peace terms to her allies and enemies alike. The New Armies were intended to win the peace for Britain, after the French and Russians had all but won the war. But the *sine qua non* of this policy was that the British could not afford to commit the great bulk of their armies to a costly continental land war until early 1917.

One of Kitchener's predictions about the likely course of the war was quickly proven to be correct. By late 1914 it was apparent that the war would not end quickly because the belligerents' economies were exhausted. However that did not put an end to the notion that the war would end through exhaustion. If the money did not run out, the men would. The casualties which the belligerents suffered were far beyond anything they had expected. In April 1906 the Director of Military Training, Major-General F. W. Stopford, had estimated that an Expeditionary Force of 140,000 men would loose 65–75 per cent of its strength during the first year of a war (i.e. 91,000–105,000 men). In fact by the end of the first battle of Ypres, after only three months of fighting, the BEF had lost 89,000 casualties.[2]

Losses on this scale provoked two reactions. The first was the comforting belief that however much Britain and her allies had suffered, the enemy's losses were always worse. In October 1914, for example, the head of the secret service at GHQ insisted that the Germans were

---

1. P[ublic] R[ecord] O[ffice] CAB 42/2/10. Lord Kitchener, Alexandretta and Mesopotamia, 16 March 1915; PRO CAB 37/127/34. Lord Kitchener, The future relations of the Great Powers, 21 April 1915.
2. PRO WO 32/8813. F. W. Stopford, Wastage in war, 26 April 1906.

390   THE MEANING OF ATTRITION, 1914–1916   April

losing three soldiers to the BEF's two.¹ The second was revulsion against the circumstances which sent British soldiers into battle with too few guns and shells to suppress the enemy's fire, coupled with the determination that the same fate must not befall the New Armies. On 9 October Asquith, Grey and Lloyd George combined to force Kitchener to accept the establishment of a Cabinet committee on munitions. Kitchener had already placed orders for guns to equip eighteen new divisions by June 1915. The Cabinet committee arbitrarily trebled his orders and asked for them to be delivered by May 1915.² This question did not have the same urgency for Kitchener that it did for his colleagues because he did not intend to commit the bulk of the New Armies to battle until early 1917 and by then even his somewhat lackadaisical methods of procuring supplies would have come good. However he never explained his timetable for the New Armies to his colleagues on the grounds that they could not keep a secret. 'If they will only all divorce their wives I will tell them everything!' he told Hankey.³ They would not, so he did not.

At the end of December 1914 several politicians, notably Churchill and Lloyd George, suggested that if the stalemate which had descended on the western front at the end of the first battle of Ypres persisted in the spring the Cabinet should consider despatching the New Armies to other theatres. By contrast Sir John French, the commander-in-chief of the British Expeditionary Force (BEF), wanted immediate reinforcements so that he could mount an attack along the Belgium coast. Once again Kitchener did not welcome their interference. In August 1914 he had promised Sir Archibald Murray, Sir John French's chief of staff, that 'he did not intend to leave the Continent until the Germans were utterly crushed',⁴ but he had not changed his mind about his timetable. And now in addition he was reluctant to send large numbers of troops abroad because of persistent rumours that the Germans were contemplating launching an invasion of Britain. He therefore sought to administer a soothing bromide which would calm his colleagues' impatience for quick action. He ordered Sir Charles Callwell, the Director of Military Operations at the War Office, to write a paper 'to prove that the Germans will run out of men within the next few months....'.⁵ As a statistical conjuring trick Callwell's memorandum was a *tour de force*. Although he estimated that the Central Powers had more men

---

1. Kirke diary entry, 29 October 1914, Kirke MSS Imperial War Museum.
2. PRO CAB 37/35/51. Asquith to the King, 9 October 1914; PRO CAB 37/35/53. Asquith to the King, 16 October 1914; PRO MUN 5/6/170/30. Notes on the supply of guns prior to the formation of the Ministry of Munitions, August 1914–June 1915; PRO T 181/65. Notes by Major General Sir S. von Donop, 6 July 1935; E. David (ed.), *Inside Asquith's Cabinet: From the diaries of Charles Hobhouse* (London, 1977), p. 197.
3. Hankey, *The Supreme Command*, i. 221.
4. PRO 79/62. A. J. Murray, Note of conversation with Lord Kitchener, Wellesley House, Aldershot, 14 August 1914.
5. Callwell to Sir Henry Wilson, 2 January 1915, Wilson MSS 73/1/18.

actually in the field than the Entente (4.2 million compared to 3.25 million) he suggested that time was on the side of the Entente because they had the greater reserves. He assumed that as the Germans were fighting on two fronts their losses had to be twice those of their enemies. He made no allowance for new classes of recruits just about to reach military age and he took too little account of the possibility that the Germans might find more soldiers by combing-out non-essential industries. These statistical sleights of hand enabled him to conclude that the Germans had only enough men to keep their armies at their present strength for between four and a half to six months. The Austrians were in a slightly better position in that although they did not have sufficient men to raise more divisions 'there seems to be no reason to suppose that the army would actually run short of men within the immediate future'. But the Entente powers were in a far superior position. The French had enough men to keep their field army up to strength for another thirteen months and the Russians, with reserves estimated to total 20 million men, could go on indefinitely. And so, he concluded

> Germany can do no more in the way of increasing her armies, and will, a very few months hence, begin to feel the want of resources in men to keep her existing armies up to strength; Austria-Hungary is far more likely to go backwards in respect to numbers than to go forward. France, on the other hand, should find no difficulty in maintaining her field [army] constantly at its present strength for many months to come, and Russia ought to begin to get over her difficulties with regard to armament in about three months, and ought to have greatly improved her position within six months. Servia and Belgium can do little, but the great expansion of the British forces in the early future has to be reckoned with, and this should prove the decisive factor in the later stages of the contest.[1]

Callwell realised that his conclusions were quite bogus. 'I could just as easily have proved that they [the Germans] were good for another two years. One must be a mug indeed if one cannot prove anything with figures as counters', he informed his friend Henry Wilson.[2] But many of Kitchener's political colleagues swallowed Callwell's conclusions whole. Asquith predicted that the war would be over by the end of the summer. Haldane told Beatrice Webb that 'By next Xmas he expects to have peace. The basis of his optimism is the exhaustion of German manpower.'[3] Perhaps only Lloyd George did not share their optimism. On 22 February he argued that the Germans had already won a string of spectacular victories which left them in occupation of large tracts of allied territory, that Russia's manpower reserves

---

1. PRO CAB 42/1/10. General Staff, War Office, The War. A comparison of the belligerent forces, 6 January 1915.
2. Callwell to Wilson, 2 January 1915, Wilson MSS 73/1/18.
3. N. and J. MacKenzie (eds), *The Diary of Beatrice Webb. Volume 3, 1905–1924. The Power to alter Things* (London, 1984), p. 223; M. and E. Brock (eds), *H. H. Asquith: Letters to Venetia Stanley* (Oxford, 1982), pp. 378, 398.

were useless unless they could be armed and that it therefore behoved the British to hasten the preparations of the New Armies.[1] Kitchener tried to administer another dose of the same bromide. He informed the War Council, a Cabinet committee which met intermittently to discuss strategy, that 'If we are victorious, the end of the war must come through one of the two following causes: (1) By a decisive victory, or a succession of decisive victories, of the Allies... (2) by attrition, for when Germany is no longer able to support her armies in sufficient strength in the field she must sue for peace.' And he concluded that 'As far as I can judge now, I think that about the beginning of 1917 this state of affairs may be reached.'[2]

In his *War Memoirs* Lloyd George claimed that Kitchener's memorandum was 'the first in which our Generals committed themselves to the idea of a "War of Attrition." Their avowed aim was to "break through" and drive the Germans back across the Rhine, a routed and broken mob, chased by cavalry.'[3] But Lloyd George's assertion was a parody of Kitchener's concept of attrition. In the spring of 1915 Kitchener doubted whether it would be possible to break through the German line and he was very reluctant to commit his New Armies to any attempts to do so. At this time Kitchener's policy of attrition meant little more than simply preparing the New Armies whilst the French and Russian armies wore down the Central Power's manpower reserves. But Sir John French was temperamentally ill-suited for any policy which required him to 'wait and see' and was under constant pressure from General Joffre, the French commander-in-chief, to assist him in expelling the Germans from France. In March Sir John used part of his existing forces in an attempt to pierce the enemy's defences at Neuve Chapelle, to prove to Kitchener that the line could be broken and to prove to the French that the British were reliable allies. The attack failed but French and Joffre decided that a second Anglo-French offensive had to be launched in May, claiming that their forces enjoyed a numerical superiority over the Germans, that their morale was higher and that the Russians needed their help. But Kitchener was adamant. Apart from two Territorial divisions already earmarked for the BEF he would not send the New Armies to France 'till the line was broken.'[4] Undaunted Sir John tried again, at Aubers ridge and Festubert, and again he failed.

The resulting 'shell scandal' was the occasion for the fall of the Asquith government and nearly cost Kitchener his job. It also made

---

1. PRO CAB 42/1/35. Lloyd George, Some further considerations on the conduct of the war, 22 February 1915.
2. PRO CAB 42/1/38. Lord Kitchener, Remarks by the Secretary of State for War on the Chancellor of the Exchequer's memorandum (G-7) on the conduct of the war, 25 February 1915.
3. Lloyd George, *War Memoirs*, i. 259.
4. H. Wilson, Notes on a meeting at Chantilly 29 March 1915, Wilson MSS 73/1/19; R. Holmes, *The Little Field-Marshal: Sir John French* (London, 1981), p. 285.

him more determined than ever not to sanction any more premature attempts to break through the German line. On 29 May he told Hankey that he had been wrong to give in to Sir John's and Joffre's importunities to send infantry to France before he had enough guns and shells to support them and he strongly deprecated another offensive on the western front. But at the beginning of May the Germans had broken the Russian front at Gorlice-Tarnow and the Russians looked to their allies in the west for help. On 22 May the Grand Duke Nicholas, the Russian commander-in-chief, asked Joffre and Sir John 'Whether we intend to "Attack" in the West or rely on a policy of "attrition"'.[1] Kitchener's preference was very much for attrition. He was afraid that if the allies launched another premature offensive they would simply exhaust their own reserves and enable the Germans to bring back their troops from Russia and inflict a serious defeat on the Anglo-French armies in the west. He left Hankey with the impression that 'Lord Kitchener's strategy is to continue for the present the war of attrition in the hope that the Germans will continue to break themselves up by costly attempts to shatter our lines – attempts which can never succeed as long as we keep proper reserves in hand to meet them.'[2]

It is only with the benefit of hindsight that it is possible to see that Kitchener was indulging in a certain amount of wishful thinking. His own past experience had taught him how effective allowing the enemy to attack a strongly defended position could be. He had made his own reputation at Omdurmann where he had allowed the Dervishes to dash themselves to pieces against his own troops. And by contrast he had almost lost it at Paardeberg when he had hurled his own infantry against well dug-in Boer positions.[3] Some substance was given to his view of an impending German attack by the fact that by April 1915 the Germans had raised fourteen new divisions and deployed them in the west. Sir George MacDonogh, French's Director of Military Intelligence, misunderstood their role and exaggerated their strength. He believed that the Germans had in fact concentrated twelve new corps in the west to mount an offensive, either towards the Toul-Epinal gap or in the Argonne. Kitchener agreed about the size and purpose of the force but thought that the offensive would come somewhere south of Arras or in Flanders. But unfortunately the Germans refused to oblige. They had no plans to attack in the west in the summer of 1915.[4]

Thus Kitchener prevaricated when he was asked to send more troops to France. On 29 May he informed the French that he would send

1. French diary entry, 22 May 1915, French MSS vol. K.
2. PRO WO 159/7. Hankey to Kitchener, 29 May 1915.
3. T. Royle, *The Kitchener Enigma* (London, 1985), pp. 128-32, 169-72.
4. Kirke diary entries, 14 and 16 July 1915, Kirke MSS; Wilson diary entry, 14 July 1915, Wilson MSS (microfilm reel 6); R. Blake, *The Private Papers of Douglas Haig, 1914-1919* (London, 1952), pp. 97-8.

no more than three new divisions to France in the forseeable future and three weeks later Joffre's summer offensive finally halted. When Joffre then asked the British to send twelve more divisions to France by mid-July to relieve French troops for another major offensive, the most that Kitchener would offer was six divisions by mid-August.[1] Kitchener's Cabinet colleagues shared his reluctance to agree to the BEF taking part in another premature and costly offensive. As Arthur Balfour, the First Lord of the Admiralty wrote, 'There is no prospect, I believe, of the Allies obtaining an old-fashioned victory over the Germans at this stage of the war'.[2]

Kitchener's unchallenged control of British strategic policy waned in the summer of 1915. This was partly a result of his close identification with the failure of the Dardanelles campaign but also because increasing numbers of disquieting reports began to reach the Dardanelles Committee from both France and Russia. Since November 1914 the British had been aware that the Germans were trying to reach a separate peace with one or more of Britain's allies and in the summer of 1915 reports also began to reach them of the growing influence of politicians like Joseph Caillaux in France and the 'reactionaries' who surrounded the court in Russia, who were disgusted by Britain's reluctance to commit herself to the continental land war and who might be ready to listen to German blandishments.[3] The British high command in France played skilfully on these reports. On 3 August Sir William Robertson, who had replaced Murray as French's chief of staff in January, sent Kitchener a memorandum insisting that if the Germans took Warsaw it 'would render Russia powerless for an indefinite time, and might conceivably lead to the conclusion of a separate peace with her', and that 'As Germany's best chance of obtaining decisive success depends on her ability to force Russia to a separate peace, it is obviously of the first importance that Russia should be afforded relief as early as possible, and no consideration of any kind should be allowed to interfere with this being done.'[4] Haig warned that unless some progress was made in driving the Germans out of France the 'peace-party may get the upper hand & peace may be made before winter',[5] whilst Sir Henry Wilson, the head of the British military mission to Joffre, told Kitchener that 'It lies with us to pull the poor French soldiers & people thro' their difficulties of Bosch in front & Caillaux behind.'[6]

This pressure gradually wore down Kitchener and his colleagues. On 2 July Balfour told the Cabinet that 'the work of attrition can

1. PRO WO 159/7. Note of a meeting held at the War Office, 8 June 1915 and Note by Lord Kitchener, 9 June 1915.
2. PRO 30/57/78/WV/49. Balfour to Kitchener, 6 June 1915.
3. D. French, *British Strategy and War Aims, 1914–1916* (London, 1986), pp. 105–8.
4. PRO WO 159/4. General Staff [Robertson], Note on the general military situation, 3 August 1915.
5. Haig to Asquith, 25 June 1915, Asquith MSS vol. 14, ff. 70–3.
6. Kitchener to Sir John French and Note by Wilson, 16 August 1915, Wilson MSS 73/1/19.

best be furthered by the allies in the West carrying on the work of attrition by means of an "active defence".[1] Churchill was prepared to support the French by 'an active defence, inflicting as much loss as possible on the enemy, & nibbling & gnawing along the whole front, but no great offensive movement until ample supplies of ammunition are available.'[2] At an Anglo-French conference held at Calais a few days later the British opted for a policy of 'nibbling & gnawing'. They gave the French a timetable showing when the New Armies would be ready and when they would be sent to France, but also pointed out that they were short of artillery ammunition, that they could only be used to hold the trenches and were not ready to take part in major offensive operations. They urged the French not to mount another offensive but agreed that if they felt that delays were impossible then Sir John would do what he could to support them but would take care that his support would not be 'unduly costly to his army'.[3]

This uneasy compromise lasted for only six weeks. It collapsed in late August in the face of the failure of Sir Ian Hamilton's second major attempt to carry the Gallipoli peninsula, the German capture of Warsaw and two political crises in Paris and Petrograd which frightened the Cabinet into believing that the very stability of the Entente alliance would be endangered unless they agreed to the BEF participating in the major offensive Joffre planned for the autumn.[4] The government's growing alarm was clearly reflected in the orders Haig was given about how he was to assist the French in the autumn offensive Joffre still insisted on launching. On 7 August Sir John ordered him to plan an attack at Loos but cautioned that it was 'to be made chiefly with artillery and I am not to launch a large force of infantry to the attack of objectives which are so strongly held as to be liable to result only in the sacrifice of many lives.' But only twelve days later Kitchener himself effectively countermanded that order. He told Haig that, because of the Russian situation, *we must act with all our energy, and do our utmost to help the French, even though by so doing, we suffered very heavy losses indeed.*'[5]

The end of the Anglo-French autumn offensive in Artois and the Champagne left the Entente no nearer victory. As Kitchener's power waned in the autumn of 1915 the General Staff's waxed. Senior officers like Haig and Robertson who had been closely associated with operations on the western front did not share the pessimism of Kitchener

---

1. PRO CAB 37/131/4. Balfour, Memorandum, 2 July 1915; French diary entry, 2 July 1915, French MSS vol. L.

2. Churchill to Lord Lansdowne, 2 July 1915, in M. Gilbert (ed.), *Winston S. Churchill*, vol. iii. *Companion*, pt. 2 (London, 1971), 1069.

3. PRO CAB 41/36/3. Asquith to the King, 3 July 1915; French diary entry, 6 July 1915, French MSS vol. L; Hankey, *The Supreme Command*, i. 349; H. Wilson, Chantilly, 7 July 1915, Wilson MSS 73/1/19.

4. French, *Strategy and War Aims*, pp. 108–11.

5. Blake, *Private Papers*, pp. 100, 102.

and many of his Cabinet colleagues that the German line in France was impregnable. They believed that with sufficient men, guns and ammunition they could break through. As Professor Travers has suggested, although the British high command was well aware of the potentially annihilating results of defensive fire-power, they nurtured notions about offensive warfare which emphasized that superior moral qualities rather than sheer weight of fire-power would lead to victories and that remaining on the defensive for prolonged periods was dangerous because it sapped their troops' offensive spirit. As Robertson wrote to the newspaper editor John St Loe Stratchey on 21 May, 'The human factor far transcends all others in war, and I think it will see us through. We are now at a critical stage, and the side will win which displays most grit and hangs together the best.'[1] Applied to the western front this meant, according to Brigadier F. B. Maurice, French's Director of Military Operations, that 'We must keep hammering away & to do that must have more & more men & more and more ammunition. If we can only keep our attacks going we shall wear Germany out & the war will be over in six months.'[2]

In the summer of 1915 members of the high command in France began to develop a new variant of attrition which bore a superficial similarity to Kitchener's concept but which was in practice radically different. Experience had taught them that they could not break through the entire German defence position in a single bound. Haig and French believed that at Neuve Chapelle, Aubers ridge and Festubert their troops had experienced comparatively little difficulty in taking the Germans' foremost trenches because they had been adequately bombarded. But the Germans now defended their positions by a succession of lines and could bring up reserves to man them much more rapidly than the British could bring their guns forward to bombard them. A successful break-through was therefore dependent on the German reserves being worn down before the British launched their major assault. In conversation with Asquith and Hankey at the beginning of July Haig explained that this might be done if the British launched an offensive on a front of twenty-five miles preceded by a heavy artillery bombardment of several days duration followed by infantry attacks all along the front to draw in and exhaust the enemy's reserves. And only when that had taken place and the commander-in-chief had discovered the weakest point in the enemy's line, should he commit his army reserves in a break-through attempt.[3]

---

1. Robertson to J. St Loe Strachey, 21 May 1915, St Loe Strachey MSS S/12/4/1; T. H. E. Travers, 'The offensive and the problem of innovation in British military thought 1870–1915', *Journal of Contemporary History*, xiii (1978), 531–53.
2. Maurice to his wife, 23 May 1915, Maurice MSS 3/1/4/167.
3. French to Kitchener, 23 June 1915, Robertson MSS I/5/2: Haig diary entry 8 July 1915 and enc., Memorandum on the strength of force required for an attack on a twenty-five mile front, Haig MSS Acc. 3155/101.

1988 THE MEANING OF ATTRITION, 1914-1916 397

The failure of the Loos offensive caused them to lay more stress on the need to prolong the 'wearing-out' stage of the next attack. On 16 October Robertson informed Callwell that 'if the supply [of ammunition] continues we can produce a very great accumulative effect here, although I am quite prepared to admit that we shall not achieve any great conspicuous success on any one occasion. The nature of the war and the general conditions do not admit of this. It is a question of exhausting and wearing down the enemy,...'.[1] The failure of Callwell's prediction that German manpower would be exhausted by the autumn also induced him to be more cautious about the time it would take to exhaust German manpower reserves. In a memorandum he wrote for the War Committee on 5 November Robertson was careful not to offer a hostage to fortune by predicting when the Germans would finally run out of men but he insisted that 'there are now many signs that Germany is finding a difficulty in providing drafts to keep up her establishments.'[2] Clearly they could not afford to slacken their efforts and on 15 November French ordered his army commanders to mount local offensive operations throughout the winter 'to wear out and exhaust the enemy's troops.'[3] When a month later Haig superseded him he pursued this policy with enthusiasm. Starting in the autumn of 1915 trench warfare came increasingly under the bureaucratic control of GHQ who tried to put an end to the unofficial 'live and let live' policy which had existed along some sections of the front in between offensives. The number of mortar batteries and machine gun companies was considerably augmented and they were used systematically to harass the enemy. Raids, which had hitherto been mounted by local commanders for a variety of tactical purposes, now had a strategic purpose and were henceforth directed by GHQ with the express objective according to the official trench warfare manual of forcing 'the enemy to keep as large or larger garrison than ourselves, and to increase his rate of wastage compared to our own.'[4]

This policy was taken a step further at the allied military conference at Chantilly between 6-8 December. The assembled allied generals concluded that the war would not be ended until the German army had been defeated and that the Germans had enough men to keep their formations up to establishment until August 1916. Their first priority was therefore to continue the war of attrition to ensure that the Germans lost an average of 200,000 men per month. The British, Russians and Italians were urged to mount a series of preliminary operations to exhaust the enemy's manpower reserves. But Joffre, whose

---

1. Robertson to Callwell, 16 October 1915, Robertson MSS I/8/24.
2. PRO CAB 42/5/6. Robertson, Memorandum on the conduct of the war, 5 November 1915.
3. Robertson to commanders of armies and the cavalry corps, 26 October 1915, Robertson MSS I/9/17.
4. T. Ashworth, *Trench Warfare 1914-1918. The Live and Let Live System* (London, 1980), pp. 18-19, 43-4, 60-6, 73-5, 179-85.

own reserves were already perilously low, declared that he would only play a limited part in this phase of the war. These operations would be followed by a co-ordinated series of allied offensives on the eastern, western and Italian fronts designed to bring the Central Powers to the peace table by the end of 1916.¹ Sir Archibald Murray, in almost his last act as chief of the imperial general staff, commended the plan to the government with the words, 'the resources of the Allies are sufficient to enable them to wear out the enemy and finally to beat him, if only the will to conquer and a sound direction of their united efforts and resources are not wanting.'²

What Murray meant by ensuring that 'resources are not wanting', was that the government had to introduce conscription. In public the conscriptionists put forward many arguments to support their case. It was necessary to demonstrate to Russia and France that Britain was totally committed to their cause. It was fairer than voluntary service because it would ensure that single men would be taken before husbands and fathers of families. But in private their most telling argument was that without conscription Britain would not be able to marshal her human and economic resources to sustain herself and her allies through a long war. As the Unionist Lord Selborne wrote on 6 August, military conscription and a rigid campaign of national economy to conserve financial and economic resources were vital because the war would last throughout 1916 and it 'will not be finished by the final and complete military success, which we have set ourselves to accomplish in the year 1916. The war will be a war of attrition, and of attrition pure and simple without annihilating military victories on either side, and the Germans will not have been reduced by the attrition of fighting by the end of next year to the point at which further resistance will have become impossible.'³ Lord Curzon's vision of the future was even more bleakly uncompromising. For him the war had become a simple matter of killing Germans 'If then two million (or whatever figure) more of Germans have to be killed at least a corresponding number of allied soldiers will have to be sacrificed to effect that object.'⁴ On 27 December Robertson, who had just replaced Murray, reminded Kitchener that French manpower reserves were now so seriously depleted that a growing burden of the land war in the west would fall on the BEF. 'We can only end the war in our favour by attrition or by breaking through the German line. The process of attrition must necessarily be slow, and will demand regular and frequent

---

1. PRO CAB 28/1. Military conference of the allies held at French Headquarters, 6–8 December 1915; PRO WO 106/1454. Note for the conference of 6 December [1915] by G.Q.G. Plan of action proposed by France to the Coalition, 6 December 1915.
2. PRO CAB 42/7/14. A. J. Murray, A paper by the General Staff on the future Conduct of the War, 16 December 1915.
3. Selborne, Memorandum, 6 August 1915, Selborne MSS file 8, fo. 34.
4. PRO CAB 37/130/19. Lord Curzon, Registration and military service, 21 June 1915.

relief of the troops fighting on the front, if the superiority of our troops in morale, vigour and efficiency is to be kept up. This demands a large and indefinite number of reserves. If the line is to be broken it is clear, from what has been said in paragraph 3, that we must take a far larger share in the attack than we have hitherto taken, so as to diminish *pro tanto* the French losses.'[1]

Their opponents, led by the Chancellor of the Exchequer, Reginald McKenna, and the President of the Board of Trade, Walter Runciman, objected that conscription, far from ensuring that Britain would win the war, would cripple her vital export industries, undermine her ability to subsidise her allies and bankrupt her before the Germans were beaten.[2] But in January 1916 the conscriptionists won because in the end a majority of Cabinet ministers were convinced by Robertson's and Kitchener's arguments that unless they agreed to conscription and participated in the plans arranged at Chantilly there was a strong possibility that one or more of Britain's allies might make a separate peace.[3] However, they agreed with considerable reluctance and without any very clear idea as to what they had agreed. The emphasis which the Chantilly conference laid on the need to wear out the enemy's reserves and the new weight which Haig placed on what he described in his official despatch of 19 May as 'raids or "cutting out parties" which are made at least twice or three times a week' had the effect of hiding the difference between Kitchener's concept of attrition and Haig's continuing belief that given the right circumstances a break-through was still possible.[4]

On 23 December Robertson asked the War Committee to agree to the Chantilly plan but Balfour, who remained fearful that any large-scale western offensive would cost the allies more men than the Germans, advised postponing any allied offensive until after the enemy had worn themselves out by attacking the allied line.[5] The War Committee therefore initially hedged their bets. On 28 December they appeared to sanction the offensive but on 13 January Balfour and Lloyd George persuaded their colleagues to alter their minds. They agreed that preparations could go forward but they postponed any decision on whether or not the operation would actually be launched.[6] Robertson protested that the allies had learnt the lessons of 1915. He admitted that

1. PRO WO 159/4. Robertson to Kitchener, 27 December 1915.
2. French, *British Strategy and War Aims*, 118–22, 128–31, 169–73.
3. Clive diary entry, 5 January 1916, Clive MSS II/2; PRO 30/57/76/WR35. Kitchener to Asquith, 11 January 1916; Kitchener to Haig, 14 January 1916, Haig MSS Acc. 3155/104.
4. Lt Col J. H. Boraston (ed.), *Sir Douglas Haig's Despatches (December 1915 to April 1919)* (London, 1919/1979), p. 4.
5. PRO CAB 42/6/14. Robertson, Note for the War Committee by the Chief of the Imperial General Staff with reference to the General Staff paper dated 16 December 1915, 23 December 1915; PRO CAB 42/6/14. Minutes of the War Committee, 28 December 1916; PRO CAB 37/139/55. Balfour to the cabinet, 27 December 1915.
6. PRO CAB 42/7/5. Minutes of the War Committee, 13 January 1916; PRO CAB 42/9/3. Minutes of the War Committee, 22 February 1916.

although their own losses were bound to be heavy and it was likely that the fighting would be prolonged, they would proceed with caution and deliberation. There would be no attempt to burst through the German line in one bound as had been tried in 1915. The allied plan called for a series of co-ordinated offensives to exhaust the enemy's reserves before the final attempt at a break-through was made. But it was Kitchener whose intervention was decisive. He explained to Balfour on 21 January that 'he did not intend to make another heavy attack in France, but merely to pursue an intensified policy of attrition in order gradually to use up the German reserves' so they would have too few men to hold their present line and would be compelled to retreat to the Meuse.[1] In the meantime the Russians would mount their summer offensive and the Central Powers would be forced to make peace by the end of 1916. The prospect that the brunt of breaking the German line would be borne by the Russians in the east, rather than the British and French in the west, was irresistible. Balfour promptly dropped his objections to the western front offensive, convinced now that the allies were not looking for a break-through but 'by the exercise of heavy pressure to compel the Germans to shorten their line'.[2]

Lloyd George's qualms were never quite overcome. He was doubtful whether the Entente armies had sufficient guns or munitions to begin their operations in the spring and to exhaust German manpower reserves by the end of the year.[3] But on 21 February the Germans launched their own variant of attrition when they began their offensive at Verdun designed to encourage the French to make peace by wearing out their manpower reserves.[4] Joffre naturally looked to his allies for assistance and on 12 March the allied commanders-in-chief or their representatives agreed that their armies would launch a combined offensive as soon as possible. On 4 April Haig sought the formal permission of the War Committee to comply with this agreement. Joffre had agreed to commit forty-five divisions to the operations and expected Haig to commit a further twenty. Ideally they would not strike until the Italians and Russians were also ready. The French commander-in-chief had, however, made one proviso; if his troops were so hard pressed at Verdun that all his reserves were absorbed in holding the city, he had asked Haig to mount an offensive to relieve him. Haig agreed 'with the proviso', he informed the War Committee, 'that any offensive undertaken in the circumstances stated in paragraph 3 above [that is

---

1. Hankey diary entry, 21 January 1916, Hankey MSS 1/1.
2. PRO CAB 42/7/12. Note by Mr Balfour, 25 January 1916; PRO CAB 42/11/6. Minutes of the War Committee, 21 March 1916.
3. PRO CAB 42/7/5. Minutes of the War Committee, 13 January 1916; PRO CAB 42/12/5. Minutes of the War Committee, 7 April 1916.
4. L L. Farrar, 'Peace through exhaustion: German diplomatic motivations for the Verdun campaign', *Revue Internationale d'Histoire Militaire*, viii (1972–75), 477–94.

1988   THE MEANING OF ATTRITION, 1914-1916   401

to relieve Verdun] would be of a strictly limited nature, not to be pushed beyond what the comparatively weak force at my disposal for offensive purposes could reasonably be expected to carry through successfully.'[1]

That caveat was enough to persuade the War Committee, with the exception of Lloyd George, to swallow their doubts. On 7 April they decided to allow Haig to co-operate in the allied offensive.[2] As French losses mounted at Verdun, the War Office moved quickly to give further reassurance. On 12 May the Adjutant General predicted that British losses in the forthcoming offensive would only amount to about 195,000 men over and above the 386,000 men they could expect to lose in the course of normal trench warfare.[3] A fortnight later, in the light of reports that because of their predicament at Verdun the French could commit no more than nineteen of the promised forty-five divisions to the Anglo-French offensive, Robertson himself stepped in to tell the War Committee that 'there was no idea of any attempt to break through the German lines, it would only be a move to *dégager* [to rescue] the French.'[4] And finally, just to emphasize the limited nature of the operation and Haig's determination to minimize his own losses, on 30 June, the day before the main assault, he told them that Haig only intended an initial advance of one and a half miles.[5] The War Committee agreed to take part in the Anglo-French offensive on the Somme not only because of the political necessity of co-operating with the French and Russians if they wanted to hold their alliance together but also because they did not really understand the nature of the operation to which they were agreeing. Since January Robertson and Haig had so blurred the distinction between Kitchener's concept of attrition and a break-through battle that they had lulled them into believing that the forthcoming operations would not seek to break through the German line but would be no more than 'nibbling & gnawing' on a large scale.

Haig himself had appeared before the War Committee on 7 June but he did not explain the exact nature of his plans, nor did he specify what his objectives were. He was already aware that his concept of the operation and that of his political masters was radically different. In February Kitchener told Brigadier Charteris, Haig's Director of Military Intelligence at GHQ, that the allied offensive would not break the German line in the west but that if they applied sufficient pressure they would force it backwards. Charteris reported their conversation

1. PRO CAB 42/12/5. Haig to CIGS, 4 April 1916; PRO CAB 42/12/5. Robertson, Future military operations, 31 March 1916.
2. PRO CAB 42/12/5. Minutes of the War Committee, 7 April 1916.
3. PRO CAB 42/14/12. Memorandum on wastage on the forces in the field prepared by the Adjutant General's branch, 12 May 1916.
4. PRO CAB 42/14/12. Minutes of the War Committee, 30 May 1916.
5. PRO CAB 42/15/15. Minutes of the War Committee, 30 June 1916.

to Haig. 'D.H. was, as always, quite unperturbed. I fancy he himself has been using the term break-through to some visitors, and it has reached K.'s ears!'[1] Charteris's supposition was correct. Haig did intend to try to break through the German line.

Haig was not blind to the importance of wearing out the Germans' reserves or of avoiding needless British casualties. Indeed in January and February he had fought a running battle with Joffre over how and when the wearing-out operations should be conducted. On 18 January he discussed with some of his senior staff officers how they should conduct the coming operation. They decided that between February and the first half of April each ally ought to conduct raids and other minor operations independently. Between the second half of April and early May the allies should co-operate to mount larger-scale wearing-down operations to weaken the enemy's line and to capture important tactical positions like the Messines–Wytschaete ridge. At the end of May these operations should be reduced to minor raids. This would give his forces time to make ready for the preparatory actions designed to draw in the Germans' reserves ten or twelve days before the decisive assault was launched. And finally, when the enemy's reserves had been absorbed he would 'throw in a mass of troops (at some point where the enemy has shown himself to be weak) to breakthrough and win victory.'[2] But Joffre wanted to stand by the Chantilly agreement, which called for the British to bear the brunt of wearing-out operations on the western front while the French conserved their manpower for the main assault. He therefore refused to co-operate and instead asked Haig to mount two preliminary offensives on his own in April and May. Haig was reluctant to do so because it meant that the main burden of these operations would fall upon the BEF who might be defeated in detail before the moment came to launch the main offensive.[3] On 1 February he informed Joffre that whilst he was ready to wear down the Germans in the spring by raids and artillery bombardments he was not prepared to mount the two preliminary offensives Joffre requested.[4] Eventually they compromised. On 14 February they agreed that although there would be no major preliminary offensives in April and May, Haig would mount minor operations on the 1st and 2nd Army fronts shortly before the main offensive, which would be launched by a combined Anglo-French force astride the Somme in July.[5]

---

1. Brigadier J. Charteris, *At GHQ* (London, 1931), p. 137.
2. Haig diary entry, 18 January 1916 and Haig [?], Some thoughts on the future, c. 18 January 1916, Haig MSS Acc. 3155/104.
3. Haig diary entry, 28 January 1916, Haig MSS Acc. 3155/104.
4. Haig to Joffre, 1 February 1916, Haig MSS Acc. 3155/104.
5. Haig diary entry, 14 February 1916, and memorandum on the note dated GQG 10 February 1916, Haig MSS Acc. 3155/104.

Haig allotted the main role of carrying out the British part in the Somme offensive to Sir Henry Rawlinson's IV Army. Rawlinson did not believe that a quick break-through was possible. On 3 April he presented Haig with a draft plan in which he sought to give some substance to Kitchener's conception of offensive attrition. The German defences on the Somme consisted of a front system, a series of strongly fortified villages, and finally, 2,000–5,000 yards behind the front system, a second line of defences. Rawlinson proposed to take the front system and then to allow the Germans to destroy themselves when they counter-attacked in an attempt to regain their lost positions. 'Our object', he wrote, 'rather seems to be to kill as many Germans as possible with the least loss to ourselves, and the best way to do this appears to me to be to seize points of tactical importance which will provide us with good observation and which we may feel quite certain the Germans will counter-attack.' Only when the Germans had dashed themselves to pieces did he intend to resume his advance.[1] Haig disliked his plan, complaining that Rawlinson merely intended to take the first two enemy trench systems and '"kill Germans"'. Instead he insisted that Rawlinson should seek to break through the German defences in his first assault by 'getting as large a combined force of French and British across the Somme and fighting the enemy in the open.'[2] The end product was a plan riddled with compromises. The infantry and artillery were spread across the entire front as if it was only intended to capture the German's first line of trenches. Some divisions expected to make a rapid break-through; others expected a hard fight.[3]

The result was the disaster of 1 July. The lesson the high command drew was not that attrition had failed but that it would succeed if only they intensified it and pursued it over a longer period. From this perception there evolved for the British the modern and now familiar notion of attrition. On 5 July Robertson wrote privately to Kiggell, Haig's chief of staff, that the main lesson of the battle so far had been that any future advance should be directed towards a strictly limited objective and must be preceded by an overwhelmingly powerful artillery bombardment.[4] On 2 August Kiggell told Rawlinson and Gough that the operations which they were now conducting 'may be regarded as a "wearing out" battle'.[5] It meant that tactically the high command now conducted a sequence of assaults each with limited objectives. Attrition was no longer the essential precursor of an offensive which

---

1. Sir James Edmonds, *History of the Great War. Military Operations France and Belgium, 1916. Appendices* (London, 1938), pp. 69, 72, 82.
2. Haig diary entry, 5 April 1916, Haig MSS Acc. 3155/105.
3. S. Bidwell and D. Graham, *Fire-power. British Army Weapons and Theories of War 1904–1945* (London, 1982), pp. 70–1, 75, 80–2; T. H. E. Travers, 'Learning and decision making on the western front, 1915–1916', *Canadian Journal of History*, xviii (1983), 87–97.
4. Robertson to Kiggell, 5 July 1916, Robertson MSS I/35/65.
5. Kiggell to Rawlinson and Gough, 2 August 1916, Haig MSS Acc. 3155/107.

404   THE MEANING OF ATTRITION, 1914-1916   April

Haig had anticipated would re-introduce mobile warfare to the western front. It was now the way in which the offensive itself was conducted. The Somme lasted until mid-November. The final casualty tolls are still a matter of dispute. Sir James Edmonds, the official historian of the war on the western front, placed total British losses at 419,654 (more than twice the figure predicted by the Adjutant General on the eve of the battle), French losses at 204,453 and German losses at 680,000. More convincingly M. J. Williams has indicated that Edmonds probably inflated German losses by about 30 per cent.[1] What was British policy, Lloyd George demanded angrily on 15 November? 'I have only heard of one. It is variously described as hammering or attrition.'[2]

The debate on the policy of attrition was about means rather than ends. The policy-making elite knew the ends they wanted to achieve, maximum victory for Britain at minimum cost, but they could not agree about the means. Attrition was an elusive concept. It meant different things to different people at different times. Asquith and Kitchener adopted it in January 1915 as a way of conserving British manpower and throwing the weight of any major offensive operations in 1915-16 onto the French and Russians. They only began slowly and reluctantly to reassess the realism of this in the summer of 1915 when it became apparent that the Germans would not oblige the allies by attacking their line in the west and that the French and Russians were not prepared to bear the burden of the land war alone. In July and early August 1915 it meant, in Churchill's graphic phrase, 'nibbling & gnawing' at the German line, mounting what Balfour called an 'active defence'. In January 1916, under ever growing pressure from the allies to participate in a combined operation which would end the war by the autumn but fearful of the cost of another attempt to break through the enemy line, Kitchener persuaded Balfour that the planned allied offensive would not be a break-through operation but 'an intensified policy of attrition'.

However since the summer of 1915 the high command in France had developed the idea that a successful break-through would have to be preceded by a 'wearing-out' phase of indeterminate duration during which the enemy's reserves would be destroyed. This concept was accepted by the Chantilly conference in December 1915. Between January and June 1916 Robertson and Haig succeeded in blurring in the minds of the War Committee the distinction between a break-through battle and a policy of intensifing attrition. In truth it was not difficult

---

1. Sir James Edmonds, *History of the Great War. Military Operations France and Belgium, 1916* (London, 1938), ii. pp. xv-xvi; M. J. Williams, 'The treatment of the German losses on the Somme in the British Official History: "Military Operations France and Belgium, 1916", vol. 2', *Journal of the Royal United Services Institute*, iii (1966), 69-74.

2. PRO CAB 28/1. Statement drafted by Mr Lloyd George as a basis for the Prime Minister's statement at the Paris Conference on 15 November 1916.

to do so. In January 1916 the Cabinet Committee on the co-ordination of military and financial effort had pointed to the fact that if the Entente did not win the war by the end of the year Britain might be bankrupt. They had to weigh up that possibility against an equally dangerous one; that if they refused to take part in the Chantilly plan France or Russia might make a separate peace. With the exception of Lloyd George they allowed Haig and Robertson to lull them into believing that somehow the BEF could attack the heavily entrenched German line on the Somme and inflict heavier losses on the enemy than they would suffer themselves. On 30 May Sir Edward Grey, the Foreign Secretary, told the War Committee that 'it would be best for the Committee not to be told, and not to know where the attacks were to be directed.'[1] They preferred to remain in the ignorance into which Haig and Robertson were happy to consign them.

In April 1916 Rawlinson proposed a new variant of offensive attrition which involved securing a lodgement in the German line and then hoping that the Germans would exhaust themselves by counterattacking. Haig rejected it and clung to his belief that a break-through on the Somme was feasible. It was only the failure of 1 July that compelled him to change his mind and resort to a series of piecemeal attacks. The British adopted attrition in 1915 as a way of conserving their military manpower. But when it was applied on the Somme in 1916 it cost them more dearly than the enemy. In the intervening months attrition had changed its meaning.

University College, London DAVID FRENCH

Acknowledgement

I am grateful to the following for permission to quote from material to which they own the copyright: Lord Esher; The trustees of the National Library of Scotland; The trustees of the Liddell Hart Centre for Military Archives, King's College, London.

---

1. PRO CAB 42/14/12. Minutes of the War Committee 30 May 1916.

[15]

German "Atrocities" and Franco-German Opinion, 1914: The Evidence of German Soldiers' Diaries*

John Horne and Alan Kramer
University of Dublin, Trinity College

INTRODUCTION

Within a few days of the German invasion of Belgium and France in 1914, rumors of atrocities abounded and rapidly found their way into print. Growing in intensity, they accompanied the entire two-and-a-half-month period of mobile warfare before the Western Front solidified. The aim of this article is twofold. First, it tries to escape the preoccupation with propaganda and the accusational attitudes that have marked the historiography of the subject by establishing the relativity of the concept of "atrocity." Second, the article seeks to establish the evidence for what happened and to explain why the two sides interpreted it so differently in 1914–15. The subject is potentially a large one, since the atrocity accusations were numerous and varied. We do not consider atrocity propaganda exhaustively, nor for its own sake, but only as evidence of the cultural values raised by the issue, and we have chosen to concentrate on a neglected but crucial source of evidence—the diaries of German soldiers. These lay at the center of one of the most acrimonious propaganda battles—an argument between intellectuals on the two sides as to the meaning of the term "atrocity"—and they allow detailed probing of the nature and causes of the conduct of the German army in the period August–October 1914. The diaries thus illuminate the relationship between event, perception, and contemporary interpretation that lies at the heart of our interest in this subject.[1]

---

* This article forms part of a continuing study of "German 'atrocities' in 1914: myths, mentalities, and realities." We would like to acknowledge the help of the Royal Irish Academy (Bicentennial Research Trust) for start-up funding in 1990, the French government for a month's fellowship (Scientific Exchange Programme) for John Horne in May 1991, and the Humboldt Foundation of the Federal Republic of Germany for granting a fellowship to Alan Kramer in 1991–92. We would also like to thank Gerd Krumeich, of the Historisches Seminar, Albert-Ludwigs Universität, Freiburg; the joint Trinity College/University College Dublin Research Seminar in European History; Fritz Fischer, Hamburg; and the Oberseminar of Wolfgang J. Mommsen, Heinrich Heine-Universität Düsseldorf, for their comments.

[1] We have discussed other aspects of the "atrocity question" of the First World War elsewhere. A discussion of the motivation of German military conduct is to be found

2 Horne and Kramer

Ironically, the complexity of this relationship has been buried by the interwar pacifist reaction to wartime propaganda and by the history of genocide in the Second World War.[2] The "German atrocities" have been regarded, at least in the English-speaking countries and Germany, as a prime example of untruthful war propaganda. The British pacifist Arthur Ponsonby, a Liberal and later Labour member of Parliament, published a book in 1928 that condemned the reports on German atrocities as pure inventions of propaganda.[3] The American historian Ralph H. Lutz considered the accusations made against the German army during the war to be falsifications designed to malign the German nation in the interest of propaganda.[4] In Germany, the defeat of 1918 was followed by rejections of the "war guilt" accusation and the associated allegations of war crimes. A book on American propaganda against Germany during the First World War, published in 1943 by a researcher at the Stuttgart *Weltkriegsbücherei* with the intention of showing that the American people had been "prepared for this war" with the same propaganda methods as for the First World War and had succumbed to "the same empty phrases and atrocity stories" as twenty-five years previously, found that the "atrocity legends" associated with the German invasion of Belgium were the main feature of American propaganda in the years 1917–19.[5]

This generally accepted consensus among historians still survives today. Thus Trevor Wilson, writing in 1979, saw the most significant aspect of the question to be the use made by the British official report of 1915 on the "German outrages" of unverified evidence from unreliable witnesses and

---

in Alan Kramer, " 'Greueltaten,' Zum Problem der deutschen Kriegsverbrechen in Belgien und Frankreich 1914," in *"Keiner fühlt sich hier mehr als Mensch . . .": Erlebnis und Wirkung des Ersten Weltkriegs,* ed. G. Hirschfeld and G. Krumeich, with I. Renz (Essen, 1993), pp. 83–112. John Horne investigates the mutilation fear in French public opinion in "Les mains coupées: Opinion française et 'atrocités allemandes' en 1914," *Guerres mondiales et conflits contemporains* 171 (1993): 29–43.

[2] The only substantial recent work published in English, J. F. Willis, *Prologue to Nuremberg: The Politics and Diplomacy of Punishing War Criminals of the First World War* (Westport, Conn., and London, 1982), is concerned essentially with a different subject: the cases dealt with in the war crimes trials following the First World War from the point of view of legal development and the diplomatic decision-making process.

[3] Arthur Ponsonby, *Falsehood in War-Time, Containing an Assortment of Lies Circulated throughout the Nations during the Great War* (London, 1928).

[4] Ralph H. Lutz, "Studies of World War Propaganda, 1914–33," *Journal of Modern History* 5 (1933): 496–516, esp. p. 506.

[5] E. Weis, *Die Propaganda der Vereinigten Staaten gegen Deutschland im ersten Weltkrieg* (Essen, 1943).

untenable accusations about cruel and sadistic behavior.⁶ Since the Second World War there have been two serious, but little-known, attempts to deal with the question of German "atrocities" in 1914 and their legacy: a case study on the destruction of Louvain published in 1958 and Lothar Wieland's book on German military conduct in Belgium in 1914 and German-Belgian relations until 1936.⁷ While both come to the conclusion that the allegations made by the Belgian authorities against the German army were in essence true, neither seeks to explain the divergent perceptions of the issue by contemporaries, including French and German intellectuals, nor do they use German military sources or the private diaries of soldiers.

Surprisingly, perhaps, atrocity tales began in Germany, where rumors circulated of armed resistance by Belgian civilians, or francs-tireurs, and of gruesome outrages against individual German soldiers and expatriate civilians. These were rapidly published by newspapers throughout the country.⁸ The stories that spread in Belgium, France, and Britain, by contrast, were of brutal conduct by the German army. Here, lurid accounts of outrages against individuals were only part of the popular apprehension, which also hinted at something more systematic and perhaps even premeditated. Pillaging on a grand scale, deliberate incendiarism, hostage taking among innocent civilians, the use of human shields in combat, deliberate firing on Red Cross and medical facilities, shooting of prisoners, the execution of civilians individually and en masse—all seemed to be the shocking hallmark of a new style of warfare practiced by the German army. The particular "barbarity" of German soldiers was also highlighted by allegations that neither women nor children had been spared and that there had been multiple cases of rape, torture, and mutilation.⁹

Rumors and newspaper stories were eventually buttressed on the Allied side by official investigations. The Belgians issued a string of reports starting as early as August 28, 1914. In the wake of the Marne the French conducted a

---

⁶ Trevor Wilson, "Lord Bryce's Investigation into Alleged German Atrocities in Belgium, 1914–15," *Journal of Contemporary History* 14 (1979): 369–83.

⁷ P. Schöller, *Der Fall Löwen und das Weißbuch: Eine kritische Untersuchung der deutschen Dokumentation über die Vorgänge in Löwen vom 25. bis 28. August 1914* (Cologne and Graz, 1958); Lothar Wieland, *Belgien, 1914: Die Frage des belgischen "Franktireurkrieges" und die deutsche öffentliche Meinung von 1914 bis 1936* (Frankfurt am Main, Bern, and New York, 1984).

⁸ F. van Langenhove, *The Growth of a Legend: A Study Based upon the German Accounts of Francs-Tireurs and "Atrocities" in Belgium* (Paris, 1916; English trans., London, 1916).

⁹ On one aspect of these forms of war atrocities, see R. Harris, " 'The Child of the Barbarian': Rape, Race and Nationalism in World War I," *Past and Present*, no. 141 (1993), pp. 170–206.

painstaking inquiry whose first fruit appeared in January 1915, and the British Bryce Committee reported in May 1915.[10] But official reports were not enough. On both sides, atrocity charges and countercharges were taken up by propagandists who published newspaper articles, pamphlets, and leaflets and drew graphic illustrations for printed posters and postcards.[11] Intellectuals and academics played a central role in this process. For as the illusion of a short war faded into the stalemate of trench combat, and as the battle for neutral opinion developed, the conflict was invested with universal values, each side seeing the identity and even the existence of the national community as being at stake. German military conduct and the atrocity question acquired a symptomatic and symbolic importance in this process as a distillation of the meaning of the war, and it came to occupy a central place in the attention of intellectuals. The clash of intellectual opinion on the subject thus establishes paradigmatically the value laden and culturally relative stances that informed the whole question of German "atrocities."

JOSEPH BÉDIER, CAPTURED DIARIES, AND THE GERMAN INTELLECTUALS

In France, the most notable academic intervention on the "atrocity" issue was that of Joseph Bédier, eminent philologist and professor at the Collège de France, who wrote two widely disseminated pamphlets based on a novel form of evidence, that of German soldiers' diaries.[12] The Second Bureau of the General Staff gave Bédier access to a collection of *Kriegstagebücher,* or individual manuscript diaries, discovered on captured or dead German soldiers during the retreat from the Marne and in the early period of trench warfare. These seemed to provide telling evidence of the actions and mentality of the German army in the opening two-and-a-half months of the war.

---

[10] Official Commission of the Belgian Government, *Reports on the Violation of the Rights of Nations and of the Laws and Customs of War in Belgium,* 2 vols. (Paris, 1915; English trans., London, 1915–16); *Rapports et procès-verbaux d'enquête de la commission instituée en vue de constater les actes commis par l'ennemi en violation du droit des gens,* 13 vols. (Paris, 1915–19); *Report of the Committee on Alleged German Outrages* (London, 1915), Cd 7894; and *Evidence and Documents Laid before the Committee on Alleged German Outrages* (London, 1915), Cd 7895.

[11] There is no comprehensive analysis of the atrocity propaganda of the First World War. J. M. Read, *Atrocity Propaganda, 1914–1919* (New Haven, Conn., 1941), is dated, limited in its coverage, and strongly influenced by the interwar conviction that German "atrocities" were largely a matter of Allied propaganda invention.

[12] J. Bédier, *Les crimes allemands d'après des témoignages allemands* (Paris, 1915), and *Comment l'allemagne essaye de justifier ses crimes* (Paris, 1915). The pamphlets were translated into English as *German Atrocities from German Evidence* (Paris, 1915) and *How Germany Seeks to Justify Her Atrocities* (Paris, 1915).

Bédier's pamphlets formed a central episode in the larger intellectual exchange over atrocities. The opening salvo had come from ninety-three German academics who signed a declaration on October 4, 1914, which denied German responsibility for the war and rejected Allied charges of brutal behavior in Belgium.[13] The ninety-three included some of Germany's most renowned and internationally respected scholars and figures from the world of culture, such as Lujo Brentano, Paul Ehrlich, Fritz Haber, Ernst Haeckel, Gerhart Hauptmann, Engelbert Humperdinck, Friedrich Naumann, Max Planck, Wilhelm Röntgen, Max Reinhardt, Gustav von Schmoller, and several professors of history and of Protestant and Catholic theology. They denied that Germany had "sinfully violated the neutrality of Belgium" and claimed that the German military had not harmed a single Belgian civilian or his property unless compelled by self-defense. The most notorious "atrocity," the destruction of Louvain, was explained as a necessary countermeasure taken by German soldiers "against frenzied inhabitants who had treacherously attacked them in their billets." The German professors claimed that the greater part of Louvain was intact and omitted mention of the incineration of the historic university library. The declaration made counteraccusations of atrocities committed by Germany's enemies who had "butchered German women and children" in the East and used dumdum bullets in the West, and had "offered the world the shameful spectacle of setting Mongols and Negroes on to the white race."[14] The declaration ended with a statement of identification of German culture and scholarship with German militarism.[15]

---

[13] "An die Kulturwelt! Ein Aufruf," *Berliner Tageblatt* (October 4, 1914). The declaration is reproduced in B. vom Brocke, "Wissenschaft und Militarismus," in *Wilamowitz nach 50 Jahren* (Darmstadt, 1985), pp. 649–719. It was published in all the main daily newspapers in Germany, translated into ten languages, and sent in thousands of private letters to correspondents in neutral countries. It was commented on instantly and extensively in France, Britain, and the United States (ibid., pp. 654–55, n. 6). On German professors during the First World War, see K. Schwabe, *Wissenschaft und Kriegsmoral: Die deutschen Hochschullehrer und die politischen Grundfragen des Ersten Weltkrieges* (Göttingen, Frankfurt, and Zurich, 1969).

[14] The German accusation of the use by Entente forces of dumdum bullets was exposed as a forgery in 1919 by a former official war reporter attached to the Grand Headquarters: H. Binder, *Was wir als Kriegsberichterstatter nicht sagen durften!* (Munich, 1919).

[15] See also the attempt of the historian Friedrich Meinecke to defend German militarism in his contribution to O. Hintze, F. Meinecke, H. Oncken, and H. Schumacher, eds., *Deutschland und der Weltkrieg*, 2 vols. (Leipzig and Berlin, 1915). Gerhard Ritter later described this publication approvingly as the "most dignified and intellectually most substantial work of German wartime journalism" and Meinecke's essay as "especially interesting" (*Staatskunst und Kriegshandwerk*, vol. 3, *Die Tragödie der Staatskunst. Bethmann Hollweg als Kriegskanzler, 1914–1917* [Munich, 1964], p. 593, n. 34).

In order to substantiate the Allied case, a select Comité d'Études et Documents sur la Guerre was established, composed of eminent French academics from the Sorbonne, the Collège de France, and the Académie Française. It was presided over by the doyen of French history in the university and school systems, Ernest Lavisse, and its secretary was no less a person than Émile Durkheim.[16] The committee thus spoke for the academic and intellectual establishment of the Third Republic. Bédier's pamphlets were part of the committee's series of brochures published in 1915. The first, *Les crimes allemands d'après des témoignages allemands,* appeared in January and was distributed both domestically and, in a variety of languages, throughout the world. Its success stung some of Bédier's erstwhile German colleagues into responding. On February 28, Professor Hollmann of Berlin disputed Bédier's interpretation of the *Kriegstagebücher* in a long article in the *Norddeutsche Allgemeine Zeitung,* and this was followed by a series of rebuttals by well-known German academic philologists that served as the basis of a German campaign of counterpropaganda in neutral countries.[17] In the spring of 1915, Bédier defended his original interpretations against Hollmann's article with a second pamphlet, *Comment l'allemagne essaye de justifier ses crimes,* in which he also presented more evidence culled from additional captured diaries.

What precisely were these *Kriegstagebücher?* They came in two forms. First, there were diaries kept by selected soldiers, from battalion to High Command level, for the purpose of later writing official war histories. By their nature and purpose, these do not contain much more than a record of troop movements, orders given, engagements with the enemy, losses, and so on. Second, there were private war diaries that the army allowed its soldiers to keep. Most of these diaries also go no further than a sterile record of military events, but occasionally one yields real insights into the actions and attitudes of German soldiers and appears to cast light on the behavior of the German army. The diaries reproduced in Bédier's pamphlets seem to be of the second provenance. But in the absence of any trace of the captured originals in French archives, there cannot be finality about this.[18] Bédier and his French

---

[16] A. Mitchell, "French History in France after 1870," *Journal of Contemporary History* 2/3 (1967): 95–97; S. Lukes, *Emile Durkheim: His Life and Work* (London, 1973), pp. 549–52.

[17] Hubert Grimme, *Ein böswilliger Sprachstümper über "deutsche Kriegsgreuel"* (Münster, [1915]); Max Kuttner, *Deutsche Verbrechen? Wider Joseph Bédier, "Les Crimes allemands": Zugleich eine Antwort aus französischen Dokumenten* (Bielefeld and Leipzig, 1915); Karl Larsen, *Professor Bédier und die Tagebücher deutscher Soldaten* . . . (Berlin, 1915). Larsen was a Danish academic.

[18] There is now reason to believe that these diaries may have been found during the German occupation of 1940–44 and possibly taken to the Reichsarchiv at Potsdam, where they presumably were destroyed in the air raid of April 1945.

contemporaries considered the value of the diaries to lie in the fact that they provided German evidence of war crimes, which was ipso facto beyond doubt of fabrication, and gave an indication of the frame of mind of those who committed or condoned the "crimes." Bédier's German opponents did not, it may be noted, challenge the authenticity of his documentation—only the use he made of it.

In his two works, Bédier drew on nearly fifty *Kriegstagebücher* in order to provide evidence of thirty-six incidents. Some topics, although they were important in more popular forms of propaganda (such as sexual and sadistic crimes), did not figure prominently in the diaries or in Bédier's pamphlets, and we do not discuss them further here. But by and large, the type of incident identified from the diaries by Bédier corresponded to those raised in the official French and Belgian reports. Half of the incidents described by Bédier concerned summary executions of civilians, frequently accompanied by the deliberate firing of buildings, from isolated farmhouses to whole villages or towns. Some of these incidents were well documented in the official reports. Lieutenant Kietzmann (Forty-ninth Infantry Regiment) describes the execution in Schaffen, northeast of Louvain, on August 18, of fifty civilians found sheltering in a church tower from which the Germans had been machine-gunned.[19] Soldier Philipp, of the 178th (Saxon) Regiment, counted over two hundred executed civilians in a burned village (almost certainly Leffe) just north of Dinant (Belgium) on the night of August 23. Soldiers Moritz Grosse (177th Infantry Regiment) and Paul Förster (108th Fusiliers) also describe the firing of Dinant and its surrounds.[20] Fischer, of the Eighth Bavarian Infantry, participated in the drama of Nomény, a substantial frontier settlement in French Lorraine, on August 20. According to his diary, the regimental commander, following a shell burst wounding seven men, ordered all male inhabitants of Nomény to be shot and the village razed "because the people had been mad enough to oppose the forward march of the German troops by arms." Fischer describes the execution of the order and the pitiable expulsion of the women and children.[21]

Diary descriptions of destruction and collective executions extend well beyond these notorious cases. An unsigned diary refers to incendiarism and the shooting of civilians at Creil, near the point of farthest German penetration into France, when the local bridge over the Oise was destroyed. Another recounts the swathe cut through the Ardennes by the 178th Saxon Regiment (noted above in connection with Dinant). Corroborating the execution of male civilians in Leffe at point-blank range on August 23, with the women and children shut in the convent from where it was alleged shots had been fired,

---

[19] Bédier, *Les crimes allemands,* pp. 10–11.
[20] Ibid., pp. 12, 26, and Bédier, *Comment l'allemagne,* pp. 17–20, 37–38.
[21] Bédier, *Comment l'allemagne,* pp. 22–23.

the anonymous diarist also noted that the priest and other inhabitants of Villers-sur-Fagne were shot on August 25 because dead and wounded German grenadiers had been found there and that the village of Gué d'Hossus was burned on August 26 and its male inhabitants thrown into the flames when a rifle was discharged, apparently innocently, by a falling cyclist.[22] Soldier Missbach (Thirteenth Reserve Battalion of Rifles) describes the valley of the Meuse alight with fires on August 23 and seventeen francs-tireurs executed in the village of Sorinne.[23] Other accounts mention the murder of individual civilians, such as the woman at Orchies (Nord) who was shot on August 25, according to soldier Bissinger (First Regiment Bavarian Pioneers), for refusing to obey an order to halt,[24] following which the village was burned, or the three women seen hanging from trees on August 22 near Longueville (Lorraine), which was burned by the Eleventh Battalion of Pioneers.[25]

Of the other half of the incidents cited by Bédier, the bulk (a third of the total) involved pillaging and incendiarism, while most of the remainder concerned the killing of wounded Allied soldiers and prisoners of war, as well as one case of rape. Several diaries registered the execution of Allied prisoners. Soldier Fahlenstein, of the Thirty-fourth Fusiliers, records that on August 28 (place unspecified) orders were carried out to finish off all seriously wounded French, while noncommissioned officer Göttsche indicated that his captain in the Eighty-fifth Infantry Regiment, before the fort of Kessel, near Antwerp, on October 6, had declared that no English soldiers were to be taken alive.[26] Bédier's pamphlet contains a version of the most notorious such order, issued verbally on August 26 by Major-General Stenger, commander of the Fifty-eighth Brigade near Thiaville (Vosges); an inquiry among German prisoners confirmed the existence of the order, and that it had been obeyed in some cases.[27]

One last type of atrocity, the human shield, was illustrated by Bédier with a published article from the *Münchner Neueste Nachrichten* of October 7, in which a Bavarian officer, Lieutenant Eberlein, recounted his use of civilian protection, leading to civilian fatalities, during the occupation of Saint-Dié in Lorraine at the end of August.[28]

---

[22] Bédier, *Les crimes allemands,* pp. 9, 11–12.
[23] Bédier, *Comment l'allemagne,* p. 15.
[24] Ibid., p. 17. (French) Ministry of Foreign Affairs, *Germany's Violations of the Laws of War* (Paris, 1915; English trans., London, 1916), pp. 123–25, gives a longer extract and supplies the author's name.
[25] Bédier, *Les crimes allemands,* pp. 15–16.
[26] Bédier, *Comment l'allemagne,* pp. 44–45.
[27] Bédier, *Les crimes allemands,* pp. 28–31.
[28] Ibid., pp. 19–21, and Bédier, *Comment l'allemagne,* pp. 27–32.

Even had Bédier displayed the scholarly detachment he claimed, his work, like any academic treatise, would have been invested with assumptions and values. As it was, he was writing polemic with passion and outrage in order to demonstrate the "crimes" committed by the German army. Yet his purpose serves all the more clearly to reveal the intellectual and moral framework on which he reconstructed the apparent facts revealed by the diaries. Likewise, the replies by Hollman and the other German philologists show their opposed moral interpretation of the "atrocity" incidents.

Bédier's German opponents accused him of editorial selectivity and mistranslation in order to supply incriminating meanings to innocent passages — charges he rebutted in the second pamphlet. In a few cases, the inference of an atrocity is, on purely internal evidence, highly dubious. Thus Bédier took a report by Delfosse, 111th Reserve Infantry Regiment, of a patrol in the forest of Saint-Rémy on September 4–5 where he came across "French corpses fearfully mutilated," to be proof of atrocities, though the presumption in the absence of other evidence must be that artillery fire was responsible.[29]

But in most cases, the controversy turned on the meanings that could be imputed to a relatively clear set of events by textual exegesis. (Bédier's pamphlets supplied transcribed excerpts from the diaries in German, usually with a photo of the original text, plus French translation.) In part, this was a bitter professional quarrel by former international colleagues over proper critical methods. Both Hubert Grimme, professor at the University of Münster, and Max Kuttner, professor at the Royal Augusta School in Berlin — two of Bédier's most eminent critics — had known Bédier (and Kuttner had taught him) when the Frenchman served his apprenticeship in "scientific" philological methods in Germany in the late 1880s. Both acknowledged Bédier's international prestige, crowned by achieving the chair of medieval French language and literature at the Collège de France while still under forty years of age.[30] The sense of betrayal with Bédier's wartime attack was all the greater. But the heart of the quarrel lay in the opposed inductive processes by which different moral and ideological presuppositions were applied to the extracts from the *Kriegstagebücher*.

Bédier invoked the Hague Convention of 1907 as his standard of military conduct. By this measure, he argued that pillaging, killing wounded or surrendered enemy soldiers, and, above all, executing civilians and firing dwellings in reprisal for acts of resistance were all abhorrent and contrary to

---

[29] Bédier, *Les crimes allemands*, p. 31.

[30] Kuttner (n. 17 above), p. 5; Grimme (n. 17 above), p. 5; C. Charle and E. Telkès, *Les professeurs du Collège de France: Dictionnaire biographique, 1901–1939* (Paris, 1988), pp. 31–32.

international law—to which Germany itself was a signatory.[31] Here, Bédier was restating the standard Allied charge, made at length in another of the Paris committee's brochures, that Germany had torn up the international attempt to devise more "civilized" codes of war suited to an era of moral progress and was reverting to barbarous practices characteristic of an earlier age or of "backward" peoples.[32]

The moral heart of the case made by the German philologists was different. They held that sniping and ambush by individuals or by irregular forces against "loyal soldiers" constituted an outrage and justified the severest repression. In effect, they upheld military authority against the specter of civilian anarchy and insurgence. In this, the philologists adopted the same position as the ninety-three German professors in their declaration of October 1914, when they denied that German conduct of the war infringed any international law and claimed the necessity of "bitter self-defense" ("bitterste Notwehr"), for "in spite of all warnings, again and again the population fired on [the German troops] from hiding." These acts of "treacherous" civilian resistance incurred "just punishments."[33]

This radical difference of view on the proper conduct of warfare explains much of the mutual incomprehension between Bédier and his antagonists. Bédier took all mention of executions and incendiarism as evidence of outrages. He admitted that occasional and legitimate resistance might have occurred, but he essentially considered the francs-tireurs to be a German invention. His German confreres clearly believed the tales of civilian atrocities against German soldiers and adduced such horrors to acquit the diarists on grounds of self-defense. Thus, Bédier reproduced the German army's open proclamations of collective sanctions against resistance and sabotage in Belgium as flagrant German self-condemnation, whereas Grimme considered them to be the only response possible.[34] In the Schaffen incident, Bédier accepted that the civilians were resisting but argued that their execution was illegal under the Hague Convention and took the phrase "all civilians" were shot ("sämtliche Zivilisten") to refer not merely to the

---

[31] Bédier, *Les crimes allemands,* pp. 8–9, 21, 28; G. Best, *Humanity in Warfare: The Modern History of the International Law of Armed Conflicts* (London, 1980), pp. 190–200.

[32] E. Lavisse and C. Andler, *Pratique et doctrine allemandes de la guerre* (Paris, 1915).

[33] Vom Brocke (n. 13 above), p. 718.

[34] Notably the announcement by K. von Bülow (commander of the Second Army) of the mass "execution" of Andenne posted in Liège on August 22 and the proclamation on sabotage by von der Goltz, military governor of Belgium, October 5, 1914 (Bédier, *Les crimes allemands,* p. 14).

supposed resisters but to the entire village. His opponents disputed the last point and judged the execution of the fifty to be legitimate. The two hundred civilian corpses noted at Leffe, near Dinant, were self-evidently a major atrocity for Bédier, whereas Grimme and Larsen assumed a case of justified repression. The latter held that "a few more or less civilians shot is a matter of complete indifference to the High Command: those people are not loyal soldiers."[35]

In another incident, reported in an anonymous diary, eight houses and their inhabitants were destroyed. In one, two men, two women, and an eighteen-year-old girl were bayoneted. The young girl's look of terror aroused the diarist's pity but he observed that against the excited mob ("die aufgeregte Menge") there was nothing to be done, since they were more animals than men. Where Bédier concluded that it was the band of soldiers who had been inflamed by blood lust, his opponents argued that, in contemporary German, *die Menge* could only designate anarchic civilian movements, never the forces of order, and that it was therefore the wild civilians who had forced the soldiers into legitimate self-defense.[36]

The German academics played down the question of pillaging, suggesting that it was inseparable from warfare and often justified by military needs, and ignored the question of drunkenness. But diametrically opposed readings of the same texts characterized the highly sensitive issues of human shields and the dispatching of wounded soldiers and prisoners of war. In a rather embarrassed response to Lieutenant Eberlein's published account of the use of civilians as a shield in Saint-Dié, Hollmann, Grimme, and Larsen all found mitigating circumstances in supposed civilian resistance. Larsen derived an ambush from the fact that one civilian, in the German account, had assured the Germans that no enemy were left in the town when in fact regular French troops had manned a barricade.[37] General Stenger's order to shoot French prisoners was dismissed by the German academics, with Grimme stating that Stenger himself had denied issuing such an order to a formal military inquiry. But Bédier's use of a sordid little account of French prisoners being finished off during a battle in late September, which appeared in a local Silesian paper the following month under the title "A Day of Honor for our Regiment," was harder to counter. Hollman and Kuttner ignored it, and Larsen considered it merely a hard-fought battle without quarter. But Grimme argued that the French were well-known for shooting the enemy in the back after surrendering

---

[35] Larsen (n. 17 above), p. 23.
[36] Bédier, *Les crimes allemands,* pp. 16–17, and *Comment l'allemagne,* p. 21. Hollmann, Grimme, and Larsen all contested Bédier's translation of *die Menge*.
[37] Larsen, p. 35.

(he produced a series of German statements to this effect) and thus upheld the German practice of preemptively finishing off "this *canaille*" (his use of the French term for an insubordinate rabble is significant).[38]

Bédier was interested in more than listing individual infractions of international law. He wished to pen a collective picture of the German army and even of the entire nation which, by diabolizing the enemy, would in turn help define the war as a struggle of good versus evil. In his portrait, he used two images—the cold, premeditated authoritarianism of the High Command and the undisciplined license of a brutal soldiery. The "crimes" in Belgium and France were seen both as the outcome of a deliberate and premeditated policy of warfare by terror and as the spontaneous outbreak of bestial passions. It was this generalized indictment for what amounted to crimes against humanity that led to some of Bédier's most imaginative inferences and that, with its implied obverse of French moral superiority, most outraged his German opponents.

Thus, Bédier ironically termed soldier Philipp's description of the mass executions at Leffe, where women and children, lamps in hand, "mußten dem entsetzlichen Schauspiele zusehen" (were obliged to witness the terrible spectacle), as a military tableau worthy of the Dresden Art Gallery. But two of Bédier's German critics argued that he had mistranslated *mußten* to mean that women and children "had to" observe the executions, in the sense of being forced to, rather than as inadvertent witnesses, thus presenting the Germans as sadists.[39] Bédier, however, was clearly convinced of a collective character that he sought to illustrate by the tone as well as the evidence of the diaries. The cryptic notation of August 23 in Dinant by soldier Moritz (177th Saxon Infantry)—"Throwing of bombs into houses. Evening, hymn in the field, 'Nun danket alle Gott' (Thank we all the Lord)"—expressed the cynicism of German culture for Bédier, while typifying the German soldier. "Few [of the crimes]," he maintained, "are the deed of isolated brutes such as are met with . . . in the noblest armies. [They] dishonor not only the individual but the entire body of soldiers, the officers, the nation."[40]

How did Bédier account for the portrait he presented? One possibility was racial characteristics, which late nineteenth-century anthropology along with social Darwinism had turned into a ready tool for explaining "national" behavior. The author of a parallel British inquiry also involving *Kriegstagebücher*, J. H. Morgan (professor of constitutional law at London University),

---

[38] Bédier, *Les crimes allemands*, pp. 31–38; Grimme (n. 17 above), p. 42.

[39] Bédier, *Les crimes allemands*, pp. 12–14, and *Comment l'allemagne*, pp. 17–19. Hollmann and Larsen contested Bédier's translation of *mußten*.

[40] Bédier, *Les crimes allemands*, pp. 26–27. "Nun danket alle Gott" was Prussia's victory hymn after the battle of Leuthen in 1757.

concluded that the ultimate explanation of German "moral perversion" was "one for the anthropologist rather than for the lawyer, and [that] there may be some force in the contention of those who believe that the Prussian is not a member of the Teutonic family at all, but a "throw back" to some Tartar stock."[41] But Bédier's explanations remained firmly cultural rather than biological.

For Bédier, language and literature were powerful forces distilling and transmitting the essence of a national identity and culture. In particular, as a leading specialist in medieval French, he felt that the literature of chivalry remained part of the French character. Neither the use of chivalry as a foil for the realities of industrial warfare nor literary definitions of national character were unique to Bédier. Many had experienced 1914 as an "escape from modernity," and the drama critic of the *Revue des deux mondes* wrote in January 1915 that "to revive our literary tradition is also part of the work of national defense."[42] Ironically, Bédier's German critics attributed what they considered his fantasies to the worst tradition of French literary licentiousness, from Rabelais to Zola. But as a specialist in troubador literature, especially the *Chanson de Roland*, Bédier had a personal vision of honorable conduct in warfare rooted in an idealized version of the French medieval past. Between writing his two brochures, he composed a show for the newly reopened Comédie Française entitled "Chivalry," which was based on the chansons de geste.[43] And he concluded *Les crimes allemands* by arguing that German military philosophy sought "to eliminate from the laws and customs of war the humanity which centuries of Christianity and chivalry had with great effort managed to instill in them."

More broadly, however, Bédier's cultural explanation of the "atrocities" stemmed from the intellectual approach to Germany and German studies prevalent in French universities. French interest in Germany after 1870 was intense but was expressed in essentially literary and philosophical terms, partly because images of Germany externalized French self-doubt faced with the multiple challenges of industrialized life and a rapidly changing European balance of power. French intellectuals in the decade before the war were by no means Germanophobes. But German evolution was explained as a dichotomy between two traditions. One was positive and varied with the intellectual's own viewpoint—social democracy for socialists, south German Catholic royalism for monarchists, *Vormärz* liberalism for moderate

---

[41] J. H. Morgan, *German Atrocities: An Official Investigation* (London, 1916), pp. 52–53; S. Wallace, *War and the Image of Germany: British Academics, 1914–1918* (Edinburgh, 1988), pp. 182–83.

[42] E. Leed, *No Man's Land: Combat and Identity in World War I* (Cambridge, 1979), pp. 58–69; *Revue des deux mondes* (January 15, 1915), p. 455.

[43] *Revue des deux mondes* (February 15, 1915), pp. 909–20.

Republicans. The other was negative and exemplified by the militarism, expansionism, and antiliberalism associated with Prussia. The intellectual doyens of this malign Germany were Hegel, Treitschke, the nationalist historian, and von Bernhardi and other theorists of the necessity of war on social Darwinist grounds. British academics shared this Manichaean vision of German culture.[44]

The outbreak of war in 1914 slotted easily into this analysis as the triumph of the negative over the positive Germany. The thesis was explicitly developed by Durkheim in another of the Paris committee's brochures. He portrayed the war as a contest between the "humanitarian morality" of a Christianized West, whose values were addressed to all mankind, and the narrowly national philosophy of the "will to power" and of the absolute right of the state over civil society, which he took to be the dominant German "mental attitude."[45] Bédier endorsed this view, accusing Treitschke, Bernhardi, and others of supplying the theories of barbaric warfare, and he castigated the ninety-three signatories of the October 1914 declaration for servility in the face of the "crimes" of the military leadership.[46] The issue of civilized conduct in warfare crystallized the moral and intellectual case against Germany.

The German philologists had a hard time opposing Bédier's overall case on German "atrocities." Faced with views like that of the Swedish *Göteborgsposten* in February 1915, which concluded that "the entire civilized world awaits the explanation of the German military authorities concerning the military diaries published by M. Bédier," the rebarbative refutation of linguistic detail (however important) made weak counterpropaganda.[47] Yet the circumstances of the war, if nothing else, deprived the Germans of the dramatic material used by Bédier. Kuttner tried to present "positive" evidence in the form of accounts by French soldiers of the sacking of French shops and some testimonies to the kindness of ordinary Germans, culled from French prisoners' correspondence. He also claimed, in response to the Stenger affair, that Joffre had issued an order on August 31 for the killing of prisoners.[48] But the essence of the German academics' case remained the franc-tireur argument, as well as a refusal to recognize the dehumanized collective character portrait with which Bédier confronted them. Bédier's picture simply did not fit the image the German academic community had of

---

[44] C. Digeon, *La crise allemande de la pensée française, 1870–1914* (Paris, 1959); Mitchell (n. 16 above); Wallace, pp. 170, 174–76.
[45] Émile Durkheim, *L'allemagne au dessus de tout* (Paris, 1916).
[46] Bédier, *Les crimes allemands*, p. 39.
[47] Quoted by Kuttner (n. 17 above), pp. 4–5.
[48] Ibid., pp. 30–37 and pp. 40 ff., esp. p. 66.

their nation, for, as Fritz Ringer has shown, Imperial Germany was regarded by the intellectuals as the fountainhead of a superior "Kultur."[49]

The cultural relativity of what contemporaries on opposing sides meant by an "atrocity" emerges clearly from the *Kriegstagebücher* controversy. The question nonetheless remains of the relationship between such radically opposed interpretations and the actual experience of the German military and of French and Belgian civilians. A complete answer cannot possibly be attempted here. But we can see whether the war diaries provide any insight into the reality of German military conduct in 1914. It is not feasible, at least for the moment, to establish the representativity of the extracts used by Bédier in relation to either the totality of captured *Kriegstagebücher* (in the absence of the originals)[50] or all extant uncaptured examples. But the published extracts can be evaluated in two ways: first, by their internal evidence and second, by their relationship with other sources concerning the same or similar incidents, and especially with a number of unpublished soldiers' diaries from German archives.

OTHER GERMAN WAR DIARIES: HOW DO THEY RELATIVIZE BÉDIER?

Among the diaries in German archives, two are particularly useful. The manuscript diary of Professor von Pezold, a conservative medical man from Stuttgart predisposed to believe in the German cause, expressed growing shock at German military conduct in 1914. He recorded the brutal treatment of French civilians and wounded French soldiers and large-scale plundering, which he either witnessed himself or heard recounted by fellow officers. The unpublished diary of another medical officer in the Württemberg army, Dr. Flammer, who was quite uncritical toward the behavior of the German army, is nevertheless useful because of its representative quality in reflecting commonly held enemy stereotypes and in condoning the harsh conduct of the troops.[51]

The official German case that the Belgians in particular had fought a savage but coordinated irregular war may have been a genuine belief or a cynical cover for preemptive action against the civilian population.[52] It was certainly

---

[49] Fritz K. Ringer, *The Decline of the German Mandarins: The German Academic Community, 1890–1933* (Cambridge, Mass., 1969), pp. 180–86.

[50] Bédier claimed that he chose forty from a much larger body of diaries quite randomly, but this is impossible to verify (*Les crimes allemands*, pp. 5–7).

[51] Württembergisches Hauptstaatsarchiv-Militärarchiv, Stuttgart (HStAS), M 660, Pezold and Flammer diaries.

[52] Notably in the kaiser's telegram of September 8, 1914, to President Wilson and in the official German reply to Allied atrocity accusations, *Die völkerrechtswidrige*

invoked by the commanders of the three main armies that swept through central and southern Belgium to justify what they admitted were harsh measures.[53] But what emerges strikingly from the diaries published by the French and from the uncaptured war diaries of Pezold and Flammer is the undoubted conviction of the ordinary German soldier that francs-tireurs really existed. Ironically, this conclusion completely escaped Bédier, since it failed to match his preconceived dual explanation of coldly premeditated brutality by the officer corps and innate bestiality by the troops. Exploration of the possibility that German soldiers suffered a collective delusion about Belgian and French civilian resistance was not on Bédier's intellectual agenda.

In fact, the ground for the rapid growth of franc-tireur fear was prepared by several factors. The image of the franc-tireur derived from the Franco-Prussian war, 1870–71, when recognizably structured bands of armed irregular soldiers formed in response to the appeal of Gambetta and the new Republican government (well after the initial invasion) and operated for a number of months. They had a high nuisance value, carrying out ambushes on the German troops already in occupation of northern and central France.[54] Soldiers' memoirs from the Franco-Prussian war, and above all those of the Count Helmuth von Moltke, chief of the Prussian General Staff, contributed to the place of the franc-tireur as a figure of fear in military and popular memory, and this image was further diabolized by a body of popular sensationalist literature on French irregular warfare in 1870–71 that was still widely read on the eve of the Great War.[55] The franc-tireur was thus readily available as a stereotype on which tension and fear could focus.

Führung des belgischen Volkskriegs (Berlin, 1915), commonly known as the German White Book (English trans. by Edward N. Bennett, *The German Army in Belgium* [London, 1921]).

[53] A. von Kluck, *The March on Paris and the Battle of the Marne, 1914* (Berlin, 1920; English trans., London, 1920), pp. 25–26. Von Kluck was commander of the First Army, on the German right flank. Von Bülow, commander of the Second Army, justified the mass killing at Andenne (see n. 34 above), as well as "reprisals" against civilians more generally in K. von Bülow, *Mon rapport sur la bataille de la Marne* (Berlin, 1919; French trans., Paris, 1921). The commander of the Third Army, Baron von Hausen, also retrospectively justified "the most serious and rigorous measures" against civilians, including the largest single mass killing, at Dinant, by reference to francs-tireurs (*Souvenirs de la campagne de la Marne en 1914* [Loschwitz, 1920; French trans., Paris, 1922], p. 134).

[54] Michael Howard, *The Franco-Prussian War: The German Invasion of France, 1870–1871* (1961; reprint, New York, 1990), pp. 249–56.

[55] Van Langenhove (n. 8 above), pp. 144–45. Compare Helmut von Moltke, *The Franco-German War of 1870–71* (Berlin, 1891; English trans., 4th ed., London, 1914), pp. 114–15. The memoirs of 1870–71 enjoyed a renaissance of popularity in 1914: cf. O. August, *Meine Erlebnisse in Frankreich, 1870/71: Kriegserinnerungen eines Füsiliers vom Inf.-Regiment Nr. 55* (Oldenburg, 1914).

In 1914, the memory of the francs-tireurs of 1870–71 was explicity called upon by the German military leadership to justify the execution of innocent civilians. A statement drafted on August 12 by the Chief of the General Staff, Helmuth von Moltke (nephew of the victor of 1871), and communicated to the world via the German Foreign Ministry and the German press on August 14 "warned" France and Belgium that resistance by civilian "francs-tireurs" was taking place, "just as was the case in 70/71," and that it would entail summary executions and the indiscriminate burning down of "towns or villages from which German troops were fired upon." Moltke explained that it was "in the nature of such things that [the military countermeasures] will be extraordinarily harsh and even, under [some] circumstances, affect the innocent."[56]

Given the widespread popular preconceptions, reinforced by promptings from the army leadership, it is not surprising that men were susceptible to the franc-tireur fear. For the mobilized soldiers the absence of news created an information vacuum that was filled by official army communications. Inevitably, rumor flourished as soldiers spread myth and fantasy by word of mouth. All this created an atmosphere in which perfectly innocent events were likely to be misread and random acts seemed part of a sinister design. Troops new to combat, many of them from an urban background, were suddenly exposed to extreme danger in unfamiliar rural surroundings. Triggering incidents were supplied by the particular circumstances of the German offensive, with enormous daily marches (especially on the German right flank) and a skilled retreat by the Allied armies, which involved the Germans in ambushes by the enemy rear guard, constant contact with hostile patrols, and scattered attacks by isolated groups of enemy stragglers.

The integral text of the anonymous diarist of the 178th Saxons (published by the French in 1916), which chronicles the regiment's march through Belgium, provides a clear example of how this combination of circumstances fanned anxiety about francs-tireurs.[57] Crossing the frontier a week after the invasion, the author felt the initial reception to be amicable, with one old woman near Gouvy telling him in French that "you are not barbarians; you have spared our crops." Sixty kilometers on, however, nocturnal nervousness about ambush was growing and hostages were taken as a "security measure." On the night of August 22, near intense fighting along the Meuse, the diarist noted a house on fire, "doubtless to betray our position," and the following

---

[56] Chief of the General Staff to the Auswärtiges Amt, August 12, 1914, Politisches Archiv des Auswärtigen Amtes, Bonn, R 20880, fol. 12–13, fol. 15; *Norddeutsche Allgemeine Zeitung, Schwäbischer Merkur,* and other papers (August 14 and 15, 1914); cf. also Wieland (n. 7 above), pp. 28–29.

[57] J. de Dampierre, *Carnets de route de combattants allemands: Traduction intégrale* (Paris, 1916), pp. 3–71.

day he was convinced that the principal opposition to the advance into Leffe had come from francs-tireurs. Two handcuffed civilians were used as either guides or shields during a night march on August 26, and the incendiarism and executions at Villers-sur-Fagne were prompted by the supposed action of the inhabitants in signaling to the French from the church tower (a detail left out of Bédier's published extract). In the forced march through the Ardennes forest toward the French frontier, there were no stragglers "for fear of francs-tireurs." But, as Bédier highlighted, the first village in France, Gué d'Hossus, was burned because of an accidental shot, and this prompted the diarist to reflect that, along with justified executions, there should be "verification of suspicions of culpability, in order to control this indiscriminate shooting of everyone."

Pezold's diary confirms the soldiers' credulity in the face of rumor and their belief in francs-tireurs. For at least the first two weeks of the war his unit received no mail and no newspapers. Only when the mobile war was succeeded by static trench warfare could the supply of mail and newspapers be resumed reliably.[58] On August 15 he noted that instead of mail and newspapers the troops were feeding on rumors. For example, a captain told his company that Belfort had been captured, Italy was said to have declared war on France and Romania on Russia, the Russian Baltic fleet had been destroyed, and Russia had sued for peace. The Metz Dragoons were said to have been wiped out. For Pezold it was clear that this was all "false news." Beyond doubt, however, and placed in the indicative, not the subjunctive used for distancing reported speech, was the "painful news" that a medical colleague, Dr. Stamer (of the Uhlans), had been "ambushed while riding behind the squadron and shot dead by a Lorraine local inhabitant."[59] Pezold went on to describe how, in consequence, "any bright, shiny items are being removed from the uniforms, the epaulettes blackened with oil paint, iodine tincture, nitric acid or sublimate, etc. . . . Numerous local inhabitants are being arrested [in Lorraine] because they had apparently been shooting. The population is filled with fear and is only gradually beginning to trust the Germans."[60] In fact, as an internal army investigation established, Stamer was not shot by francs-tireurs but by French army snipers on bicycles.[61] But

---

[58] On August 17 Pezold noted that he had still received no mail (HStAS, M 660, Pezold diary, p. 3).

[59] HStAS, M 660, Pezold diary, August 15, 1914, p. 2. On August 31 Pezold reported further similar rumors, which he termed "unverifiable": Belfort had been captured; America, Italy, and Holland had declared war on Britain; the Belgian king had been captured (Pezold diary, p. 15).

[60] HStAS, M 660, Pezold diary, August 15, 1914, p. 2.

[61] Graf von Pfeil, 27th Division (2d Royal Württemberg) to Generalkommando, August 14, 1914, transcript in Grand Headquarters to Reichskanzler, August 29,

meanwhile Villers la Montage and a neighboring village in which Stamer was killed were set on fire by the 123d Infantry Regiment, and the priest and mayor were turned over to a court-martial on suspicion of shared guilt, after having been beaten thoroughly with rifle butts.[62]

Captain Meyer, a member of a squadron of Uhlans attached to a Landwehr Regiment, told Pezold how tense the German soldiers were at the beginning of the war. He himself had very frequently been shot at by his own troops, and he had seen how salvos were fired into empty houses. He had just arrived on the scene once when a seventy-five-year-old man was about to be shot. All inhabitants (at a place not named) had been ordered to hand in their weapons, and the old man arrived late with his useless rifle. First he was shot at by the guard, then taken prisoner, and would have been killed for bearing a weapon, but Meyer prevented the execution.[63]

Flammer's diary provides additional corroboration of the nervousness of the German troops. At Barancy, on the evening of August 25, several dead officers were buried with military honors. After the usual salvo of shots a number of further shots were fired near the field hospital, giving rise to the impression that a planned attack was taking place. Flammer and his men immediately seized their weapons and the hospital guards started shooting in the direction they thought the shots had come from. Heightening the panic, a cyclist arrived, reporting that on the road from Signeulx to Barancy he had been shot at twenty-five times. Patrols, however, found no sign of the enemy. The column telephoned the command post in Signeulx for help; the commander, Captain von Puttkamer, immediately moved out, shot a suspicious-looking farmhouse into flames, and hurried to Barancy. General merriment and drinking of wine ensued in relief.[64]

The area Signeulx-Musson-Barancy was clearly one that had experienced high tension and several cases of savage reprisals against the civilian population for what were perceived as franc-tireur attacks. On August 22, according to the war diary of Generalmajor Christof von Ebbinghaus, commander of the 125th (Württemberg) regiment, shots were fired from the fruit orchards near Signeulx by individual French army snipers and civilians. The first house from which the regiment was fired on was set on fire. In

---

1914, Politisches Archiv des Auswärtigen Amtes, Bonn, R 22382. Nevertheless, the incident may still have represented a breach of the laws of war, for according to the division's report the French soldiers must have seen Stamer's Red Cross armband.

[62] Diary of Generalarzt Dr. Max Erwin Wilhelm Flammer, August 20, 1914, HStAS, M 660, pp. 6v, 7.

[63] HStAS, M 660, Pezold diary, October 29, 1914, p. 81.

[64] HStAS, M 660, Flammer diary, August 25, 1914, p. 10v. The typed transcript has "Ligneulx," but there is no village of that name in the area, and this is probably a misreading for "Signeulx," a village three kilometers west of Barancy.

Musson there were reportedly francs-tireurs involved in fighting, and likewise in Barancy. Ebbinghaus was honest enough to record that in Barancy there was a French machine-gun emplacement in the church tower and French infantry in the village, but he did not seem to be aware of the unlikelihood of civilians using a machine-gun. Near the station in Signeulx shots were fired from the houses and Ebbinghaus ordered the houses to be burned down, but they failed to catch fire.[65] Ebbinghaus was not such a skeptical observer as Pezold, but he too was aware of the ease with which civilians could be wrongly suspected of engaging in battle. He reported how on the next day, August 23, his regiment was advancing toward Fresnois-Montigny without coming under attack. Suddenly, at a distance of 500–600 meters, there was heavy firing from the first houses in Montigny. Ebbinghaus, who had thrown himself to the ground and taken cover behind a haystack, saw how his men, assuming that the shots must have been fired by the local inhabitants, "stormed wildly into the village." The men set Montigny on fire.[66] It should be noted that at a distance of 600 meters it is almost impossible to distinguish soldier from unarmed civilian.

A junior officer, Captain Fauser, leader of the Seventh Company, 121st Regiment, clearly felt no doubts about the culpability of the civilian population. He recorded how, on August 22 in the village St. Pancré, the women offered the passing soldiers water, which they gladly drank. Then, "Hardly had we and a following company left the village of St. Pancré [when] furious shooting by the inhabitants began, aimed at our machine-gun company which they must have taken to be our field kitchen. This mean treachery! First water and then franc-tireur shooting! But these fellows chose the right one by picking on Captain Sprösser: immediate machine-gun fire and the glow of burning soon showed us that the machine-gun company was taking thorough revenge."[67] Here the lack of any evidence of civilian resistance is noteworthy. But the assumption of civilian culpability was not restricted to the soldiers and junior officers. Fauser's company came under fire, allegedly from francs-tireurs, from Fresnois la Montagne. The consequence, he wrote, was that the Sixth Company was ordered to attack Fresnois, round up the francs-tireurs, and kill them.[68] Such an order can only have come from the officer

---

[65] Diary (handwritten manuscript, corrected after the war) of Generalmajor Christof von Ebbinghaus, HStAS, M 660, NL Ebbinghaus, Heft 4, August 22, 1914, pp. 8–9.

[66] Ibid., August 23, p. 22. In 1917 Christof von Ebbinghaus published *Kriegserlebnisse im Herbst 1914 in Frankreich* (Stuttgart, 1917), in which he quoted extensively from his diary. The last passage was quoted as it stands, but the final sentence dealing with the burning of Montigny was left out.

[67] Kriegsbericht des Hauptmanns d.R. Fauser, typescript, August 22, 1914, in HStAS, M 660, NL Ebbinghaus, Heft 8, p. 18.

[68] Ibid., p. 21. A pencil-written marginal addition after the word *erschießen* reads "twenty men," which might mean the number killed.

commanding the 121st Regiment, or possibly even a more senior commander. Again, no evidence was cited to prove that civilians were involved in the fighting. But the fear of francs-tireurs was real enough, as countless other diary entries show. Despite evidence to the contrary—for example, that casualties in the German ranks were often caused by nervousness and "friendly fire"—Fauser was not alone in believing in the existence of the francs-tireurs. When the divisional staff marched through the town of Longuyon, the battalion of which his company was a part was given the task of securing the route. The battalion commander divided the companies into two rows and ordered them to march with their rifles aimed at the houses to the right and left of the road. Any male citizen showing himself at a window and any armed woman was to be shot immediately.[69]

There were, however, some skeptical minds in the German army who, although not able to prevent the commission of "atrocities," preserved a record for future generations. Lieutenant-Colonel Gleich, a member of the General Staff until 1913 and in 1914 the commander of the Twenty-fifth Dragoon Regiment (First Württemberg) noted at several points his doubt as to the assumption by his men that unexpected shooting must have come from francs-tireurs.[70] With breathtaking honesty he recorded how the nervousness and inexperience of his men could lead to tragic results, as the following incident revealed. In the town of Blâmont, although most inhabitants had fled, his troops were nevertheless on high alert because they had sighted a French patrol and felt that the remaining civilians were hostile. In the evening of August 10, a reserve lieutenant, Loos, was checking that the order to keep a light on in all windows and the doors open was being obeyed. He found one door locked; despite repeated knocking it was not opened until at last a man in shirtsleeves appeared in the doorway with a raised rifle. Loos, who took the man to be a franc-tireur, shot him with his pistol. The man, who died of his wound, was in fact a German soldier who thought he was being attacked by francs-tireurs.[71]

The fear engendered by the chaos of the invasion and the specter of francs-tireurs thus emerges as a major cause of the reprisals against civilians, of whose ferocity the *Kriegstagebücher,* unpublished as well as published, leave little doubt. Soldier Philipp and his anonymous comrade of the 178th (Saxon) Regiment were, as we have seen, both eyewitnesses of the execution of 150–250 civilians in Leffe, immediately north of Dinant. Both men believed, in common with the German White Book of May 1915 (the response

---

[69] Ibid., August 24, 1914, p. 24.

[70] For example, in an incident in which a dragoon was fatally wounded near Verdenal (near Blâmont) on August 9 (diary of Gleich, HStAS, M 660, NL Gleich, Heft 153, pp. 24–25).

[71] Ibid., August 10, pp. 37–38.

to the official Belgian and French reports), that withering fire by francs-tireurs had been responsible for the regiment's losses, where Belgian official reports and independent testimony held that the shooting came from the French army on the far bank of the Meuse.[72] But both diarists also convey, almost casually, the severity of the reprisal, with "every house in the entire valley overturned [and] the men shot. . . . This perfidious war arouses a boundless rage in our men, and they want to put everything to the torch."[73] Over six hundred civilians were executed in Dinant as a whole.

In Lorraine, soldier Fischer recorded his shock at the destruction of Noményand its menfolk in response to supposed franc-tireur resistance, by order of his regimental commander. The French official report concluded a few months later that no such resistance had occurred but that the Germans had fired on each other. One prisoner suggested, however, that officers had stoked such a mood of anxiety with tales of the French mutilating captured Germans that the Second and Fourth Bavarian Regiments simply fell on the hapless village. Over fifty civilians perished.[74] Overall, about 5,500 civilians were deliberately killed by the German army in Belgium in 1914.[75] No estimate exists for France, but on a minimum reckoning the figure would bring the total for both countries to well in excess of six thousand and perhaps substantially more. Dinant and Nomény, moreover, were only two of a number of incidents that involved the simultaneous execution of tens, and sometimes hundreds, of civilians.

The status of the civilian resistance claimed by so many of Bédier's diary extracts and clearly credited by Pezold and Flammer is thus a central issue. The franc-tireur anxiety, amounting to a kind of mass paranoia, that swept Germany in the autumn of 1914 with its tales of mutilations, shooting in the back, curés signaling from church towers, and so on, and that was sanctioned by the official German texts justifying military repression, was discredited by two contemporary inquiries within Germany, one Catholic and one in the Social-Democratic daily *Vorwärts*. The franc-tireur fear was also pronounced by the only scholarly study during the war to be a "cycle of legends" without any substance in reality.[76]

---

[72] The eleventh Belgian report dealt with Dinant, as did the Belgian reply to the White Book (n. 52 above), *Réponse au livre blanc allemand du 10 mai 1915* (Paris, 1916), pp. 199–289. Both the inquiry by the bishop of Namur in October 1915 (ibid., p. 216) and an independent investigation in the winter of 1914–15 (J. Chot, *La fureur allemande dans l'entre-Sambre-et-Meuse* [Charleroi, 1919], p. 75) concluded that there had been no civilian resistance.

[73] Dampierre (n. 57 above), pp. 22–23.

[74] *Rapports et procès-verbaux d'enquête* (n. 10 above), no. 1 (December 17, 1914).

[75] H. Pirenne, *La Belgique et la guerre mondiale* (Paris, 1928), p. 64.

[76] See van Langenhove (n. 8 above), which examines the Catholic and socialist criticisms in detail; Pirenne, esp. p. 56, for a similar conclusion to that of van Langenhove; and Wieland (n. 7 above).

German "Atrocities" and Franco-German Opinion 23

This is not to deny that scattered Belgian and French resistance may have occurred, especially under the initial shock of invasion. But there seems little evidence of the organized and widespread character claimed by the Germans and for which the British editor of the German White Book, Edward N. Bennett, produced evidence by citing Belgian newspapers of August 5–8, 1914.[77] Only in one instance, the defense of the arms factory at Herstael, does there appear to have been concerted resistance.[78] In both the Belgian and French cases there was insufficient time to organize this, and the authorities strenuously warned the population against any such action. The one detailed case study undertaken, of the sacking and massacre of Louvain from August 25 to August 30, endorses the contemporary Belgian and neutral conclusion that there was no evidence of the civilian resistance blamed by the Germans for the incident—the likely cause being a mistaken clash between the German garrison and German troops falling back under attack by the Belgian army.[79]

If it is true that there was no substantial irregular or civilian opposition to the German invasion, this means, paradoxically, that atrocity hysteria in the German army (i.e., the fear of francs-tireurs) had as its first and grimmest consequence savage reprisals that, in the eyes of the Allies, at least, amounted to real, and major, "atrocities." Yet in trying to elucidate further the nature of German military behavior in 1914, it is necessary to ask whether franc-tireur paranoia and mythology suffice as an explanation, especially since the "crimes" explored by Bédier through the evidence of the *Kriegstagebücher* covered more than reprisals against civilians, including use of human shields and the execution of wounded and prisoners. The evidence of published and unpublished war diaries suggests at least three additional categories of explanation for German military conduct in 1914, some of which touch on these additional types of "atrocity."

FURTHER EXPLANATIONS OF GERMAN MILITARY CONDUCT

First, some diaries reveal a substratum of more permanent mentalities that served to make harsh reprisals appear morally permissible, even necessary. Among these was a fierce anti-Catholicism and an almost phobic fear of

---

[77] Bennett (n. 52 above), pp. vii–ix.

[78] Ibid., p. viii. However, according to the Belgian newspaper *Le XXe siècle* of August 14, the reports of the civilian resistance at Herstael were based on a story by the correspondent of the Amsterdam *De telegraaf* and were greatly exaggerated. The idea of the entire population, including women and children, fighting the Prussians to the death was "une belle page de roman ou une émouvante scène de drame." The shooting came from a few civilians exasperated by the insolence and brutality of the invaders and who paid for their resistance with their lives (newspaper file in Bundesarchiv Koblenz, NL 15 Schwertfeger 106).

[79] Second official Belgian report, Antwerp, August 31, 1914; Schöller (n. 7 above).

priests among non-Catholic elements of the German army. From the outbreak of war, one form assumed by the spy mania that afflicted Germany, as all other belligerent societies, was that of supposed French agents dressed in religious habits.[80] The idea of a conspiratorial Catholicism, exercising total authority over its superstitious believers, found sharper focus as an explanation for the atrocities allegedly being committed against German troops on the clearly Catholic territories of Belgium and French Lorraine. The idea that Belgian and French priests were inciting their followers to resist legitimate military action by Germany became a key element of the German "atrocity" mythology and a source of bitter contention between the Belgian, French, and German Catholic churches.[81]

Anti-Catholicism thus tinged many of the incidents that constituted "atrocities" in Allied eyes. Convents and monasteries were rumored to be diabolical places where, behind a religious facade, mutilations were practiced on hapless wounded German soldiers. Priests were commonly arrested on suspicion of orchestrating resistance, while churches, and especially church towers, acquired an almost mystical role as the source of secret communication with the French and Belgian forces (by signal or telegraph) and as sites of deadly machine-guns.[82] The Belgian bishops identified fifty priests assassinated by the invaders.[83]

A Hamburg soldier who published his diary after the war recorded his first encounter with the fearful figure of the Belgian priest on August 13, 1914, thus: "Here we see the first Belgian prisoners in uniform and in civilian

[80] Telegram of the German abbot of Maria-Laach to Cardinal Mercier, primate of Belgium, on August 11, 1914, quoted in *Les evêques de Belgique aux évêques d'allemagne et d'Autriche-Hongrie* (November 1915), p. 4.

[81] Cardinal Mercier, primate of Belgium, conducted a campaign of protest against German "atrocities," including the sack of Louvain, which was addressed to his German coreligionists as well as to the German government and military authorities. H. Davignon, *Belgium and Germany* (London, 1916), pp. 82–83; I. Meseburg-Haubold, *Der Widerstand Kardinal Merciers gegen die deutsche Besetzung Belgiens, 1914–1918: Ein Beitrag zur politischen Rolle des Katholizismus im ersten Weltkrieg* (Frankfurt am Main, 1982). In France, a Catholic committee to disseminate anti-German propaganda was established early in 1915. Its first publication, A. Baudrillart et al., *La guerre allemande et le catholicisme* (Paris, 1915), dealt centrally with Germany's claim to be innocent of "atrocities" (pp. 280–86). It prompted a strong reaction from the German catholic hierarchy, notably Cardinals von Bettinger of Munich and von Hartmann of Cologne, and a German committee (lay dominated) was set up to rebut the French claims. Its first publication, *Der deutsche Krieg und der Katholizismus: Deutsche Abwehr französischer Angriffe: Herausgegeben von deutschen Katholiken* (Berlin, 1915), signed by one hundred distinguished Catholics, was a justification of legitimate self-defense for German actions in Belgium.

[82] Van Langenhove, pp. 66–84.

[83] *Les evêques de Belgique*, p. 10.

clothing, that is, *monsieur le curé*, this sinister figure of Belgium."[84] Bédier recorded the disgust of one diarist at the desecration of a Catholic sacristy by his fellow soldiers, as well as the account by soldier Thomas, of the 107th (Saxon) Infantry, of the execution of the priest of Spontin, Belgium, on August 23, along with thirty of his male parishioners.[85] Wladyslaus Ossowski, a Polish medical orderly with the Thirty-fourth Infantry Regiment (from Stettin), was shocked by his fellow soldiers' willful destruction of figures of the Virgin Mary in a Belgian shop and noted other manifestations of anti-Catholicism.[86] Of course, many of what the Allies took to be "atrocities" were committed by Catholic troops. This was notably the case with the Bavarian regiments in Alsace and Lorraine. But religious myths that had long expressed internal antagonisms within Germany (as during the Kulturkampf of the 1870s) seem now to have been exported as one explanation of illegitimate civilian resistance to the German army—and they colored German reprisals accordingly.

A second additional explanation for German military conduct in 1914 lies in the rapid blurring of the German army's own distinction between "true" and "treacherous" forms of warfare, and thus between soldiers and civilians. Underlying German military thinking in 1914, including the entirely unrealistic timetable of the Schlieffen Plan, was the institutionalized memory of 1870 with its consequent belief that the French army was militarily worthless and incapable of offering serious resistance.[87] Added to an unwillingness to accept that the Belgians were even entitled to oppose the traversal of their territory by a foreign army, this predisposed the German High Command (and

---

[84] W. Nau, *Beiträge zur Geschichte des Regiments Hamburg*, vol. 1, *Der Marsch auf Paris* (Hamburg, 1924), p. 16 (diary entry for August 13, 1914). Another, posthumously published, diary is also indicative of these often-voiced sentiments among Protestant Germans. Recording his lone trips on horseback through the Flemish part of Belgium in March 1915, Lieutenant Otto Ahrends noted that these were dangerous because of francs-tireurs. On Easter Sunday, he wrote, a soldier was found unconscious, with three serious wounds. In a moment of consciousness the injured soldier said he had been attacked by three *Pfaffen* (the contemptuous word for a priest or pastor). Thereupon several dozen priests were arrested. "It is the priests (Pfaffen) above all which Belgium can thank for its fate, for instead of carrying out their duties in the interests of harmony, the priests are whipping up fanaticism" (*Mit dem Regiment "Hamburg" in Frankreich, 1914–1916: Kriegs-Tagebuch* [Munich, 1917], p. 62).

[85] Bédier, *Comment l'allemagne* (n. 12 above), pp. 33, 35.

[86] Archives générales du royaume (AGR), Brussels, 3, 374 B1, Commission d'enquête sur la violation du droit des gens, file 34, signed deposition by Wladyslaw Ossowski, entitled "Die deutschen Barbaren in Belgien—ich selbst der Augenzeuge," handwritten in poor German and Polish, with a typed transcript in French.

[87] Gerhard Ritter, *The Schlieffen Plan: Critique of a Myth* (Munich, 1956; English trans., London, 1958), pp. 58–59.

quite possibly the ordinary soldier) to blame the fighting retreat and extremely heavy casualties they in fact encountered on underhanded tactics.

In some respects, this attitude was deeply contradictory. For if the notion of "honest," open battle between professionally led troops was obsolete even at the time of the Franco-Prussian war, failing as it did to allow for the tactics of ambush by regular troops or the role of irregular military forces, such as Gambetta's Republican levies in 1870–71 or the Belgian civil guard in 1914, the Germans themselves recognized this by attempting to criminalize and punish "treacherous" forms of combat. Moltke's "warning" published in the German press on August 14 was backed up a few days later by the War Ministry's instruction that anyone caught resisting who was "not unquestionably a member of the armed forces" was to be shot without court-martial, while a German Foreign Office note of August 13 accused Belgium of conducting warfare in breach of international law—with civilians fighting, the German wounded being mutilated, and cruelty toward medical staff and German civilians.[88]

Official policy underwrote, and thus helped to cause, the escalating harshness of reprisals. From August 12 to the end of the month, the number of collective executions involving tens or hundreds of civilians rose rapidly, before subsiding as the main body of fighting troops moved out of Belgium (and to a lesser extent, Lorraine) to converge on the Marne. At the same time, the dividing line between francs-tireurs, who in the original perception of German soldiers were armed civilians, and regular enemy troops who were also held guilty of "treacherous" tactics became obscure. By the end of August, whatever the status of the individual, soldier or civilian, prisoner or wounded, the treatment meted out was equally ruthless.

Thus, a wounded lieutenant in Pezold's field hospital told Pezold that he thought at first that the burning down of villages and shooting of inhabitants was extraordinarily cruel. But now (August 31, 1914) "he realized that this was the only way to end the franc-tireur war and the treacherous murders. The francs-tireurs did not dare to attack the infantry; they mainly attacked machine-gun units and ammunition columns. The ferocity [*Erbitterung*] with which the Germans fought on account of this minor war was [the lieutenant said] astonishing. A company of sappers which had been attacked killed the enemy soldiers with their axes. The wounded were killed by bayonet thrusts, for they often still fired."[89] In the case of Arlon, in Belgium, both alleged franc-tireur activity and mutilation of German wounded were used as justification for a mass execution of civilians. An apparently reliable German

---

[88] Directive, signed by von Falkenhayn, from the Prussian Ministry of War to Grand Headquarters, August 26, 1914, HStAS, M79/11b; Meseburg-Haubold, p. 47.

[89] HStAS, M 660, Pezold diary, August 31, 1914.

source told Pezold that he had heard that the franc-tireur fighting in Arlon was so heavy that 123 inhabitants were subsequently shot dead in groups of ten (the official Belgian report confirmed 121 victims). "They were then dragged by the legs and thrown onto a pile, and the corporals shot with their revolvers all those who had not been killed by the infantry. The whole execution was witnessed by the pastor, a woman, and two young girls, who were the last to be shot, for they had put out the eyes of wounded soldiers."[90]

The indiscriminate confusion of combatant and noncombatant, soldier and civilian, in the generalized charge of "treacherous" conduct also helps explain the significance of "human shields" and the dispatching of captured and wounded Allied soldiers, which figured so prominently in Bédier's *Kriegstagebücher* evidence. The use of civilian cover against the enemy in combat was at best justified on the grounds that civilians were guilty by association with the retreating enemy forces. But more typically, in the multiple examples in the French and Belgian official reports, it was a matter of pure military expediency, in which the German troops simply ignored the noncombatant status of the civilian population. In the case of Bédier's example, Lieutenant Eberlein's use of civilian cover under fire in Saint-Dié, the official French inquiry contested the German defense that the civilians were complicit in setting an ambush. Faced with a rear-guard action by the *chasseurs-alpins,* the Germans seized four civilians, one of whom was Visser, accountant in a local factory and undoubtedly the man who, according to Eberlein, assured him that there were no French soldiers left. But according to Visser's account, he was simply forced at gunpoint to precede the Germans toward the French barricade, after a German soldier had fallen, and in so doing he and one of his cohostages were wounded and the other two were killed.[91] In none of the statements gathered by the French committee is there any mention of French civilian resistance.

Dispatching wounded soldiers and prisoners was a practice clearly opposed to the German soldier's self-interest (in case of his own capture) and to the code of regular military warfare supposedly upheld by the Germans. But the French official reports endorse the suggestion of Bédier's examples that this was something that happened on a wide scale. In raising the Stenger case as a particularly notorious example at a senior level in the military hierarchy, Bédier could not reveal the full extent of the French government's proof without endangering its sources. In fact, the French embassy in Switzerland

---

[90] Ibid., October 18, 1914, pp. 67–68; *Commission d'enquête sur les violations des règles du droit des gens, des lois et des coutumes de la guerre, rapports et documents d'enquête* (Brussels, 1922), 1, pt. 1:249–50.

[91] *Rapports et procès-verbaux d'enquête* (n. 10 above), no. 5 (December 1915), pp. 171–72.

had been informed of the verbal order to finish off French soldiers as early as September 1914 by an Alsatian medical officer, Zimmerman, mobilized with the 112th (Baden) Regiment.[92] The form of the order he reported supports that indicated by the 1915 French inquiry among sixteen prisoners from the 112th and 142d Regiments.[93] A war diarist, Anton Rothacher of the 142d, confirmed the order and also provided some insight into its motivation or excuse, noting on August 27 that "French prisoners and wounded are all shot because they mutilate and maltreat our wounded."[94] This suggests how atrocity hysteria reinforced a readiness to accuse ordinary French soldiers of "treacherous" conduct, resulting in a sharp departure by German troops from accepted norms of military conduct. The French government brought Stenger's order as one of its cases before the abortive war crimes tribunal, organized less than enthusiastically by the German government at Leipzig in 1921. Although Stenger was acquitted, sufficient extra evidence was gathered—notably from Alsace-Lorrainers like Zimmerman, who were now free to give full rein to their dissidence—to make it quite clear that such an order had been issued and executed.[95]

The third additional explanation for German military conduct comes from the ambiguous status of Alsace-Lorraine. France and Belgium were not the only enemy territories on the Western Front. Partly because of the ethnic tensions within the German army, Alsace and German Lorraine were dangerous areas. Not only were local inhabitants especially untrustworthy (often German speaking, but equally often Francophile) but the German divisions deployed there also contained many soldiers from these same "unreliable" peripheral regions of the Reich. The situation was made more tense by the French invasion of upper Alsace in the first week of the war, which exposed the local population to accusations of treason on the return of the Germans. On August 14, houses in the suburbs of Mulhouse (briefly occupied by the French) were burned and civilians executed on the grounds that the inhabitants had fired on the German troops.[96] Alfred Fried, the founder of the German Peace Society, recorded in his (civilian) diary on

---

[92] Archives Nationales, Paris (AN), BB 18 2568/4 (Stenger dossier), report of French embassy, Switzerland, to the government in Bordeaux, September 22, 1914, and note from the French ambassador, Berne, to the French Foreign Office, August 16, 1921, with a retrospective account of how the information was acquired. Zimmerman copied the order, and it was relayed by his brother-in-law to the Berne embassy. The families were from Mulhouse, very close to the Swiss frontier.

[93] *Rapports et procès-verbaux d'enquête*, no. 3 (May 1, 1915), pp. 10–11, 66–73.

[94] Ibid., p. 72.

[95] AN, BB 18 2568/4 (Stenger dossier), depositions by Geisser, Schaffhauser, Haberetser, and Gisié.

[96] AN, 4AJ 7 (Besançon), deposition of Marcel Schoff, mayor of Pfastatt, a commune on the outskirts of Mulhouse.

August 20 that because of franc-tireur activity the commanding general in upper Alsace had issued a proclamation that stated that if the inhabitants of a community took part in fighting against the German troops, not only they but also the mayor of the community would be shot and the place demolished. The troops had received the order to shoot any householder affording shelter to a French soldier.[97] This harsh policy created severe tensions within the German forces in the region. The French authorities received a report from a woman who had witnessed a mutiny in Dornach by troops who were almost certainly Alsatian and who, when forced to shoot civilians, turned and killed their officer. The same woman overheard other German troops say that before they left they would smash Alsace to smithereens.[98]

The extent of contempt for, and mistrust of, the Alsatian population within the German military had already been revealed in the Zabern Affair of 1913, in which a Prussian officer offered a reward to encourage his men to use their sabers against civilians in cases of quarrels or disturbances.[99] During the war Alsace was the only part of Germany on the Western Front that was in the immediate war zone. Although most citizens of Alsace and German Lorraine professed their loyalty to the German cause, General Gaede, the commanding officer responsible for upper Alsace, regarded every Alsatian as a potential spy. The German press and the army leadership contributed to the construction of an image of the Alsatian as an enemy, and German soldiers were led by the press and the inhabitants of the border regions in Baden to believe that the population on the other bank of the Rhine were all *Franzosenköpfe* who were thoroughly untrustworthy.[100]

Such an attitude doubtless helps to explain why the worst cases of collective reprisals against civilians in France mainly occurred in the nearby area of French Lorraine and the Vosges, where the population was also seen as unredeemably treacherous and hostile to Germany. Amid widespread accusations of collusion with the French forces and franc-tireur activity, the civilian population was treated harshly, especially by the Bavarian army. The prefect of the Meurthe-et-Moselle (Lorraine) reported to the Ministry of the Interior that "on Friday, August 21, from early morning, the city of Nancy was in violent turmoil. It was learned that the Germans were approaching

---

[97] Alfred H. Fried, *Mein Kriegs-Tagebuch* (Zurich, 1918–20), 1:26–27.

[98] Declaration by a woman from Alsace before Sous-Lieutenant Suran, August 20, 1914, on events at Burzwiller and Dornach, August 14/15 and 19, in Archives du Ministère des Affaires Etrangères, Paris, Guerre 1914–18. Droit de la Guerre sur Terre, microfilm P1463, vol. 1097, pp. 101–2.

[99] D. Schoenbaum, *Zabern 1913: Consensus Politics in Imperial Germany* (London, 1982); D. Richert, *Beste Gelegenheit zum Sterben: Meine Erlebnisse im Kriege, 1914–1918,* ed. A. Tramitz and B. Ulrich (Munich, 1989), p. 399, postscript.

[100] Richert, p. 403.

from the north and east, in the north via Nomény where they were committing atrocities (executions, incendiarism, rapes) and from where the terrified population had in part come to take refuge in Nancy."[101] Not only the Nomény incident, for which Bédier, of course, provided diary evidence, but also other incidents such as those in Lunéville and in Gerbéviller (where at least fifty inhabitants died) caused significant numbers of civilians to perish, while random shootings and widespread incendiarism helped provoke a substantial civilian exodus into the French interior.

The *Kriegstagebücher,* then, published and unpublished, provide a considerable body of evidence not only about the nature and evolution of German military reprisals against French and Belgian civilians but also about the mentality in which these were carried out. The framework of this mentality was formed by atrocity hysteria, by the military view of "treacherous" enemy tactics and civilian resistance, and by internal divisions of German society, both religious and regional, that were externalized onto invaded populations. The degree to which the fears of ordinary German soldiers were manipulated by officers and perhaps by the High Command (as some war diaries and other sources hint) cannot be pursued here. What does stand out is the apparent consensus within the German army, from official declarations to ordinary soldiers' diaries, that what Bédier (and Allied opinion) took to be "atrocities" constituted both necessary and legitimate action—as it did for the philologists who contested Bédier's reading of the captured *Kriegstagebücher* and for German intellectuals generally.

Yet German opinion on the issue was more complex than this. Some dissonant German voices clearly felt that what was occurring in invaded Belgium and France was morally worrying, if not indefensible, although in the German diaries we consulted the concepts "atrocities" and "war crimes" are not used. Bédier, in making his case for the collective brutality of German soldiery, found some opposing voices that threw the general argument into sharper relief by criticizing comrades and signaling disquiet at civilian repression. A certain Glöde, of the Ninth Battalion of Pioneers, painted a vivid picture of the "fury" of the German soldiers early on in the Belgian campaign. He deemed a measure of anger to be justified but condemned wanton "vandalism" and reflected that the inhabitants, who were only defending their country, had been savagely punished for their cruelties. Kuttner hinted, wrongly, as it turned out, at a forgery.[102] Bédier quoted a

---

[101] AN F7 12938, report of August 27, 1914.

[102] Bédier, *Les crimes allemands* (n. 12 above), pp. 36–38; Kuttner (n. 17 above), p. 8; (French) Ministry of Foreign Affairs (n. 24 above), no. 54. Kuttner claimed that the German military authorities could find no record of Glöde. But the Ministry of Foreign Affairs volume, on the advice of Glöde (a prisoner of war in Casablanca), ascribed probable authorship to another, presumably dead, soldier, Dannehl, of the same regiment.

number of other diarists (withholding their names to spare them disciplinary sanctions) who used terms like "barbarians" and "vandals" in referring to pillage and arson by the German army. Again, Kuttner's response was an open accusation of forgery, as if such sentiments were inconceivable. He dismissed X (Forty-sixth Infantry Regiment), for example, on the grounds that no German noncommissioned officer would be so unpatriotic as to suggest that Germany's conduct in France was "direkt barbarisch" (purely barbarous) and much worse than that with which the Germans charged the Russians.

Yet there is little reason to accept the forgery charge. Rather, these were symptoms of doubt among some German soldiers (how many, it is impossible to say) about the discrepancy they experienced between draconian military repression and the civilian offenses that supposedly justified it. Bédier's examples are corroborated by the evidence of unpublished diaries. Pezold echoed the sentiment that crimes committed by German soldiers dishonored the German army and nation. Reporting on the pillage by German soldiers of two small châteaus at Landreville, near Rémonville, he directly contradicted Kuttner's assumptions about German patriotism precisely by suggesting that the Russians could not have behaved any worse in East Prussia. "Again I was ashamed [of ourselves] before the population."[103]

Pezold also noted in his diary on November 6 that a medical officer in the western army was disciplined for making remarks in a letter that could be used by the enemy to attack the Germans. He thought it was probably about German soldiers plundering and noted that he himself had certainly also made such remarks and that "at every step" one heard officers "and especially doctors" making such remarks.[104] The question of plundering was a constant topic of conversation among officers, as Pezold noted in his diary on November 12, 1914. One fellow officer, Lieutenant Veiel, said that "the pharisaical tone of the German newspapers made him sick and the Russian depredations can hardly have been any worse than those committed by our soldiers." Veiel went on to say that "many sins had been committed when villages were set on fire because of shooting from the houses by isolated French soldiers [*Versprengte*] and then even the women and children became the victims of the firing of our infantry against the will of the senior commanders."[105]

Unsurprisingly, those elements of the population least integrated into the Reich (and deemed hostile, or "reichsfeindlich," by the authorities), were well represented among these dissonant voices. The Alsatian Dominik Richert, whose diary written shortly after the war has recently been

---

[103] HStAS, M 660, Pezold diary, September 15, 1914, p. 26.
[104] Ibid., November 6, 1914, p. 92.
[105] Ibid., November 12, 1914, p. 102.

discovered and published, was a peasant from Alsace conscripted into a Baden regiment who from the start had profound misgivings about the behavior of German troops. As early as August 9, 1914, he prevented a Baden soldier in his regiment (112th Infantry) from finishing off a wounded Frenchman, and he not only confirmed the existence of the Stenger order to finish off the French prisoners of war but also, and more significantly, suggested that it was unpopular with most soldiers, although some welcomed it.[106] Wladyslaus Ossowski, who felt intimidated as a Pole and offended as a Catholic by his fellow soldiers, burned his uniform and deserted to Holland in 1915, where he related his account, "The German Barbarians in Belgium," to the Belgian authorities.[107]

CONCLUSION

These countercurrents of German military opinion significantly deconstruct the image of treacherous and hostile civilians that was projected by the bulk of German soldiers onto the population whose territories they were invading. Furthermore, skeptical humanitarianism and a critical attitude toward the conduct of the German armies were not confined to Pezold and his circle of like-minded officers or to *reichsfeindlich* diarists like the Alsatian Richert. Kurt Riezler, private secretary to Chancellor Bethmann Hollweg, wrote in his diary on a visit to Belgium on October 11, 1914, after describing the mass executions of thousands of civilians for allegedly resisting the German army, that the events of this war would never be forgotten. A cavalry officer had told him of the shootings in the small towns of all men aged sixteen to sixty years, thousands lying in the fields, every tenth corpse one pace forward. "No one dares to say anything against military necessities. . . . Horrendous misunderstanding because of the *levée en masse* prepared by fools without a conscience. . . . There is a terrible tragedy in the war, perhaps also in the destiny of the German people. There can be no doubt that if it is victorious it will be ruined intellectually by its system of political rule."[108] Riezler's prescient analysis foretold military dictatorship if Germany were to win the war, the final victory of militaristic Germany over the "other Germany."

In a curious way, these dissonant voices and consciences echoed the distinction between two German nations made by French and British intellectuals, even if the distinction was repudiated by the German academic community. They underline the fact, moreover, that while the term "atrocity"

---

[106] Richert, p. 77.
[107] See n. 86 above.
[108] Kurt Riezler, *Tagebücher, Aufsätze, Dokumente*, ed. Karl Dietrich Erdmann (Göttingen, 1972), pp. 216–17.

German "Atrocities" and Franco-German Opinion 33

is a culturally relative concept, and one not employed as such by the critical German diarists, the latter shared Bédier's moral outrage. The Allies were not alone in considering German military conduct to be a case of morally indefensible "barbarism."

[16]
Tactical Dysfunction in the AEF, 1917-1918

by Timothy K. Nenninger

TACTICAL performance in the American Expeditionary Forces during World War I did not always match tactical pronouncements and intentions. Some historians have recently taken an increasingly critical view of this problem, particularly focusing on the doctrinal, organizational, and operational shortcomings of the AEF.[1] James Rainey, for instance, has demonstrated how the unsettled, "ambivalent" tactical doctrine in the AEF, based partly on the "open warfare" pronouncements of John J. Pershing and partly on the trench warfare experiences of the Allies, led to inadequate training and ultimately to failures on the battlefield. This lack of a sound doctrine, that sought to adjust organization, equipment, and tactics, to overcoming the stalemate on the Western Front, was a significant shortcoming that adversely affected American effectiveness in France. It was but one of several factors, however, that coalesced in 1917 and 1918 to determine how American troops fought and how well they performed. The ideas and self-perceptions of the officer corps of the U.S. Army, as well as pressures from the French and British Allies, helped shape American tactics. Battlefield performance was also directly affected by Army personnel practices, by the individual and unit training system in the United States and France, and by logistics and support afforded American combat units.

American commanders, particularly Pershing, believed that three years of trench warfare had eroded the offensive spirit of the French and British and led them to accept a defensive attitude which resulted in an indecisive war of attrition. Pershing concluded that if his troops adopted the trench warfare tactics of the Allies, their offensive spirit would also wane. He wanted aggressive American troops capable of driving the Germans out of their trenches and of defeating them in a war of movement and pursuit. He believed that the traditional skills of American infantrymen, as marksmen and scouts, and the experience of the U.S. Army operating in the vastness of the American West, contributed to mark the AEF with a "special genius" for what he termed open warfare.[2] Pershing continually stressed the importance of the infantry rifleman in achieving success against the Germans: "The rifle and the bayonet are the principal weapons of the infantry soldier. He will be trained to a high degree of skill as a marksman both on the target range and in field firing. An aggressive spirit must be developed until the soldier feels himself, as a bayonet fighter, invincible in battle."[3]

Despite Pershing's faith that the American rifleman was the key to success on the Western Front, other aspects of AEF planning took cognizance of the effects of modern weapons on warfare. In July 1917 the Operations Section (G-3) at GHQ rejected recommendations that the AEF adopt light, mobile howitzers for its artillery regiments. Choosing firepower over mobility, the G-3 determined the AEF should use heavy French weapons, 75-mm and 155-mm guns. The size and organization of American infantry divisions also indicated the AEF expected battles of attrition against German defenses organized in depth. AEF divisions were twice as large as European, were rich in infantry, and had a full artillery brigade for fire support.

From shortly after Pershing arrived in France in June 1917, the AEF based its planning, organization, and training on an offensive role for U.S. troops, with the main effort to come in 1919 by an independent American field army. But it took time and assistance from the Allies to create the sort of force and

155-mm. guns of Battery E, 56th Artillery, Coast Artillery Corps, supporting the 1st Division in the Meuse-Argonne; near Baulny, France, October 1918. (Photo courtesy National Archives.)

train it in offensive tactics that the Americans wanted. While open warfare was the ultimate tactical goal, all American divisions received extensive training in trench warfare. In fact, most U.S. troops first saw action occupying trench positions, on the defensive, usually closely supervised by the French or British.

Indeed, some in the AEF believed the Allies exerted too much influence on American tactical development. One staff officer in July 1918 articulated a commonly-held view among AEF professionals: "Berlin cannot be taken by the French or the British. . . . It can only be taken by a thoroughly trained, entirely homogeneous American Army."[4] The American insistence on their own tactical methods was consistent with the political and strategic objective of emphasizing a unique U.S. contribution to the war effort.

BESIDES political considerations and national pride, there were valid tactical reasons why the AEF opposed amalgamating companies and battalions into French and British divisions as the Allies wanted. After four years of war, Allied interoperability was far from perfected. At the tactical level, the French and British remained remarkably ignorant of each other's language, doctrine, organization, and methods. There was little reason to suppose the Americans would have any more success in such matters, especially with the French. The language problem alone frequently proved insurmountable. American experience with French staff work and command methods was sometimes exasperating and costly. For instance, on three occasions in the Summer of 1918 during Aisne-Marne counteroffensive, on the Marne, on the Ourcq, and at Fismette, units of the 28th Infantry Division, while attached to French divisions, suffered heavy casualties directly as a result of faulty French tactics. French commanders repeatedly changed orders, often with little advanced warning, and paid little attention to the logistical needs of the American units serving under them. The experience of the 28th Division made Allied criticism of American training, tactics, and competence all the more difficult for Pershing and his subordinates to accept. It reinforced their faith in American methods and their opposition to amalgamation.[5]

Doctrinally, American offensive tactics emphasized the close integration of infantry with supporting arms and the need for infantry to use fire and maneuver when attacking hostile positions. Performance was inconsistent, with most divisions seldom achieving the level of tactical proficiency Pershing expected. Rigid plans of attack, lines of infantry advancing over open ground without regard for concealment or cover, little use of fire and maneuver, and improper employment of infantry supporting arms, were typical of American infantry in the offensives through much of the Summer and Fall of 1918. During the three day (18-21 July) attack at Soissons, for instance, the 1st and 2d Divisions advanced six to seven miles but at a cost of 12,000 casualties. The 26th Infantry Regiment alone lost 3000 men; only 200 from the regiment survived the battle unscathed. The Americans had advanced in steady lines across open wheat fields as German machine-gunners shot them down. Soissons demonstrated the passion, courage, and aggressiveness of American troops, all characteristics that, as one Frenchman observed at the time, were "too apt to get them killed." But at Soissons the Americans also demonstrated a lack of tactical acumen. Formations were too dense; little use was made of fire and maneuver; infantry cooperation with the supporting French tanks was poor; and artillery support was equally lacking.[6]

Infantry attacks on the Western Front seldom could carry beyond the limit of the range of the field artillery. Thus any army contemplating offensive oriented tactics needed to find a means to extend the range of artillery support. Most simply, this required firing batteries to displace forward as the infantry advanced; the process required planning, training, and coordination. Some batteries had to remain in place to continue fire support for the infantry while others were on the move. Engineers had to make roads passable so the guns would have unhindered, rapid movement to their new firing positions. And the infantry had to stay in touch with the gunners so the advance would not be deprived of support at critical moments. Few American divisions trained to accomplish such complicated movements. Division artillery, in fact, normally trained separately from the other combat elements. Furthermore, American divisions in the latter stages of the war had artillery

A unit of the 2d Division, the 16th Company, 6th Marines, practicing offensive tactics near Harmonville, France, August 1918. (Photo courtesy National Archives.)

regiments from other divisions attached, rather than their organic units. Tactical effectiveness suffered because the AEF did not take steps to maximize coordination and integration of the infantry and artillery within combat divisions.[7]

A tactical system that was supposed to rely on offensive combat by combined arms in open warfare should have put a premium on junior leadership, unit cohesion, and morale. Heavy dependence on inexperienced infantry made such requirements even more necessary. Personnel policies in the U.S. Army, however, did not give sufficient attention to the needs of its tactical units. In a few cases, procedures in the AEF were actually destructive of the required results.

The quantity and quality of manpower from which the Army drew its small unit leadership was generally adequate, possibly of even higher quality than was available to it during World War II. By most accounts, American junior officers were "gallant and brave," but many platoon leaders lacked tactical skills.[8] Part of the problem was training and accountability. Instruction at the Officer Training Camps, from which most of the platoon leaders had been commissioned, had in some cases been too rudimentary. Equipment shortages, inadequate housing, and not enough instructors experienced in dealing with civilians, plagued the OTCs. As a result, officer training too closely resembled recruit training without sufficient development of leadership qualities and tactical skills.[9]

Other personnel policies did not compensate for the shortcomings of the officers. Unlike some European armies, for instance, the U.S. Army tended to undervalue the importance of its noncommissioned officers. NCOs were not a class apart from other enlisted ranks, with distinct privileges, duties, responsibilities, and prestige. Such distinctions could have enhanced their role as small unit leaders, especially in combat. Promotion to noncommissioned rank was often a casual affair — easily won and easily taken away. Wartime NCO training tended to be on-the-job, and stressed the vocational aspects of an NCO's duties. The training neglected the leadership role of noncommissioned officers and their status in the hierarchy of command. This is not to say that some American NCOs did not rise to the occasion when required by circumstance of battle, even assuming command of platoons and companies when the officers became casualties.[10] But the system of NCO selection, training, and promotion neither emphasized nor inculcated such performance.

Particularly destructive of unit cohesion in the AEF was the practice of relieving officers from their commands for detached service, often to attend army schools, on the eve of major operations. Long after the war George C. Marshall complained that just before the Meuse-Argonne attack several of the inexperienced assault divisions "were absolutely scalped . . . in order that the next class at Langres [the AEF-Staff College] might start on scheduled time. The amount of confusion and mismanagement resulting from this was tremendous."[11] The staff at AEF GHQ, specifically the Training Section, was principally responsible for these practices. Thus that element of the command structure that should have been most cognizant of troop needs and unit cohesion was fostering practices destructive of them.

The replacement system also created personnel turbulence and was not conducive to fostering unit cohesion. Because the War Department wanted to ship full strength units to France, it broke up established organizations to provide fillers and replacements for divisions ready to embark for overseas. Many units were cannibalized in this manner, some more than once; morale and unit esprit could hardly develop under such circumstances. A similar situation obtained later in France when the AEF broke up some of the newly-arrived combat divisions in an effort to replace casualties and maintain experienced divisions at near fighting strength. Despite these expedients throughout much of the war available replacements fell short of the needs of AEF combat divisions. Frequently American divisions had to stay in action at strengths considerably below tables of organization. Replacement shortages began occurring early in 1918 and persisted until the Armistice. In February, long before most AEF formations saw sustained combat, the system was functioning so poorly that the four combat divisions of the 1st Corps were short 8500 men. The 41st Division, a depot division responsible for furnishing replacements to the corps, was itself short 4500

Road congestion northeast of St. Mihiel during the St. Mihiel offensive, September 1918. (Photo courtesy National Archives.)

men. By October AEF combat units needed 80,000 replacements, but only 45,000 were available. Combat divisions had to reduce their strength by 4000 men, mostly riflemen.[12]

Late in the war, particularly in the Meuse-Argonne, evidence of the weak personnel practices became clearer. After the Armistice one AEF inspector reported: "Discipline, as shown by inattention and carelessness in saluting, straggling, lack of proper measures in sanitation, carelessness in observance of traffic regulations, etc., seemed to grow more lax as the offensive went on." Straggling was an especially pernicious problem, sapping combat strength and effectiveness. Hunter Liggett, First Army commander during the last month of the war, believed there were as many as 100,000 stragglers throughout his army's zone in mid-October. One division in the Meuse-Argonne had reported an effective front line strength of only 1,600 men. Yet when the division came out of the line and arrived in its rest area, the infantry regiments alone had over 8,400 men; returning stragglers had accounted for most of the newly added numbers.[13] The AEF used expedients such as straggler posts of military police to keep the troops moving toward the front. But these had only limited effect and did not address the root causes of the problem.

During World War I the U.S. Army organized a system of training that dwarfed all its previous efforts. The 1.4 million soldiers who actually fought in France were supposed to pass through a progression from individual, to small unit, to division training. Officers and specialists attended schools that covered a range of subjects from general staff duties to proper use of the Stokes mortar. Although the magnitude of the training effort was considerable, a number of problems hampered the overall effectiveness of the program.

Neither the Training Branch of the War Department General Staff nor the Training Section (G-5) of AEF GHQ had full responsibility or authority for training. Both organizations, in fact, published some training literature, supervised some aspects of individual training, and issued unit training schedules. Neither the Training Branch nor G-5 supervised all American troops in any single aspect of the training cycle. Although there was some liaison between the two organizations, neither had the resources required to supervise properly individual and unit training in their areas of responsibility. Many departmental, camp, and unit commanders, consequently exercised their own initiative in carrying out various training functions. That most American units upon reaching Europe initially trained and served in quiet sectors under French and British supervision only further exacerbated the diffusion of responsibility.

THE original AEF training plan anticipated complete divisions arriving in France on a regular basis. After arrival each infantry division was to have three months training in France before commitment to combat. The three one-month phases included preliminary small unit training; integration of U.S. battalions into quiet defensive sectors with French or British units "to harden and accustom them to all sorts of fire"; and finally regimental, brigade, and division maneuvers in the attack. The German 1918 Spring offensives, necessitating early commitment of American units, forced curtailment of the divisional training program. After April 1918 few divisions had a full four weeks in any phase; for some the entire cycle was only a month.[14]

The necessity to speed troops to the front likewise affected individual training. Many untrained replacements, for example, reported to combat divisions in the latter stages of the war. In late September 1918 the 77th Division received 2100 replacements. Over half lacked rudimentary infantry skills. Many had not been issued weapons prior to reporting to the division and did not know how to care for or use a rifle. Yet the day after receiving these replacements the infantry jumped off at daylight as part of the Meuse-Argonne attack.[15]

Many of the AEF recognized the shortcomings of the training system. The G-5 section in particular tried to inculcate doctrinal uniformity on American units and troops. To that end, G-5 had observers with nearly all frontline divisions during combat. Based on their observations, G-5 produced a series of "lessons learned" for dissemination throughout the AEF.[16] Units not yet in combat could adjust their training regimens and gain some benefit from the experience of veteran outfits. Seasoned units too, after their periods in the line, withdrew to rest areas where they resumed training. For instance, after its hard battles in June and July 1918 the 2d Division, one of the best in the AEF, practiced "open order warfare" in its rest area in Lorraine eight hours a day through most of August. The training emphasized small unit tactics with one squad of a platoon utilizing maximum firepower, from rifles, grenades, and automatic rifles to attack an enemy position while the other squads used cover and maneuvered against the enemy's flanks.[17]

Given time, veteran AEF units could profit from their combat experience, conduct realistic training based on that experience, and improve overall tactical effectiveness. For most units, however, the rapid expansion and early commitment of the AEF prevented the orderly training required.

The AEF also had other serious problems with the human and material aspects of combat support and sustainability. Although some weaknesses were apparent even before U.S. troops entered combat, the sustained fighting in the last two months of the war magnified them. The large 28,000-man American divisions did not meet the expectations of AEF planners for staying power in battle. Moreover, American divisions proved difficult to supply, transport, and manage. They had difficulty getting into battle and once engaged had difficulty distributing food, ammunition, and other supplies.

Division transport depended on primitive motor trucks and especially on horse and mule drawn wagons. Because shipment of animals from the U.S. to France was considerably reduced in the spring of 1918 to make room for infantry replacements, severe shortages of transport animals occurred later. By the end of the war, because of overwork and poor care the condition of horses and mules in many divisions was very bad, contributing to the already difficult transport problems. Congestion within division areas was another hindrance. Traffic conditions throughout the First Army during much of the Meuse-Argonne offensive "became a severe impediment" to movement. Division engineers worked almost solely on repair and construction of roads. It took 3 to 5 trains daily just to bring in materials to maintain the existing road system. The AEF clearly underestimated the difficulties of transporting troops and supplies in close proximity to the battlefront.[18]

Late in the war, in some combat units there were shortages of crucial supplies. Again, a contributing factor was the shipping schedules during the Spring and Fall of 1918. To sustain a high rate of troop shipments, the shipment of other supplies was cut drastically. In a few units troops went hungry in the first weeks of the Meuse-Argonne. After they had finished the two days of iron rations they carried, frontline infantry could get little resupply. Field kitchens could not get far enough forward, and carrying parties had difficulty getting over the rough, shell-pocked terrain to ration dumps in the rear. One platoon leader described a ration dump in the 2d Division sector: "just what the name implies — a dump." Ration wagons had deposited great heaps of bread and canned goods into a huge hole caused by the collapse of a dugout. There was no system, no issue — anyone could carry away what he wanted.[19]

Despite the huge size of its infantry divisions, the AEF did not have sufficient service troops to carry rations, bury the dead, evacuate casualties, and perform other direct combat support functions. Too often the infantry, already strained and exhausted from combat, had to do these tasks. Commanders sometimes did not appreciate the effects that sustained combat had on individual troops. The weaknesses of the AEF's combat support and sustainability became manifest in the Meuse-

Argonne. As one historian has put it, "The 'staying' power of a division often was reduced to replacing exhausted troops who had suffered casualties with exhausted troops who had not."[20]

Despite these negative signs, by the Armistice American tactical performance was improving. In the last weeks of the war, the division, corps, and army commanders were more sure-handed — Pershing relinquishing command of the First Army to Hunter Liggett clearly helped here. The extensive efforts of AEF GHQ to analyze and disseminate "lessons learned" were beginning to take hold. Units were making better use of supporting arms, employing less dense attack formations, using fire and maneuver, and taking advantage of cover."[21] Several divisions exhibited considerable tactical skill in the final week of the war. A few demonstrated dramatic improvements — the 5th Division, for example, nearly fell apart in the hard fighting of mid-October; but in the first days of November, under new leadership, the 5th made a series of dramatic assaults across the Meuse River that contributed significantly to breaking open a large section of the German front. Other divisions were similarly improving.

TWO largely uncontrollable factors had a significant negative impact on American tactical performance in World War I. First, U.S. combat troops had to be committed on a large scale in the Spring of 1918, nearly a year earlier than originally planned; the resultant curtailed training regimen led to many green soldiers and units entering combat woefully unprepared. Second, the short period of American participation, basically five months of active combat by divisions and corps, allowed little opportunity for commanders or troops to learn from experience; in terms of its organizational development, in November 1918 the AEF was in many respects the equivalent of other belligerent armies in early 1916.

But other factors, over which the Americans had some control and which could have been rectified, also contributed to the weak tactical performance. These included the doctrinal ambiguity, between Pershing's faith in open warfare and other aspects of AEF preparation emphasizing trench warfare; the split training responsibilities between the General Staff in Washington and AEF GHQ in France; personnel practices that did not pay sufficient attention to morale, unit cohesion, and leadership; and weak combat support capabilities, especially at the division level.

REFERENCES

1. The best overall account of how the AEF organized, trained and fought, remains Edward M. Coffman, *The War To End All Wars: The American Military Experience in World War I* (New York: Oxford Univerversity Press, 1968.) Donald Smythe's recent *Pershing: General of the Armies* (Bloomington: Indiana University Press, 1986), provides an excellent critical view from the "Commander-in-Chief's" perspective. Of particular interest on doctrinal developments are James W. Rainey, "Ambivalent Warfare: The Tactical Doctrine of the AEF in World War I," *Parameters*, 13 (Sept. 1983), 34-46, and James W. Rainey, "The Training of the American Expeditionary Forces in World War I" (MA Thesis, Temple University, 1981). Although Allan R. Millet, *The General: Robert L. Bullard and Officership in the United States Army, 1881-1925* (Westport, CT: Greenwood Press, 1975), is essentially a biography, it includes particularly cogent analysis of AEF tactical and operational performance because Bullard commanded in turn a brigade, a division, and a corps, as well as, for a brief period, the AEF schools. Other recent works with critical accounts of AEF tactics include I.B. Holley, Jr. *General John M. Palmer, Citizen Soldiers, and the Army of a Democracy* (Westport, CT: Greenwood Press, 1982); Paul M. Kennedy, *Over Here: The First World War and American Society* (New York: Oxford University Press, 1980); Charles Douglas McKenna, "The Forgotten Reform: Field Maneuvers in the United States Army, 1902-1920" (PhD Dissertation, Duke University, 1981); and, Richard Lee Pierce, "A Maximum of Support: The Development of US Army Field Artillery Doctrine in World War I" (MA Thesis, Ohio State University, 1983).

2. Smythe, *Pershing*, 72-73.
3. Pershing quoted in Maj. Harold B. Fiske, "Training in the AEF" (21 April 1920), Army War College Lecture, RG 165, National Archives.
4. Col. Harold B. Fiske to Chief of Staff AEF (4 July 1918) AEF AG File 16875-5, RG 120, NA.
5. H. Essame, *The Battle for Europe* (New York: C. Scribners Sons, 1972), 97; Louis Felix Ranlett, *Let's Go!* (New York: Houghton Mifflin Co., 1927), 86-87; John Kennedy Ohl, "The Keystone Division in the Great War," *Prologue* (Summer 1978), 83-99.
6. Millet, *The General*, 382-83; Coffman, *War To End All Wars*, 235-48.
7. Pierce, "A Maximum of Support," using the 1st Division as a case study, details the organization, training, and operations of AEF field artillery.
8. Brig. Gen. M.G. Spinks to Chief of Staff AEF, "Notes Made By the Inspector General AEF" (11 Dec. 1918), Folder 1115-A, G-3 Correspondence, RG 120, NA.
9. John Garry Clifford, *The Citizen Soldiers: The Plattsburg Training Camp Movement, 1913-1920* (Lexington: University of Kentucky Press, 1972), 256.
10. Ernest F. Fisher, "The American Noncommissioned Officer in World War I," Center of Military History draft paper in author's possession, 1984.
11. Marshall to Pershing (24 Oct. 1930), in Larry I. Bland (ed.), *The Papers of George Catlett Marshall, Volume I* (Baltimore: Johns Hopkins University Press, 1981), 360.
12. Leonard L. Lerwill, *The Personnel Replacement System in the United States Army* (Washington: Department of the Army, 1954), 180 and 212.
13. Spinks to Chief of Staff AEF (11 Dec. 1918), G-3 Folder 1115-A, RG 120, NA. On the straggling problem see Smythe, *Pershing*, 217-18 and Coffman, *War To End All Wars*, 332-33.
14. Brig. Gen. Harold B. Fiske, "Report of G-5 GHQ AEF" (30 June 1919), Folder 215, Commander-in-Chief Reports, RG 120; Maj. Harold B. Fiske, "Training in the AEF," Army War College Lecture (21 April 1920), RG 165, NA.
15. Spinks to Chief of Staff AEF (11 Dec. 1918), G-3 Folder 1115-A, RG 120, NA.
16. "Memorandum for Corps and Division Commanders" (5 Aug. 1918), G-5 Document 1325; "Combat Instructions" (5 Sept. 1918), G-5 Document 1348; "Notes on Recent Operations: No. 1" (7 Aug. 1918), G-5 Document 1322; "Notes on Recent Operations: No. 2" (2 Sept. 1918), G-5 Document 1346; "Notes on Recent Operations: No. 3" (12 Oct. 1918), G-5 Document 1376; "Notes on Recent Operations: No. 4 (22 Nov. 1918), G-5 Document 1417, RG 120, NA.
17. Ranlett, *Let's Go!*, 162.
18. Millett, *The General*, 347; James A. Huston, *The Sinews of War: Army Logistics, 1775-1953* (Washington: GPO, 1966)), 383; Smythe, *Pershing*, 207.
19. Spinks to Chief of Staff AEF (11 Dec. 1918), G-3 Folder 1115-A, RG 120, NA; Ranlett, *Let's Go!*, 280.
20. Millett, *The General*, 347.
21. The steady tactical improvements can be seen in the four "Notes on Recent Operations" issued by the GHQ Training Section based on experience in the battles of the Summer and Fall of 1918; cited in note 16. Smythe, *Pershing*, 225, also cites several examples of the increasing tactical prowess of American divisions in the last two weeks of the war.

Timothy K. Nenninger has been an archivist at the National Archives since 1970 and is currently Chief of the Military Projects Branch. A graduate of Lake Forest College, he received his Ph.D. from the University of Wisconsin-Madison. He is the author of The Leavenworth Schools, 1881-1918 (1978) and the co-editor of Soldiers and Civilians: The U.S. Army and the American People (1987). This article was accepted for publication in December 1986.

[17]
Why the British Were Really on the Somme: A Reply to Elizabeth Greenhalgh

William Philpott

In recent years a 'revisionist' view of Britain's political and strategic role in the First World War has developed. Works by David French, Keith Neilson, David Dutton and this author have stressed the coalition nature of the First World War and the constraints which it placed upon Britain's policy makers and military commanders.[1] These authors have moved the debate on Britain's wartime policy and strategy away from the school of historiography which studies British political and military decision making in a vacuum,[2] and have attempted to evaluate the extent to which a 'national' policy was possible in the context of a close military alliance, developing what Neilson characterizes as 'a new "alliance" view of British strategy'.[3]

Elizabeth Greenhalgh's *War in History* article, 'Why the British Were on the Somme in 1916',[4] reflects both this revisionist trend and another revisionist trend in First World War historiography, the re-evaluation of the battlefield performance of the British army, by scholars including Tim Travers, Gary Sheffield, Robin Prior and Trevor Wil-

---

[1] D. Dutton, *The Politics of Diplomacy: Britain and France in the Balkans in the First World War* (London, 1998); D. French, *British War Aims and Strategy, 1914–1916* (London, 1986) and *The Strategy of the Lloyd George Coalition, 1916–1918* (Oxford, 1995); K. Neilson, *Strategy and Supply: The Anglo-Russian Alliance, 1914–1917* (London, 1984); W.J. Philpott, *Anglo-French Relations and Strategy on the Western Front, 1914–1918* (Basingstoke, 1996), 'Kitchener and the 29th Division: A Study in Anglo-French Strategic Relations, 1914–1915', *Journal of Strategic Studies*, XVI (1993), pp. 375–407, and 'Squaring the Circle: The Higher Co-ordination of the Entente in the Winter of 1915-1916', *English Historical Review*, CXIV (1999), pp. 875–98.

[2] While of course British policy in the First World War could never entirely ignore the alliance factor, earlier works such as P. Guinn, *British Strategy and Politics, 1914–1918* (London, 1965) take a decidedly Anglocentric view of the decision-making process. This narrow focus persists in the otherwise valuable B. Millman, *Pessimism and British War Policy, 1916–1918* (London, 2001).

[3] Neilson, *Strategy and Supply*, p. viii.

[4] E. Greenhalgh, 'Why the British Were on the Somme in 1916', *War in History*, VI (1999), pp. 147–73 (hereafter cited Greenhalgh).

son.⁵ Greenhalgh's stress on the coalition nature of the battle of the Somme is a long overdue corrective to the habitual perception that the battle was fought by the British army and directed by Sir Douglas Haig. The Somme is the coalition battle *par excellence*, with the British Fourth and French Sixth Armies fighting side by side on a common front in a manner that was not to be seen again until 1918. Curiously, her recognition that the Somme was a coalition battle directed by the French commander-in-chief, General Joseph Joffre, and his subordinate General Ferdinand Foch, has led Greenhalgh to deny the historiography of the 1916 offensive, and of Anglo-French politico-military relations in general. She makes the forceful assertion that:

> historians have failed to understand the nature of the Franco-British military alliance in 1916. First, for more than 80 years they have accepted at face value Sir Douglas Haig's own assessment of the Battle of the Somme ... namely that it was a battle fought to relieve the French at Verdun. Secondly, they have not established what the overall relationship between the two alliance partners actually was.⁶

This claim represents both an unwarranted criticism of recent secondary literature, and a misreading of the available primary evidence. Moreover, Greenhalgh does not present a clear alternative view of the Anglo-French relationship. While effectively analysing Haig's independence in the operational planning and conduct of the Somme battle,⁷ her inference from this would seem to be that the British army was an independent actor at all levels of war. This article has been prepared as both a rejoinder to Greenhalgh's assertion and an analysis of the recent historiography of the Anglo-French alliance which, when it has been read, is inappropriately treated in Greenhalgh's article.⁸

I.

Revisionist writings on the Anglo-French relationship in the First World War have reached the conclusion that Britain's political and

---

⁵ See, for example, T. Travers, *The Killing Ground: The British Army, the Western Front and the Emergence of Modern Warfare, 1900–1918* (London, 1990); R. Prior and T. Wilson, *Command on the Western Front: The Military Career of Sir Henry Rawlinson, 1914–1918* (Oxford, 1992); G. Sheffield, *Forgotten Victory* (London, 2001).
⁶ Greenhalgh, p. 147.
⁷ Existing historiography of the alliance has never suggested that Haig did not retain operational independence in the conduct of individual battles. For discussion of this see Philpott, *Anglo-French Relations*, pp. 103–106; W.J. Philpott, 'Haig and Britain's European allies', in B.J. Bond and N. Cave, eds, *Haig: A Reappraisal 70 Years On* (Barnsley, 1999), pp. 133–40; W.J. Philpott, 'Britain and France go to War: Anglo-French Relations on the Western Front', *War in History*, II (1995), pp. 43–64.
⁸ This author's work is the most directly challenged. It has certainly been misinterpreted, and in part misrepresented. Greenhalgh is not afraid to take on respected experts in the field. Both Brian Bond and John Gooch, identified as failing to understand the Anglo-French relationship (p. 147), base their conclusions on this author's work. John Gooch was external examiner for, and Brian Bond read the final draft of, W.J. Philpott, 'British Strategy on the Western Front: Independence or Alliance, 1904–1918', DPhil. thesis (Oxford University, 1991).

448 William Philpott

strategic freedom of action were both severely constrained by the need to sustain the alliance with France – essential as France both was the main theatre of military operations for the Anglo-French forces and, before 1917 at least, provided coalition leadership and the majority of the coalition's land forces. This meant that in practice Britain's freedom was restricted to battlefield operational and tactical matters. Greenhalgh demonstrates this in her analysis of the battle itself, while ironically proving that if the British had followed French tactical guidelines during the preparatory phase of the battle they would have done much better on the Somme![9] Of course it was in the nature of the Anglo-French military alliance – a coalition of an overbearing senior partner and a powerful, overconfident and self-assured junior, with ill-designed structures for liaison and exchange of ideas – that the exchange of tactical doctrine was, where it existed at all, on an ad hoc and very limited basis.[10] Yet while Greenhalgh's analysis of the tactical preparation and execution of the battle is a valuable corrective to the uninformed view of the Somme as a British battle in which there was only one significant day of fighting, and although she stresses 'the *inter-Allied* nature of the 1916 campaign', she fails to engage with the historiography of the political and strategic rationale for the battle.[11] Consequently her broader thesis, that politically Britain was obliged to fight in 1916, and that therefore Haig was willing to fight on the Somme, seems an ill-founded oversimplification.

Greenhalgh's thesis relies on her refutation of two 'perceptions' about the British in 1916: first, that the British did not want to fight in 1916, but preferred to wait until 1917 to win a decisive victory and impose peace on defeated enemy and exhausted ally together; second, that the British did not want to fight on the Somme, but in Flanders, where their maritime interests were threatened by a German naval presence in the Belgian Channel ports.[12] These 'perceptions' are a rather simplistic summation of essential factors – the readiness of Britain's New Armies for offensive action, and the real strategic threat in the Channel – in the complex politico-military situation with which Britain's leaders wrestled in that year.[13] That neither of these strategic

---

[9] Greenhalgh, pp. 156–57. The same unfavourable comparison was made at the time. Maurice Hankey diary, 18 October 1916, Hankey papers, Churchill College Archives Centre, Cambridge, HNKY 1/1.

[10] Such an interchange of tactical ideas was never formalized. Both armies may have learned as much from their own mistakes and from the successes of their enemy as from each other's experience. P. Griffith, *Battle Tactics of the Western Front: The British Army's Art of Attack, 1916–1918* (London, 1994), pp. 52–53.

[11] Greenhalgh, p. 147, Greenhalgh's italics.

[12] Ibid., p. 149. The perceived threat was not submarines, the 'traditional' menace which Greenhalgh presumes, but the destroyer flotillas which posed a threat to Britain's Channel communications with her army on the continent. Philpott, *Anglo-French Relations*, pp. 144–45.

[13] The broader issues and complexities of strategic decision-making are evaluated in D. French, 'The Meaning of Attrition, 1914–16', *English Historical Review*, CIII (1988), pp. 385–405; H. Strachan, 'The Battle of the Somme and British Strategy', *Journal of Strategic Studies*, XXI (1998), pp. 79–95.

options proved possible, and might therefore be dismissed as 'counter-factuals', does not mean that at the time these lines of action were not considered viable and desirable – the obvious inconsistency between not wanting to fight in 1916, and wanting to fight in Flanders in 1916, would in itself suggest that there were tensions and points of disagreement in the strategic debate.[14] Consequently it is with Greenhalgh's analysis of these two 'perceptions', closely intertwined with the French army's difficulties at Verdun in Haig's preparations for the Somme, that this reply will be primarily concerned.

Before addressing in detail the two 'perceptions' of the British army in 1916, and Haig's own point of view, it is necessary to outline broadly the nature of the coalition war in which Britain was involved. Identification and analysis of the relationship between policy and strategy lie at the heart of this author's assessment of the Anglo-French relationship in the First World War; from it derives the idea of Britain's 'strategic paradox' – 'British strategy was an unsuccessful and perhaps misguided attempt to balance traditional strategic interests with novel military obligations.'[15] In practical terms this paradox meant that any desire Britain had to pursue an independent strategic path had in the final analysis to be subordinated to the obligation, adopted as policy in August/September 1914, to support France militarily.[16] Central to Greenhalgh's misunderstanding of how the alliance worked for Britain is her failure to appreciate the nature and significance of this politico-military dilemma, and her rejection of the idea of a 'strategic paradox' out of hand.[17] It is one aspect of a general failure to distinguish between policy and strategy, particularly at the theatre or operational level,[18] that runs throughout the article.

Greenhalgh's assessment of Britain's reason for going to war, 'in order to maintain its own interests – to maintain its status as a great power',[19] and her strategic rationale, that 'British policy had always been to prevent any one power from dominating the Low Countries', and that 'Britain's strategic interest lay in supporting France's great-power status in the face of German aggression', should not raise too many objections.[20] However, maintenance of a European balance of power, while an axiom of British foreign *policy*, or 'grand strategy',

---

[14] While not immediately attributing to them specifically, Greenhalgh makes the presumptuous inference that these are historiographical interpretations (or 'claims') rather than contemporary 'perceptions', the first attributed to David French, the second to this author. David French's and this author's own work have explored these contemporary perceptions and their significance in British policy and Anglo-French relations in detail.

[15] Philpott, *Anglo-French Relations*, pp. 163–64.

[16] Ibid., pp. 25–26.

[17] Greenhalgh, p. 151.

[18] For example, the operational problems Haig and Joffre experienced in conducting the joint battle are casually characterized as issues of 'strategy'; Greenhalgh, pp. 166–67.

[19] Ibid.

[20] Ibid.

remained before 1914 – in the eyes of the director of military operations, Brigadier-General Sir Henry Wilson, at least – out of alignment with British military *strategy*, which despite Wilson's best efforts pursued an unrequited desire for operations in Belgium. In practice no pre-war decision was made between 'a limited independent "northern flank" commitment or a potentially unlimited continental alliance strategy'.[21] Any possibility that after war broke out Britain could pursue an independent line in policy, strategy and operations was surrendered when Britain decided to dispatch her small regular army to France, and specifically to the French left wing, in August 1914 – as Haig acknowledged, 'our best policy at the present time was to do as the French wished us'.[22] Had this military strategy contributed to the quick decisive defeat of Germany that Henry Wilson and other 'short war delusionists' anticipated,[23] then Britain's great power status would have been maintained at minimum cost – her *policy* of supporting France against German aggression, belatedly reconciled with an 'alliance' military *strategy*, would have paid off. When it did not, the real cost to Britain of adopting an alliance policy and strategy slowly became apparent. The paradox was that British statesmen and soldiers, uncommitted to an alliance policy and strategy before 1914, still felt that they were free to pursue an independent military strategy within the coalition, both on the Western Front and more widely, yet time after time the need to sustain the alliance with France obliged them to abandon an independent strategic line for higher policy goals.

II.

Turning to the 'perceptions' which Greenhalgh purports to refute, the idea that the British 'did not want to fight at all in 1916',[24] when stated in such a glib form, is certainly untenable. Nevertheless, there was a long-standing politico-military debate in British, and allied, councils on when and how the British would fight, the preliminaries to determining where they would fight. 'Fighting to the last Frenchman'

---

[21] Philpott, *Anglo-French Relations*, pp. 2–9; W.J. Philpott, 'The Strategic Ideas of Sir John French', *Journal of Strategic Studies*, XII (1989), pp. 458–78; W.J. Philpott, 'The General Staff and the Paradoxes of Continental War', in D. French and B. Holden Reid, eds, *The British General Staff: Reform and Innovation* (London, 2002, forthcoming); K.M. Wilson, *The Policy of the Entente: Essays on the Determinants of British Foreign Policy, 1904–14* (Cambridge, 1985), pp. 125–33. The 'Belgian option', as it was known, was an unsuccessful attempt to reconcile an alliance policy with an independent strategy. However, another paradox, it was admitted from the start that operating in Belgium was impossible without a French alliance. 'Records of a Strategic Wargame, 1905', Directorate of Military Operations, General Staff, War Office: Reports and Miscellaneous Papers, Public Record Office, Kew (PRO), WO 33/364.

[22] 'Secretary's Notes of a War Council Held at 10 Downing Street, 5 August 1914', Cabinet Office: Cabinet Papers, 1915–16, PRO, CAB 42/1/2.

[23] The phrase is borrowed from H. Herwig, *The First World War: Germany and Austria-Hungary, 1914–1918* (London, 1997), p. 36.

[24] Greenhalgh, p. 149.

is a common but unjustified calumny levelled against the British in the First World War. On the contrary there is a clear and consistent theme running through British military policy on the Western Front throughout the early years of the war, that Britain's forces ought not to be committed prematurely to an offensive for which they were not yet thoroughly trained and which was unlikely to prove decisive, *unless* the political consideration of supporting the French dictated it.[25] This policy was separate from, but naturally fed into, Britain's strategy, at both grand and theatre strategic levels. That the British would fight to preserve Frenchmen and the French alliance, even if it was considered strategically and operationally unsound, because ultimately Britain's own existence – its status as a great power – depended on it, was an axiom of Britain's war policy from the start.[26] Kitchener and Haig, against whom Greenhalgh fires her heaviest salvoes, were always of that view when policy had to be balanced against strategy.[27] Nineteen-sixteen was no exception; strategy, overall and in the western theatre, had to be developed with due regard to this 'alliance' policy, severely restricting Britain's freedom of action. Therefore, while it is right to conclude that the British were willing to fight in the summer of 1916, this was because policy necessitated it, whatever the strategic advantages and disadvantages of Joffre's Chantilly plan.

Having established the nature of British policy and its broad relationship with strategy, it is appropriate to analyse the contemporary view of Britain's position in 1916. The first 'perception' or 'claim', that Britain did not want to fight in 1916, is attributed in the historiography of the war to David French, and historically to Lord Kitchener, secretary of state for war from August 1914 until his untimely death in June 1916. Here it is not so much what Greenhalgh says, but the way that she says it, that invites comment. Her cursory dismissal of this perception, while broadly justified, suggests a rudimentary and erroneous appreciation of Kitchener's talents as a strategist and coalition politician, and in particular of how his conception of the war evolved between 1914 and 1916. The wisdom of calling upon a soldier with an 'imperial' perspective to run Britain's alliance war effort has rightly been questioned, and indeed was done so by the French at the time. Colonel de la Panouse, military attaché in London when war

---

[25] As the war progressed and the balance of military influence on the Western Front changed, a third consideration – could the French offer effective support to a British offensive – also had to be factored into the decision-making process.

[26] This policy, with its inherent renunciation of politico-military independence, was effectively adopted at the war councils which took place at 10 Downing Street on the outbreak of war, when it was decided, on Kitchener's suggestion, to consult the French before determining Britain's line of military action. 'Secretary's Notes of a War Council Held at 10 Downing Street', 5 and 6 August 1914, PRO, CAB 42/1/2 and 3; Philpott, *Anglo-French Relations*, pp. 8–11.

[27] R. Williams, 'Lord Kitchener and the Battle of Loos: French Politics and British Strategy in the Summer of 1915', in L. Freedman, P. Hayes and R. O'Neill, eds, *War, Strategy and International Politics: Essays in Honour of Sir Michael Howard* (Oxford, 1992), pp. 117–32; Philpott, 'Haig and Britain's European Allies', pp. 128–44.

452   William Philpott

broke out, immediately got the measure of Kitchener: 'un homme de grande volonté et excessivement entêté... tout à fait ennemi de l'offensive... [et] imbu des principes de la guerre coloniale'.[28] Certainly he took time to adjust this perspective to the reality of the politico-military situation, but the man who in the first 18 months of the war had to coordinate British military policy and strategy with that of the French came in time to appreciate and accept Britain's strategic paradox. From the start it was certainly Kitchener's policy to sustain the *entente* with both France and Russia;[29] As he left for the continent he informed the chief of staff of the British Expeditionary Force (BEF) that he 'did not intend to leave the continent till the Germans are completely crushed'.[30] However, in baldly listing the pivotal moments when Kitchener acted decisively in pursuing this policy in the western theatre, Greenhalgh makes no acknowledgement that this was directly contrary to Kitchener's own perception of the best strategy for the *entente*, or of the difficult juggling act which Kitchener, in the absence of any formal alliance directive machinery, had to conduct with Britain's growing military forces.[31]

Greenhalgh does not acknowledge, and may be unaware of, this author's and Keith Neilson's 'revisionist' assessments of Kitchener as a strategist, which explain the conversion, or perhaps more accurately reconciliation, which Kitchener experienced during the first year of the war.[32] Kitchener's plans, Neilson argues, 'were based on a sophisticated understanding of the two front nature of the war and upon a shrewd assessment of the relative strengths of Britain and her allies'.[33] The idea that Britain could sit on the sidelines while building up her forces to intervene decisively after three years of conflict rightly proved untenable. But there is little evidence to support the contention that this is what Kitchener had in mind in 1914, let alone 1916.[34] It is certainly clear that from the outset Kitchener rejected the prevailing view of Britain's military planners that the war would be short, and anticipated a three-year conflict.[35] This would allow Britain plenty of time to raise, train and equip a continental-scale army, something which Liberal sentiment had prevented in peacetime. The view that Kitch-

[28] Panouse to *ministre de la guerre*, 19 August 1914, Service Historique de l'Armée de Terre, Vincennes, 7N1228.
[29] Neilson, *Strategy and Supply*, p. 8; K. Neilson, 'Kitchener: A Reputation Refurbished?', *Canadian Journal of History*, xv (1980), pp. 207–27.
[30] Note, 14 August 1914, Murray papers, PRO, WO 79/62, quoted in G. Cassar, *Kitchener: Architect of Victory* (London, 1977), p. 231.
[31] Greenhalgh, p. 153.
[32] Neilson, 'Kitchener'; Philpott, 'Kitchener and the 29th Division'. The former evaluates Kitchener's grand strategic perspective, the latter his dealings with Joffre and the Western Front in 1915.
[33] Neilson, 'Kitchener', p. 207.
[34] David French's own analysis acknowledges that Kitchener's initial perception was evidently unrealistic by the end of 1915. French, *Strategy of the Lloyd George Coalition*, p. 4.
[35] Haig shared this view. Haig diary, 5 August 1914, *The Private Papers of Douglas Haig, 1914–1919*, ed. R. Blake (London, 1952), p. 69.

ener intended to use this army to win the peace in 1917, rather than fight the war between 1914 and 1917, cannot be sustained. The overall perception that he gave in his early interview with *The Times*'s military correspondent, Colonel Charles à Court Repington, before hostilities had begun in earnest, indicated that his intention was to use Britain's growing manpower to support her allies, who were throwing all their weight in at the start, over time – 'il est décidé à conduire la lutte jusqu'au bout' as the French military attaché reported positively.[36] That did not, however, mean that he intended to use Britain's forces indiscriminately as Britain's allies dictated, but appropriately as in his own judgement the military situation warranted. He had always been suspicious of the general staff's pre-war collaboration with the French – 'it will mean inevitably that we shall be tacked on to a French plan which might not suit us' he declared in 1909.[37] The instructions which he drafted for Sir John French, the BEF's commander-in-chief, that he should consider himself an independent field commander,[38] indicate an obvious failure to acknowledge the reality of the military position which Britain had placed herself in, and provide clear evidence that, whatever British policy, Kitchener was unwilling to countenance military subordination to France. His caution manifested itself right away in the three-hour argument he had on 12 August 1914 with representatives of the British and French general staffs, before reluctantly conceding that the BEF should concentrate on the French left rather than in reserve at Amiens.[39] It was soon apparent that Kitchener's position was untenable. As early as 1 September 1914 Kitchener, representing the cabinet, found himself in Paris effectively countermanding his own instructions to Sir John French, who had taken the warning offered by Kitchener, that in the event of an initial French setback the BEF ought to retreat on its line of communications rather than expose itself to destruction, literally. Political considerations would not allow the British to abandon the French army at such a crucial point.[40]

Kitchener's initial call had been for 100 000 men, six additional divisions to reinforce the BEF, although he immediately became aware that supply far exceeded demand. But as the nature of the war became apparent, demand from the voracious Western Front soon exceeded supply – demand from both the British army and Britain's French allies. Sir John French demanded troops to plug the gaps in his increasingly stretched defensive line, and later for his own ambitious 'Zeebrugge plan' to break out along the Belgian coast. Joffre, forcefully

---

[36] Panouse to *ministre de la guerre*, 19 August 1914; C. à C. Repington, *The First World War*, 2 vols (London, 1920), I, p. 21–22. It is to Kitchener's credit that even before France's early reverses he rejected the so-called 'British way in warfare', limited military effort and 'mercenary' subsidies to her allies.
[37] Cassar, *Kitchener*, p. 160.
[38] Quoted in Philpott, *Anglo-French Relations*, pp. 15–16.
[39] Wilson diary, 12 August 1914, Field Marshal Sir Henry Wilson papers, Imperial War Museum, London; Panouse to *ministre de la guerre*, 19 August 1914.
[40] Philpott, *Anglo-French Relations*, pp. 10, 15 and 22–26; Cassar, *Kitchener*, p. 231.

454   William Philpott

backed by Kitchener's opposite number at the *ministère de la guerre*, Alexandre Millerand, pressed for Britain's impressive new formations to come as quickly as possible to the Western Front to support his own offensive plans.[41] Kitchener never intended to keep the New Armies from the Western Front – in pursuance of British policy he had promised Joffre in November 1914 that they would go there when ready the following summer.[42] However, Kitchener came to regret this morale-boosting promise made at the height of the defensive crisis, for by early 1915 he was clearly at odds with Joffre on the coalition's strategy. From the relative detachment of the War Office, Kitchener could form a broader, more balanced view of the coalition's strategic position than the principal theatre commander. While acknowledging the primacy of the Western Front for the coalition's military effort, like several of his cabinet colleagues he concluded that the Western Front would not produce the quick decisive victory Joffre sought, and that Britain's new formations would not produce any significant change in the military stalemate on that front in the short term; in the spring of 1915 he judged that victory could only be secured there following a three-year war of attrition, starting in May 1915 when the first New Army would be ready.[43] Meanwhile he favoured a holding strategy of 'active defence' on the Western Front while the Russians stoked up their spluttering steamroller.[44] This, it was acknowledged, was a threat to Anglo-French cohesion: 'Even at considerable risk we must convince France (still the predominant partner on land in the Western theatre) that we are ready and willing to do our utmost to cooperate with her'.[45]

Clearly in the spring and early summer of 1915 Kitchener had to face Britain's strategic paradox directly, struggling to balance the most effective strategic use of Britain's growing military reserves with the commitment already made to Britain's principal military ally on the main front.[46] It was his hope that, with limited but regular British reinforcements, France could hold the Western Front, while the general coalition position could be improved by an initiative in the east. Naturally Kitchener's stance was unacceptable to the French, who from the start had rejected the idea of any British forces being held back from the decisive battles.[47] The result was the under-resourced and piecemeal Dardanelles misadventure; its deficiencies were epitomized in Kitchener's original briefing to General Sir Ian Hamilton, when it

---

[41] Philpott, 'Kitchener and the 29th Division', pp. 379–387, *passim.*
[42] F. Foch, *The Memoirs of Marshal Foch*, trans. T. Bentley Mott (London, 1931), p. 184.
[43] A very percipient judgement, as it turned out. Notes of a conversation between de Broqueville and Kitchener, 16 February 1915, De Broqueville papers, *Archives Générales du Royaume*, Brussels, file 391. For an analysis of Kitchener's broader strategic analysis, see French, 'The Meaning of Attrition', pp. 390–92.
[44] Neilson, 'Kitchener', pp. 211–18, *passim.*
[45] 'An Appreciation', [?] January 1915, Kitchener (Creedy) papers, PRO, WO 159/3/2.
[46] Philpott, 'Kitchener and the 29th Division', pp. 385–399, *passim.*
[47] Panouse to *ministre de la guerre*, 19 August 1914.

was made clear that British forces for the Dardanelles would be limited 'for big demands would make his position difficult with France'.[48]

Kitchener's position was already difficult with France. Nevertheless, he hoped to impose some restraint on the flow of troops to the French front, both to maintain an independent strategic reserve in his own hands, and for the practical reason that they lacked equipment and training. That 25 British divisions went to France in 1915 is true, but this fact is not proof in itself of Kitchener's commitment to a western offensive strategy[49] – while the majority of new British divisions went west, some went east. Indeed Kitchener made the dispatch of the first New Army to France conditional on Joffre's spring offensive breaking the German line. When it did not, the order was rescinded, and three of its divisions went to break the stalemate at the Dardanelles, even at the risk of trouble with the French.[50] Eventually, against the background of failure at the Dardanelles and stalemate on the Western Front, Kitchener surrendered to French importuning in the interests of the alliance, reversing the thrust of British grand strategic policy from an 'imperial' to a 'coalition' orientation as the true nature of the war, and the effort required for Britain to remain a great power, became clear. At the important Calais conference on 6 July 1915 he presented a timetable of British reinforcements for the Western Front.[51] By the end of August he was also forced to concede the point that the British army should attack to support Joffre's renewed offensive in the autumn – 'we must wage war as we must, and not as we would like to', he informed his sceptical cabinet colleagues.[52] Policy was now to 'try to finish off the Dardanelles and then concentrate our strength in France',[53] contrary though it was to Kitchener's strategic judgement. As the prime minister reported to the king: 'Lord Kitchener, while far from sanguine that any substantial military advantage will be achieved, is strongly of the opinion that we cannot, without serious and fatal injury to the alliance, refuse the cooperation which General Joffre invites and expects.'[54] By 1916 Kitchener's conversion was total: 'I feel very strongly that unless we make every effort this year

---

[48] Hamilton diary, 15 March 1915, in General Sir Ian Hamilton, *Gallipoli Diary*, 2 vols (London, 1920), I, p. 9; Philpott, 'Kitchener and the 29th Division', pp. 391–95.

[49] Greenhalgh, p. 150. Kitchener's continued opposition to an offensive on the Western Front is clear from the minutes of the war council, 14 May 1915, and Dardanelles committee, 5 July 1915, PRO, CAB 42/2/19 and 42/3/7.

[50] Philpott, 'Kitchener and the 29th Division', pp. 395–98.

[51] R.A. Prete, 'La conflit stratégique Franco-Britannique sur le front occidental et la conference de Calais du 6 juillet 1915', *Guerres Mondiales et Conflits Contemporains*, CLXXXVI (1997), pp. 17–49, p. 46.

[52] Minutes of the Dardanelles committee, 20 August 1915, PRO, CAB 42/3/16, quoted in Greenhalgh, p. 150. Greenhalgh claims this comment is made in reference to sending 'half-trained and ill-equipped' troops to the Western Front, but in fact it refers to the likelihood that the offensive may prove as indecisive as those which had preceded it.

[53] Ibid.

[54] Asquith to King George V, 20 August 1915, Asquith papers, box 8, Bodleian Library, Oxford. For Kitchener's reasoning see Williams, 'Kitchener and the Battle of Loos'.

456 William Philpott

we may either lose the war or drift into a most dangerous peace for this country', he cautioned the prime minister in January, adding that all British divisions should be prepared for action as soon as possible.⁵⁵

Greenhalgh attests that 'Kitchener knew the effects of fighting as part of ill-prepared formations from his experience in the French army during the Franco-Prussian war', shortly after asserting that Kitchener sent divisions to France 'as soon as they had received a modicum of basic training'.⁵⁶ This is a misrepresentation of the position in which Kitchener found himself and his army in 1915. In early 1915, as newly formed regular divisions and territorial battalions sent to France proved ill-prepared for the new style of warfare, it became clear that new formations sent from Britain would have to be accustomed to the methods of trench warfare through practice, and so tactical training would have to take place behind and in the line.⁵⁷ Kitchener reluctantly agreed, recognizing full well that any troops sent to the Western Front would be lost permanently for 'indirect' operations elsewhere. British divisions did go out to Flanders in dribs and drabs during the course of 1915, as Kitchener increasingly acknowledged the obligations of an alliance policy, contrary as this was to his own perception of strategy. But these raw divisions were not thrown into the offensive that Joffre championed. Given their shortage of equipment and lack of experience, it was acknowledged by both armies that new British formations were primarily to be sent out to allow experienced French divisions to be relieved for offensive operations on their own front, not to attack on the British front.⁵⁸ That the New Armies had yet to develop offensive élan became only too apparent at Suvla Bay and in the Loos offensive, their first independent engagements.

This would have to be addressed before the 1916 campaign, and this is the main factor which explains Kitchener's reluctance to blood the New Armies in an indecisive Western Front offensive. If there is a reason why the British did not wish to attack in 1916 it is that they did not consider their troops ready. Greenhalgh presents it as a 'generally accepted fact that it takes two years to raise, equip and train an army'.⁵⁹ It was 23 months after the outbreak of war that the New Armies went

---

⁵⁵ Kitchener to Asquith, 11 January 1916, Asquith papers, box 16.
⁵⁶ Greenhalgh, p. 150.
⁵⁷ French diary, 19 February 1915, Field Marshal Viscount French of Ypres papers, Imperial War Museum, London. Although Kitchener opposed the idea of breaking up new divisional formations raised in England and redistributing their subunits among experienced formations, once New Army formations started to arrive Sir John French promptly redistributed his experienced regular army brigades to induct and strengthen the new divisions. Kitchener to French, 20 January 1915, and French to Kitchener, 23 January 1915, Kitchener Papers, PRO, 30/57/50/69 and 70.
⁵⁸ Clive diary, 6 July 1915, 'Cabinet Office: Correspondence Used in the Compilation of the Official History', PRO, CAB 45/201.
⁵⁹ Greenhalgh, p. 150.

over the top on the Somme,⁶⁰ and their real training was only just beginning. Haig had been disappointed by his New Army reserves at Loos,⁶¹ and the deficiencies of the New Army divisions' offensive training were one of the refrains in his diary and correspondence as he prepared for the Somme battle.⁶² He had warned Joffre of this concern at their first meeting,⁶³ and it was the principal reason why he delayed launching the offensive for as long as possible, despite French importuning for relief of the pressure on their army at Verdun. In practice it was to take a further two years for this army to learn from experience successful offensive methods to break the trench deadlock, and much of that experience was gained on the Somme, after the salutary lesson of 1 July.

III.

How then did the British army come to that fateful summer day? To understand why the British attacked on the Somme on 1 July 1916, strategy in the western theatre must be analysed in greater depth than Greenhalgh's article offers. On the Western Front the 'strategic paradox' meant that the British army found itself engaged in offensive operations that, while serving the allied cause, did not directly serve Britain's own strategic need to ensure maritime security in the Channel and North Sea, the strategic rationale for Haig's other great flawed offensive, the third battle of Ypres.⁶⁴ This is at the root of Greenhalgh's second 'perception', that the British would have been better off fighting in Flanders rather than on the Somme. This is not a perception that Greenhalgh attributes to Haig or others at general headquarters (GHQ), but indirectly to 'some British historians', who think, throwing objectivity aside, that the British 'should have been fighting on the northern flank, not in France'.⁶⁵ This author's analysis of Haig's and the general staff's papers produced in the first half of 1916 makes it clear that the British *wanted* to fight there, either instead of or after

---

[60] Four regular and seven New Army divisions went over the top in the first wave on 1 July 1916. The New Army divisions committed had arrived in France between July 1915 and February 1916. Two of the New Army divisions had been bolstered by the incorporation of an experienced regular brigade.

[61] Haig felt obliged to withdraw the 21st and 24th Divisions from the battle for 'training' after three days. Haig diary, 28 September 1915, Haig papers, National Library of Scotland, Edinburgh.

[62] 'I have not got an army in France really, but a collection of divisions untrained for the field. The actual fighting Army will be evolved from them.' Haig diary, 29 March 1916, *Private Papers*, ed. Blake, p. 137.

[63] Haig diary, 23 December 1915, Haig papers.

[64] Significantly, it had been an element of the strategic rationale for the first proposed 'independent' British offensive on the Western Front, Sir John French's 'Zeebrugge plan' of January 1915, and had preoccupied GHQ planning staff ever since. Philpott, *Anglo-French Relations*, pp. 53–149, *passim*.

[65] Ibid. In practice, while geographically in Belgium not France, the 'northern flank' was still part of the coalition front and subject to the vagaries of coalition warfare.

458   William Philpott

the Somme, if the political and strategic situation allowed or necessitated it.[66]

Paradoxically, in her analysis of the Somme as a coalition battle, Greenhalgh dismisses the coalition rationale for the battle, that it was fought to relieve the hard-pressed French at Verdun – 'Haig's excuse for failure', invented after the battle, as Greenhalgh has it.[67] Greenhalgh's conjecture does not stand up to critical scrutiny. At best her analysis represents a misreading of this author's own research, at worst a misrepresentation, with selective use of sources and confusion in ideas. Her alternative rationale for Haig's willingness to fight on the Somme, the desire to win a victory to sustain his position,[68] invites the pointed observation that no general was likely to contemplate a battle unless he expected to win a victory, except of course where policy overrode strategy, and there are clear examples – Loos, the Nivelle offensive – of policy requiring the British army to fight at times and in places which GHQ's strategic appreciations judged inappropriate, in the interests of alliance cohesion. Whether Greenhalgh accepts this broader rationale for British offensive operations before mid-1917, and judges the Somme to be an exception, is unclear. But the broad interpretation that she gives is that Haig was attacking for reasons of personal prestige – to secure his position by winning the victory that had eluded his predecessor, Sir John French.[69] This would suggest that the actual point of attack – tactical and operational considerations – counted for little in Haig's thinking. Even for the much maligned Haig, that is to oversimplify his approach to battle to the point of absurdity.

Considering the possible fronts of attack, Greenhalgh further asserts that in 1916 'A joint battle with the French gave greater chance of success than going it alone in Flanders', although her aside, tinged with hindsight, that Passchendaele demonstrated that a victory could not be won by the British army fighting alone in Flanders in 1916 is no evidence for GHQ holding this view in the winter and spring of 1916.[70] There is also the question of the sort of victory that Haig expected to gain on the Somme. Greenhalgh indicates that Haig expected the battle he agreed to fight on 14 February to be 'decisive', although there is strong evidence that the scale of Haig's expectations

---

[66] Technological and terrain limitations were unlikely to have produced any greater success in Flanders than on the Somme. See J. Terraine, *The Road to Passchendaele* (London, 1977). One perceived advantage of a northern flank offensive was that the British army would not have had to work in close tactical cooperation with the French army. In early 1916 the possibility was, however, negated by another awkward ally, the Belgians. W.J. Philpott, 'Britain, France and the Belgian Army', in B. Bond et al., *Look to Your Front: Studies in the First World War by the British Commission for Military History* (Staplehurst, 1999), pp. 121–35.
[67] Greenhalgh, pp. 147 and 155.
[68] Ibid., p. 154.
[69] Ibid. Of course if Haig had won this decisive victory he would no longer have had a position to sustain!
[70] Ibid.

was revised downwards in the light of military events elsewhere in the four and a half months of planning and preparation that preceded the offensive.[71] When Haig met Joffre on 31 May for their final planning meeting it was agreed that, while still an element in the wider allied strategy of simultaneous offensives on all the allied fronts, the Somme attack itself would have the important subsidiary objective of relieving the pressure on the French army at Verdun.[72] On 10 June Haig confirmed to his chief of staff, General Kiggell, 'the object of our attack is to *relieve pressure on Verdun*'.[73] It is surprising that Greenhalgh has not noticed Haig's 'post-battle excuse for failure' written into the scaled-down strategic objectives of the offensive before it started.

Important elements of the planning processes – the decision on the point of attack, and the subsequent evaluation of the strategic prospects for the coming battle – receive no sustained analysis in Greenhalgh's article. This author has made this detailed analysis elsewhere. Excepting a few selective and poorly contextualized quotations from contemporary documents, it is not acknowledged or evaluated by Greenhalgh, and is incompatible with her own reinterpretation. Her bland statement that 'the battle began *as planned* several months previously on 1 July' flies in the face of the contemporary evidence.[74] It is therefore necessary to reiterate here this author's earlier analysis as a counterpoint to Greenhalgh's ill-documented point of view, and to invite a reply based on the sources produced by Haig and GHQ in the first half of 1916.[75]

It has been outlined above how Kitchener had determined by 1916 to throw the full weight of Britain's military and industrial resources behind the French offensive effort in the west. Kitchener's armies were ready, if not experienced, and it now seemed necessary to use them to win the final victory and bring about a satisfactory peace: 'we ought to make them ask for terms by August and accept them by November', he confided to Lieutenant-Colonel Clive, the chief of Haig's mission at *grand quartier général* (GQG), at the beginning of the year; 'if another winter come on us the peace would be a bad one, especially for England'.[76] The war seemed to be going as he had predicted. 'Indirect' and 'breakthrough' strategies had failed to break the western stalemate in 1915. The alternative, as Kitchener recognized, was a strategy of

---

[71] That Haig's perception had changed over the course of 1916 is evident from the title of his dispatch on the Somme, 'The Opening of the Wearing Out Battle'.
[72] 'Memorandum pour la réunion du 31 mai', by GQG, 30 May 1916, GHQ correspondence and papers, PRO, WO 158/14/118B; Haig diary, 31 May 1916, *Private Papers*, ed. Blake, p. 145. This important meeting left no formal written record, and whether Joffre shared Haig's impression is not recorded.
[73] Haig to Kiggell, 10 June 1916, Haig's italics, PRO, WO 158/14/122.
[74] Greenhalgh, p. 148, my italics.
[75] For this analysis and full documentary references from British and French sources see Philpott, *Anglo-French Relations*, pp. 112–28.
[76] Clive diary, 6 January 1916, PRO, CAB 45/201.

460 William Philpott

pure attrition, Joffre's *guerre d'usure*, with the losses that it entailed.[77] This was the reality of Britain's military and strategic position in 1916, and the dissenting voices which were heard in London were those of 'business as usual' politicians. Kitchener's conversion came shortly before the British military command was reorganized, and Joffre was finally confirmed in his hitherto unofficial role as strategic director of the coalition.[78] Kitchener backed the new regime wholeheartedly; having conceded that British policy should be unequivocal support to France, he took on and defeated the dissenters in the war committee who balked at the prospect of further indecisive offensives on the Western Front.[79] His new policy is indicated in the private advice he gave to Haig when he assumed command, 'to keep friendly with the French ... in France we must do all we can to meet the French C[ommander]-in-C[hief]'s wishes, whatever may be our personal feelings about the French Army and its Commanders'.[80] It was a lesson that Kitchener had learned in the course of 1915, and one which Haig was to take to heart, having reached similar conclusions on the alliance.[81]

Haig's actions in the first half of 1916, when he was learning by practical experience the methods and trials of cooperating with the French, must be judged in the dual context of his general attitude to coalition warfare and the strategic position of the *entente*. Like Kitchener, Haig did have a broad multinational and multi-front conception of the policy and grand strategy of the war, even though it might compromise his own freedom of action in the west, which he always judged the principal theatre for Britain. When Haig took up the command of the British army in December 1915 the broad lines of coalition strategy had already been agreed at Chantilly, and Haig readily accepted them. Significantly, Haig's second stated objective in the Somme battle was 'To assist our Allies in the other theatres of war by stopping any further transfer of German troops from the Western front',[82] an element of the initial agreement of December 1915 for 'combined offensives on the Russian, Franco-British and Italian

---

[77] French, 'The Meaning of Attrition', argues that from the start of the war Kitchener had conceived the Western Front campaign in terms of a long attritional struggle, although in February 1916 he still showed a certain reluctance to rush ill-equipped British divisions across the Channel when the French were attacked at Verdun. J. des Vallières, *Au Soleil de la Cavalerie avec le Général Des Vallières* (Paris, 1962), pp. 143 and 147.
[78] Philpott, 'Squaring the Circle', *passim*; R.A. Prete, 'Joffre and the Question of Allied Supreme Command, 1914–16', *Proceedings of the Annual Meeting of the Western Society for French History*, XVI (1989), pp. 329–38, 333–34.
[79] Philpott, *Anglo-French Relations*, pp. 83–85.
[80] Haig diary, 3 December 1915, *Private Papers*, ed. Blake, pp. 115–16.
[81] For detailed analysis of Haig's views on the alliance, see Philpott, 'Haig and Britain's European Allies', *passim*.
[82] 'The Opening of the Wearing Out Battle', GHQ, 23 December 1916, *Sir Douglas Haig's Despatches*, ed. J.H. Boraston (London, 1920), p. 20.

fronts'.[83] In practice, for Haig coalition warfare meant ensuring effective cooperation with the French army on a day-to-day basis – it boiled down to the fact that 'if France drops out we not only cannot continue the war on land, but our armies in France will be in a very difficult position' – even if his relations with individual Frenchmen were changeable and produced regular frictions and differences of opinion.[84]

Whether Haig retained any operational independence in the western theatre was yet to be tested. Greenhalgh does not acknowledge the complexities of the strategic assessments made at GHQ over the winter of 1915/16, the simultaneous debate over operations going on with GQG, and the ultimate compromise which resulted. Greenhalgh cites the minutes of Haig's conference with the responsible army commander, General Allenby, on 28 December 1915, as the moment when Haig decided that the Somme offered the best prospects of success for a British offensive. From that point she implies (there is no analysis of the intervening decision-making process) that it was a straightforward and natural path to the final agreement made with Joffre for 'an offensive on or about 1 July in conjunction with the French on the Somme', finally agreed some six weeks later on 14 February 1916. 'Moreover', she adds, 'the Belgians would not fall in with Haig's projected Flanders operation against Ostend', a passing acknowledgement that GHQ did have an alternative operational plan, a plan which she admits Joffre had actually agreed to support with French troops as late as 20 January.[85] Whether or not Britain '[lacked] the resources to pursue an independent strategy',[86] Haig's Flanders plan, an independent *battle*, was conceived as an operational component of the broader alliance theatre and grand military strategies, and for a time was accepted by Joffre as such.

Joffre's strategic plan for the Western Front in 1916 had contemplated two operations, a 'wearing-out battle' (*usure*) in the spring to defeat the enemy's reserves, followed by a decisive blow in the summer when the other allied armies would be ready to attack. Haig was broadly in agreement, although he felt that in order to draw in the enemy's reserves the wearing-out phase of the operations should come immediately before the decisive blow on another part of the front. Joffre considered the British army's fresh but untrained divisions more

---

[83] Conclusions of Chantilly conference, quoted by Greenhalgh, p. 148. While, as Greenhalgh states (p. 149), strictly speaking this objective did not 'necessarily require action on the date or in the place agreed', with a Russian offensive already under way, a new Italian offensive being prepared and indeed a French offensive ready to launch on the immediate right of the British army, it would have been a foolish and selfish commander who went back on this long-standing and politically sensitive agreement.

[84] Notes by Haig, 22 July 1917, *Private Papers*, ed. Blake, p. 247; Philpott, 'Haig and Britain's European Allies'.

[85] Greenhalgh, p. 154.

[86] Ibid.

suited for holding the line, and the wearing-out phase of the operations, and hoped to husband his own experienced but weary divisions for the decisive blow.[87] This was the first point of disagreement between Haig and Joffre. The former judged the resilience of the French army to be uncertain, yet clearly wanted the British army to be preserved intact for the final decisive blow if possible – but for practical reasons rather than personal glory.[88] General Sir William Robertson, chief of the imperial general staff, was to caution him against a British 'wearing-out' battle that cost lives with little obvious gain, which would have a harmful effect on the home front and political support for the high command,[89] and this became an axiom of Haig's preparations for the battle. In May he reassured Robertson 'that I deemed it unwise (for the reasons I have often stated in the diary) to attack until all our resources had been developed and our Army in France was as strong as possible'.[90] This is certainly evidence that Haig wanted to maximize his chances of victory, but it also suggests that Haig himself did not wish to attack until the British army was ready to deliver the final blow that won the war and placed Britain at an advantage at the peace conference. The desire to deliver the final blow on the British front was ill-disguised at GHQ, much to the disgust of the French; Major-General Davidson, Haig's director of operations, indicated as much to Haig's French liaison officer, Colonel des Vallières, who commented wryly, 'C'est ... le même calcul toujours de l'Angleterre pour dicter finalement par la force à des partenaires épuisés une paix à sa convenience'.[91] Whether the blow was ultimately to be delivered on the Somme or in Flanders, however, depended not on the British army, but on the state of the French army, and his knowledge of GHQ's ambitions undoubtedly influenced Joffre's determination to attack on the Somme while the French still had fresh divisions, even though the British divisions were not fully trained. A policy of winning the final victory on the French front was equally strongly entrenched at GQG, and Joffre was still the military director of the coalition in 1916.

At both headquarters operations were still in the *étude* stage. That there was 'some argument' before the Somme was chosen as the front of the British attack on 14 February, Greenhalgh acknowledges, with-

---

[87] 'Memorandum for the Meeting of Representatives of the Allied Armies on 25 November 1915', by GQG, November 1915, PRO, CAB 42/5/1; Haig diary, 14 January 1916, *Private Papers*, ed. Blake, p. 125.

[88] 'There is no doubt to my mind but that the war must be won by the forces of the British Empire'; Haig diary, ibid.

[89] Robertson to Haig, 28 January 1916, *The Military Correspondence of Field-Marshal Sir William Robertson, Chief of the Imperial General Staff, December 1915–February 1918*, ed. D.R. Woodward (London, 1989), pp. 32–33.

[90] Haig diary, 6 May 1916, *Private Papers*, ed. Blake, p. 142.

[91] Des Vallières, *Au Soleil de la Cavalerie*, pp. 149–50. Kitchener's early pronouncements, if abandoned, had clearly not been forgotten. The view that it was now or never if Britain wanted to 'win the peace' was certainly prevalent in early 1916. See, for example, Robertson to Wigram, 12 January 1916, *Military Correspondence*, ed. Woodward, p. 27.

out elaborating.⁹² In fact it is in the detail of this argument that the determinants of British military strategy can be ascertained, and the reality of her second 'perception' can be judged. In December 1915 and January 1916 Haig was engaged in preliminary consultations with all his army commanders to get an overall view of the situation on the front for which he had just assumed responsibility. His meeting with Allenby on 28 December was only one of a series of conferences with his army commanders, who were all instructed to review the options for offensive action – both for drawing in the enemy's reserves and delivering the decisive blow – on their respective fronts.⁹³ Joffre was at the same time undertaking a similar review with his own army commanders, and informed Haig on 25 December that if he chose to make the decisive attack on the French front south of the Somme a British attack north of the river would offer considerable assistance.⁹⁴ While Greenhalgh appropriately cites Haig's meeting with Allenby on 28 December 1915 as the point at which Haig, following up Joffre's request, reviewed the arguments in favour of an attack on the Third Army front on the Somme, no immediate decision was taken on the front of attack. That, Haig noted in early February, depended on 'circumstances and dates'.⁹⁵ Both commanders appreciated that a joint attack offered the advantages of an extended front of attack, but the proven disadvantages of close tactical cooperation between the allied armies.⁹⁶ Attacking on the Somme offered no obvious tactical objectives, although it was good fighting country, and an attack there could be mounted in the spring. An attack on the Second Army front in Flanders offered contrasting advantages and disadvantages; an operation against the Belgian coast had support in London; there would be less tactical cooperation with the French;⁹⁷ although the ground was more difficult and an offensive could not realistically take place there until the summer, there were clear tactical and strategic objectives which were perceived to be within the reach of a sustained advance by the British army. Significantly, as Haig pointed out to des Vallières

---

⁹² Greenhalgh, p. 148.
⁹³ See, for example, Haig diary, 4 and 8 January 1916, Haig papers.
⁹⁴ Joffre to Haig, 25 December 1915, Haig papers, 104.
⁹⁵ 'Plans for Future Operations', by Haig, 10 February 1916, Haig papers, 104.
⁹⁶ J. Joffre, *The Memoirs of Marshal Joffre*, trans. T. Bentley Mott, 2 vols (London, 1932), II, 461–62. Haig diary, 11 February 1916, Haig papers. Greenhalgh, pp. 163–70, offers clear evidence for the latter in the offensive itself.
⁹⁷ Though Haig never considered 'going it alone in Flanders' (Greenhalgh, p. 154). In practice the Flanders offensive was never anticipated as an independent operation by the British army. In January 1916 Joffre planned for a French force to play a part between the British and Belgian armies, and in the actual Flanders offensive in 1917 (which the French official history of the war calls 'l'offensive franco-anglais'!) the French First Army participated on the British left. Then the problems of tactical coordination meant a vital six days were wasted waiting for the French army to register its artillery – to give the demoralized French army the opportunity to fight as Haig and Robertson acknowledged in presenting the plan to the war cabinet. Once again the policy of sustaining the alliance had a clear influence over British operational strategy. Philpott, *Anglo-French Relations* pp. 145–47.

464 William Philpott

at their first meeting, the Flanders front offered the public more tangible rewards than the Somme front[98] – he could be seen to win a clear victory *in Flanders*. As planning proceeded it became clear that Haig judged the Somme the best place for a decisive spring offensive, and Flanders best for a summer attack. As it was becoming apparent that the Russian army would not be ready to participate in the coordinated offensives agreed at Chantilly before the summer, Joffre accepted that the decisive offensive would have to be delayed. In the meantime, despite Haig's misgivings, wearing-out attacks should take place on the Western Front. It was the basis of the agreement made by the commanders-in-chief on 20 January that the British should undertake a wearing-out attack on the Somme in the spring followed by a decisive attack in Flanders in the summer, with French support on both occasions. GQG had judged that, since the fresh British divisions were expected to carry the weight of the offensive in 1916, GHQ should determine the general line of operations. Joffre was willing to concede to the British on the point of their decisive attack, in return for Haig's agreement to mount a wearing-out offensive.[99]

That this was an uncertain compromise was soon obvious, as both Haig and Joffre tried to modify the agreement. Joffre pressed for more British wearing-out attacks during the spring, while Haig, cautioned by the war committee against 'an attack on our part which is independent of a general allied offensive', and the planned spring attack in particular, tried to avoid any limited operations that did not immediately precede the decisive attack.[100] At the start of February he proposed to Joffre preliminary operations elsewhere in the summer immediately before the decisive attack in Flanders. The British and French were only to attack together on the Somme in the spring if the Russians were attacked.[101] GQG had also hardened its opinion. Des Vallières's alarming reports from GHQ that, under pressure from London, Haig was wavering in his support for an offensive convinced the French staff that to keep the British in hand they should insist on a contiguous offensive on the Somme in all circumstances.[102] It was at this point that King Albert threw his royal spanner into the workings of Haig's Flanders plan. It was one thing for Haig to contemplate a Flanders offensive as part of the general plan agreed with Joffre, quite another for him to go it alone without the support of the two allied armies whose cooperation was essential to success in Flanders. Hence his agreement at his next conference with Joffre to attack alongside the French on the Somme around 1 July – a necessary concession in the

[98] Des Vallières, *Au Soleil de la Cavalerie*, pp. 139-40.
[99] Notes of and interview with General Joffre at St Omer, 20 January 1916, Haig papers, file 213d; Philpott, *Anglo-French Relations*, pp. 116–18.
[100] Robertson to Haig, 28 January 1916; Joffre to Haig, 23 January 1916 and Haig's note on this letter for Kiggell, 25 January 1916; Haig diary, 28 January 1916, Haig papers, 104.
[101] Haig to Joffre, 1 February 1916, Haig papers, 104.
[102] Haig diary, 11 February 1916, Haig papers, 104.

face of allied intransigence, not a recognition that this was preferable to attacking in Flanders, whatever the operational merits of the Somme front.[103] In return Joffre conceded that there should be no separate wearing-out attack by the British army unless it immediately preceded the decisive attack.[104]

Although this is what was agreed on 14 February, it was mere coincidence that the battle actually started on the suggested target date of 1 July. In the interim the general expression of intent of 14 February had to be developed into a practical plan of action taking into account the military situation on the Western Front, and of the coalition as a whole. This changed significantly, mainly as a consequence of the German offensive against the French army at Verdun, the prospect of which was already starting to exercise the French even as the agreement was made.[105] In the coming months roles on the Somme were reversed, and Haig rethought the operation accordingly. The decisive Anglo-French offensive to win the war soon took on a much less conclusive character.

The state of the French army was a particular concern of Haig's throughout his period of command.[106] In 1916 specifically it was the effect of the Verdun 'mincing machine' on their offensive capability, and their capacity to remain in the fight, which preoccupied him. His avowed objective 'to relieve the pressure on Verdun' may perhaps be judged a crude and rather symbolic way of defining the consequences of this preoccupation, but it was a straightforward summation of Haig's perception of the coalition's military situation at the time nonetheless, not an *ex post facto* 'excuse for failure'. A perceived decline in French fighting power, to which his own official correspondence and diary, and that of his French liaison officer, testify, undoubtedly had an important influence on Haig's perceptions of the coming battle.

It is this preoccupation with the state of the French army, and his consequent re-evaluation of the nature and purpose of the battle in the intervening months, that Greenhalgh fails to acknowledge in her rejection of Haig's subsequent assessment of the battle. In reality, the prospects of a decisive success diminished as the French army's offensive capability was ground down. Haig's third objective, 'to wear down the strength of the forces opposed to us',[107] actually marked a return to the concept of an attritional wearing-out battle that Haig had rejected out of hand in the initial planning stage. This reassessment derived from the conjunction of his awareness of the decline of the French contribution to the battle, and his appreciation of the

---

[103] 'Plans for Future Operations', by Haig, 10 February 1916, Haig papers, 104.
[104] Haig diary, 14 February 1916, Haig papers, 104; Philpott, *Anglo-French Relations* pp. 118–20.
[105] Haig diary, 19 February 1916, Haig papers.
[106] This aspect of Haig's strategic thinking is thoroughly analysed by Blake, *Private Papers*, pp. 51–58.
[107] 'The Opening of the Wearing Out Battle', 23 December 1916, *Sir Douglas Haig's Despatches*, ed. Boraston, p. 20.

unreadiness of his own army, even before the tactical disaster of 1 July removed any possibility of decisive victory.

In February 1916 Joffre anticipated engaging 40 fresh French divisions in the summer offensive. However, Haig immediately came to doubt this probability, as the opening of the Verdun offensive threw Joffre into a panic and produced the immediate demand for a British counter-attack or the relief of French divisions on the Tenth Army front. Haig and Kitchener took vicarious satisfaction when the French were attacked at Verdun. This would allow the *usure* to take place on the French front, and the British army might still deliver the decisive blow in the summer.[108] However, the 14 February agreement had not included the possibility of an isolated British offensive to disengage the French, nor were Haig's divisions ready for such an operation. Although it would reduce his offensive strength, to husband his forces for the summer offensive Haig reluctantly opted to extend the British line.[109]

More generally, Haig's growing anxiety about the French army's morale, obviously shaken by Verdun, became a factor in his calculations over the ensuing four months of preparation. He was obliged to continue a careful juggling act between training his divisions, preventing French collapse at Verdun and ensuring French support for the Somme attack. At the end of March, Kitchener cautioned that the French appeared anxious to economise men and wished to leave the real fighting in France to the British army – hence they might not try to force a decision in the summer. Haig accepted Kitchener's advice that in the changed circumstances he should try to 'husband the strength of the British army in France'.[110] Although he was determined 'In every way we possibly can [to] take the lead, or at any rate refuse to be led against our own judgement',[111] Haig could not unilaterally rescind his earlier arrangement with Joffre while the French still planned to attack. Nevertheless, he prepared a contingency plan, for a British offensive in Flanders, should the French army be so worn out at Verdun that it was unable to attack alongside the British on the Somme. Although Haig was always ready to attack 'in an emergency to save the French from disaster',[112] by the end of April the situation on the French front appeared more stable, and Joffre reverted to his original intention to attack in the summer. Haig now favoured attack-

---

[108] For his part, Haig felt that the French were panicking because Verdun would deny their army the honour and profit of winning the victory and (as des Vallières foolishly let slip) having a strong voice in the peace. Haig diary, 2 and 20 February 1916, Haig papers; Haig to Esher, 22 February 1916, Esher papers, ESHR 4/6, Churchill College Archives Centre, Cambridge.

[109] Philpott, *Anglo-French Relations*, p. 121.

[110] Haig diary, 29 March 1916, Haig papers; for details see Philpott, *Anglo-French relations*, pp. 121–26.

[111] Robertson's words, quoted in Haig diary, 8 March 1916, *Private Papers*, ed. Blake, p. 135.

[112] Ibid.; des Vallières, *Au Soleil de la Cavalerie*, p. 150.

ing in mid-August, when the British divisions would be fully trained, but Joffre for his part would not delay beyond 1 July because of the need to relieve pressure on Verdun. Moreover, Joffre's position was becoming increasingly shaky: there now appeared the distinct possibility that the French government would refuse to allow the French army to attack,[113] or that if it did attack it would only amount to a counter-attack on the Verdun front. Although information received from GQG was contradictory and uncertain, it was becoming clear that, as Verdun ground down the French army, Joffre's perception of the offensive had changed, especially as the number of French divisions available for the offensive was being reduced week on week. It mutated from the decisive war-winning blow to a relief operation, which might develop into a lengthy attritional battle to keep the Germans in the west while the Russians advanced in the east.[114] Weighing up all these factors, Haig opted to throw his weight behind Joffre and the plan he had agreed on in the spring. Hence his agreement on 31 May that the immediate strategic objective of the joint offensive on the Somme would now be to relieve the pressure on Verdun, which was judged unlikely to hold out beyond the beginning of July..[115] Haig's 'post-battle excuse for failure' was written into the Anglo-French agreement on the objectives of the battle before the offensive was launched, and the war council was well aware that the battle's objective was now to '*dégager* the French', and that it would be 'a battle of "durée prolongée"'.[116] One might judge with hindsight that Verdun would not have fallen if the Somme attack had not taken place; nevertheless, Joffre's repetitive pleas in June to advance the date of the attack because of the situation at Verdun made Haig very aware that something would have to be done to aid his ally sooner or later. That it was done on 1 July was merely a coincidence;[117] that it was done sooner than Haig would have preferred was of more significance.

It would be fair to deduce that the success which Haig anticipated on 1 July was far less than he had expected in February. His policy by the summer, he informed the British ambassador in Paris, was to:

> 1) train my divisions and collect as much ammunition and as many guns as possible. 2) To make arrangements to support the French by [?] attacking in order to draw off pressure from Verdun, when the French consider that the military situation demands it. 3) But

---

[113] Haig diary, 20 May 1916, *Private Papers*, ed. Blake, p. 142.
[114] Ibid., 2 May 1916, p. 141; minutes of the war committee, 30 May and 7 June 1916, PRO, CAB 42/14/12 and CAB 42/15/6; des Vallières, *Au Soleil de la Cavalerie*, p. 158.
[115] Haig diary, 31 May 1916, *Private Papers*, ed. Blake, p. 145.
[116] Minutes of the war committee, 30 May; Haig diary, 9 June 1916, *Private Papers*, ed. Blake, p. 149. Haig conveyed the second of these facts privately to the prime minister rather than to the war committee as a whole.
[117] In fact the day of attack had been delayed from 29 June because of bad weather. There was much toing and froing about the actual day between GHQ and GQG in June. Joffre Journal, 9–28 June 1916 *passim*, *Journal de Marche de Joffre, 1916–1919*, ed. G. Pedroncini (Vincennes, 1990), pp. 12–29.

468 William Philpott

while attacking to help our allies not to think that we can for a certainty destroy the power of Germany this year.[118]

Since there would be fewer (or possibly no) French divisions in the attack, and Haig felt that his own divisions were inadequately trained, there was no longer any real expectation that it would be the decisive blow that would win the war. But it would be an important blow; one that would inspire his allies and draw in German reserves. In fact Haig now perceived it as the preliminary wearing-out battle that he had agreed to conduct on 14 February.[119] This is evident from his plan of attack.[120] Having drawn in the enemy's reserves, there remained the possibility of switching the British offensive to the Flanders front to deliver a decisive blow. If the British wanted to attack in Flanders in 1916, it was not as an alternative to attacking alongside the French on the Somme, but it was an option if the French were unable to attack on the Somme, or to follow up a successful Somme offensive.[121] Joffre knew nothing of this. Haig clearly did have an alternative military strategy (centred on an offensive in Flanders), based on his perceptions at the start of the year, which he would have tried to pursue if the agreed coalition strategy had collapsed, but he could never have carried it out against the wishes of the French commander-in-chief.

'For Britain the Somme was a battle fought for intangible strategic gains, to sustain an ally as much as defeat the enemy.'[122] This conclusion is borne out by the contemporary documents that chart the development of GHQ's conception of the coming offensive as the military situation changed over the spring and early summer of 1916. The desire not to attack until the British army was ready – for practical military as well as realistic political reasons – and the option to attack in Flanders if the French abandoned their joint effort on the Somme were elements of British strategic planning in the first half of 1916. These, it needs to be emphasized, are not simply the subjective 'perceptions' of later historians, but, in the objective judgement of those managing British policy at the time, viable, if politically sensitive, mili-

---

[118] Haig to Bertie, 5 June 1916, Haig papers, file 214.
[119] Charteris diary, 1 May 1916, J. Charteris, *At GHQ* (London, 1931), p. 143.
[120] Much ink has subsequently been spilt over this plan. It is not possible to reconsider its details here, but it is worth commenting that Haig undoubtedly wanted to be ready to exploit tactical success – he had not expected to break through at Loos and had no reserves at hand to exploit that unanticipated success. Since the 'hoped-for breakthrough' (Greenhalgh, p. 163) on the Somme did not materialize, he has been criticized for being overambitious, rather than commended for learning from his mistakes.
[121] If there was a post-battle excuse for failure on the Somme it was provided by Lt-Col. J. H. Boraston, Haig's private secretary at the time and a post-war defender of Haig's reputation, who edited Haig's dispatches. He noted on Haig's dispatch of 23 December 1916: 'The choice of front for the allied offensive was governed by the consideration that neither the French nor ourselves were at the moment deemed strong enough to undertake unaided an offensive on a really large scale. It was therefore necessary to deliver a combined attack.' *Sir Douglas Haig's Despatches*, ed. Boraston, p. 19, n. 2.
[122] Philpott, *Anglo-French Relations*, p. 128.

tary options. Although both proved impossible given the needs of coalition warfare, these possible strategic alternatives exercised considerable influence over Haig and GHQ between January and June 1916 – maybe if the British army had retained complete freedom of action they would have been judged preferable.

IV.

Greenhalgh writes that 'the preparation of the battle of the Somme reveals no domination by the French of the British, either in terms of plan of attack, tactical doctrine or date'.[123] Certainly the French had no say in determining Haig's operational and tactical objectives.[124] Operational control on the battlefield does not, however, amount to operational independence in the theatre. Far from being a battle in which the British asserted their strategic independence, the Somme was the coalition battle *par excellence*. When it came to the date, the place and the strategic objectives of the operation Joffre took the lead, and Haig and Kitchener paid careful attention to coalition concerns. Had GHQ asserted themselves they would have attacked later, and probably elsewhere. On the battlefield, where Haig was able to retain some independence, Greenhalgh rightly concludes that this contributed to the initial disaster, and in this analysis her article has some merits. But her barrage against the historiography of the higher direction of the coalition is deficient.

Much has been done in recent years to rehabilitate the reputations of Britain's higher military leadership in the First World War. Both Kitchener and Haig, the central figures of Greenhalgh's narrative, and more directly the historians who have returned to the archives to assess their perceptions and actions free as far as possible from the justifications and misrepresentations of postwar memoirs and critiques,[125] are denigrated by Greenhalgh's article, while in no way refuted. Greenhalgh makes some crude assumptions about this author's perspective in particular.[126] In Greenhalgh's post-revisionist article the 'butchers

---

[123] Greenhalgh, p. 162. Contrarily, she acknowledges elsewhere (pp. 171–72) that 'Haig agreed to the timing and the place of the Somme battle in accordance with the proposed and agreed French plans'. This seems directly to contradict her earlier (p. 151) challenge to this author's argument that 1916 represented 'The Ascendancy of French Strategy'.

[124] Greenhalgh is, however, mistaken if she thinks this has been argued in the historiography of the coalition.

[125] For a survey of the extensive literature on the war see B.J. Bond, ed., *The First World War and British Military History* (Oxford, 1991).

[126] Greenhalgh makes the bizarre assertion (p. 151) that 'The ... perception – that Britain was forced to fall in with French aims and strategy, rather than following its own, different ones independently – would appear to derive from the horror inspired by the excessive slaughter on the Somme'. Her own summation of the battle is revealing (p. 148) – 'The overwhelming feature of the battle was not, however, these high points, but the costly and futile local actions which took place betweentimes, in the increasingly horrendous conditions caused by the appalling weather.'

and bunglers' school of historiography rears its head once more.[127] Its argument is weakened by suppositions, misconceptions and hindsight, and it presents a very meagre alternative rationale for British policy and strategy, offering the trite generalization that Haig attacked on the Somme because he wanted to achieve a military success. What general would launch an offensive without the prospect of success? In practice, only the general who placed the political needs of an alliance over the military needs of his army, as Kitchener had recently demonstrated when, against his own military judgement, he agreed for the good of the coalition to British support for Joffre's autumn 1915 offensive, even at the risk of heavy casualties. This need was impressed on Haig when he took command in December 1915, and it informed his judgement throughout 1916 and beyond. Haig's decision to attack at the time and place he did in 1916, in February based on a sound balance of policy and strategy, came by June to depend more on the former than the latter. British policy did not allow Haig an operational free hand, before or after the Somme. It was this author's conclusion from analysing carefully GHQ's preparation for battle in 1916 that:

> Haig's claim that he mounted and prolonged the Somme battle for the broader interests of the alliance is borne out by the analysis of the decision making process. This in not incompatible with his desire to mount an independent offensive in Flanders, but simply further evidence that in strategic matters Britain had to give priority to alliance obligations over national interests.[128]

This is an explanation for the 'strategic paradox' of Britain's Western Front campaign; it is not an argument that Britain should not have been attacking, or should have been attacking in Flanders. Ultimately, policy determined that the British offensive would take place on the Somme, alongside the French, when the general situation of the coalition necessitated it.

It is true that Haig hoped in June for more from the 1916 campaign, both tactically on the Somme and strategically on the Western Front, than the allied offensive achieved. The British army's tactical plan, the one area in which Haig retained his independence, was generally a failure – Haig's assessment that the British army was not yet adequately trained or equipped for offensive warfare was proved tragically correct. It is from this, and the attrition and casualties which followed, that Greenhalgh concluded that Haig failed on the Somme – there was no clear victory which she argues he sought. Her own measure of success – 'a significant breach in the German lines on the Somme, or a cavalry pursuit of fleeing German infantry'[129] – is tactical at best, and does not reflect Haig's own assessment of the operation. It is, moreover, surpris-

---

[127] Evident in the citation of Liddell Hart and Peter Liddle (p. 171, n. 90) to back her case.
[128] Philpott, *Anglo-French Relations*, p. 127.
[129] Greenhalgh, p. 149.

ing given recent scholarship that Greenhalgh can still justify evaluating attritional operations against such criteria.[130] Haig's own record of the battle's preparation suggests that he had significantly scaled down his expectations in the light of developments on the French front in the intervening months. If the achievements on the Somme were not what the allies expected in February, the battle did accomplish their scaled-down and more realistic expectations which had been set out in the planning stage of the battle, when it became clear that the French army was worn out by Verdun and the British army insufficiently trained. On this basis the Somme cannot be judged a failure, despite the small territorial gain to show for the casualties sustained. In a strategy of attrition, success is measured in less tangible ways: the coalition survived; the French army's morale revived with offensive success on the Somme and at Verdun; the British army learned to fight an offensive battle; German forces were held on the Western Front while other allies attacked; the German army sustained casualties at such a rate that its morale plummeted, its commander was sacked and the following spring it was obliged to carry out a strategic retreat; Romania joined the *entente*; Germany made serious peace overtures to the allies. This is what the British, or more accurately the Anglo-French forces, were doing on the Somme in the 1916 campaign – not winning the war, but wearing down the enemy, and serving the strategy of attrition which had replaced the quest for decisive military victory between February and June 1916.

Acknowledgement

The author would like to thank Claire Herrick, John Hussey and Gary Sheffield for their valuable comments during the preparation of this article.

---

[130] For a more balanced assessment of the strategic significance of the battle see Strachan, 'The Battle of the Somme and British Strategy'.

[18]

Madelon and the Men—in War and Memory

Charles Rearick

One French song of the era of the First World War stands out as *the* hit of the war and long remained in popular memory as such: the music-hall march entitled "Quand Madelon." It became for French soldiers an identifying theme song, as "It's a Long Way to Tipperary" was for British infantrymen and "Over There" was for the Americans. During the war soldiers and their entertainers sang it on or near the front. Civilians heard it and sang it in music-halls behind the lines. Recent research on the common soldier—the *poilu*—and on civilians has added much to our knowledge of daily life during the war, but it has not addressed a number of historical questions which still surround that celebrated song.[1] Why and when did it become popular? And what did it mean to soldiers and civilians? Answers to those questions are to be proposed here not as mere details about a song, but as a contribution to the understanding of French mentalities and culture of the wartime era. In

---

Charles Rearick is professor of history at the University of Massachusetts/Amherst. His publications include "Song and Society in Turn-of-the-Century France," *Journal of Social History* 22 (Fall 1988), 45–63, and *Pleasures of the Belle Epoque: Entertainment and Festivity in Turn-of-the-Century France* (New Haven, 1985). He is currently writing a history of French culture—with a focus on social representation—in the era of the world wars.

For suggestions and criticisms of earlier drafts, I wish to thank Bruce Saxon, Mary Rearick, Professors Kathy Peiss and David Glassberg of the University of Massachusetts, and a particularly helpful anonymous reader.

[1] Memoirs, newly published correspondence, studies of *journaux de tranchées* and postal inspectors' notes have yielded valuable insights into mentalities of the mass of soldiers who were not writers or otherwise members of a cultural or social elite. See, for example, Gérard Canini, *Combattre à Verdun: Vie et souffrance quotidiennes du soldat, 1916–1917* (Nancy, 1988); Louis Barthas, *Les Carnets de guerre de Louis Barthas, Tonnelier, 1914–1918* (Paris, 1978); Gérard Bacconnier et al., eds., *La Plume au fusil: Les Poilus du Midi à travers leurs correspondance* (Toulouse, 1985); Stéphane Audoin-Rouzeau, *14–18, les combattants des tranchées à travers leurs journaux* (Paris, 1986); Françoise Thébaud, *La Femme au temps de la guerre de 1914* (Paris, 1986); and David Englander, "The French Soldier, 1914–18," *French History* 1 (March 1987): 49–67. On George Cohan's "Over There" (1917), see Sigmund Spaeth, *A History of Popular Music in America* (New York, 1966), 342, 402–20. Spaeth notes that "Quand Madelon" in English translation was also popular with Americans.

writing on French responses to the war experience, historians have given much attention to the importance of nationalism, duty, and hatred for the "Boches." This article examines other important cultural idioms of that time: namely, prewar myths and memories encoded in popular songs and in "Quand Madelon" in particular.

The song's importance after the war has received even less attention than its wartime history has. Through the troubled decades between the wars "Quand Madelon" persisted as one of the most familiar and emotionally charged songs. It figured routinely in plays and movies set in the period of the war, and it inspired numerous sequels and legends. Developed in its own right, apart from the music, the Madelon motif recurred in literature, plays, and films. Even when the Second World War ended preoccupation with the Great War, Madelon did not disappear. She enjoyed revivals at a time of the Liberation and again in the mid-1950s. In the course of this long period of the twentieth century Madelon had become a basic myth, a commonly known collective representation, in French popular culture. This article attempts to provide fuller understanding of that myth's development and meanings by examining the song in its successive contexts of prewar, wartime, and subsequent culture. Like Marianne (the feminine representation of the Republic analyzed so well by Maurice Agulhon),[2] Madelon was historically polysemous and complex, subject to a variety of interpretations; yet, her story remained tied to specific historic associations. After the armistice the song about her became what Pierre Nora has called a *lieu de mémoire*, a "site" around which memories of the "Great War" crystallized. It was one of the elements with which the French constructed their memories not only of the war, but also of the social world of 1914. With its familiar images and multiple associations it was invoked to serve present needs in France over a period of almost a half century.[3]

"Quand Madelon" made its debut in the spring of 1914 in the Paris music hall Eldorado where a star comic soldier-singer (*comique troupier*) with the stage name Bach sang it as part of his set. The song was just one of many light songs about soldiers' camp life in peacetime. Its sketchy lyrics form a narrative told by common soldiers. In the first verse they describe a "young and nice" barmaid named Madelon who

---

[2] For the period of La Madelon, see Maurice Agulhon's most recent volume, *Marianne au pouvoir, l'imagerie et la symbolique républicaines de 1880 à 1914* (Paris, 1989).

[3] See Nora's theoretical essay, originally an introduction to his volumes entitled *Les Lieux de mémoire* (Vol. 1, 1984), reprinted and translated as "Between Memory and History: *Les Lieux de mémoire*," trans. Marc Roudebush, *Representations* (1989): 7–25. A recent, clear summary of historical reflection on memory may be found in David Thelen's "Memory and American History," *Journal of American History* 75 (March 1989): 1117–29.

MADELON AND THE MEN

works at a pastoral drinking spot named "Aux Toulourous" ("To the Grunts," we might say—or to the foot soldiers). Madelon is "light like a butterfly" and has an eye that sparkles like the wine she serves to her admiring, indeed adoring, soldier friends.

> *Pour le repos, le plaisir du militaire. / Il est là-bas, à deux pas de la forêt, / Une maison aux murs tout couverts de lierre, / "Aux Tourlourous" c'est le nom du cabaret. / La servante est jeune et gentille, / Légère comme un papillon, / Comme son vin son oeil pétille, / Nous l'appelons la Madelon. / Nous en rêvons la nuit, nous y pensons le jour, / Ce n'est que Madelon, mais pour nous, c'est l'amour.**

In the second verse the men speak of their distant sweethearts whom they will one day marry. Meanwhile there is Madelon, who is gentle and kind as she listens to the men telling her what they cannot say to their favorites back home. She is also there for a quick embrace, as the men imagine her to be the absent woman.

> *Nous avons tous au pays une payse / Qui nous attend et que l'on épousera, / Mais elle est loin, bien trop loin pour qu'on lui dise / Ce qu'on fera quand la classe rentrera. / En comptant les jours on soupire, / Et quand le temps nous semble long, / Tout ce qu'on ne peut pas lui dire / On va le dire à Madelon. / On l'embrass' dans les coins. Ell' dit: Veux-tu finir . . . / On s'figur' que c'est l'autr', ça nous fait bien plaisir.*

In the last verse she refuses the proposal of a smitten officer—out of fondness for all the soldiers of the regiment.

> *Un caporal, en képi de fantaisie, / S'en fut trouver Madelon un beau matin / Et fou d'amour, lui dit qu'elle était jolie / Et qu'il venait pour lui demander sa main. / La Madelon, pas bête en somme, / Lui répondit en souriant: / Et pourquoi prendrais-je un seul homme / Quand j'aime tout un régiment. / Tes amis vont venir. Tu n'auras pas ma main, / J'en ai bien trop besoin pour leur verser du vin.*

After each verse there is the chorus, which returns to the essential relationship:

> "When Madelon comes to serve our drinks, / Under the arbor we brush against her petticoat / And each one tells her a story, a story in his own way. Madelon doesn't give us a hard time, / When we take her by the waist or her chin, / She laughs, that's all the trouble she knows how to make."

*"QUAND MADELON"
(Camille Robert, Louis Bousquet)
© 1916 WB MUSIC CORP. (Renewed)
All Rights Reserved. Used by Permission.

1914. When the song first appeared only months before the outbreak of war, its sheet-music cover featured jovial peacetime soldiers smiling and singing as they march past Madelon, standing in front of her "cabaret." Detail of the cover. Drawing by Pousthomis. Private collection. All rights reserved.

> *Quand Madelon vient nous servir à boire, / Sous la tonnelle on frôle son jupon, / Et chacun lui raconte une histoire, / Une histoire à sa façon. / La Madelon pour nous n'est pas sévère, / Quand on lui prend la taille ou le menton / Elle rit, c'est tout l'mal qu'ell' sait faire.*

Then this chorus culminates in a triple invocation of her name, each time rising higher: "Madelon! Madelon! Madelon!"

The tune of this light march was eminently singable—with an upbeat, regular 2/4 rhythm. Yet neither the lyrics nor the music was enough to make it an instant hit. In prewar 1914 this song was just one of many music-hall marches and just one of many songs about men admiring and desiring an attractive young woman. "Quand Madelon" was so ordinary that it went almost unnoticed.

When war broke out only months later, the Madelon march encountered neglect for another reason: it did not fit the mood of "la patrie en danger." Stridently nationalistic and martial songs now became standard in the music halls. Old ones, like "Le Chant du départ," "Le Clairon," and above all "La Marseillaise" resounded anew. Revanchist songs in the spirit of super-patriot Paul Déroulède now flourished, and new ones quickly proliferated: "Gloire aux alliés," "Gloire à nos canons," "Jusqu'à Berlin," "Marche anti-Boche," "1915 on les aura." Military bands played the "Chant des Girondins," also known as "Mourir pour la patrie," whose lyrics proclaimed that to die for the fatherland was the most beautiful of fates—"le sort le plus beau, le plus digne d'envie." "All of France wants to sing and to die for liberty to the accents of 'La Marseillaise!'," maintained Comédie française star M. de Max in his poem "Mourir en Chantant," which was recited in Paris in late November 1914. A *Grande marche patriotique* launched by singer Lise Canti on 23 December 1914 stated the notion as an imperative: "Die for France." Typically, it also expressed reassurance of victory: "Be patient, for the day is near when we will go to the home of the Alboches."[4]

In the spirit of the *Union sacrée* both Leftist and Rightist singers trumpeted hymns to the French cause. The anarcho-syndicalist, former antimilitarist Gaston Montéhus now championed the soldiers in songs like "Les poilus qui passent!," comparing them to the revolutionary "gars of the Year II." Yet he still expressed sympathy for the suffering of the poor and of striking workers, enough so that the censors suppressed lines and whole verses in such songs as "Les Sacrifiés."[5] Right-wing nationalist Théodore Botrel fared better with the censors and received much more publicity from the general press. When the war broke out, the minister of war charged the well-known singer with the mission of

---

[4] The Bibliothèque de documentation internationale contemporaine at Nanterre University has a good collection of the patriotic songs and poems of the war period. Works like "Meurs pour la France" and "Mourir en chantant" are to be found there (4 Δ1508–1509). Even more sheet music of the Paris music halls is available in the Archives of the Paris Prefecture de police (hereafter cited as APP). The music of the "Chant des Girondins" is by Alphonse Varney, the words by André Chenier.

[5] Copies of censored songs, with the crossed out lines usually still legible, are in the same police archives. Struck out of "Les Sacrifiés" was a verse about strikers going to the foot of a cross and telling how the poor are shot and how the rich and the priests would condemn Jesus if he came back to earth. Having censored those lines, the police cleared the song for performance (granted a visa) on 23 Jan. 1917. APP BA 735. Montéhus' *Chants de la Grande Guerre* (Paris, 1916) is a representative anthology of his war songs.

entertaining front-line troops and spurring them on with his chauvinist talks and songs. In late 1914 in Alsace he composed what became one of his best known new creations, "Rosalie." In this song the soldiers sing to the glory of Rosalie, punctuating each new detail about her with the command "pour the drinks"—*verse à boire*—and a concluding "let's drink then." Rosalie is so pretty that she has millions of admirers [galants]. "Irresistible when she surges, terrible," "fully nude," "she pierces and pricks [pique] and cuts [taille]." So she nails the routed Austrians and Prussians.

> She started out all white, but by the end of the party,
> Pour the drinks!
> She is bright red.
> So let's drink!
> So vermilion and so rosy
> That we have baptized her
> Pour the drinks!
> "Rosalie" in unison.
> So let's drink."

Verse à boire also suggests the spilling of blood: "And, with the impure blood of the Boches / *Verse à boire!* / drench again our fields! / So let's drink!" / We are thirsty for vengeance." Rosalie was the *poilu*'s bayonet.

Botrel's song expressed well not only the freshly aroused sense of martial aggression, but also widespread male ambivalence toward women. Fear of the "fatal female" is well known.[6] In this case the threat of feminine cruelty is directed at the enemy and is controlled by the Frenchmen who sing. Yet, as Peter Gay and others have made clear, that threat made men in general uneasy. That uneasiness is doubtless a part of the reason why Frenchmen did not take this song as a favorite. After the war went on for more than the expected few months, the song's heroics about an offensive were also disturbing to many fighting men, as we shall see. For its part the general public responded favorably to bellicosity in many songs, yet it made no song of such graphic bloodthirstiness into a hit. In contrast to "Rosalie," the still little known "Quand Madelon" offered a view of soldiers and women that avoided these troublesome issues.

In 1915 Botrel went on to create a rival for Rosalie called Mimi. In this recasting of the prewar hit "La petite Tonkinoise" a soldier sere-

---

[6] See Peter Gay, *The Bourgeois Experience: Victoria to Freud* (New York, 1984), 201–7; George Mosse, *Nationalism and Sexuality* (New York, 1985), chap. 6; Bram Dijkstra, *Idols of Perversity: Fantasies of Feminine Evil in Fin-de-siècle Culture* (New York, 1986).

nades his love, his "little Mimi," otherwise known as his machine-gun or *mitrailleuse*.

> My *mitrailleuse*, oh happiness!
> Becomes, for me, Soul-Sister!
> When she sings in her manner: "Ta ta ta ta, ta ta ta ta, ta ta ta tère!"
>
> Ah! how her refrain enchants me.
> It's like a bird that sings!
> I call her my Glorious one, my little Mimi, my little Mimi, my
>   *Mitrailleuse*.
> Rosalie makes sweet eyes to me,
> But it's she [Mimi] I like the best.[7]

The press did its part to encourage that kind of spirit by reporting stories about musicians playing "La Marseillaise" in a trench under fire and soldiers joining in such songs as "Chante petit pioupiou" (Sing, simple soldier) while mounting an assault.[8] "Sing, *pioupiou*/Gaiety, it's life," the men reportedly sang as they fought. The courageous singing during attacks was a telling detail supporting the journalists' basic view of the war in its early years—a war in which the men were experiencing the joy of attacking, were maintaining ever high spirits, were indifferent to danger, and were always exemplifying heroism.[9]

Within months, *poilus* on the front began to criticize that view as despicable propaganda, *bourrage de crâne*. Front-line soldiers who wrote in trench newspapers and improvised revues expressed a less blithesome experience of the war. "[The *poilu*] doesn't call [the bayonet] Rosalie," wrote one trench journalist in April 1915. "The bayonet is called Rosalie only in a song of Théodore Botrel that no one sings and in *Le Bulletin des armées de la République* that no one receives."[10] The *poilus* themselves dwelled on lice and mud and essential rations of wine and food, as they vented resentment of the privileged who managed not to be with them on the front. In a revue entitled "Débochons-nous," [a characteristic double-entendre: let's rid ourselves of the Germans—or let's get debauched] that front soldiers performed on 18 April 1915, one song pours scorn on the despised shirkers

---

[7] Entitled "Glorieuse," "Chanson des mitrailleurs," it appeared in the trench newspaper *Rigolboche*, 20 Nov. 1915.

[8] See, for example, *Paris qui chante*, 1 Dec. 1915, p. 9—for a story about a regiment singing *Chante petit pioupiou* while rising to charge in the battle of the Yser. *Le Miroir*, 17 Oct. 1915, reports on musicians courageously playing on during an attack. Numerous other reports of this kind appeared in the press.

[9] Audoin-Rouzeau, *14-18*, 108, 114.

[10] *Le Poilu*, 30 April 1915, cited in Audoin-Rouzeau, *14-18*, 111.

of military service—the *embusqués*—as well as the politicians who helped them stay out. In the same revue a wounded soldier sings bitterly of those like himself who went to fight: "We the little ones, the humble [*obscurs*], the non-ranking [*sans-grades*]/ We have marched dead tired, covered with mud, wounded, sick,/ without hope of dukedoms and endowments. . . ." These sentiments became central to the mentality of the *poilu* but were usually leavened with some joking—about women, for example. One song of the revue told of the soldiers finding women (*poulettes*) for secret night rendez-vous in the village where the performance was taking place.[11] Humor and irony abounded in the *poilus'* own songs. In particular, lyrics lending sexual meanings to the military vocabulary—rising to the assault, pointing one's bayonet, going into little trenches—were common through the war years.[12]

Meanwhile in Paris the wartime censors purged songs of bawdy phrases along with the criticisms of politicians, *embusqués*, and the cruelties of the war. That left many heavy-handed attempts at lightheartedness. "Le Polka des tranchées" (1915) has the *poilus* making "a true salad of the Boches" in the trenches and charging forward with bayonets, of course winning the battle. In "La Valse des Marmites" *poilus* play the card game of *Manille* in the trenches, unmindful of the falling shells. The "Marche des Totos" tells how "our brave men" on the front amuse themselves and pass the time between attacks by hunting lice and counting them while singing the song's refrain. In addition, old mainstay genres persisted—notably sentimental romantic songs and "realist" or melodramatic narratives. Many prewar favorites continued to figure regularly in wartime programs. Songs of the *comique troupier*, too, continued to have an important following in wartime audiences, both civilian and military. Performed by men in clownishly ill-fitting uniform, these songs comically recounted such common situations of military life as problems with superiors and pursuits of women.

Two prewar songs of this genre, "Avec Bidasse" and "La Caissière du Grand Café," were often heard in Paris music halls in the early years of the war, when "Quand Madelon" was not. In both these songs the soldier appears as a silly simpleton from the country. In the song about the cashier, the soldier admires the pretty young woman as others do in "Quand Madelon," but it is only one individual who describes his at-

[11] Henri Chapron, "Les Chansons composées au front," *Bulletin de l'Ile de France*, July–Sept. 1962, 582–83. The village was Brebis in the commune of Mazingarbe (Pas-de-Calais).
[12] See, for example, the songs in Pierre Chaffange's *L'Humour au front: Chansons de poilus* (Paris, n.d.—clearly after Verdun, probably 1917 or 1918).

traction, and the relationship is not developed. In the early half of the war one romantic relationship that frequently appeared in song was that between an English soldier and a French woman—such as "Tommy et la Petite Française, Tommy and the French Girl" (1915) and "Miss Tipperary." These happy-ending tales, reflecting general satisfaction with the English allies fighting on French soil, entertained Paris music-hall audiences but offered little to the fighting men who commonly worried about the fidelity of their women back home.

For any show in the first two years of the war the surefire applause-getter remained "La Marseillaise." It served commonly as a climax in music-hall programs and was heard regularly in concerts and benefit galas. New topical verses appeared, and new songs were written about the anthem. In "Si les pierres pouvaient parler," for example, the refrain concludes fatuously that "if the stones could speak they would sing 'La Marseillaise'."[13] The strains of "marchons, marchons" filled the air, but the day of glory was agonizingly slow to dawn.

"Quand Madelon" was virtually unknown in Paris during 1914 and 1915. In April 1916 it received a boost when both words and music were published in the *Journal de l'Université des Annales*. Not long before, music-hall star Polin had brought it to the attention of the *Annales* editors, among others, by including it in his comic-soldier repertory in special concerts in the capital, but it still did not become a "hit" with civilians that year. The music-hall programs preserved in the Paris Police Archives do not show any wartime performance of the song before February 1916.[14] It became a regular part of such programs only in the summer and fall of 1917—well *after* it had become popular with the troops.

Since early in the war Bach had been singing it in all sectors on the front as specially delegated "singer to the armies." Bach and Polin had also been performing the song in behind-the-lines camps and hospitals. Like the composer and lyricist of "Quand Madelon," those two

---

[13] "Les Stupidités du café-concert," *La Renaissance*, 5 Aug. 1916, p. 22. Numerous other examples of "stupidities" are given. The first Bastille day of the war, 14 July 1915, saw an apotheosis of the national hymn and its composer. With imposing ceremony the ashes of Rouget de l'Isle were enshrined in the place of highest military honor, the Invalides.

[14] *Journal de l'Université des Annales*, 1 April 1916, p. 263. For the music-hall programs, see APP, B/A 738. The earliest wartime performance in Paris was at the music hall La Fauvette, 58, ave. des Gobelins (13th arrond.) in the week of 18-24 Feb. 1916. The singer was Mlle Gaby de Fradas. The song does not show up on any other program in 1916 at La Fauvette. At the Concert de la Poste, 99 rue St. Domingue (7th arrond.) "Quand Madelon" was performed in the program for 19-21 May 1916. The singer is not identified. It appeared on the program there only one other time in 1916, for performances given 28-30 July. APP, B/A 740. Clearly, performances of the song in Paris were extremely rare before 1917.

singers were well known and popular. Indeed, they were France's leading *comiques troupiers*, and because they chose to perform this song, its chances of becoming a hit no doubt greatly increased.[15]

Did *poilus* sing it on the Front? Did they sing much at all? With machine gun fire and cannon barrages ever threatening, it was dangerous to make any sounds in many trenches. Yet there is ample testimony that soldiers sang on many occasions, even on the front, though most of the singing was done in shelters and rest camps behind the front lines.[16] The men sang folk songs from their home region, old army standards like "Auprès de ma blonde," songs from the repertory of urban music halls, and their own compositions. There is no direct contemporary testimony that soldiers sang "Quand Madelon" from the early months of the war, contrary to later memory, but there is evidence that by the middle of 1916 it had become familiar to the men in the trenches. In June 1916 a soldier sending in his own lyrics to the army's newspaper remarked that the editors would already know the tune because it was the "devilishly catchy" one for "Quand Madelon," so widely known on the front.[17]

Marching, Wine, Women, and Song

By 1916 a resentment of superpatriot blustering had spread widely among the *poilus*. Trench newspapers and even Paris journalists' reports made clear the soldiers' disgust with the exploitation of "La Marseillaise" and other martial hymns. Songwriter and singer Jean Deyrmon's "Une Soirée au beuglant" put the complaint into a song

[15] The French state made Bach a member of the *Légion d'honneur* in July 1933 for entertaining the troops and popularizing "Quand Madelon." In numerous interviews in the 1920s Bach told of having been sent to the front by General Gallieni to sing and of having sung "Quand Madelon" often; see, for example, "L'histoire de la 'Madelon,' racontée par Bach, son créateur," by Henri Jeanson, *Belgique-spectacles*, 18 June 1926. War veteran Jacques Meyer writes that the song was first popular with the troops; see his *La Vie quotidienne des soldats pendant la Grande Guerre* (Paris, 1966), 347. In *La Vie quotidienne des civils en France pendant la Grande Guerre* (Paris, 1966), 318, Gabriel Perreux maintains—without offering any evidence—that Polin popularized the song first with civilians in cafés-concerts and then they "imposed it on the soldiers."

[16] Albert Thierry, "Carnets de guerre," *La Grande Revue* (July 1918): 95, entry for 19 April 1915, describing Maurice Thierry singing songs of the cafés-concerts and another comrade singing in Breton. Chapron, "Les Chansons composées au front," 582–83. In his *Une Heure de musique avec les chansons de guerre* (Paris, 1930), 7–13, former poilu José Germain observed that soldiers did not sing going to battle or in the trenches, but did sing *chansons de route* on leaving the trenches for rest camps and while staying there.

[17] In a letter dated 5 June 1916 a soldier named André Laphin wrote a letter to the editor of the *Bulletin des Armées de la République* offering his own new lyrics. The soldier serving with the 12th Artillery wrote: "You know the devilishly catchy [*entrainant*] tune of [my song] since it's the one for 'Quand Madelon,' so widespread today on the front (I know something about this)." Laphin entitled his song "Le Chant de marche des Armées Pétain." Archives de l'Armée de Terre, Château de Vincennes, 5N 566–567.

that was sung in Parisian music halls in 1916–17; the subtitle called the abuse of the anthem "the sabotage of 'La Marseillaise' in the Caf'-conc's." After Verdun and the Chemin des Dames, after the carnage of 1916 and April 1917, vainglorious lyrics lost their appeal to most fighting men. Rosalie and Mimi were less entertaining than ever before. The growing popularity of "Quand Madelon" signaled a yearning for old pleasures dissociated from the war. After the troop mutinies in the spring of 1917 and the subsequent repression, it also served as a safe alternative to revolutionary songs like the "Internationale" and antiwar songs like "La Chanson de Craonne."[18]

"Quand Madelon" evoked no martial or nationalistic ardor, but rather the ordinary soldierly preoccupations of peacetime service—first of all, marching, for the music is a lively, cheery march. Along with marching went lighthearted singing, associated with military routine and camaraderie—at least in the music-hall version of military life. This particular march also offered an easy, catchy refrain, which even first-time listeners could quickly pick up and sing with others.

It also resembles a drinking song and centers on drinking, an essential social rite of soldiers. Sharing Madelon's wine could suggest a will to forgetfulness—of the hardships of military life and loneliness, but the more manifest meaning is the celebration of a pleasant moment. Many new songs about wine appeared in the war period: "Vin de la Victoire," "Le Vin 1915," "Le Vin du Général Joffre," "Verse, Bistro," "Verse Margot," "Vive le pinard," "Pinard Valse," "Le Pinard" are some typical ones. Virtually all stressed the role of drink in preparing men for battle, in chasing away depression—the famous *cafard*—or in celebrating victory. "Quand Madelon" contained none of those associations. Rather, it refers to wine simply as a part of fraternal ritual in an idyllic rural cabaret where even the thought of war is missing.

And it was about an admired and desired young woman. Madelon, it was often stressed after the war, represented to many *poilus* a young sweetheart back home (as she did to the prewar soldiers, according to the lyrics). Her innocence may seem a strange or unlikely feature of a woman idolized by hard-bitten combat troops often separated from women for months on end. According to some accounts of soldiers' lives on the front, sexual drive diminished greatly or virtually disappeared under conditions of fatigue and remoteness from female com-

---

[18] On the mutinies, see Guy Pedroncini, *Les Mutineries de 1917* (Paris, 1967). He frequently notes the singing of the "Internationale" (43, 87, 114, 122, 131, 177) but does not mention "Quand Madelon." A combat veteran of the war, Irénée Manget, does associate the "Madelon" with the post-mutiny period. See Manget's *En Chantant la Madelon!* (Paris, 1930), 225–26.

pany;[19] yet there is evidence of abundant sexual desire and energy. Popular song shows unmistakable sexual interest in several categories of women: wives and fiancées or sweethearts, "godmothers" (*marraines*)—patriotic women who corresponded with lonely soldiers and received them during leaves, and army canteen-keepers (*cantinières*). In "real life" soldiers' sexual acts most often took place with prostitutes. Brothels near the camps were more than busy with prostitutes "doing" fifty to sixty men a day, sometimes working eighteen hours a day.[20] More rarely did the soldiers have flings with young women—like Madelon—in villages near the front.

In traditional popular culture of the military, the most talked about sexual recourse for soldiers was to pursue *la cantinière*. From the time of Napoleon's armies such women had become legendary as heroic fighters and as generous dispensers of "tenderness" as well as of alcohol and meat. Their lot was also commonly one of alcoholism, poverty, and venereal disease, realities not evoked by popular songs.[21] In music halls of the fin-de-siècle the song "L'Amant de la cantinière" became one of the great hits made popular by the inventor of the genre *comique troupier*, the elder Ouvrard. His talented son renewed its popularity at the beginning of his own career in 1909.[22] In the very same year army authorities forbade *cantinières* from going on campaigns, adding to numerous restrictions placed on their activities in the late nineteenth century. Despite that drastic reduction of their role, ribald songs about them continued to appear and to be sung during the First World War (for example, Bach's "Cantinière-Mazurk," in which the soldier narrator tells of dancing her into bed with him), though most songs that made her sexual role too clear were censored in Paris.[23] The legendary *cantinière* prefigured Madelon in several regards: as dispenser of drink, celebrated for her generosity, and as common object of the soldiers' affections.

But there were important differences. Madelon was a figure of youthful love, a young woman not taken. She was all smiles and laughter, indulgent and open to flirtations, but she drew the line there. As the second verse makes clear, she was a symbol of each *poilu*'s beloved back

---

[19] J.-H. Lahy, "La Notion de temps chez les combattants," *La Grande Revue* (July 1918): 48.
[20] Thébaud, *La Femme au temps de la guerre de 14*, 137.
[21] Bruno Dufaÿ, "Les Cantinières," *Revue historique des armées* 2 (1980): 95–98, 106.
[22] Pascal Servan, *Le Music-hall français de Mayol à Julien Clerc* (Paris, 1978), 24.
[23] Censored, for example, was "Marie . . . j'ai vu"—words by L. Benech and V. Telly, copyright 1910. APP, BA 716. Another example is Bach's "Chez la cantinière," from which a couple of too explicit words were censored, while leaving the general notion that she satisfied the singer's diverse needs.

home. Now about half the combat troops came from the peasantry, and that second verse seems to capture their situation of having a sweetheart back in the *pays*. They were home-centered, and they missed their beloved. They also worried about women's infidelity; stories about *embusqués'* success with women on the home front spread resentment and anxiety.[24] Bousquet's lyrics conjured up for them a woman who served soldiers well and was lovable but had no pretension to substituting for a prior primary attachment. She was almost motherly in her caring and giving to the "boys," warm and playful but nothing more.

She was an idealized figure, but she was not perfect nor socially beyond reach. "It's only Madelon," the soldiers sing. "We dream of her at night/We think of her all day/It's only Madelon, but for us it's love." Young and untaken, she was a woman whom all the men could love. Of course, many of the *poilus* who joined in singing of the imaginary scenes were older married men. For them the song must have evoked not only prewar good times, but also their youth and common youthful romantic experiences. Such experiences often coincided with men's early military service when they typically felt great solidarity with their fellow soldiers who were at the same time classmates.[25] In sum, the situations and feelings presented in "Quand Madelon" could resonate with many men.

Altogether, then, the song's common male perspective on an idealized young woman, the evocation of peacetime marching and drinking, and the easy group singing of at least the refrain were, understandably, appealing to the *poilus*. By 1916, when so many other songs resembled the same old *bourrage de crâne* or were simply stale, "Quand Madelon" expressed the common soldier's autonomy from official culture and from the authorities running the government and the war.[26] As its popularity grew, it became a ritual anthem of soldierly bonding.

In light of the war situation it is also understandable why civilians and authorities responded favorably to the song when they did. In the last two years of the war, when "Madelon" became popular in Paris, the song suited and reinforced the image of the *poilu* maintained by the dominant culture. "Quand Madelon" portrayed the soldier as good-natured, flirtatious, and romantic, but not sexually predatory. It por-

---

[24] Audoin-Rouzeau, *14–18*, 145–50.
[25] For a discussion of the common conscript's experience and mentalities, see Daniel Roche and Fanette Roche, "Le Carnet de chansons d'un conscrit provençal en 1922," *Ethnologie française* 9 (1979): 15–28.
[26] In the postwar years, Bach, among others, made observations that support this analysis. See his comments in the interview "Au pays du caf'conc', 'La Madelon.' " *Eclair*, 26 July 1923, by Marcel Espiau. See also Georges Ricou, "La Musique de camp," *Conferencia* (1 Dec. 1921): 513–25.

trayed a prewar joviality that was in dangerously short supply in the spring of 1917, when tired, embittered troops refusing to fight were singing the "Internationale" as their song. It was in that very spring of crisis in the army that "Quand Madelon" began appearing regularly on programs in Paris after receiving a Police visa on 11 April 1917.[27] Without a hint of discontent in the military it evoked comforting scenes of soldierly solidarity in amusement and love. In 1917 it was widely performed in Paris music halls as a song that was popular with the *poilus*. The number of police authorizations that were issued for it and the frequency with which it was performed rose through the spring and summer of 1917 and peaked in November.[28] At last the French public had a counterpart to "Tipperary," which had been established in Paris music halls within the first six months of the war as *the* emblematic song of the English soldiers.

"Quand Madelon" also depicted a woman congruent with the dominant values of society. She was pure and devoted to the soldiers, playful but innocent, beneficial to the soldiers' morale and hence the war effort. Yet one of the striking features of the song is Madelon's refusal of the marriage proposal by an officer. More common was sentimental romance like that in the often performed song "Quand le soir" (copyright 1915). It tells of a young man who notes a pretty, poor young woman wandering despondently along the banks of the Seine one spring evening. He falls in love with her; they marry; then the man

---

[27] APP, BA 723.

[28] In his *Cahiers de guerre* (p. 483) Louis Barthas makes it clear that the song about Madelon was well known in 1917, when he reports that after the revolts in the army in May and June 1917 the military authorities forbade singing "even 'La Madelon.'" That severity of repression appears to have been limited to the time and areas of revolt. According to the records in the Paris Police Archives (BA 737–740), only two music halls asked for authorization of programs including "Quand Madelon" in April with a total of fourteen performance days involved. The period of the song's greatest popularity in Paris is seen in the following table:

No. of authorizations		No. of performance days	No. of authorizations		No. of performance days
May 1917	5	24	Sept. 1917	22	82
June 1917	5	13	Oct. 1917	16	71
July 1917	9	40	Nov. 1917	24	91
Aug. 1917	17	57	Dec. 1917	11	12

Few authorizations (4) are in the files for 1918, but the records do not appear to be complete.

In the fall of 1917, when the song was at its height of popularity in music halls, it also entered into history as a painting. In a work dated October 1917 Roger de La Fresnay painted a watercolor depicting the famed waitress and some soldiers in a café. The painting is now in the Philadelphia Museum of Art. See Kenneth E. Silver, *Esprit de Corps: The Art of the Parisian Avant-Garde and the First World War, 1914–1925* (Princeton, 1989), 254.

leaves for war and dreams of his *jolie brune* and their nights of love in "their little Paris nest."

Madelon does not find one man to love, but neither is she promiscuous, as women in music-hall military songs often were. Such a woman was "Marie-Margot," for example, who "in a day relieves [*soulage*] a batallion." This song was totally censored.[29] Another song about a camp follower named "Margot" described her more discreetly as "une belle fille qui est complaisante et gentille"; this one was given a visa on 18 December 1917 only after offensive lines were cut out. Even depictions of one-on-one relationships ran into trouble with the censor. In the song "Quand un poilu" (When a *poilu* meets a *belle fille*) the lines detailing the man's expressed designs and moves on her body were censored on 16 March 1916. In Vincent Scotto's "Quand y r'viendra mon homme" the woman sings that she will let her man have his way "even if he asks me the moon." That too was censored. So were references to pregnancy out of wedlock, as in "Sidonie" (1913), references to prostitutes (as in "Sa Majesté l'argent"), or to wives' infidelity—in fact, to anything that censors deemed immoral or morale damaging.[30]

Madelon, then, was an alternative to the *cantinière*/prostitute motif, on the one hand, and the individual sweetheart or wife, on the other. She also contrasted starkly with the hard-pressed women workers who went on strike in 1917, even striking in the munitions factories in wartime. Conservatives found shocking and outrageous not only what they considered a sabotage of national defense, but also what they regarded as the women's unfeminine attitudes and language.[31] In the summer of 1917 antiwar feminists such as Hélène Brion also aroused much fear and anger in the press and in public officials. Schoolteacher Brion was suspended without pay in July and charged with making pacifist propaganda (the same month accused spy Mata Hari was put on trial). In November Brion was arrested, and the following March a Conseil de guerre sentenced her to three years in prison. Although the sentence was suspended, she was fired from her job.[32] By contrast, Madelon was an old-fashioned young woman, who evoked patriotic devotion along with uncomplicated youthful flirtation. The relation-

---

[29] The song was advertised as part of Bach's repertory. The lyrics were by Mellinger and the music by Camille Robert.

[30] PPA B/A 735—for all these censored songs. The lyrics of "Margot" were by Marc-Hély. "Quand un poilu" was a new version of "Quand un soldat," a march made famous in 1911 by Polin.

[31] Mathilde Dubesset, Françoise Thébaud and Catherine Vincent, "Les Munitionnettes de Seine," in *1914–1918: L'Autre Front*, ed. Patrick Fridenson (Paris, 1977), 213. The dominant strike demand was for better pay.

[32] Maïté Albistur and Daniel Armogathe, *L'Histoire du féminisme français du Moyen Age à nos jours* (Paris, 1977), 363.

ship between her and the soldiers highlighted youthfulness, good humor, and solidarity in the army in a critical period of the war. Altogether the song served at once the dominant political culture and traditional male dominance. While conceding male emotional submission, it celebrated woman in a traditional servant role. It also celebrated her as congenial companion and young romantic figure serving a convivial fraternity of soldiers.

What did the song mean to women? Women in music-hall audiences heard it, women often performed it on stage, and some joined in singing it among celebrating crowds when the war ended. Women's journals, memoirs, and war publications by and about women, unfortunately, do not provide specific testimony on "Quand Madelon." It is not clear whether women simply did not choose to write about such a light song in that time of grave worries and war efforts, or whether the particulars of such songs were truly unimportant to them—at least to those who have left records. What is clear is that it was a song overtly aimed at men, framed in a male perspective, and first made popular by men. All in all, one can surmise that among women "Quand Madelon" elicited neither strong disapproval nor noticeable approval. By that era's standards it was innocuous and not particularly remarkable. Historical studies of French women make it clear that in that time the great majority of women shared the attitude of patriotism that was the public's early response to the war. They wanted to do what they could to boost the soldiers' morale, as Madelon was doing. But by 1917 they were also dissatisfied with the seemingly endless war—more so than men generally, historians have found. The majority of women were neither pacifist nor chauvinist, but they were discouraged, tired of anxious waiting, and eager for peace. Performed most often in 1917, "Quand Madelon" was a reminder of better times—a simple song refreshingly free of overblown war heroics and disturbing references to infidelity or prostitution. Madelon was a traditional consoling woman, yet she worked outside the home and kept her independence of any man, as so many working women were doing in the wartime. And she was far from being a passive, suffering, martyred heroine like the many cultural models that women like young Simone de Beauvoir then found themselves offered by religion, history, and mythology.[33]

---

[33] James F. McMillan, *Housewife or Harlot: The Place of Woman in French Society, 1870–1940* (New York, 1981), 103–15. See also Margaret Higonnet et al., eds., *Behind the Lines: Gender and the Two World Wars* (New Haven, 1987) (esp. essays by Margaret and Patrice Higonnet and Steven Hause); and Thébaud, *La Femme au temps de la guerre*, esp. the third part. On authorities' fear of women's desire for peace, see also J. J. Becker, *Les Français dans la Grande Guerre* (Paris, 1980), 223. On the plethora of feminine images used to heighten patriotism, see

Further, it is noteworthy that as performers, women sang the song more often than men, according to the programs in the police archives. They sang the same lyrics as men, words written from a male point of view (some songs included variant lyrics for female performers).[34] While singing of Madelon, the woman on stage seems to have represented the heroine of the song. In any event, when spectators (women as well as men) applauded, they expressed appreciation for the singer, the song, and Madelon (in unknowable proportions). As performers and spectators alike, women were evidently ready to accept the song that so clearly pleased the men and offered tension-relieving moments to themselves as well.

In April 1918, an article in the theatrical journal *La Rampe* reviewed songs of the war (a "facile abundance") and concluded that "up to now the popular song 'Quand Madelon' seems to be the only one which has truly reached the mark."[35] Through the last year and a half of the war Madelon appeared as a stock character in revues and even made a cinematic debut in a short film pantomiming the song.[36] New lyrics were put to the now well-known melody. Some added to the Madelon story, telling of her marriage or her praise for war bonds, for example. Others only mentioned her in passing ("Sérénade à nos poilus," and "Les Marraines des journaux," for example). Meanwhile on the front, too, new versions appeared: "Le Chant de marche des armées Pétain," for example, and "La Chanson du pinard," which a stretcher-bearer named Damien wrote on the "Madelon" melody (reportedly to the delight of the troops).[37] Some versions circulating on the front were ribald

---

Laurent Gerverdau, "La Propagande par l'image en France, 1914–1918," in *L'Image de 1917* (Paris: Le Musée d'histoire contemporaine et la B.D.I.C., 1987), 150–69. Camille Clermont's *Souvenirs de Parisiennes en temps de guerre* (Paris, 1918) reports on the views of women of a range of classes but clearly is patriotically motivated and seems unlikely to include anything not serving that cause. The same ardent wartime patriotism informs similar books of reportage on women written by men sympathetic to the women's suffrage movement and the equality of women generally—notably, Léon Abensour, *Les Vaillantes: Heroïnes, martyres et remplaçantes* (Paris, 1917); and Gaston Rageot, *La Française dans la guerre* (Paris, c. 1918). Memoirs by such notable women as Gyp (Sibylle Martel de Janville), Colette, Louise Weiss, Mistinguett, and Simone de Beauvoir, as well as by little known women like Bonnie Smith's concierge (*Confessions of a Concierge*, New Haven, 1985) and Emilie Carles (*Une Soupe aux herbes sauvages*, trans. as *A Life of her Own*, New Brunswick, N.J., 1991) offer few references to songs, and those few are, unfortunately, cursory and made in passing. On the heroines generally celebrated in French culture, see Simone de Beauvoir, *Mémoires d'une jeune fille rangée* (Paris, 1958), 57. Beauvoir was eighteen years old at the end of the war.

[34] In the programs kept in the Paris Police archives (BA 737–740), I count sixty-eight performances authorized for women's performances, forty-four for men, and eleven not clearly identified.

[35] Jean d'Astorq, "La Guerre et la chanson," *La Rampe*, 18 April 1918, 30.

[36] Georges Lordier invented the new "filmed song" shorts, of which "Quand Madelon" was one of the first. See the column "La Rampe du cinéma," *La Rampe*, 29 Nov. 1917.

[37] "François Signerin, "Le Théâtre au front," *La Rampe*, 22 Nov. 1917, reporting that the troops called for "La Chanson du pinard" "again and again." Another new version appearing in

and mocking, expressions of *poilu* rebellion against homefront pomposity and pap. Improvised new lyrics ridiculed the depiction of such innocent, attractive young barmaids serving the soldiers and maintaining strictly platonic relationships with the men.[38]

One sign that an important part of the public knew the song well by late 1917 and early 1918—and was perhaps even approaching the point of satiety—was the appearance of parodies in music-hall revues. In the revue "Tu viens avec?" at the Cigale on 18 January 1918, the officer sings new lyrics to the tune of "Quand Madelon." In this version, although each soldier has a promised one back in the village, none of the men hesitates to take up with a *jolie fille* met while strolling. "But since one thinks of the other/there's no harm in that!" [Mais comme on pense à l'autre/Y a pas de mal à ça!]. In the last years of the war, with large numbers of military men of several nations filling the music halls, the Paris censors became more tolerant. In March 1918 a Cigale revue entitled "On en parle" featured a *cantinière* called Margoton who bluntly explains to the soldiers that she dispenses "not wine but love." She adds that she hears now the men in each regiment singing (the chorus that follows): "Night and day/in turns/when one dreams of his belle/One comes to her [Margoton]/And one finds love!" At the Ba-Ta-Clan in November 1918 a revue entitled "Dans les nues" (in the skies—or nudes) went further: the *contrôleur des charmes* sings to the tune of "Madelon" a lyrical description of *mamelons*, a word for either little hills or a woman's nipples. He goes on to tell of a soldier saying that he will take the pair in his hands—"a good thing [*filon*] that the Boches won't have." The chorus is a rousing final tribute not to Madelon but to *mamelons*: "Beautiful *mamelons* which serve us drink [qui nous servent à boire]. When the *poilus* will parade as victors/To the balconies, set yourself out for their glory/Mamelons, mamelons, mamelons!"[39]

Madelon and the "Victory"

On the eve of the day of the Armistice, 11 November, songwriter Lucien Boyer worked hard to create a new version of the wartime hit. Setting

---

late 1917 substituted *tobacco* as the main theme. Archives of the Army, Vincennes, 5N566. The lyrics to "Madelon et l'emprunt," praising saving and subscribing to war bonds, were written by Léo Lelièvre; it appeared in November 1917. "Sérénade à nos poilus" and "Le Mariage de Madelon" were both by Bachet-Lemonnier.

[38] For a sample of such lyrics see Guy Breton, *Le Cabaret de l'histoire* (Paris, 1973) 1:128. See also Germain, *Une Heure de musique*, 7–8, and the axiom (p. 5): "La chanson du soldat français sera gauloise ou ne sera pas."

[39] PPA B/A 856—for the Cigale revues and B/A 723 for the Ba-Ta-Clan revue.

his words to music by Borel-Clerc, he produced the "Madelon de la victoire." His Madelon now presides over the celebration of the victory of all the allied peoples. In the humblest *guinguette* people call to her and ask her to fill their glasses and to sing with the *poilus*: "We have won the war." Requesting no water in the wine, they explain, "It's to celebrate the Victory!/Joffre, Foch and Clemenceau!" In the second verse, the heroic General Gouraud walks in and asks for drink—to the waitress's great surprise. The last verse is addressed to children, asking them to remember those who "have saved us." "But while speaking of your fathers/Don't forget Madelon/Who poured on their troubles/The sweetness of a song./Sing Madelon/The muse of the front!" Lyrics in English have the soldiers singing "Hourrah [sic] for the great victory/ For Wilson, Foch and Pershing!"

Boyer's victory version was quickly introduced in leading music halls and became a widely known song over the next nine months as the Versailles peace was being made. It was sung in the streets on the first postwar 14 July festival, which was celebrated as a great victory rite. When the government awarded Lucien Boyer a medal of the Legion of Honor in January 1920, some journalists reported that the authorities had made a mistake and had intended the honor for the author of "Quand Madelon." The Legion of Honor dossier shows that it was no mistake,[40] but the credibility of such confusion and the new song's immediate success indicate that the young woman had become a familiar personage existing independently of any particular song. For several years after the war a number of lyricists and composers capitalized on her vogue, as Boyer had. Even Louis Bousquet and Camille Robert produced sequels.[41] But none achieved the fame that the "victory Madelon" did in 1919. The victory version itself passed from the scene within months of its topical apogee, leaving the original "Madelon" as the song of an enduring familiarity.

About twelve thousand songs came out of the war years,[42] but it

---

[40] AN, Legion of Honor dossier 67999D; Boyer is *matriculé* no. 93,706.

[41] For example, Bousquet and Robert's "Madelon, j'attends la classe" (copyright 1923) failed to catch on. The lyrics are about a young soldier writing to his beloved Madelon, urging her to wait for him and describing the joys of their life together after his service—in a postwar army. Among other postwar lyrics for the Madelon melody are A. Margal's "La Madelon Mancelle" (undated) and "Grève des Tramways de Lille, musique de marche"—February 1920. The tune of "Madelon de la Victoire" was also used for new songs on the same theme: for example, Bachet-Lemonnier's "La Madelon des ouvriers" and Henry Moreau's "La Madelon de la Paix," both of 1919. Still others, such as the song "Clémence" (1918 copyright; words by Georges Arnould, music by A. Chantrier) continued the story with a new melody and—in this case—a new female protagonist, successor to Madelon. The motif of a woman cheering the men, serving them wine, and grateful praise runs through all these songs.

[42] Louis-Jean Calvet, *Chanson et société* (Paris, 1981), 119.

was "Quand Madelon" that remained in public memory as the essential song of the 1914–18 experience. Just after the war singer and songwriter Xavier Privas made the point with telling hyperbole: "What remains of the terrible war which just convulsed the world? A song— *'La Madelon'*!"[43] After so much death and destruction the song lived on; associated in memory with the men who fought and died, it was a way of remembering them without being overwhelmed by grief. When the president of the Republic held a *fête* in the Palais de l'Elysée for blind war veterans in 1920, Polin concluded his concert with "Quand Madelon," and everyone present, including President Deschanel, joined in what the reporter called "the immortal refrain of our Poilus." A few years later it was reported that the only thing known about the unknown soldier was that he had sung "La Madelon."[44] The remark passed as a truism.

The song most often identified with the Great War in France contained no reference to the war, but postwar memory created tight links. After the armistice, legends about "Quand Madelon" being sung in battle cropped up in memoirs and histories. As Marc Bloch noted about his comrades in arms, the widespread distrust of everything printed and official opened wide the springs of oral tradition, the mother of legend.[45] The battle stories about "Quand Madelon" were new versions of old traditions about other songs in other wars: ancestral Gauls had purportedly sung while fighting to victory. The revolutionary war hymn "Le Chant du départ" lodged in popular memory the very phrase "la victoire en chantant" (victory while singing or even *by* singing). So, according to a song of 1918, the "heroes of Verdun"—with "valiant heart and sword on fire"—sang the national anthem in battle in 1916.[46] An early October 1918 issue of the cartoon weekly *La Baïonnette* featured the phrase "victoire en chantant" as its theme, with a lead article by Léo Claretie reaffirming: "music prepares for victory by singing." The back cover showed soldiers marching through a liberated town while singing of none other than "La Madelon," named in a cartoon-strip bubble over their heads (see illustration). The caption reads: "And this evening there on the front they will sing too."[47] The

---

[43] Preface to Maurice Hamel, *Nos Artistes de café-concert et de music-hall et de cabaret* (Paris, n.d. [circa 1919]).

[44] See Marcel Espiau, "Au pays du caf'conc', 'La Madelon'," *Eclair*, 26 July 1923.

[45] Marc Bloch, *The Historian's Craft*, trans. Peter Putnam (New York, 1964), 107–9. Paul Fussell notes this skepticism and develops the point with regard to English soldiers; see his book *The Great War and Modern Memory* (New York, 1975), 115.

[46] The song is entitled "La Marseillaise de Verdun"; PPA Police Visa 18 Jan. 1918. Jules Romains's novel *Verdun* (1938) also has the soldiers singing "La Marseillaise" in the great battle.

[47] *La Baïonnette*, 3 Oct. 1918, 627. "La Victoire en chantant" is also the title of Claretie's arti-

In the fall of 1918 war-weary *poilus* are shown singing the now famous "La Madelon" as they march through a liberated, battle-damaged village. *La Baïonette,* 3 October 1918. Drawing by Gus Bofa. Courtesy of Widener Library. All rights reserved.

image of singing to victory was a French equivalent of the British legend of fearless soldiers launching offensives by kicking the soccer ball across no-man's land.[48]

---

cle. The back cover caption is: "Et ce soir là, au front, ils chanteront aussi." The drawing is by Gus Bofa.

[48] On the British stories and actual incidents, see Colin Veitch, " 'Play up! Play up! And Win the War!' Football, the Nation and the First World War," *Journal of Contemporary History* 20 (July 1985): 363–78.

Less than a year after the armistice, when the magazine *Paris qui chante* interviewed notable writers and songwriters about the role of popular music in the war, the director of the "Foyer du soldat," poet Alphonse Huau, declared unreservedly that "the favorite pastime of our dear *poilus* was song." Songwriter Maurice Boukay, like the other respondents, affirmed that "song had a positive influence on the morale of the *poilu*" and went on to cite "La Madelon" in particular, describing it as having "joyously and gloriously" "gone the round of the trenches and of the world." Writer Georges Montorgueil, too, singled out only "Quand Madelon," praising its sprightly rhythm and its successful evocation of the image of the men's loved ones—without any *bourrage de crâne*. Songsmith Georges Millandy went further and asserted what he took to be a consensus: "People have said it: 'La Madelon,' the true one, has done more for victory than all the fine speeches and all the fine official verses."[49] Although no one could cite polls as evidence, Millandy and others felt quite certain not only that "Quand Madelon" was the most popular song of the war, but also that it had contributed to the French success. As people professionally associated with songs, these people were of course quite ready to give the greatest possible credit to the wartime role of songs—indeed, to overestimate it. What is noteworthy is that they considered "Quand Madelon" the obvious case in point and that they considered their assessment of its impact credible.

One postwar story attributed to General Gouraud gives a specific case in which singing that song made the difference. The incident purportedly took place in the early fall of 1918 when the French Fourth Army under Gouraud was pushing back the Germans from the heights of the Champagne. In an area near Moronvilliers one day a strong German surprise attack broke through the center of the French line and created a "pocket." The French had to retake the terrain. With so many trenches in the area they found it difficult to know where the enemy was dug in and hiding. The problem was solved when the troops on the left began singing "Quand Madelon" and those on the right responded. It became clear where the enemy was, and the pocket was soon eliminated. The first-hand, day-by-day *Journal des marches et opérations* in the Army Archives has nothing in it to confirm this account, nor do any of the authoritative histories of the war.[50]

---

[49] *Paris qui chante*, 15 July 1919, 1–2; 1 Aug. 1919, 2; 15 Aug., 1919, 2.

[50] Nor does this story appear in the popular war chronicle found in *L'Illustration* in 1918. Like other battle stories about "La Madelon," it has been reprinted many times without a source given. For example, it appeared in a booklet accompanying records entitled *La Grande Guerre* written by Frédéric Robert (p. 46; no date given—probably in the 1960s), and André Gauthier repeats it in his *Les Chansons de notre histoire* (Paris, 1967), 189.

MADELON AND THE MEN

The most deliberate, most open spinning of legend was popular writer Joseph Deltheil's *Les Poilus, épopée*, published in 1926.[51] In this illustrated, nationalistic "epic" of the *poilus*, the chapter on Verdun is a storyteller's embroidery on the Madelon tale now set during the heated battle of 1916 in a village just behind the Verdun front. There "one day in April, between two assaults, the *Poilu* and Madelon make love," Deltheil declares provocatively early in the chapter. The full account has it that the *poilus* fill the cabaret of the "Toulourous" and lovingly sing "La Madelon" to the young waitress, and in turn she loves not just one man but a whole regiment. The *poilus* also sing the song in battle. On 9 April they fight at Verdun while singing it and by the evening drive back the enemy. Pétain proclaims confidently: "On les aura!"—the famous cry of 1915 that was also the title of a popular song. On 7 June, the story continues with deceptive precision, a remarkable incident occurred in the battle at the fort of Vaux. Deltheil recounts that there a lieutenant, wounded while bounding to attack, sings "La Madelon" to encourage the troops. At the refrain, he dies, but the *poilus* counterattack with jagged bayonets while singing "La Madelon." Discreetly Deltheil does not claim that the singing attackers enjoyed victory but nonetheless leaves them and the song with an aura of glory.

The legend showed up in the movies a few years later. In 1931 Léon Poirier's early sound movie *Verdun* did not place the song in the battle itself but did include what *Ciné-miroir* magazine called "the scene of La Madelon": the embattled soldiers of Verdun enjoy a bit of rest seated at a table outside a café where a young woman serves food and wine. And decades later the *Grand Larousse encyclopédique* stated flatly in edition after edition that the soldiers sang "La Madelon" while retaking the fort of Vaux in 1916.[52]

Madelon and the Veterans of War

Would-be legend-makers were less successful in adding to the life story of Madelon after the war. As we have noted earlier, songwriters made

[51] Joseph Deltheil, *Les Poilus, épopée* (Paris, 1926), chap. 7, "Verdun," 101–20.
[52] *Ciné-Miroir*, 6 Nov. 1931. *Grand Larousse encyclopédique*, tome 6 (Paris, 1962—first edition and still in the 1975 edition), no pagination. Jules Poirier's memoir *La Bataille de Verdun, 21 février–18 décembre 1916* (Paris, 1922) tells of two occasions when French units sang "La Marseillaise" as they attacked—one 6 May 1916 against le Mort-Homme and the other 8 May on *la côte* 287 to the south of Haucourt. On 24 Sept. 1916, Poirier also reports, during a battle in the Thiaumont-Fleury sector a unit of Alpine troops sang "la Sidi-Brahim" and forced the Germans to pull back. See pp. 187–88, 244. He does not mention "Quand Madelon." Another postwar memoir tells of *poilus* singing "La Cocarde de Mimi Pinson" after having taken a German position in the battle of Verdun; see the "notes du capitaine Guy Schlesser" in *Histoire de la guerre par les combattants*, (Paris, n.d. [1921]), 3:388.

An illustrated postcard from the war era highlighting an officer's marriage proposal and Madelon's (negative) response. This part of the story was of particular interest to the civilian population toward the end of the war and in the immediate postwar period (the date 1919 is handwritten on the back of the card). Courtesy of Le Musée d'histoire contemporaine—BDIC. Illustrator anonymous. All rights reserved.

numerous attempts to give her a husband (preferably a *poilu*) and children—in what seemed to them a natural continuation of the story. But none caught on; that kind of ending eliminated the distinctive and essential characteristic of the barmaid: her egalitarian warm relationship with a large number of men at once. Yet the forces pushing for the traditional maternal, home-centered role of women were patently powerful in postwar France. They continued to deny the vote to women (until 1945), and in 1920 they gave the nation a strict law banning abortion and the dissemination of birth control information. Women workers lost most of the ground they had gained in the war when industrial jobs were reclaimed by the returning men. Even so, conservatives still had much to worry about: the "new woman" rejecting the ideology of domesticity was much in the news. In 1922 the scandal-producing, best-selling novel *La Garçonne* made most vivid that widely feared new social type: the short-haired, sexually liberated "bachelor girl."[53]

In the mid-1920s, with the relations of the sexes thus problematic in new ways, playwright Jean Sarment probed the darker side of the Madelon story, showing the long-term course of a woman's habitual relationships described only briefly in the song. Sarment's 1925 play *Madelon*[54] carries into the postwar period the loving and mothering sides of Madelon as friend of soldiers and lover of young men.

Living in the United States some years after the war, Sarment's Madelon/Madeleine has a favorite, and he is not even a soldier; he is a young musician named Marc-Adolphe, who has just arrived in New York. There the young man met not only Madeleine but also a group of her friends, older Frenchmen. The men are veterans of the war, and so in a sense is Madeleine. She admits readily to having been "ten times a good comrade and ten times a mistress." She has been a "lover, dreamy and naturally disappointed," an excellent but unfortunate wife, and a divorced woman. Still she cannot stand to see men suffer and believes it necessary to always console them, "these children." Now Marc-Adolphe is the lonely young man-child who wants Madeleine as a mistress. He tells her so and even admits that he does not believe he could love her. For her part Madeleine is willing. She has no illusions about him but gives herself to him as she did before to the soldiers. Faithful to her legendary role, she serves all the men drink and sings the famous

---

[53] For the text of the 1920 law, see Susan Groag Bell and Karen M. Offen, eds., *Women, the Family, and Freedom, 1880–1950* (Stanford, 1983), 2:309–10. See McMillan, *Housewife or Harlot* on the war's aftermath and "the new woman," chapter 8—and Dubesset et al., "Les Munitionnettes de la Seine," 218–19. See also Anne-Marie Sohn, "La Garçonne face à l'opinion publique," *Le Mouvement social*, no. 80 (July–Sept., 1972): 3–27.

[54] *La Petite Illustration*, May 1925.

song with them but now has only Marc-Adolphe as lover. Her veteran friends resent the success of the intruder who is too young to have fought in the war. Undeterred, Madeleine comforts and encourages the musician to the point where his career begins to be successful, and then she sadly leaves. Her mission in life is to give pleasure to her men, who are always needy of comfort and love, driven by desire, and sooner or later unfaithful. Her generosity contrasts with their egoism. A woman of striking 1920s modernity, she chooses to love young men even while knowing the outcome. No one is deceived. Yet through her successive loves she maintains respectability, strength, and a poignant dignity.

This was Sarment's first play for the general public of the boulevard theaters; his earlier works were written for the Comédie française. Clearly he did not offer that broader audience an easy, ingratiating sequel to the light story of the song. The mixed reviews indicate that both main figures came across as having serious character flaws. The play brought out the sorrows and hurt involved in both the older model of feminine virtue and the "modern" course of individual freedom. It was a disturbing work, satisfying to neither the partisans of the old nor those of the new.

To many who felt a revulsion against the slaughter of the war it was not the woman's story that was most disturbing but the original song now enmeshed in embellished memory of that war. To them the song was a painful reminder and part of the glorified view of war as a great adventure. In a book entitled *Le Cabaret de la belle femme* (1919), published in the spring after the armistice, veteran and famed antiwar writer Roland Dorgelès ridiculed the credulous veterans and conscripts singing "Madelon" and believing stories about the "beautiful women on the front" and the love affairs that developed. To Dorgelès these were pathetic fictions that would someday end up as part of a bigger story about how beautiful the war was. "The truth, the sad truth," he wrote, "is that there was no love, there were no women on the front, any more than there was butter in the cantine wagon or carpets in the shacks [*gourbis*]." Then, correcting himself, he added that soldiers did on rare occasion glimpse a woman, but she was neither available nor beautiful. The usual large country girl with missing teeth, he added, was not at all thrilled to find herself pursued by hundreds of men in ill-fitting, muddy uniforms who as civilians would never even have looked at her.[55]

Antiwar sentiment in the 1920s and 1930s produced not only at-

---

[55] Roland Dorgelès, *Le Cabaret de la belle femme* (Paris, 1928), 21, 26–27.

tempts to deromanticize the song, but also hostile reactions to everything about it. "The pathetic *Madelon* is too entangled with atrocious memories for us to hold onto the memory of her," wrote an interviewer of Bach in 1926.[56] In 1929 veteran and writer Pierre MacOrlan asserted that the song was never sung much in the army, although marching bands adopted it for its lively beat. "It smelled like an official song, and the soldiers were rather distrustful," he maintained.[57] Twice-injured war veteran Jean Renoir shared those views and so chose not to include "Quand Madelon" in his film *La Grande Illusion*. In an interview at the time the film appeared in June 1937, Renoir acknowledged that "most of my fellow veterans have completely adopted 'La Madelon' "— understandably, he added, because "it is a charming song." But he went on to disparage it as "the perfect type of the song of the rear, composed in a spirit of the rear and sent to the combatants in the same way that people sent them inedible *pâté de foie gras*."[58]

In the 'thirties "Quand Madelon" reemerged in the public limelight only episodically, but it continued to be widely known. Parents and grandparents kept it alive through singing at home, passing it on to youth. In a poll of about a hundred people toward the end of the decade it came out second best known (first was "Le Temps des cerises").[59] And it continued to evoke strong emotions and memories. Above all, it was the song's associations with the Great War that produced reactions in this period—divergent reactions of hope and bitterness.

A play of 1938 makes clear how troubling the song was in that time of widespread antipathy to war. Grégoire Leclos' play *Quand Madelon*, first presented at the Théâtre Athéna on 5 June, carried the story down to the present some twenty years after the war and put the focus back on the *poilus*. The drama centers on a moral conflict between a grandfather, who was a veteran of the 1870 war, and his son, Jules Arnaud, who fought in the "Great War." The first two acts show how the war affects the family in 1917. The wife of Jules is assuming great responsibility in her husband's absence and successfully runs the family busi-

[56] Henri Jeanson, "L'Histoire de la 'Madelon' racontée par Bach," *Belgique-Spectacles*, 18 June 1926.
[57] Pierre MacOrlan, "Essai sentimental sur la chanson populaire," preface to Champigny, *Le Grand Vent* (Paris, 1929), 15–16.
[58] Jean Renoir, "En tournant *La Grande Illusion* j'ai essayé de me reporter vingt-cinq ans en arrière," *Paris-soir*, 4 June 1937. Instead of "Quand Madelon" Renoir used such songs as "Frou-Frou," "Le Petit Navire," and "La Marseillaise," See Alexander Sesonske, *Jean Renoir: The French Films, 1924–1939* (Cambridge, Mass., 1980), 291, 306, 318.
[59] Writing on popular songs in 1933 Pierre Dufaÿ testified to the persistent emotional impact of "La Madelon"; see his article "De l'Alcazar au cinéma," *Mercure de France* 246 (1 Sept. 1933): 327. On the opinion poll, see André Coeuroy, *La Musique et le peuple en France* (Paris, 1941), 75.

ness. Jules, home on leave, cannot stand the nationalist heroics of his old father. When Jules wants to hear a tune from before the war, he suggests "Sous les ponts de Paris" and "Caroline, Caroline." His father suggests "something gay, something French — 'La Madelon'." Bitterly Jules responds, "Oh! good, then, we'll go back to that!" The family is then interrupted by a soldier wanting to see the grandfather. He brings the terrible news that Jules's son Jean has been killed in the Champagne. The truth about his death is that Jean refused to rise to attack, threw away his rifle, and offered his life in protest against *"la guerre, this useless horror."* Jules finally explodes in angry response to his father: "You present . . . [death] to us as a seductive slut [*catin*], you call her 'La Madelon.' " With impassioned eloquence he denounces war with "all its tortures, moral and physical." Grandfather's concern is to keep the truth about Jean's death secret forever. Jules returns early to the front, knowing that his comrades will understand. The rest of the play takes place in the mid-thirties. Jules is an embittered, lame veteran. He receives a visit from a family friend, Dussaux-Malet, a man who is a politician and a president of a veterans' association, though he never saw action. This man's current project is to prepare for the dedication of a new monument to the war dead. Jules quickly tires of the crass jingoist and tells him to get out; Dussaux calls him a dirty pacifist. Then Jules angrily learns that his twenty-year old son Claude is embarking on a military career. Jules had not told his son about the war, but the grandfather had filled in and imparted his super-nationalist attitudes. The play closes with a brass band playing "La Madelon." "Like someone hallucinating," Jules exclaims: "She is back!" In anguish he goes to a portrait of Jean and stares at it while crying out "Help, my little boy . . . help, help."[60]

As the twentieth anniversary of the armistice approached, moviemakers chose to continue the Madelon story with a contemporary happy ending, which no doubt seemed most likely to draw and please large audiences in the continuing depression and darkening international situation. The 1937 film *La Fille de Madelon* plays on the now blended memories and legends of *poilus* with their beloved waitress— without any reminder of battle horrors. The scenario is a love story about a young woman who is the daughter of a Madelon, running an inn now named "Aux anciens combattants." The daughter loves a young officer of high social status. There is a complication: she has a rival for his affections, the daughter of a rich Jewish merchant named

---

[60] Grégoire Leclos, *Quand Madelon, Comédie dramatique en quatre actes* (Paris, 1939).

Abraham Goldberg. In the end the young man's father, a Pétain-like general named Cassagne, finally intervenes to assure that his son married the daughter of the waitress of '14–'18, explicitly disapproving any alliance of the Goldbergs with the Cassagne. The film ends with a happy crowd in front of the inn, a scene which then fades into shots of parades, the Arc de Triomphe, the "Marseillaise" of Rude, and a flag.[61] Spectators were thus offered the satisfaction of seeing love and nationalist sentiments triumph over certain social barriers—pleasing at least those of a rightist and antisemitic cast. This was but one of a number of films of the period offering tales of social reconciliation and national unity—a message especially appealing after the bitter divisions of the Popular Front period.[62]

Madelon in War Again

With the coming of a new war there was great reason for nostalgia about the last one, or rather about certain cheery mythical associations. Entertainers were not slow to offer young soldiers opportunities to identify with the *poilus*. After the declaration of war on 1 September 1939 and the quick fall of Poland, the French troops on the Western front soon found themselves idle, but this time within the early weeks of the conflict the military began presenting entertainment. One of the first shows of the *Théâtre aux armées*, presented in a little village of the North, featured Madelon of 1914–18 as its heroine. Played by a soldier with a shrill voice, she admits that she is a bit old but hopes that the soldier will say to himself: "She pleased my papa, so she will please me." The audience responded enthusiastically with loud cries and clapping.[63]

In late 1939 a new version of the myth appeared in film but without explicit reference to Madelon and the first World War. The film entitled "Let's Sing Anyhow"—*Chantons quand même*—was another bit of upbeat entertainment for a tense population well into an eerily quiet war that was indeed strange. Like *La Fille de Madelon*, this movie focussed on a single relationship—between a soldier of 1939 and a young woman he had come to love the summer before the war. While the company enjoys good wine and songs and thinks back fondly on peace

---

[61] Jean-Pierre Jeancolas, *15 ans d'années trente, le cinéma des Français, 1929–1944* (Paris, 1983), 245–46. The film, the work of G. Pattu and Jean Mugeli, came out the fall of 1937.
[62] Joseph Daniel, *Guerre et cinéma: Grandes Illusions et petits soldats, 1895–1971* (Paris, 1972), 157–58.
[63] Hervé Le Boterf, *Le Théâtre en uniforme* (Paris, 1973), 54–55. See *Mach*, 14 Oct. 1939.

time, Sergeant Jacques makes plans for the future with his beloved.[64] The let's-whistle-in-the-dark title expressed well the posture that was to be a guiding rule for many—most conspicuously those in the entertainment industry—through the tragic next five years.

In the same period of the *drôle de guerre* the song "Victoire, la fille à Madelon" played more squarely on hope and wishful thinking about parallels with 1914–18. The time evoked is exactly twenty years after Armistice Day. In the victory parade a lieutenant, the corporal of the earlier version, asks Madelon for her hand. This time she marries him and has a daughter called *Victoire*: "Victory, it's Madelon's daughter." In the last verse Victory has just had her twentieth birthday and, beloved by the whole army (like her mother), is somewhere on the front. "To all our victorious soldiers Victory has promised her heart." The refrain states that all the men are in love with her and "have only one hope: that's to carry off *la Victoire*/Victoire . . . Victoire/She's the daughter of Madelon."[65]

The *original* song of Madelon also served in the phony war to conjure up victory—at least that of the last war. In early May 1940 on what turned out to be the eve of the German invasion of Belgium, star Marie Dubas chose to sing once more the old hit of the Great War as part of a benefit performance. It provided her listeners a last opportunity under the Third Republic to lose themselves in the peaceful scenes of Madelon with her admiring soldiers and in comforting memories of the heroic *poilus*.[66]

The German masters of the occupied North and the Vichy regime in the rest of France had no interest in encouraging memories associated with the Madelon myth. Entertainers gave the entertainment-hungry public a stream of sunny songs devoid of historical references.[67] But in 1944 the Liberation and victory of the Allies brought new occasion to gloss over differences and highlight parallels with the First World War. A song entitled "La Madelon de 44" and its English version "Our Madelon of 44"—printed in April 1945—evokes the past and makes the song timeless: "When a Frenchman goes off to make war, the Madelon is always there. To give the soldier ardor and mettle [*du cran*] La Madelon of 44, joyous reminder of the old days, pours her wine and

---

[64] Raymond Chirat, *Catalogue des films français de long métrage: Films sonores de fictions (1929–39)* (Brussels, 1975).
[65] "Victoire . . . la fille à Madelon," Words by Marcel Travers et Cyrleroy, music by Frédo Gardoni and Francis Salabert, in Roland Erbstein, *Les Chemins de la Victoire* (Nancy, 1986), no pagination.
[66] Le Boterf, *Le Théâtre*, 29.
[67] See André Halimi, *Chantons sous l'Occupation* (Paris, 1976), esp. 145–46.

her love to our soldiers." In the English version the soldiers address the young woman as the daughter of the heroine of the earlier war. "Oh Madelon just like your mother Love us the way she did before. You know the world is calling for you/ Deep in your heart here's worm [sic] for more/ You know that all of us adore you Our Madelon of 44." Where the French soldiers sing of her love and wine, the English words speak of her smile, her laughter, and her wine.[68]

Another song occasioned by new peace, "La Madelon de la Délivrance," is addressed to "Madelon, fille de France." A loftier figure than her namesake, she is less a real woman than a symbol of France on the glorious day of deliverance. There is no mention of her beauty or of serving wine. But the lyrics do refer to her being with the soldiers "in the last one": "With you we were victors/ And the words that our fathers sang have remained engraved in our hearts." The refrain moves away from any reference to the *poilu*'s favorite, warmly evokes a good future, and expresses satisfaction with having France back under French control: "Madelon, the sky of France today will take on the three colors: blue of love, white of hope, the evening red of heart. Now we can live at home [*chez nous*] in our country."[69]

In the same period the song of 1914 was not forgotten. Sung in the context of the Liberation, it too could help tie the new victory to the more fully French effort of the Great War. In a songbook published for interallied troops in November 1944, "Quand Madelon" was the first entry—with lyrics in English and French.[70]

By the 1950s, as France recovered from the Second World War and as the First War became a kind of remote prehistory to a fast-growing new youthful population, the occasions for references to a pre-1914 waitress grew rare, but there was one that is certainly noteworthy. In 1955 on the day of remembrance, 11 November, a new film entitled *La Madelon* made its debut. The director was Jean Boyer, the son of the author of the 1918 song "La Madelon de la Victoire." The scenario was a basic love story. The young beautiful Madelon was a good comrade to all the soldiers she served, but she was in love with only one, Corporal Beauguitte. His rival was a rich, politically powerful *embusqué*; yet, after a few complications true love triumphs in the end.

Why exhume this story in 1955? asked a reviewer in *Libération*.

---

[68] French words by Bob Chalard et René Mars, English words by L. Robert and H. Fetterly. Copyright 1945. Paris: Editions Raymond Jouve.
[69] Words by Lucien Lagarde, music by Maurice Denous. Editions musicales, n. d.
[70] Ministère de la Guerre, Direction de la Presse, Service du Théâtre aux armées et de liaison artistique auprès les troupes interalliées (Paris, 1944).

With memories of the First World War so faded or nonexistent for most and with the horrors of the Second War fresh in memory and the Algerian war simmering away, this romantic story set in the shadow of the distant war was—now more clearly than before—an evasion. The film won the "grand prix du cinéma pour le prestige de France," but critical opinion in the press was divided. Some saw it as only light entertainment, an upbeat musical comedy, a sure commercial success. Others made harsher judgments. In *Le Figaro* Louis Chauvet summed it up as "nicely needless" and "nicely weak." The reviewer for *Libération* saw it as a sad trivialization of the war experience.[71]

France soir critic Andrew Lang, who considered the film "a great success," made the telling observation that it had a quality of "image d'Epinal" about it.[72] So did the song and its essential narrative—from the very beginning. That is to say, the story had a simplicity and directness about it that helped make it a powerfully appealing myth of an era. It was about a woman who corresponded to a number of feminine types well established in French life. It was about relationships familiar to many: between lonely men in uniform and a desired young woman who is giving, but not yet taken by an individual. The song tapped springs of nostalgia and hope. It played on reveries about unfulfilled and untroubled relationships, but left open possibilities for development of complications, usually followed by a happy denouement.

In 1960 singer Charles Trenet composed a kind of requiem for the beloved young woman of the Great War and included a mournful comment on the movie by Jean Boyer. Madelon and the *poilus* had great personal meaning for Trenet, whose father was away fighting during the entire war—from 1914, when Charles was only one, to the armistice, when he was five. His song "Qu'est devenue la Madelon" asks if she still has her amazed blue eyes and her figure, if she still affably gestures with her hand to admonish men admiring her bust, and in what village or region she lives. He wonders if he has sometimes passed her in the street and if she has a little girl who resembles her. "Seeing at the cinema yesterday evening a story of this ancient time," he muses, "I said to myself that in our atomic age it is sad that that epoch has become comic." After the movie, the song of 1960 continues, the narrator Trenet "went out into the street rediscovering vanished images of his childhood, of the youth of his father, of his mother, and also of the war." The

---

[71] *Le Parisien*, 15 July 1955, reported the prize. *Le Figaro*, 7 July 1955. *Libération*, 12 Dec. 1955. Favorable reviews also appeared in *Express* (13 Dec. 1955), *Franc-Tireur* (22 Dec. 1955), and *France soir* (7 Dec. 1955).

[72] Lang, *France Soir*, 17 Dec. 1955.

song concludes with "visions of these images that were those of a beautiful age and of its farces—fire on a thatched roof and the Kaiser Wilhelm."

Madelon had become a memento and a dreamlike specter of a distant past. In 1960 the song about her had little appeal for the millions of young people of the baby boom begun in the Second World War, and it dated Trenet himself, who had emerged as a youthful star in the 1930s and who was now in his late forties. French popular culture was entering a decidedly new era. To French youth that was just discovering rock 'n roll, Charles Trenet was a "fossil" and an "ancestor" whose nostalgia for images of the First World War only confirmed how "out of it" he was.[73]

In contemporary France, Madelon is indeed a historic relic, virtually unknown to the younger part of the population, but for older people she is a sure activator of memories of aged or dead fathers and grandfathers. For the French army the music-hall march has attained the honorable and venerable status of a "chant de tradition," categorized thus alongside military songs of the French Revolution in an official army songbook published in 1986.[74]

In the generally fast-changing popular culture of the twentieth-century, Madelon has had a remarkably long, rich life. Born in prewar popular culture, the myth of Madelon and her adoring soldiers enjoyed a period of youthful vigor as a part of wartime and postwar folklore. Her song was charged with nationalist and military associations, yet the young woman was less overtly political and more humanly lovable than the august and maternal Marianne. After the armistice the song now known as the *poilus'* favorite became a trigger of strong emotions about the Great War—the innocence and the good nature of the beloved men who fought and died, the unexpected horror of the drawn-out slaughter, and the outcome celebrated and remembered by optimists as victory. At the end of the Second World War it was used to link the French liberation to the *poilus'* accomplishments, skirting the shame of collaboration.

Through carefully wrought plays and mass-audience movies, the myth gained syncretistic strength and more depth than it had in the songs. When the young woman was put in up-to-date situations with contemporary men, postwar imaginations explored power relations between the sexes and the question of greater liberty for women as opposed to a traditional maternal role. The most common and most pop-

---

[73] Richard Cannavo, *Le Siècle en liberté* (Paris, 1989), 410, 412.
[74] *Carnet de chants* (Pussay: Librairie de L'Armée, 1986), 29.

ular treatment, however, continued to be that of a romantic love story. Over more than four decades, the essential fable with its highly sentimentalized sex roles played a conservative part in the politics of gender, in which gains for French women were so notoriously slight.[75] Under her protean forms Madelon remained a largely old-fashioned, nonpolitical figure, a woman *hors du combat,* as real-life women were no longer.

[75] On the failure of French women to gain the vote until decades after most Western countries had enfranchised women—and on the relative weakness of the French women's rights movement in general, see Steven G. Hause with Anne R. Kenney, *Women's Suffrage and Social Politics in the French Third Republic* (Princeton, 1984), chaps. 8–9. See also Higonnet, *Behind the Lines,* essays 1–2, 7. An article not yet available to me promises to offer a revisionist argument: Karen Offen, "Body Politics: Women, Work, and the Politics of Motherhood in France, 1920–1950," in Gisela Bock and Pat Thane, eds., *Maternity and Gender Politics: Women and the Rise of the European Welfare States, 1880s–1950s* (London, 1991). On French song several very recent books are noteworthy: Serge Dillaz's *La Chanson sous la IIIe République* (Paris, 1991) and Nicole and Alain Lacombe's *Les Chants de bataille: 1900–1920* (Paris, 1992). Helpful also is Jean-Claude Klein's *Florilège de la chanson française* (Paris, 1990).

[19]

The Battle of the Somme and British Strategy

HEW STRACHAN

Recent interpretation of the First World War have argued that from 1916 Germany adopted 'machine warfare', by contrast Britain favoured a manpower-dominated form of war. This article suggests that the British, because of their commitment to colonial operations with small armies, and to naval and economic warfare in European conflict, were already developing machine warfare before 1914. At the beginning of 1916 British strategy was still developing along traditional lines – naval and economic pressures, supplemented by a limited (even if growing) liability on land. Planning for the Somme was predicated on a version of machine warfare. Indeed it was Britain's use of its which fuelled Germany's. But British approaches to war were radically revised in 1916, because the adoption of conscription involved the incorporation of manpower-dominated warfare for the first time.

On 6 September 1916 General Erich Ludendorff visited the Western Front for the first time in two years.[1] In the opening days of the war he had taken a personal hand in storming the fortified city of Liège and had won the *Pour le Mérite* for his actions. Apparently, heroic deeds and personal initiative could still, at this early stage of the war, subdue heavy artillery and reinforced concrete. In the subsequent months on the Eastern Front Ludendorff directed campaigns of comparatively high mobility punctuated by seemingly decisive battles. Fighting over a rural landscape against an enemy that was not among the most advanced of Europe's industrialised powers, Germany made considerable territorial gains. These experiences in the war against Russia proved compatible with the intellectual framework of pre-war military doctrine. Some illusions at least could remain intact.

Ludendorff's amazement at what he found in the West was near total. As he and Hindenburg toured the battlefields of the Somme and Verdun, they confronted troops in moral crisis. Savaged within the space of six months by the two battles which have had such a large part in defining warfare in the twentieth century, the German Army was, reportedly, close to collapse.[2] What had brought it to this nadir was the experience of industrialised war – of defensive battles fought in fixed positions, dominated by weight of artillery. The courage of the individual soldier, the genius of the great commander – qualities apparently still crucial at Liège and Tannenberg –

seemed less significant given the tyranny of the timetabled bombardment, and its rapid replenishment by rail.

What Ludendorff and Hindenburg saw on the Somme acquired a new descriptive vocabulary. It was dubbed a *Materialschlacht*, a battle of *matériel*.[3] Shocked, they set about the reorganisation of Germany's war industry with the zeal of new converts, Hindenburg immediately announcing his so-called programme for doubling the production of shell and tripling that of guns. Much of this was rhetoric, and its impact on actual output was confused. But the conjunction of these initiatives with the new tactical methods evolved by German stormtroops out of the experiences of 1915–16 has led Michael Geyer to attribute to the German surpreme command the development of what he has called machine warfare.[4] One of the most effective of recent critics of the British high command, Tim Travers, has followed Geyer, using his model as a yardstick by which to compare – and to denigrate - the work of Field-Marshal Sir Douglas Haig and his *confrères*. According to Travers the British failed to shift from a paradigm that was manpower-centred to one that was machine-centred: new technology was grafted on to old tactical forms rather than used as the basis for a doctrinal rethink.[5]

That the Somme represented a caesura in the history of modern war is not in dispute. That it was, to all intents and purposes, a battle fought with old methods is more contentious. Attributing the advent of machine war to what the Germans learnt from the fighting is to confuse the chicken and the egg. The main brunt of the attack in the late summer of 1916 was borne by the British Army: if what transpired can be called a battle of material then its origins must, as Ludendorff himself acknowledged,[6] be found with the British rather than the Germans.

For students of the history of war in Europe the notion of the British Army as a chicken sits ill – not just for the absurdity of the metaphor (or the crassness of the pun), but also because it bestows on British military thought an unwonted fertility. After all, for the hundred years preceding the Battle of the Somme, the British Army was a small, regular force committed to the conduct of limited conflicts in the pursuit of empire. Ideas as to how to fight European war were derived at second hand from the precepts of Napoleon and Moltke, not from firsthand experience. Indeed the significance of the Somme for the British Army lies precisely in the seismic shift which it represents – the move to a mass army taking the main burden in war on the Continent.

In this sense 1916 is more significant even than 1914. Britain's entry to the First World War did not at the time mark an immediate change in Britain's strategic assumptions. When Sir Edward Grey told the House of Commons on 3 August 1914 of the background to Britain's ultimatum to

THE SOMME 1916 AND BRITISH STRATEGY

Germany, he suggested that for Britain the difference between neutrality and belligerence was slight. His justification for such seeming insouciance was his belief that Britain's contribution would be primarily maritime. As a neutral crosstrader, Britain would find its shipping, insurance and financial services seriously affected; as a belligerent in a naval war its commitment would still be limited. Not even the dispatch of the British Expeditionary Force to the Continent necessarily ruptured this sense of continuity: by contributing a small regular army and yet leaving the main burden of land warfare to the forces of France and Russia, British strategy ran along grooves familiar from eighteenth-century practices.

These continuities persisted until the winter of 1915–16. At sea, the Royal Navy, or more specifically its battlecruisers, sought a major naval battle, and got three – Coronel, the Falklands, and Dogger Bank. For all the frustrations felt within the Admiralty, the first two years of the war witnessed the principal surface engagements of the conflict, culminating at Jutland in May 1916. Second, the British Army and its colonial adjuncts, although supporting their allies in Europe, also embarked on operations on its periphery. They fought Germany for control of the Cameroons and East Africa, and they attacked Turkey through Mesopotamia and Gallipoli. This last was the operation that captured the strategic imaginations of the cabinet in 1915. In August, the Prime Minister, Asquith, although intellectually convinced of the primacy of the Western Front, nonetheless described the failure to rekindle the Dardanelles offensive at Suvla Bay as his biggest disappointment of the war.[7]

Until 1916, Britain's strategy was one of limited liability. It appreciated that Europe was the decisive theatre of the war, and it accepted that ultimately it would have to make a major military contribution to the achievement of victory there. But Lord Kitchener, the War Minister, for one aimed to postpone making that commitment until 1917.[8]

Limited liability was not, however, the same as limited effort. The adjectives used to describe British strategy in European war – naval, amphibious, peripheral – convey an implicit criticism. Britain's geographical position and its maritime supremacy enabled it to take as much or as little of the war as it wanted; its cities were not prey to the depredations of invading armies; it spilt the blood of its allies in preference to the lives of its own soldiers. But it is misleading to conclude that Britain was therefore unmilitary. At the beginning of the twentieth century Britain's defence spending was the highest per capita in the world. Between 1900 and 1913 Germany spent each year on defence an average of 77 pence per head of its population, France 85 pence, and Britain £2.04.[9] Britain's military effort required the expenditure of money, not men.

That this was so was primarily the consequence of its determination to maintain its maritime supremacy. From the launching of HMS *Warrior* in 1861 to the construction of dreadnoughts and super-dreadnoughts, Britain committed itself to the acquisition of the most advanced naval technology in the world. From the precision tools required for the manufacture of 15-inch guns to the electrical systems on which the ships' signalling and fire-control mechanisms depended, battleships represented a massive investment in sophisticated engineering. When Jackie Fisher became First Sea Lord in 1905, his initial brief was to control the consequent costs. His idealised answer was a navy of few ships but of extraordinary capabilities: by 1914 he was pushing for battlecruisers capable of 32 knots and armed with 15-inch guns, and in 1915 he was planning on speeds of 35 knots and 20-inch guns. But in the event quality did not oust quantity. The imperatives of the Anglo-German naval race in the North Sea, and then the emergence of new dreadnought fleets in the Mediterranean, insured that the navy got both.[10]

Over the long haul British navalism was a more expensive option than Prussian militarism. Men, the basic resource of an army, were cheaper, especially if conscripted, than big-gun battleships. However, Britain's massive defence costs were not just the consequence of its reliance on the Navy. Britain's Army was also comparatively dear. Between 1815 and 1895 it actually cost more than the Navy.[11] And until the final decade before the First World War its financial demands were comparable with those of major European armies. This was not because of its manpower: its size was about a quarter of that of most of its European comparators. One reason for such outgoings was the need to enter an open job market. Britain's soldiers were not richly rewarded, but they were not conscripts. Voluntary enlistment and long service had attendant consequences for pay, pensions, and the Army's infrastructure. Men were not easily enlisted or easily replaced: their lives and health, particularly in tropical climates, were a source of constant concern. This emphasis on long service was a consequence of imperial obligations. Therefore, the Army was, thanks to the colonies, effectively on a continuous war footing. In many, if not most, of the so-called small wars that empire engendered the Army was outnumbered. As a result it put its faith in more advanced technology. Kitchener himself had defeated the numerically much superior forces of the Mahdi at the Battle of Omdurman in 1898 through disciplined firepower. Hilaire Belloc's famous lines, penned in the same year – 'whatever happens, we have got the Maxim Gun, and they have not' – carry fraught implications for the acceptability of Travers's thesis. By 1904, Britain alone of the major powers had incorporated machine guns within their standard military formations.[12] Colonial warfare constantly required the British Army to maximise its manpower through the application of science and technology. At the micro

THE SOMME 1916 AND BRITISH STRATEGY

(and microbe) level quinine cured malaria; at the macro the railway enabled small numbers to garrison an empire while not forfeiting the capacity for rapid concentration.

Therefore, the First World War did not require Britain to shift from a manpower-dominated paradigm of warfare to a machine-dominated one. The British way in warfare already put its weight on high technology solutions. Indeed, the fact that Britain was not only the world's pre-eminent seapower but also the world's first industrialised nation points to the logic of such an outcome. What the First World War forced Britain to do was not to abandon a manpower-dominated form of warfare but to move towards one. This was not the opposite of what it had done hitherto: men and machines were not alternatives. Rather, it was an addition: it had to do both.

Britain's entry to the First World War did not therefore occasion any doubts about the need to maximise the production of war materials. In fact the reverse happened. The Chancellor of the Exchequer, Lloyd George, criticised the War Office for not going far enough in its placing of orders. As a result he was himself appointed Minister of Munitions at the end of May 1915. Britain was thus the first belligerent to establish a separate ministry charged with the task of industrial mobilisation. It also accepted sooner and more fully the need for state intervention in its regulation. The shortage of shells suffered by all armies in the winter of 1914–15, and throughout much of 1915 itself, was a manifestation of the difficulties of conversion from peace production to war production. What is instructive is the difference in the priorities evident in the programmes pursued by each of the belligerents.

Both France and Germany emphasised the need to sustain their holdings of field artillery. By the end of 1915 France had produced 1,010 new 75mms, 700 of them in the last quarter of that year.[13] Germany's holdings of field guns rose from 4,200 in 1914 to 5,700 in 1915.[14] To draw in new plant both powers lowered specifications, particularly in the manufacture of shell, and both promoted the use of low technology weapons like mortars and grenades. In pursuing these policies they accepted two penalties. First they postponed any improvements in quality in the interests of ensuring quantity. Second, and relatedly, they neglected heavy artillery. France drafted into the field obsolescent heavy guns from forts and coastal defences: only 250 new heavy guns had been passed to the Army by the end of 1915.[15] Germany deferred any serious consideration of its heavy artillery programme until 1916.[16]

Britain adopted many of the same expedients in the pursuit of short-term quantities. But, significantly, it did not simultaneously forfeit quality. Above all, it put the weight in new manufacture not on field guns but on heavy artillery.

Before the war the Royal Artillery had, to a degree even greater than the artilleries of the other powers, committed itself to mobile warfare, emphasising field artillery to the detriment of heavy artillery, and shrapnel shell rather than high explosive. One possible reason for the Germans' complacency concerning heavy artillery over the first two years of the war was their pre-existing superiority in pieces of larger calibre. The British, starting from massive inferiority, began the revision of their thinking in the autumn of 1914. Again and again Sir John French hammered home the message that what he needed was more guns. The battles of spring 1915, Neuve Chapelle, Aubers Ridge and Festubert, confirmed for GHQ that what would win the war on the Western Front would be long bombardments by heavy artillery. The guns' task was not to storm and surprise but to destroy: they could ravage the German defences before a single British soldier had to lift his head above the parapet. Thus the infantry would advance against a broken enemy. Massive material superiority would save lives. This was machine warfare as understood by Geyer and Travers: the British had taken a weapons system and reworked their methods in the light of it. The achievement of these tactics depended also on the application of cartography and meteorology, and the British would not reap the full benefits until 1917–18, particularly in the last hundred days of the war. But the approach was not just tactical; it was also strategic. Its purpose was the exploitation of scientific acumen, technological capabilities, and industrial resources.

The implications of these methods for production were immense. In 1915 the artillery had to operate on a narrow front if it was to be sufficiently concentrated to achieve the desired levels of destruction. But attacks on narrow fronts were exposed to the flanking fire of the defence. Therefore the ideal offensive would be conducted on a broad front. But attacks on broad fronts against deep defensive positions required many more guns.

In the summer of 1915 GHQ developed a programme for an additional 1,090 heavy guns, so that the army would have a total of 8,881 guns of all calibres, of which 7,240 were to be in the field by March 1916. This was Gun Programme A, communicated to Lloyd George by the BEF technical adviser, Major-General J.P. Du Cane, at the Allied munitions conference in June 1915. By July Gun Programme B had added an additional 325 heavy guns, and in August Gun Programme C set a target of 2,825 new heavy guns by the end of 1916.[17] Du Cane told Lloyd George that the army needed as many heavy guns as light: between the summer of 1915 and the summer of 1916 the Ministry of Munitions reduced the production capacity for lighter calibres by 28 per cent, and increased that for medium calibres by 380 per cent and for heavy guns by 1,200 per cent.[18]

The Somme was therefore planned as a battle of machine warfare.

THE SOMME 1916 AND BRITISH STRATEGY

Perhaps the most potent symbol of Britain's commitment to innovation in this respect was the deployment of the first tanks in the attack on Flers on 15 September 1916. However, the key aspect of that assault was not the tank itself but the effectiveness, or otherwise, of its integration with the artillery.[19] The British Army, as several recent scholars have made clear, was working towards combined arms tactics in which the driving force was less the infantry and more the artillery.

The failure on 1 July was therefore primarily a gunnery failure. Between the outbreak of the war and the end of 1915 Britain produced 208 new heavy guns; by the end of 1916 it had manufactured a further 1,714.[20] But the targets of the 1915 gun programmes were not met in time. Ostensibly the concentrations achieved by the British Fourth Army for 1 July 1916 were the greatest of the war thus far. A total of 1,538 guns compared favourably with 1,204 committed by the Germans to the opening of Verdun. However, of the German total 654 were heavy pieces and only 550 field guns; of the British 468 were heavy and 1,070 were field guns.[21] Furthermore the British front was more than twice as long. Thus the effects of the bombardment were dissipated. Efforts to expedite production had undermined quality control. Design faults and inferior materials put 25 per cent of guns out of action, and about 30 per cent of shells were duds. Much of the firing that was done was inaccurate - due to poor fuses, barrel wear, inadequate survey techniques, and insufficient training.[22] Far from saving the lives of the infantry, the artillery – through the as yet unresolved imperfections of its new methods - was indirectly responsible for the highest losses suffered by the British army in a single day's fighting.

It was not at the tactical level but at the strategic that the pay-off for Britain's emphasis on material was to be found in July 1916. What it secured was the ability to mount the offensive in the first place. When the Germans chose Verdun for their main attack in the West in 1916 they were guided not least by that sector's relative logistic and territorial advantages; the French had no main railway into the salient which was exposed to German fire on two sides, and which was as close to Germany's bases as any sector of the front. Picardy, by contrast, was distant from the railway lines and Channel ports on which the British Army depended for its supply in 1916. Supply considerations pointed to an offensive not here, but at Ypres: Flanders was therefore Haig's preferred theatre of operations. The case for the Somme rested on the pressures of the alliance, and the presumption of major French co-operation. The sector was chosen in deference to General Joseph Joffre's wishes; in this respect the Somme is symbolic of the continuity between the BEF's role in 1916 and that of 1914–15, and indeed of earlier wars.

The terrain north of the Somme required the British Army to create virtually from scratch the infrastructure of a major city, with its attendant traffic and housing problems. The British Fourth Army needed 31 trains per day, rising to 70 when there were many wounded. Eight new railheads had to be built. Wells were sunk to ensure fresh water supplies. Over 7,000 miles of cable were buried underground, and a further 43,000 miles were erected above ground.[23]

Thus at the outset British strategy on the Somme could be construed in terms of continuity. Machine warfare, a battle for material – both were compatible with possible interpretations of the commitment to limited liability. Furthermore, the operations themselves were conceived according to a pattern set by Britain's senior continental partner. But in practice the battle developed differently. As 1916 unfolded the incompatibility between the preparations for the offensive and the continuance of limited liability became increasingly evident. The realisation that the Somme contained elements of strategic change created deep division in the Cabinet.

First, the effects of Verdun reduced the French contribution. Thus the British Army was acting less in direct support of its continental ally and more on its own account. That being the case, it would have made more sense for the British to be fighting on their preferred ground to the north, round Ypres. Instead the British Expeditionary Force was committed to the wrong battle in the wrong place. Nor was the timing of its choice. If we accept Kitchener's initial calculation, Britain would have reserved its major military contribution until 1917; by then, it is worth noting, its artillery would have been a much more finely-honed instrument of machine warfare.

What enabled the British army to shoulder the burden now thrust upon it was the creation of Kitchener's New Armies. They had been formed by voluntary enlistment, without recourse to conscription. But having expanded its military establishment, Britain was confronted with the problems of maintaining it. Voluntary recruiting declined in the second half of 1915: 135,263 men enlisted in May, but only 95,413 in July. In October the Army said it needed 35,000 men a week in order to keep its existing units up to strength.[24] It did not get them. At the end of February 1916 the army was 250,000 men below establishment and it anticipated a deficit of 400,000 by the end of April.[25] Assuming the major responsibility on the main front in a European war would confront the army with the seeds of its own disintegration. By late 1915 both Kitchener and General Sir William Robertson, the Chief of the Imperial General Staff, had become advocates of conscription. Thus it was the manpower-driven model of modern war that represented innovation, and which pitched the Cabinet into crisis: compulsion was not only a radical departure in British strategy, it was also an affront to the individualist traditions of British Liberalism. The key

THE SOMME 1916 AND BRITISH STRATEGY

debate in Britain in the winter of 1915-16 was not about where in the world to concentrate British efforts but about now best to do so.

The 'Easterner'/'Westerner' division in strategy, which should by now have been consigned to the historiographical waste-paper basket, is particularly inappropriate in any consideration of strategic decision-making in the winter of 1915-16. The only viable eastern option for the Entente was an active Russian front. There was nothing more that the British Army could do. It was in the throes of abandoning the Dardanelles; in Mesopotamia Major-General Sir Charles Townshend was falling back from Baghdad to Kut; in the Balkans the Serb Army had been crushed and the war committee in London favoured the evacuation of Salonika. The primacy of the Western Front was not in doubt.

Both the machine warfare and the manpower models of strategy focus on resources. The concern of those who opposed the introduction of conscription was that a manpower-driven strategy would undermine Britain's ability to sustain either machine warfare or the battle of material. In their view Britain's policy of limited liability enabled it to develop its role as the armourer and financier of the Entente. To do that it needed to retain its productive capacities, not only to ensure deliveries of munitions to its allies as well as to the BEF but also to maintain the trade on which its international credit depended. The ability of the Entente to place orders for arms in the United States in particular rested on the dollar-sterling exchange rate. If Britain adopted conscription and thus drew even more of its workforce into the army, it would be unable to sustain the output so vital not only to the armies of the Entente but also to its balance of trade.

The primary spokesmen for this approach to strategy were to be found at the Treasury and the Board of Trade. Within the Cabinet, they included W. R. Runciman, Sir John Simon and, above all, Reginald McKenna, the Chancellor of the Exchequer. The strategy which they advocated – primarily naval and economic in its application – can be described as traditional. As should by now be clear this traditional strategy implied an adherence to machine warfare, not its rejection. By the time Britain faced the manpower implications of the First World War it had already accepted and largely resolved the industrial aspects.

The hinge that linked the military and industrial dimensions of Britain's war effort was financial. Indeed it was more than a hinge, it was a pivot. Students of economic mobilisation in the two world wars have become adept at explaining victory or defeat in terms of the balance of raw materials and productive capacity. But these were not the primary economic preoccupations of British Liberals in 1914-16. Physically close to the City of London, accustomed to seeing the reconciliation of Britain's balance of trade achieved by its invisible exports, and unable or reluctant to grasp the extent to which war could be funded through credit, they saw strategy in gold reserves, foreign exchange and interest rates.

Standing against McKenna was his predecessor as Chancellor, Lloyd George, never a spokesman for fiscal rectitude and now convinced that Britain could sustain both a mass army and war production. Standing behind McKenna was his adviser at the Treasury, John Maynard Keynes. Keynes argued in August 1915 that 'the labour forces of the United Kingdom are so fully engaged in useful occupations that any considerable further diversion of them to military uses is *alternative* and not *additional* to the other means by which the United Kingdom is assisting the Allied cause'.[26] If Britain withdrew more workers and so failed to produce sufficient to meet the demands of domestic consumption, Keynes feared, then civilian demand would find an outlet either by competing for the produce of war industry or by generating pressure for increased imports. The pursuit of too few goods by too much money would stoke price inflation. The decline in domestic munitions production through the loss of labour would increase the Entente's reliance on American production and so erode the value of sterling on the international exchanges.By November 1915 the pound had fallen to $4.56 from a pre-war par of $4.86. Britain could shore up the exchange rate in two ways. One was to export gold, a heterodoxy which Keynes strongly supported. The other was to increase its overseas borrowings, not least in order to use their fruits to hold the price of sterling. But the US money market was not accustomed to negotiations on the scale which the war was forcing the Entente to envisage. Allied loan stock sold at 98 in August 1915 was trading at 94 by the end of the year, with £187 million unsold. On 6 January 1916, with the conscription crisis at its deepest, Keynes wrote under a nom-de-plume in the *Daily Chronicle*: 'Nothing but the fact that we remained content for a considerable time with an army of a reasonable size, has deprived Germany of victory. Nothing but military megalomania on our part can still save her from defeat. For, whether the view of the past, expressed above, is true or not, any army which we now start to create absorbs resources at once, but cannot take the field for many months.'[27]

The debate between McKenna and Lloyd George was not one over the issues of free trade and state intervention. The notion that the Liberals in the coalition government still cleaved to pre-war orthodoxy, expressed in such misapplied catchphrases as 'business as usual' , has been well and truly scuppered by David French among others.[28] From the outset of the war Asquith and his colleagues pursued policies which responded to the needs of the war itself rather than to the cherished convictions of their party. In September 1915 McKenna himself had imposed minor duties on imports. The choice was therefore betweeen alternative strategies, for which economic policy was a means not an end.

THE SOMME 1916 AND BRITISH STRATEGY

Confirmation of this interpretation is provided by the groupings that the debate promoted and which bore little relationship to pre-war approaches to economic policy. Ranged alongside McKenna was Arthur Balfour. As the last Conservative prime minister he had had to contain an intra-party debate on tariff reform and 'fair trade': he had done so by obfuscation, not by a public declaration for or against free trade. He did not now position himself because of any predilection for liberal orthodoxies, but because of his long-standing involvement in British defence policy. Both as premier and as prime mover in the Committee of Imperial Defence, his pre-war military concerns had focused on the defence of India: his worries were thus the pith of continuity in British strategy. Moreover, when he was brought into the coalition in May 1915 it was as First Lord of the Admiralty. This was a post which McKenna too had held. Like McKenna, Balfour could not but be exposed to naval views. Balfour was therefore a traditionalist in strategy, emphasising Britain's economic and maritime strengths, preferring a limited liability on the continent, and displaying a marked enthusiasm for machine warfare. He opposed conscription; he supported the development of the tank (even riding in one, as he had also flown in an aeroplane and submerged in a submarine). The only ground on which he could justify a major British role on the Western Front in 1916 was the need to save Britain's allies.[29]

Most of Balfour's Unionist colleagues stood not with him but with Lloyd George. They were persuaded by the arguments of Robertson and the general staff. The alliance they produced was a strange one. Lloyd George, the most radical of the pre-war cabinet, the man who fused the 'old' Liberal roots of Celtic non-conformity with the semi-socialist doctrines of 'new' Liberalism, was not a natural colleague for Bonar Law and his Conservative Party. But such a sense of what was logical presupposes that what drove politics in 1915–16 was peacetime party ideologies. It was not; it was the war, and ultimately it would enable Law and Lloyd George to construct a government.

The fact that the Cabinet conducted the compulsion debate in terms of strategic necessity does not mean that those were the terms in which the issue was addressed outside government. Within the Liberal press and on the Liberal backbenches the introduction of conscription went to the heart not only of what the war was about but also of the Liberal Party. Asquith avoided a split in his government when he took Britain into the war. But many, particularly on the Liberal backbenches, felt betrayed. Their palliative, and the basis for party reconciliation, was the conviction that Britain had taken up the cudgels of Liberalism in a struggle against Prussian militarism. Belgium's rights as a neutral power were fundamental to this justification for Britain's part in the hostilities. But the corollary of a war for Liberalism was that it should be fought with Liberal methods. Britain had to show the superiority of individualism and voluntarism by using both for the achievement of victory. If it had to achieve victory by way of Prussian methods then it had forfeited Liberal principles and had thus effectively lost the war. To adopt the manpower-driven model of warfare was therefore tantamount to defeat.

For those who cleaved to such ideas McKenna was the standard-bearer. The blow to free trade embodied in his September 1915 budget was offset by his commitment to fiscal prudence. In the same package he introduced a wartime excess profits tax, thus making Britain the first belligerent to adopt one, and he also committed himself to levels of taxation sufficiently high both to cover the interest on Britain's borrowings and to establish a sinking fund on the debt. Thus the pragmatic nature of his opposition to conscription did not necessarily occlude the appearance of high principles. McKenna had the power and the opportunity to split the coalition if he wished to exercise them. In the end the Lloyd George faction was victorious on all counts – it formed the government in December 1916, it associated itself with an all-out commitment to the struggle, it won the war in November 1918, and it dominated the memoir literature thereafter. But this triumphalist hindsight should not obscure the reality of the choice in late 1915 or the evenness with which the issues seemed to be balanced. J. L. Garvin, the Conservative newspaper editor, told C. P. Scott, editor of the Liberal *Manchester Guardian*, in November that so great was McKenna's ascendancy over Asquith that 'In fact we were now living under a McKenna regime.'[30]

In the end McKenna did not force the issue, much to the dissatisfaction of his Liberal supporters. Only Sir John Simon publicly embraced the issue of principle – that an individual should not against his own will be required to bear arms – and only Simon resigned. Both McKenna and Runciman, reflecting the strategic issue and not the Liberal one, elected to fight Lloyd George on the overall size of the Army not on the precise manner of its enlistment. In August Lloyd George had talked airily of an army of 100 divisions: this was the origin of Gun Programme C. Even the War Office had balked at that, and preferred a target of 70 divisions – the basis of Gun Programme B and of the demand of 35,000 men per week. McKenna preferred Kitchener's initial target of 50 divisions, which he reckoned would require 20,000 men a week, a level compatible with the needs of industry.[31]

That the Cabinet did not split was largely due to its secretary, Maurice Hankey. Hankey's skills were those of reconciliation and emollience, but his own opinions and prejudices were aligned with McKenna and Balfour. A Royal Marine officer, he was convinced that Britain's strengths were 'naval, economic and financial':[32] his continuing and pervasive influence in British

THE SOMME 1916 AND BRITISH STRATEGY

strategic counsels throughout the war is evidence of how persistent traditional approaches to strategy remained despite their apparent defeat in 1916. To Hankey Asquith attributed McKenna's decision not to resign,[33] and his willingness instead to join a committee on the coordination of Britain's military and financial effort. Asquith and Austen Chamberlain also served on this committee and Hankey was its secretary. The result of its deliberations was a compromise – a field army of 62 divisions, not 70 (let alone 100), with 5 more for home defence. Thus was the manpower model of strategy grafted on to that of machine warfare.

The precondition on which the creation of the committee and the production of its compromise rested was an understanding between McKenna and Sir William Robertson brokered in advance, also by Hankey. Robertson was not unresponsive to the financial approach to Britain's strategy – a point made clear to McKenna at the end of December and which persuaded the Chancellor that the adoption of conscription did not necessarily mean an army of unlimited size.[34] A private letter which Robertson wrote to Haig on 31 December 1915 gives the flavour of his flexibility: 'There is dreadful need of superior control of the war & our money though plentiful has its limits. There has been no coordination of the different departments. K. has been working up to 70 Divisions. L. George has ordered material for 100 Divisions. The Chancellor of the Exchequer did not till yesterday know either of these things! Now he says the money will not run to it & I do not think it will. Clearly he cannot do impossibilities and the Government must decide what force they will maintain. There is great waste going on.... In many ways we are using our resources in the worst possible way. We have heaps of men as it is, but there is no intelligent plan for using them. What I am now aiming at is to find what number of men we can raise & *pay for.*'[35]

For Robertson the manpower model and the material model were not alternatives. In November and December 1915 he stressed that the defeat of the Central Powers could only be obtained by the exhaustion of Germany. At one level this was a manpower-dominated strategy. The Allies' conference at Chantilly in December 1915 set as the target for their strategy for 1916 the exhaustion of Germany's reserves by the mounting of simultaneous attacks on all fronts. 'The process of attrition', Robertson wrote to Kitchener at the end of the same month, 'must necessarily be slow, and will demand regular and frequent relief of the troops fighting on the front, if the superiority of our troops in morale, vigour and efficiency is to be kept up. This demands a large and indefinite number of reserves.'[36]

But Robertson's strategic vision was wide enough to see the other dimensions to attrition.[37] At the tactical level, it meant making machines do the work of men if the manpower balance was to remain favourable. It meant, as he wrote to Haig on 28 May 1916, an increase in artillery and a reduction in cavalry.[38] It meant too limited attacks designed in accordance with the capabilities of the artillery.[39] At the highest level, attrition marched in step with the naval and economic appreciations of the war's strategy. In theory at least, it was a limited and gradualistic approach to the fighting on the Western Front, exploiting Britain's inherent strengths to wear down the enemy.

Robertson's strategic picture certainly required a bigger army than McKenna and others would have liked. But it could be construed as a difference of degree, not of kind. It was also a vision which Kitchener shared: hence the surprising lack of friction between the Secretary of State for War and the man who had effectively usurped his position as the Cabinet's principal strategic adviser. Both were at pains to stress that Britain's effort would be set within bounds: the aim was to encourage the Allies and gradually use up Germany's reserves through 'active defence'.

In many respects, therefore, the Somme, despite its revolutionary aspects, followed logically from the imperatives of traditional British strategy. It rested on the notions of limited liability, the need for strong European allies, and the primacy of material superiority in the conduct of war. In the event of course it did not represent a limited liability. Rather, it ensured that Britain took the main burden of continental warfare from its Allies, and its material preparations were inadequate to prevent the battle becoming a trade-off in manpower.

This was not entirely a product of accident or mismanagement. What underpinned the whole debate on resources, whether material or human, was the question of the war's length. Robertson's evolving ideas of attrition and McKenna's naval-financial strategy could merge in large part because neither was predicated on victory in 1916. Both were methods of eking out Britain's comparative strategic advantage over a long haul. The Treasury's worry concerning conscription was that in curbing domestic production it demanded a quick victory. As Keynes put it in September 1915: 'If by flinging our resources lavishly we could be sure of finishing the war early next spring, I estimate that they might be about equal to our needs.'[40] Both McKenna and Robertson knew that the condition would not be fulfilled. Thus each in his respective sphere accepted that the logic of the situation demanded a more conscious pacing of Britain's effort.

But this was a view of the war that commended itself neither to Lloyd George nor to Haig. The former was temperamentally averse to the cautious and realistic prognostications of Robertson; it made him more vulnerable to the certitude and optimism of Haig than he cared to admit or the public appearance of their later relationship revealed.[41] Haig saw the Battle of the Somme in very different terms from those embraced by Robertson or

THE SOMME 1916 AND BRITISH STRATEGY

Kitchener. For him the offensive had the potential to win the war; he reckoned on achieving breakthrough and so restoring manoeuvre to the battlefield. The difference in operational outlook between himself and Henry Rawlinson, the Fourth Army's commander, and an advocate of more restricted and artillery-led attacks, produced a plan for the battle that was fatally compromised at the tactical level. Uncertain whether its objectives were limited or not, it mixed concepts without matching them, and contributed in no small measure to the casualty bill from which the manpower model of war can derive its damning evidence. But the consequences of such confused objectives were also felt at the strategic level, for they made a mockery of any suggestion that the Somme was compatible with a strategy of limited liability, resulting in a use of resources so prodigal as to create havoc with any notions of gradualism inherent in the thinking of either Robertson or McKenna. The strategy of the Somme made some sort of sense while it was shaped by the idea that victory was not on offer in 1916; it became deeply flawed when it set off in pursuit of an illusion.

What the Somme therefore exposed was the paradox at the heart of McKenna's approach to strategy. Orthodox finance required a quick victory in 1916, but neither he nor Keynes saw how such a victory could be achieved. Certainly Robertson's ideas on attrition held out no such prospect. Furthermore, as a former First Lord, McKenna's faith in naval pressure implied the acceptance of a long war. But if there was no quick victory, then orthodox finance would fail, and its demise would put in jeopardy the survival of Liberalism itself. Like it or not, Asquith's Cabinet had to tie itself to Haig's star because his bid to achieve the seemingly impossible, a major British victory in 1916, would accomplish at least one of two objectives – and possibly both. First, it might restore Britain's credit: its ability to continue to float the loans on the US stock market which paid for its American imports and sustained the dollar-sterling exchange rate rested on the probability of an Entente victory. Second, it would prolong the life in government of the Liberal Party, riven by the contradictions created witnin it by the strains of war and now dependent on a coalition for its political survival.

Whatever the pluses and minuses of the British Army's efforts on the Somme, it failed to deliver on either count. By August Britain was spending $250 million a month in the United States: this represented two-fifths of total war expenditure.[42] At the end of November the Federal Reserve Board warned its member banks against the purchase of foreign bills. Allied shares plummeted, and a run on the pound ensued. As the financial crisis developed, simultaneously the political bonds broke. In the first days of December Asquith's coalition finally ruptured, and Lloyd George became prime minister. By then Britain was no longer fighting a war of limited liability with Liberal methods. The main political struggles over strategy had already occurred. But the credit (if credit it be) for the change in strategy would go not to Asquith but to his successor. The division in the party's leadership may have been promoted by the conduct of the war, not by peacetime ideologies, but it would persist beyond the Armistice. It was at least one element in consigning the Liberals to perpetual political opposition.

NOTES

1. General Ludendorff, *My War Memories 1914–1918*, 2 vols (London: Hutchinson 1919) I, p.265, gives 5 Sept.; Reichskriegsministerium, *Der Weltkrieg*, XI (Berlin: Mittler 1938) p.10, gives 6 Sept.
2. Friedrich Altrichter, *Die seelischen Kräfte des Deutschen Heeres im Weltkriege* (Berlin: Mittler 1933) pp 91–2; Erich Otto Volkmann, *Der Marxismus und das Deutsche Heer im Weltkriege* (Berlin: Hobbing 1925) p.161.
3. For the use of this word see Reichskriegsministerium, *Der Weltkrieg*, X (Berlin: Mittler 1936), p.384; Ernst von Wrisberg, *Wehr und Waffen* (Leipzig: Koehler 1922) p.90.
4. Michael Geyer, *Deutsche Rüstungspolitik 1860–1980* (Frankfurt: Suhrkamp 1984) pp.13, 91–2, 99–103; also 'German strategy in the age of machine warfare, 1914–1945', in Peter Paret (ed), *Makers of modern strategy from Machiavelli to the nuclear age* (Oxford: Clarendon Press 1986).
5. Tim Travers, *The Killing Ground: the British Army, the Western Front and the Emergence of Modern Warfare, 1900–1918* (London: Allen & Unwin 1987).
6. Reichskriegsministerium, *Der Weltkrieg*, XI, pp.2–3.
7. George H. Cassar, *Asquith as War Leader* (London: Hambledon 1994) p.119.
8. David French, 'The Meaning of Attrition, 1914–1916', *English Historical Review* 103 (1988) pp.385–405.
9. Lance E. Davis and Robert A. Huttenback, *Mammon and the Pursuit of Empire: the Political Economy of British Imperialism 1860–1912* (Cambridge: CUP 1986) p.160; David Stevenson, *Armaments and the Coming of War: Europe, 1904–1914* (Oxford: Clarendon Press 1996) p.6 points out that defence expenditure in relation to net national product is a more realistic indication of the actual defence burden. By this standard Britain lagged behind the other great powers.
10. Jon Tetsuro Sumida, *In Defence of Naval Supremacy Finance, Technology and British Naval Policy, 1899–1914* (Boston: Unwin Hyman 1989) esp. pp.290–3; Sumida, 'British capital ship design and fire control in the *Dreadnought* era: Sir John Fisher, Arthur Hungerford Pollen and the battle cruiser', *Journal of Modern History* 51 (1979) pp.205–30.
11. David French, *The British Way in Warfare 1688–2000* (London: Unwin Hyman 1990) p.120.
12. David Herrmann, *The Arming of Europe and the Making of the First World War* (Princeton, 1996) p.20.
13. C. Reboul, *Mobilisation industrielle; tome 1. Des fabrications de guerre en France de 1914 à 1918* (Paris 1925).
14. Volker Mollin, *Auf dem Wege zur 'Materialschlacht'. Vorgeschichte und Funktionen des Artillerie – Industrie – Komplexen im Deutschen Kaiserreich* (Pfaffenweiler 1986) p.329.
15. Reboul, *Mobilisation industrielle* (note 13) p.50.
16. Wrisberg, *Wehr und Waffen* (note 3) pp 53–5.
17. *History of the Ministry of Munitions*, 12 vols (London: HMSO 1922) X, Part 1, pp.6–27.
18. R.J.Q. Adams, *Arms and the Wizard: Lloyd George and the Ministry of Munitions* (London: Cassell 1978) p.172.
19. Robin Prior and Trevor Wilson, '15 September 1916: the dawn of the tank', *Journal of the*

Royal United Services Institute 136/4 (Autumn 1991) pp.61–5; J.P. Harris, *Men, Ideas and Tanks: British Military Thought and Armoured Forces, 1903–1939* (Manchester UP 1995) pp.58–9, 63; David Childs, 'British Tanks 1915-1918: Manufacture and Employment', Glasgow University PhD, 1996; Jackson Hughes, 'The Monstrous Anger of the Guns: the Development of British Artillery Tactics 1914–1918', Adelaide University PhD 1992.

20. *Ministry of Munitions* (note 17), X, Part 1, p.96.
21. J.E. Edmonds, *Military Operations: France and Belgium 1916*, Vol. I (London: Macmillan 1932) pp.300–1; Reichskriegsministerium, *Der Weltkrieg* X (note 1) p.62.
22. Shelford Bidwell and Dominick Graham, *Fire-Power: British Army Weapons and Theories of War 1904–1945* (London: Allen & Unwin 1982) pp.98–9; John Terraine, *The Smoke and the Fire Myths and Anti-Myths of War 1861–1945* (London: Sidgwick 1980) p.113; Travers, *Killing Ground* (note 4) pp.138–42.
23. Edmonds, *Military Operations: France and Belgium 1916* (note 21) I, pp.273, 286.
24. Cassar, *Asquith* (note 7) pp.151, 154.
25. David French, *British Strategy and War Aims 1914–1916* (London: Allen & Unwin 1986) p.187.
26. Elizabeth Johnson (ed.) *The Collected Writings of John Maynard Keynes*, Vol. XVI (London: Macmillan 1971) pp.110–11. Much of what follows has been developed in discussion with my doctoral pupil, Martin Farr, who is working on McKenna as Chancellor of the Exchequer.
27. Ibid. p.159.
28. David French, *British Economic and Strategic Planning 1905–1915* (London: Allen & Unwin 1982).
29. Sydney H. Zebel, *Balfour: A Political Biography* (Cambridge: CUP 1973) p.215.
30. Trevor Wilson (ed.), *The Political Diaries of C.P. Scott 1911–1928* (London: Collins 1970) p.157.
31. Ibid. pp.144–5; Keith Grieves, *The Politics of Manpower, 1914–18* (Manchester UP 1988) p.20.
32. Hankey, 29 April 1916, quoted in Stephen Roskill, *Hankey: Man of Secrets*, I (London: Collins 1970) p.269.
33. Ibid. pp.240–1.
34. French, *British Strategy and War Aims* (note 25) p.172.
35. David Woodward (ed.), *The Military Correspondence of Field-Marshal Sir William Robertson, Chief of the Imperial General Staff, December 1915–February 1918* (London: Army Records Soc. 1989) p.25.
36. French, *English Historical Review* (note 8) pp.397–8; also David Woodward, *Lloyd George and the Generals* (Newark, NJ: U. of Delaware Press 1983) pp.76–7.
37. Robertson to A.J. Murray, 8 March 1916, in Woodward, *Military Correspondence of Robertson* (note 35) p.41.
38. Ibid. p.53.
39. Robertson to Kiggell, 5 July 1916, ibid. pp.64–5.
40. Johnson, *Collected Writings of Keynes*, XVI, p.124; see also Robert Skidelsky, *John Maynard Keynes* I (London 1983) pp.312–13.
41. This is also developed in relation to 1917 by Trevor Wilson, *The Myriad Faces of War: Britain and the Great War 1914–1918* (Cambridge: Polity Press 1986) pp.462–4.
42. Kathleen Burk, *Britain, America and the Sinews of War, 1914–1918* (Boston: Allen & Unwin 1985) pp.81–2.

[20]

The Road to Ypres: The Beginnings of Gas Warfare in World War I*

Ulrich Trumpener
University of Alberta

On the afternoon of April 22, 1915, a large volume of compressed chlorine, probably close to 150 tons, was released from thousands of storage cylinders in the German trenches along the northern arc of the Ypres salient. Within minutes, dense clouds of the asphyxiating gas drifted with the wind into a four-mile-wide sector held by units of the French Forty-fifth (Algerian) and Eighty-seventh (Territorial) Divisions, killing some soldiers outright, seriously incapacitating many more, and causing hasty withdrawals of the others in much of the affected area.[1] Although a broad gap was thereby temporarily opened in the Allied lines, the Germans did not fully exploit their advantage. By the end of the day their infantry had overrun part of the Ypres salient and captured over fifty French and British guns, but no strategically decisive breakthrough was attempted or achieved.[2]

---

* The preparation of this paper was facilitated by a Canada Council leave fellowship and the cooperative attitude of many West German archivists and librarians. I am also indebted to Dr. L. F. Haber, University of Surrey, and Professor Gerald D. Feldman, University of California, for valuable advice and information. Finally, I wish to thank Colonel Hurbin and his colleagues at the Service historique de l'armée, Vincennes, who answered some of my questions and provided me with copies of two declassified French army documents.

[1] Some recent accounts, e.g., Seymour M. Hersh, *Chemical and Biological Warfare* (London, 1968), p. 5, list French gas casualties as over 5,000 killed and another 10,000 injured. Both of these figures are far too high. Contemporary German reports indicate that few bodies were found in the gassed area, and the death rate among about 200 seriously incapacitated French soldiers who were later taken to German hospitals was well below 10 percent. See Lt. Gen. Waldorf to HQ XXVI Reservekorps, April 27, 1915, Nachlass Otto Freiherr von Hügel [hereafter Hügel papers], Württembergisches Hauptstaatsarchiv Stuttgart [hereafter WHA]; XXVI Reservekorps to A.O.K. 4, April 29, 1915, ibid.; and Rudolf Hanslian, *Der deutsche Gasangriff bei Ypern am 22. April 1915* (Berlin, 1934), pp. 64, 70, 104 and passim. For similar findings by medical officers on the Allied side of the line, see Sir Andrew Macphail, *The Medical Services*, Official History of the Canadian Forces in the Great War (Ottawa, 1925), p. 300; and a French casualty report by the medical inspector Sieur, dated April 25, 1915, which refers to 625 gassed soldiers counted as of the previous day, of whom three died of congestion of the lungs (information supplied by Dr. L. F. Haber, who found the report in Box 16 N 826 at the military archives, Vincennes).

[2] See the official accounts in Reichsarchiv et al., *Der Weltkrieg 1914 bis 1918: Die militärischen Operationen zu Lande* [hereafter RA, *Weltkrieg*], 14 vols. (Berlin,

The release of "poison gas" against Allied troops, which was repeated two days later during an assault on Canadian positions in the adjacent sector, near Saint-Julien, provoked great indignation in the Western world and was denounced by many Allied leaders as a flagrant breach of the rules and customs of war and an offense against all humane principles.[3] Although a number of historians and military men have since pointed out that the "illegality" and "inhumanity" of the German gas attacks were not really all that clear, many Western authors have continued to take a very dim view of what the Germans did at Ypres. There is widespread agreement, in particular, that their resort to gas weapons was completely unprovoked and, furthermore, that the German high command did not even have the wit to use the odious new technique for a strategically significant purpose but wasted it, and thus the all-important surprise effect, on a limited offensive with inadequate reserves.[4]

The purpose of this essay is to probe into the background of the Ypres operation and to reassess the military, technical, and moral aspects of imperial Germany's pioneering role in the development and use of "chemical warfare" devices during the opening stages of World War I. Although many important documents bearing on these questions were unfortunately lost when the Potsdam Heeresarchiv burned down in 1945, some valuable records did survive in other places, making it possible to take a fresh look at this controversial subject.

* * *

Contrary to general belief, gas warfare in World War I did not begin at Ypres. Attempts to break the resistance of enemy troops

---

1925–44), 8:39–41; Ministère de la Guerre, *Les armées françaises dans la Grande Guerre*, 11 vols. (68 subvols.) (Paris, 1922–39), 2:699–700; and G. W. L. Nicholson, *Canadian Expeditionary Force, 1914–1919*, Official History of the Canadian Army in the First World War (Ottawa, 1964), pp. 61 ff.

[3] See, e.g., *The Times History of the War*, 21 vols. (London, 1915–20), 5:53 ff.; Sir John French's statement of June 15, 1915, in *The Great Events of the Great War*, ed. Charles F. Horne, 7 vols. (n.p., 1923), 3:139–40; Viscount Grey of Fallodon, *Twenty-five Years*, 2 vols. (London, 1926), 2:102; Joseph Joffre, *Mémoires du Maréchal Joffre*, 2 vols. (Paris, 1932), 2:32 ff., 72; and Maxime Weygand, *Mémoires: Idéal vécu* (Paris, 1953), pp. 224–25.

[4] See Victor Lefebure, *The Riddle of the Rhine* (New York, 1923), pp. 22 ff., 31 ff.; J. E. Edmonds et al., *Military Operations: France and Belgium, 1915*, History of the Great War Based on Official Documents, 2 vols. (London, 1927–28), 1:193–94; B. H. Liddell Hart, *The Real War, 1914–1918* (Boston, 1930), pp. 130, 175 ff.; Sir Llewellyn Woodward, *Great Britain and the War of 1914–1918* (London, 1967), p. 127; and Field-Marshal Viscount Montgomery of Alamein, *A History of Warfare* (London, 1968), p. 548.

462   Ulrich Trumpener

through the diffusion of noxious vapors had actually been started much earlier in the war—both by the French and by the Germans themselves.

While no definitive assessment of French front-line experiments with gas munitions prior to April 22, 1915 is possible until all relevant files in the military archives of France have been opened, some tentative conclusions on this subject can be drawn now.[5] To begin with, it is now beyond question that small gas-diffusing projectiles of prewar design and manufacture, so-called *cartouches suffocantes*, were used by French troops in some sectors of the Western front as early as 1914.[6] Intended primarily for attacks on fortifications, these projectiles were filled with ethyl bromo-acetate (in liquid form), weighed approximately half a pound, and were launched by special twenty-six-caliber rifles (*fusils lance-cartouches éclairantes*).[7] By February 1915, hand grenades containing the same chemical agent, but of greater weight and volume and thus more suitable for assaults on open trenches, had been added to the stock of French gas munitions, and there are strong indications that some of these *grenades suffocantes* were used against German troops in the Argonne sector from mid-March on.[8]

According to a confidential circular issued by the French war ministry on February 21, 1915, the vapors released by these two types of *engins suffocants* were "irritant" to the eyes, the nose, and the throat but, "at least in small dosage," not actually "deleterious."[9] While this was certainly an accurate summary of the effect

---

[5] For an introduction to the historical controversy which erupted after World War I on the subject of French gas munitions, see the Swiss contribution by W. Volkart, "Der Giftgaskrieg und seine Entstehung," *Allgemeine schweizerische Militärzeitung*, no. 2 (1926), pp. 69–78.

[6] This was confirmed by Colonel Hurbin, adjoint au chef du Service historique de l'armée, Vincennes, in a letter to the author, March 26, 1971.

[7] Information derived from ibid.; a follow-up communication from the Vincennes office, May 12, 1971; and the text of a French war ministry circular, "Notice sur les engins suffocants," February 21, 1915. (An original of this circular fell into German hands during the war and was widely publicized in German postwar publications, but most Western authors either ignored it altogether or dismissed it as spurious. I wish to thank the Service historique de l'armée for confirming the authenticity and supplying me with a copy of the document.)

[8] For a detailed description of the grenades and advice on their proper use in attacks on trenches, see Ministère de la Guerre, "Notice . . . ." According to Colonel Hurbin, the grenades, as distinct from the less powerful *cartouches suffocantes*, were "not used" until after the Germans had staged their first chlorine attack. However, this information is hard to reconcile with the text of the "Notice . . ." and conflicts directly with German reports from the front in March and April which refer explicitly to French attacks with "hand grenades" or "bombs" of the gas-diffusing type.

[9] See Ministère de la Guerre, "Notice . . . ," last section.

produced by the detonation of individual missiles, it should be added that the chemical agent as such was not entirely harmless; that is, extended exposure to the vapor could cause severe choking and under some exceptional circumstances even prove lethal.[10]

Early in April 1915, General Joffre's staff notified French senior commanders that a new type of chemical hand grenade, the "Bertrand No. 1," was being placed "at the disposal of the armies," and that the older *engins suffocants* were henceforth to be identified as the "1.914" (*sic*) models. While it is fairly certain that the new Bertrand grenades were filled with chloracetone,[11] no reliable information is as yet available as to when they were first used in actual combat.

As for the "1914" models, it appears from German reports that, because of their limited size and volume, they rarely caused more than temporary discomfort (irritation of the eyes, a choking sensation, etc.) among troops who were attacked with these missiles. Nevertheless, the very use of such devices by one of the Allied armies from the fall of 1914 did set a precedent of sorts, making it psychologically easier for the Germans to try out their own, and far more potent, gas weapons at the earliest opportunity.

Just as in France and Britain (where the War Office had started tests with chemical "irritants"—chloracetone and benzyl chloride—in the spring of 1914),[12] some military experiments with chemical agents had been conducted in Germany before the outbreak of the war. However, according to an extant memorandum by Colonel Max Bauer—the well-known artillery specialist in the Prussian general staff who later, in 1916, became General Ludendorff's principal adviser on economic and political questions—the results of these German prewar tests had been "negative" throughout. Indeed, Bauer complained, not only was it necessary to start all over again during the war, "but the negative outcome of the experiments made before the war actually impeded the acceptance of the new results,

---

[10] On the physiological effect of ethyl bromo-acetate vapors in various concentrations and time periods, see Ulrich Müller-Kiel, *Die chemische Waffe im Weltkrieg und jetzt* (Berlin, 1932), pp. 47–48; and Morris B. Jacobs, *War Gases: Their Identification and Decontamination* (New York, 1942), pp. 21–22, 26–27, and passim.

[11] See Order no. 781, Grand quartier général, April 3, 1915, signed by Hellot (copy furnished by Service historique de l'armée). The reference to the chloracetone filling and other technical data are found in a penciled annotation on the original.

[12] The British prewar tests are described in a typescript "Historical Account of Offensive Chemical Warfare Research up to the Date of the Formation of the Chemical Advisory Committee in February 1916," prepared by J. Davidson Pratt. I am indebted to Dr. Haber for bringing this material in the Public Record Office, MUN 5/385/1650/9, to my attention.

464 *Ulrich Trumpener*

for one believed that the subject was already known and that it had been found unsuitable."[13]

Judging from Bauer's papers and other sources, the decision to reopen work on chemical munitions was taken by the German high command (Oberste Heeresleitung [OHL]) in the second half of September 1914, that is, shortly after the great German setback at the Marne and the de facto replacement of the hapless von Moltke as chief of the general staff by the Prussian minister of war, Lt. Gen. Erich von Falkenhayn. While rumors and unconfirmed reports about Allied experiments with chemical munitions seem to have played some part in the deliberations at the OHL, the final decision was triggered primarily by concern over Germany's rapidly dwindling powder and shell reserves and mounting complaints from the front that conventional high-explosive shells were relatively ineffective in dislodging the enemy from well-prepared trenches and other earthworks.[14]

On personal instructions from General von Falkenhayn, Max Bauer—who was then a major and chief of the Heavy Artillery and Fortresses section in the Operations Branch at the OHL—early in October 1914 convened a small group of scientists and army officers on the Wahn artillery range near Cologne. The assigned task of the committee, which included Walther Nernst (a future Nobel laureate) and the director-general of the Leverkusen Farbenfabriken, Carl Duisberg, was to develop a chemical shell—of the "incendiary, smoke, irritant, or stink" type—that could be used to drive enemy troops from house cellars and other inaccessible places. Apparently at the suggestion of one member who had previously served at the front, the committee eventually decided to try out a nontoxic sternutator, double salts of dianisidine, and recommended that the powdery substance be put into the standard shrapnels used by German field howitzers.[15]

---

[13] "Denkschrift betreffend den Gaskampf und Gasschutz" (n.d., probably late 1918), p. 2, Nachlass Max Bauer [hereafter Bauer papers], Bundesarchiv Koblenz. On Bauer's career and activities before and during the war, see his "Niederschrift über amtlichen Werdegang," June 30, 1921, ibid.; Frhr. Ludwig Rüdt von Collenberg's article on Bauer, in *Deutsches biographisches Jahrbuch für 1929* (Stuttgart, 1932), pp. 16–32; and Gerald D. Feldman, *Army, Industry, and Labor in Germany, 1914–1918* (Princeton, N.J., 1966), passim.

[14] See "Der Gaskrieg 1914–1918" (typescript draft, n.d.), pp. 1–2, Bauer papers; Erich von Falkenhayn, *Die Oberste Heeresleitung, 1914–1916, in ihren wichtigsten Entschliessungen* (Berlin, 1920), p. 40; and RA, *Weltkrieg*, 8:35–36. On the German munitions crisis, see ibid., 9:390 ff.; Feldman, pp. 52 ff.; and Hans-Joachim Flechtner, *Carl Duisberg: Vom Chemiker zum Wirtschaftsführer* (Düsseldorf, 1959), pp. 269 ff.

[15] See "Denkschrift betreffend den Gaskampf . . . ," p. 3, Bauer papers; and

Production of these so-called Ni-shells must have begun very quickly, for about 3,000 of them were first used on October 27 in the area around Neuve-Chapelle. The effect of the sternutatory dust, however, appears to have been so slight that the Allies did not even know about its use until the matter was revealed in German postwar publications. Nevertheless, approximately 17,000 additional Ni-shells were turned out by German factories before the project was abandoned.[16]

Early in November, chemist Hans Tappen—whose brother Gerhard, at that time a colonel, was one of Falkenhayn's closest advisers in his capacity as chief of the Operations Branch at general headquarters—proposed to the OHL that artillery shells be filled with xylyl bromide, a liquid which could be turned into an "irritant" vapor quite similar to that produced by the French *engins suffocants*. Major Bauer, it appears, initially rejected the proposal on the grounds that it was technically not feasible to fire shells with a liquid filling, but subsequent tests ordered by Colonel Tappen indicated that premature detonations and other malfunctions of such shells were unlikely to pose too much of a problem.[17]

Prototypes of the new ammunition (eventually code-named "T-shells" in recognition of Hans Tappen's contribution) were initially tried out on the Kummersdorf artillery range near Berlin and subjected to various technical modifications. After a "large-scale" test at Wahn on January 9, 1915, which was attended by Falkenhayn, his quartermaster general, Adolf Wild von Hohenborn, and other top figures from the OHL, the new chemical shells (fifteen-centimeter caliber) were formally approved for use in the field.[18]

Hermann Geyer, "Wie sich der Gaskrieg entwickelte," in *Was wir vom Weltkrieg nicht wissen*, ed. Friedrich Felger (Berlin, 1930), p. 300. (Geyer was a captain in the Operations Branch during the war and assigned to Bauer's section.)

[16] See "Denkschrift betreffend den Gaskampf . . . ," p. 4, Bauer papers; Rudolf Hanslian, *Der chemische Krieg*, 2 vols., 3d ed. (Berlin, 1937), 1:12; and Liddell Hart (n. 4 above), p. 129. The "Ni" stood for *Niespulver* (sneezing powder).

[17] See personal war diary, November 6, 8, 9, 1914, Nachlass Gerhard Tappen [hereafter Tappen papers], Bundesarchiv-Militärarchiv Freiburg i.B. [hereafter BA-MA]; Hans Tappen to Reichsarchiv, November 1923, ibid.; and Gerhard Tappen's "Stellungnahme zu dem Buche des Obersten Bauer . . . soweit meine Person darin erwähnt wird" (undated draft), ibid. Cf. Max Bauer, *Der grosse Krieg in Feld und Heimat* (Tübingen, 1921), pp. 33–34, for the allegation that Tappen had been completely disinterested in technological questions and various other uncomplimentary remarks by Bauer about his former superior.

[18] See Bauer, *Der grosse Krieg*, p. 68; Hanslian, *Der chemische Krieg*, 1:48 ff.; "Denkschrift betreffend den Gaskampf . . . ," pp. 4–5, Bauer papers; personal war diary, December 8, 11, 14, 1914, and January 9, 1915, Tappen papers; and Wild von Hohenborn to his wife, January 8, 1915, Nachlass Adolf Wild von Hohenborn, BA-MA. On the physiological effect of xylyl bromide vapors in various concentra-

While laboratory work on the T-shell was still under way, sometime in December, one of the scientific consultants on that project, Fritz Haber, pointed out to the military authorities that chlorine gas, a potent "lung irritant," might be an even more effective weapon for breaking the deadlock of trench warfare. As the director of the Kaiser Wilhelm Institut for physical chemistry in Berlin, Haber had already established a close working relationship with the Prussian war ministry during the opening months of the war. This relationship was now formalized by his appointment as head of a new "chemicals" section in that ministry and his advancement from a noncommissioned rank in the militia (*Landwehr*) to that of captain by a special imperial patent.[19] Starting with the supervision of the chlorine project, both at home and at the front, he gradually emerged as the chief authority on all chemical warfare matters in Germany and received several high decorations, including the Iron Cross First Class, for his accomplishments in this field.[20] The Allies, on the other hand, took a rather dim view of his activities. In 1919, shortly after Haber had been awarded the Nobel Prize for his prewar work on the synthesis of ammonia, his name was placed on an Allied list of Germans who were to be handed over for trial. Although proceedings against him were subsequently quashed, feeling over his role as the "inventor" of chemical warfare remained strong in some circles. When Haber left Germany after Hitler's rise to power and was given an opportunity by Sir William Pope, of the Cavendish Laboratory, to continue his work at Cambridge, Ernest Rutherford, for instance, let it be known that he did not wish to meet Haber because of his wartime record.[21]

---

tions and the potential for lethal dosages, see Müller-Kiel (n. 10 above), pp. 49 ff.; and Jacobs (n. 10 above), pp. 24–25.

[19] See Haber's postwar testimony in *Das Werk des Untersuchungsausschusses der Verfassunggebenden Deutschen Nationalversammlung und des . . . Reichstages . . .* (Berlin, 1925 ff.), ser. 3, *Das Völkerrecht im Weltkrieg* [hereafter *UA/Völkerrecht*], 4 vols., 4:13 ff.; Richard Willstätter, *From My Life* (New York, 1965), pp. 264 ff., 279 ff.; Feldman (n. 13 above), pp. 54–55, 170 ff.; Hanslian, *Der chemische Krieg,* 1:16; Bauer, *Der grosse Krieg,* pp. 61–62, 67 ff.; and Erna Jaenicke and Johannes Jaenicke, "Fritz Jacob Haber," *Neue deutsche Biographie* (Berlin, 1953–), 7:386–89.

[20] See Ernst von Wrisberg, *Wehr und Waffen, 1914–1918* (Leipzig, 1922), p. 168; Hermann Geyer, "Der Gaskrieg," in *Der Weltkampf um Ehre und Recht,* ed. Max Schwarte, 10 vols. (Leipzig, 1921–33), 4:493; and diary, September 30, 1917, Nachlass Gerhard von Nostitz-Wallwitz, BA-MA.

[21] See Karlheinz Lohs, "Fritz Haber und der chemische Krieg," *Zeitschrift für Militärgeschichte* 10 (1971): 432–45; Otto Hahn, *Mein Leben* (Munich, 1968), p. 131; and Max Born, *My Life and My Views* (New York, 1968), pp. 194–96. For a more sympathetic recent assessment of Haber's wartime work, see Wyndham D. Miles, "Fritz Haber: Father of Chemical Warfare," *Armed Forces Chemical Journal* 14 (1960): 28–29; and Morris H. Goran, *The Story of Fritz Haber* (Norman, Okla., 1967), pp. 66 ff.

Because of the still-existing bottlenecks in the German shell production program,[22] Haber came up with the idea of releasing the chlorine from specially fitted containers in the German trenches and letting the wind push the gas into the opposing lines. Aside from the ready availability of industrial storage cylinders that could be adapted for that purpose, the "cloud gas" technique proposed by Haber offered the additional advantage that it could be used against those Allied positions which were too close to the German lines to permit their bombardment with high-explosive shells.[23] The most serious drawback of the whole system, as the Germans soon found out, was of course its complete dependence on suitable wind conditions.

On December 18, shortly after testing of the new T-shells had commenced on the Kummersdorf artillery range, General von Falkenhayn got in touch with Emil Fischer, a renowned chemist at the University of Berlin. According to Fischer's account of the meeting, Falkenhayn pointed out that the new *Stinkstoffe* were not altogether satisfactory in their effect, and that he wanted something which would incapacitate the enemy "permanently." Fischer (who apparently had never been consulted before) thereupon replied that it was very difficult to develop chemical agents which would produce a lethal effect, though he subsequently confided to Duisberg that he actually knew of a substance that was "very bad" indeed. However, since the "necessary raw materials" for its production were not available in Germany, he, Fischer, thought it best not to pursue the matter, particularly since the enemy might get wind of it and use the idea to his own advantage.[24]

About two weeks after Falkenhayn's meeting with Fischer, the first experiments with chlorine discharges from cylinders were carried out on the Wahn artillery range. However, for security reasons, no "large-scale" test was attempted; as General Tappen later put it, one could hardly afford to have the smell of chlorine spread out for miles and miles.[25] On the basis of the preliminary test results, the OHL decided in mid-January to clear the new weapon for use at the

---

[22] See "Denkschrift betreffend den Gaskampf . . . ," p. 13, Bauer papers; and Hanslian, *Der deutsche Gasangriff bei Ypern* (n. 1 above), p. 77.

[23] See "Der Gaskrieg . . . ," p. 2, Bauer papers; Geyer, "Der Gaskrieg," pp. 499–500; and Friedrich Seesselberg, ed., *Der Stellungskrieg, 1914–1918* (Berlin, 1926), p. 405.

[24] Emil Fischer to Carl Duisberg, December 20, 1914. (The text of this letter, from Fischer's *Nachlass*, was kindly furnished by Prof. Gerald D. Feldman.)

[25] See personal war diary, January 9, 1915, Tappen papers; Tappen to Wohlenberg, March 1922, ibid.; Tappen to Reichsarchiv (draft), March 19, 1927, ibid.

front, though its "unchivalrous nature," according to Tappen, was "initially repugnant" to everyone concerned.[26]

At the Hague Peace Conference of 1899, many nations, including Germany, had formally agreed to a number of rules and limitations in the conduct of war. Among other things, they had pledged not to "employ poison or poisoned weapons," or "arms, projectiles, or material calculated to cause unnecessary suffering," or to make "use of projectiles the sole object of which is the diffusion of asphyxiating or deleterious gases."[27] By interpreting these clauses very literally, General von Falkenhayn and his advisers satisfied themselves that, quite apart from the "provocation" already offered by the French with their *cartouches suffocantes,* both the T-shells and the chlorine cloud gas were permissible weapons under the Hague Convention.[28]

As far as the prohibition of "poison or poisoned weapons" was concerned, the OHL took the position that this clause applied only to the deliberate poisoning of food or water, the use of missiles steeped in a poisonous substance, and the like, but that it clearly had no bearing on "gas" warfare, since the matter of "asphyxiating or deleterious gases" had been dealt with in an entirely separate agreement. The wording of that agreement, in turn, made it possible to maintain that the prohibition expressed therein did not apply to the particular gas weapons the OHL intended to use. The T-shells, at Falkenhayn's insistence, contained both a gas-producing compound and an explosive charge for fragmentation effect (hence they could be said to serve a dual purpose), while the release of chlorine gas from stationary cylinders did not involve "projectiles" at all. Finally, it could be and was argued that the new German gas weapons did not inflict "unnecessary" suffering on the enemy, since they were used solely to break, or at least reduce, his capacity for fight.[29] Indeed, Haber both then and later took the position that

---

[26] See Tappen to Reichsarchiv, July 16, 1930, ibid.; and RA, *Weltkrieg,* 8:38.

[27] See the Annex to the Convention respecting the Laws and Customs of War on Land, article 23a, 23e; and the "Declaration concerning Asphyxiating Gases" of July 29, 1899. Britain and the United States did not sign the latter declaration, but Britain later, in 1907, formally "adhered" to it. See *The Reports to the Hague Conferences of 1899 and 1907,* ed. James B. Scott (Oxford, 1917), pp. 126 ff., 170 ff., 891, and passim.

[28] See RA, *Weltkrieg,* 8:36–37; and Haber's postwar testimony in *UA/Völkerrecht,* 4:13.

[29] See "Denkschrift betreffend den Gaskampf . . . ," Anlagen 5, 6, Bauer papers. On the legal merits of the German case, see Morris Greenspan, *The Modern Law of Land Warfare* (Berkeley, Calif., 1959), p. 355; and Hans Kruse, "Gaskrieg," in *Wörterbuch des Völkerrechts,* ed. Hans-Jürgen Schlochauer et al., 3 vols., 2d ed. (Berlin, 1960–62), 1:615–16.

gases were actually less cruel in their effect than high-explosive shells and other conventional weapons—a judgment which was eventually supported by many Western historians.[30]

* * *

Because of various technical problems, more than three months were to elapse before the first chlorine cloud gas attack was actually carried out. The T-shells, on the other hand, were tried out at the front only a few weeks after testing had been completed.

The first contingent of T-shells, approximately 18,000 in all, was assigned to Colonel-General August von Mackensen's Ninth Army on the Eastern front. After bitter fighting in central Poland during the late fall, Mackensen's troops had been forced to dig in along the Bzura and Rawka Rivers, roughly halfway between Lodz and Warsaw. To screen Field Marshal von Hindenburg's preparations for a major strike against the Russians in East Prussia,[31] Mackensen was urged to stage diversionary attacks in his own sector and did so on a rather massive scale at the end of January. In the area near Bolimow, the attack by several of Mackensen's divisions was preceded by an extensive bombardment of the Russian positions with the new T-shells, but the chemical irritant had little discernible effect on the enemy and the advancing German infantry quickly ran into fierce resistance. Only later was it realized that the volatility of the xylyl bromide had been severely reduced by the extreme cold at the time of the battle, a problem which really ought to have been foreseen by the chemical experts on the German side.[32]

As a result of the costly lesson learned at Bolimow, the chemical charge of the T-shells was subsequently changed to a mixture of xylyl bromide and bromoacetone, which seemed more suitable for cold-weather use.[33] Some of these new shells were shortly thereafter

[30] Cf. Fritz Haber, *Fünf Vorträge aus den Jahren 1920–1923* (Berlin, 1924), pp. 35 ff.; Liddell Hart (n. 4 above), p. 130; Lefebure (n. 4 above), chap. 11; C. R. M. F. Cruttwell, *A History of the Great War*, 2d ed. (Oxford, 1936), pp. 153–54; and Corelli Barnett, *Britain and Her Army* (London, 1970), p. 398.

[31] Hindenburg's offensive, which began on February 7, led to the grim "Winter Battle of Masuria."

[32] See RA, *Weltkrieg*, 7:161–67; Geyer, "Der Gaskrieg," p. 497; and the eyewitness account of the Oberost representative, Lt. Col. Max Hoffmann, in *Die Aufzeichnungen des Generalmajors Max Hoffmann*, ed. Karl Friedrich Nowak, 2 vols. (Berlin, 1929), 2:92–93. On the background of the operation, see also *Mackensen: Briefe und Aufzeichnungen des Generalfeldmarschalls . . .* , ed. Wolfgang Foerster (Leipzig, 1938), p. 125; and Ludendorff to Moltke, January 27, 1915, in Egmont Zechlin, "Ludendorff im Jahre 1915: Unveröffentlichte Briefe," *Historische Zeitschrift* 211 (1970): 328–30.

[33] See Hanslian, *Der chemische Krieg*, 1:57; and Carl Duisberg to Bauer, March 3, 1915, Bauer papers.

assigned to the Fourth Army, which, under the command of Duke Albrecht of Württemberg, held the Flanders sector of the Western front. It appears that the shells were first tried out there some time in March, particularly in the area near Nieuport, but the effect of the irritant gas seems to have been as minimal as it had been at Bolimow. One month later, the T-shells were used on a more massive scale during the German attacks in the Ypres region, though even then their impact appears to have been very limited.[34]

While the T-ammunition, upon its clearance by the OHL in mid-January 1915, was initially tried out against Russian troops, Falkenhayn and his advisers decided that the chlorine cloud gas system—code name "Disinfection"—should first be used on the Western front. According to later testimony by Gerhard Tappen, this choice was very much influenced by the OHL's intention at that time to seek a "decision" in the West before long, but all available evidence points to the conclusion that such grand strategic considerations were quickly lost sight of. Indeed, it is obvious from subsequent events and Tappen's own papers that the leading men at the OHL were doubtful from the start that the cloud gas system, requiring difficult and easily detectable preparations close to the enemy lines and depending completely on suitable weather conditions, could actually be used in a strategically decisive fashion.[35]

Having been assured by "the experts"—presumably Haber and other German chemists—that the Western Allies did not have the technical capability to respond very quickly with cloud gas discharges of their own, Falkenhayn and his advisers at the OHL between January 14 and 25 called in senior staff officers from various parts of the Western front (including the Verdun sector) to determine where the new weapon could best be used.[36] In a conference with the chief of staff of the Fourth Army, Major-General Emil Ilse,[37] and the commander of the Fifteenth Army Corps, General

[34] See RA, *Weltkrieg*, 7:54; Hanslian, *Der chemische Krieg*, 1:15; "Denkschrift betreffend den Gaskampf . . . ," p. 4, Bauer papers; and Edmonds et al. (n. 4 above), 1:184, 192, 198, and passim. A more "effective" German gas shell (which contained mono-chlor-methyl-chloroformate as the principal chemical agent) had been developed by April, but these so-called *K-Granaten* apparently did not become available for front-line use until the early summer. See RA, *Weltkrieg*, 9:394, n. 5; "Der Gaskrieg . . . ," p. 5, Bauer papers; Carl Duisberg to Bauer, July 24, 1915, ibid.; and Geyer, "Der Gaskrieg," p. 497.

[35] See Tappen to Wohlenberg, March 1922, Tappen papers; Tappen to Reichsarchiv, March 19, 1927, ibid.; Hans von Zwehl, *Erich von Falkenhayn* (Berlin, 1926), p. 104; and RA, *Weltkrieg*, 8:38.

[36] See personal war diary, January 14, 25, 1915, Tappen papers; Tappen to Reichsarchiv, March 19, 1927, and July 20, 1930, ibid.

[37] Unlike most other senior general staff officers who served as *Chefs* in the principal front-line *Oberkommandos*, Ilse was a heavy artillery specialist by

Berthold von Deimling,[38] final agreement was reached that the chlorine cylinders would be assigned to the Fourth Army in Flanders and initially tried out in Deimling's corps area, that is, on the southeastern side of the Ypres salient.[39]

To instal and operate the gas cylinders at the front, several special troop units were formed and placed under the command of an officer from the engineers corps, Colonel Peterson, while Haber took over the technical supervision of their work. Ultimately designated as the Pionierregiment 35, the new units were made up of regular combat engineers and a number of scientists who were recruited from other branches of the army or from civilian life. Among the newly recruited men were physicists James Franck and Gustav Hertz and chemist Otto Hahn (all future Nobel Prize winners), as well as several other scientists of great distinction.[40] Hahn, according to his recently published memoirs, initially was very reluctant to become involved in a military activity which seemed to be violating the rules of the Hague Convention, but Haber pointed out to him that the French, through their use of gas-diffusing rifle grenades, had already begun to do just that, albeit in an "inefficient manner." Moreover, Haber emphasized, "countless lives would be saved if the war could be ended more quickly in this way."[41]

Toward the end of February, Colonel Peterson's newly trained units began with the placement of chlorine cylinders in General von Deimling's corps area near the village of Gheluvelt. The difficult job of moving the heavy steel cylinders (code name "F batteries") into

---

background. His keen interest in technological innovations may well have contributed to the OHL's decision to assign the new weapon to the Fourth Army. See Dr. Karl Heber, "Gasangriffe im 1. Weltkriege" (undated typescript), pp. 2 ff., Nachlass Friedrich von Tempelhoff [hereafter Tempelhoff papers], BA-MA; Tappen to Reichsarchiv, July 20, 1930, Tappen papers; and the biographical sketch of Ilse in Hanns Möller, *Geschichte der Ritter des Ordens pour le mérite im Weltkrieg*, 2 vols. (Berlin, 1935), 1:527–28.

[38] A Badensian of bourgeois origin, Deimling in the course of his prewar career had acquired the reputation of being a particularly zealous "Prussian militarist"—notably at the time of the Zabern Affair. His attitude changed very drastically toward the end of the war; in contrast to most other generals, he became an active supporter of democratic and pacifist causes and later played a prominent role in the republican Reichsbanner organization.

[39] See personal war diary, January 25, 1915, Tappen papers; and Berthold von Deimling, *Aus der alten in die neue Zeit: Lebenserinnerungen* (Berlin, 1930), p. 201.

[40] See Hanslian, *Der chemische Krieg*, 1:16; and Hahn (n. 21 above), p. 118 and passim. Like Haber, Franck left Germany when Hitler came to power. He eventually continued his research in the United States, where, in 1945, he warned against a rash use of the atomic bomb ("Franck Report"). Hertz worked in the Soviet Union after World War II and received the Stalin Prize in 1951.

[41] Hahn, pp. 117–18, 130. Hahn speaks of his being trained in the Pionierregiment 36, but this particular "gas regiment" actually was not formed until May. See RA, *Weltkrieg*, 8:133; and Heber, "Gasangriffe . . . ," p. 7, Tempelhoff papers.

the forward trenches and embedding them there under a layer of earth had to be done mostly at night and was not completed until about March 10. To everyone's consternation, wind conditions in the area during the next two weeks either proved clearly unsuitable for a release of the gas into the opposing, British-held, lines or changed just before a scheduled attack was to get under way. As a result, the German troops in the sector were placed repeatedly on fruitless alerts. To make matters worse, several cylinders were punctured by enemy shells or bullets, causing a growing number of gas casualties among the unprotected infantrymen in the German trenches.[42]

In view of the problems encountered in the Gheluvelt sector, Duke Albrecht of Württemberg and his advisers at Fourth Army headquarters decided on March 25 that an alternate "gas front" should be prepared on the northern side of the Ypres salient. While most of the chlorine cylinders eventually used for that new front seem to have come from newly delivered stock, there are indications that some F batteries were also taken from the contingent originally assigned to the Gheluvelt area. In any event, it is clear that because of continued adverse wind conditions no gas was actually released in Deimling's sector until the beginning of May, that is, a full two months after the cylinders had first been readied for action there.[43]

Both in Deimling's sector and later in the alternate gas front farther north, most German infantrymen, and their officers in particular, reacted to the arrival of the F batteries with distrust and displeasure. Their antipathy toward the eerie new weapon was soon heightened by occasional gas leakages from damaged cylinders in their own trenches and the additional work and danger to which they were subjected in assembling repeatedly for attacks which then had to be canceled because of adverse weather conditions.[44] Misgivings about the new weapon were shared by several senior commanders in other parts of the Western front. Crown Prince Rupprecht of Bavaria, whose Sixth Army was deployed immediately to the south of Duke Albrecht's sector, told both Falkenhayn and Haber that the impending cloud gas attacks in the Ypres region seemed to him not only distasteful but also militarily unsound. If the technique proved effective, the enemy would certainly adopt it too, and since the

[42] See RA, *Weltkrieg,* 7:55; Hanslian, *Der chemische Krieg,* 1:87; Deimling, p. 202; and Hahn, p. 118.
[43] See RA, *Weltkrieg,* 7:63–64; and Deimling, pp. 202-4. Hahn, p. 119, claims that all chlorine cylinders in the Gheluvelt sector were moved to the northern gas front in mid-April, but this is obviously in error.
[44] See Deimling, p. 202; "Der Gaskrieg . . . ," p. 4, Bauer papers; and the detailed analysis in Heber, "Gasangriffe . . . ," pp. 2 ff., Tempelhoff papers.

prevailing winds on the Western front came from the west, the Allies would be able to blow off gas "against us ten times more often than we could" against them.[45] Despite Falkenhayn's and Haber's reassuring reply that the chemical industry of the Allies "was simply not capable of producing gas in the quantity needed," Rupprecht's concern did of course prove justified before long—by September the British were ready to stage a major cloud gas attack of their own, and Rupprecht's Sixth Army was in fact the first to be hit.[46]

Colonel-General Karl von Einem,[47] who commanded the Third Army in the Champagne, was similarly unhappy about the introduction of the new weapon. "I fear it will produce a tremendous scandal in the world," he wrote to his wife shortly after he had heard about the first gas attack at Ypres. Though the Allies "supposedly cannot imitate the device, I presume nonetheless that they will soon have something similarly diabolical. . . . War has nothing to do with chivalry any more. The higher civilization rises, the viler man becomes."[48] Two years later, after both sides had introduced ever more toxic gases on the battlefield, Einem would express himself even more strongly about Falkenhayn's initiative in using such an "unchivalrous" weapon which was "repugnant to me from the very start." "Now our enemies have it too, and many a good man on our side has died a hero's death from poison."[49]

On April 2, 1915—over four weeks after the first chlorine cylinders had been placed in the German trenches in the Gheluvelt sector—a large-scale test of the F batteries behind the front was at long last undertaken. In the course of the experiment, which was conducted on the Beverloo troop training grounds in eastern Bel-

---

[45] See Kronprinz Rupprecht von Bayern, *Mein Kriegstagebuch*, ed. Eugen von Frauenholz, 3 vols. (Berlin, 1929), 1:304–5.

[46] "Now there we have got the reply to our *chlorreichen* [a pun on *glorreichen* (glorious)] attacks," was General Groener's sarcastic reaction when he first heard about the British operation (personal diary, September 25, 1915, Nachlass Wilhelm Groener, BA-MA).

[47] One of Falkenhayn's predecessors as Prussian minister of war (1903–9).

[48] Einem to his wife, April 23, 1915, Nachlass Karl von Einem gen. v. Rothmaler, BA-MA. Four days later, after hearing that the cloud gas had only "stupefied" the enemy, Einem agreed with the "very sensible proposal" by his chief of staff that the latter should visit the Fourth Army area to gain some experience with the new weapon. See Einem to his wife, April 24, 1915, ibid.; and Einem's war diary, April 27, 1915, ibid.

[49] Einem to his wife, February 1, 1917, ibid. Many other prominent German officers serving on the Western front were more ambivalent in their reactions. See, e.g., *General Erich von Gündell: Aus seinen Tagebüchern*, ed. Walther Obkircher (Hamburg, 1939), p. 169; and Albrecht von Thaer, *Generalstabsdienst an der Front und in der O.H.L.*, ed. Siegfried Kaehler (Göttingen, 1959), p. 33.

gium, Bauer and Haber rode their horses too close to a drifting gas cloud and paid for their recklessness with near suffocation and several days of illness.[50] Three days later, Colonel Peterson's men started work on the alternate gas front north of Ypres. By April 11, over 5,500 gas cylinders had been moved into the forward trenches from a point near Steenstraat to the vicinity of Poelcappelle. Of the four German divisions holding this part of the front and the adjacent sectors on either side, two belonged to the Twenty-third Reserve Corps of General Hugo von Kathen, the other two to the Twenty-sixth Reserve Corps, which was headed by General Otto Freiherr von Hügel, a Württemberg officer who had been recalled to active duty at the beginning of the war. Both corps commanders, after witnessing the Beverloo test, were informed that the impending cloud gas discharges in their sectors were to be used for gaining ground on both sides of the Yser Canal, with the high ground near Pilckem serving as the prime objective for General von Hügel's attack.[51]

According to the official history prepared at the Reichsarchiv after the war, Fourth Army command assumed that with the capture of the Pilckem heights the positions of the Allies in the remainder of the Ypres salient would become untenable and Ypres itself would thus fall into German hands.[52] However, there is considerable evidence that most of the principal figures involved in the operation did not expect very much more than a purely local success. To begin with, no major reserves were allocated for the operation; indeed, General Ilse initially turned down an offer of two regiments which the Naval Infantry Corps on the Channel coast was prepared to send down to Ypres for that purpose.[53] Perhaps even more indicative of the limited objectives pursued by the Germans are General von Hügel's instructions to his troops. On April 8, for instance, he notified his subordinates that the objective of the

[50] See Bauer, *Der grosse Krieg* (n. 17 above), p. 69; Haber, *Fünf Vorträge* (n. 30 above), p. 88; and an eyewitness account by Lt. Col. Count von Tattenbach, in Hanslian, *Der deutsche Gasangriff bei Ypern* (n. 1 above), p. 99.

[51] See RA, *Weltkrieg*, 7:64; Seesselberg (n. 23 above), p. 408; and personal diary, April 1–2, 1915, and subsequent undated entries, Hügel papers.

[52] See RA, *Weltkrieg*, 7:64, 8:39.

[53] See ibid., 8:38–39 and n. 1; and the testimony of the Naval Infantry Corps's (Marinekorps's) chief of staff, Col. von Hülsen, in Hanslian, *Der deutsche Gasangriff bei Ypern*, pp. 93–94. General Ilse's handling of the Ypres operation, including the belated and piecemeal use of the available Naval Infantry Corps units, subsequently caused some criticism in circles close to the kaiser, but no action was taken to remove him from his *Chef* position. See personal war diary, May 27, 1915, Nachlass Georg Alexander von Müller [hereafter Müller papers], BA-MA; and Col. Holland, A.O.K. 4, to Marchtaler, July 11, 1915, Nachlass Otto von Marchtaler, WHA.

impending operation was to seize the "ridge along the road Boezinge-Pilckem-Langemarck-Poelcappelle," following which all units were to "dig in immediately and establish mutually covering strong points."[54] Eight days later, Hügel cautioned his two division commanders that the effect of the cloud gas might prove insufficient to get the German infantry to the Pilckem heights without great losses; if so, the attack was to be halted and everyone was to dig in until the enemy's resistance had been softened up further by a bombardment with T-shells.[55]

On April 10, that is, shortly before the placement of chlorine cylinders in the Steenstraat-Poelcappelle sector had been completed, Falkenhayn summoned General Ilse to his headquarters and impressed upon him that the gas attack should be carried out as soon as possible, since the Twenty-sixth Reserve Corps and several other units in the Ypres region might soon be needed elsewhere. Faced with this pressure from the OHL, Fourth Army command ordered that the gas attack be launched on April 15, but a complete lack of wind on the morning of that day once again, as in the Gheluvelt sector before, made it necessary to cancel the operation.[56]

In view of the tense situation on the Eastern front, where the Austro-Hungarian ally was under mounting Russian pressure in the Carpathians, General von Falkenhayn had meanwhile arrived at a rather drastic change of plans. Whereas it had hitherto been intended to use Germany's newly created strategic reserves either in France or in Belgium, he now decided to transfer at least eight divisions to Galicia for a major strike against the Russians in the Gorlice-Tarnow area.[57] As a result of this shift of forces, which started on April 17, a new army—the Eleventh, with Mackensen in command and Colonel Hans von Seeckt as chief of staff—was formed on the Eastern front, while the German armies in the West were left with just enough strength to maintain their positions or, at most, to conduct local attacks here and there.[58]

Although the chances for a strategically significant exploitation of a successful gas attack in the Ypres area thus became even more

[54] "Korpsbefehl zur Wegnahme von Pilkem, Langemarck in Zusammenwirken mit dem XXIII. Reservekorps," April 8, 1915, Hügel papers.

[55] Order no. 4/16.4., to 51st and 52d Reserve-Divisionen and commander of the heavy artillery, April 16, 1915, ibid.

[56] See personal war diary, April 10, 1915, Tappen papers; and RA, *Weltkrieg*, 7:64.

[57] See RA, *Weltkrieg*, 7:301–23, 346–62; Karl-Heinz Janszen, *Der Kanzler und der General* (Göttingen, 1967), pp. 102 ff.; and Gerhard Ritter, *Staatskunst und Kriegshandwerk*, 4 vols. (Munich, 1954–68), 3:84–85. Cf. Gerard E. Silberstein, *The Troubled Alliance* (Lexington, Ky., 1970), pp. 282–83.

[58] See personal war diary, April 17, 1915, Tappen papers; Tappen to Reichsarchiv, March 19, 1927, ibid.; and RA, *Weltkrieg*, 8:34–35.

remote than they had been previously, both Falkenhayn and Tappen insisted that the gas fronts prepared by the Fourth Army be activated as soon as possible. According to Falkenhayn's memoirs, continued German activity along the Western front was necessary to screen the troop transfers to Galicia, and the Ypres operation was therefore quite useful.[59] Moreover, according to Tappen's testimony, it was felt that the hoped-for elimination of the Ypres salient was worthwhile in itself, in terms both of shortening the front and of seizing an area which had been fought over so "ardently" in the fall of 1914.[60]

On April 21, one day after a second attempt to activate the gas front in the Steenstraat-Poelcappelle sector had had to be canceled because of a lack of wind, Falkenhayn and Tappen personally called on Duke Albrecht at his headquarters in Thielt. Both visitors made it clear to the Duke that the often-postponed gas attacks in the Ypres region were to be launched as soon as a "halfway favorable opportunity" presented itself, and that the objectives of the whole enterprise should not be set too high.[61] Since weather conditions in the Steenstraat-Poelcappelle sector seemed to be improving, Fourth Army command thereupon scheduled the attack for the very next morning. As so often before, however, wind conditions early on April 22 proved clearly unsuitable, and the attack was eventually rescheduled for the late afternoon—despite serious reservations on the part of General von Kathen.[62]

After weeks of anxious waiting by the Germans, during which period Allied military authorities had received, but largely ignored, several specific warnings about the new German weapon,[63] the F batteries in the Steenstraat-Poelcappelle sector were finally activated about 5:00 P.M. local time (6:00 P.M. German time). Advancing

---

[59] Falkenhayn (n. 14 above), p. 72. General Ludendorff at Oberost, long since a severe critic of Falkenhayn's conduct of the war, promptly disagreed with that decision as well. See Ludendorff to Moltke, April 27, 1915, in Zechlin (n. 32 above), p. 339.

[60] See Tappen to Reichsarchiv, March 19, 1927, and July 20, 1930, Tappen papers.

[61] See personal war diary, April 21, 1915, ibid.; RA, *Weltkrieg*, 8:38; and Hanslian, *Der chemische Krieg*, 1:88.

[62] See RA, *Weltkrieg*, 8:39. According to Hanslian, *Der chemische Krieg*, 1:88, the hour for the attack was actually changed three times.

[63] For an up-to-date account, see Nicholson (n. 2 above), pp. 60–61. Perhaps the most valuable information was supplied by a soldier from Hügel's corps, August Jäger, who deserted on April 13–14 and was picked up by the French Eleventh Division. After his name was revealed in 1930 by the former commander of that division, General Ferry, an investigation was started in Germany, and Jäger eventually, in December 1932, received a ten-year prison term from the Leipzig Reichsgericht. See Hanslian, *Der deutsche Gasangriff bei Ypern*, p. 24, n. 30, and p. 80.

behind the drifting gas clouds, the German infantry made rather uneven progress during the following hours. While the thrust in the center, toward the Pilckem heights and the Yser Canal between Het Sas and Boesinghe, succeeded very well, the advance on either wing ran into considerable resistance. The village of Langemarck, where whole regiments of young German volunteers had been decimated in futile attacks the previous fall, was taken by the Fifty-first Reserve Division of Hügel's corps within an hour, but both in this area and during its subsequent advance toward Saint-Julien, the division was slowed down by flanking fire from Canadian troops in the adjacent sector and resistance from French units which had survived the gas attack with little or no harm. As a result, the Fifty-first Reserve Division did not catch up with its sister division on the right (the Fifty-second Reserve) until late in the evening, and the advance was subsequently halted.[64] Shortly before midnight, General von Hügel issued instructions that the corps artillery be brought forward immediately and simultaneously advised his infantry to prepare their newly won positions for the "most tenacious defense."[65] Farther to the west, in General von Kathen's sector, too, the advance by the Forty-fifth and Forty-sixth Reserve Divisions was halted or bogged down late in the evening following the capture of some bridgeheads on the western bank of the Yser Canal and of the fiercely defended village of Steenstraat.[66] The Allies thus gained precious time to recover from the initial shock and to rush their reserves into the area.[67]

The effectiveness of the cloud gas in opening a hole in the French lines and the ensuing rapid advances by some of Hügel's and Kathen's troops initially produced considerable excitement at German general headquarters. The Kaiser, when he heard of the success the next day, embraced Falkenhayn three times and promised Colonel Tappen a bottle of pink champagne. His enthusiasm would probably have been less pronounced had he known that no sig-

---

[64] See RA, *Weltkrieg*, 8:39–41; and Hügel papers, personal diary, April 22, 1915. Cf. the eyewitness accounts in Hanslian, *Der deutsche Gasangriff bei Ypern*, pp. 87 ff., and in *Das Ehrenbuch der Deutschen Pioniere*, ed. Paul Heinrici (Berlin, 1932), pp. 565 ff.

[65] "Korpsbefehl für den 23.4.15," issued at 11:50 P.M., April 22, 1915, Hügel papers.

[66] See RA, *Weltkrieg*, 8:40–41.

[67] See Ministère de la Guerre, *Les armées françaises* (n. 2 above), 2:700 ff.; Edmonds et al. (n. 4 above), 1:178 ff.; and Nicholson (n. 2 above), pp. 66 ff. On the first reactions at the headquarters of the French Army Group of the North, see Foch to Joffre, April 23, 1915, in Ministère de la Guerre, *Les armées françaises*, annex vol. II/2, no. 1422; and Weygand to his wife, April 26, 1915, in Jacques Weygand, *Weygand: Mon père* (Paris, 1970), p. 110.

nificant reserves were left in the Ypres area to exploit the initial tactical success, and that all further offensive thrusts would have to be improvised.[68]

The lack of systematic planning became evident already on April 23. It was only late in the morning that specific directives concerning the continuation of the offensive were issued by Fourth Army command. While Hügel's corps was instructed to push on southward toward Ypres, General von Kathen was given some reinforcements and told to advance "in the direction of" Poperinghe, a town west of Ypres which lay over ten kilometers behind the salient. Duke Albrecht's and General Ilse's apparent intention to send a major part of Kathen's corps farther toward the west immediately aroused the misgivings of the OHL, and a hasty reminder was sent to the Fourth Army that for the time being the operation should be aimed solely at "pinching off" the remainder of the Ypres salient.[69]

But by now even this more modest goal could no longer be attained without a severe struggle, for Allied efforts to seal off the holes in their lines had already progressed too far and Allied counterattacks were mounting in strength. Although the German line of attack was progressively broadened toward the south during the following days, the whole operation quickly turned into a typical battle of attrition. A small-scale discharge of chlorine cloud gas early on April 24 against Canadian-held positions near Saint-Julien pushed back but failed to crush the defenders (who had meanwhile been issued makeshift respirators),[70] and even though a series of further cloud gas discharges was staged in the early part of May, practically all further gains of ground by the Germans were achieved at an increasing cost to themselves. When the offensive in most parts of the salient finally ground to a halt in the second week of May, Ypres and its immediate environs were still in Allied hands and the German casualty rate had climbed to a total of over 35,000 men.[71]

Although the total losses of the British Empire troops and of the

---

[68] See the report by Maj. Gen. von Magirus of the Württemberg war ministry on "Meine Reise auf den Kriegsschauplatz 22.4.–1.5.1915," Nachlass Adolf von Magirus, WHA; personal war diary, April 23, 1915, Tappen papers; and personal war diary, April 23, 1915, Müller papers.

[69] See RA, *Weltkrieg*, 8:41–43; the report by Magirus cited in n. 68 above; and Order no. 5/23.4., April 23, 1915, 5 P.M., Hügel papers.

[70] I.e., cotton bandoliers which were to be wetted and tied over mouth and nose if a gas cloud approached. Other men saved themselves by applying a wet handkerchief to the face. See Nicholson (n. 2 above), pp. 71 ff.; and Macphail (n. 1 above), p. 299.

[71] See RA, *Weltkrieg*, 8:42–49. Cf. personal war diary, April 25–May 2, 1915, Tappen papers; personal diary, April 23–May 10, 1915, Hügel papers; and Deimling (n. 39 above), pp. 203–4.

French and Belgian units in the Ypres region were even higher, and although the Allies' long-standing plans and preparations for a great "Spring Offensive" in Artois were seriously disrupted by the German onslaught in the Flanders sector,[72] the "premature" disclosure of the cloud gas technique for such a "paltry prize" has often been interpreted as a major blunder on the part of the German high command.[73] It is now clear, however, that General von Falkenhayn and his advisers at the OHL "wasted" the new weapon on a local operation with limited goals not so much because they were "scientifically hidebound" and muddleheaded, but because they had justifiable doubts that a large-scale offensive based on prior cloud gas discharges could actually be prepared with the necessary degree of secrecy. While it was difficult enough to conceal the installation of thousands of bulky gas cylinders in the forward German trenches, the leading men at the OHL were even more concerned about the likely prospect that the masses of troops needed for any kind of major offensive might have to wait in their jump-off positions for weeks on end before suitable wind conditions for a cloud gas discharge materialized.[74] It was this specter of perpetual delays, and the attendant risk that the enemy would discover the buildup of forces against him, which induced Falkenhayn and his staff in mid-April to prepare the great German-Austrian strike against the Russians in the Gorlice-Tarnow area with conventional weapons only[75]—a decision which would be fully vindicated by the smashing success of that offensive early the next month.[76]

---

[72] See Cruttwell (n. 30 above), pp. 157–58; and Jean Perré, *Les mutations de la guerre moderne* (Paris, 1962), p. 155.

[73] See Liddell Hart (n. 4 above), pp. 178–79. Cf. Hanslian, *Der deutsche Gasangriff bei Ypern*, pp. 80–81; Brian Bond's summary of the case in *The New Cambridge Modern History*, 2d ed. (Cambridge, 1968), vol. 12, p. 181; and S. L. A. Marshall, *World War I* (New York, 1971), pp. 164–65.

[74] For a review of the deliberations at the OHL, see especially Tappen to Reichsarchiv, March 19, 1927, Tappen papers.

[75] See ibid.; and RA, *Weltkrieg*, 7:360–63, 367 ff.

[76] About five days before Mackensen's offensive started, the OHL actually changed its mind and dispatched a battalion of gas troops to the Gorlice area. However, both the men and their equipment arrived there much too late to serve any useful purpose. In mid-May, the battalion was therefore reassigned to the Ninth Army in central Poland, where, together with other units, it subsequently prepared a major gas front (with 12,000 cylinders) in the area northeast of Bolimow. That front was activated on May 31—exactly four months after the first T-shell attack had been staged against the Russians in the very same region. See Heber, "Gasangriffe . . . ," pp. 7–9, Tempelhoff papers; Hahn (n. 21 above), p. 119; RA, *Weltkrieg*, 8:133–35; and Hanslian, *Der chemische Krieg*, 1:17, 100. Both Erich Ludendorff, *Meine Kriegserinnerungen* (Berlin, 1919), pp. 109–10, and Hoffmann's *Aufzeichnungen* (n. 32 above), 2:107–8, list May 2 as the date of the first cloud gas attack by the Ninth Army, but this is obviously in error.

480 Ulrich Trumpener

As for the traditional commemoration of April 22, 1915, as the birthday of modern chemical warfare, that designation is obviously quite misleading. Attempts to break the resistance of enemy soldiers by chemical "irritants" had been made on both the Eastern and Western fronts long before that day. What happened at Ypres was thus not an abrupt departure from all existing norms and practices but rather the escalation of a combat technique which had been used before, albeit ineffectually. The "success" of the German gas attack at Ypres, it should be emphasized, was only in part attributable to the fact that chlorine gas was more harmful in its effect on the human organism than the irritant vapors previously tried by Germans and French alike. Far more important was the quantitative dimension of the operation, that is, the enormous volume of gas that was effectively diffused on that day. In fact, it was above all the high concentration of gas over a wide area (something which the French had never tried and the Germans had never achieved before) which made the attack of April 22 militarily "effective"—in terms both of incapacitating a large number of enemy soldiers and of killing some of them for good measure.[77] In the course of the next three years, Germans and Allies alike were to introduce ever more toxic chemical agents on the battlefield and to use them on a truly gigantic scale; but thanks to the rapid development and continuous improvement of face masks and other protective devices, only a few gas attacks of this later period would have quite the same impact as the one that opened the "Second Battle of Ypres."[78]

[77] While the German chemical warfare experts were well aware that chlorine gas could be made even more "effective" by mixing it with phosgene, the use of that highly toxic pulmonary irritant was initially deemed too provocative, and the Ypres cloud gas discharges on April 22 and 24 were therefore staged with chlorine only. This restraint, however, was soon abandoned. In the first cylinder attack on the Russian front, on May 31, a phosgene "supplement" (*Zusatz*) of "about 5 percent" was used along with the chlorine, and the death rate in the gassed Russian trenches was accordingly much higher. See Heber, "Gasangriffe . . . ," pp. 2-9, Tempelhoff papers; Hanslian, *Der deutsche Gasangriff bei Ypern*, p. 70; idem, *Der chemische Krieg*, 1:100; and RA, *Weltkrieg*, 8:135, n. 1.

[78] For an introduction to the extensive monographic literature on these subjects, see especially Hanslian, *Der chemische Krieg*. Useful statistical assessments of the gas casualties on both sides may be found in Harry L. Gilchrist, *A Comparative Study of World War Casualties from Gas and Other Weapons* (Washington, D.C., 1928); and in the *Handbuch der neuzeitlichen Wehrwissenschaften*, ed. Hermann Franke, 3 vols. (Berlin, 1936-39), 1:104.

Part IV
Other Fronts

[21]

FRANCE, AFRICA, AND THE FIRST WORLD WAR

BY C. M. ANDREW AND A. S. KANYA-FORSTNER

BY 1914 France possessed the largest Empire in African history. Yet that Empire was of only trivial interest to both French people and their governments. As the diminutive colonialist movement complained: 'l'éducation coloniale des Français demeure entièrement à faire'.[1] Though few Frenchmen suspected it in August 1914, however, World War I was to mark a turning point in their relations with Africa in four ways. The War brought with it the final phase of French colonial expansion; it led to the recruitment of French Africa's first great conscript army; it launched the first concerted campaign for the *mise en valeur* of the Empire; and, at least at the moment of victory, it seemed to have begun 'l'éducation coloniale des Français'.

I

The great territorial question raised in Africa by the war was the disposal of the German Empire. British war aims in German Africa were discussed by both the cabinet and several cabinet committees. In France the cabinet seems never to have discussed African war aims at all.[2] The official mind of French imperialism, non-existent at the cabinet level, was weak and fragmented even at the ministerial level. The colonial ministry did not administer all French Africa. Algeria came under the ministry of the interior; the Moroccan and Tunisian protectorates were the responsibility of the quai d'Orsay. Until almost the end of the war, no government department developed war aims for Africa as a whole. For most of the war the foreign ministry's African war aims were limited to strengthening the French hold on Morocco; but in its order of priorities North Africa came clearly behind the Middle East and far behind the Rhine. Only for the colonial ministry was Africa a major priority. The colonial ministry, however, still remained—along with the ministry of public works—'la

---

[1] C. M. Andrew and A. S. Kanya-Forstner, 'The French "Colonial Party": Its Composition, Aims and Influence, 1885–1914', *Historical Journal*, XIV (1971), 99–128; C. M. Andrew, 'The French Colonialist Movement during the Third Republic: The Unofficial Mind of Imperialism', *Transactions of the Royal Historical Society*, 5th series, XXVI (1976). C. M. Andrew, P. Grupp, and A. S. Kanya-Forstner, 'Le mouvement colonial français et ses principales personnalités, 1890–1914', *Revue Française d'Histoire d'Outre-Mer*, LXII (1975).

[2] For a more detailed analysis of France's African war aims see: C. M. Andrew and A. S. Kanya-Forstner, 'The French Colonial Party and French Colonial War Aims, 1914–1918', *Historical Journal*, XVII (1974), 79–106; idem, 'France and the Repartition of Africa, 1914–1922', forthcoming in *Dalhousie Review*.

cendrillon des ministères', at the bottom of the ministerial pecking order. By the outbreak of war the ministry, with its fiercely independent yet overlapping departments (*services*), staffed in general by *fonctionnaires* of only modest abilities, had become a byword for confusion. The report of the Chamber of Deputies' budget commission in 1917 summed up many earlier criticisms of the ministry:

> Chaque service, *constituée comme une forteresse*, traite, pour les colonies qu'il administre, ses affaires à un point de vue particulier. Il advient ainsi le plus souvent ... que trois ou quatre services s'occupent simultanément, *et en leur donnant parfois des solutions différentes*, du règlement d'une question de principe qui appellerait une direction unique.[3]

Not until October 1917 did the colonial ministry take steps to remedy the chaos of its post-war planning by establishing a *commission de documentation coloniale*, in order to collate 'tous les documents relatifs aux problèmes politiques coloniaux d'après-guerre'.

The unofficial mind of French imperialism was far quicker off the mark than the official mind. Unlike the government, the colonialists lost no time in debating their African war aims. Immediately after the outbreak of war, the *Comité de l'Afrique Française* turned its attention to the 'vastes réorganisations ... africaines qui en résulteront'. During 1916 representatives of the main colonialist societies met at the *Société de Géographie* in a first attempt to agree on the 'vastes réorganisations' which were needed. The African reorganization proposed by Auguste Terrier, secretary-general of the *Comité de l'Afrique Française*, was vast indeed. The peace settlement, in Terrier's view, would provide an opportunity for acquiring territory not merely from a defeated Germany but also, by negotiation and barter, from allies and neutrals. His aim was to unify French West Africa by acquiring all foreign enclaves between Senegal and Dahomey. The report prepared for the colonial ministry in November 1917 by Albert Duchêne of the *commission de documentation*, though slightly less unrealistic in its expectations, had the same general aim. While less hopeful than Terrier that Britain could be persuaded to part with the Gold Coast, Duchêne was hopeful of acquiring the Gambia and Sierra Leone as well as Portuguese and Spanish possessions, and at least informal control of Liberia.

The elaboration of France's African war aims was thus the work not of the cabinet nor even of the 'official mind' of the colonial ministry, but of two overlapping groups: the leaders of the colonialist movement and a handful of African enthusiasts in the colonial and foreign ministries (almost all linked, like Duchêne, with the colonialist movement). On the two occasions during World War I when the French government was forced to acquire some African war aims, it was these two groups which jointly supplied them.

[3] *Journal Officiel, Documents Parlementaires* (*Chambre des Députés*), 1917, no. 3476 (emphasis shown as in the original).

The first occasion arose during the winter of 1915–16 when the British attempt to provoke an Arab rising against the Turks and the allied conquest of German West Africa forced the French to negotiate with Britain provisional partitions of both the Middle East and the Cameroons. On the French side the same man, François Georges-Picot, conducted both sets of negotiations. Picot was both a diplomat and a member of a famous colonial dynasty which had played a prominent part in the *Comité de l'Afrique Française* and its Asian counterpart, the *Comité de l'Asie Française*. The French cabinet took no part in Picot's negotiations. On the Middle East Picot was told to draft his own instructions which were then signed without amendment by Briand, the prime minister. Not till Sykes and Picot had initialled their celebrated accord did Briand outline its terms to the Cabinet. And he did so then with what the President rightly described as 'une spirituelle imprécision'. During the negotiations which followed for a provisional partition of the Cameroons Picot stressed the demands not of the cabinet but of the colonialists. 'The French Colonial Party', repeated the French ambassador, 'are very excited'. In the event, the final agreement, which gave nine-tenths of the Cameroons to France, exceeded the expectations of both the colonialists and the colonial minister.

During 1918 the French government was obliged to furnish itself with a more general set of African war aims as part of French preparations for the peace conference. In February 1918 the cabinet simply passed the colonial buck to the new and inexperienced colonial minister, Henri Simon, whom it made president of a *Commission d'étude des questions coloniales posées par la guerre*. Simon in turn then passed the buck to the commission whose meetings he modestly declined to attend on the grounds that its competence in the matter of war aims greatly exceeded his own. In Simon's absence the commission was dominated by the colonialists, aided and abetted by the more energetic officials of the colonial ministry. Its war aims, once decided, became the war aims of the French government.

The ultimate ambition of the colonial war aims commission was the same as that of the *Comité de l'Afrique Française*: 'faire régner la paix française sur la totalité de l'ouest africain'. But it recognized that the American entry into the war and President Wilson's well-advertised aversion to the old diplomacy of imperialism would make impossible the vast repartition of the African continent at the peace conference for which colonialists had earlier hoped. In West Africa the peace conference simply made France and Britain mandatories of those parts of the German Empire they had already partitioned between themselves (though France's share was slightly enlarged).[4] But the post-war negotiations which the colonialists had hoped would remove at least some of the foreign 'enclaves' in French

---

[4] The smaller of Germany's two West African colonies, Togo (one-ninth the size of the Cameroons) had been provisionally partitioned on the spot by the British and French commanders after its conquest in the first month of the War. At the Peace Conference France's share was enlarged to include the port of Lomé and all the railway lines.

West Africa never materialized. Attempts to extend French control of Morocco were also unsuccessful. Protracted negotiations over Tangier during the 1920s ended not, as the colonialists and the foreign ministry had wanted, in a French Tangier, but in confirmation of its international status.

II

Before August 1914 no government of the Third Republic had given serious thought to the potential contribution of French Africa, in either men or raw materials, to a war in Europe. And yet the idea of an African army was an old one. 'Ce que l'Afrique peut produire de plus utile à la France', Napoleon III had declared, 'ce sont des soldats'. Algerian troops had been used in the Crimean War. The *tirailleurs sénégalais*, whose first battalion was founded in 1857, distinguished themselves in the Franco-Prussian War. But successive republican governments failed to build on the foundations left by the Second Empire. Even during the decade before the World War I the vigorous campaigns led by Adolphe Messimy and Charles Mangin in favour of, respectively, an Algerian army of 100,000 men and an even larger *force noire* from tropical Africa met with indifferent success.[5] In August 1914 there were only 30,000 *tirailleurs sénégalais* and 35,000 Algerians under arms.[6]

The enormous early losses on the Western Front led to the first mass recruitment in French Africa. By the time Clemenceau became prime minister in November 1917, French Africa had provided a further 270,000 men, with the largest contingents coming from A.O.F. (90,000) and Algeria (85,000).[7] The colonial troops most valued by the high command were the Moroccans. According to a racist army proverb, 'the Algerian is a man, the Tunisian a woman, the Moroccan a warrior'. The most decorated unit in the French army was a Moroccan regiment.[8] But because the 'pacification' of Morocco was still incomplete, only 23,000 Moroccan troops had been sent to Europe by November 1917.[9] Though generally satisfied also with the quality of Algerian recruits, most of the high command had grave doubts about the suitability of the *force noire* for the Western Front. Black troops, used at Gallipoli and to garrison the Empire during 1915,

[5] C.-R. Ageron, *Les Algériens musulmans et la France, 1871–1919* (Paris, 1968), II, ch. 38. M. Michel, 'Un mythe: la "Force Noire" avant 1914', *Relations Internationales*, I (1974), 83–90.

[6] M. Michel, 'Le recrutement des tirailleurs en A.O.F. pendant la première Guerre mondiale. Essai de bilan statistique', *Revue Française d'Histoire d'Outre-Mer*, LX (1973), 645. Ageron, *Les Algériens musulmans*, II, 1165.

[7] 'Recrutement indigène fourni à la Métropole du début des hostilités au 15 novembre 1917', ANSOM (Archives Nationales, Section Outre-Mer), Affaires Politiques 533 (3); cited by M. Michel, 'La genèse du recrutement de 1918 en Afrique noire française', *Revue Française d'Histoire d'Outre-Mer*, LVIII (1971), 437–8.

[8] S. C. Davis, *The French War Machine* (London, 1937), ch. 7. A. Guignard, 'Les troupes noires pendant la guerre', *Revue des Deux Mondes*, 15 June 1919, 849–79.

[9] See note 7.

FRANCE, AFRICA, AND THE FIRST WORLD WAR 15

did not appear in the trenches in large numbers until 1916. Even their valour at Verdun did not overcome the doubts of the high command. Instead, those doubts were confirmed by the inability of the black battalions to withstand winter on the Western Front, and by their poor performance (due to inadequate training and leadership) in the disastrous Nivelle offensive of April 1917. Even the manpower crisis at the end of 1917 did not persuade the general staff of the need for more black troops.[10] The colonial administrations themselves, disturbed by the revolts provoked by conscription in both West Africa and Algeria, were either lukewarm or actively hostile to further recruitment. After the Batna rebellion in Algeria at the end of 1916, the pace of recruitment slackened during 1917.[11] In A.O.F. Van Vollenhoven, the governor-general, declared that a further call-up, however small, could not fail to produce 'une révolte générale': 'La colonie est arrivée à la limite de ce qu'il lui est possible de faire: peut-être même cette limite a-t-elle été dépassée'.[12]

Ironically, the man responsible for a further mass recruitment in French Africa, Clemenceau, was, by his own reckoning, 'le moins colonialiste de tous les Français'. Though Clemenceau was an anti-colonialist, his decision owed much to the influence of the colonialists. Soon after he became prime minister in November 1917 he was persuaded by Mangin, the leading advocate of the *force noire*, that many more troops could be levied in tropical Africa.[13] And he was persuaded by Jonnart (president of the *Comité de l'Afrique Française*) and Flandin (president of the *Réunion des Etudes Algériennes*) that, if reforms were promised, the same was possible in Algeria.[14] Clemenceau's decision to follow their advice was, nonetheless, an act of desperation rather than of faith in the Empire. In order to hold out until the Americans arrived in force, France, in his view, needed more troops from every possible source, even at the cost of provoking a mass revolt in her African Empire:

Les insurrections? Je ne m'en soucie pas pour le moment. Mieux vaut courir des risques en Afrique que sur le front. Ce que nous devons éviter par-dessus tout, c'est une défaite sur le Rhin.[15]

In the event, the colonial call-up of 1918 proceeded without serious difficulty. At least 72,000 men were recruited in A.O.F. and A.E.F., and

[10] Michel, 'La genèse du recrutement de 1918'. Marc Michel's thesis, 'L'A.O.F. et la Grande Guerre: contributions et réactions', now nearing completion, will represent a major contribution to West African history. It will include a detailed analysis of A.O.F.'s military and economic involvement in the War, as well as the African and European consequences of that involvement. On French Guinea see also the article in this issue by R. Johnson and A. Summers.
[11] Ageron, *Les Algériens musulmans*, II, 1162–3.
[12] Van Vollenhoven to colonial ministry, 25 Sept. 1917, ANSOM, Affaires Politiques 533 (2).
[13] Michel, 'La genèse du recrutement de 1918', 436–8.
[14] See the correspondence between Jonnart and Flandin for the period Nov. 1917 to Jan. 1918. in the Flandin MSS (uncatalogued) at the Archives Nationales.
[15] Ageron, *Les Algériens musulmans*, II, 1163.

more than 50,000 in Algeria.[16] In all, French Africa sent 450,000 soldiers to Europe during the War.[17] Mangin claimed later that their numbers could have been 'easily trebled or quadrupled' if African recruitment had been planned before the War began.[18]

Africa also provided 135,000 wartime workers (most from the Maghreb) for French factories.[19] Even during the manpower crisis of 1918 they were received with something less than enthusiasm. In January 1918 the ministry of labour asked the colonial ministry (whose responsibilities by now included North African recruitment) to ensure that the French labour force was insufficient before seeking further workers from the Empire.[20] Some at least of the colonial ministry officials shared the apprehensions of the ministry of labour. A report in January 1918 by Fauchère, *inspecteur d'agriculture coloniale*, on the colonial labour force in French factories concluded: 'Il faut trois, quatre indigènes pour fournir le travail d'un Européen'. Further colonial workers would, in Fauchère's view, be badly received by the French working class. They would be accused of keeping down wages. And they would provoke sexual jealousy: 'Que l'indigène fréquente nos ouvrières et le sentiment ou plutôt l'instinct national n'en sera-t-il pas offensé?' Furthermore, besides depriving the Empire of a labour force it could ill spare during the war, the immigrant workers would cause trouble on their return:

Les conditions de la vie en France permettront à l'indigène de jouir peu à peu d'une familiarité qui n'est pas d'usage aux colonies entre blancs et jaunes ou noirs. Ayant noté nos faiblesses, lorsqu'il sera de retour dans son pays, il contribuera considérablement par ses racontars à nuire à notre prestige.[21]

France's first mass recruitment of African soldiers and workers had inevitable political consequences. From the first the *Jeunes Algériens* and *Jeunes Sénégalais* supported conscription partly as a means of winning political concessions. Most *colons* opposed African conscription, again partly for fear of its political consequences. In December 1914 Lutaud, governor-general of Algeria, exempted from the *indigénat* (the system of summary native jurisdiction), all army volunteers, their fathers, and migrant workers who spent more than a year in France.[22] A series of parliamentary bills (none translated into law), tabled in a flush of patriotic enthusiasm during the first six months of 1915, declared the right of all native soldiers to citizenship: 'Ils se sont élevés à la dignité supérieure de sauveurs de

---

[16] Michel, 'La genèse du recrutement de 1918', 443. Ageron, *Les Algériens musulmans*, II, 1165.
[17] The official statistics compiled by the French general staff are to be found in: P. Varet, *Du concours apporté à la France par ses colonies et pays de protectorat au cours de la guerre de 1914* (Paris, 1927), 40.
[18] *Dépêche Coloniale*, 16 July 1920.   [19] Varet, *Du concours*, 45.
[20] Ministry of labour to colonial ministry, 21 Jan. 1918, ANSOM, Affaires Politiques, 19.
[21] Fauchère, 'Rapport sur l'utilisation de la main-d'oeuvre coloniale dans l'industrie métropolitaine', 12 Jan. 1918, ANSOM, Affaires Politiques, 19.
[22] Ageron, *Les Algériens musulmans*, II, 1141.

FRANCE, AFRICA, AND THE FIRST WORLD WAR 17

la patrie. Nous devons à nous mêmes de les élever à la dignité de citoyen'.[23] The extension of conscription to the 'Four Communes' of Senegal in 1915 was followed by formal recognition of the *originaires*' French citizenship. The West African recruiting drive of 1918 was accompanied by the appointment (despite the opposition of commercial interests and most of the local administration) of the black deputy, Blaise Diagne, as *commissaire de la République* to lead a propaganda mission promising 'un ensemble de réformes'.[24] The Algerian recruitment of 1918 was similarly accompanied by Jonnart's appointment as governor-general, and by the promise of a reform of the *indigénat* which eventually materialized, despite violent opposition from the *colons*, as the Jonnart law of 1919.[25] With the gift of hindsight both the hopes and fears aroused by the reforms in North and West Africa appear greatly exaggerated. In the four years after the Jonnart law only 256 Algerians gained French citizenship.[26]

III

Just as World War I emphasized the military potential of French Africa, so, though in a lesser degree, it also drew attention to its economic potential. Before 1914 remarkably little use had been made of the Empire's resources. Whereas India was Britain's largest export market and the mainstay of her balance of payments, the French Empire actually contributed proportionately less to the French economy before World War I than before the French Revolution. In 1787 30 per cent of French foreign trade was with the French West Indies. During the years 1909–13 the whole of France's Empire, despite its enormous size, accounted for only 10 per cent of her foreign trade. Joseph Chailley-Bert, secretary-general of the *Union Coloniale*, the main business wing of the colonialist movement, described colonial production at the outbreak of war as 'véritablement misérable pour un Empire colonial si vaste et pour un métropole si riche'.[27] In 1914 only 9 per cent of France's foreign investment was in the Empire, as compared with 25 per cent in Russia alone. As du Vivier de Streel, wartime

[23] *Journal Officiel, Documents Parlementaires, (Chambre des Députés)*, 1915, no. 935. Cf. Ageron, *Les Algériens musulmans*, II, 1191.

[24] G. Wesley Johnson Jr., *The Emergence of Black Politics in Senegal: The Struggle for Power in the Four Communes, 1900–1920* (Stanford, 1971), ch. 10. M. Michel, 'Citoyenneté et service militaire dans les quatre Communes du Sénégal au cours de la Première Guerre mondiale', in *Perspectives nouvelles sur le passé de l'Afrique noire et de Madagascar. Mélanges offerts à Hubert Deschamps* (Paris, 1976); idem., 'La genèse du recrutement de 1918'.

[25] Jonnart had persuaded Clemenceau that a new recruitment would necessitate 'la mise en pratique d'une politique indigène d'une grande bienveillance'; Jonnart to Clemenceau (copy), 27 Dec. 1917, Archives Nationales, Flandin MSS (uncatalogued). For details of the reforms, see Ageron, *Les Algériens musulmans*, II, ch. 43, and V. Confer, *France and Algeria: The Problem of Civil and Political Reform, 1870–1920* (Syracuse, 1966), ch. 7.   [26] Ageron, *Les Algériens musulmans*, II, 1223.

[27] C. M. Andrew and A. S. Kanya-Forstner, 'French Business and the French Colonialists', *Historical Journal*, XIX (1976), 982–6. C. Régismanset and E. du Vivier de Streel (eds.), *Conférence Coloniale instituée par M. Maginot, ministre des colonies* (Paris, 1917), 169.

leader of the colonialist campaign for the *mise en valeur* of the Empire, complained:

> Nos capitalistes ont toujours été très méfiants à l'égard des entreprises coloniales, en raison de leur ignorance d'une part, et par suite aussi des conseils peu encourageants qui leur ont été donnés par les établissements financiers dont ils suivaient les inspirations, et qui préféraient les entraîner vers des placements étrangers de plus grande envergure.[28]

The greater part of France's colonial trade was conducted with her oldest colonies. Algeria was her main colonial trading partner. By contrast, the huge tropical Empire acquired during the late nineteenth-century scramble for Africa remained remarkably neglected. The French Congo attracted only a small fraction of the investment which had poured into the Congo of Leopold II.[29] Even in West Africa, despite the long history of French commerce with Senegal (which continued to account for well over half the foreign trade of A.O.F.), French businessmen were notoriously less enterprising than their British and German rivals. Production of cocoa, coffee, and tropical fruits had scarcely begun in A.O.F. In 1913 cocoa production in the Gold Coast already amounted to 51,000 metric tons; in the neighbouring Ivory Coast it was only 47 tons. After the outbreak of war British merchants were far quicker to take over the German share of African commerce even in French Africa. Owing to the superiority of the British merchant navy, by 1916 Britain had actually replaced France as the main supplier of A.O.F.[30]

Before the outbreak of war the French government had not even considered the possibility of an economic contribution by the Empire to the war effort. In keeping with its incompetent organization the colonial ministry as yet possessed no department concerned with the economic development of the Empire. After the outbreak of war conscription, the occupation of the northern departments, and the shortage of fertilizers and machinery quickly ended France's agricultural self-sufficiency. But the government was slow to seek help from the colonies. An unwieldy 56 man *Commission consultative coloniale* set up in September 1914 to consider trade with the Empire ground to a halt within a year. In November 1915 the colonial ministry at last established a *Service d'utilisation des produits coloniaux pour la défense nationale*, to coordinate the supply of colonial products. In December 1916 colonial governors were asked to encourage production of all foodstuffs which could be shipped to France.[31]

---

[28] E. Du Vivier de Streel, 'Une grave question de l'après-guerre', *Revue de Paris*, 1 Feb. 1916, 3.

[29] C. Coquéry-Vidrovitch, *Le Congo au temps des compagnies concessionnaires, 1890–1930* (Paris, 1972), 15.

[30] See chapters 7 and 8 of the forthcoming thesis by Marc Michel referred to above (note 10).

[31] Varet, *Du concours*, 9–13. D. Heisser, 'The Impact of the Great War on French Imperialism, 1914–1924', unpublished dissertation (University of North Carolina, 1972), 14 ff., 121 ff.

FRANCE, AFRICA, AND THE FIRST WORLD WAR 19

No more, in the view of the *Service d'utilisation des produits coloniaux*, could be done.³²

Many colonialists disagreed. By 1917, with a wheat harvest less than half the pre-war level and domestic sugar production even harder hit, France was faced with a crisis of food supply. That crisis gave added weight to the colonialist campaign for the *mise en valeur* of the Empire. In April du Vivier de Streel wrote to the colonial ministry:

J'estime qu'en obtenant le concours de tous nos colons pour créer les exploitations nécessaires et si les Administrations locales interviennent pour exiger des populations indigènes l'activité laborieuse qu'elles ne donnent pas toujours spontanément, on peut arriver en un an à intensifier dans des proportions extraordinaires notre production coloniale.³³

Maginot, the new and inexperienced colonial minister, was seduced by the colonialist campaign. In June 1917 he summoned a *Conférence Coloniale* attended by 250 delegates representing the colonialist movement, the colonial administration, and business interests, with du Vivier de Streel and an official of the colonial ministry as joint secretaries-general. Their task, Maginot told them, was to find means not merely to overcome the present crisis of food supply but also to draw from the Empire vast quantities of raw materials to ensure post-war France 'une puissante renaissance économique': 'Pour tirer de notre admirable empire colonial le parti que nous devrions normalement en tirer, il nous reste à faire dix fois, vingt fois plus que nous avons fait jusqu'à présent'.³⁴ After two months' discussions, Maginot set up a *commission executive* in August 1917 to act as liaison between the colonial administration and the colonial movement and work for 'la réalisation des voeux émis par la Conférence coloniale'. In May 1918 the *Union Coloniale* organized a *Congrès d'Agriculture Coloniale* with much the same kind of membership as the conference of the previous year. This conference, too, gave birth to an action committee of colonialists and colonial officials to implement its resolutions.³⁵

As Lyautey observed in January 1918, the campaign for the *mise en valeur* of the Empire was by now in conflict with the attempt to recruit more troops:

La France demande au Maroc de lui fournir des soldats, des ouvriers et des céréales. Il y a antagonisme entre ces diverses demandes dont les deux premières absorbent presque toutes nos possibilités et ne laissent à la main-d'oeuvre agricole que le déchet.³⁶

---

³² Rheinhart, 'Note pour M. le chef du service du secrétariat et du contresigne', 15 May 1917, ANSOM, Affaires Politiques 2613 (2).
³³ Du Vivier de Streel to Maginot, 15 Apr. 1917, ANSOM, Affaires Politiques 2613 (2).
³⁴ Régismanset and du Vivier de Streel (eds.), *Conférence Coloniale*, 1–7.
³⁵ Heisser, 'French Imperialism', 130–2, 180–7.
³⁶ Lyautey, 'Rapport mensuel', Jan. 1918, ANSOM, Affaires Politiques 899 bis (1). A similar point was made during 1917 in the monthly reports from Algeria and—with particular force—in dispatches from A.O.F.

There was thus a conflict of priorities within the colonialist movement between those for whom the most urgent necessity was more soldiers and those whose main aim was the *mise en valeur*. For the *Union Coloniale* and the business wing of the colonialist movement, as for most of the colonial administration, the overriding need to intensify colonial production made it vital to preserve what remained of the colonial labour force. As one of the reports to the *Congrès d'Agriculture Coloniale* concluded: 'on aboutit à un dilemme simple et précis, ou bien renoncer à mettre en valeur nos colonies, ou bien conserver intégralement la faible main-d'oeuvre dont elles disposent'.[37]

The wartime achievements of the campaign for the *mise en valeur* of the Empire were, however, slight. By 1918 the French merchant navy had lost almost half its pre-war tonnage. Even where colonies were able to increase wartime production, the ships were not available to bring it to Europe. In A.O.F. the administration was left with the problem of disposing at the end of the War of substantial stocks of foodstuffs it had been unable to ship to France.[38] Even in Morocco, André Fribourg, secretary of the *groupe colonial* in the post-war Chamber of Deputies, complained of 'des milliers de sacs de blé pourrissant sur les terres pleines de Safi tandis qu'on manquait de pain en France, à trois jours de mer de là'.[39] In the short term World War I produced no major shift in the pattern of French trade with her African Empire. Indeed, partly because of the continuing shipping problem, the Empire was marginally less important as a supplier of major foodstuffs in 1920 than in 1913.[40] The real importance of the wartime campaign for the *mise en valeur* of the Empire was not its contribution to the war effort but the stimulus it provided for post-war investment.

IV

In the aftermath of victory it was possible to believe that the War had transformed popular attitudes to Empire, and above all to French Africa. As Chailley-Bert told the *Conférence Coloniale* in 1917: 'Cette guerre a enseigné à la France qu'elle a des colonies. Elle l'ignorait complètement.'[41] The lesson had been begun by the colonial troops who had helped to bring victory on the Western Front. Bitter German complaints against the post-war occupation of the Rhineland by black soldiers made these soldiers more popular still. But an even more important reason for the Empire's newfound popularity was its potential contribution to post-war recovery.

[37] Fauchère, 'Rapport sur l'utilisation de la main-d'oeuvre coloniale dans l'industrie métropolitaine', 12 Jan. 1918, ANSOM, Affaires Politiques 19.
[38] See chapters 13 and 18 of the forthcoming thesis by Marc Michel.
[39] *Dépêche Coloniale*, 25 Feb. 1920.
[40] C. Fidel, 'La part des colonies dans nos importations de matières premières', *Bulletin de Renseignements Coloniaux*, no. 474, Jan. 1923.
[41] Régismanset and du Vivier de Streel (eds.), *Conférence Coloniale*, 159.

Once victory had ended wartime demands on the Empire's manpower, the whole colonialist movement was able to unite in a campaign for the *mise en valeur* of the Empire. The colonies, so the colonialists claimed, would free France from dependence on foreign imports and provide an inexhaustible reservoir of raw materials to supply her industries. Those arguments persuaded one third of the deputies elected in 1919 to join the parliamentary *groupe colonial* which thus became the largest group in the Chamber of Deputies. When Albert Sarraut, the leader of the *groupe colonial*, became minister of colonies in January 1920 (a post he was to retain in successive cabinets until the 1924 elections), the colonialist programme seemed about to become government policy. In April 1921, after long preparation, the 'Sarraut plan' for the *mise en valeur* of the Empire was finally tabled as a parliamentary bill. The plan suffered, however, from one simple and insuperable defect. Its cost was (probably optimistically) estimated by Sarraut at four billion francs, and the bill came before parliament at a time of financial crisis.[42]

Many of the deputies who had joined the *groupe colonial* had only the vaguest idea of the colonial resources they were so anxious to exploit. For most deputies, as for most Frenchmen, enthusiasm for the *mise en valeur* of an Empire of which they knew little was, like reparations, a way of taking refuge from the appalling economic realities of post-war France. And when the limitless resources of the Empire proved even harder to obtain than reparations, the Empire quickly lost its newfound popularity. As soon as the rhetoric of the *mise en valeur* was translated into a programme costing billions of francs, the enthusiasm of taxpayers and their parliamentary representatives disappeared. The Sarraut plan, introduced amid fanfares in April 1921, was then sidetracked by a parliamentary committee which did not report until the end of 1923. The report had still not been debated when parliament was dissolved in May 1924.[43] The first comprehensive study of the Empire's contribution to the war effort, published in 1927, gloomily concluded that the imperial enthusiasm generated by the war had almost disappeared: 'Le "Français moyen" s'imagine volontiers que les colonies servent uniquement à faire vivre des fonctionnaires et "coûtent cher" au budget de la métropole.'[44]

The apparent return to pre-war apathy, however, concealed at least three significant changes in attitude. The most easily discernible, despite the demise of the Sarraut plan, was among French investors. The loss of half France's foreign investment during the war (including, notably, all her Russian loans), the rapid decline of the franc in foreign exchanges, the various post-war restrictions on investment outside French territory, all combined to make colonial investment more attractive than in 1914. At the end of 1920 the colonial ministry reported:

[42] C. M. Andrew and A. S. Kanya-Forstner, 'The *Groupe Colonial* in the French Chamber of Deputies, 1892–1932', *Historical Journal*, XVII (1974), 842–5.
[43] Ibid. See also: Heisser, 'French Imperialism', ch. 6.
[44] Varet, *Du concours*, 5.

un afflux récent de capitaux nouveaux porté vers les colonies et la création presque quotidienne d'un grand nombre d'entreprises ou de sociétés qui se proposent l'exploitation, la mise en valeur et l'apport sur le marché français des ressources coloniales.[45]

The Empire's share of French foreign investment grew from 9 per cent in 1914 to 45 per cent in 1940, with the main movement of private capital coming in the 1920s. Of France's colonial investment in 1940, about 60 per cent was in North Africa and 14 per cent in tropical Africa. Trade with the Empire grew more slowly. But with the Depression its relative importance increased dramatically and Algeria, with only seven million inhabitants (most of them impoverished), became France's main trading partner.[46]

Secondly, colonialist propaganda achieved a degree of success, if not among French adults, then at least among French schoolchildren. By ministerial regulations of 1923 and 1925 the history and geography of the Empire became for the first time a compulsory part of the school curriculum. School textbooks began to portray France as 'l'héritière de Rome', reviving the Empire of the Romans on both shores of the Mediterranean, though now with an African hinterland stretching southwards to the Congo.[47] Many later supporters of 'Algérie française' first learned the myth that 'the Mediterranean runs through France as the Seine runs through Paris' in the schoolroom. The *Ligue Maritime et Coloniale*, most of whose members came from the schools, grew from modest beginnings to claim a membership of half a million in 1925 and 700,000 for most of the 1930s.[48]

Finally, World War I left behind it an imperial myth which the approach of World War II was to revive. Faced in 1939 with the enormous demographic and economic superiority of Greater Germany, the colonialists argued once again that the resources of the Empire would make good the weakness of the metropolis. And once again, though dormant for most of the years between the wars, the imperial myth struck a popular chord. The wartime governments of Daladier and Reynaud eagerly seized on the colonialist slogan, 'La France de 110 millions d'habitants fait face à l'Allemagne'. Georges Mandel, once an anti-colonialist, now minister of colonies, boasted that 'notre Empire pourra lever 2 millions de soldats et 500,000 travailleurs'.[49] Imperial France would conquer continental Germany. That myth was brutally destroyed in the six-week blitzkrieg of 1940.

---

[45] Untitled memo [late 1920], ANSOM, Affaires Politiques 2613 (1).

[46] J. Marseille, 'L'investissement français dans l'Empire colonial: l'enquête du gouvernement de Vichy (1943)', *Revue Historique*, CCLII (1974), 409–32. Andrew and Kanya-Forstner, 'French Business', 986–7.

[47] M. Semidei, 'De l'Empire à la décolonisation à travers les manuels scolaires français', *Revue Française de Science Politique*, XVI (1966), 56–86.

[48] Membership figures were published intermittently in the *Ligue*'s official bulletin, *Mer et Colonies*.

[49] *France Outre-Mer*, 29 Sept. 1939.

FRANCE, AFRICA, AND THE FIRST WORLD WAR

SUMMARY

World War I marked the final phase of French colonial expansion. France's African war aims were determined not by the cabinet but by the leaders of the colonialist movement and by a handful of African enthusiasts in the colonial and foreign ministries. Most of these men harboured the unrealistic aim of acquiring not merely German territory but also other foreign 'enclaves' in A.O.F. At the peace conference, however, France's African gains were limited to mandates over the greater part of German West Africa.

Before August 1914 no government had given serious thought to the potential contribution of French Africa, either in men or raw materials, to a war in Europe. The enormous losses on the Western Front led to the recruitment of French Africa's first great conscript army. By the end of the War French Africa had sent 450,000 soldiers and 135,000 factory workers to Europe. The crisis of French food supply also led in 1917–18 to the first concerted campaign, mounted jointly by the colonialists and the colonial ministry, for the *mise en valeur* of the Empire. But France's shipping losses made it impossible to increase her African imports.

In the aftermath of victory French Africa appeared genuinely popular in France for the first time. The main reason for that popularity was the naïve belief that the resources of the Empire would free France from dependence on foreign suppliers and speed her post-war recovery. When the resources of the Empire proved even slower to arrive than reparations, the Empire quickly lost its newfound popularity. The War nonetheless left behind it the myth of the Empire as a limitless reservoir of men and raw materials: a myth which, though dormant for most of the inter-war years, was to be revived by the coming of World War II.

[22]

THE NORTH-WEST FRONTIER IN THE FIRST WORLD WAR

LAL BAHA

Dr. Lal Baha is a Lecturer in History at the University of Peshawar, West Pakistan. For reasons of space the very full documentation of her mainly unpublished sources has had to be omitted, but she (or the Editor) will be glad to supply particulars on request.

DURING the First World War, the situation on the North-West Frontier of India, which had been a perennial source of danger for the British Government of India, gave them many anxious moments. They feared that the attitude, already far from cordial, of Habibullah Khan, the Amir of Afghanistan—he had been enraged at not being consulted over the Anglo-Russian Convention of August 1907—would take a turn for the worse, events in Europe providing him with an opportunity to declare a "preventive war" against the British. An Anglo-Afghan war would be certain to arouse the frontier tribes and involve them in a tribal conflagration. Should large-scale tribal raids be made on British territory in the hope of finding the frontier denuded by the despatch of troops overseas, then the Government might be forced to launch a campaign into tribal territory, the consequences of which would be unforeseeable. The situation was all the more dangerous for the Government because of serious internal troubles caused by increasing terrorist activites in Bengal, Western India and the Punjab. There was the further fear that Indian Muslims might be incited by pan-Islamic propaganda from Turkey, and by frontier uprisings.

Lord Hardinge's policy as Viceroy was to keep on good terms with Amir Habibullah, who was promptly informed of the outbreak of the war, advised to maintain neutrality and requested to take special steps for the preservation of order on the Indo-Afghan border. To the relief of the Government of India, the Amir assured them of his neutrality, an assurance which he repeated in November 1914 when Turkey entered the war. Throughout the war the Amir remained true to his pledge, although this was by no means an easy task. The anti-British and pro-Turkish faction at Kabul, headed by Nasrullah Khan, the Amir's younger brother, and supported by priests and fanatical elements, made no secret of their opposition to the Amir's neutral policy, and exerted strong pressure on him to enter the war on Turkey's side. The arrival at Kabul in August 1915 of a Turco-German mission, allegedly bearing messages from the Sultan of Turkey and the Kaiser of Germany, and the intrigues of Indian "seditionists" with the anti-British elements at Kabul, made the situation all the more difficult for the Amir; there were rumours of rebellion against him, and even of his assassination. Habibullah handled the situation with consummate tact: he listened to the advice of the pro-Turkish elements in his court but never acted on it, he welcomed the Turco-German mission but kept it guessing about his intentions, and he kept an effective control over the frontier tribes. He restrained his subjects from committing offences in British territory, sent troops to recall those assisting in raids, reproved the most influential Afghan *mullas* for directing these operations, and discouraged the tribes on the Indian side of the Durand Line from hostility towards the British Government. The Amir's influence was of vital political importance, for it helped in steadying the situation on the frontier. Hardinge had the "firmest confidence" in Habibullah's good faith, and so had the Home Government. In September 1915 George V sent the Amir a letter of thanks, and the Government of India increased his subsidy by two lakhs of rupees.

Towards the tribes Hardinge had meanwhile, with the concurrence of Crewe, the Secretary of State, maintained a "watchful policy". In August 1914 three divisions of infantry and a cavalry brigade were maintained on the frontier on a "mobilised footing", with three other frontier brigades at Kohat, Bannu and Derajat. Their particular task at the commencement of the war was to watch the Mohmands and the Mahsuds, both of whom were restless. From the adjacent Afghan district of Khost, over which the Amir's authority had through maladministration slackened, incursions on the Kurram and Tochi valleys were apprehended. However, there were in the tribal territory some important loyal elements such as the Mehtar of Chitral, the Nawab of Amb, the tribes of Swat and the Khyber Agency, all of whom offered their services and cooperation to the British. So, too, did the Bhittanis of Jandola and the Waziris of Tochi; the Khyber Rifles and the North Waziristan Militia volunteered contingents for active service.

The uneasy balance of forces on the frontier was threatened in November 1914 by Turkey's entry into the war. Increased vigilance over Indian Muslims, who were reported to be in a state of "considerable bitterness and some unrest", was called for. Yet at the same time more and more Indian Army units had to be despatched to Mesopotamia and other theatres of war in the Middle East. As a result, for several weeks in 1915 the number of troops for the maintenance of internal security in India fell "dangerously below the safety level", the total British garrison in India being less than 15,000 men. The mutiny of the 130th Baluch Regiment and the suspected disaffection of other Indian troops added to the Government's worries.

War with Turkey also furnished the *mullas* in the tribal territory with an admirable opportunity to incite the local population to *jihad*. "Hopes of a great Islamic renaissance were at once aroused." It was fondly expected that Persia would join the war on the side of Turkey and that the Amir, notwithstanding his present neutrality, would ultimately join Persia. The tribal *mullas* were reinforced by the *mullas* of southern Afghanistan in urging the tribesmen to rise in the name of the Sultan of Turkey and to take advantage of the drain on government troops caused by the war. The return of sick and wounded soldiers from France gave rise to stories of German invincibility, and hundreds of trans-border tribesmen serving in the Indian Army deserted their ranks, and joined the *mullas*. In 1914 there were nearly 5,000 trans-border Pathans in the Indian Army, of whom about half were Afridis. By June 1915, over 600 Afridis had deserted; there were many dismissals and discharges for misconduct. In November 1915 all recruitment of trans-border Pathans was stopped, and by the end of 1918 there were less than 1,800 trans-border Pathans in the Indian Army.

To this situation among the frontier tribes the Government of India, with depleted and in some cases wavering forces, was compelled to respond as much with political as with military measures. The attitude of the Afridis, "the keystone of the frontier arch", was of paramount importance. Roos-Keppel, the Chief Commissioner of the North-West Frontier Province, in emphasising this stated:

> In the Muhammadan crisis, which there is reason to believe is approaching rapidly, their [Afridi] friendship will be of incalculable value. So long as we hold Afridis, who can form a fireproof curtain between northern and southern Islam on this frontier, no *Jehad* or rising can be general.

The Mohmands, Orakzais and other neighbouring tribes, he pointed out, were eagerly awaiting a lead from the Afridis. He therefore urged that the Afridis' allowances be increased forthwith; an Afridi petition to that effect was already before the local government. The Government of India actually doubled the allowances, and the Home Government endorsed this decision, agreeing that the "wisdom of this concession at the present time can hardly be disputed". On 13 February 1915 Roos-Keppel held a representative *jirga* of 3,000 men in the Victoria Memorial Hall, Peshawar, where he announced the grant of increased allowances on condition of "loyalty, good conduct, ratification of past agreements and equitable distribution of whole of subsidy" by the tribe. The announcement was received with a satisfaction which led Roos-Keppel to hope that "the maliks, the elders and the tribe as a whole will be with us and that nothing but a general upheaval of the Islamic World, including Afghanistan, will shake the Afridis". Further, as a measure of support and encouragement to the loyal trans-border chiefs, Roos-Keppel recommended a gift of rifles and ammunition to the Mehtar of Chitral and the Nawabs of Amb and Dir.

Simultaneously military measures were taken which though they strengthened forward positions along the frontier were intended to be "purely defensive". Preoccupied with the war in Europe and the Middle East, the Government had to be content with what Hardinge described as "necessarily a hand to mouth policy" on the frontier. This policy, as Roos-Keppel later elaborated it, was

> to keep on as good terms as possible with the tribes who are behaving well, freely to use force in crushing any incipient outbreak, to encourage and support the people of the districts in resisting transfrontier raids and, generally, to carry on as well as possible until the cessation of other preoccupations enables us to initiate a definite policy of setting our house in order.

The development of the war made the maintenance of this policy increasingly difficult. In 1915 a number of raids on British territory took place, and incitement to *jihad* by the *mullas* continued unabated. There were attacks on Miranshah and Spina Khaisora in the Tochi valley by the Afghans of Khost, repulsed by the North Waziristan Militia and the Bannu Brigade, and five attacks on the Peshawar border by the Mohmands and Bunerwals, repulsed by the First Division, part of the Second Division and the Frontier Constabulary. Though outside India little was known about these frontier incidents, Hardinge claimed to have quietly and successfully carried out "the greatest military operations on the frontier since the frontier campaign of 1897".

That these *jihad* campaigns and disturbances did not escalate into a general uprising in the tribal territory may be ascribed to three causes. First, the Amir's attitude had a generally restraining influence on the tribes. Hardinge kept Habibullah informed about the movements of his Afghan subjects and urged him to hold them in leash. Habibullah made genuine though not uniformly successful efforts to check his subjects from taking part in the *jihad* or otherwise creating trouble for the British. Roos-Keppel was sure that

> but for the Amir's prompt action, the flame of *Jehad* would have spread and that there would have been a whole rising of Ningrahar and of the Mohmand and Bajaur countries. His Majesty has displayed unprecedented boldness in his attitude towards the mullas and the *Jehad* party and has incurred much unpopularity, but his attitude and action have been of incalculable value to us.

It was, indeed, a most striking admission on the part of a Chief Commissioner who, as the India Office noted, had "seldom ... a good word to say for the Amir", and who appeared to Chelmsford, Hardinge's successor, as "confessedly an Afghanphobe".

The second favourable factor for the Government was the continued loyal behaviour of the Afridis, which, true to Roos-Keppel's anticipation, drove an effective wedge between the tribes of the northern and southern borders of the province. Apart from the increased allowances, one factor which contributed notably to the quiet in the Afridi country was the remarkable influence of Sahibzada Abdul Qaiyum, the then Assistant Political Agent of Khyber, who, in Roos-Keppel's words, was the "anchor to which Tirah is moored". "If we get through this critical year [1915]," Roos-Keppel informed Hardinge, "this will be more due to Abdul Qaiyum than to any other individual, I include myself."

The third factor in the Government's favour was the loyalty and cooperation of the *Khans* and *Nawabs* of the settled districts who volunteered to help the local government put down tribal disorders.

It was fortunate that the Amir and the Afridis did hold firm, for, from the military point of view, 1915 was a very trying year for the Government of India. Their military strength was waning as a result of Kitchener's ceaseless demands for troops from India to which Hardinge's government responded with increasing reluctance. The efficiency of the three frontier divisions was greatly affected when good Indian battalions from these divisions were sent overseas and replaced by inferior Indian battalions, "under-officered, under-gunned" and composed chiefly of new recruits and reservists. This the tribesmen soon came to know about. They had the "utmost contempt" for Indian battalions, especially those having Brahmin elements: it was only British battalions, so Hardinge believed, whom the tribesmen feared.

The Government of India's anxiety over the draining away of good troops was reinforced by the war situation in Mesopotamia and Persia and its effect on Afghanistan and the frontier. In July 1915, when Kitchener asked for more British regular battalions from India, both Hardinge and Beauchamp Duff, the Commander-in-Chief, flatly refused to send any. There were then only eight British battalions in India, all stationed on the frontier. It was impossible, in Hardinge's opinion, "to play with the situation on the frontier", where peace hung in the balance. If Persia were involved in the war that balance, Hardinge feared, could no longer be maintained, and this the Viceroy clearly pointed out to the Secretary of State, Austen Chamberlain.

The Home Government saw Hardinge's point. In December 1915 Chamberlain apprised the War Committee of the Cabinet of the Viceroy's anxiety about the military situation on the frontier. The War Committee decided to send "without delay" reinforcements for the British regiments in Mesopotamia and on the Indian frontier. Accordingly, four garrison battalions sailed forthwith for India.

Meanwhile, Roos-Keppel was becoming concerned over the situation at Kabul. Reports of the German intriguers consolidating their influence came thick and fast; Nasrullah's influence, too, was on the increase; he was now being addressed as "Amir Nasrullah Khan". In January 1916, an apparently forged letter purportedly signed by the Amir, by Nasrullah and by the pro-Turkish elements in the Afghan court was circulated in the frontier areas asking the *"mullas, maliks* and *kazis* of the Tirah *ilaka"* to prepare for a *jihad* in the spring of 1916. Stories of German plans for the invasion of Egypt, Persia and Afghanistan gained wide currency and ready credence in the Frontier Province. Roos-Keppel feared that under pressure from Nasrullah and his men the Amir was "showing signs of wavering" from his neutral policy.

Hardinge, reporting Roos-Keppel's anxiety to Chamberlain in January 1916, made it clear that he still regarded the Chief Commissioner's views as rather too pessimistic. Nevertheless the Viceroy himself was uneasy, and he waited impatiently for the Amir's reply to the letter from King George sent three months back, speculating meanwhile on whether the recent British setback in Mesopotamia had compromised British prestige so much as to force Habibullah to abandon his neutrality, and even on what would happen if he were assassinated. In order to strengthen the Amir's hand the Viceroy intended to write him a farewell letter, using the announcement of his impending retirement to cover a veiled warning that any hostile attitude towards the British would be dangerous for Afghanistan. However, in February 1916 the tension relaxed: the long-awaited reply of the Amir to the King's and the

Viceroy's letters reached Delhi, and in addition Habibullah saw the British agent at Kabul. These were encouraging signs. Hardinge could now "feel confident that he [the Amir] means to maintain his neutrality, provided that he can do so, and I think he can". Meanwhile, the Russian successes in Persia and the Caucasus had restored the Allies' prestige in Afghanistan and proportionately strengthened Habibullah's position.

The Government of India's military position had also improved by the beginning of 1916. In January the four garrison battalions from England arrived in India. Quietly but steadily territorial battalions had been moving up to the frontier, and two flights of aircraft were also sent there, which could not but profoundly impress the tribes, the *mullas* and the Afghans. On 17 February 1916, at a garden party at Peshawar, 25,000 tribesmen with many Afridi *maliks* and chiefs among them, together with a good number of Afghans, saw an aeroplane flight organised by Roos-Keppel. The effect was tremendous. One Afridi elder asked Roos-Keppel: "What do these things cost? The two that you have there are worth twenty thousand men to you." And one Mulla Doda Jan, in an intercepted letter to Babra Mulla, wrote thus:

> I have heard wonderful things from the Mulla of Khema who says that the wicked British have got aeroplanes in Peshawar district where they fly in the sky. God knows whether we can fight against them or not. The Mulla of Khema is sent on to you in order to relate the account to you personally. But the grace of God is greater than such deeds of devils.

As a further demonstration of British military might armoured cars and mechanical transport were also kept on the frontier. Lastly, in March 1916 the War Office in London provisionally earmarked two divisions in Egypt as a reserve for the Indian frontier.

The maintenance of peaceful relations with the frontier tribes during the war was made still more difficult by the presence within tribal territory of anti-British elements both from India and from abroad. These elements were the *Mujahidin* (holy warriors), called by the British the "Hindustani Fanatics"; the Indian "seditionists"; agents from Turkey; and the Haji Sahib of Turangzai, a prominent religious leader of the Peshawar border. The tribal regions provided both a rendezvous and a base of operations for these elements.

The *Mujahidin* colony at Sittana in Buner had long been a centre of unrest in the tribal territory. The *Mujahidin* were followers of Syed Ahmad Shahid (1786–1831), a native of Rai Bareilly in Oudh and a spiritual disciple of Shah Abdul Aziz of Delhi. Their aim was the reestablishment of a Muslim state as conceived by Shah Wali-ullah (1703–62),a renowned Muslim scholar and reformist, and to deliver the Muslims from the bondage of the "infidels". "They faced formidable opponents: the Marathas in the south, Sikhs in the Punjab and the British who were to overthrow all."

Syed Ahmad had appeared on the Yusufzai border and soon stirred up the local population to holy war against the Sikh rulers of Peshawar. The conflict with the Sikhs met with varying fortunes, but thenceforward the *Mujahidin* on the frontier were regularly "associated with deeds of blind fanaticism against the non-Islamic rulers of India, and no period of political stress . . . [had] passed without attempt on their part, attended with varying success, to engender religious excitement among the border tribes". The *Mujahidin* had always maintained a secret communication with their sympathisers in India who sent men and money to the colony. In the nineteenth century the *Mujahidin* had several armed conflicts with British troops. However, during the last quarter of the century the fighting spirit of these "professional fanatics" —as dubbed by Roos-Keppel—deteriorated, and thereafter their activity was confined to "occasionally making a noise" in the tribal region with the object of keeping up "the supply of presents from the Amir [of Afghanistan] and of offerings from the dupes in India".

From 1914 the *Mujahidin*, no doubt seizing the opportunity of British involvement in the war, stepped up their activity. Their colony moved in 1915 to Samasata in Buner. In the middle of that year, a branch colony was set up at Chamarkand in Bajaur. This provided a rallying point for intriguers against the British and eventually became the *Mujahidin* headquarters. In April 1915 the *Mujahidin* were directly implicated in a tribal attack on the village of Rustam on the Peshawar border. The Government retaliated by blockading the *Mujahidin;* the blockade pressed hard on them and reduced them to sore straits. In April 1917 two Bengali Muslims were arrested at Peshawar while carrying 8,000 rupees for the *Mujahidin*. This strengthened the Government's decision to continue the blockade, though at the same time the *Mujahidin* leader Niamatullah Khan was led to hope that the Government would accept his overtures for a settlement. In October 1917, after four months of negotiations, in which Abdul Qaiyum acted as intermediary, an understanding was reached, the Government giving Niamatullah certain allowances on condition that he kept his men away from anti-British elements in the tribal territory. Niamatullah was thus won over. Later, in recognition of his friendliness to the Government during the Third Afghan War (1919) Roos-Keppel recommended a reward of 25,000 rupees and twenty-five squares of good land in the Punjab for his family. Niamatullah's attachment to the Government made him unpopular with the extremists among his followers, and on 4 May 1921 he was assassinated.

The *Mujahidin* were a Muslim body whose opposition to the infidel rule in India was of long standing and cast in a traditional mould. But, besides them, there was a small but well-organised group of Indian "seditionists", composed of Hindus and Sikhs as well as Muslims, whose aim was to overthrow the British Government in India by violent means. They took their models from Europe and looked for support there as well as in India. They saw in the war an opportunity to stir up trouble by appealing to the "ignorance and fanaticism" of the frontier tribes. During the war years the "seditionists" from the Punjab, East Bengal and even the Far East, together with eight students from the North-West Frontier Province, found their way into the tribal territory. In August 1915 the famous Indian anarchists, Barakatullah and Mahendra

Pratap, reached Kabul along with the Turco-German mission, and were presently joined by Obaid Ullah Sindhi, one of the leaders of the *Mujahidin*. The three men formed a "Provisional Government of India", with Mahendra Pratap as its President, and sought an alliance with the Turkish Government against the British; this was the "silk letter plot", discovered by the Government of India in August 1916, and so called from the yellow silk on which Obaid Ullah wrote letters to his contact in Mecca. They also urged the Amir to declare a holy war against the British, and were in close touch with the *Mujahidin*, the Haji Sahib of Turangzai and all important *mullas* on the northern sector of the border. The "seditionists" remained active on the border until the early 1920s.

The "seditionists" made use of Turkish agents to intrigue with the tribes, and their operations had the financial support of Nasrullah Khan. The most serious attempt to incite the tribes was made in the Tirah (an area in the Khyber) where in June 1916 two emissaries were sent; one was Khired Bey, a staff colonel of the Turkish Army, and the other was Mohammad Abid, alias Abidin, an Arab, formerly employed by the Turks as a drill instructor in Kabul. Turkish agents also operated in Bajaur and the Mahsud country.

Before the Turkish emissaries arrived in the Tirah, one of their agents, Mir Mast by name, had already been intriguing with the Afridis. Mir Mast was a Kamber Khel Afridi and an ex-Jamadar of the 58th Rifles, from which he had deserted in France and then accompanied the Turco-German mission to Kabul. The "uneasy feelings" in the tribal area as a result of the intrigues of the mission were further intensified by Mir Mast's activities in the Khyber. On their arrival in the Tirah the Turkish emissaries declared themselves to be the Sultan's plenipotentiaries and offered the Afridis his protection and assistance against the British. The Afridis were also promised concrete support in the shape of arms, ammunition and money. In the middle of 1916 deserters and dismissed Pathan sepoys from the Indian Army swelled the ranks—mainly pro-Afghan Afridi—of the emissaries. The latter started recruiting for what they gave out to be sometimes a "Turkish army" and sometimes the "Amir's army". By July 1916 the total number of Afridi recruits so enlisted was reported to have reached about 400.

Roos-Keppel kept a close watch on these developments. According to him the Turkish agents had succeeded in creating a schism in the tribe, which was slowly being divided into two camps: the one in favour of maintaining peace and friendship with the Government, and the other advocating the opposite policy. The Chief Commissioner could not take action against the Turkish agents and their Afridi supporters for fear of disturbing what he saw as "a very delicate equilibrium" in the tribe, and most probably straining the Indian Government's relations with Habibullah Khan. In such circumstances he considered it better to "leave the Turks alone". It was only in the middle of September 1916 that, under "gentle pressure" from the British officers in the Khyber, the pro-Government faction of the Afridis drove off the Turks to Rajgal near the Afghan border, and in June 1917 the Turks were reported to have finally left the tribal territory and crossed over to Afghanistan.

Turkish machinations were more successful in the Mohmand country and in Bajaur. Two Pathans, who had lived for a long time in Berlin and then accompanied the Turco-German mission to Kabul, acted as Turkish agents in these areas. Already the Haji Sahib of Turangzai and other local *mullas* were fomenting intrigues. The Haji was "probably the most respected and trusted" *mulla* in the triba territory, his influence being strongest in the Peshawar district and its tribal border where he enjoyed a "reputation for sanctity and unselfish benevolence". The Haji intermittently visited the Swatis, Bajauris and Mohmands to preach *jihad*. He also established contact with the anti-British party at Kabul and set up a press from which he issued a series of "rousing *jihad* leaflets". Influenced by this preaching, the Mohmands began carrying out extensive raids in the Peshawar district; and in October 1916 the Government was forced to impose a blockade of the tribe. This continued until July 1917, when a settlement was reached.

The Government made peace with the Mohmands because of troubles with the Mahsuds. Since the Tank outrage of April 1914—in which they killed Major Dodd, Political Agent for South Waziristan, two other officers and three sepoys—the Mahsuds had been openly hostile to the Government. This hostility was fanned by the pro-Turkish and anti-British elements from Kabul, and in January 1916 Roos-Keppel informed the Viceroy that

> no village is safe, and the Mahsuds raid from their hills right down to the banks of the Indus and kill, entrap and abduct Hindus. Altogether the position of the people is pitiable, and we can do very little to protect them or even to alleviate their sufferings.

In the first half of 1917 the Mahsuds attacked government pickets, garrisons and convoys, inflicting heavy losses. To restore the Government's prestige, the Chief Commissioner pressed for an immediate punitive expedition; and in June 1917 the tribe was subdued by the so-called Waziristan Field Force, under the command of Major-General Beynon. On 10 August 1917 an agreement was arrived at with a Mahsud *jirga*. This brought the Mahsud affair to an end, to the great relief of the India Office: "The North-West Frontier of India," the Political Secretary hopefully commented, "is now free from trouble."

In November 1918 the war ended. The North-West Frontier appeared to Roos-Keppel to be settling down to a quieter and quieter state: there was, in his opinion, "no history" for the year 1918-19. His optimism soon proved mistaken. In May 1919, the Third Afghan War broke out, setting the tribal area once more aflame. Meanwhile, however, those who served the Government loyally during the war had been rewarded. A free bonus of one year's allowances was given to the Afridis. The Nawabs of Amb and Dir and the Mehtar of Chitral were paid handsomely. Abdul Qaiyum had, in 1917, received a K.C.I.E. and in May 1918 he was appointed Political Agent in the Khyber. Finally, Roos-Keppel himself had, in 1917, earned a G.C.S.I. for his war services.

[23]

The South African Rebellion, 1914

'THIS meeting is . . . of the opinion that there is no reasonable ground to expect that by carrying on the war the People will be able to retain their independence, and considers that, under the circumstances, the People are not justified in proceeding with the war, since such can only tend to the social and material ruin, not only of ourselves, but also of our posterity.'[1] In these terms, the Boer commandants agreed by 54 votes to 6 to accept the British peace offer in 1902. They had not found the decision easy. Some, like Botha and Smuts, were resigned to the hopelessness of continued resistance.[2] Others found the surrender of independence so bitter a pill that they spoke in favour of fighting on unless their freedom could be assured.[3] The unfolding of Milner's anglicizing policy in the immediate post-war years filled many Afrikaners with the idea that peace had been bought at too high a price, and a nationalist revival within Afrikanerdom resulted,[4] only to have its impetus blunted with the grant of self-government to the ex-republics and the development of a conciliation policy by Botha and Smuts which carried South Africa to the successful achievement of union in 1910. The 'convention spirit' of 1910 infected perhaps a majority of Afrikaners; but Botha had not been at the head of the first Union ministry for long before it became clear that there were substantial groups among the Afrikaner people who still resented their exposure to British influences and Imperial pressures. Hertzog, in whom the opposition found a leader, was driven out of Botha's government in December 1912. A year later his Nationalists broke away from Botha's South African Party, and when the European war broke out in August 1914 they were busy establishing branches in the Union's rural constituencies, especially in the Orange Free State.

South Africa was committed to belligerent status by the king's declaration of war against Germany;[5] but the degree of her active

[1] J. D. Kestell and D. E. van Velden, *The Peace Negotiations between Boer and Briton* (London, 1912), p. 205. [2] *Ibid.* pp. 180-91.
[3] This view was for a long time held by the following, among others: C. F. Beyers, J. B. M. Hertzog, J. C. G. Kemp, C. R. de Wet, J. H. de la Rey, P. J. Liebenberg and President Steyn. All of them play prominent parts in the following narrative.
[4] L. M. Thompson, *The Unification of South Africa* (Oxford, 1960), pp. 4-30.
[5] R. M. Dawson, *The Development of Dominion Status, 1900-1936* (Oxford, 1937), p. 17.

participation was a matter for the Union Government to decide. Botha did not hesitate to accept responsibility for South Africa's defence, thus releasing 6,000 Imperial troops for service elsewhere; and when, on 7 and 9 August, he received requests from London to conduct an invasion of German South West Africa, the Cabinet agreed to do so, acting on its own responsibility, for parliament was not then in session, but with the reservation that it would take no action until a special session of parliament had approved the decision.[1] Parliament eventually did so, by overwhelming majorities, between 9 and 12 September.[2] But within five weeks of the end of the session armed rebellion had broken out on the northern frontier of the Cape, under Lieutenant-Colonel S. G. ('Manie') Maritz, the district staff officer in command of the German frontier region. Soon afterwards, it spread to the northern Free State, under the leadership of C. R. de Wet, another Boer ex-general and close political associate of Hertzog; and to the Transvaal under the leadership of C. F. Beyers, Commandant-General of the Union Defence Force till 15 September, and Major J. C. G. Kemp, district staff officer of the western Transvaal until the same date. The rebellion was easily quelled, for the rebels lacked proper organization and supplies; but it had its moments of high drama, it rocked the state severely while it lasted, and it cast a long shadow over the South African political scene, reaching backwards to the days of Vereeniging, for the rebel leaders came from among the *bittereinders* of 1902, and forwards into the nationalist mystique of modern times.

The rebellion presents difficult problems of interpretation because the source material, though voluminous, is tantalizingly incomplete. The records of the special treason courts set up in 1915 are not available. This is a major gap, because the three official inquiries which were held—that conducted by Professor Leo Fouché in 1915,[3] that by a select committee of the House of Assembly under Patrick Duncan in the same year,[4] and that of a judicial commission under Judge J. H. Lange in 1916 [5]—heard relatively little evidence from the rebel side. This has led some,

---

[1] For correspondence between the Imperial and South African Governments, see the Report of the Lange Commission (U.G. 46-'16), pp. 111-13, and for an account of the Cabinet's discussion, Botha's evidence before the Lange Commission in U. G. 42-'16, pp. 349-50.

[2] By 92 votes to 12 in the lower house and 24 to 5 in the upper.

[3] *Report on the Outbreak of the Rebellion and the Policy of the Government with regard to its Suppression* (U.G. 10-'15), hereafter referred to as the Fouché Report. Leo Fouché was professor of history at the Transvaal University College.

[4] *Report of the Select Committee on Rebellion* (S.C. 1-'15), hereafter referred to as the Duncan Report. Twenty-four witnesses were examined.

[5] *Report of the Judicial Commission of Inquiry into the Causes and Circumstances relating to the recent Rebellion in South Africa* (U.G. 46-'16), and *Minutes of Evidence* (U.G. 42-'16), hereafter referred to as the Lange Report, and the Lange Report (Minutes) respectively. One hundred and thirty-six witnesses gave evidence.

notably G. D. Scholtz,[1] to discount the value of the blue book evidence—excessively in my view, but not altogether without reason. The Fouché Report made a forthright condemnation of the rebel leaders, but it was unsupported by details of the evidence to which Fouché had access. Fouché was himself examined by the Duncan committee, and substantiated some but by no means all of his earlier allegations. The Duncan committee was handicapped by the paucity of witnesses it was able to call, and prudently refrained from delivering judgment; but it did secure the evidence of General Hertzog, achieving in this respect greater success than the Lange commission, which heard many more witnesses, but only such as would voluntarily appear, and was in fact boycotted both by the rebel leaders, who were given the opportunity to appear before it, and by the Nationalist Party. The gap on the rebel side has meanwhile been filled by a plethora of works by or about the leading participants,[2] which in general contradict the conclusions in the official reports. But the effect of these later writings has been to clarify the questions rather than to provide satisfactory answers to them.

What are these questions? Some concern the motives of the rebels. Here, interpretations vary from that of Fouché, who contended that the real aim was a *coup d'état* for the sake of restoring republican independence, to that of certain rebel leaders and their apologists, who have since asserted that there was no rebellion in the proper sense of the word, but only isolated outbursts of spontaneous defiance arising out of the Government's decision to invade South West Africa. Other questions concern the degree of co-operation between the various leaders. The Fouché and Lange commissions, on the one hand, concluded that Maritz, Beyers, de la Rey, Kemp and others attempted to develop a co-ordinated plot, whereas Scholtz maintains that the Maritz rebellion was essentially a separate, disconnected event. Arising out of this disagreement, there have naturally followed rival theories as to the parts played by the individual leaders. None have disputed the treasonable nature of Maritz's aims and actions, least of all Maritz himself. But Beyers has been cast in the roles of arch-plotter and innocent victim; de la Rey and Kemp alternatively as traitors, heroes, or slaves of a pathetic delusion. There is, finally, considerable controversy over the propriety of the Government's conduct, not only in relation to its war policy, but also to the manner in which it handled the rebellion.

[1] G. D. Scholtz, *Die Rebellie* (1942), p. 8. He refers to the Fouché Report as ' niks anders as 'n apologie vir die optrede van die destyds regering nie ', and the Lange Report as ' Objektiewer opgestel, maar ... ook gekleurd, [wat] doen aan die standpunt van die rebelleiers geen reg nie.'

[2] See especially J. D. Kestell, *Christiaan de Wet* (1920); G. D. Scholtz, *Generaal Christiaan Frederik Beyers, 1869–1914* (1941); J. C. G. Kemp, *Die Pad van die Veroweraar* (1946); S. G. Maritz, *My Lewe en Strewe* (1939); C. H. Muller, *Oorlogsherinneringe* (1936).

Reassessment is therefore necessary. It is a moot point how far the historian of today can legitimately assert detachment as a counterweight to the advantage of examining witnesses in the flesh which the original investigators possessed. His only possible *modus operandi* is to trust the words of those who uttered from first hand knowledge, on the presumption that these witnesses were trying to tell the truth, and to endeavour to harmonize statements which on the surface appear incongruous in such a way that the story as a whole hangs together. The following interpretation of events derives from an attempt to apply this method; but the gaps remain, and must still be filled by conjecture.

Government apologists, whose views were largely reflected in the Fouché and Lange Reports, represented the rebellion as basically an attempt to re-establish a republican regime on the part of war veterans with an undying hatred of the British connection. The strongest evidence in their favour was the existence of undoubted unrest in the Union, especially in the western Transvaal, before the Government had even made up its mind to recommend the invasion of South West Africa. The far western Transvaal had been a restless frontier district in living memory, and even in 1915 one of its magistrates could fail to notice whether the citizens turned up to a public meeting with or without arms, because at Lichtenburg 'people carry their arms ... as anyone else would carry a walking-stick'.[1] They were, in general, a poor community: the district received a great deal of attention from the Carnegie Poor White Commission in 1932.[2] The members of this 'very ignorant community', as the same magistrate described them, scratched an unscientific living from the soil, and were more ready to listen to the oracles of the diviner than would have been the case had they been more cultured, more prosperous, and less absorbed in biblical ways of thought.

Hence the enormous reputation of the prophet van Rensburg.[3] This old seer, who lived in the Wolmaransstad district, had a record of inspired guesses since the days of the Anglo-Boer war. He was said to have forecast the capture of Methuen, and to have rescued de la Rey from capture on at least one occasion. He had foretold the coming of the Anglo-German war years before its outbreak (though he was wrong as to its result). On another occasion he was supposed to have had a vision of 'the number 15 on a dark

[1] Duncan Report, p. 184 (J. C. Juta).
[2] *Report of the Carnegie Commission of Investigation on the Poor White Question in South Africa* (1932). See especially the map opposite p. 14 in each volume.
[3] Fouché Report, pp. 5–6; Lange Report, pp. 4–5; Sybrand Botha, *Profeet en Krygsman: Lewensverhaal van Siener van Rensburg* (n.d., c. 1941); Kemp, pp. 123–37. References to van Rensburg in the minutes of evidence are numerous. See especially Duncan Report, pp. 218–20 (Hertzog's experience); Lange Report (Minutes), pp. 351 (Botha), 252 (Capt. H. T. Watkins) on his influence on de la Rey.

cloud, from which blood issued, and then General de la Rey returning home without his hat' followed by a carriage covered with flowers: this he had interpreted as a sign of some triumph for de la Rey, the uncrowned king of the western Transvaal, who by all accounts came under the influence of this modern Artemidorus to a remarkable degree, as did many others. Van Rensburg believed in the coming of the republic, and made appropriate forecasts which were readily taken up. This meant, to him and his followers, a restoration of independence through the removal of the British yoke. The Transvaal, men urged, had been freed by divine intervention in 1881. This would happen again. Even Botha and Smuts, for all their acceptance of the British connection, could be expected to pronounce in favour of independence when the time was ripe—in other words, when Britain's hands were tied up elsewhere. A secular version of the kingdom of heaven was at hand.

These were the kind of anticipations which seem to have inspired the calling of a meeting at Treurfontein for 15 August.[1] At first, the burghers were required to appear armed, with horses saddled and provisions for eight days, because de la Rey, in whose name the meeting was called, was expected to lead a march to Pretoria which would result in the establishment of a republic with the full co-operation of Botha and Smuts. Botha half-killed the demonstration by summoning de la Rey to Pretoria and talking him out of his extraordinary plan. But the idea of a march on Pretoria, once planted, bore fruit, even if it no longer seemed likely after mid-August 'to promise a peaceful outcome. It reappeared in the context of more reckless proposals during the month of September; and again, this time as a counsel of desperation, among rebels who had burned their boats in October.

Botha told Beyers and de la Rey about the plan to invade South West Africa in the middle of August, and thereafter, though officially secret, the news spread quickly. The military reasons for it were plain enough, above all the necessity of neutralizing radio stations and harbours which could have been of use to the German fleet, while there may have been more than political propaganda in Botha's statement made at Bank on 28 September that if the Union's armed forces were not used, Australians or Indians would be.[2] But the thought of taking part in an invasion of the territory of hitherto friendly neighbours evoked immense emotional and moral repugnance among a large section of Afrikanerdom. South West Africa had its own Afrikaner community (placed at over 400 adult males by one of them [3]); there was a good deal of friendly traffic

[1] Lange Report, pp. 5–6; *ibid.* (Minutes), pp. 233–5 (D. J. Louw, a Lichtenburg farmer, gives a typical account, with more detail than most).
[2] F. V. Engelenburg, *Gen. Louis Botha* (1929), p. 295; Sir J. Rose Innes, *Autobiography* (ed. B. A. Tindall, 1949), pp. 259–60. [3] Lange Report (Minutes), p. 73 (P. G. de Wet).

across the border; Germans had responded generously to the appeals of the Boer generals for relief in 1902; there was little danger of an invasion of the Union by the small German garrison; and the war would in any case be won or lost in Europe, whatever happened locally. The argument advanced by some, for example by Kemp,[1] that the conduct of an offensive campaign was a violation of the Defence Act, need not be taken seriously and has been dismissed by Scholtz;[2] but the moral argument used by de Wet,[3] and by some but by no means all of the Dutch Reformed clergy,[4] that Botha was committing the sin of trying to move his neighbour's landmark, was given a great deal of weight. The Nationalist Party condemned the invasion policy on 26 August, and when Botha introduced the policy motion in the Assembly, Hertzog moved its rejection. When Kemp and Beyers resigned in mid-September, they gave the decision to invade as their public reason. De la Rey, one of Botha's most loyal supporters, could not bring himself to vote for the policy in the Senate, even if he would not vote against his leader.

This unanimity among the later rebel leaders and their Nationalist sympathizers gave them impressive grounds for contending that the rebellion had arisen purely out of opposition to the invasion plan; but unfortunately this simple explanation leaves too much unexplained. The balance of probability must be taken to lie against the view that three remarkable disturbances in public opinion—mystic republicanism in August, alarming demonstrations of seditious talk in scattered military camps in September, followed by armed rebellion in much the same districts and under much the same leadership in October—had no intimate connection with each other. The obvious connections between these three manifestations are slight; but on balance it can be taken as probable that there was collusion between Maritz in the northern Cape and Beyers and his associates in the Transvaal, preparatory to a proposed *coup* in mid-September; that the aim of this *coup* was to overthrow the existing regime; and that it failed for two main reasons: the shooting of de la Rey, and the failure of Maritz to make the necessary arrangements in time.

[1] Lange Report (Minutes), p. 229 (Lieut. Col. P. D. A. Roux). Maritz used the same argument.

[2] Scholtz, *Rebellie*, pp. 106–8.   [3] Kestell, p. 177.

[4] Numbers of the clergy felt that opposition to the invasion was justifiable on conscientious grounds, and several were to play an active part on the side of the rebels when the rebellion got under way—Ds. H. van Broekhuizen, for example, who went into the field with Beyers, and the Ds. Ferreira, whose parsonage was the venue for the Kopjes meeting of 13 Oct. (see below). On the other hand, there were many prominent clergy, especially in the Cape Church, who opposed the rebellion so strongly that they came out in public against it. See J. C. Hefer, *Kerk en Rebellie* (1915) for the open letter from Cape Church leaders to their fellow clergy, dated 13 Oct., urging them 'om deze heilloze beweging tegen te gaan', quoted also in Lange Report, pp. 36–37. The Dutch Reformed synods all refused to take sides.

The question of whether or not the rebel leaders in the Transvaal and the Orange Free State were in collusion with Maritz has often been taken as the acid test of their political guilt; but this line of argument is quite worthless unless it is related closely to the time factor. To prove collusion between Beyers and Maritz before 15 September would not make Beyers in any way responsible for the overt acts committed by Maritz, which belong mainly to a later date; but it would throw light on the ramifications of the so-called 'September plot',[1] and perhaps implicate Maritz in schemes associated with the name of Beyers. But the logical line of cleavage, as I shall try to show, is not a line dividing Maritz from the other leaders which Scholtz has tried to establish, but a line dividing the events before 16 September from those after that date.

On 14 August, a week before the chiefs of staff met to plan the South West African campaign, Botha and Smuts called the Transvaal commandants together in Pretoria to brief them on their wartime obligations and make arrangements for the training of citizen force men at various centres from the beginning of September. The commandants pressed Botha and Smuts for information regarding a possible plan to invade German territory; but instead of giving them a direct answer, Botha lectured to them on discipline: 'Look here, you are officers ..., and I must say it is an amazing thing for me to come here this morning and to hear you asking where you must fight. The duty of an officer is to obey the dictates of Parliament ... no matter what his private feelings may be.'[2] Was Botha presuming too much on their loyalty? 'I must confess', he told the Lange commission, 'that to my surprise I could plainly see that day a decided spirit of unrest and irritation among a certain section of the commandants, who were evidently opposed to our views; namely, Beyers, Kemp, [General C. H.] Muller, Maritz and [Major J. J.] Pienaar. They assumed an altogether hostile attitude towards the Government.'[3]

It may be urged in Botha's favour that the dissident officers appear to have been a small minority, and that Beyers and Kemp both covered up when Botha put leading questions to them; but in the light of his quoted comments, and others which he made before the Lange commission, it is extraordinary that he should have left men of doubtful loyalties in positions where they were able to do so much harm—Kemp in command of the citizen force camp at Potchefstroom, scheduled to start on 2 September; Maritz, a man who had been appointed to the north-west Cape command on Beyers's recommendation and against Smuts's better judgment,[4] in charge of the camps at Upington and Kakamas; and Beyers

---
[1] Fouché's term.   [2] Lange Report (Minutes), p. 350.
[3] Lange Report (Minutes), p. 351.
[4] Duncan Report, p. 7 (Fouché); Lange Report (Minutes), p. 355 (Botha).

himself, who remained Commandant-General until he voluntarily resigned for his own reasons on 15 September. If rebellion was intended, Botha and Smuts helped to create the opportunity.

Maritz was in Pretoria for the commandants' meeting (though Botha wondered why Beyers had summoned him), and conferred with the dissident coterie while he was there.[1] This was the last occasion on which he saw them before the outbreak of the rebellion; but the fact that plans were then made between him and Beyers for liaison with the Germans was stated by Maritz himself, and by General P. J. Liebenberg in the Duncan and Lange Reports.[2] Liebenberg told, not his own story, but that of Major J. J. Pienaar, as allegedly related to him in October when the two men were travelling together to a meeting at Kopjes in the Free State. It was to the effect that Maritz was to 'start rebellion' on 15 September, having been sent to the German frontier for this purpose by Beyers. The purpose of the rebellion was to set up a provisional government with Beyers as president,[3] de la Rey as Commandant-General of the Union, de Wet as Assistant Commandant-General in the Free State, and Maritz holding the same position in the Cape. Kemp, as was in any case publicly known, was to 'call the Defence Force to Potchefstroom in September';[4] de la Rey was to attend the parliamentary session in Cape Town and return to Potchefstroom on 14 September, where he would be met by Beyers and Pienaar. Potchefstroom was to be taken and the Vierkleur raised on the 15th; de la Rey, Kemp, and Lieutenant-Colonel Kock were then to raise revolt in the western Transvaal; Beyers and Pienaar were to seize the railway and Krugersdorp; they were then to combine forces, release the German prisoners at Roberts Heights, and with their help take Pretoria. Meanwhile de Wet was to start rebellion in the Free State (though it is not clear how well informed he was of the plan). The setting up of a republic would crown the proceedings.

[1] Fouché Report, p. 12; Lange Report, p. 4; Maritz, pp. 69-70.

[2] Maritz, p. 70: 'Die verstandhouding was dat ek 'n bestelling met die Duitse Goewerneur sou maak, en dan sou genl. Beyers, nadat hy met die ander generaals onderhandel het, self afkom en die Duitse Goewerneur ontmoet en onderhandel.' Liebenberg's evidence is to be found in the Duncan Report, pp. 139-49, and in the Lange Report (Minutes), pp. 114-21. The two accounts should be considered together.

[3] It is noteworthy that, when Maritz drew up a provisional government for an independent South Africa in December, Beyers was relegated to a humbler role (Lange Report, pp. 67-68). That Maritz was reluctant to accord any sort of priority to Beyers is suggested also in the evidence of Maj. J. W. G. Leipoldt (Duncan Report, p. 119).

[4] Scholtz, *Rebellie*, p. 165, comments: 'Nòg een van hulle nòg genl. Kemp het die mag daartoe gehad. Die persoon wat vir die oefenkamp verantwoordelik was, was niemand minder as genl. Smuts.' This is true, so far as responsibilities were concerned; but the point is trivial, and Liebenberg may be interpreted as recording a decision which had already been taken by the proper authorities to call a camp over which Kemp had been given command. To assume, as not even Scholtz appears to do, that Kemp was to call the entire Defence Force to Potchefstroom, would be preposterous.

Scholtz has subjected Leibenberg's evidence to searching criticism, but he has failed to knock it down.[1] His *argumentum ad hominem* falls once it is realized that Pienaar, so far from being a complete outsider (*buitestaander*) almost certainly had knowledge of the existence of a plot.[2] He fails to note that Beyers was primarily responsible for Maritz's appointment; he gives a misleading impression of the view of the Lange commission by stating that it considered there was 'no satisfactory evidence' that Maritz had been in league with de Wet, Kemp and Beyers before 9 October;[3] and he neglects to relate Liebenberg's evidence to the testimony of those who watched developments in the Potchefstroom camp from the inside.

The meetings of 14-15 August were the last occasion on which Maritz saw the other leaders of the movement; but the evidence that he maintained contact with them is suggestive, if not as detailed as could be desired. It hinges on the movements of P. J. Joubert, a resident of South West Africa, whom Maritz appointed as his staff captain in August.[4] Joubert, whose movements in the Free State during July have not been plotted in detail, is known to have visited South West Africa at the beginning of August. Maritz met him at Kakamas, after returning from the commandants' conference, on the 24th, and at the end of the month Joubert was in Pretoria, ostensibly to advise Botha and Smuts about the South West African campaign, but in reality—on his own evidence referred to by Fouché [5]—to see Beyers and de la Rey. On his return from Pretoria, Joubert went again to South West Africa, met Maritz again on 13 September, boarded the train for Bloemfontein on which

[1] Scholtz, *Rebellie*, pp. 160-6.
[2] Scholtz, *Rebellie*, p. 164. General Pienaar (as he subsequently became) has done the writer the courtesy of reading and commenting on the present article. He denies having had any connection with the rebel organization in the western Transvaal or the Free State, and disclaims a major role in the conspiracy itself, though not in the subsequent rebellion, when he was elected rebel Commandant-General for the northern and central Transvaal. His evidence is important because, both through Liebenberg and through Fouché, he linked Maritz's actions in the Cape with plans for a simultaneous rising in the Transvaal in September, about which he apparently had some knowledge. He was the 'prominent conspirator' mentioned at pp. 10, 12 and 14 of the Fouché Report, as is plain from the Duncan Report, p. 22.
[3] Lange Report, p. 102. The commissioners stated: 'The majority of your Commissioners are of the ... opinion ... (b) That there is no satisfactory evidence as to the extent to which, or the period at which, Maritz communicated to Beyers, Kemp and De Wet definite plans for rebellion; but that there is strong ground for believing that he did communicate his intentions to them before he went into open rebellion on October 9th 1914.'
[4] References in the evidence to Joubert are scattered, but numerous. See especially Duncan Report, pp. 38-40; Lange Report (Minutes), pp. 1-2, 344-5 (A. E. Trigger, Assistant Provost Marshal of the Union); and *ibid*. pp. 135-8 (Maj. F. S. van Manen, staff officer to General Beyers, who witnessed Joubert's visits to the Commandant-General's office). Trigger interviewed Joubert after his capture, and found him 'very communicative indeed' on the wrongness of the invasion policy, but cagey on the subject of his conversations with Beyers. [5] Fouché Report, p. 10.

de la Rey was returning from the parliamentary session at De Aar on the 14th, and travelled through to Johannesburg. He was travelling to keep an appointment with Beyers, who had wired Maritz to go to Pretoria or send Joubert.[1] Therefore on the day before the alleged rising was due to take place in the Potchefstroom camp (this had been put back from 15 to 16 September) Beyers, through this intermediary, had up-to-date information from Maritz.

The known evidence concerning Joubert's movements can be related intelligibly both to developments in the Transvaal and to the build-up of Maritz's negotiations with the South West African authorities. Beyers's invitation to Maritz to visit Pretoria in mid-September seems to have been part of an attempt by Beyers to get Maritz, de la Rey, Kemp and perhaps de Wet to Pretoria shortly before the middle of the month. De la Rey, who had urged the troops at Potchefstroom to be loyal to their officers on his way to Parliament on 5 September, was expected to return direct to Potchefstroom after the parliamentary session; but Beyers persuaded him instead to return first to Pretoria 'on important business'.[2] De Wet did not go to Pretoria at this time, though apparently he had intended to do so earlier in the month, for Beyers put him off on the 8th with the information that 'our friend [presumably de la Rey] will not be here'. Kemp arrived in Pretoria with Lieutenant-Colonel Bezuidenhout, one of his supporters in the Potchefstroom camp, on 12 September in response to telephonic instructions from Beyers. Before returning to Potchefstroom the next day, they held a consultation with Beyers, during part of which Pienaar was apparently present, for he made the following statement at the time of his eventual capture by Government forces:

> 'During my stay in the office a discussion took place about Kemp's camp at Potchefstroom, and it was decided to keep the camp on till the following Wednesday,[3] to enable De la Rey to address the men. The camp was to have broken up on the Monday. I heard Kemp tell Beyers that Manie Maritz had made all arrangements down there, and it was understood that Maritz was to start the trouble, and as soon as he started De la Rey and Kemp were to start in the Transvaal. Kemp, I understood, was to act under de la Rey, and I gathered that the organization in the Western Transvaal was of old standing and all arrangements seemed to have been made; and I think the idea was to use the camps as a nucleus to get the men together'.[4]

[1] Fouché Report, p. 14 (text).   [2] Fouché Report, p. 13 (text).
[3] This was not true. According to the Lange Report, p. 7, which draws mainly on the evidence of A. E. Basden, chief clerk of the Department of Defence, Pretoria, ibid. (Minutes) pp. 209-13, 340-2, the Potchefstroom camp was in any case scheduled to continue until 16 September.
[4] Fouché Report, p. 14; Duncan Report, p. 22. The Lange Commission had Pienaar's statement before them, though they did not publish it. See Lange Report (Minutes), p. 345 (A. E. Trigger).

A common factor in both of Pienaar's stories was the assertion that the signal for the rising to start was to be some action by Maritz in the Cape. This did not happen, and the fact that it did not happen has been used to discredit Pienaar's evidence; but there is no reason why it should, if two further considerations are borne in mind—the fact that Pienaar's evidence, just quoted, relates to a meeting *before* Beyers's final interview with Joubert, at which a change of plan could have been agreed upon, and the very strong probability that Maritz's plans for a rising in the Cape had not worked out as he had hoped, so that a change of plan was necessary.

Information is extremely scrappy as to the actual date of commencement of the Upington and Kakamas camps, which Maritz was supposed to use as bases for his operations. Some activity seems to have started at Upington on 2 September,[1] but the impression created by witnesses before the Lange tribunal is that these camps were by no means in efficient working order by 15 September. If Maritz had arms and ammunition, as his subsequent correspondence with defence headquarters suggests, it is by no means clear that he yet had sufficient men.[2] Furthermore, he had failed to make satisfactory arrangements with the Germans.[3] When he met Joubert at Kakamas on 24 August, he also made contact with P. G. de Wet, another Afrikaner who lived in South West Africa, who had been sent by Seitz, the Governor, together with a certain Teinert from Windhuk, to make contact with Maritz. Teinert stayed on German soil while de Wet crossed into the Union. Maritz and de Wet, perhaps accompanied by Joubert, then went to Schuit Drift, where a small engagement had taken place on the 21st, found the Union police post temporarily empty, and crossed unobserved to the German side. Maritz then spoke to Teinert on the telephone, and arranged that de Wet should proceed to Windhuk to obtain artillery and trained personnel and try to arrange for a meeting between Seitz and Beyers. Next day he wired Beyers to visit his

[1] Fouché Report, p. 59 (affidavit by S. Malan).

[2] According to A. E. Basden (Lange Report, Minutes, pp. 209, 340), Maritz had received verbal instructions on 14 August to mobilize 1,000 A.C.F. men for peace training and in fact brought together 773; but it was impossible in Maritz's district (by contrast with Kemp's) to concentrate the men quickly. Basden referred to the men having to battle through 'heavy rains and snow'. D. P. Rousseau of Van Rhynsdorp (*ibid.* p. 4) reached Kakamas on 16 September, a day or so after his men. Compare the evidence of S. J. Heyns (*ibid.* p. 11) who was only commandeered on 17 September and barely reached Upington before the end of the month. The men of Calvinia, Van Rhynsdorp, Nieuwoudtville and Brandvlei reached Kakamas on about 12 Sept., having travelled since the 3rd (*ibid.* p. 19, evidence of K. D. C. van Zyl).

[3] The following sources have been used for Maritz's negotiations with the Germans during August and September 1914: Fouché Report, pp. 7-10; Lange Report, pp. 11-16, 93-4; *ibid.* (Minutes), pp. 1-4, 344-6 (A. E. Trigger), 72-80 (P. G. de Wet), and 323-6 (I. J. Minnaar); Maritz, pp. 68-70. No attempt has been made to trace Maritz's relationship with the Germans back into the pre-war period, though it seems quite clear that he had entered into negotiations with them at that time.

district after 7 September, by which time he probably expected arrangements with the Germans to be finalized. De Wet secured an interview with Seitz and the German commander-in-chief, von Heydebreck. Seitz said he was prepared to meet Beyers; but the Germans equivocated over the supply of arms and men, mainly because von Heydebreck did not trust Maritz. All they were prepared to do was to set up a Vrij Korps of Afrikaners living on German soil and under German control, which they did eventually on 9 September, placing it under Piet's brother, Andries de Wet.[1] Neither Piet de Wet nor Teinert resumed contact with Maritz, who may well have been kept in the dark regarding the Windhuk negotiations until the Vrij Korps was actually formed. It is most improbable that Joubert knew of the failure of the negotiations when he went to Pretoria at the end of August, as he later told Trigger, to tell Beyers that Maritz was 'all right'. Maritz clearly desired a quiet frontier between the Union and South West Africa, across which the sinews of war could flow in a southerly direction to aid a rising in the Union—hence his concern to apologize to the Germans for the shooting at Schuit Drift. But his calculations were upset, not only by the opposition of von Heydebreck, but also by the unexpectedly early start of the South African attack on German territory, which began with General Lukin's seizure of Raman's Drift on 14 September. The Vrij Korps was of no use to him, because its existence constituted a form of provocation from the German side, and when it attacked and took Nakob on 16 September, instead of welcoming its success he was highly indignant. At a first glance, the Nakob attack may seem like the signal from the Cape which, according to Pienaar's statement, was expected to precede the rising at Potchefstroom. But Maritz did not have prior knowledge of it; its propaganda value, as an attack on Union soil from the outside, was poor; and Maritz had in any case sent Joubert, in response to a summons from Beyers, who knew the invasion plans,[2] on a hasty journey to Pretoria beginning on the night of the 13th, to make new arrangements in the light of the new developments. The impression left by Maritz in his memoirs is that, notwithstanding this setback, on 15 September Beyers, de la Rey and Joubert agreed that the Potchefstroom plans should go ahead without a prior signal from the Cape.[3]

So far as activities in the Potchefstroom camp were concerned, there is abundant testimony that in the first fortnight of September

[1] For the constitution of the Vrij Korps, see Lange Report, pp. 136–7.
[2] Fouché Report, p. 14. Beyers even sent a telegram of good wishes to General Mackenzie, whose force was due to attack Lüderitzbucht—a blind?
[3] Maritz, p. 70, states that Joubert, Beyers and de la Rey together agreed to start the rebellion at 4 a.m. on 16 September, and that Joubert was pressed to accompany the generals on their fateful car journey; but Joubert preferred to leave immediately for the Cape by train.

a most abnormal atmosphere prevailed.[1] The evidence admits of no reasonable doubt that, under the inspiration of Kemp, Bezuidenhout and Kock, an organized movement was on foot not only to prevent the use of citizen force trainees in a campaign against South West Africa, but also to win independence by a *coup d'état*, perhaps—though this rests on slenderer evidence—with the aid of weapons procured from the Germans.[2] The republican objective is quite indisputable, particularly in the purposes of Kemp, who, like de la Rey, was clearly obsessed by the ideas of the prophet, and lived in high hopes—indeed expectations—that the restoration of independence was just round the corner.[3]

Then, at a critical moment, occurred the shooting at Langlaagte. The killing of de la Rey by a Johannesburg policeman on the evening of 15 September was, beyond reasonable doubt, an accident. It was considered to be so by Judge Gregorowski after careful examination of the evidence, and the presumption must lie in favour of this interpretation despite suggestions made at the time and since that de la Rey was shot on Government orders.[4] Its effect was decisive: the Potchefstroom *coup*, scheduled to begin in the early hours of 16 September with the arrival of Beyers and de la Rey at the camp, fizzled out. Kemp looked upon the event as a sign of divine disapproval of the proposed rising,[5] and tried to withdraw his resignation. Beyers, who was understandably 'speechless' at the time, likewise felt that the plans had collapsed beyond repair. When he spoke at de la Rey's funeral at Lichtenburg on the 20th, he went so far towards advising his fellow Afrikaners to obey the decision of parliament, if necessary by taking part in the invasion of South West Africa, that even Botha was impressed.[6] Armed resistance, he now said, would be false to the memory of de la Rey.

In mid-September the conspiracy ended, but the underlying and immediate causes of it remained—the folk memory, the new war, the invasion, and the resentment of the malcontents at Botha's

[1] Fouché Report, pp. 16–18; Lange Report, pp. 7–10, and *ibid.* (Minutes): evidence of Lt. Cols. P. D. A. Roux, N. J. Pretorius, and Capts. H. T. Watkins, I. J. Geyser, W. J. van Graan, J. F. Terblanche and P. A. Vermaas.

[2] Lange Report (Minutes), pp. 14 (Geyser), 61–62 (Pretorius), 266 (van Graan), 272 (Terblanche).

[3] E.g. Lange Report (Minutes), pp. 252–3 (Watkins). Scholtz (*Rebellie*, p. 99) finds that on 15 September de la Rey intended a republican rising, but is not prepared to assume that Beyers, who set out with him for Potchefstroom that evening, knew this.

[4] *Report of the Judicial Commission of Inquiry into the Circumstances leading up to and attending upon the deaths of Senator the Honourable J. H. de la Rey and Dr. G. Grace* (U.G. 48–'14). Gregorowski's conclusions are supported in substance by Scholtz, *Rebellie*, p. 101, *Beyers*, p. 319. Beyers believed that the bullet was intended for himself (Duncan Report, pp. 214–15: evidence of P. G. Beyers, his brother). Hertzog suspected 'snaakse dinge' (C. M. van den Heever, *Generaal J. B. M. Hertzog*, 1929, p. 377). Kemp, pp. 177–86, tried to leave the impression that the shooting was not accidental.

[5] Lange Report (Minutes), pp. 14 (Geyser), 63 (Pretorius), 230 (Roux), 253 (Watkins), 267 (van Graan). [6] Lange Report, p. 11.

refusal to accede to their demands, which was aggravated rather than lessened by parliament's endorsement of Botha's policy. What claim had such a parliament to be representative of the nation, they began to ask, since Botha had refused to ask for a dissolution either after the dismissal of Hertzog or on the outbreak of war?[1]

It would have been prudent for the Government to decide from the start that the invasion of South West Africa would be carried out by volunteers alone. This was not their original intention; but Botha and Smuts declared it to be their policy on 21 September, in a somewhat equivocal proclamation which invited misunderstanding.[2] A public meeting at Lichtenburg on the same day carried a resolution requiring the Government to withdraw its troops from South West Africa, and appointed a committee consisting of Beyers, de Wet, Kemp and Liebenberg to receive the Government's answer by 30 September and call a further meeting to consider it.[3] The volunteer proclamation did not appear to be genuine to many, for two days later Maritz was asked by Smuts whether he would move a strong force to the frontier to take part in the invasion. His own feelings quite apart, Maritz was able to point out in his refusal that his men had been called up for peace-time training, and that not all of them were volunteers.[4]

If Smuts was trying, as he probably was, to test Maritz's loyalty, it would have been wiser to avoid leaving this sort of loophole. Maritz, given a plausible reason for disobeying this informal instruction, at first adopted an evasive attitude; but after the beginning of October he concentrated his men and supplies at Van Rooyens Vlei, between Upington and Kakamas, concluded an agreement

[1] '... that the Government has decided to attack German South West Africa... without an opportunity being given to the people of the Union to express their opinion about it' (Resolution carried at Lichtenburg, 21 Sept.); '... and as Parliament has taken this step without consulting the nation, whereby the rights of the people have been outraged...' (from Beyers's Steenbokfontein manifesto, 28 Oct.). Both these documents are referred to below. Parliament, '... that concoction of so-called constitutionalism' (J. H. Schoeman, *The other side of the Rebellion*, c. 1915, p. 13).

[2] Lange Report, p. 31. The proclamation regretted 'disquietude' at 'the impression gaining ground that it was the Government's intention to commandeer citizens of the Citizen Force Reserve and National Reserve for war service... outside the Union', and concluded with the statement that 'it is quite improbable that the Government will find it necessary to call out any *more* regiments of the Active Citizen Force for service outside the Union' (my italics).

[3] Lange Report, p. 30. Though the Lichtenburg meeting was ignorant of the proclamation, it seems that Botha had told the people on the previous day, at de la Rey's funeral which he and Smuts attended, that only volunteers would be used in South West Africa (Lange Report, Minutes, p. 108: evidence of J. C. Juta, magistrate of Lichtenburg).

[4] Lange Report, pp. 16–17: '... if the Germans advance owing to action of Government and the volunteers cannot repel them, the public will unanimously refuse to fire a shot.'

with the Germans on about the 8th,[1] and next day declared his open defiance of the Union Government.[2] He then tried to turn his dispute with the Government to his own advantage by posing as a true South African patriot, telling the Government that he would lay down his arms if Beyers, Hertzog, de Wet, Kemp and Muller were allowed access to his camp and told him to surrender.[3] Botha was prepared to let Beyers visit him, but not Hertzog. Hertzog was prepared to go, and Beyers was not; but it is hard to view Maritz's request as anything but an attempt to outmanoeuvre the Government, for his mood was far from abject.[4]

Maritz made no bones about linking Beyers's name with his own schemes at this time, and he was almost certainly right to do so; but Maritz was a rather unattractive exponent of *Realpolitik*, and he was not trustworthy.[5] Can we therefore believe the affidavit of Captain A. S. Louw, the officer in charge of the Kakamas camp, when he used Maritz's words to implicate Hertzog in the movement— 'I was always led to understand by Maritz that he was in constant communication with Generals de Wet, Hertzog and Kemp with a view to regaining our independence'?[6] Corroborative testimony is very weak, and not for want of efforts by supporters of the Government to bring Hertzog into the open. Botha gave press publicity to Maritz's request to see him, probably with the object of forcing Hertzog to take sides or lose face,[7] and the Duncan committee pulled no punches.[8] But Hertzog, if he had anything to hide, left no traces. Nothing can be proved from his slight political

[1] For the text of Maritz's agreement with the Germans, see Lange Report, pp. 26–27.

[2] For Maritz's negotiations with the Union authorities which preceded his rebellion, see Lange Report, pp. 16–27, 137–40; *ibid.* (Minutes), evidence of Lieut. Col. B. D. Bouwer, Brig. General B. G. L. Enslin, Capt. P. E. Erasmus; and Duncan Report, pp. 114–29, 136–9 (evidence of Maj. J. G. W. Leipoldt).

[3] Lange Report, p. 21; *ibid.* (Minutes), pp. 39 (Bouwer), 274–8 (J. H. Conradie, superintendent of the labour colony at Kakamas, who acted as messenger between Maritz and the Union authorities).

[4] Lange Report, p. 30; *ibid.* (Minutes), pp. 355–6 (Botha); Scholtz, *Beyers*, p. 346, for Botha's approach to Beyers. Scholtz's statement, drawn from Ds. C. A. Neethling's wife's memory, that Botha told Beyers that an Afrikaner rising 'in sy guns sou wees, aangesien hy dan aan die Britse regering kon sê dat hy niks kon doen nie' (*i.e.* invade South West Africa) is, frankly, incredible. For Hertzog's willingness to go, and Botha's refusal to send him, see Duncan Report, pp. 234–9 (Hertzog); Lange Report (Minutes), pp. 363–4 (Botha). For Maritz's attitude, see his own memoirs and the evidence of Colonel Bouwer.

[5] The tone of *My Lewe en Strewe* is anti-black, anti-British and anti-semitic, traits which witnesses detected in Maritz at the time. He claimed to have proposed to Beyers the kidnapping of Botha and Smuts and all British officers, which offended Beyers's sense of honour, and to have justified such a plan on the ground that war is war (Maritz, p. 69).

[6] Fouché Report, pp. 61–62. Fouché believed the statement.

[7] Lange Report, pp. 23–24, 114. Botha did not have to distort Maritz's statement to embarrass Hertzog; but that Hertzog was embarrassed, perhaps unfairly, can be seen from his evidence before the Duncan committee, and from van den Heever, pp. 379–82.

[8] Duncan Report, pp. 218–93—a most persistent cross-examination.

association with Maritz before the war, or from their telephone conversation on 16 August.[1] Hertzog would not make a public statement condemning Maritz's rebellion, as Botha challenged him to do; but he would no more take part in a meeting of the malcontent leaders at Kopjes in the Free State on 13 October, though pressed to do so by de Wet, because he did not wish to provide Botha with political ammunition against himself, or turn the rebellion into a party issue.[2] In the end he worked hard behind the scenes, trying to prevent rebellion in the Free State. The fact that when full scale rebellion broke out in the Union, by far the largest number of rebels came from the Free State, which was Hertzog's stronghold, prompts the suggestion that the Nationalist Party was behind the unrest.[3] But there is no more ground for implicating the Party than there is for implicating its leader. What party members did may be a different question altogether.

The Kopjes meeting of 13 October was a follow-up of the campaign begun at Lichtenburg on 21 September. It was held to consider the Government's failure to reply to the Lichtenburg demands, which had in the meantime been reiterated at further meetings in the Transvaal and Free State.[4] Maritz and Beyers[5] were not available, but most of the leading malcontents were present, and the decision which they had to make—though the majority still refused to face the fact—was absolutely clear cut: either to associate themselves with Maritz, or to acknowledge the authority of the Government and desist from law-breaking activities. A few, notably de Wet and Kemp, were provoked by Botha's proclamation of martial law and his conscription order of the previous day,[6] and urged an immediate link-up with Maritz, de Wet complaining bitterly that the martial law regulations would drive discontent underground.[7] But the majority favoured a further approach to the Government. They accordingly appointed a deputation which saw Botha in Pretoria on the 14th, and, as might have been antici-

[1] Duncan Report, pp. 221–2, 225–7 (Hertzog); Maritz, p. 70; Lange Report (Minutes), p. 90 (H. J. Nel, referring to an earlier description of the conversation by Maritz).
[2] Duncan Report, pp. 230–2 (Hertzog); van den Heever, p. 379; Kemp, pp. 247–9.
[3] Official figures for numbers of rebels going into the field were: from the O.F.S. 7,123; from the Transvaal 2,998; and from the Cape 1,251 (Lange Report, p. 135).
[4] At Kopjes (24 September), Klerksdorp (28 September) and Potchefstroom (2 October). For accounts of the Kopjes meeting of 13 October, see Lange Report (Minutes), pp. 116–18 (Liebenberg); Kestell, pp. 194–5; Kemp, pp. 247–52.
[5] Beyers had been a victim of public violence when addressing a Kruger Day meeting on 10 Oct. in Pretoria, as a result of which he had left Pretoria for hiding in the northern Transvaal, believing himself no longer safe in the capital. For this episode, one of the rare occasions during the rebellion period when rebel leaders faced a predominantly English-speaking mob, see Lange Report, p. 33, and Duncan Report, pp. 205–8 (evidence of P. G. Beyers).
[6] Lange Report, p. 114.
[7] Kestell, p. 195: 'En so is die weg afgesny om op konstitusionele weg te werk te gaan.'

pated, found him quite unwilling to listen to their demand for the withdrawal of forces from South West Africa.[1] De Wet, who was not a member of the deputation, went with it to Pretoria in order to seek out Beyers.

The leaders, minus Liebenberg who had in the meantime changed sides, met again at Kopjes on 22 October and plucked up the bravado which they had lacked on the 13th, agreeing to leave decisions on future action to Beyers in the Transvaal and de Wet in the Free State.[2] Kemp makes it clear that this involved a decision to rebel: de Wet was to mobilize the Free State commandos and march to Maritz, Kemp to make contact with Beyers and take a Transvaal commando across the Kalahari.[3]

During the final week of October, de Wet enjoyed immense success in the northern Free State, many of the commandos joining the rebellion, and he celebrated his success with a fiery speech at Vrede on the 28th, when he listed the establishment of a republic among his objectives.[4] But in the Transvaal the rebellion developed more slowly, largely owing to the greater restraint of Beyers, who might well have refrained from cutting the traces but for the fight at Commissie Drift on the 26th. Botha's attempt to seize Beyers was unfortunate in its results, and there is reason to believe that it was premature. The Lange commission justified Botha's action on the ground that his earlier conciliatory approaches had met with rebuff;[5] but the testimony of one of his envoys, Commandant S. F. Alberts, whose loyalty seems to have been mainly towards the Government, does not altogether bear this out. Alberts told the Lange commission:

> It might have been possible to have suppressed this rebellion without bloodshed, but at Commissie Drift the Government did not use commonsense. ... I am ... satisfied that if only the authorities on the Government side had sent a letter saying 'I want you to do this, that or the other', I could then have used the influence which I possessed ... I think that if General Botha had sent a letter they would all have surrendered.[6]

The question to which Botha supplied no answer was why he and Smuts failed to make full use of Alberts, a man who, against his own inclinations, had been sent to Beyers as a 'hostage', as an earnest of the Government's good faith. Commissie Drift did not

[1] Lange Report, pp. 34–36; Kestell, pp. 195–6.
[2] Lange Report, p. 38; Kestell, pp. 197–8; Kemp, pp. 252–9.
[3] When de Wet objected to the weight of responsibility, states Kemp, ' die algemene antwoord daarop was: " Ja, Generaal, maar ons sal u bystaan." '
[4] On the Vrede speech, see Lange Report, pp. 44–45; *ibid.* (Minutes), pp. 284–5 (C. J. Fraser, magistrate of Vrede); Kestell, pp. 204–5. ' My intention is to go through and join Maritz ', he is reported to have said, ' where we shall all be armed. From there we shall trek to Pretoria to pull down the British flag and to proclaim a free South African Republic.' [5] Lange Report, p. 39.
[6] Lange Report (Minutes), pp. 156–62 (Alberts), 355–6 (Botha).

turn Beyers into an irreconcilable rebel, though it sent him on the run. On the day of de Wet's Vrede speech he issued a much more moderate manifesto at Steenbokfontein, with no republican demands in it, and defining his stand as that of passive resistance under arms to the Government's South West African policy.[1] The most unfortunate effect of Commissie Drift was that it caused de Wet to reject an offer by Steyn for a parley at Onze Rust: Hertzog had with great difficulty tracked him down at Bezuidenhouts Drift on the 29th, and had already persuaded him to visit Steyn when the news of the attack on Beyers made him change his mind.[2]

When Smuts offered an amnesty on the 30th to rebels who laid down their arms and returned home,[3] its effect on both Beyers and de Wet was encouraging. Beyers met a Government emissary at Katbosfontein on 4 November, and as good as accepted the amnesty offer. Further hostilities resulted owing to unfortunate delays in finding him to deliver the Government's reply; but he still accepted a safe conduct to visit Steyn and did so on the 10th.[4] Should the Government then have granted his further request, and allowed him to make personal contact with de Wet? Steyn thought so, and pressed Smuts.[5] But by this time de Wet, who had responded favourably to an offer of safe conduct to visit Steyn, had also been involved in a fight with Government troops on the 8th, at Doornberg on the Sand River, during which his son Danie had been killed.[6] Said to have been 'maddened with rage', de Wet would not go to Steyn now save under the armed escort of his own commandos, and on the condition that he be allowed to see Beyers. He would

[1] Lange Report, p. 40 (text). 'Whereas', ran this manifesto, the Government has 'decided to conquer German South-West Africa' for reasons which are unacceptable and 'deprived the public of its right to protest peacably by proclaiming Martial Law and regulations, now therefore we continue to protest, arms in hand....' But the intention of the signatories was 'not to shed innocent blood' and 'under no circumstances to assume the offensive'. They urged burghers 'to refuse to be used by the Government to fight against us with weapons'. De Wet's signature appeared at the foot of the document, above that of Beyers. Conceivably it was drawn up by Beyers and de Wet together when de Wet visited Beyers on 14 October. Kestell has shrewdly observed that parts of it, notably the reference to a 'godless' attack on South West Africa, suggest de Wet's influence (p. 202); but de Wet can have had nothing to do with its issue. His mind had in any case advanced beyond the idea of a passive protest, as his Vrede speech shows. [2] Duncan Report, pp. 251–3 (Hertzog).
[3] Lange Report, p. 42. [4] Lange Report, pp. 58–60.
[5] Lange Report, pp. 128 (Steyn to Smuts, 10 November, no. 43), 129 (Smuts to Steyn, 11 November, no. 47), 60 (Steyn to Smuts, 12 November), 61 (Smuts to Steyn, 12 November). For the fullest justification of Steyn's actions, see N. J. van der Merwe, *Marthinus Theunis Steyn* (1921), ii. 297–325.
[6] Fouché Report, p. 40; Duncan Report, p. 253 (Hertzog), referring to document marked *Very Confidential* in Fouché Report (English edn.), p. 33; Lange Report, p. 124 (Smuts to Cols. Brand and Botha, 31 October, no. 13); Kestell, p. 209; van den Heever, p. 383. For the delays in de Wet's progress to Bloemfontein to visit Steyn, culminating in the Doornberg fight, see Lange Report, pp. 124–8 (Smuts-Steyn telegraphic correspondence, 5–9 November), 50–51; Kestell, pp. 209–12. As was the case at Commissie Drift, both sides claimed that the other had fired first at Doornberg.

not bend even after his defeat at the hands of Botha in Mushroom Valley on the 12th, though his officers urged him to do so.[1] Steyn again interceded with the Government to allow an interview between de Wet and Beyers;[2] but Botha now knew that he had the situation under control, and rejected the plea. During November the resistance in the Free State collapsed, in December that in the Transvaal, in January that in the northern Cape. De Wet was caught by Government forces near Kuruman on 2 December, as he was trying to make his way to Maritz. Beyers was drowned while in flight across the Vaal on 8 December. Kemp, after an epic journey across the Kalahari, made contact with Maritz and helped him to take Upington on 25 January; but he realized that the cause was hopeless and surrendered within a week. Maritz alone, the first to rebel, withdrew into South West Africa, and on the occupation of that territory by Union troops in 1915 he crossed the border into Angola.

The October rebellion presents fewer problems of interpretation than the September conspiracy. There is less controversy about the motives of the leaders during this phase, because there seems to be no doubt that their aims would have expanded or contracted in direct relation to the degree of their success. It seems hardly necessary to attribute the republican references in de Wet's Vrede speech to the anger of a man provoked by a local magistrate,[3] for it was essentially the speech of a man whose fortunes were improving. The aims of Beyers are less easy to discern, for it is hard to imagine what he hoped to achieve by sitting down under arms and waiting to resist capture: his restraint had its pathetic side, as if he was courting martyrdom in what he never considered after mid-September to be anything but a lost cause. The strategy of the rebels was forced upon them by circumstances, and depended on making contact with Maritz who was thought (probably erroneously) to possess adequate military supplies, as a preliminary to a full-scale trial of strength with the Government.

The handling of a situation of this kind presented the Government with almost as difficult policy decisions as those which confronted the rebels. Though it is possible, as in the case of Commissie Drift, to criticize Botha for too precipitate action, it is not true to say that he and Smuts closed the door to negotiation. The volunteer proclamation of 21 September and the amnesty offer of 30 October must be considered alongside the proclamation of martial law and the conscription order; and although Botha embarrassed Steyn and Hertzog by pressing them to make public

[1] Lange Report, p. 51; Kestell, p. 216.
[2] Lange Report, pp. 129–30 (Steyn to Smuts, 16 November, no. 52), 62–63 (Smuts to Steyn, 17, 19 November; Steyn to Smuts, 18, 20 November).
[3] As Kestell does, pp. 204–5.

92 SOUTH AFRICAN REBELLION, 1914 January

statements condemning the action of Maritz, which both refused to do, he did not on that account refuse to make use of their services in a mediatory capacity. If Steyn failed, and attributed his failure to the Government's refusal to allow Beyers and de Wet to meet in November, this refusal must itself be considered in the light of the military situation, above all the necessity of preventing Beyers and de Wet from co-ordinating their strategy.

The Government handled the rebels with considerable leniency and tact. The stage-managing of the only execution, that of Jopie Fourie, was poor; but it must be urged that a commissioned officer who went into rebellion without resigning his commission, and was responsible for considerable loss of life, could hardly expect a light sentence.[1] The Government put the rebellion down, so far as it could, with Afrikaner forces alone, so as to avoid the risk of evoking renewed Anglo-Boer antagonism. The rank and file rebels, who seem to have taken up arms for a multitude of causes,[2] had all been released by the middle of 1915, and were further penalized only by the refusal of the rebellion losses commission to consider their claims.[3] The leaders, of whom 281 were tried by special treason courts, were fined or given sentences of between two and seven years; but all were in fact released by the end of 1916.[4]

[1] Lange Report (Minutes), pp. 236–7 (H. Rose-Innes, magistrate of Pretoria, desscribed Fourie as ' really responsible for I should say about forty per cent of the total casualties in the whole rebellion '). See below, p. 93, n. 3.

[2] For views on the reasons why the rank and file went into rebellion, see Duncan Report, pp. 187 (J. C. Juta, Lichtenburg), 63 (J. M. Carpell, Intelligence Dept., Kroonstad), 195 (W. Whipp, Memel). These observers listed, variously, a desire to regain independence, opposition to the South West African campaign, intimidation by rebel commandos, indignation at the exclusion of Hertzog from the Cabinet, all of which are fully attested in other evidence. The informality of the commando system, which gave local commandants considerable initiative in the calling up of their men, undoubtedly facilitated the raising of rebel armies: for the Treurfontein meeting of 15 Aug., for example, most of the men seem to have been commandeered without written authority at all. Some, called up by the Government to put down Maritz, seem to have gone into rebellion because they thought they were being conscripted to fight in South West Africa. Poverty and drought were certainly conditioning factors. Van den Heever refers, p. 371, to ' die jammerlike toestand wat in die Vrystaat heers as gevolg van die droogte '. Compare Lange Report (Minutes), p. 23 (Ds. J. A. Viljoen, on distress in the north-western Cape). Speakers at the Dutch Reformed Church conference on the Poor White question at Cradock in Nov. 1916 gave the number of poor whites in the Union at between 70,000 and 107,000, of whom the vast majority were Afrikaners. References to poor white-ism as a cause of the rebellion are few, but they exist; *e.g.* Duncan Report, pp. 134 (J. H. Conradie, who, as superintendent of the Kakamas Labour Colony, reported the loss of some of his protégés to Maritz), 202 (E. Reading, Heilbron). Kopjes, the scene of a good deal of rebel activity, was also the site of a poor white agricultural settlement established in 1912 (See R. W. Willcocks, *The Poor White*, Report of the Carnegie Commission, 1932, ii. 107; Kemp, pp. 247–59, has references to crowds outside the Kopjes meeting places). But one looks in vain for attempts to exploit economic grievances in the speeches of the rebel leaders.

[3] *Report of the Rebellion Losses Commission* (U.G. 40–'16) (chairman M. S. Evans), p. 9.

[4] Scholtz, *Rebellie*, pp. 289–90; Kestell, pp. 233–44; Kemp, pp. 390, 405–6. De Wet was sentenced to six years' imprisonment and a £2,000 fine; but he was released

The cumulative impression left by the Government's actions is that of a preparedness to bury the hatchet.

It would, however, be an exaggeration to say that this effort was successful. Nationalist Afrikanerdom has always thrived on the blood of martyrs, and the rebellion added the names of de la Rey, Beyers and Fourie to their roll of honour. De la Rey had some title to be there already, but the uncertainties surrounding his death assured him of a special place.[1] Beyers provided the image of an innocent sufferer who had never intended violence, and who, though fired on as he crossed the river, died with a full bandolier.[2] The circumstances of Fourie's execution inspired a biographer to even greater extremes of hagiographic sentimentality than those achieved by S. J. du Toit in the case of the Slagters Nek victims, or by Gustav Preller in his work on Gideon Scheepers.[3]

The pathos of the rebellion lies mainly in its character as a civil war between Afrikaners, in which heroes of the war of liberation played the leading roles on both sides. Botha and Smuts, from the point of view of the rebels, had sold themselves to the English. Old wounds had been reopened, and the psychological gulf created which would make it impossible thereafter for many Afrikaners to vote 'SAP'. Hertzog might succeed for a while in holding the two wings of Afrikaner opinion together in the 'twenties and early 'thirties; but fusion in the later 'thirties, between the Hertzogite Nationalists and the South African Party, followed by the outbreak of a second world war against the same enemy, would impose too great a strain on Afrikaner unity. It can hardly have been accidental that the outbreak of the second World War should have caused the Malanite hard core Nationalists to turn their attention

---

after eleven months and confined to his home district, while the *Volksblad's* appeal for funds to assist him was vastly over-subscribed. Kemp records how he was sentenced to seven years' imprisonment and a fine of £1,000, but goes on to state that his fine was paid out of de Wet's surplus, that he was released in November 1916, and that he was able with impunity to ignore a ban on participation in politics for the remainder of his sentence. [1] See above, p. 85, n. 4.

[2] Scholtz, *Beyers*, pp. 381-2. There is a considerable literature on how Beyers met his death, the question being whether he was shot by Government forces or merely drowned. See J. J. van Heerden, 'Die Dood van Kommandant-Generaal C. F. Beyers' (the memoirs of a Government officer, Major H. S. Uys, with annotations) in *Historiese Studies*, June 1947, pp. 54-60; S. J. van der Walt, 'Die Rivier was vol. Hoe Generaal Beyers verdrink het', in *Die Brandwag*, 24 Aug. 1947; S. P. E. Boshoff, *Vaalrivier, die Broederstroom*, pp. 116-18. 'General Beyers', said the Lange Report, p. 64, 'though undoubtedly fired at, was not hit, as the inquest proceedings disclosed that there were no wounds on his body, and that his death was caused by drowning.'

[3] J. M. de Wet, *Jopie Fourie: 'n Lewensskets* (1940) (1st edn. by C. A. Neethling and J. M. de Wet, 1915). The account of Fourie's last hours reads not unlike the Passion according to St. John. A characteristic of the traditional Afrikaner folk hero is his loyalty to his religion. The stress on Fourie's religious loyalty, together with the attribution of irreligion to his opponents, can be compared in the realm of fiction with A. J. Bruwer's play, *Gert Vosloo, die Egte Rebel* (1918), in which Vosloo is captured by the 'English' while reading his Bible, which is summarily snatched from him.

again to the events of 1914—though few were prepared this time even to consider risking their necks in rebellion—or that a spate of literary and historical works on the rebellion should then appear after two decades of relative quiescence.[1] Malan no doubt recalled the efforts which he had made to rescue Fourie from the firing squad, to which a recent historian of the Nationalist Party has drawn special attention.[2] *Hereniging*[3] was brought about under circumstances not unlike those of 1914, concerning which both Hertzog and Malan had bitter memories to recall.

The rebellion greatly stimulated the subsequent development of ideological nationalism among Afrikaners. This was partly a result of the great effort of group self-help launched in 1915 to pay the fines imposed on the rebels by the courts. The *Helpmekaar* (co-operative) movement spread far beyond the ranks of rebel sympathizers, achieved prodigious feats of fund-raising and competitive giving among people not over-endowed with wealth, and raised enough money not only to pay the fines of convicted rebels but also to endow various Afrikaner cultural organizations into the bargain.[4] It was especially strong in the Orange Free State, and surprisingly strong in the Cape.

The stimulus given to the Nationalist Party by the rebellion becomes apparent from the 1915 general election onwards, when it made a net gain of twenty seats and almost achieved a grand slam in the Free State. There was no republicanism in the Programme of Principles of the Party on its establishment in 1914, and Hertzog, though he was certainly a republican at heart, concerned himself less with nomenclature than with the actual legal relationship between South Africa and Great Britain, in a political campaign which reached its climax with the passage of the Status Act in 1934. But pressure from the Malanites for the right to preach republicanism within the fold of the Nationalist Party had the effect of making it a permissible article of faith in 1919. In 1936 the *Gesuiwerdes* under Malan, having broken their ties with Hertzog, made the profession of a republican faith a condition of party membership. Republican associations in the mind of the Afrikaner grew rather than iminished with the passage of time.

University of Cape Town   T. R. H. DAVENPORT

[1] Nearly all the published works on the rebellion pre-date 1920 or post-date 1939.

[2] J. J. van Rooyen, *Die Nasionale Party: Sy Opkoms en Oorwinning—Kaapland se Aandeel* (1956), pp. 26–29.

[3] *I.e.* the reunion of Malanite and Hertzogite Nationalists in 1940.

[4] Kemp, c. xxiii, gives details. According to Sheila Patterson, *The Last Trek* (1957), p. 164, *Helpmekaar* raised £180,000 in two months. See Gert Pretorius, *Man van die Daad: 'n Biografie van Bruckner de Villiers* (1959), c. 6, for an account of the analogous efforts in 1916 to raise funds to establish the *Nasionale Pers*—an interesting insight into the Nationalist *élan vital*.

SOUTH AFRICAN REBELLION, 1914

SUGGESTIONS FOR FURTHER READING By T.R.H. Davenport

Please note that some articles have postdated this article and modified its approach by laying more emphasis on the broad socioeconomic background without altering the political and military aspects.

Swart, Sandra (2000), 'Desperate Men: the 1914 Rebellion and the Politics of Poverty', *South African Historical Journal*, 42, pp. 161–75

Hyslop, Jonathan (1995), 'The Prophet can Rensburg's Vision of Nelson Mandela: White Popular Religious Culture and their Responses to Democratisation', *Social Dynamics* (A University of Cape Town), 21, pp. 23–55

Grundlingh, Albert (1996), 'Probing the Prophet: the Psychology and Politics of the Siener van Rensburg Phenomenon', *South African Historical Journal*, 34, pp. 225–39

Bottomley, J. (1992), 'The O.F.S. and the Rebellion of 1914: the Influence of Industrialisation, Poverty and Poor Whites' in ed. R. Morrell, *'White but Poor: essays in the History of Poor Whites in South Africa, 1880–1940'*. Pretoria: University of South Africa

Spies, Burridge (1986) in, *'A New Illustrated History of South Africa'*, pp. 236–38

Snyman, D.S. Adriaan, *'Stem van 'n profeet'*, Hugenote Publikasies; 1. uitgawe edition, 1993

Kemp, J.C.G (1946), *'Die pad can die Veroweraar'*, Ons Geskiedenis-Serie, Nasionale Pers, Cape Town, 1942

Scholtz, G.D., *'Generaal Christiaan Frederik Beyers: 1869–1914'*, Johannesburg: Voortrekkerpers, 1941

De Wet, J.M., *'Jopie Fourie: 'n Lewenskets'*, Voortrekkerpers, Tweede hersiene druk, Johannesburg, 1940

Maritz, Manie., *'My Lewe en Strewe'*, Johannesburg, 1939

Meintjies, J., *'De la Rey: the Lions of the West'*, H. Keartland, 1966

[24]

Black Men in a White Man's War: The Impact of the First World War on South African Blacks*

Albert Grundlingh

The past decade in European and Anglo-American historiography has witnessed a steady growth of literature in what is generally termed 'war and society' studies. This development is largely a reaction against the 'drum and trumpet' school of military history, a field of inquiry that may be valid in its own right, but one that often degenerates into a discussion of uniforms and badges and seldom rises above campaigns and battles — the major weakness being an inclination to divorce the fighting side of war from its socio-economic and political context. Practitioners in the field of 'war and society' therefore seek to place warfare in its total historical milieu and they share *inter alia* a common interest in war as an agent of social change.[1]

In comparison with the position in Britain, America and Europe, the historiography of 'war and society' in Africa is relatively underdeveloped. Although the subject has not necessarily been neglected in African historiography, certain deficiencies remain. The full complexities of war-related change as opposed to mere change over time have only been partially unravelled and the uneven regional impact of the two World Wars still awaits detailed comparative treatment. More specifically, the quality of analyses regarding the nature, degree and implications of wartime political and socio-economic change has yet to reach the standard attained by the best works in the European and Anglo-American field. However, the outlook is not completely bleak and there are indications that the 'ideas about war and society that are familiar to European history are now being moved south into Africa.'[2]

As far as South Africa is concerned, the Anglo-Boer War of 1899-1902 has consistently attracted scholarly attention, but despite the numerous works on this conflict it is only in a recent publication edited by Peter Warwick and S.B. Spies that some of the wider effects of the war on the various societies involved have been investigated in a systematic way.[3] Whilst certain advances have been registered in the studies of the Anglo-Boer War, the same cannot be said of South Africa's involvement in the First World War. For a background to the war period one is dependent

---

* The terms 'Blacks' and 'Africans' are used as synonyms in this article.

on general, though stimulating, overviews by S.E. Katzenellenbogen[4] and N.G. Garson.[5] Given the lack of interest in South Africa and the First World War, it is not surprising to find that black participation in the conflict has passed almost unnoticed. Except for a pioneering article by Brian Willan on the South African Native Labour Contingent which served in France,[6] little is known about black involvement and even less about the responses that such a cataclysmic event as World War I elicited from various African groupings.

This article develops some of the issues mooted by Willan and furthermore attempts to evaluate the general consequences of the war as they relate to the black population in South Africa. The topic is being dealt with by focussing on the following aspects: first, the effect of war-time service on the socio-political consciousness of those South African Blacks who served as labourers in France and the related question, namely, whether veterans acted as catalysts for resistance against white rule on their return to the Union; second, the wider ramifications of the war as it affected the political perceptions and expectations of those Africans outside of the military sphere; and third, the implications of war-related socio-economic changes for certain African groupings. The essay concludes with an assessment of the nature of change wrought by the war and the hypothesis — common in some studies of 'war and society' — that underprivileged groups in society tend to benefit from war-time changes is considered. Within this admittedly arbitrary framework, only the more salient features are high-lighted; the article makes no claim to be exhaustive and to have covered the total impact of war.

The South African Native Labour Contingent (SANLC) was formed by the South African government in September 1916 in response to urgent requests from the Imperial authorities for manpower to expand the military infrastructure for the gigantic Somme offensive. A suggestion by the Colonial Office that the Union government might also consider arming Africans for service in France was summarily rejected since the South African authorities feared the implications of training Africans in the use of firearms and allowing them to fight against Europeans. Blacks therefore only served in a non-combatant capacity, and up to January 1918, when the decision was taken to disband the SANLC, 21,000 men left for France where at one stage they constituted almost twenty-five per cent of the total military labour force.

Recruitment for the contingent met with considerable black resistance; partly because Africans did not consider the military wage of £3 per month (approximately ten per cent higher than the average mining wage) as sufficient compensation for the dangers inherent in war-time labour, but more pertinently because the South African government, which did the recruiting on behalf of the British, had through its repressive policies alienated the African population. Various coercive measures were employed to induce Africans to enlist, but obviously certain recruits also had their own reasons for joining. A prevailing drought in some rural areas and attendant poverty assisted the authorities to swell the ranks of the SANLC, whilst a criminal element, on the run from the police in the Witwatersrand area, found a relatively safe haven in the contingent. For the educated African elite, who enrolled in numbers disproportionate to the size of their class in the total black population, the idea to prove their loyalty to the 'civilising' Imperial power in an hour of need, as well as the notion that service abroad was an educative experience, were important considerations.

The bulk of the contingent consisted of poverty-stricken African peasants, whilst criminals formed a minority and the educated elite comprised approximately a quarter of the total number of recruits. The educated elite was, in the main, a product of English mission schools and had integrated the values of a Christian-British education with their own African consciousness. They shared a common ideological outlook and at the time of the First World War the effects of their socialization were discernible in their support of the British Empire — a symbolic embodiment of 'justice and fairness' — and the perception that their own future was linked to that of the Empire. Moreover, integral to this world-view was the belief in 'progress' and that recognition depended in part on their unflagging efforts to develop and improve their own abilities. The value system of this class was of central importance in their decision to serve the Empire.

In France the various companies of the SANLC were used mainly for loading and unloading ships in the channel ports, though some were also employed for work on the railways, roads, quarries and forests. On the insistence of the South African government they were isolated and housed in closed compounds — the only unit in France to be accommodated in such a way. This extreme measure of social control – a direct transplant from, in particular, the diamond mines in Kimberley — was instituted to ensure that members of the SANLC would not come into contact with 'harmful social conditions' in a foreign country experiencing total war and was regarded as an essential safeguard to prevent Africans acquiring ideas which the authorities considered detrimental to white South African interests.[7]

The white officers and non-commissioned officers who accompanied the contingent were carefully selected. They were mainly officials from the Native Affairs Department and compound managers drawn from the mines; men who were either intimately involved in the implementation of the Union government's race policies or who were well versed in controlling the black labour force on the mines. Their reports on the effects of war service on the black members of the contingent reflect an almost obsessional tendency to present the venture as an unqualified 'success', with the Africans returning to South Africa 'uncontaminated' and 'unspoilt'. Because of their own prejudices and vested interests in the matter, their impressions are heavily biased towards a sanitised version and the African voice is only audible when it has been decoded, and even then very rarely.[8]

Service overseas nevertheless presented Africans with an opportunity to contrast the crass, or at best, paternalistic racism prevailing in South Africa, with the way in which Whites abroad behaved towards them. Although the officers tried to ensure that members of the contingent had limited contact with the civilian population, some of them did on the odd occasion manage to acquaint themselves with life outside the compounds. Such encounters with French civilians gave them sufficient reason to question in a more searching manner the rigidity of South African society. 'Coming from South Africa, we had fixed ideas about black/white relationships, so we were surprised that some of the French would mix freely with us', declared R. Mohapeloa. Similarly, P. Mabathoana was impressed that 'we were treated with dignity by white people.'[9] Moreover, Jason Jingoes drew a fine distinction between paternalistic racial attitudes and involvement on the basis of equality. The way in which white women received them with tea and other refreshments when they stopped at Liverpool in England before embarking again for France, caused him to remark: 'They were so friendly and we warmed to their concern for us .... Although white women had served us with tea in Cape Town, we know they were only doing it because we were going to war. These girls were different.'[10]

The South African authorities were particularly concerned about the possibility that members of the contingent might establish intimate relationships with French women; in fact, this was one of the main reasons for the compound system. However, some Africans devised resourceful plans to abscond from the compounds and a few were involved with French prostitutes who frequented the dockyard areas. The very nature of such affairs made them momentary and superficial, but there is also evidence to suggest that certain members formed somewhat more enduring relationships with French women that went beyond casual sexual flirtation. It is instructive to note that after the return of the SANLC to South Africa, the chief censor, J.M. Weaver, intercepted and destroyed ten letters from French women to members of the contingent. Weaver argued that such letters 'will give the natives a wrong impression as to their relative position with regard to Europeans.'[11] Liaisons between black males and white females were not completely unknown in South Africa; however, white public 'morality' ensured that they were often clandestine, and when revealed, such relationships met with near hysteria as a dangerous aberration that threatened the status quo.[12] In wartorn France a relatively more permissive atmosphere prevailed amongst the civilian population,[13] and it can be surmised that particularly those members of the SANLC who were involved in Black/White affairs became more acutely aware of the discrepancy and less inclined to view the racist ideology in South Africa as an immutable force.

Through the exigencies of war-time service certain companies of the SANLC also came into occasional contact with white labour battalions which did exactly the same manual work as Blacks. This exposure, which was in sharp contrast to the position in South Africa where Whites left most of the hard labour for Africans to perform, did not fail to leave an imprint. What impressed some Blacks even more though, was that the Whites in labour battalions displayed little colour prejudice and treated them as equals.[14] Jason Jingoes even struck up a friendship with a British labourer, William Johnstone, and it was in this respect that he noted: 'It was our first experience of living in a society without a colour bar.'[15] The implications of black labourers identifying with their white counterparts caused considerable distress amongst the white officers in the contingent — those ever watchful custodians of vested South African interests. It is therefore not surprising that the policy adopted was that only in the most pressing circumstances should Blacks be allowed to work alongside Whites and that they otherwise should be kept completely separate in the work-place.[16]

In one respect the carefully controlled labour regimentation of the SANLC in France differed from the standard procedures usually followed in South Africa. Whereas it was normal practice on the South African mines to divide the black labour force along ethnic lines, in France it was decided to integrate the various 'tribes'. Practical considerations dictated this course of action, and it was also argued that such an arrangement would prevent the possibility of sympathetic strikes amongst members of the same ethnic group.[17] This had an unintended consequence. The continuous contact between workers from the different 'tribes' in the work situation and the fact that they were all exposed to the same conditions in a white man's war, meant that at least for some Africans the ethnic affiliations became distinctly blurred. In an unambiguous statement Z.F. Zibi revealed: 'We are not here as Mfengu, Xhosa and other tribes. We are conscious of the fact that we Blacks are united in staying together.... Therefore we shall never be deceived.... Otherwise it would mean that we are like people who share mat but quarrel — in such cases one never sleeps well.'[18] The exact degree and intensity of solidarity is difficult to determine, but it seems clear that to some extent a common consciousness of their position as workers, as opposed to members of an ethnic group, began to develop in France.

In a more generalised sense the war-time experiences of some members also meant an expansion of their world view. On the way to France several troopships called at Sierra Leone, where M. Mokwena was particularly impressed by the fact that he met 'some pure black negroes of very high educational attainments equal to that of the best Europeans....'[19] Similarly, certain Africans regarded the sea voyage and what they were allowed to witness abroad as formative influences. Thus D.S. Makoliso, who came from a small Transkeian village, Cala, wrote: 'I am glad to say that my experiences are more than any man's in Cala.... My head is full up with new things and the wonders of the world.'[20] Likewise, E. Mdlombo viewed the period spent in France as 'an education' which provided him with new insights and knowledge.[21]

One outstanding event in France left a very marked impression. On 10 July 1917 the British king, George V, inspected and addressed the contingent. For many of the educated Africans it was an unforgettable experience to see the king in person — the supreme symbol of Imperial supremacy and British 'justice' which loomed so large in their imagination. 'We saw him, George V, our king, with our own eyes.... To us it is a dream, something to wonder at', mused M.L. Posholi.[22] What made this visit even more memorable, is that the king in his address not only praised them for their labour, but also assured them: 'You are also part of my great armies fighting for the liberty and freedom of my subjects of all races and creeds throughout the empire.'[23] The implications of these words were not lost on Posholi. 'We are indeed in the midst of great wonders', he wrote, 'because we personally heard that we blacks too are British subjects, children of the father of the great Nation, trusted ones and helpers, and that we are cared for and loved.'[24]

For some Africans at least, the cumulative effect of their wartime experience and observations, as well as a hopeful expectancy that their assistance to the white man in troubled times might yet yield rewarding dividends, found expression in greater self-esteem and a less deferential attitude towards Whites. Jason Jingoes strikingly revealed that 'we were aware, when we returned that we were different from the other people at home. Our behaviour, as we showed the South Africans, was something more than they expected from a Native, more like what was expected among them of a white man.'[25] Jingoes was not the only one to experience a change in outlook and to adopt a more assertive attitude. The commanding officer at the demobilization depot in Cape Town, Major H. Dales, who was in a unique position to witness the demeanour of time-expired Africans returning from France, testified from a white point of view that 'the conduct of these natives left much to be desired, great laxity of discipline being apparent, and their behaviour in general being a great contrast to that of recruits in training for overseas.'[26]

Although the period spent in France undoubtedly sensitised certain members, it is of prime importance in a general assessment of the effects of war-time service on the socio-political consciousness of the participants to consider also those factors which counteracted the development of increased militancy. Apart from the fact that the impact of military service obviously differed according to individual temperament, personality and the pre-existing degree of socio-political awareness, members of the contingent were also exposed to influences which undermined their confidence. In this respect they had occasion to witness the almost inexhaustible armed resources of the white man and the techniques of modern warfare in France. This caused some of them to realize that in the face of the ever increasing military potential of the Whites, an African uprising in South Africa stood even less chance than before of succeeding. One veteran summed up the situation succinctly when he said: 'Our assegais are no good now; they could not reach an aeroplane.'[27]

Moreover, it was the avowed policy of the South African authorities to stifle the potential 'harmful' effects of war-time service and the closed compound system was the salient feature of this policy. Although this system was not completely successful — black opposition and the practical military demands caused its imminent breakdown and were the major considerations in the disbanding of the contingent in January 1918[28] — it nevertheless severely limited the intensity of exposure to new conditions in a foreign country. Colonel S.M. Pritchard, commanding officer of the contingent, probably had sufficient reason to declare in a self-congratulatory statement in November 1919:

> Knowing as he did the conditions under which they [the Africans] were employed, knowing the restrictions placed on their movements, and the strict discipline enforced, it would be a remarkable thing if these natives came back any the worse.[29]

From a different perspective, what is indeed remarkable under these circumstances, is that at least some Africans, as indicated, used the restricted opportunities in the way they did.

This analysis points to the need to maintain a fine balance in evaluating the effect of participation in a white man's war. For every participant who returned from France with a changed outlook, there might have been another who was less affected. In addition, virtually all the factors in overseas service which had the potential to broaden the social and political perception of black members were consciously emasculated by the South African authorities.

Related to the war-time exposure of SANLC members were grievances about the callous treatment meted out to them by South African officers in France and resentment about the paucity of post-war recognition. Veterans received no war medals or gratuities. Furthermore, the inflated promises made to lure the unsuspecting into the recruiting net during 1916-17 were simply brushed aside; promises that they would be relieved from paying poll tax, be exempted from pass laws and be given free grants of land as well as cattle remained unfulfilled. To add insult to injury, former members were even expected to pay poll tax for the period they had been absent from South Africa.[30] A disillusioned A.K. Xabanisa certainly echoed the sentiments of a considerable number of veterans when he wrote: 'I am just like a stone which after killing a bird, nobody bothers about, nor cares to see where it falls.'[31] It was in this context of post-war disillusionment amongst veterans of the contingent that Edward Roux claimed in his seminal work on black resistance in South Africa: 'After 1918 there were thousands of black men in the country who were not willing any longer to endure the anti-Native laws, men who were prepared to stir up their fellow Africans to revolt against the system.'[32]

Did they, however, in practice act as political catalysts? It remains to explore the links between military service in France and tangible opposition to white rule in South Africa. The fact that some members of the SANLC returned from France with a sharper awareness of their relative deprivation and were discontented over their post-war treatment, does not necessarily mean that their feelings and insights were actually translated into active resistance. It is therefore essential to consider whether the stimuli of service abroad and all that accompanied it, were sufficient to galvanise veterans into political action.

Some ex-members did become active in formal black politics. Shortly after the war Doyle Modiakgotla joined the Industrial and Commercial Workers' Union of Africa (ICU) and later became secretary of the Griqualand-West branch. In 1920 S.M. Bennet Ncwana also became a member of the ICU and in addition initiated a shortlived publication, *The Black Man*.³³ Although it is significant that they became overtly involved in the black cause, there is no firm evidence to suggest that their war experiences were the prime motivating force. It can only be surmised that to some extent their exposure in France must have had a contributory influence.

Other veterans were not to be found in formally organised political opposition, but nevertheless influenced their compatriots in more subtle ways. Shortly after his return from France, L. Molife addressed rural peasants in the Rustenburg district in the western Transvaal and assured them in the following terms that their plight would soon be relieved: 'The Germans were building powerful airships, capable of moving an army — they must not worry, that shortly a German army would be in Africa and would help them gain their freedom.' This message, endorsed by similar statements from other ex-members, was received with considerable acclamation.³⁴ The factual accuracy of Molife's account is of course besides the point; what is important is its strong millenarian element. Millenarianism usually reflects a pessimism about the efficacy of human agencies to effect change and is grounded in a belief that social transformation can only come about by cataclysmic extraneous means.³⁵ In this particular case Germany was cast in the role of the saviour who would liberate them from white oppression. There were, it is true, no large scale post-war millenarian movements in the Transvaal, but it is nonetheless revealing that certain veterans of the SANLC were instrumental in the dissemination of millenarian ideas.

In contrast with the Transvaal, millenarianism was an outstanding characteristic of rural resistance in the Eastern Cape and Transkei during the twenties. Here America featured prominently as the country which would deliver Africans from bondage.³⁶ There is some tantalising evidence to suggest that a few former members of the contingent were involved in these movements; however, it seems as if they could only have played a very marginal role.³⁷

On a more individual and personal level some veterans did not hesitate to demonstrate their sharper perception and increased self-confidence in everyday and practical South African situations. In the Pietersburg district in the northern Transvaal an anonymous ex-member refused to accept passively what he regarded as exorbitant prices in the local trading store. He confronted the shopkeeper, named Williams, and a subsequent police report on the incident strikingly reveals (though this was obviously not the intention) the way in which this particular veteran asserted himself:

> A native who had recently returned from France came to his [Williams'] store and stated that the Europeans were responsible for the high prices of foodstuffs. He then asked Williams to whom the ground on which he was trading belonged; on receiving a reply that the ground belonged to Williams, the Native replied, 'the ground belongs to the natives and we will show you.'[38]

Such instances could be multiplied, but there is no satisfactory evidence that ex-contingent members were in the vanguard of sustained and coherent black resistance to white domination. For example, no indication could be found that former members were involved in the black industrial unrest on the Witwatersrand during 1918-19. Nor does it appear, on a somewhat different level, that veterans acted as 'modernisers' in rural societies. Immediately after his return, Jason Jingoes found (and one can readily assume that this was not an isolated case) that 'he was thrown back into the old traditional ways.'[39]

The evident lack of involvement on the part of ex-members in overt resistance seems to prove that war service as such, for the reasons already mentioned, was not sufficient either to jolt veterans into revolt or for them to encourage others to do so. However, it must be borne in mind that even those who possibly contemplated such action, had to consider the formidable power of the state to crush any uprising. It is nevertheless clear that in the South African case the general assumption that service in a white man's war is often a catalyst for vigorous black resistance, cannot be taken for granted. When Africans did resist, as they did on the Witwatersrand in 1918-19, it was not because they were influenced by 'new ideas' emanating from abroad, but because of the fundamental oppression built into the South African system of white domination – and they did not have to go to France to become aware of that.

The impact of the war was obviously not only restricted to those who actually participated. It is therefore important to delineate the wider effect of the war as it was manifested in African political responses and perceptions.

Immediately prior to the war, the South African Native National Congress (SANNC) — founded, as is well known, in 1912 as an African political organization and composed of the educated elite — was involved in sustained protest against the 1913 Land Act which left numerous rural Blacks destitute in the northern provinces and denied Africans the right to purchase land outside certain limited scheduled areas. As an important part of their campaign the SANNC had sent a deputation to England in the early months of 1914 in an attempt to persuade the Imperial government to intervene on their behalf and to influence the policy being pursued by the South African government. Although it was abundantly clear even before the outbreak of war in August 1914 that the British government was not prepared to pressurise the Union cabinet, the belief nevertheless persisted amongst certain SANNC members that the deputation 'might have had a real effect had not the First World War been declared in the midst of that agitation.'[40] Besides the obviously wishful element in this claim, it can also be viewed as an indication that at the time of the outbreak of war members of the SANNC were in their own minds still hopeful that Britain would not completely abandon African interests in South Africa.

The SANNC was in session in Bloemfontein when the news was conveyed that hostilities had broken out in Europe. They immediately affirmed their loyalty to King and Empire, pledged to suspend all public criticism of the Union government, and to refrain from agitation in connection with the 1913 Land Act. A delegation from Congress further informed the authorities of African support for the duration of the conflict.[41] However, one dissenting voice was heard. J.T. Gumede, a more militant member of Congress, considered it essential to keep up criticism of the South African government despite the war. He argued in March 1915 that such a policy would be more beneficial to African interests 'than the present attitude of folding their hands in idle talk of the war, which they have no right to claim as theirs....'[42]

Although Gumede's argument was an exception to the overwhelming loyalist response, it nevertheless points to the precarious position of a middle-class constitutionalist body like the SANNC. Since they operated through constitutional channels, they were ultimately dependent on official goodwill and could hardly have afforded to alienate the authorities on such a major issue as the war. It would be wrong, however, to construe their loyalist response and co-operative stance as an indication of passive acceptance of their subservient position. Given their limited range of options to bring about constitutional change, they regarded loyalty during the war as an additional method to be utilised in the unequal struggle. In identifying themselves with the white ruling class in a common cause and openly proclaiming a common allegiance to the British crown, they expected in due course to be rewarded for their loyalty. They also hoped that such an attitude might enable them to pressure the authorities into granting meaningful recognition. In addition, they had implicit trust in the ability of the British government to effect favourable change. This clearly influenced their view that an event as cataclysmic as the First World War would change the nature of the Empire with corresponding benefits accruing to the African population.[43] During the war the SANNC consistently adhered to this policy. They did, it is true, express criticism on various issues and gave half-hearted support to strike action on the Rand in 1918, but their loyalty as such was never in doubt.

Towards the closing stages of the war black participation in the hostilities had further raised the level of expectancy amongst African political leaders and they became more strident in their demands. 'We expect to be rewarded for our work after the war when prizes are distributed to the brave who were in battle', insisted D.S. Letanka, an influential SANNC member, in February 1918.[44] In April 1918 his colleague, L.T. Mvabaza, made a similar point and furthermore located African aspirations within the context of freedom and democracy — the declared war aims of the allied forces. Unambiguously he stated:

> That in consideration of the sacrifices the Bantu have made during this war which we are continually being told is for democracy and freedom, the British and the white people of this land should redress our grievances and give the freedom for which we lost thousands of men in this struggle.[45]

It was basically such beliefs — reinforced by statements of the American president, Woodrow Wilson, and the British prime minister, David Lloyd George, to the effect that the post-war settlement should allow sufficient scope for the self-determination of subjected peoples — that prompted the SANNC to sent yet another deputation to Britain in 1919. The efforts of this delegation are documented elsewhere and need no recounting here;[46] suffice to say that despite sympathetic remarks by Lloyd George, the deputation was a dismal failure. In retrospect their attempts to bring about British constitutional intervention may appear unrealistic and even naive. This however, would be too harsh a judgment. Viewed in their own terms and the overall historical context it becomes clear that in the more hopeful post-war climate their attempts amount to a resolute move by constitutional minded men to effect favourable change through the only avenue they deemed promising and available. 'The Great War has . . . opened a chance to us, . . . let us not lose the chance', argued L.T. Mvabaza on the eve of their departure to Britain.[47]

The failure of the deputation left the SANNC disillusioned and eroded their earlier trust in the British government. Even Lloyd George's sympathetic attitude was no consolation. 'Lloyd George said he did not know the black people were so badly treated in Africa, but Lloyd George is a white man and cannot be trusted...', was the reaction of J.D. Ngoja, a Cape member of the SANNC.[48] In his study of the African National Congress Peter Walshe regards the fruitless visit to Britain as a watershed in the history of Congress. Its constitutional efforts frustrated, the organization found it difficult to realign itself and to adopt decisive new strategies; consequently its support declined in the post-war years.[49]

In assessing the effect of the war on the SANNC it is clear that increased expectations brought about by the war only buttressed the aspirations of Congress for a limited period. When it became evident that there would be no concessions on account of black loyalty and sacrifices, the organization lapsed into a mood of political cynicism which contributed towards its relative stagnation in the twenties. It would thus appear that viewed from the perspective of the twenties the war actually had a detrimental effect on the position of the SANNC. However, the subsequent decline of the SANNC can obviously not be attributed to post-war disillusionment only; other factors, such as the rise of the more populist ICU, also played their part.

It further remains to explore the way in which the war affected the political perceptions of African groupings other than the SANNC. Often the loyal rhetoric of the African elite conceals the ferment in the rest of society. To dispel a notion of general and undisturbed tranquillity it is necessary to look beyond the utterances emanating from a few, not necessarily representative, African leaders.

In contrast to the loyal response of the educated elite at the outbreak of war, dissenting views were expressed by the African working class on the Witwatersrand gold mines. They were quick to draw their own conclusions from the European struggle and relate them to their experiences as an exploited labour force on the mines. Britain was associated with the oppressive system in which they found themselves and therefore Germany was seen as worthy of their sympathies. On the Nourse Mines L. Ralitane informed his fellow labourers that 'the Germans are beating the English, and you boys are foolish to work for the English when the Germans are giving them a hiding.' Ralitane's 'inflammatory' views earned him the option of a £25 fine or six months' imprisonment.[50] Another labourer even more clearly directed his animosity against the British. 'God be with Germany and clear out all Englishmen on earth', was his fervent wish. 'Indeed', he continued, 'if the German came out in South A.[frica] we shall be glad if we can help them too.'[51] Moreover, some mineworkers also perceived that the war held out opportunities for resistance against the repressive system in which they found themselves. The chief compound manager at the Crown mines reported in September 1914:

> I notice a great change the last weeks in the attitude of the natives towards Europeans, the natives being very cheeky and insurbordinate. They appear ... to have the idea that the Government are in difficulties owing to the war and are in consequence weak and frightened of the natives ....[52]

Lack of organization on the part of these Africans, as well as the effective controlling agencies of state and industry — which were particularly pronounced during war-time — prevented such resistance from taking the form of concerted mass actions in 1914. Manifestations of African resistance and their perception of the war as having liberating potentialities were however no less real.

These responses were not confined to the working classes in industrial areas. From rural Natal pro-German sympathies were very much in evidence amongst the Zulu peasant communities. They associated the British with the white colonization of Natal; if Britain could be defeated, it was argued, their position might also change. From their perspective any change of the status quo was regarded as preferable to the existing dispensation.[53] Not surprisingly, these desperate expectations found expression in millenarian fantasies. In the Pietermaritzburg district S. Nkabindi gained a considerable following as a prophet predicting that the Whites in South Africa would be annihilated by the Germans who would then restore the land to their rightful African owners.[54] Likewise, in the Dundee district an anonymous prophet claimed that Dinuzulu (former head of the Zulu Royal House who had died in 1913 after being deposed in 1909 and sentenced to four years' imprisonment for his part in the Zulu rebellion of 1906) was still alive and that the Germans would bring him to South Africa and reinstate him as the supreme African ruler.[55]

Others did not look to the Germans, but perceived the war as an opportunity to deliver themselves from bondage. The magistrate of the Greytown district declared explicitly:

> Certain natives are going amongst the tribes ... saying that now the English are at war with another nation, you have a good chance to fight them, as England cannot send men to assist. Why should you forever be under a contract to a white man ... ? What are you to do? Your chance to ease your burdens is to fight the white man and get your country back.[56]

Although it must be kept in mind that at the outbreak of the war Whites were prone to exaggerate the possibility of African uprisings — a psychological overreaction which had more to do with stereotyping and fears than the actual African response — in this particular case there is no reason to doubt the veracity of the report.

In the Transkei — where the impact of white rule and settlement was less pervasive — some Africans did not merely indulge in speculation on the opportunities offered by the outbreak of war, but actually used the occasion to come out in revolt. Between 12 and 19 November 1914 an uprising occurred in the Matatiele district where the Hlubi destroyed dipping tanks and burnt and looted a number of trading stores. The situation seemed critical at the time and the Whites in the countryside hastily fled into the town for protection. The Chief Magistrate, W.T. Brownlee, immediately acted to re-assert white dominance in the district; every available member of the Citizen Force was called out, armed and rushed by motor car to the scene of disaffection. Confronted by the armed might of their white overlords, open resistance on the part of the Hlubi petered out. A subsequent report revealed that they were seriously aggrieved by the way in which the authorities applied compulsory cattle dipping regulations against East Coast Fever. Although Matatiele was not a fever-stricken area, African peasants in the district were nevertheless forced to comply with the dipping regulations. Moreover, they had to make weekly payments for such dippings, whilst white farmers of greater financial means managed to evade these regulations with impunity. Dipping regulations were admittedly the focal point of the revolt, but the timing of the Hlubi resistance to these measures is of considerable significance in assessing the African response to the outbreak of the Great War. The revolt took place at a time when white authority in the Transkei was particularly vulnerable since many policemen had been drafted into the South African Defence Force. It is clear from a series of meetings held prior to the revolt that the withdrawal of a substantial section of the police had not gone unnoticed amongst the Hlubi. With the white man's attention diverted by hostilities elsewhere, the opportunity for meaningful resistance had, as they were clearly aware, presented itself. To their suprise, however, more armed men turned out to quell the revolt than they had anticipated. It is nevertheless clear that the Hlubi reaction to the outbreak of war represented a definite and organised attempt to rid themselves of the obligations imposed by white rulers.[57]

The Hlubi revolt was the only rural African uprising in the Transkei, or for that matter in South Africa, that can be related to the war. Perhaps less dramatic, but not necessarily less important, was the way in which the wider ramifications of the conflict exerted an influence on post-war millenarian movements in the Transkei. These movements, already alluded to, which were connected with the war as far as black disillusionment with the failure of the British government to intervene in South Africa, shifted the attention to America. In 1927 W.D. Cingo, a Transkeian journalist, graphically explained this strand in millenarianism and its relation to the war:

> The Great European War also had its contribution to these illusions. The moral and military power of America came into prominence. Her declaration for the 'Self determination of smaller nations'... caught the tender ears of the unsophisticated natives in these parts. They regard the voice of America as that of a mighty race of black people overseas, dreaded by all Europeans.... Hopes for political and economic emancipation were revived and today the word America (iMelika) is a household word symbolic of nothing but Bantu National freedom and liberty.[58]

Furthermore, another occurrence related to the war — the death of 615 members of the SANLC who lost their lives when the troopship, the S.S. *Mendi*, sank off the Isle of Wight on 21 February 1917 after being rammed by the S.S. *Darro* — featured in post-war African thinking. The memory of the sinking of the *Mendi* was kept alive by the Mendi Memorial Club, formed by African ex-servicemen, and the annual commemoration of 21 February as 'Mendi day'. In course of time the actual events of that fateful night were related in exaggerated heroic terms and assumed a mythological nationalistic dimension in African group-memory.[59] Related to this was the 'Mendi Memorial Bursary Fund' founded in 1936 to sponsor promising black pupils. A distinct characteristic of this fund was the perceived need to increase black self-esteem through education and the importance of education in the struggle against white domination. During a Mendi memorial meeting in Johannesburg in 1946, attended by 20,000 Blacks, it was argued: 'The white men are clever people and the only way to oppose their oppressive measures is by education and cleverness.'[60]

It is clear that the wider effects of the war on African perceptions and responses are evident in a number of disparate ways, reflecting the complex diversity in African society itself. Nevertheless, one overriding impression that remains is that several African groupings viewed the war as an event that could be used for expressing their opposition to white rule. The war, however, did not constitute a turning point in this respect; to claim that would mean that the preceding and subsequent process of African resistance would be distorted. Neither would it be correct to assume that all African groupings were affected by the hostilities conducted beyond the South African borders. Some Africans paid scant attention to the white man's quarels. 'The feeling came to be pretty common amongst them', it was reported, 'that this was only one more of those wars to which the Europeans, who ought to know better, were accustomed, and that it was not in any vital sense a Bantu concern.'[61]

Apart from the impact of the war on African political perceptions, certain war-related socio-economic changes also affected the black population. It was particularly in the industrial areas of South Africa that these changes made themselves felt and where the effects were starkly visible.

Shortly after the outbreak of war the directors of De Beers decided to suspend all their mining operations on the diamond fields. The mining magnates argued that the uncertain war conditions in Britain and Europe would have a detrimental effect on the international demand for diamonds. Beside cheap labour, the profitability of the industry was dependent on the careful marketing of diamonds and it was therefore essential to avoid flooding the market at a time when the international prospects for luxury items like diamonds appeared decidedly bleak. The possibility of continuing mining operations and stockpiling diamonds to market at a later stage was also considered unfeasible because of the considerable capital investment and high risk involved. Consequently some 5000 Whites and 45,000 Blacks were dismissed from the various diamond mines and mining operations were only resumed on a limited scale in July 1916.[62]

For the mining magnates such a policy made sound financial sense, but the summary cessation caused considerable resentment amongst the unemployed workers. After the Jagersfontein mine had been closed down, an indignant white worker asked:

> Is it right that a few men who have obtained their wealth by the labour and sweat of their employees in Jagersfontein, can stop a whole industry and plunge a whole town into the miseries of starvation, to save themselves not from ruin but from the temporary loss of their fat dividends and profits?[63]

And, one may very well ask, how much more applicable must these sentiments have been to the black workers who found themselves on the bottom rung of the labour ladder?

Whilst white workers were offered some financial assistance to tide them over, no such provision was made for African workers. Having served their purpose, they were repatriated without any further ado. Many of them were in dire distress; without food and little money they streamed back to poverty-stricken areas which they had actually left in the first place to supplement their meagre income. This was particularly the case with the Sotho who had left Basutoland on account of a shortage of food during 1914. Not surprisingly the police on the border between South Africa and Basutoland reported that 'a disquieting feature is the behaviour of the natives who are returning from the diamond fields. Their attitude is mutinous and quite unlike their usual behaviour.'[64] Equally clear is the motivation which prompted a number of labourers returning from Kimberley to Basutoland to plunder a shop in Brandfort and remove the food supplies in it.[65]

In contrast to the diamond mines, the production of gold was uninterrupted by the war; gold being sold at the fixed price of 85/- per fine ounce. During the war though, a situation arose on the gold mines which could have had far-reaching effects for the black labourers. Approximately twenty-five per cent of the skilled or semi-skilled white labour force left for active service,[66] and the opportunity therefore existed for Blacks to replace them. The Chamber of Mines was in favour of such a move — not on account of any 'liberal' considerations — but only because skilled or semi-skilled black labour would be cheaper than similar white labour.[67] However, this did not materialise to any great extent since the white Mineworkers Union ensured that the places of those who had left for the front were filled by 'poor white' Afrikaners.[68] Thus, although a few Blacks did move up in the labour hierarchy during the war, it was hardly of any significance for the great majority of the African working class who made no gains during the war.

The labour supply to the gold mines was not seriously affected by the military recruitment of Blacks; although it caused a slight drop, this was off-set by unemployed workers from the diamond fields finding their way to the gold mines.[69] In the closing stages of hostilities though, the labour supply became insufficient to satisfy the demands of an expanding industry and in the aftermath of the war increased production costs, due to war-time inflation, contributed to a serious profitability crisis.[70] This had, as we shall see later, important implications for black wage rates and war-time inflation also contributed to a few 'wildcat' strikes during the war years which foreshadowed the extensive strike of February 1920 involving 71,000 black workers.[71]

Strained industrial relations were of course not confined to the gold mines. Outside the mining industry considerable labour unrest occurred during 1918-20: the demands for higher wages in Bloemfontein in February 1919; the large scale revolt against passes in Johannesburg in March and April 1919; the dock strike in Cape Town in December 1919 which launched Clements Kadalie's ICU; and the agitation for wage increases in Port Elizabeth in January 1920. These upheavals, which were particularly sustained in Johannesburg during 1918-19, have been well documented by other historians and will not be further discussed here.[72] However, several writers have briefly hinted at or merely assumed that the war contributed to the rising tide of militancy. Although this assertion is undoubtedly valid, it has not been demonstrated, except for rather vague statements,[73] how hostilities conducted mainly in Europe influenced black workers in a country 10,000 kilometres removed from the seat of war. Within the context of this article it is therefore important to establish the links between the war and labour unrest.

In this respect it is essential to note the rapid secondary industrialization which occurred during the war years. There was a brief decline in trade and industry at the outbreak of war, but soon after that remarkable growth took place. From 1915-16 the number of factories and other manufacturing enterprises increased from 3998 to 6890 in 1919-20 — an increase of seventy-two per cent.[74] Basically this development was related to the war in that South Africa was unable to import articles not usually produced locally and local manufacturers were induced to take advantage of the opportunity created by diminishing foreign competition whilst the natural protection which South African industries enjoyed as a result of being thousands of kilometres from Europe and America was increased during the war by the rise in freight, insurance and other import charges as well as the severely reduced commercial output of the belligerent nations.[75] The industrial take-off was closely allied with accelerated urbanization. During and immediately after the war, the number of unskilled workers (mainly Africans) employed in urban industries (excluding mines) rose dramatically by eighty-three per cent; from 61,654 in 1915-16 to 113,037 in 1919-20.[76] The vast majority of these workers were concentrated in the industrial heartland of South Africa, the Witwatersrand area, where they were housed in appalling conditions. The rapid proletarianization clearly had important implications for labour unrest and indirectly the war thus provided the broad socio-economic context for strained industrial relations. This connection did not go unnoticed amongst the officials of the Native Affairs Department. In a memorandum of May 1919, dealing with the position of Africans on the Witwatersrand, it was explicitly pointed out:

> The disorganisation of the commercial world ... has thrown the British Dominions on their own resources, and one is amazed at the strides that have been made in local manufacturing during the past four years. In short, the war has put the hand of time forward many years ... and this is perhaps most noticeable in regard to the

natives.... They have been awakened by the roar and noise of a universal war.... Johannesburg had become the centre in which native thought has developed most during the war, and from which native political movements will radiate.... It is on the Witwatersrand that the native has had the opportunity of realising what industrial labour strikes mean.[77]

Important as war-time industrialization might have been in accelerating proletarianization, it was of course, not the only contributory factor. Underdevelopment of the reserves — an ongoing process which drove Africans off the land — as well the effects of droughts in the rural areas also loomed large in this transformation. Once again the necessity of balancing war-related developments with other trends in society is evident.

A further consideration in examining the links between the war and labour unrest, is that of inflation. As a result of war conditions in Britain, demand for goods exceeded supply and consequently prices increased drastically. Since South Africa had intimate trade links with Britain, this also affected the price structure in the Union. Moreover, banking and credit facilities were considerably extended during the war-time industrialization and the unproductive debt almost doubled between 1910 and 1920. The cost of living, according to official statistics, increased by 15.07 per cent between 1914 and 1918, but there are indications that retail prices for the same period rose between thirty-one and thirty-nine per cent.[78] Although white salaries were adjusted accordingly, black wages were either pegged at pre-war levels or only increased marginally.[79] Not surprisingly, the issue of wages became a burning grievance and the focal point for industrial unrest.

In addition to these developments, the sacrifices made by African participants in the war also impinged on the ideological consciousness of Blacks during the unrest on the Witwatersrand. Thus a black women, E. Mallela, declared at the time of the so-called one shilling strike: 'King George in France said to the natives you are my soldiers. Why should we be arrested and killed under the Union Jack? We have helped. We must be free, why should we be slaves? Think of the blood of our boys in France.'[80] Essentially the same point was made by an anonymous African at more or less the same time: 'Some of our brothers are in France today. Some of us are dying for Botha's Government which do[es] not give us anything.'[81] These were not isolated examples and it can be readily assumed that this awareness must have had a stimulating effect. However, despite the significance of these war-related ideas actually surfacing on the Rand during 1918-19, there is no satisfactory evidence that these were important considerations for spurring either black workers or petty bourgeoisie elements into revolt.

The links between the war and labour unrest are therefore mainly confined to industrialization, proletarianization and inflation. Of these, the effects of inflation on black wages were directly connected with the primary cause for agitation. However, as P.L. Bonner has noted in his article on the unrest on the Rand, it would be wrong 'to exaggerate the importance of this factor [black wages] at the expense of the wider range of repressive, discriminatory mechanisms....' The iniquitous pass system, poor housing and inadequate educational facilities were all interrelated and integral to the system of labour repression which evoked such sustained resistance.[82] In evaluating the effect of the war on urban discontent, these inherent structural inequalities are obviously of overriding and paramount importance; war-related developments only served in an oblique way to expose and emphasise the exploitable position of African workers.

In his seminal work on war and social change in the Anglo-American and European context Arthur Marwick has generalized that 'in modern war there is a greater participation on the part of larger underprivileged groups in society, who tend correspondingly to benefit, or at least develop a new selfconsciousness.' More specifically he contends that participation in the war effort involves 'a strengthened market position and hence higher material standards for such groups; it also engenders a new sense of status, usually leading to a dropping of former sectional or class barriers.'[83] In the southern African context few historians have provided an overall assessment of the impact of war, but S.E. Katzenellenbogen has nonetheless ventured to suggest: 'Generally, all social groups in southern Africa benefitted economically from the war. Wages were driven up by the greater shortage of labour....'[84]

Katzenellenbogen's assertion can be readily dismissed; as indicated the economic position of South African Blacks actually declined during 1914-18 as a result of war-time inflation. Although Marwick's generalization is more subtle than the foregoing extract would suggest, it is also largely unacceptable when applied to war-related development in South Africa. Admittedly participation in the war did serve to increase the self-esteem and consciousness of certain Africans, but apart from the enduring effect of the *Mendi* disaster, little, if any, practical advances were achieved.

Obviously a key question in determining the impact of war is whether the war itself actually initiated new trends or reinforced existing ones. For

South Africa it would be claiming too much to aver that the war was responsible for a completely original departure. However, particularly in the field of war-time manufacturing and commerce, decisive changes did occur. 'While imperial capital's influence declined', B. Bozzoli has recently shown, 'that of national capital rose; while the elements that constituted imperial capital were shaken by the war, those of national capital seized the opportunity to grow and become firmer....'[85] Closely allied to growth of local capital was the extension of social and political control over urban Africans in the post-war period — formally embodied in the 1923 Natives Urban Areas Act. This legislation, as Peter Kallaway has interpreted it, was 'the basis of a much tougher political creed, namely the foundation of a stable urban African community in the towns of South Africa, which would because of its stake in the status quo, form a bulwark against labour unrest and political agitators.'[86] Thus, even from this cursory discussion of the nature of changes effected by the First World War, it is clearly evident that the white man's war not only brought greater hardships for Africans during the war-period, but that war-related developments outside their control also had detrimental longterm implications.

Notes

1. See for instance M.R.D. Foot (ed.), *War and Society* (London 1973); A. Marwick, *War and social change in the twentieth century: a comparative study of Britain, France, Germany, Russia and the United States* (London 1974); A. Marwick, *Women at war, 1914-1918* (London 1977); M.A. Nettleship, R.D. Givens and A. Nettleship (eds.), *War, its Causes and Correlates* (The Hague 1975); R.F. Weigley (ed.), *New dimensions in military history* (New York 1975); B. Bond and I. Roy (eds.), *War and Society*, I and II (London 1975 and 1977); M. Howard, *War in European history* (Oxford 1976); V.G. Kiernan, *European empires from conquest to collapse, 1815-1960* (London 1982).
2. D. Killingray, 'War and society in British colonial Africa: themes and prospects' in D.I. Ray, P. Shinnie and D. Williams (eds.), *Into the 80's: the proceedings of the eleventh annual conference of the Canadian Association of African Studies*, I (Vancouver 1981), 251.
3. P. Warwick and S.B. Spies (eds.), *The South African War, 1899-1902* (London 1980).
4. S.E. Katzenellenbogen, 'Southern Africa and the War of 1914-18' in Foot (ed.), *War and Society*, 107-21.
5. N.G. Garson, 'South Africa and World War I', *The Journal of Imperial and Commonwealth History*, VIII: 1 (1979), 68-85.

6. B.P. Willan, 'The South African Native Labour Contingent, 1916-1918', *Journal of African History*, XIX: 1 (1978), 61-86. For a recent article focusing on Lesotho see R.R. Edgar, 'Lesotho and the First World War: Recruiting, Resistance and the South African Native Labour Contingent', *Mohlomi, Journal of Southern African Historical Studies*, III, IV, V (1981), 94-108.
7. The formation, recruitment and composition of the contingent as well as the closed compound policy are discussed in detail in A.M. Grundlingh, 'Die Suid-Afrikaanse Gekleurdes en die Eerste Wêreldoorlog' (unpublished DLitt. et Phil. diss., University of South Africa 1981), 113-48, 164-218, 269-88.
8. The composition of the white personnel is discussed in Grundlingh, 'Suid-Afrikaanse Gekleurdes', 262-6. For examples of their reports see for instance Public Record Office (PRO), War Office (WO) 107/37, 'History of the S.A.N.L.C.,' Lt.-Col. A. Barnard, 1918; Letter from Capt. L.E. Hertslett, *Imvo Zabantsundu*, 27 November 1917; Central Archives Depot Pretoria (CAD), Government-General (GG) 545/9/93/56, Report on the South African Native Labour Corps, 31 July 1918.
9. Transcripts from interviews with R. Mohapeloa, Maseru, 9 May 1980 and P. Mabathoana, Maseru, 22 April 1980. (I am indebted to Robert Edgar from Howard University, Washington, DC, for these transcripts.)
10. J. Perry and C. Perry (eds.), *A Chief is a Chief by the People; the Autobiography of Stimela Jason Jingoes* (Oxford 1975), 80.
11. South African Defence Force Documentation Centre (SADFDC), Secretary of Defence (DC) 1136/2/1997, Chief Censor to acting Secretary of Defence, 23 April 1918. For further evidence of Black/White affairs see PRO, WO 95/4115, SANLC General Hospital Diary, 1917; 'White women and Black men', *Western Morning News*, 22 October 1917 (cutting in Aborigines Protection Society Papers [APS], S 23 H2/1).
12. Compare C. van Onselen, *Studies in the social and economic history of the Witwatersrand, 1886-1914*, 2, *New Nineveh* (London 1982), 45-50.
13. The Officer commanding the Cape Auxiliary Horse Transport Company (a Cape 'Coloured' unit which served in France as drivers) reported in this respect that some 'white women showed partiality towards the Cape men and no matter how strict the control, found means of communicating with them, as was evidenced by a number of venereal cases.' PRO, Colonial Office (CO) 551/117/39492, Report on the Cape Auxiliary Horse Transport Company, 13 June 1919.
14. 'Letter from F.H. Kumalo', *Native Teachers Journal*, October 1920; SADFDC, Union War Histories (UWH) 89/34, Report on the SANLC, 8 March 1919.
15. Perry (eds.), *Jingoes*, 93.
16. PRO, WO 107/37, 'History of the SANLC', 1918.
17. SADFDC, UWH 89/34, Report on the SANLC, 8 March 1919.
18. 'Letter from Z.F. Zibi', *Imvo Zabantsundu*, 18 September 1917 (translated from Xhosa).

19. CAD, J (Department of Justice) 258/3/127/20, Report on a meeting of the Transvaal Native Congress in Johannesburg, 24 August 1921. Mokwena informed the meeting of his experiences in France. See also Willan, 'South African Native Labour Contingent, 1916-1918', 78.
20. Cape Town Archives Depot (CTA), Chief Magistrate Transkei (CMT) 3/930/778/2, D.S. Makoliso to Magistrate Cala, 24 February 1917.
21. Jagger Library, University of Cape Town (UCT) Stanford Papers BC 293/Frr/2, E. Mdlombo to Stanford, 3 March 1918.
22. Lesotho National Archives, Maseru (LNA), Secretary to the Government (S) 3/13/2/3, M.L. Posholi to P. Griffiths, 12 July 1917.
23. Quoted in S.M. Bennet Ncwana, *Souvenir of the Mendi Disaster* (Johannesburg 1942), 26-7.
24. LNA, S 3/13/2/3, M.L. Posholi to P. Griffiths, 12 July 1917.
25. Perry (eds.), *Jingoes*, 92.
26. SADFDC, OC Records 44/22/81, Report on the SANLC, 12 April 1918.
27. 'What the Native is thinking', *Cape Times*, 18 April 1921.
28. Black resistance against the closed compound policy and the reasons for the disbandment of the contingent are discussed in Grundlingh, 'Suid-Afrikaanse Gekleurdes', 280-8, 297-300.
29. 'Natives' Proud Record', *South Africa*, 8 November 1918.
30. See Grundlingh, 'Suid-Afrikaanse Gekleurdes', 322-5.
31. CTA, CMT 3/925/778/2, A.K. Xabanisa to Chief Magistrate Transkei, 28 December 1919.
32. E. Roux, *Time longer than Rope: a history of the Black man's struggle for freedom in South Africa* (Madison 1972), 114.
33. Grundlingh, 'Suid-Afrikaanse Gekleurdes', 314; Willan, 'South African Native Labour Contingent, 1916-1918', 83.
34. CAD, South African Police (SAP) file 6/592/18, Report from detective P. Mokhatla, 7 March 1918.
35. See for instance G. Shepperson, 'The comparative study of millenarian movements' in S. Thrupp (ed.), *Millennial dreams* (The Hague 1962), 44.
36. For a detailed analysis of these movements see R.R. Edgar, 'Garveyism in Africa: Dr Wellington and the American Movement in the Transkei', *Ufahamu*, VI: 3 (1976), 31-57; R.R. Edgar, 'The Fifth Seal: Enoch Mgijima, the Israelites and the Bulhoek Massacre 1921' (unpublished PhD diss., University of California, Los Angeles 1977), esp. 151-81.
37. Evidence for this is marshalled in Grundlingh, 'Suid-Afrikaanse Gekleurdes', 318-19.
38. CAD, J 255/3/527/17, District Commandant Pietersburg to Assistant Commissioner of Police Pretoria, 21 December 1917.
39. Perry (eds.), *Jingoes*, 93.
40. 'Interview with H. Selby Msimang', *Contact*, 3, 7, 2 April 1960. See also P. Walshe, *The Rise of African Nationalism in South Africa: The African National Congress, 1912-1952* (London 1970), 50-1 for this deputation.
41. Walshe, *African Nationalism*, 52; 'S.A.N.N.C. resolutions', *Tsala ea Batho*, 22

42. 'The Native Question', *Izwe La Kiti*, 17 March 1915.
43. Compare 'The Native disposition', *Ilanga Lase Natal*, 5 March 1915; 'Native Loyalty', *Ilanga Lase Natal*, 9 October 1914; 'Native Loyalty', *Tsala ea Batho*, 12 December 1914; CAD, Government Native Labour Bureau (GNLB) 187/1217/14/D110, Report of an interview with the acting Minister of Native Affairs, 31 October 1914.

August 1914; S.T. Plaatje, *Native Life in South Africa* (London 1917), 260-1.

44. 'Our position', *Abantu-Batho*, 14 February 1918.
45. 'Notes and Comments', *Abantu-Batho*, 25 April 1918.
46. A detailed discussion of the work of this deputation is to be found in Grundlingh, 'Suid-Afrikaanse Gekleurdes', 339-48; B.P. Willan, 'The role of Solomon T. Plaatje (1876-1932) in South African society' (unpublished PhD diss., University of London 1979), 211-21.
47. CAD, J 256/3/527/17, Report of a meeting of the Transvaal Native Congress, 17 December 1918.
48. CAD, J 257/3/727/17, Report of a meeting of the Transvaal Native Congress, 8 February 1920.
49. Walshe, *African Nationalism*, 65.
50. CAD, GNLB 192/1329/14/D48, Copy of a report by the compound manager, 18 November 1914.
51. CAD, GNLB 192/1329/14/D48, Anonymous letter intercepted by Native Affairs Department, 6 September 1914.
52. CAD, SAP file 6/245/14/37, Copy of a report by the compound manager, 4 September 1914.
53. See Grundlingh, 'Suid-Afrikaanse Gekleurdes', 54-5.
54. Natal Archives Depot (NAD), Chief Native Commissioner (CNC) 247/1196, Chief Native Commissioner to Attorney-General, 10 August 1916 (copy).
55. CAD, SAP file 6/245/14/37, District commandant Dundee to Commissioner of Police Pietermaritzburg, 6 September 1914 (copy).
56. CAD, J 205/4/467/14, Report from the magistrate at Greytown, 18 August 1914.
57. This revolt is discussed in detail in Grundlingh, 'Suid-Afrikaanse Gekleurdes', 59-62.
58. Quoted in Edgar, 'Garveyism in Africa', 37.
59. Willan, 'South African Native Labour Contingent, 1916-1918', 85.
60. 'Mendi Memorial Service', *The Bantu World*, 2 March 1946.
61. R.H.W. Shepherd, *Lovedale, South Africa: the story of a century* (Lovedale 1941), 323.
62. H.A. Chilvers, *The story of De Beers* (London 1939), 209-13; 'Report on the annual meeting of shareholders', *Diamond Fields Advertiser*, 29 July 1915; CAD, Mines and Industries (MNI) 258/2195/14, Memorandum on the closing of the mines, 15 August 1914.
63. 'Letter from Anti-Capitalist', *The Friend*, 14 August 1914.
64. CAD, J 208/5/314/14, Lt. E. Hardiman to Staff Officer Bloemfontein, 13 August 1914 (copy).

65. 'Basuto and the war', *Tsala ea Batho*, 12 September 1914.
66. F.A. Johnstone, *Class, Race and Gold: A study of class relations and racial discrimination in South Africa* (London 1976), 95, 104-5.
67. Johnstone, *Class, Race and Gold*, particularly 120. This is also stated quite explicitly in CAD, MNI 939/1738/19, Chamber of Mines to Acting Prime Minister, 19 May 1919 (copy).
68. Johnstone, *Class, Race and Gold*, 105-7, 116; CAD, MNI 427/2270/18, Inspector of Labour to Chief Inspector of Labour, 4 July 1918.
69. *Annual Address of the President of the Transvaal Chamber of Mines*, 1916, 1917, 1918, 7, 17, 8 respectively.
70. This is discussed in detail in Johnstone, *Class, Race and Gold*, 93-118.
71. For these developments see P.L. Bonner, 'The 1920 Black Mine-workers Strike: a preliminary account' in B. Bozzoli (ed.), *Labour, Township and Protest* (Johannesburg 1979), 173-297; Johnstone, *Class, Race and Gold*, 172-4, 181-4.
72. See for instance P.L. Bonner, 'The Transvaal Native Congress, 1917-1920: the radicalisation of the black petty bourgeoisie on the Rand' in S. Marks and R. Rathbone (eds.), *Industrialisation and social change in South Africa: African class formation, culture and consciousness, 1870-1930* (London 1982), 270-313; P.L. Wickins, *The Industrial and Commercial Worker's Union of Africa* (Cape Town 1978), 23-38, 43-4, 52-7; Walshe, *African Nationalism*, 70-4, 89; F.A. Johnstone, 'The I.W.A. on the Rand: socialist organising among the Black workers on the Rand, 1917-18' in Bozzoli (ed.), *Labour, Township and Protest*, 248-72; Johnstone, *Class, Race and Gold*, 174-9.
73. For example the statement by Walshe, *African Nationalism*, 89 that 'a combination of economic development and social unrest, allied to the impact of new ideas in the aftermath of World War I, produced an increased level of political awareness within African society....'
74. D.H. Houghton and J. Dagut (eds.), *Source material on the South African Economy, 1860-1970*, 2, *1899-1919* (Cape Town 1972), 209, Industrial Census, 1915-1916, 1919-1920.
75. C.W. Pearsall, 'Some aspects of the development of secondary industry in the Union of South Africa', *The South African Journal of Economics*, 5 (1937), 414; M.H. de Kock, *Selected subjects in the economic history of South Africa* (Cape Town 1924), 130, 290. See also B. Bozzoli, *The political nature of a ruling class: capital and ideology in South Africa* (London 1981), 143-5.
76. Houghton and Dagut (eds.), *Source Material*, 2: 210, 226, Industrial census 1915-1916, 1919-1920, National resources of South Africa.
77. NAD, Secretary for Native Affairs (SNA) 1/4/26, Memorandum relating chiefly to Native political affairs on the Witwatersrand, 14 May 1919.
78. 'The cost of living', *Cape Times*, 18 January 1918; De Kock, *Economic history*, 131; Houghton and Dagut (eds.), *Source material*, 2: 192, 214, 233, Cost of living, Report of the trade commissioner, National resources of South Africa.

79. Bonner, 'The Transvaal Native Congress, 1917-1920', 273; 'The major grievances of the labour', *Abantu-Batho*, 20 June 1918; 'Natives and the Unrest', *Rand Daily Mail*, 4 April 1919.
80. CAD, J 256/3/527/17, Report of a meeting of the Native Women's League, 7 July 1918.
81. CAD, J 256/3/527/17, Report of a meeting of the Industrial Workers of Africa, 28 May 1918.
82. Bonner, 'The Transvaal Native Congress, 1917-1920', 274.
83. Marwick, *War and social change*, 12-13.
84. Katzenellenbogen, 'Southern Africa and the War of 1914-1918', 115.
85. Bozzoli, *Political nature of a ruling class*, 172.
86. P. Kallaway, 'F.S. Malan, the Cape liberal tradition and South African politics', *Journal of African History*, XV: 1 (1974), 124.

[25]
The Far East at the end of the First World War

Geoffrey Hudson

It has become standard usage to speak of the two wars which began in 1914 and in 1939 as the first and second world wars, but it is a usage which can be misleading unless the actual geographical scope of serious military and naval operations in each war is kept clearly in mind. In neither war was there any fighting in the Western Hemisphere; as far as the Americas were concerned, the Seven Years War of the eighteenth century has a better claim to universality. In the second world war from 1941 to 1945 there was an armed struggle in East Asia and the Pacific Ocean comparable in scale and violence to the struggle which raged on the continent of Europe. But the war of 1914–18 was throughout its course essentially a European war with an extension to the territory of the Ottoman Empire in Asia and areas close to its borders. Outside the theatre of war reaching from the Yser to the Tigris there were only the minor operations required for the liquidation of Germany's overseas colonial empire, and these, except for the campaign in German East Africa, were not only minor, but trivial. It is difficult to regard a struggle in which the range of major hostilities was so circumscribed as really entitled to be called a world war.

The effects of the struggle, however, were not limited to the regions in which important fighting fronts were located. The political and economic repercussions of the gigantic armed conflict were felt all over the globe, and nowhere more than in the Far East, where during the two decades before 1914 the enfeebled Manchu-Chinese empire, replaced in 1912 by the Republic of China, had been the object of a complicated international diplomacy with a rivalry for influence among six Great Powers – Britain, France, Germany, Russia, the United States, and Japan. The fourth month of the war saw the elimination by an Anglo-

CONTEMPORARY HISTORY

Japanese expeditionary force of Germany's only colonial *point d'appui* on the mainland of Asia, the leased territory of Kiaochow with the harbour and port of Tsingtao; the remaining German presence in China was for the time being wiped out by China's declaration of war on Germany in August 1917, which was followed by the internment of German nationals, the sequestration of their property, and the abrogation of their rights of extraterritorial jurisdiction. But this obliteration of Germany was not the only, nor even the most important, Far Eastern consequence of the armed struggle which had broken out in Europe. An even greater change was brought about through the concentration of the energies and resources of Britain, France, and Russia in Europe, which meant a weakening of their positions in the Far East in relation to Japan. Japan was their belligerent ally in the war against Germany, but was not involved directly in the hostilities in Europe, and retained her full power for support of her regional foreign policy in East Asia. Moreover, for the time being the war gave a great economic advantage to Japan. Except for the trifling expenditure incurred in the capture of Kiaochow, Japan suffered no costs of war, and was able to expand her trade both by meeting needs of her more deeply war-involved allies and by replacing them in markets which they could no longer hold because of diversion of their industrial resources to war production.

Until the spring of 1917 the United States was not a belligerent in the European war, and the power and attention of the American government were not diverted from the Far East in the same way as were the policies of Britain, France, and Russia. Washington was thus able to pursue in the Far East from 1914 to 1917 a policy no less vigorous than it had been before the outbreak of the war in Europe. But there were strict limits to its vigour imposed by the prevailing aversion of the American people to any course of action outside the Western Hemisphere likely to involve a risk of war. The State Department might wish to play an active part in the international diplomacy of the Far East, but was always aware that it could not count on support from Congress or public opinion if taking a strong line were to lead to dangerous complications. The United States gave China a degree of political support when the latter was confronted with the Japanese 'Twenty-one Demands' in January 1915, and was indeed the only Great Power to do so; the American government declared in notes sent both to

166

THE FAR EAST AT THE END OF THE FIRST WORLD WAR

Tokyo and Peking that it could not 'recognize any agreement or undertaking... impairing the treaty rights of the United States and its citizens in China, the political or territorial integrity of the Republic of China, or the international policy relative to China commonly known as the Open Door'. The American attitude had the effect of causing Japan to drop certain of the demands which were most obviously designed to give her a position of paramountcy in China, but when Japan enforced compliance with the rest of the demands by an ultimatum with the threat of war, there was no American reaction and China had to submit. This was a situation which was quite different from what it would have been if Japan had taken such action a year earlier; a Japanese move of this kind at the beginning of 1914 would certainly have met with a combined opposition of all the other Great Powers, with the possible exception of Russia, and Japan would not have dared to press it to the point of war with China.

Apart from a number of miscellaneous provisions of minor importance, Japan achieved two major objectives through her pressure on China in the spring of 1915, one being the prolongation of the leases of the Kwantung Territory and the South Manchuria Railway, and the other China's acceptance in advance of any treaty which might subsequently be concluded between Japan and Germany with regard to the German rights in Shantung. The issue in Manchuria had no connection with the war in Europe. As spoils of victory in the Russo-Japanese war of 1904-5, Japan had taken over the Russian leases of Dairen and Port Arthur and the railway as far north as Changchun, but as these were only twenty-five-year leases, they were due to expire in 1923 and 1928 respectively, and already in 1914 there was apprehension in Tokyo that China, when the time came, would refuse any extension, thus removing the legal basis of Japan's special political and economic position in Manchuria. By the ultimatum of 1915 Japan compelled China to substitute ninety-nine-year for twenty-five-year leases, so that they would run to 1997 and 2002 instead of expiring in the 1920s. The effect of the new treaty thus imposed on China was not to give Japan anything she did not already possess, but simply to deprive China of the prospect of recovering the ceded rights at an early date; even this, however, was enough of a blow to the developing nationalist sentiment of China to make it likely that after the war the Chinese would make every effort to

167

revise or abrogate the agreement, or at least do what they could to thwart the promotion of Japanese enterprises in Manchuria based on the Kwantung Territory. In such policies they might well receive the active diplomatic and financial support of the USA; the Japanese had not forgotten the attempt of Secretary Knox to 'neutralize' the Manchurian railways in 1911. Fear of trouble ahead in Manchuria caused the Japanese to draw still closer to the Russians, with whom they already had an agreement dividing Manchuria into spheres of influence to the exclusion of all third parties. The common interest of Russia and Japan in the restriction of Chinese sovereignty in Manchuria now, in July 1916, led the two powers to conclude a secret treaty of alliance, which had nothing to do with the war against Germany, but was undoubtedly, though without specific reference by name, directed against America. This treaty the Bolsheviks not only repudiated, but published, when they came to power in Russia; otherwise its existence might never have become known. It was kept secret from Britain not because a post-war conflict with Britain over Manchuria was anticipated – Britain over a period of years had tacitly acquiesced in Japanese encroachments there – but because Britain could not be expected to approve of the formation of an anti-American combination by her Japanese ally; she had already made it clear to Japan in 1911 that the Anglo-Japanese alliance was not applicable to the case of a Japanese–American war.

The issue in Shantung differed from that in Manchuria in that, whereas the Manchurian question was one between Japan, Russia, and China, with other powers involved only in so far as they chose to regard their interests as affected, the Japanese capture of the German holdings in Shantung had been an episode in the coalition war against Germany and must therefore be subject to the decisions of a general post-war peace conference. When Japan had entered the war against Germany she had declared that she was taking the leased territory of Kiaochow 'with a view to its eventual restoration to China' and could not claim a simple transfer of the German lease for the remainder of its term. The Japanese aim, therefore, was to obtain the cession of the leasehold and related properties in Shantung from Germany by the peace treaty, and then drive a hard bargain with China for concessions in return for the promised 'eventual restoration', which could other-

THE FAR EAST AT THE END OF THE FIRST WORLD WAR

wise be indefinitely delayed. China herself, as already mentioned, had been compelled by the ultimatum of May 1915 to give assent in advance to whatever post-war settlement Japan might make with Germany about Kiaochow. But Japan had still to obtain the agreement of her European allies, and neither Britain nor France regarded with favour an extension of Japanese power southward from Manchuria into the northern region of China proper. Moreover, in August 1917 China herself declared war on Germany and terminated all German treaty rights in her territory, so that it could be claimed that the lease had already reverted to Peking. Had the war been going favourably for Britain and France in 1917, they might well have resisted Japanese pressure and supported China's claim at the Peace Conference. But this was the period of war when the heavy toll of shipping taken by the German submarine campaign had created an urgent demand for additional naval forces for purposes of convoy, and the Western Allies were obliged to ask Japan to send naval units to the Mediterranean. Japan complied and sent a cruiser and three destroyer flotillas to help in the protection of the Mediterranean shipping routes, but took the opportunity to obtain from both Britain and France secret treaties promising their support for Japan's claims in Shantung – and also to the German islands in the Pacific north of the Equator – at the Peace Conference.

These treaties, however, did not bind the United States, and were not indeed disclosed to Washington before the Peace Conference. It was from this quarter that Japan could anticipate the most serious opposition to her claims. But even the USA, after her entry into the war, became subject to pressure from Japan. The Americans were in need of additional shipping to transport and supply their expeditionary forces in Europe, and Japan was the only country from which such a supplement could be obtained. A mission headed by Viscount Ishii was sent to Washington to negotiate on this matter, and it did not fail to obtain a political *quid pro quo* for Japan's aid. In an exchange of notes dated 2 November 1917, known as the Lansing-Ishii agreement, the American Secretary of State recognized that 'territorial propinquity creates special relations between countries and consequently the government of the United States recognized that Japan has special interests in China, particularly in that part to which her possessions are contiguous'.

CONTEMPORARY HISTORY

This document was vague enough in its wording, and unlike the agreements which Japan had concluded with Britain and France, did not specifically endorse the Japanese claim to the German rights in Shantung, but it was to prove a potent diplomatic instrument in the hands of the Japanese and a serious embarrassment to President Wilson when he wished to oppose the Japanese demands at the Peace Conference. On a broad view of the diplomatic history of the war years it must be admitted that Japanese foreign policy was conducted with great tactical skill and a keen instinct for grasping the opportunities of the moment. Japan emerged from the war, in which the cost of her participation had been negligible in men or money, as a belligerent member of a victorious coalition of Great Powers, with specific commitments from Britain and France and an imprecise, but substantial, declaration from the USA to support her claims in the peace settlement. The alliance with Russia had meanwhile lapsed as a result of the Bolshevik revolution, and this involved in the long run a serious weakening of Japan's international position, but it did not affect the issues at the Paris Peace Conference, since the new Soviet regime, by concluding a separate peace with Germany, had detached itself from the anti-German coalition and was not represented in the making of the peace treaties.

But in spite of – and partly because of – Japan's successful coercion of China in 1915, it was still necessary to reckon with China as a hostile element at the Peace Conference, and Shantung was indeed to prove one of the most explosive issues in the postwar peacemaking. The Chinese delegation was to play a most active and effective part in the proceedings in Paris. It was the first time that China had thus emerged as an actor in the arena of *Weltpolitik*; she was of course attending the Conference as of right in consequence of her entry into the war against Germany, but what was extraordinary in her diplomatic representation was that it was appointed, not by a single internationally recognized government of China, but jointly by two authorities, each claiming to be the only legitimate Chinese government and each in a state of civil war with the other. The actual condition of China in 1919 was indeed even more confused than was indicated by the co-existence of these two rival governments, for neither of them exercised more than a limited local power, and a number of provinces enjoyed complete *de facto* independence. This disintegration of the Chinese

THE FAR EAST AT THE END OF THE FIRST WORLD WAR

state was something which had happened during the war of 1914–18 and partly as a consequence of it; it is necessary to understand how it happened in order to appreciate the peculiar international status of China in the immediate post-war period, as a nation which conducted a vigorous foreign policy through a team of patriotic diplomats while its internal state authority collapsed in a welter of anarchy and civil war.

It had been a basic contradiction in the Chinese Revolution of 1911 that, whereas the aim of the young nationalist and republican revolutionaries had been to build up China as a strong modern state in place of the loosely organized archaic autocracy of the old imperial system, the short-term effect of the upheaval was to strengthen the forces of provincial particularism. The crucial issue was the lack of central control over the units of the national army due to the deficiency of revenue available to the central government. The army reorganization programme of 1907, adopted four years before the fall of the monarchy, had provided for an army of 36 divisions, but of these only five were to be directly paid and controlled by the central government; the rest were to be financed by the provinces in which they were stationed, and this gave a great quasi-feudal power to the provincial military commanders, who came to have a vested interest in the decentralized system. Nearly all of them came out for the Republic in 1911, but for them the overturn of the monarchy meant not the creation of a unitary modern state, but an increase of their own local independence. As against these anarchic, centrifugal tendencies, the republican intellectuals and bourgeois politicians who followed Sun Yat-sen were powerless to unite China; the only prospect for consolidation of a central authority seemed to lie in a decisive supremacy of the strongest of the military leaders who would curb the provincial commanders – who came to be known to western journalists as 'war-lords' – and gradually bring all armed forces on to the budget of the central government, using his power to increase the revenue raised from the provinces. In 1914 it seemed that President Yuan Shih-k'ai would be able to perform this task. The year before he had obtained from abroad a 'reorganization loan' which enabled him to pay his troops, and he had begun to organize a new disciplined force of so-called Standard Regiments under his own command. He was ruthless and dictatorial in his methods, and never at any time of his life had any sympathy for the ideals of political democracy which were the theoretical basis of the new Republic; but if war had not broken out in Europe in 1914 he might well have succeeded in giving China an effectively centralized state administration. His personal ambition went beyond the Presidency of the Republic, even with eligibility for re-election; he hoped to found a new dynasty, to be enthroned as emperor and to transmit the sovereignty to his son. It is now the fashion to regard Yuan's scheme for a restoration of the monarchy in his own person as an absurd anachronism which could not possibly have succeeded. It must be remembered, however, that in 1914 the Republic was only two years old and meant nothing to the masses of the Chinese people outside a small western-educated elite; the communists with their potent doctrine of social revolution had not yet appeared on the scene, and the influence of western political ideas was still extremely restricted; what most Chinese wanted was stability and order, and traditionally these were restored after the decline and fall of a dynasty by the emergence of a new one. It should be remembered also that of the eight nations of the world which ranked as Great Powers in 1914 six were monarchies, so that the foreign models which the new generation of Chinese sought to imitate for the regeneration of their country were by no means unanimously arrayed in favour of republican principles. Had the European powers been as well able to lend money to China in 1915 as they were in 1913, there is no reason to suppose that Yuan Shih-k'ai would have been deemed less credit-worthy as he consolidated his power, or that his project of making himself emperor would have deprived him of access to the international money market. Britain, then still the foremost financial power in the Far East, had no bias against monarchy as such, and Sir John Jordan, the British Minister in Peking, was personally favourable to Yuan's design. But the war in Europe cut off all possibility of financial support for the Chinese government from European nations, and Japan, a country which, being itself a monarchy, might have been expected to have sympathy for a monarchical restoration in China, was in the event deeply hostile to it, partly because of an old antipathy to Yuan going back to the time when he had thwarted Japanese policy in Korea in the 1880s, but even more because the very idea of a strong central government in China was regarded in Tokyo with

THE FAR EAST AT THE END OF THE FIRST WORLD WAR

alarm and apprehension. Japanese statesmen always had in the back of their minds the thought that if China in the twentieth century were to modernize her economy under a strong central government, as Japan had done in the Meiji era, China's greater size and population and more abundant natural resources would soon make her wealthier and more powerful than Japan, not to mention such things as the Kwantung Leased Territory which a strong China would soon try to get back. What suited Japan was a weak, decentralized, faction-ridden China, in which Japan could exert influence by playing off one faction against another. The war in Europe left Yuan face to face with Japan without any of the balancing diplomatic and financial support which would otherwise have been available to him. His mistake was in going on with his dynastic project when circumstances had changed so radically to his disadvantage. His ambition combined against him both the doctrinaire republicans among China's new intelligentsia and a number of generals who were not moved by any enthusiasm for the Republic, but by fear of the loss of their semi-independent military commands and of the possibility of succeeding to the Presidency on Yuan's death. Meanwhile Yuan's prestige was irreparably damaged by his forced submission to Japanese demands in 1915; how could a man who thus proved unable to defend his country against foreign aggression be supposed to have received the 'Mandate of Heaven'? Shorn of prestige as a national leader and unable to raise money from any quarter, he was overthrown by a revolt of disaffected generals, and the Japanese, who would do nothing to ease the financial difficulties of his government, provided money and arms for his enemies. Already in poor health, he was overwhelmed by his misfortunes; he died in June 1916, and for twelve years after his death China had no central government worthy of the name.

After Yuan there was nobody who could effectively control the provincial war-lords; those in the remoter provinces set themselves up as independent despotic rulers, while those who had forces near Peking grouped themselves into factions which aimed at imposing their nominees as President or Prime Minister in the capital. From 1916 to 1920 the so-called Anfu Club, headed by General Tuan Ch'i-jui, was the strongest of the factions, and Tuan held the office of Prime Minister, deposing two Presidents with whom he came into conflict; he was thus nominally at the head of the

CONTEMPORARY HISTORY

recognized government of China in Peking at the time of the Paris Peace Conference. But the government in Peking was in 1917 challenged not only *de facto* by the lawless insubordination of the provincial war-lords, but also *de jure* by an authority established in Canton, which claimed to be the only legitimate government of China because it was based on a gathering of members of the parliament which had been sitting in Peking in June 1917 and had then been dissolved as a move in a civil war between the President and the Prime Minister. These politicians were for the most part members of the Kuomintang, the political party led by Sun Yat-sen. The Kuomintang had originated in Canton and had its greatest strength there; it denounced the generals of the Anfu and other factions as usurpers, and demanded a restoration of the original constitution of the Republic. But although it at least stood for certain political principles, in contrast to the undisguised self-seeking of the war-lords, and although theoretically committed to control of the army by a civilian government, it found itself in practice unable to exert authority even in Canton itself except by making alliances with provincial commanders in South China whose main concern was to enhance their own independence by profiting from the new rivalry between Canton and Peking. Not until the Whampoa Military Academy, with the aid of Russian political and military advisers, produced from 1924 onwards a Kuomintang army, did the Canton regime have any soldiers who were really under its own control, and its early history was marked by a series of mutinies and revolts.

Such was the China which presented itself to the gaze of western nations when, after four years of preoccupation with events in Europe, they were again able to spare attention for the affairs of the Far East. A country in such a state of confusion and chaos was hardly to be taken seriously as a factor in international politics. Yet China asserted herself with an unexpected vigour at the Paris Peace Conference. The reason for this was the growth in China of a national consciousness which was quite independent of the various military factions contending for governmental power. The Chinese diplomatic service, staffed by men of western education with a wide experience of the world outside China, was capable of functioning almost as an autonomous organization, with a strong *esprit de corps* and a sense of responsibility, not to this or that army

THE FAR EAST AT THE END OF THE FIRST WORLD WAR

general, but to the public opinion of the new nationally minded intelligentsia. There was thus a Chinese foreign policy which was in a curious way quite detached from the factional strife of Chinese domestic politics. The Chinese delegation to Paris was composed of three nominees of Peking and two of Canton; in spite of having to represent two Governments at war with one another, they acted as a united team. They demanded that the German rights in Shantung should be returned to China direct and not transferred to Japan for 'eventual restoration' to China. President Wilson's sympathies were with China on this issue; he claimed that he was in no way bound by the war-time secret treaties concluded by Japan with Britain and France. As a compromise Lansing proposed that the German rights be ceded to the Allied and Associated Powers which would subsequently make a just disposition of them. But this was quite unacceptable to Japan and the Japanese delegation declared that it had instructions from Tokyo not to sign any treaty unles the Shantung claim was met. In the end the Japanese pressure prevailed, and on 30 April 1919 the Council of Three agreed to transfer the German rights to Japan.

Five days later, however, something happened in China which was to have far-reaching consequences and is now regarded as a principal landmark in modern Chinese history. A great wave of nationalist indignation swept the universities of China and burst out on 4 May in student riots in the streets of Peking. The student upheaval received encouragement and support from bankers and merchants. The Peking government and the local warlords, in spite of their possession of the means of armed force to quell the disturbances, hesitated to take action, and three government ministers, denounced as 'national traitors' for their pro-Japanese inclinations, were dismissed from office and fled abroad. It was a formidable demonstration of a new spirit in China which was to become a great political force in the future, though it brought no immediate change in the existing political order – or lack of order – in the country, and the faction fighting of the warlords went on as before. In Paris, however, it had its effect; the Chinese delegation refused to sign the Treaty of Versailles which contained the unacceptable provisions about the transfer of the German rights in Shantung to Japan.

The question of Shantung was the main subject of dispute between China and Japan at the end of 1918 and was the principal

CONTEMPORARY HISTORY

Far Eastern question discussed at the Paris conference. But there was another situation, involving both China and Japan and also the leading western powers which, from the nature of the case, was not on the agenda of the conference; this was the state of affairs produced by the Russian Revolution in eastern Siberia and the Russian spheres of influence in North Manchuria and Outer Mongolia. When the Bolsheviks seized power in Petrograd in November 1917, Siberia, like other parts of the Russian empire, at first accepted the new government, but more from the habit of obeying all orders that came from the capital than from attachment to the Bolshevik cause; for in Siberia, a thinly inhabited territory which contained neither great landed properties nor a substantial industrial proletariat, support for Lenin's party was minimal. Soon there were manifestations of dissent, partly in Russian and partly in Chinese territory; General Horvath, commanding the Russian troops acting as railway guards on the Russian-owned Chinese Eastern Railway in Manchuria, defied the new regime and there were revolts in the Siberian Cossack settlement; then came the clashes between the Soviet authorities and the Czech Legionaries, who refused to be bound by the Treaty of Brest–Litovsk and sought to extricate themselves from Russia by transporting themselves over the Trans-Siberian railway to Vladivostok. Britain, France, and the USA were ready to help the Czechs to get out of Russia, and were also afraid that some of the quarter of a million German and Austrian prisoners in Siberia set free after the conclusion of the Treaty of Brest-Litovsk might acquire arms from the stocks sent to Russia via Vladivostok by her allies before she withdrew from the war. Over and above these motives for intervention there was an imaginative, though ill-conceived, idea of reconstituting an Eastern Front against Germany with the aid of anti-Bolshevik Russians who did not accept the Brest–Litovsk Treaty. The policies of Japan and China in the new situation produced by Russia's disintegration were much less related to the war in Europe and much more to their regional national interests. China hoped to take over the Russian rights in North Manchuria and to suppress the autonomy of Outer Mongolia, which Russia had guaranteed but was no longer able to preserve; Japan intended, through co-operation with the Chinese Anfu faction, which was supplied with Japanese money and arms, to extend her preponderant influence into the Russian sphere of

THE FAR EAST AT THE END OF THE FIRST WORLD WAR

Manchuria, and some at least among the Japanese military leaders hoped to detach a part of eastern Siberia from the Russian empire and set up a satellite state there under Japanese tutelage.

This diversity of motives soon became manifest in the intervention undertaken jointly in Siberia by Britain, France, Japan, and the USA from August 1918 onwards. When the war in Europe was ended by the November armistice, this intervention could no longer be related to strategy against Germany, and Britain, France, and the USA sought to terminate it except for such moral and material aid as they continued to give to the White Russian government set up in Omsk. The western Powers hoped to see a restoration of Russia as a unified state under a non-Bolshevik government, and in 1919 they regarded Kolchak as the leader most likely to achieve such a result. Both Japan and China, on the other hand, wished to accentuate, if they could, the disunity of Russia in order to achieve their special objectives. The Japanese supported, not Kolchak, but two Cossack adventurers, Semenov and Kalmikov, who were willing to set themselves up as local rulers in Transbaikalia and the Siberian Maritime Province under Japanese protection. The Chinese disarmed Horvath's troops in Manchuria and sent a large military force into Outer Mongolia to suppress the Russian-sponsored Mongol state established there since 1912.

In the end all these policies came to nothing because the decisive victory of the Bolsheviks in the Russian civil war was followed by an effective reassertion by the Soviet regime not only of Russia's territorial sovereignty in Asia, but also, under new forms, of the sphere of influence established under the Tsars in North Manchuria and Outer Mongolia. Semenov and Kalmikov proved to be liabilities rather than assets to Japan, and it was found to be impossible to separate any Russian-inhabited territory from the main body of Russia without a greater military effort than post-war Japan was willing to undertake and a greater defiance of world opinion than she was then willing to sustain. After a heavy expenditure for little or no profit, Japanese forces were withdrawn by stages from Siberia; they evacuated Transbaikalia in August 1920 and the Maritime Province in 1922, and finally got out of North Sakhalin in 1925. The fiasco of the Siberian expedition greatly diminished the prestige of the army within Japan, which had been

CONTEMPORARY HISTORY

enormously inflated by the great victories in the wars against China and Russia. The desultory and futile operations carried on in Siberia for no aims which could be publicly avowed brought only discredit on the expansionist military leaders who had promoted them. The 1920s were to be the era of the liberal tide in Japanese politics, and it was not until 1930 that changed circumstances again played into the hands of the militarists.

In Manchuria the Chinese abandoned the idea of simply expropriating Russia as the owner of the Chinese Eastern Railway, although the Karakhan manifesto of July 1919 fully authorized China to do so. It was realized in Peking that if Russia were not to be given once more a stake in North Manchuria, China would not be able to resist the expansion of Japan in that quarter, and it was hoped that, with the bad relations between Japan and Russia which continued even after the end of the Siberian expedition, Russia would serve as a check on Japan in Manchuria. The Soviet representative, Leo Karakhan, who negotiated the Sino–Soviet Treaty of 1924, was more than willing to give China the appearance of a great advance on the original railway contract of 1896; it was now to be a joint Russo–Chinese enterprise, with equal Russian and Chinese representation on the Board of Directors, and there were no longer to be any Russian railway guards (in contrast to the Japanese railway guards still maintained in South Manchuria). In practice, however, the Soviet Union ran the railway through the Russian General Manager.

The Chinese reconquest of Outer Mongolia in 1919 – or perhaps conquest, since the Mongols held that they had previously been subject to the Manchus but not to China – was destined to be of even shorter duration than the sequestration of the Chinese Eastern Railway. Mongol rebels aided by White Russian forces under General Ungern von Sternberg drove the Chinese army from Urga in 1921; Russian Red Army troops from Siberia then entered Mongolia, captured and executed Ungern, and gave power to a new organization, the Mongol Revolutionary People's Party, which henceforth ruled the country under Russian protection. The Chinese were effectively deterred from attempting any further expedition across the Gobi, and it was a mere matter of form when in the Treaty of 1924 the Soviet Government recognized Outer Mongolia as 'an integral part of the Republic of China'.

It would, however, be misleading in a survey of the Far East in

THE FAR EAST AT THE END OF THE FIRST WORLD WAR

1919 to take note only of the Japanese and Chinese governmental attempts to exploit the temporary weakness and disunity of Russia – attempts which ended in failure because of the subsequent revival of Russian power. Far more important in the long run was the deep impression made on the national consciousness of China by the contrast between the principles of Soviet policy as proclaimed in the Karakhan Declaration and what the Chinese regarded as the intolerable humiliation inflicted on them at the Paris Peace Conference. Since Britain, France, and America had accepted the Japanese claims there, they were all included in the anger and resentment directed against Japan; only Russia, the new revolutionary Russia, could be regarded as a friend. This was more than a passing mood and it was by no means limited to those who became communists; it was the background to Sun Yat-sen's agreement with Joffe at the beginning of 1923 and all that flowed from it. Whatever were to be the subsequent quarrels between Russia and China, the influence of the Russian Revolution in the period immediately following the end of the war in Europe was greater in China than in any other country, not because China was ripe for a dictatorship of the proletariat, but because Russia was accepted by the greater part of Chinese educated and patriotic opinion at that time as the sole true champion of anti-imperialism.

[26]

World War I and the Rise of African Nationalism: Nigerian Veterans as Catalysts of Change

by James K. Matthews, Historian, Department of the Air Force, Headquarters Strategic Air Command, Offutt Air Force Base, Nebraska[1]

The enlistment and conscription of combatants and non-combatants in Nigeria during World War I represented an unprecedented mobilisation of the country's labour force. In September 1914, the Nigeria Regiment supplied shock troops for the Cameroons Expeditionary Force, and in December 1917 the Nigeria Overseas Contingent entered the campaign in Tanganyika. By September 1919, when Nigeria's military recruitment drive ended, 17,000 combatants, 2,000 enlisted carriers, and some 35,000 non-enlisted carriers had participated in the Southern Cameroons and German East Africa campaigns. In addition, the British recruited thousands of Nigerians for military service along Nigeria's northern and eastern borders, and for related duties inside the country.[2]

These tens-of-thousands of Nigerian veterans acted as catalysts of change on their return home. Their experiences had altered ideas, attitudes, and habits during the war, and made them not only receptive to additional changes in the post-war years – especially socio-economic, military, and political – but also inclined to compel others to follow suit. The returned soldiers and carriers were, however, more accelerators of changes already under way in pre-war Nigeria than a force for new directions.[3]

---

[1] The author was greatly assisted during his stay in Nigeria by Obaro Ikime and Robert Smith of the History Department of the University of Ibadan, and wishes to dedicate his article to the memory of John Barrett, whose study of 'The Rank and File of the Colonial Army in Nigeria, 1914–18' was published in this *Journal*, Vol. 15, No. 1, March 1976, pp. 105–15.

[2] For somewhat conflicting statistics on Nigerian and other British West African World War I combatants and non-combatants, see Public Records Office, Kew Gardens, Colonial Office, 'Reorganization of the WAFF and KAR', 5 May 1919, CO 445/48/27111; A. H. W. Haywood to Secretary of State for the Colonies, London, 'Manpower – Native Races of West Africa', 3 July 1923, CO 537/954; and Minute by Major Beattie, 27 September 1917, CO 445/44/48141. One difficulty, unresolved by the Colonial or War Office, was how to distinguish between 'enlisted' and 'recruited' carriers, between 'porters' and 'carriers', and between 'labourers' and 'carriers' – Sir Hugh Clifford to Colonial Office, 11 March 1921, CO 445/56/16908.

For a discussion of the rôle played by West Africans during World War I, see James K. Matthews, 'Nigerian Military Experiences in the First World War: recruitment, service, and postwar change', Ph.D. dissertation, University of California, Santa Barbara, March 1981; also David Killingray and James K. Matthews, 'Beasts of Burden: British West African Carriers in the First World War', in *Canadian Journal of African Studies* (Ottawa), XIII, 1–2, Winter, 1979, pp. 6–23.

[3] Similar conclusions have been reached by other scholars of Third-World nations. See Melvin Eugene Page, 'Malawians in the Great War and After, 1914–1925', Ph.D. dissertation, Michigan State University, 1977, and DeWitt C. Ellenwood, 'The Indian Soldier, the Indian Army, and Change, 1914–1918', in Ellenwood and S. D. Pradhan (eds.), *India and World War I* (Columbia, 1978).

Socio-Economic Changes

The war experiences of the veterans indubitably helped to accelerate linguistic change in Nigeria. At the minimum, soldiers and carriers had to learn commands in English. They adopted these and other words, which expanded and moulded their indigenous languages. For example, Hausa soldiers and carriers who went overseas 'on ships...learnt the words "down below" for the vast holds in which bunks had been knocked up for them...and a "dambelo" became a large barge on the Benue', and eventually 'a cheap prostitute who takes any number of men each night'.[1] Many soldiers also received advanced instruction in English. In September 1917, in a report on training centres, Major G. W. Moran noted that 'a large number of men are rapidly acquiring English, and company commanders appear to take great pains in instructing and encouraging progress in this direction'.[2] Some, in time, even conquered the mysteries of reading and writing.[3]

Knowledge of the English language obviously benefited those seeking employment with the Government or European businesses, and the experiences of World War I had other important economic ramifications. Military service introduced thousands of veterans, their families, and other Nigerians to the money economy. After returning to their villages, some squandered their accumulated pay on gambling, gifts for women, and drink, while others invested wisely in land, homes, businesses, and wives.[4] Regardless of how they spent their money, the veterans popularised its use.[5] The appearance of coins and notes in the hinterland, where there had been little or none prior to 1918, signalled the arrival of a new element in economic life. For Nigerians, it created a fresh form of wealth, one that offered the possibility of greater control over their own labour.

War service whetted appetites for a new range of foodstuffs and consumer goods. Tea, coffee, milk, sugar, flour, soda water, whisky, brandy, kerosene, soap, drugs, toilet preparations, and especially bicycles and European clothing were all very popular.[6] Most of these could be found only in urban areas such as Lagos, Ibadan, Kano, and Calabar, where veterans were most likely to find wage-earning jobs comparable to those to which they had become accustomed. For many Nigerians, the allure of the city was too much to resist, and war service facilitated such geographical mobility. Thousands of Nigerians had not only been exposed to foreign travel for the first time, but they had encountered Europeans, Asians, and other Africans who had travelled from their homes as well. Men realised that there was a world beyond their villages and outside

---

[1] Stanhope White, *Dan Bana* (London, 1966), p. 186.

[2] G. W. Moran, 'Report on Training Centres', 3 September 1917, Nigeria National Archives, Ibadan, 20/5 NC 158/17.

[3] Samson Ukpabi, 'Military Recruitment and Social Mobility in Nineteenth Century British West Africa', in *Journal of African Studies* (Washington, D.C.), II, 1, 1975, pp. 87–107.

[4] Interviews conducted in July 1979 with No. 23411, ex-Sgt. Major Gbadamoshi Adedeji, Iwo; No. 15307, ex-Private Oyeleke, Ibadan; No. 1325, ex-Corporal Afalabi, Ibadan; No. 4463, ex-Private Baba Tunde, Ibadan; and No. 32584, ex-Private Adeyemi, Ibadan.

[5] Ukpabi, loc.cit.

[6] Interviews, Adedeji, Oyelek, Afalabi, Baba Tunde, and Adeyemi.

their lineage groups. Consequently, migration to the city became an alternative to a comparatively uneventful life as a farmer.¹

Wartime travel brought soldiers and carriers into contact with foreign ways of life, resulting in cultural exchange. F. W. H. Migeod later noted the arrival of the 'metallophone' in Sierra Leone:

> I found a biscuit tin was used as a sound box and the half dozen steel notes were made from...knife blades ground down thin. This instrument does not belong to this country...The idea was brought back by natives who had been to East Africa in the war.²

There is evidence also of Hausa 'experiments in architecture of grass and bamboo construction' while the troops were in East Africa, as well as enthusiasm for gathering souvenirs such as cowries and other East African shells 'with the intention of presenting necklaces and waist belts to their womenfolk'.³ There were, undoubtedly, elements of cultural diffusion from West to East Africa, but their effect on African society needs to be studied more carefully. It would be equally interesting to determine what became of the West African carriers who, following the war, acquired relatively well-paid jobs as lorry drivers in Kenya.⁴

Contact with European science and technology was another factor that contributed to change in Nigeria. Before the war, the men knew only the casual, nature-oriented time-sense of the village; army life taught them a new concept of punctuality, compatible with reveille, parades, drills, and deadlines. Many Nigerians took their first ride on a train and saw their first car, aeroplane, and motion picture. Large numbers learned to shoot and care for modern weapons – not only rifles, but machine-guns and artillery. Also, soldiers and carriers learned basic hygiene, water sterilisation, and other methods of disease control and health care. Thousands of Nigerians received their first vaccination and took their first pill during the war.

Some African soldiers became especially familiar with European technology, The Nigerian Railway Department gave one month's intensive training in driving and mechanical maintenance to 280 Yoruba in preparation for their service with the West African Motor Transport Division.⁵ In December 1916, 500 Southern Nigerians were recruited by the Royal Engineers for the Inland Water Transport Section and sent to Mesopotamia in early 1917 as boatmen, mechanics, and dock hands.⁶ Other Nigerians received special traning as operators and linesmen for the Signal Section; as sappers, miners, and engineers for the Pioneer Company; and as medical assistants for base and field hospitals. The high incidence of casualties during the war meant that large

---

¹ Page, op.cit. and Ellenwood, loc.cit. have made similar observations.
² F. W. H. Migeod, *A View of Sierra Leone* (London, 1926), p. 186.
³ 'A Reader of *West Africa* in East Africa', in *West Africa* (London), 11 January 1919.
⁴ Ibid.
⁵ Railway Department to Central Secretary, 16 January 1918, CSO 19/6 N 446/18; Central Secretary to AG Base, Dar es Salaam, 25 March 1918, CSO 19/6 N 607/18; Treasury Department (Hyatt?) to Central Secretary, 31 December 1919, CSO 19/8 N 49/20. This unit, which included men from the Gold Coast, sailed to Dar es Salaam in late 1917 and returned to Lagos and Accra in mid-1919.
⁶ Lugard to A. B. Law, 1 December 1916, CO 583/50/844.

numbers of men spent time in hospitals, where they witnessed advanced medical techniques, including amputations, prosthetics, and plastic surgery.

Most Nigerians accepted the new technology in a professional, workmanlike way, and those on leave in Durban, for example, seemed to display no cultural shock. According to one of their officers:

> the men, who could never in their lives have conceived the existence of such a town as Durban with its harbours, shops, electric tram, cinema theatres...were to all appearances less impressed by what they saw than were the inhabitants of Durban themselves at the unusual sight of such a body of fully trained African troops.[1]

Although the men may not have been as enthusiastic about European technology as their officers expected, most were definitely impressed. When asked what the English had taught him during the war, ex-Private Oyeleke replied: 'They taught me to shoot by lying down and standing. How to use rifles and machine-guns, and how to take them apart and put them together again...I liked it very much'. Following the war, he bought some mechanic's tools with his savings and made money 'fixing things'.[2]

Testimonials by veterans showed that Nigerians also reacted favourably to European medical practices. Baba Tunde, who spent four months in a hospital in Dar es Salaam with a foot wound, was forever grateful to English doctors for allowing him to 'walk like a man again'.[3] The 90-year-old Oyeleke was equally convinced of the benefits of European medicine: army doctors taught him 'how to live long'.[4] In fact, access to European medicine was one reason why the soldiers were healthier as a group than the population as a whole. In a letter to the Acting Governor-General explaining why relatively few military men had died from influenza during the devastating epidemic of 1918, Dr J. Beringer, Medical Officer of Health at Lagos, reported: 'Soldiers are compelled or accustomed to have skilled medical treatment with consequent lessening of the death rate'.[5] It seems a valid conclusion, then, that the military experience of Nigerians made them, and perhaps their families and friends, more likely to accept modern technology in general, and western medicine in particular.

The Military Institution

A tight post-war budget hindered the army's modernisation programme, initiated in 1914 with the creation of the Nigeria Regiment.[6] Previously, for instance, the colonial authorities had wished to increase the number of British N.C.O.s in the Regiment to improve army training. Following the war, however, funds were unavailable for additional British sergeants or even replacements for those whose term of service had expired. The way in which the British solved this problem resulted in a 'Nigerianisation' of the Regiment's

---

[1] E. St. C. Stobart, 'A Record of the Doings of the Nigeria Regiment during the Campaign in German East Africa, December 1916 – December 1917', 12 April 1919, CO 445/47/28875.

[2] Interview, Oyeleke.   [3] Interview, Baba Tunde.

[4] Interview, Oyeleke.

[5] J. Beringer, Medical Officer of Health, Lagos, to Andrew Boyle, Acting Governor-General, 30 October 1918, CO 583/74/28850.

[6] Colonel A. H. W. Haywood and Brigadier F. A. S. Clarke, *The History of the Royal West African Frontier Force* (Aldershot, 1964), p. 319.

WORLD WAR I AND RISE OF AFRICAN NATIONALISM 497

non-commissioned officers. Prior to demobilisation, more Nigerian sergeants and corporals than were authorised in the Regiment's peace-time establishment made it known that they wished to remain in the service. According to the Acting Governor-General, it was

> hardly conceivable that these NCOs who have gained their rank by virtue of good work in the field should be forced to choose between serving as Privates or a lower rank than which they previously held. I submit that the only fair way to deal with these cases would be to allow the NCOs to retain their rank and make them 'supernumerary' until the time they can be absorbed.[2]

The Colonial Office agreed, adding that the increase in Nigerian N.C.O.s would be paid for by a corresponding decrease in British staff.

To ensure uniform instruction, the British opened a school at Zungeru in early 1918 to train many of these young Nigerian N.C.O.s as teachers. British personnel and senior Nigerian N.C.O.s staffed the school, and introduced a syllabus of instruction for a six-week course based on their experiences in the Cameroons and East Africa campaigns. By the end of the year, nearly 200 Nigerians had qualified as instructors in drill, musketry, bayonet, machine-gun, signalling, and lower-standard English.[3] Thus, during the post-war era Nigerians began to fill many posts previously held by British N.C.O.s, a process that gave increasing numbers of them positions of leadership in the army and helped to reduce the Regiment's payroll expenditures.

There was another important post-war change in the army's training programme. The superb work done by Africans during the war reinforced the Colonial Office's belief that the West African Frontier Force and the King's African Rifles should make a greater contribution to the defence of the Empire. In fact, between the two world wars a variety of influential officials and public lobbies in London argued that African troops should be used as combatants and non-combatants in limited theatres, and that an African force should be created as a parallel to, or a replacement for, the Indian Army.[4] Consequently, when funds permitted, Nigerian units were concentrated for war games in preparation for the Regiment's possible rôle as an imperial force outside of Africa.[5]

Post-war financial straits influenced miliary modernisation in other ways. Late in 1918, General Frederick Cunliffe requested that his officers should draw upon their war experiences and submit recommendations for improving the effectiveness of the Nigerian military.[6] Medical officers were unanimous in their desire to have Africans trained as stretcher-bearers, and medical assistants become part of the Regiment's permanent establishment.[7] Because of the

---

[1] Andrew Boyle to Secretary of State for the Colonies, 20 October 1918, CSO 19/6 N 2736/18.

[2] Colonial Office to Lugard, 27 March 1919; ibid.

[3] G. W. Moran, 'Report on Training Centres', 26 January 1918, CO 445/44/18468; Cunliffe's 'Recommendations for Reorganization of the West African Frontier Force', in Boyle to Milner, March 1919, CO 445/47/23456.

[4] David Killingray, 'The Idea of a British Imperial Army', in *The Journal of African History* (Cambridge), 20, 3, 1979, pp. 421–6. See also his Ph.D. dissertation, 'The Colonial Army in the Gold Coast: official policy and local response, 1890–1947', University of London, 1982.

[5] Haywood and Clarke, op.cit. p. 323.

[6] E. C. Feneran to Cunliffe, 26 December 1918; T. Sargent to Cunliffe, 9 February 1919; and G. D. Mann to Cunliffe, 26 December 1918; CO 445/47/23456.

[7] T. M. Russell Leonard to Cunliffe, n.d., ibid.

excellent work done by the Gold Coast Pioneers in the Cameroons and by the Nigeria Pioneer Section in East Africa, military officers believed that an engineering unit composed of Nigerians should form part of an expanded colonial army. They also emphasised that any modern military force needed Lewis and Stokes gun-sections.[1] All these suggestions were sound but impossible to implement because of lack of finance. Instead, the mounted infantry and one of the gun batteries were disbanded in 1922 for reasons of economy.[2]

The budget did, however, allow improvements in the Regiment's weaponry, clothing, and rations. Leather packs, for instance, were replaced by web haversacks, which were less likely to crack, resisted weather, and needed no saddlesoap, an item rarely available during the war.[3] The rifles carried by machine-gunners in the Cameroons and Tanganyika tended to get caught on low branches, delaying assembly of their Maxims for action. Consequently, machine-gun crews were issued with revolvers instead of rifles.[4] Also, the length of the bayonet often proved a handicap in the forest, so the British devised a special shortened 'bush' bayonet that became part of the infantry's standard equipment. The Nigerian's traditional weapon of close combat, the *machete*, proved its usefulness during the war, and it too became official weaponry.[5]

Problems created by inadequate foot-and-leg protection during the war led the British to conduct a field test of new footgear in 1921. Medical officers in the First Battalion and the Battery issued their men with several different types of canvas and leather-topped boots. These were worn on duty and parade for 18 days, after which the experiment was discontinued. Both the canvas and leather boots 'were found to be clumsy and made the wearers awkward and slow in movement. They complained that the large toe-cap hurt, and bruised the toe joints and the foot between the toes and the instep'. The guiding principle in the selection of footgear, the study concluded, must be that it provide protection when circumstances necessistated its use, yet not require regular wear for a comfortable fit.[6] In 1923, the Inspector-General announced that the official foot-and-leg gear of the W.A.F.F. was light-leather sandals with 'chupplies' over a grey worsted sock, although the men could still go barefoot on drill and patrol if they wished.[7]

The hunger that the men experienced in the Cameroons and Tanganyika caused the British to make major improvements in their war rations. By World War II West African troops and carriers were on an official daily diet of 4,300 calories, which included pork, beef, beans, and chocolate, as well as rice and yams. Transport officers were even estimating the number of cigarettes, kola nuts, and sheets of toilet paper required for men in the field.[8]

[1] E. C. Feneran to Cunliffe, 26 December 1918; T. Sargent to Cunliffe, 9 February 1919; and G. D. Mann to Cunliffe, 26 December 1918; CO 445/47/23456.
[2] Haywood and Clarke, op.cit. p. 319.
[3] Lt. Colonel Gibb to Cunliffe, 1 March 1919, CO 445/47/23456.
[4] Major Commanding 4th Training Centre, Ibadan, to Jenkins, 13 April 1917, CSO 19/5 N 1079/17.
[5] Cunliffe to Boyle, March 1919, CO 445/47/23456; and Haywood to Clifford, 25 May 1920, CO 445/58/29804.
[6] J. Sargent, Acting Commandant, to Governor-General, 18 July 1921, CO 445/56/4228.
[7] 'Report of the Inspector General for 1922', Kaduna (?), 28 May 1923, CO 4 5/62/26548.
[8] F. A. S. Clarke, 'Recollections of an Area Commander in Africa', in *Journal of the Royal United Service Institute* (London), XCIV, 1949, pp. 20–45; also Haywood and Clarke, op.cit. pp. 331–480.

WORLD WAR I AND RISE OF AFRICAN NATIONALISM 499

Political Ramifications

The nature of military life held the potential for radical political change. By mixing diverse peoples in the army, the British helped break down barriers between ethnic groups and replace them with bonds of friendship. This was especially true during the war, when it became impossible for the British to segregate ethnic groups by company. Men from Nigeria's north, east, and west not only spent time together on board ship, in hospitals, and on leave, but also found themselves fighting side by side in the same units. Yoruba Baba Tunde of B. Company, Third Battalion, for example, took orders from Hausa and Igbo N.C.O.s whom he called 'brothers', while Yoruba Sergeant Major Adedeji of C. Company, Fourth Battalion, issued orders to Hausa, who gave him 'no problems'.[1]

Specialised units, such as the Artillery, the Pioneers, the Signals, the Machine Gunners, and the Mounted Infantry, were even more heterogeneous. The latter had been almost exclusively Hausa before the war, but by 1916 were recruited from dozens of different ethnic groups.[2] To facilitate communication within this unit and others, the British were forced to put increasing emphasis on English-language training, which also fostered Nigerian unity both in and out of the ranks.

Although the British were aware that increased contacts between different Nigerian ethnic groups were inconsistent with the colonial policy of 'divide and rule', they were much more concerned about the prospect of thousands of Nigerians – instilled with military discipline, organisation, and perhaps political ideology – returning to the Colony following the war. Disarming demobilised soldiers did not alleviate their fears. According to Colonel A. H. W. Haywood in 1920, 'considerable quantities of arms and ammunition' had made their way into West Africa from the north. 'Owing to the circumstances of the war', he continued, 'a number of inhabitants of Nigeria have been trained to arms. We [the Regiment's Officer Corps] are thus led to the conclusion that in any future risings...the rebels are likely to be better armed and trained than they were in the past'.[3]

Surprisingly, Nigerian veterans, who had been exposed to the cosmopolitan worlds of Lagos, Durban, Dar es Salaam, Bagdhad, and Bombay, who had established friendships that helped to break down the parochialism of ethnicity and provincialism, and who had been trained to arms and inculcated with army discipline and methods of organisation, did not attempt to overthrow their colonial masters. Apparently they did not even form political lobbies or self-help organisations.[4] The fact that governments in general discouraged such

[1] Interviews, Baba Tunde and Adedeji.
[2] *Nigeria and the Great War* (Lagos, n.d.), CSO 19/5 N 1735/17. On p. 20 there is a photograph entitled 'The Tower of Babel – 12 men from one company, MI all of different tribes. Top row: Dekkakerri, Zeberma/Arriwa, Berri-Berri, Senegalese, Fulani. Bottom: Bauchi, Pagan, Barbarimis, Buzu, Hausa, Shewa Arba, Beddi'.
[3] Haywood to Clifford, 22 April 1920, CO 445/51/29803.
[4] My research disclosed no documentation on the existence of a veterans association, and none of those I interviewed had ever joined or even heard of such a group. In addition, Chief Olyonu of Ibadan, who was instrumental in establishing the Nigeria Legion, which brought together a number of post-World War II ex-servicemen's organisations in 1964, and Colonel Akafar, the Secretary of the Nigeria Legion, Ibadan, told me that they had been unable to find any record of post-World War I veterans associations.

activity among veterans helps to explain their basically apolitical nature, a common characteristic of ex-soldiers in both Europe and British Africa.[1]

The Nigeria Regiment's reputation among the civilian population also helps explain why veterans did not become political leaders. While Nigerians were winning *kudos* overseas, the garrison troops at home were perpetuating the Regiment's negative image.[2] Their punitive behaviour, ostensibly justified because of the delicate internal situation precipitated by the war, convinced many Nigerians that the Regiment was an oppressor, the instrument of British imperial policy. This image acted as a counterbalance to the unity achieved by various ethnic groups within the Regiment while fighting overseas. Ironically, it was this *camaraderie*, forged on the battlefield, that might have helped transform the Regiment into a respected mechanism of national integration, the antithesis of indirect rule.

Although Nigerian veterans were not highly political, they did help to build a new political order. Their military discipline and foreign travel, plus their exposure to the English language, the money economy, modern technology, and other aspects of European culture, accelerated the country's move into the twentieth century. In addition, their war experiences increased their self-confidence and sense of self-worth, character traits inextricably linked with the growth of a national consciousness.

A new unity based on race also emerged; Nigerians were proud of their contributions to victory and their ability to excel in battle as a modern military force. A letter to the editor of *West Africa*, criticising the tendency of Europeans to attribute African successes in the Cameroons and East Africa to white leadership, clearly expresses this new-found pride in race:

It is in no vaunting or glorifying spirit that I remind the European that the race which smashed the British squares at the Soudan, and the race which, with bare hands and assegais, charged in a frontal attack the British machine guns and got to within 17 yards of those deadly weapons in South Africa, and the race whose fighting qualities compelled General Smuts to advise Europe to make a cardinal law of the League of Nations...the definite non-arming of the African, has defensive instinct which can successfully function without European leadership.[3]

Nigerian participation in the world conflict encouraged national identity in other ways. The mobilisation of Nigeria's manpower during World War I forced very many Africans, previously ignorant of any political unity outside their own village, to recognise the existence of a much larger territorial entity and to participate for the first time in Nigerian affairs. There was also a shared sense of suffering. Demobilised veterans returned home to relate their trials and tribulations to family and friends. Those who were maimed served as visual reminders of Nigerian sacrifice, and the families of men who did not return grieved together.

Nigerian veterans hastened, directly and indirectly, the decline of the old political order. They witnessed, at first hand, Europeans fighting among themselves. They no longer regarded whites as a monolithic race, but instead

---

[1] See Steven R. Ward (ed.), *The War Generation: veterans of the First World War* (New York, 1975), for studies of British, American, French, Italian, and German veterans associations.

[2] Samson Ukpabi, 'The Changing Role of the Military in Nigeria, 1900–1970', in *Afrika Spectrum* (Hamburg), 76/1, pp. 61–77.

[3] Victor Allen of Lagos, *West Africa*, 17 January 1920.

WORLD WAR I AND RISE OF AFRICAN NATIONALISM

saw them as 'tribes' quite capable of being divided. Some Nigerians had killed Europeans in and out of battle. When asked what became of German officers captured in the field, Adedeji replied, 'We poured petrol or kerosene over them and set them on fire while alive'.[1] Although this is probably an exaggeration on the part of an old man hoping to impress his interviewer, grandchildren, and neighbours, it illustrates how the war changed Nigerian perceptions of Europeans. Like other men, Europeans were vulnerable and in the long run could be defeated. In general, Nigerians were less likely to fear men simply because of their colour or nationality.

Ironically, World War I, fought by Britain to maintain and strengthen its power world-wide, helped erode its might and prestige in Nigeria. The educated élite, who had expected that their steadfast support of Britain would be rewarded by the recognition that Africans were adults entitled to be treated as such, had to wait until after World War II for any meaningful share in their government. They were not alone in feeling cheated. Thousands of Nigerians, after years of faithful service in the Regiment, received no back pay, gratuities, or medals; Nigerians, rich and poor, contributed generously to various relief funds without any apparent benefit to the veterans or their dependents.[2] When asked what the British did for the families of dead soldiers, Baba Tunde answered: 'The Government did not care about the families...did not even take care of living soldiers...The British could not be trusted'.[3]

World War I served in other ways to discredit the British in Nigeria. Colonial officials, military officers, and the British press heaped praise upon the men of the Nigeria Regiment; yet 30 years passed before a Nigerian was promoted to the officer corps. The educated élite was quick to point out that Africans in the French territories served as officers, even generals: 'These men have only risen by their brave endeavours, but we who are under the British flag cannot get above the rank of Sergeant Major, and what we were entitled to we did not get'.[4]

Although the British refusal to grant commissions to West African veterans incensed the educated élite, one particular post-war injustice convinced many West Africans that they would not share in the fruits of victory. The Nigeria Regiment, sent to the East Africa theatre to replace white troops suffering severely from the effects of the tropical climate, was not given any opportunity to take part in the London Peace Parade; the Colonial Office concluded that it would be 'impolitic to bring [to England] coloured detachments to participate in the peace processions'.[5] A letter by Victor Allen of Lagos to the editor of *West Africa* articulated the righteous indignation felt by those who were stung by this insult:

In your issue published the week after the Victory march in London, you asserted that Africans could not be in the march because there was no time to get them to England owing to lack of

---

[1] Interview, Adedeji.
[2] See James K. Matthews, 'Clock Towers for the Colonised: demobilisation of the Nigerian military and the readjustment of its veterans to civilian life, 1918–1925', in *International Journal of African Historical Studies* (New York), 14, 2, 1981, pp. 254–71.
[3] Interview, Baba Tunde.
[4] Victor Allen, *West Africa*, 11 October 1919.
[5] Colonial Office minute by Colonel Jenkins, 15 October 1919, CO 583/76/51430.

transport. You do not mean to say that Great Britain could not afford to send out two men-of-war to bring them if they had been wanted?...They were fit to assist in breaking the aggression of Germany but they were not fit to be in the Victory march...We live and learn.[1]

Indeed, Nigerians would long remember this 'petty and penny-pinching piece of trivial racism'.[2]

British methods of recruitment during World War I also lowered their prestige in Nigeria.[3] For instance, people in the North were heard saying in 1916: 'Here have these...Christians been for twenty years preaching and legislating against slavery, and they themselves are slave-raiding our villages and taking children to fight for them'.[4] The impressment of soldiers and carriers not only exposed the hypocrisy of European religion, but also struck at the heart of indirect rule. Throughout Nigeria, the British pressured chiefs and headmen into meeting manpower quotas, a process that alienated the people from their traditional leaders. E. M. Falk, the District Officer at Owerri, in south-eastern Nigeria, reported in May 1919 that the 'relatives of men who have not come back from military expeditions or railway work invariably consider the chief who recruited the men to be guilty of a species of homicide or slave dealing'.[5] Consequently, the families of soldiers and carriers who failed to return from the war inevitably held the chiefs responsible, and in some cases claimed compensation from them.

In 1918, chiefs and headmen had to confront the demobilised military men they had sent to war. These cocky and sometimes hostile veterans, many of whom had held positions of responsibility in the military, challenged the authority of their traditional leaders. On his return to Iwo following the East Africa campaign, Adedeji found his chief unable to command the respect of the town's young men. When asked what the chief did to regain his authority, Adedeji replied: 'Nothing. The people would not listen'.[6] By discrediting traditional authority, the British undermined the foundation of their own rule. Unwittingly, they helped create a political vacuum, to be filled by the increasingly nationalistic élite.

Conclusion

World War I created a commonality of experience in Nigeria that included both the erosion of traditional power and values and the building of pride and self-worth. Nigerians shared not only the suffering brought on by the fighting, but also – for the first time – a knowledge of European weaknesses and an understanding of what it meant to be colonised. In addition, many acquired a new and fundamental awareness that they belonged to a larger political unit. This conflict, in which the military man played the protagonist, was Nigeria's first national experience.

[1] Victor Allen, *West Africa*, 11 October 1919.
[2] Akinjide Osuntokun, *Nigeria in the First World War* (Atlantic Highlands, 1979), p. 297.
[3] See James K. Matthews, 'Reluctant Allies: Nigerian responses to military recruitment, 1914–1918', in Melvin E. Page (ed.), *Black Men in a White Men's War* (forthcoming).
[4] Palmer to Lugard, 2 March 1917, CO 583/63/3057.
[5] Memorandum from E. M. Falk to Resident, Owerri, 20 May 1919, NNA, Owerri Provincial Papers.
[6] Interview, Adedeji. For similar accounts in West Africa, see Roger Thomas, 'Military Recruitment in the Gold Coast during the First World War', in *Cahiers d'études africaines* (Paris), xv, 57, 1975, pp. 57–83.

[27]

WORLD WAR I AND AFRICA: INTRODUCTION

BY RICHARD RATHBONE

THE study of the history of Africa during World War I raises two major problems of synthesis and a host of smaller problems. First of all, the sheer diversity of the continent and the extremely uneven nature of its precolonial development,[1] let alone the patchy and differentiated modes of imperial and colonial penetration, make it difficult to see its experience, even of so ostensibly cataclysmic an event as World War I, as a unified whole. Indeed, the diversity of the continent was mirrored in the diversity of its experience of the war, which combined the actual agony of the battlefield for many thousands of black troops both in Africa and in Europe at one extreme, with the undoubted uneventfulness of those same years for many others.

Secondly, there is a problem of periodization. Unlike World War II, World War I does not mark a turning point in anything like so clear a fashion. Whereas after World War II it is surely true that 'nothing was ever the same', the lines between cause and effect before and after World War I are far from neatly drawn, and not merely because less is known about the period as a whole.

Apart from the directly obvious changes in Africa consequent upon the war itself, such as the East African campaign, the transfer of the German colonial possessions under the League of Nations mandate after the War, the recruitment of Africans and the emphasis on 'war production', the key question of cause and effect, of whether what we observe after the war came because of the war, remains hazy in the minds of historians. It was this, above all, that prompted the selection of this theme—'The impact of World War I on Africa'—for a two-day conference held at the School of Oriental and African Studies, London, in 1977, at which the papers in this issue of this Journal were first presented. The conference, naturally, solved few of the problems but it did draw attention to some major themes which ran through many of the papers and which, it is hoped, will provide others with ideas for future research.

Before attempting to tease out some of these, it is important to note the areas of darkness. We learnt little about colonial policy in war-time and little about the economic history of Africa between 1914 and 1918. If anything we were left with a general impression that the problems of communication during the period, coupled with the grander preoccupations of metropolitan governments, led to a period of almost maximal local, pro-consular initiative with minimal metropolitan inter-

[1] Under which head I include factor-endowment, demography, the spread of pre-colonial cash production, etc.

ference. To some extent it is clear that local colonial authorities used the war in Europe as a convenient smoke-screen behind which they could pursue cherished goals unhindered. Lugard, for example, seems to have been behaving thus in rushing through the Provincial Court, Supreme Court and Criminal Procedure Bills in Nigeria in the two months following the outbreak of European hostilities. World War I was certainly a smoke-screen which blinded both metropolitan critics of colonialism and, as one could see in many of the conference papers, many of the African modern elite whose 'loyalty' and 'goodwill' towards the metropoles appears to have been relatively general.

These generalities aside, it is important to recapture the marginality of Africa in overall imperial war strategy, particularly in the case of Britain. Although it looms large in our consciousness, and was to figure prominently in metropolitan concern in the inter-war period, a dogged hunt through the numerous memoirs of the period reveals that those in high places thought little about the 'colonies' and even less about Africa at the time. Empire meant pre-eminently the 'white Dominions' and India; throughout 1914–18, Africa was reserved, as on pre-war agendas, for 'any other business'. This is a rude discovery for an Africanist, but the very transformation of that situation, the growth of the perceived need to be better informed, instanced by the burgeoning committees of experts working for the Colonial Office in the inter-war years, owed a great deal to the alteration in circumstances in metropolitan-African relations following World War I.

A substantial degree of this transformation can, in the case of Britain, be seen in economic terms. In 1913, for example, only about 22 per cent of all United Kingdom exports had Imperial (including African) destinations; by 1938 that percentage had doubled. Of those figures, of course, both India and the 'white Dominions' enjoyed the lion's share and Africa accounted for only a minute proportion of such flows. A non-economist cannot satisfactorily account for such changes and the secondary literature seems still to be debating them. Imperial markets obviously become more important relative to non-Imperial markets after 1918. And part of the reason for this lies within the metropole itself. British goods found it harder to compete within the markets of the industrialized world after 1918; Britain's industrial efficiency had not kept abreast with the strides made in German and North American industry, for example. Moreover, after 1918 the industrialized world played a rougher and tougher game, first using tariffs and later even more direct methods.[2] In import terms, Britain's imperial dependence increased dramatically after 1918. In 1913 something like 80 per cent of British imports derived from non-imperial sources. By 1938 that percentage had been reduced to about 60 per cent.[3] In sum, it seems that the Empire as a whole began to make a dramatic

---

[2] See A. R. Hall (ed.), *The Export of Capital from Britain* (London, 1968).
[3] See Ian Drummond (ed.), *British Economic Policy and the Empire, 1919–39* (London, 1972).

'contribution' as a supplier and as a market in the inter-war period. Part of the explanation for this, and much of the explanation for the far greater concern with colonial matters after the War, lies in the extensive 'sharing' Britain enjoyed in the relative domestic prosperity achieved in the Empire after 1918.

In many areas of the colonial world, then, considerable economic expansion occurred between the wars and it seems likely that Africans were highly significant in the process, though the precise size and nature of their contribution remains a subject for further research. Capital investment and exports appear to have risen, with a grinding interlude during the Depression; even in those parts of Africa where Britain enjoyed no tariff preference, Britain 'shared' the market response of Africans, the growth of local markets and the creation of wealth. It is clear from many of the conference papers, and from discussion they provoked, that this expansion was closely related to the War itself. First, the war-time measures of the metropoles included an intensification of the production drive in cash-crops and minerals. This in turn was reinforced by the clear relationship between military recruitment and labour recruitment. It is evident that the extent of social and political control over Africans was increased under war-time conditions, accelerating processes of change implicit in the introduction and encouragement of new modes of production before 1914. Before 1914 Africa was for the most part a dream for the greedy speculator. From 1918 it seems likely that her role was more centrally related, or at least perceived to be more centrally related, as part of the empire, to the very heart of the metropolitan economies themselves.

By 1914, although the metropoles were inescapably imperial powers in Africa, the shape of that colonial domination was by no means set. In Britain the contest between those loosely described as liberals and Imperialists as to that shape was not completely ended. It is a contest complicated by the political crises of the first decade of the twentieth century. But it is tempting to see the 1914–18 War as a period in which the liberal conscience abdicated in favour of more imperially minded figures like Curzon, Milner and, even more importantly for the future of southern Africa, Jan Smuts, all of whom served in the War Cabinets. But that abdication pre-dates 1914 in many respects. Dilke was clear, for example, about the escape and evasion exercise that had ensued in the House of Commons debate on the South African Union Bill.[4] While he and others may have striven for what they perceived as the preservation of African interests, the resolution of the white war in South Africa involved *voltes faces* and retractions which left the critiques of colonialism in less and less well-placed hands well before 1914. But as Sir Keith Hancock has shown[5] the Rhodes–Chamberlain ideal of a protectionist imperialism gained ground amongst Conservatives through the course of World War I.

[4] House of Commons, *Debates*, 4H 188.13:V:1908.1229.
[5] *Survey of British Commonwealth Affairs, 1918–39. Vol. II Problems of Economic Policy* (London, 1942), Part I, 94–110.

RICHARD RATHBONE

At the other extreme, as Professor P. S. Gupta explains,[6] the British Labour movement was confused on colonial matters.

But 1914–18 were crucial years in that throughout Europe they were not years of debate and theory, but rather years of practice, a time of short-term actions rather than long-term planning. Opponents of colonialism were in a trap they themselves perceived. War was inseparable from imperialism, and Empire. To oppose war was to be unpatriotic, and patriotism and Empire became more and more synonymous. This closing of ranks, the take-over of the commanding heights by imperially minded statesmen, and, no less importantly, civil servants and diplomats, in some senses completed colonialism in fundamental fashion.

In the circumstances it seems odd that some historians persist in calling World War I a 'European War'. Lloyd George himself concluded that 'it is not one continent that is engaged—every continent is affected'.[7] As he admitted to Colonel House, it *was* an imperialist war.[8] Securing German colonies, for example, *was* amongst allied war aims. No power was capable of significantly altering the victors' chosen paths. Although a fair amount of attention has focused on American influence in the imperial sphere, particularly over the initiation of the mandates system,[9] that influence seems to have been severely limited. More significant in the long term, perhaps, was the early appreciation and exploitation of the Allied shipping shortage during 1914–18, when American freighters became more and more regular callers at West African ports. Although W. H. Page, the American Ambassador in Britain, wondered whether the imminent collapse of 'this England and Empire' would 'put the leadership of the race in our hands'[10] his musing was thirty years premature.

Fundamentally World War I seems to have accelerated the process of political and economic change in colonial Africa. It was a period in which a largely haphazard colonial world became an increasingly centralized affair. The widening scale of the African empires both in terms of space and, more importantly, of economic, political and social penetration forced a radical change in the 'style' of colonialism, and all the contributions to this conference seem to have been agreed upon this point. In many ways the War marked the period in which 'pacification' of both African and metropolitan critics of colonialism ends and colonial rule proper begins.

This is perhaps rather a negative standpoint. One can assuredly set against it Harry Johnston's trenchant comments to the African Society in March 1919. World War I, he argued, had seen the 'beginning of revolt

[6] Partha S. Gupta, *Imperialism and the British Labour Movement 1914–1964* (London, 1975), cap. 2.
[7] *War Memoirs*, vol. II (London, 1938), 1355.
[8] C. Seymour (ed.), *The papers of Colonel House* (London, 1926), vol. III, p. 240.
[9] See, e.g., Gaddis Smith, 'The British government and the disposition of the German colonies in Africa', in P. Gifford and W. R. Louis (eds.), *Britain and Germany in Africa* (Yale, 1967) and W. R. Louis, 'The United States and the African peace settlement of 1919', *J. Afr. Hist.*, IV, 3, 413–34.
[10] B. Hendrick, *Life and letters of W. H. Page* (London, 1923), vol. I, p. 174.

against the white man's supremacy'. If he had been as well informed by nearly sixty years of ensuing African studies he would have found ample evidence for his polemical assertion. The period had seen innumerable cases of opposition to European rule, from outright resistance—the Kwale Ibo or the Egba rising of June 1918, for example—to the newer and more subtle forms of hostility evidenced by the clear signs of crop retention by Gold Coast cocoa farmers in reaction to low cocoa prices. But the role of the War itself as either an immediate case of new social movements or as a period in which the form of social movements radically changes was hotly debated at the conference. And, in general, the tentative conclusion again was that continuity and discontinuity were finely balanced. In line with perhaps the most important shift in African historiography in the past twenty years, the conference papers bore strikingly upon the absolute importance of focusing on *all* African social groupings, and not merely the 'westernized elite', whose relative passivity in this period conceals the ferment in the rest of the society as Killingray shows for the Gold Coast.

The period is one of striking contrasts. It is apparent that Africans were being presented in their everyday life with an infinitely more intensive and sometimes brutal form of repression than they had experienced in the early years of colonial rule. The French West African recruiting drive of 1915–16 clearly deserves its awful reputation for harshness. As Ann Summers and R. W. Johnson show, few of its recruits were volunteers in any of the accepted senses of that word, and the methods employed in impressing men both by administrative officers and chiefs rank alongside some of the worst horror stories of the epoch. Similarly, as Cross sought to emphasize in a paper on social movements during and after the war, examples abound throughout Africa of arbitrary and uncompensated crop requisitioning, and cavalier treatment (to put it mildly) of entire areas with the misfortune to be cast as war zones. Robert Archer's interesting paper on Madagascar rebutted the 'inevitability' of all this. His account singularly lacked the oppressive thread of both the West and East African stories. (Unfortunately both these last papers have had to be omitted from the collection of papers published here for reasons of space). It is at any rate clear that the economic impact of the War on southern Africa was a great deal more equivocal than Katzenellenbogen has acknowledged; increased demand for strategic minerals, for example, did not necessarily 'drive up' wages, for as Charles Perrings has shown recently in the case of Katanga, the response to labour 'shortage' might simply be to tighten the screws on African villagers.[11]

Many of the papers presented to the conference contributed to the erosion of simplistic views of change in Africa. However frightful many of

---

[11] S. E. Katzenellenbogen, 'Southern Africa and the War of 1914–18', in M. R. D. Foot (ed.), *War and Society* (London, 1973), 107–22; C. Perrings, ' "Good lawyers but Poor Workers": Recruited Angolan Labour in the Copper Mines of Katanga, 1917–21,' *J. Afr. Hist.* XVIII, 2 (1977), 237–59.

the induced changes occasioned by the War were, African society had by no means lost all of the initiative. African society was not being simply crushed. Cross's paper was wisely insistent upon this; Archer's paper stressed the continuity in Madagascar in this period. Paradoxically, as Summers and Johnson show, the crushing pressure of conscription in Guinea actually appears in some cases to have frozen the *status quo ante bellum* and even to have restored the power of chiefs who had been under severe French pressure in the years before 1914.

Part of the explanation of this must lie in a theme which appeared marginally in a number of the papers, but which needs to be more fully explored. This period of rapid change occurred at a time of significantly lower administrative and commercial white staff-numbers in almost all colonial states. The percentage of white administrators and *commerçants* to total populations fell throughout Africa throughout 1914–18, as it was to do during the Depression and again in 1939–45, as the priorities of great matters in Europe lured them away. Thus the deeper and ultimately most pervasive penetration of the fabric of African life occurred when there were fewer visible 'colonialists' upon the ground. In South Africa, both African and Afrikaner were to benefit from the absence of English-speaking workers on the front—though the former were only to do so temporarily. Elsewhere, one of the results of this was the simple substitution of blacks in roles previously earmarked for whites, which in turn goes some little distance towards explaining elite quiescence.

But the very staff shortages signalized a crisis of considerable dimensions both for colonial powers and for commercial concerns. For both, the short-term solutions were to prove to be of long-term significance. To put it at its simplest level, there was a clear fusion of these two spheres. Government was to play a greater role in the economies, in the forms of controls and intervention in general, and business, as Killingray shows for the Gold Coast, was to play a greater role in government as adviser and as lobby.

Colonial authority was digging itself in, an inevitable consequence of the demands for conscripted troops and labour, the general increase in taxation and the rising demands being made upon rural producers. But it was doing so in a period of weakness. Killingray cites Clifford's fears about the 'Combine's' near monopoly, but the Gold Coast's revenues depended vitally upon the unencumbered activity of firms taking full advantage of the death of laissez-faire. In more simple form, colonial governments were also bound to respect the local equivalents of Chambers of Mines and Chambers of Commerce who were 'doing their bit' in terms of producing the materials the Empire Resources Development Committee demanded.

It was not only this leverage that increased the power of European business. The growth of European oligopolistic enterprise, or at least oligopolistic aspirations, certainly antedates 1914. But World War I greatly facilitated its success. First, and not unimportantly, the War removed Germany from its powerful trading position in Africa. French and particularly British enterprise was greatly encouraged by the elimination of major competition. As is well known, German commercial houses before 1914 dominated not only their own colonial trade but played a very large part in the trade of French and British colonies as well.

That windfall accelerated trends already in train. The war certainly stimulated, sometimes in crude fashion, African production. But to conclude from the figures that prosperity resulted goes too far. Despite the appearance of a boom in most sectors between 1915 and 1917, the external trade of most African colonies in real terms was depressed. Despite the complexities of the situation, there are grounds for hazarding that World War I rehearsed the mode by which African entrepreneurs and rural producers were to be out-gunned during World War II by the European competitors. Between 1914 and 1918, as between 1939 and 1945, severe shipping shortages created bottlenecks which adversely affected African business to the gain of European concerns who through their closeness to Government had more access to shipping space. In West Africa it can be clearly seen how the West African Shipping Conference, which of course had linkages with British commercial concerns, kept non-British concerns out of trade by its virtual monopoly of freight space. It also, logically from its own point of view, blocked African access to shipping for both import and export purposes. This occurred, as it did in 1939–45, when commercially minded Africans knew that they could have benefited from the considerable profits accruing from the common practice of 'marking-up' prices of imported goods at a time of their relative shortage. European commerce reaped a rich reward partly because producer prices were being kept down by the state while no matching controls were placed upon retail prices. Other institutions reinforced this tendency. Certainly the reputation of the banking sector for prejudice in the granting of credit owed something to the particularly tight controls placed upon Banks in war-time. But there is little doubt that the favouring of 'old' customers, more particularly firms in which they had large stakes, blocked Africans in a further way.

The significance of inflation in provoking African discontent during and after World War II has received more attention than that of inflation between 1914 and 1920, which appears to have been no less important. Although the figures are confusing, it appears that the amount of money in circulation increased in British African colonies by about 500 per cent between 1913 and 1918. Because of the short supply of import goods, the cost of these rose enormously. In addition it appears that many areas also saw great increases in food prices, not least because of shortages occasioned by the removal of labour from food cultivation through conscription and the diversion of food cultivators into non-edible cash crops. In much of Africa by 1914, many imported goods were no longer classifiable as luxuries. Kerosene, cloth, matches, matchets and many other western industrial products were part of African everyday life. Thus the overall situation of real decline in prices paid for export crops was mirrored in the high cost of imported goods and probably locally produced goods as well.

The financial implications of war for most colonies worsened this situation and underlines the governmental role in circumscribing African opportunity. In many colonies the war increased taxation and decreased development expenditure. Some colonies like the Gold Coast or Kenya actually funded colonial war, the bill for the invasion of Togoland being £60,000. In addition, most colonial governments voted sums as war 'contributions' to metropolitan governments. To meet these bills taxation was increased and services declined, not least because the low energy of colonial economies made revenue hard to raise in other fashions. This did not stop colonial governments increasing specific duties on a number of significant imports, sometimes by several hundred percent. At the same time, public sector capital expenditure in most colonies, which in any case was very modest before 1914, fell by as much as a third between 1914 and 1918 in money terms and in real terms of course a great deal more dramatically. Africans paid a heavy price for maintaining the colonial governance of their countries in war-time. And when the burden appeared to fall on expatriate companies, as it appears to do in the raising of revenue through, for example, cocoa export duty, it is clear that the burden of this was shifted onto the farmers by price-lowering.

The press of war-time measures, from labour-recruitment through price manipulation for producers and the obstruction of African traders, affected all levels of colonial society. They gave the previous abstraction of the 'colonial state' a thoroughly concrete reality. Africans did not of course simply lie down under this onslaught. In many respects their reactions were remarkable for their doggedness. Beyond the sphere of open revolt lay powerful attempts to outflank European encroachment. Africans, as Killingray shows, adopted subtle methods to evade the European shipping and banking lock-outs. Cash farmers went on buying land throughout the war in many areas despite the drop in world prices. On the eve of the lorry revolution the optimistic maximizers are to be found energetically building their own roads and their own bridges, usually without central revenue support and frequently voluntarily. Similarly, 1914–18 seems to have heralded a vast increase in demand for western education. Most African colonies had many more schools in 1918 than they had in 1914. Both in West Africa and, as Louise Pirouet shows, in East Africa, schools and missions were most certainly the product of African demand, and some were financed and run by Africans. To this more positive picture must be added the role of the ex-servicemen, some of whom do appear to have been significant 'modernizers'. They also appear to have been an importantly disappointed group whose inducements to serve were seldom honoured. Their political consciousness was to be significant in the history of nationalism in the following three decades.

WORLD WAR I AND AFRICA

This rather more positive and redressive picture needs to be set beside a somewhat more equivocal penetration of Africa by survey. Physically Africa was more exhaustively surveyed for its mineral and other wealth than ever before. Some of the most notable mineralogical surveys date from this period, such as Major Kitson's famous Gold Coast survey which *inter alia* resulted in the discovery of and immediate exploitation of its bauxite reserves. Agricultural research was similarly energetically pursued, particularly where it could be followed up with development based upon war requirements: hence a widespread devotion to rubber and oil production. But African society no less than African topography was also under the microscope. Systematic official, as opposed to missionary, research into language and society seems to have its origins in this period. While one is in the debt of the Rattrays and the Cardinalls, the process of increasing information carried with it the essential message of the permanent nature of colonial rule.

It seems clear that the War itself, and its direct consequences, were of enormous significance to Africa. The conference by no means tied up all the loose ends. Strikingly absent in terms of systematic treatment was, for example, the influenza epidemic of 1919–20, which Kuczynski himself is vague about. It does seem likely on his figures, and others, that mortality of the order of 5 per cent was common. It is an odd comment on our priorities that we know more about cattle epidemics than we do about human disasters. In conclusion it seems clear that the period of World War I is not a Eurocentric time capsule which we artificially introduced into the African context. The War was very much a reality for Africa, a period of immense and significant change of which we have only just scratched the surface.

[28]

FIXING HISTORY:
NARRATIVES OF WORLD WAR I IN FRANCE

ANN-LOUISE SHAPIRO

ABSTRACT

For nearly a century, the French have entertained an unshakable conviction that their ability to recognize themselves—to know and transmit the essence of Frenchness—depended on the teaching of the history of France. In effect, history was a discourse on France, and the teaching of history—"*la pédagogie centrale du citoyen*"—the means by which children were constituted as heirs and carriers of a common collective memory that made them not only citizens, but family. In this essay, I examine the rhetorical and conceptual effects on history writing that emerge out of this preoccupation with the elaboration of a continuous, coherent national identity.

Focusing on schoolbooks, I begin by looking at the dominant, nearly hegemonic model of French history created by Ernest Lavisse in the 1890s—a model informed by the dream of a unified, unitary French nation, embodied in and articulated through the history of France—and at the disruption of this paradigm in the aftermath of the Great War. I then consider a text written in the 1990s specifically to repudiate the kind of nationalist narratives that prevailed for most of this century—a new supranational history of Europe. I argue that, in their different experiments with fixing history, both Lavisse and the contemporary textbook authors did not so much repair a deficient history as produce a historical fixation, creating mythicized histories that are complete, closed, predictable, and at bottom ahistorical. Finally, I turn to a recent World War I novel, *A Very Long Engagement* by Sébastien Japrisot, in order to suggest ways in which the narrative strategies of a fiction writer may be useful to historians in thinking about a different kind of historical project.

Several months ago, the headline of a *New York Times* article announced in large type: "Lacking Barricades, France Is in a Funk." The article went on to discuss a widely reported malaise generated by contemporary challenges to France's sense of itself—challenges posed by the conditions of a global market and the ambiguities of its position in the emerging European Community. France is, according to these reports, "disoriented," "a society unmoored," and, in the words of philosopher André Glucksmann, "in a crisis with respect to its own history and ... its place in the world."[1] While it is not surprising to find that the French perceive no clear models by which to address current economic

---
1. *New York Times* (29 December 1996), E5.

and geopolitical shifts, I want to draw attention to the allusive historical quotation of the headline—the reference to barricades that invokes an assumed relation between the French nation of the present and the history of France.

In an immediately transparent shorthand—condensed in an icon that at once identifies national character and commitments, points to former times when both were threatened, and demonstrates their staying power—the lack of barricades produces a sense of the French adrift, unhinged from their past, without direction for the future. By this reference to a resonant national image, the headline is able to conjure up the "imagined community" of the French, drawing a continuous line from the great revolutionary moment of 1789 to the present. Even in the unlikely circumstances of 1944—a time considerably less celebratory than that of 1789—the French raised barricades, tying their sense of themselves in the ambiguous context of World War II to a comforting, continuous national tradition.[2] As part of a national system of references, barricades, like other national icons and memories, constitute the historical frame within which events become meaningful, able to explain the past, guarantee the present, and produce the future.

As Pierre Nora has argued, until quite recently in France, "the relationships between history, memory, and the nation were ... shown to involve a reciprocal circularity, a symbiosis at every level."[3] For nearly all of the hundred years since Jules Ferry introduced compulsory, free, secular education (1880), an unshakable conviction has persisted that the ability of the French to recognize themselves—to know and transmit the essence of Frenchness—depended on the teaching of the history of France. To this day, scholars continue to explain the fortitude of the French in the Great War, the collapse of France in 1940, and the success of DeGaulle with reference to specific interpretations of history.[4] Shortly after becoming President, Mitterand warned his ministers: "The bankruptcy of history teaching in our schools has become a national danger.... A people who loses its memory, loses its identity."[5] Pushing the point even further, Alain Decaux, historian and popular television commentator, identified a love of history as an essential aspect of French culture—something that makes the French different from the English and Germans in the ways in which a special feeling for history is "second nature" for the French, generating the sale of nine million history books per year, four-to five-hundred thousand issues of history journals per month, and guaranteeing the success of historical works on television and in film.[6] In his terms, history is in some sense the lifeblood of France—natural, fundamental, formative.

In effect, history in France has been a discourse on France, and the teaching of history *"la pédagogie centrale du citoyen"*—the means by which children have been constituted as heirs and carriers of a common collective memory

---

2. Robert Minder, *Manuels d'histoire et inconscient collectif* (Nancy, 1952), 6.

3. Pierre Nora, "Between Memory and History: Les Lieux de mémoire," *Representations* 26 (Spring 1989), 10.

4. Alain Kimmel and Jacques Poujol, *Certaines idées de la France* (Frankfurt am Main, 1982).

5. Mitterand in Jean-François Fayard, *Des enfants sans histoire* (Paris, 1984), 9.

6. Decaux in *ibid.*, 14.

that made them not only citizens, but family. As one critic wondered apocalyptically in 1984: "If it happened by some cataclysm that we would become deprived of all reference to the past, if we would become ignorant of all that came before us, what would we be if not orphans?"[7] In practice, the ideal of history as a legacy between generations was often quite real, as elementary school texts remained largely unchanged from the end of the nineteenth century to the 1960s, with children typically using the schoolbooks of their parents and, in poorer areas, those of their grandparents.[8] Given the high degree of uniformity assured by official programs of instruction and the overwhelming popularity of certain key texts—in this example, Bruno's 1877 *Tour de la France par deux enfants*—the Minister of Education could draw out his pocket watch at 8:05 AM and proclaim, "All of our children are [now] crossing the Alps"[9]—an observation that might have been equally true for several generations.

Not surprisingly, the linking of history lessons to national self-consciousness has led to recurrent "crises of teaching" and "wars of the schoolbooks." Who, then, is to identify the specific, defining outlines of the history of France? How is this history to be conveyed to schoolchildren? What exactly should they learn (and, of course, equally important but entirely unspoken, what should they forget?) And how can this history lesson be transmuted into the desired sense of national belonging and national pride? I will explore this persistent conviction about the mission of schoolbooks (*manuels scolaires*), looking specifically at different renderings of the history of World War I, in order to reflect more broadly on the relationship between the specific understanding of the project of writing history and the type of history produced.

I begin by looking at the dominant, nearly hegemonic model of French history created by Ernest Lavisse in the 1890s—a model informed by the dream of a unified, unitary French nation, embodied in and articulated through the history of France—and at the disruption of this paradigm in the aftermath of the Great War. I then consider a text written in the 1990s specifically to repudiate the kind of nationalist narratives that prevailed for most of this century—a new supranational history of Europe. I argue that this new text ironically reproduces in its structure, if not its content, the very model it has sought to supersede: in their different experiments with fixing history, both Lavisse and the contemporary textbook authors create a wished-for version of national memories, mythicized histories that are complete, closed, predictable, and at bottom ahistorical. Finally, I turn to a recent World War I novel, *A Very Long Engagement* (*Un long dimanche de fiançailles*) by Sébastien Japrisot, in order to suggest ways in which the narrative strategies of a fiction writer may be useful to historians in thinking about a different kind of historical project.

---

7. Decaux in *ibid.*, 17.
8. Antoine Prost, *Histoire de l'enseignement en France, 1800–1967* (Paris, 1968), 485; Suzanne Citron, *Enseigner l'histoire aujourd'hui* (Paris, 1984), 14.
9. Nora, "Between Memory and History," 20.

ANN-LOUISE SHAPIRO

I. THE SECULAR CATECHISM

Beginning with an 1890 decree requiring the teaching of French history, France was represented in school texts as "the envelope" in which history happened. Primary schools disseminated histories that, above all, elaborated the genius of France—*la France éternelle*, indestructible and continuous. So, for example, in recounting the conquest of the Gauls by the Romans, one text declared: "Here we are, more than two thousand years ago, in the period when France was still called Gaul."[10] France is less a nation here than an essence projected backward and presumably forward as well. It was the task of the text to secure the incorporation of the child within this envelope, to engage the student in continuing the tradition. Listen to one version of this appeal as presented in a 1934 text:

> A century ago, we had a quarrel with the Russians, and we went to meet them in the Crimea. There was a battle; in the evening, two wounded soldiers found themselves lying side by side on the battlefield; there had not been time to pick them up. One was a Frenchman and the other a Russian. They suffered cruelly; they tried to speak, and even if they could not understand very much, they showed friendship that at least relieved their pain. Night came; one of the two fell asleep. In the morning when he awakened, he saw a coat over him that he did not recognize. He looked for his neighbor [and saw that] he had died, and that at the moment of death, he had placed his coat over his companion in misery. Do you know which one did this? I see it in your eyes; you want it to be the Frenchman. Well, you can be pleased: It was the Frenchman.[11]

With this image of the maternal soldier, the text invokes a canonical representation of France—strong, but vulnerable—a France that joins maternal caring to paternal responsibility, France endowed with a civilizing mission, a nation apart, exemplary, different from all others. But what is equally typical in this story is its style and presentation—the direct address ("Do you know which one did this?") and the use of first person pronouns ("I can see it in your eyes . . ."). Schoolbooks spoke directly to the students of "our" strength, "our" values, "our" sorrows, and "our" recovery and regeneration.

A more directive, more ideologically explicit example of this strategy may be seen in the letter to students offered by Ernest Lavisse in the conclusion to his 1921 history text. He has just finished narrating the events of the Great War and stops to address his readers:

> Students of our schools: The war that I have just related to you is one of the greatest events in universal History. Germany, arrogant and rapacious, sought to dominate the World in order to exploit it. The great free peoples joined to defend the World's liberty. . . . Never was a generation so indebted to its elders [as yours]. To repay this debt, you must devote yourselves, body and soul, to the recovery of France. . . . It is necessary that you work longer and harder than anyone has ever worked in France. . . . It is no longer war, but it is a battle that will decide the future of Nations. A Frenchman who is nonchalant and soft [flabby, limp] is the equivalent of a bad soldier, an idler, a deserter. . . .

---

10. Citron, *Enseigner l'histoire aujhourd'hui*, 17.
11. Antoine Lyonnais, *Le Français par les choses et par les images: Cours élémentaire* (Paris: Istra, 1934), quoted in Alain Choppin, *Les Manuels scolaires: Histoire et actualité* (Paris, 1992), 171.

NARRATIVES OF WORLD WAR I IN FRANCE

Lavisse continues in an even more personal vein, noting that he is an old man about to reach his seventy-seventh birthday:

> During nearly fifty years, since the disastrous [defeat by Prussia in 1870], I have lived in a vanquished France, a France dismembered, humiliated. I have suffered from defeat, from dismemberment, from humiliation! ... Without desiring war, I have always hoped that a day would come when France would take its just revenge and when Humanity, thanks to her, would be assured of its liberty and its dignity; for France and Humanity are not two words that are opposed one to the other; they are joined and inseparable. Our fatherland is the most humane of Fatherlands! Vive la France![12]

For Lavisse to be drawing his readers into the project of fulfilling an old man's fondest wishes is entirely characteristic. He had become, after all, "the name best known to all the schoolchildren of France."[13] It was Lavisse who created the model for an aggressive pedagogy that would turn peasants into Frenchmen, boys into citizen-soldiers, and the Third Republic into the idealized incarnation of the principles of the Revolution of 1789, making the school, and especially the subject of French history, into an instrument for securing ideological integration and social order.[14] In response to the humiliating defeat of 1870, Lavisse provided a template for texts that were to be part of a "work of reparation," designed to inculcate a love for the institutions and (bourgeois) values of the Republic while preparing the French to retrieve their lost sense of grandeur (and, less explicitly, to reclaim the lost provinces of Alsace and Lorraine as well). Noting the preeminence of Lavisse's voice in this national project, Pierre Nora has observed that his *manuels scolaires* are as much the history of France as they are the narration of that history.[15]

II. THE NATION ARMED

Following Lavisse's lead, schoolbooks typically featured the lives of French heroes, promoted the achievements of Republican governments, celebrated French culture and style, mourned the loss of Alsace and Lorraine, and emphasized the overarching solidarity among Frenchmen that overcame differences. (Omitted entirely were references to class conflict. The Commune, for example, was described not as a civil war, but as a republican uprising; texts lauded the social legislation of the Third Republic, but made no reference to labor unions or labor conflict.) While France was apparently incapable of unleashing war (colonial adventures became vehicles for extending the benefits of French civilization), the nation was represented as ready should war be thrust upon her. A 1908 text captured this modality of restrained belligerence: "Suppose that the tragic moment comes: ... that the bad faith and the barbarity of a neighboring

---

12. Ernest Lavisse, *Nouveau cours d'histoire. Histoire de France: cours moyen* (Paris: Librairie Armand Colin, 1921), 266.
13. Jacques and Mona Ozouf, Preface to Ernest Lavisse, *Souvenirs* (Paris, 1988), viii.
14. In 1895, Lavisse's three-volume history of France was already in its seventy-fifth edition.
15. Pierre Nora, "Ernest Lavisse: Son rôle dans la formation du sentiment national," *Revue historique* 228 (July–December 1962), 89.

government drives us to war; what enthusiastic energy would be that of our army to fight for the fate of our Fatherland and the future of civilization."[16]

What is most striking in these accounts of French history is the intense focus on France itself, complemented by the ever lurking presence of Germany, the Other to French civility and style, the standard against which to measure French accomplishments. French patriotism was fueled not only by invoking the great figures and moments of French history but by the shadow presence of an hereditary enemy. The *manuels scolaires* from the 1890s into the immediate postwar period—that is, into the mid-1920s—preserve and extend this fixation. In explaining the causes of the war, for example, an elementary school text claimed that Germany had persistently dreamed of world supremacy, "actively pursuing its military readiness, waiting only for a favorable occasion to crush *us*."[17] France, for her part, was represented as fighting for Civilization, a destiny the texts compared to the French mission to bring liberty to the rest of Europe in 1789:

> France [in 1914] had military leaders and soldiers who were full of ardor and confidence because they had right on their side and were fighting, as in the time of the Revolution, not only for France but for the freedom of the World.[18]

> The France of the Crusades, the France of Joan of Arc and of Henri IV, the France of the Revolution, could not become, would never be, the slave of another people! In a sublime *élan*, France of 1914 resuscitated the France of the year II of the Revolution, [renewing] . . . the patriotic miracle of the [general mobilization] of 1792.[19]

With the predictable parallelism that juxtaposed French humanity against German brutality, the texts of the early 1920s—some merely continuing earlier models, others written in the emotional heat of the immediate postwar world—typically depicted the Germans as "Huns," "a people of prey," "the Barbarians of the twentieth century," relentlessly pursuing world hegemony. In fact, the nationalist catechism promoted by Lavisse was not the only kind of historical narrative available from the prewar period; there were schoolbooks that tried to articulate a less emotional message, drawing a line between good and bad versions of patriotism, just and unjust aggression. But as Jacques and Mona Ozouf have argued, the dream of universal peace is more difficult to animate and make vivid for students than descriptions of heroic actions in a just war; noble actions have a greater purchase on the imagination than abstract principles.[20]

III. FIXING HISTORY: THE NATION DISARMED?

World War I, however, effectively forced a remaking, not only of buildings and villages, of the patterns of everyday life, of values and commitments, but of

---

16. Payot, *Cours de morale* (Paris: A. Colin, 1908), quoted in Jacques and Mona Ozouf, "Le thème du patriotisme dans les manuels scolaires," *Le Mouvement social* 49 (October–December 1965), 30.
17. E. Segond, *Histoire de France des origines à nos jours* (Paris: Librairie A. Hatier, 1920), 173. Emphasis mine.
18. Lavisse, *Nouveau cours d'histoire* (1921), 250.
19. Gauthier and Deschamps, *Cours d'histoire de France* (Paris, 1923), 232.
20. Ozouf, "Le thème du patriotisme," 20.

historical consciousness. In its enormity it was both a trauma of history and a crisis of historical thinking, seeming simultaneously to confirm and unravel dominant beliefs about French national identity and the legacy of French history. While France did emerge victorious, the decimation of a generation called into question Lavisse's paradigm of the uninterrupted transmission of a beneficent national inheritance, forcing an anguished reexamination of the place of history in elementary education and of the specific history that ought to be taught.[21] Part of the attack on older methods of teaching (rote learning, memorization) and older curricula (*l'histoire-bataille*) reflected a new sense of radical discontinuity, a rejection of the institutions and values of the prewar world. But on a deeper and more troubling level, schoolteachers wondered how to assess their responsibility for the catastrophe they had just endured. Had the kind of vigorous patriotism that lay at the core of *manuels scolaires* prolonged the killing? Were *instituteurs* to blame for the crushing human losses and the debilitating disillusionment of the war? Henri Barbusse, the author of France's most popular war novel, angrily characterized history texts as "deformed by nationalistic and retrograde prejudices,"[22] a charge emotionally delivered by Anatole France in 1919 to a congress of schoolteachers: "Burn! Burn all books that teach hate! Exalt work and love! Shape for us rational men who can topple the vain splendours of barbarous glories and resist the bloody ambitions of nationalism and imperialism that led their fathers astray."[23] Teachers were themselves making the same accusations. At a meeting of educators in 1924, for example, one teacher announced that "It is not the nations that are responsible for the slaughter, but the teachers...,"[24] while a syndicalist teacher concluded without hesitation, "In order to secure a definitive peace, stop teaching history."[25]

In the less-fraught climate before the war, the mission of history teaching had seemed clear, even when secular and lay authorities, or the political left and right, divided over specific interpretations. For example, the following general precepts introduced the 1910 instructions on history teaching that accompanied the Ministry of Education's regulations for primary schools:

---

21. In the 1920s, many teachers appealed to the *Société des professeurs d'histoire et de géographie*, asking where they could find lessons on the war. Warning against the pervasive propaganda, *lycée* professor Jules Isaac recommended the novels of Henri Barbusse and Roland Dorgelès and the correspondence of Pierre-Maurice Masson, *Lettres de guerre*, as the most reliable sources. Hubert Tison, "La mémoire de la guerre 14–18 dans les manuels scolaires français d'histoire, 1920–1990," in *Guerre et Cultures 1914–1918*, ed. J. J. Becker *et al.*, Colloque international de Péronne (Paris: A. Colin, 1994), 295.

22. Barnett Singer, "From Patriots to Pacifists: The French Primary School Teachers, 1880–1940," *Journal of Contemporary History* 12 (1977), 421.

23. *Ibid.*

24. Jacques Girault, "Instituteurs syndiqués et enseignement de l'histoire entre les deux guerres," *Revue d'Histoire moderne et contemporaine, numéro spécial* (1984), 142. In fact, anxieties about bellicose *manuels scolaires* had been expressed since the beginning of the century, particularly among socialist educators. For a full treatment of this subject, see Christian Amalvi, "Les Guerres des manuels autour de l'école primaire en France (1899–1914)," *Revue historique* 532 (October–December 1979), 359–398.

25. Girault, "Instituteurs syndiqués," 142.

When it is well taught, history shows the young generation the path taken, the progress realized, the liberties obtained by comparing the actual situation to that of their ancestors; [it shows] as well the suffering endured, the battles fought, and the efforts expended to attain the advantages that we find today to be natural: we take possession of the present in rendering justice to the past and we become conscious of the duties that are incumbent upon us for the future.[26]

Such directives were standard; they typically prompted comments like those addressed to student readers by the editor of a 1914 history of the nineteenth century:

To our readers,
The editors of *The History of France* want to give the present generation the most honest image of our past that is available, glorious in every way, crossed by hours of darkness, sometimes desperate, but from which France always emerged stronger, in search of a new fate and leading the nations toward a better civilization.[27]

When actualized in individual texts, these pedagogical commitments articulated, as we have seen, both a national personality and a national mission, what historian Etienne Balibar has called a project and a destiny, "the two symmetrical figures of the illusion of national identity."[28] But the unprecedented trauma of the war dissolved the clarity and complacency on which this pedagogy had been predicated. The effects of unrestrained patriotism seemed readily and horrifically apparent; at the same time, it seemed evident that the nation needed some renewed, acceptable sense of itself in order to begin the process of physical and emotional recovery. The tension inherent in these potentially contradictory concerns is captured in the instructions that accompanied the 1923 regulations of the education ministry, in which we can hear echoes of the intense doubts about history teaching that had emerged to challenge dominant paradigms of civic education. These instructions worried over the implications of promoting a mythologized national past:

It is sometimes asked what ought to be the character of history instruction in elementary schools: [this question] sets in opposition the scientific point of view and the civic perspective, some arguing that the historian, even in primary school, ought to have no concern other than to tell the whole truth, others believing that the teacher ought especially to address himself to cultivating patriotic sentiments, by the story of the glories of our country and by the description of its beauties.[29]

Not surprisingly, the instructions judiciously concluded that the problem cannot be posed in terms of an opposition between patriotic lessons and the "whole truth." But just how to insure that the schoolbooks reflected both "the scientific point of view" and an uplifting message about the glories of France remained vague:

---

26. *Programmes Officiels des écoles primaires élémentaires*, 2d ed. (Paris: Hachette, 1910), 133.
27. Albert Malet, *L'Epoque contemporaine* (Paris: Librairie Hachette, 1914).
28. Etienne Balibar, "The Nation Form: History and Ideology," in *Becoming National*, ed. Geoff Eley and Ronald Grigor Suny (Oxford, 1996), 132.
29. *Programmes et instructions officiels des écoles primaires élémentaires*, 3d ed. (Paris: Hachette, 1923), 53.

NARRATIVES OF WORLD WAR I IN FRANCE

We refuse to oppose the rights of science to the rights of France. French patriotism has nothing to fear from the truth. . . . The teacher is able, without hesitation, to recount the history of our country in conformity with the results of the impartial research of scholars. The place of France in the world is sufficiently grand, its role sufficiently noble, that an honest education, rigorously careful of the truth, encourages the blossoming and expansion of patriotic sentiments. Such ought to be the goal of history education in the primary school.[30]

At issue here is not merely the goal of harmonizing scholarship and patriotism, but of keeping in play a national identity that is grounded in a particular image of France—familiar, even familial, and unchanging through time. What is occluded by these directives is any recognition of the kinds of questions that might put scholarly research at odds with conventional representations of the French past. Nor did these directives provide answers as to how the war itself should be represented. Some critics argued that the war should not be a part of the curriculum at all; other authors produced texts that reduced the space allotted to the battles, maps, and strategies of war, focusing instead on its unacceptable material and human costs and the need for world peace. Addressing the experience of the infantry soldier in some detail—that is, the experience of the vermin- and mud-filled trenches, poison gas, continuous shelling, and physical destruction—one 1927 text urged: "This war should make you detest war," and concluded with a short reading on the League of Nations.[31]

The war had initiated a project of fixing history. The challenge for schoolbooks was to preserve national understandings of eternal France, articulated through appropriate moral and civic lessons, while suppressing what had come to be seen as unacceptable bravado, dangerous nationalist rhetoric. More typical than expressly pacifist sentiments were efforts to purge the most bellicose texts of their provocative language and their most inflammatory interpretations. What this meant especially was a reexamination of the motives attributed to Germany in the prewar decades, a rewriting of the language on the causes of the war, careful rewording of the account of the German invasion of Belgium, deletion of the most graphic and colorful accusations of German barbarism, and a more restrained narration of the victory.

Many texts struggled valiantly, for example, to find an appropriate representation of Germany's invasion of Belgium. Angry language charging the rapacious violation of neutrality disappeared; a canonical anecdote recounting Germany's cavalier dismissal of the treaty guaranteeing Belgian neutrality as a mere "scrap of paper" was expunged. Instead, authors searched for an acceptable verb. Giving up images of rape and penetration, they showed the Germans as having "passed through" (*passer*) Belgium, "crossed over" (*traverser*) Belgian territory. Whereas texts of the early 1920s tended to insist that the war was

---

30. *Ibid.*
31. P. Besseige and A. Lyonnet, *Histoire de France, cours moyen* (Paris: Librairie Istra, 1927), 238. In the changed context of post-World War II France, this sentence carried a different emotional charge and was omitted from the 1948 edition of the text.

the result "of the determined will of Germany to dominate the world,"[32] later editions spoke less of Germany and more of William II, less of world domination than of William's desire to extend his influence. In the popular text written by Malet and Isaac, for example, the 1925 edition had claimed that "in order to realize this program of domination and spoliation, Germany conceived of only one means: war"; the revised 1948 edition instead explored Austro-Serbian tensions and the outbreak of the war without mentioning German ambitions or directly attributing blame.[33]

The 1921 Lavisse account of the Great War had been positively jubilant about the Treaty of Versailles, emphasizing the theme of deserved punishment, while above all setting this moment of victory against the earlier embarrassment of the treaty that had concluded the humiliating defeat of 1870 in the same room: "The 18th of January 1871 had been a day of triumph for the strength and pride of Germany. Since that time Germany expanded its strength and pride. The 28th of June 1919 is the day of chastisement."[34] By contrast, the 1948 edition did not mention this emotionally-charged history. Similarly, a 1923 text by Gauthier and Deschamps had exulted in victory: "We've got them! Finally, everywhere—tracked down, distraught, decimated, exhausted, vanquished—the Germans asked for mercy."[35] In a nearly complete reversal, the 1931 edition substituted a grim quantification of damage for the celebration of victory: "In this war of 1500 days . . . [France] emerged admired, but in the most difficult situation: 1.4 million dead, one-and-a-half million disabled, 350 billion in expenses and damage, with 10 departments devastated. . . . *war is not worth it. . . . Such disasters impose the same duty on all the French . . . to work to establish peace between nations in dignity and honor.*[36]

One last example: In his final chapter of a 1925 text,[37] Jules Isaac, *lycée* professor and war veteran, brimmed with anger and recrimination. He wrote extravagantly about German arrogance and aggression, laying full responsibility for the cataclysm on an explicit menu of unrestrained German appetites. He described in detail the atrocities perpetrated by a uniquely German savagery, representing the German soldier as a barely human instrument of butchery: "I have watched the passing of great armies. They were armies of men; this [German] one is a machine, without end, without pause, precise as a watch, brutal as a steamroller.[38] Later, however, Isaac came to reject the sustained belligerence of his war chapter. Subsequent editions of the text emphasized the different perspectives that each nation brought to the divisive issues in the prewar period, and specifically sought to remove nationalist language.

32. Gauthier and Deschamps, *Cours d'histoire de France*, 233.
33. A. Malet and P. Grillet, *XIXe Siècle: Histoire contemporaine (1815–1920)* (Paris: Librairie Hachette, 1925), 1065; Jules Isaac and Henri Béjean, 1948 edition, 446.
34. Lavisse, *Nouveau cours d'histoire*, 1921, 264.
35. Gauthier et Deschamps, *Cours d'histoire de France*, 1923 edition, 244.
36. *Ibid.*, 1931 edition, 257. In neither the early texts nor in the revised, less bellicose editions was there any mention of the 1917 mutinies in the French army.
37. Malet and Grillet, *XIXe Sicle: Histoire contemporaine.*
38. *Ibid.*, 1082.

Isaac is a particularly interesting figure because he agreed to serve, in the mid-1930s, on a Franco-German commission, initiated by German historians, to discuss and revise objectionable sections of history schoolbooks.[39] This meeting produced a document in thirty-nine sections that identified specific interpretations of historical events on which consensus had been reached, while noting points that could not finally be resolved. The document is odd in the mixture of levels on which it addresses the problem of historical interpretation, and the effect of the negotiated language seems to emphasize as much the limits of the consensus as the desired agreement. For example, in each of the propositions there is an element of a trade: Section X announces agreement that 1) French texts exaggerated the importance of German expansionism in the period after 1870, and 2) German books exaggerated the import of "the idea of revenge" in France. Acknowledging these mutual excesses placed both nations on an equal playing field—attributing to each some role in the suspicions and aggressions of the prewar world. The Commission goes on to hope (Section XII) "that French and German *manuels scolaires*, instead of focusing on manifestations of Franco-German antagonism, will also signal the periods when the two nations enjoyed good relations. . . ." It then specifies the periods of good relations, "in particular from 1878 to 1884 as well as between 1894 and 1898. . . ."[40] This addition—locating a six-year and a four-year zone of comfort—seems a good deal less than a conceptual or interpretive breakthrough. The achievement of this kind of consensus can hardly have become the basis for transforming mutual misunderstanding, and points, rather, to the limits of history-by-consensus. But even these carefully crafted reinterpretations were checked by the quite different goals of the new Nazi regime. It was not until the mid-1950s and 1960s that efforts resumed to reform the content of schoolbooks.[41]

Both domestic French efforts to modify the tone and content of schoolbooks and the reform efforts of the Franco-German commission proceeded by examining specific themes and interpretations that had exacerbated conflict, substituting instead more neutral interpretations, different themes. As I will argue, this level of revision—one that fails to address the underlying teleology of the typical narrative of French history—preserves even as it revises. We can see this pattern of continuity-preserved-through-change in the conclusion to a 1936 edition of a history by Gauthier and Deschamps. Following an exhortation to the students to work for world peace, the authors offer a final reflection on the state-of-the nation that evokes eternal France while renouncing the bellicose image of the preceding decades:

With colonies, France in 1936 is a country of 100 million inhabitants and is twenty times larger than in the reign of Henri IV. Thanks to the progress in its communication and

---

39. *Bulletin de la Société des Professeurs d'Histoire et de Géographie de l'Enseignement public*, n. 85 (1935).

40. *Ibid.*, numéro spécial 91 bis (1937), 8–9.

41. Between 1965 and 1979, the discussion about the place of history in the school curriculum was again heated. For the decade of the 1970s, history was in fact removed from the elementary school curriculum, but was replaced again in the 1980s along with suggestions for a more interactive pedagogy.

transportation systems, to the schools, and to military service, the French know each other better. They have become more like brothers; they love a fatherland that shows itself to be just toward its sons and improves the condition of the most humble among them. If the world no longer fears France as in the time of Louis XIV and Napoleon, it admires our country for its valor and its intellectual grandeur. France is always for other nations the "land of Liberty."[42]

The text has indeed transformed the story of World War I (this is, in fact, the text that concluded "war is not worth it"). Nevertheless, the contours of the (familial) familiar narrative are readily apparent: it is the story of an exemplary nation, united by fraternal bonds that are supported by a (maternal) beneficent state, preserving and extending liberty for the rest of the world—in effect, history as a discourse on France. The "project and destiny" of the nation are preserved. Some of the details that underpin this conception have been changed, but the message itself and the unbroken continuity that it invokes suffuse this text as clearly as in earlier, more disturbingly nationalist incarnations.

IV. REPRISE: FIXING HISTORY AGAIN

In the past decade, scholars and educators have begun to revisit, once again, the question of the meaning and legacies of the Great War. Rejecting a tradition in which historians were effectively "partisans in a nationalist consensus," and seeking a pluralist approach to European history, a group of some of the most renowned historians of the war—including Jean-Jacques Becker, Jay Winter, Gerd Krumeich, Annette Becker, and Stéphane Audoin-Rouzeau—presided in 1992 over the opening of the Historial de la Grande Guerre in Péronne, France, an international museum and research center dedicated to promoting supranational perspectives on the war. In keeping with their conviction that World War I must be understood in all its facets as a *European* phenomenon, all of the museum exhibits are labeled in French, English, and German, the documentary film images represent all three nations (often shown simultaneously), as do all of the material artifacts on display. In a volume of essays published to celebrate the opening of this project, Fritz Stern observed that "those who conceived the project of the Historial are thinking of the new Europe. . . . it ratifies the process of reconciliation that has taken place. . . . the new Europe needs a common past."[43] In keeping with this perspective, the editors of the Historial volume locate the causes of the war not in the particular actions of any one nation or in any specific events, but in a Europe-wide "culture of war"—in representations, mentalities, and practices overinvested in conflict—whereby the marriage of Judeo-Christian religious fervor to escalating nationalism culminated in a shared vision of a war to end all wars. Their goal is to explore and critique this common culture.

In the context of such wide-ranging efforts to reconceive European history in supranational terms, twelve historians from different nations collaborated

---

42. Gauthier and Deschamps, *Cours d'histoire de France*, 1936 edition, 299.
43. Fritz Stern, "Reflexions à propos de l'inauguration de l'Historial, 13–20 juillet 1992," in J. J. Becker et al., eds., *Guerre et Cultures*, 24.

on a history of Europe published by Hachette in 1994 and translated into at least ten languages.[44] The editors billed the publication of this *euromanuel* as itself a historic event that would provide a new prototype—one which would not neglect, but rather complement, national history. The preface by the organizer of the project, Frédéric Delouche, delineated the motivating objectives:

To the extent that Europe is trying to feel its way toward its destiny, something imperceptible seems to inhibit its peoples on the way to their rapprochement. This something is constituted, to different degrees, by economic interests, by linguistic practices, by cultural traditions, as well as by irrational prejudices. These prejudices are durable and are transmitted from generation to generation by families, but also too often by certain aspects of the history that is taught in schools. . . . The national idea has only existed for several centuries and it is often education that has played an essential role in its establishment, also occasionally perverting national consciousness. Can history today play a comparable role in the construction of Europe?[45]

Given its unifying mission, the *euromanuel* begins with a discussion of the possibility of a European identity, speculating about the meaning of European civilization, *l'esprit européen*, seeking to call into being, or make real, the notion of Europe.[46] Without directly providing exact definitions, it lays out a set of themes that produce an image of diversity within integration, charting a line of defining qualities from the ancient Greeks to the Europeans of the present. The parallels to Lavisse are striking. The model is one of continuity in which differences (named "variety," "diversity") are subsumed within a broad, overarching consensus. Although an international framework substitutes here for a national one, the effect is analogous to that created by Lavisse: the authors envisage children all over Europe reading the same schoolbook, metaphorically "crossing the Alps" together.[47]

Again, echoing Lavisse and earlier texts, the editors make an explicit commitment to provide schoolchildren with the kind of history that is needed, writing in the foreword the following rationale of their effort: "Democratic states have an obligation to educate their citizens. As a nineteenth-century writer wrote,

---

44. *Histoire de l'Europe, écrit par 12 historiens européens* (Paris: Hachette, 1994). The editor was Frédéric Delouche. The authors included: Jacques Aldebert (France); Johan Bender (Denmark); Jiri Grusa (The Czech Republic); Scipione Guarraccino (Italy); Ignace Masson (Belgium); Dr. Kenneth Milne (Ireland); Foula Pispiringou (Greece); Dr. Juan Antonio Sanchez y Garcia Sauco (Spain); Antonio Simoes Rodrigues (Portugal); Ben W. M. Smulders (The Netherlands); Dieter Tiemann (Germany); Dr. Robert Unwin (United Kingdom).

45. *Ibid.*, Preface, 5.

46. A survey conducted in 1991 found that 80% of the people polled were in favor of European union, but most said that they did not feel "European." In response to the question, "As well as feeling your nationality, how often do you feel European?" 49% of EC residents responded "never"; 33% said "sometimes"; 15% responded "often," with elite groups indicating a stronger sense of Europeanness than non-elites.

47. While it is clear that this *euromanuel* seeks to make real, in intellectual and especially affective terms, the notion of Europe, it is also possible that this *manuel*—with the same cover, the same format, and the same content in every country in which it is published—is very like other commodities circulating in the common market with a new European label (same packaging, same format, same logo), and that what we are looking at here is as much the production of a new consumer as a new citizen.

'Although God is omnipotent, he is not able to change the past. He therefore created the historian.' "[48] No gloss is provided for this highly ambiguous quotation—one that unhesitatingly embraces "*l'histoire mobilisée*"—by which the historian is invested with the task of making a past that will most directly serve a quite specific vision of the future.

The *euromanuel*'s representation of World War I illustrates the implications of this charge. It describes the prewar period as a time of "nationalist exaltation" in which "the fatherland is judged worthy of every sacrifice" and military power is the currency of international competition. But the text matches each reference to aggression with a counterexample of a persistent internationalist spirit. So, for example, while it introduces the period 1900–1945 as "a march toward self-destruction" in which states were little disposed to seek peaceful solutions to conflicts, the next paragraph seeks to bring the reader back to the concept of international cooperation: "Nevertheless, this period witnessed the pursuit of a durable peace acceptable to all Europeans, and the idea of a European unity based on equal states and free peoples also made its mark." Similarly, following a paragraph on intense imperialist rivalries the text asserts that "[T]his mounting nationalism did not hinder the durability (*pérennité*) of a sentiment of European solidarity. . . ." And finally, the description of the early twentieth-century system of armed alliances is immediately succeeded by the observation that "all voices were not raised in favor of war. The workers' International and pacifist associations within bourgeois circles sought peace," a claim the text confirms with the examples of the creation of the Nobel peace prize in 1901 and the work of the International Red Cross.[49] This somewhat strained swinging between the different possibilities of the prewar period is less the reflection of alternative explanations than an unwillingness of the authors ultimately to address and evaluate contradictions. Rather than producing a new interpretation, there is a refusal of interpretation that ultimately rewrites the past not, as is common, in light of the present, but *as* the present.

The presentation of the war itself reveals the same principles of selection that downplay conflict and enhance common ground. There is no discussion of battles (Verdun gets less than a sentence); the text diffuses responsibility for the origins of the war ("The responsibility for the outbreak [of the war] is still the object of discussion. Historians agree on the fact that politicians and heads of state were prepared to take the risk of armed conflict. Each belligerent considered its cause just and its interests legitimate."); civilian hardships and military mutinies receive greater attention; the postwar world is discussed as a moment when a fragile, endangered peace, an emerging "*euroenthousiasme*," sustained repeated challenges from the recurrence of virulent nationalism; and the report of the return of hostilities in 1939 is followed immediately by the reassurance that visions of greater cooperation survived the war and would be taken up again after 1945.[50]

48. *Histoire de l'Europe (euromanuel)*, 6.
49. Ibid., 328–330.
50. Ibid., 331; 333; 339; 340.

I wish to emphasize here not just the content of this new schoolbook—although the relationship between goal and content is indeed part of the point. Even more, I want to draw attention to the less obvious ways in which the structure of this account, the way the narrative unfolds, replicates to a quite striking degree the structure of the texts of nearly one hundred years earlier. Beginning with Lavisse, France was represented not only as the repository of Liberty for the world, but as a (female) figure, civilized, generous, "giving to other nations the example of every liberty, of devotion, of the spirit of sacrifice,"[51] vulnerable to predatory threats from without, the prey of vicious others. In the words of one commentator, French schoolbooks present France as a "threatened mother.... The child is invited to merge with this primordial object and to direct its destructive impulses toward the mother's enemies."[52] Readers were thus enlisted in a highly charged mission to protect and defend that which is most dear and inevitably fragile. This image of the vulnerable nation is reproduced, or reincarnated, in the 1994 text as the spirit of pacifism, continuously present, but always in danger. At each critical juncture, the text posits a persistent pacifist current repeatedly under attack by malignant forces.

The similarities continue. In recounting French defeats and losses in 1870 and in 1914, early twentieth-century schoolbooks typically are also at pains to preserve eternal France, the entity that rises, renewed, from the ashes, that is never extinguished: from Lavisse, "the recovery (*relèvement*) after crisis is a habit, a law of our history."[53] In like manner, the *euromanuel* represents a spirit of international cooperation as the pulsing undercurrent that is inevitably sustained through the darkest moments of belligerency. Both the earlier patriotic texts and the *euromanuel* posit an essential pattern of continuity—interrupted, yes, but quickly resumed—that moves toward a goal (the nation; international cooperation) that was always already present, always waiting to be realized. Both readily use the word "destiny" without irony or self-consciousness; in each case, history becomes both the fulfilling of this destiny *and* the account of the unfolding of that inevitable process.

I do not want to condemn efforts to produce a transnational history, a history that focuses on a region in which the interests, cultures, and histories of each nation were and are, of course, inextricably linked. It is more appealing (if less entertaining) to read this *euromanuel* than the inflamed nationalism of the earlier texts. But not much. I wonder, indeed, whether this contemporary group of twelve historians are, in effect, Lavisse's true heirs?

---

51. D. Blanchet and J. Toutain, *Histoire de la France et notions d'histoire générale de 1852 à 1920* (Paris: Belin, 1923), 230. The way gender works in such descriptions is a bit more complicated because this feminized vision of France is typically followed by an invocation of (male) national heroes who then complete the idealized couple that is France.

52. Pierre Ansart, "Manuels d'histoire et inculcation du rapport affectif au passé," in *Enseigner l'Histoire: des manuels à la mémoire. Travaux du colloque Manuels d'histoire et mémoire collective*, ed. Henri Moniot, Université de Paris VII, April 1981 (Berne, 1984), 61.

53. Lavisse, cited in Besseige and Lyonnet, *Histoire de France* (1927), 248–249.

Beginning in the 1960s, the determination to exorcise *"l'histoire mythologique"* resulted in a new policy that required that authors of *manuels scolaires* be informed of the results of current scholarship, thereby enlarging, qualifying, remaking the conventional (and often aggressively nationalist) story. The objective was to tilt the balance toward professional history, to institute research as a corrective to mythical thinking. But it is not clear what such a prescription means in practice, or how it speaks to the limitations of a book like the 1994 *euromanuel*. This text does, in fact, incorporate contemporary scholarship: it includes a discussion of the kinds of social and economic issues absent from earlier histories; it restores subjects intentionally "forgotten"; it resists nationalist bravado. But, as I have argued, it is precisely its implication in the project of producing a benign past, an anodyne for contemporary memories, on which it founders. Like the earlier model of consensus history attempted in 1935, the determination of this text not to offend—to ignore the issues most problematic for its desired thematic unity—is its most striking feature.[54] The articulation of an already present European unity results, in the end, in familiar distortions and, even more, in new kinds of systematic forgetting that effectively close the gap between the past and the present.

Is it possible to produce a history that is both analytic and critical, attentive to the difference and heterogeneity of the past, and, at the same time, able to satisfy the desire of educators for a history that contributes to a democratic public culture grounded, at least in part, in a knowledge of history?[55] I am not, in fact, attempting to provide a definitive answer to this question, but want to suggest that we need to think more about the relationship between the form and structure of the narrative—as an aesthetic and conceptual whole—and the kind of history that is produced. I will conclude with another history, which emerged contemporaneously with the publication of the *euromanuel*, in order to open up these issues.

---

54. Perhaps the clearest example of the effects of what I am calling a consensus model may be seen in the discussion of World War II. It is very difficult to discover in this text anything about what happened to France. After noting Nazi military successes, the text states that on "10 May [1940], the Wehrmacht penetrated the French line of defense, thanks to aviation and tanks. On 17 June, Marshall Petain announced the armistice which became effective on the 25th. In the meanwhile Italy entered the war on the side of Germany." There is no mention of the Vichy regime, no discussion of France as having a unique wartime experience (350–351). With reference to the problem of collaboration, the text states: "A certain number of individuals and governments, in particular the France of Marshall Petain, hoped for the victory of Germany and were prepared to collaborate with the occupier. *However, the majority of people preferred not to take any risk and to wait. But as the war dragged on, resistance became organized.*" (Emphasis in original, 355). After a sentence on French, British, and Eastern European resistance, the text devotes several sentences to the efforts of Germans to resist the Nazi regime: "In Germany even, many were aware of the crimes committed in their name. The totalitarian regime made action very difficult and particularly dangerous for these men and women from every stratum of the German population who decided to try something against the Nazi madness. In July 1944, an assassination attempt organized by officers of the Wehrmacht failed" (355). As presented in this sequence of statements, the officers here were, in essence, acting for the German nation.

55. See *Learning History in America: Schools, Cultures, and Politics*, ed. Lloyd Kramer, Donald Reid, and William L. Barney (Minneapolis, 1994), especially the introduction by Kramer and Reid.

NARRATIVES OF WORLD WAR I IN FRANCE

VI. CODA

In 1991, the well-known mystery writer, Sébastien Japrisot, published a World War I novel, *A Very Long Engagement*, that remained a national bestseller in France for over six months and was awarded the prestigious Prix Interallié. The novel recounts the unrelenting effort of a young woman, Mathilde, to discover the details of the fate of her fiancé, Manech, or Cornflower as he was called by his regiment, reported to have "died in the line of duty." Structured around this search for the truth, the novel is part mystery story, part quest; it sometimes reads like a fable (witness the first sentence: "Once upon a time, there were five French soldiers who had gone off to war, because that's the way of the world"), and sometimes like a realistic novel, attentive to the minute details of life in the midst of war. The story unfolds around the following incident: Cornflower is one of five men court-martialed in 1917 for self-mutilation. As punishment, the men are led, with their hands bound behind their backs, to a part of the front closest to enemy trenches, thrown over the top into No-Man's Land, and left to die in the ensuing crossfire. While it appears that all five died, there is no definitive confirmation of this—in fact, all official records were destroyed and the witnesses dispersed, silenced, or dead. Mathilde nevertheless determines to follow all the ambiguous traces left by this incident to uncover exactly what happened to her fiancé.

A Very Long Engagement is a richly-textured story—a gripping mystery, a powerful rendering of the mood, events, and particular insanities of the First World War. But it is also a profound meditation on history itself—history here as both the practice of producing the past and the narrative that is the result. Mathilde's investigation enacts the historian's search: she repeatedly reaches dead ends; many of her best leads leave her in blind alleys. In following up every trace, she must evaluate very different versions of what happened on that January morning, sorting through conflicting testimonies, intentional lies, moving beyond the gaps left by partial memories. The epigraph that Japrisot has chosen for his story is from Lewis Carroll: "'I see nobody on the road,' said Alice. 'I only wish I had such eyes,' the king remarked in a fretful tone. 'To be able to see nobody. And at that distance, too! Why, it's as much as I can do to see real people, by this light.'" Playing on the inversion of what is seen and unseen, Mathilde's investigation invokes the historian's task of seeing something different from that which appears self-evident—of going beyond the official/conventional version in order to find what has previously been invisible, neglected, distorted, disguised, or unquestioned.

Both Japrisot and Mathilde are engaged in the production of a narrative, a layering that enables the novel to speak to the process of historical revision. Just as Mathilde continuously rewrites her understanding of events, the novel replays old and new versions of the war experience. There are the familiar themes from canonical descriptions dating from the 1920s: the hopelessness of the assault; the absence of purpose behind military strategy; the camaraderie among the men and the brutality and sadism of some of the officers; the alienation and madness of the trenches; the pain of the women left behind. Many of the most important shifts in the plot are produced through ironic juxtapositions—the most typical trope through which the World War I story has been told. At the same time, it moves beyond these themes, incorporating information and perspectives that have emerged in recent scholarship, including references to the corrosive disillusionment that began to be expressed in the French army in 1917, and the pervasive censorship and passing of misinformation that lasted for decades after the war. It replicates recent efforts by historians to complicate the "myth" of the war experience: in its presentation of five very different men (a carpenter, a union activist, a pimp and petty criminal, a farmer, and Cornflower, a nineteen-year-old innocent) from different regions of France, it demonstrates the different investments, different emotional registers, and diverse backgrounds that provided the interpretive filter through which each participant ordered the chaos of lived experience. We might read this as a rewriting of older representations of France, the mythical homogeneous hexagon, that preserves France the nation while remaking the national community.

Japrisot seems to be as interested in the construction of an adequate narrative of the past as in the details of the mystery that his novel unravels. He is palpably aware of the kind of systematic suppression of information required for the sake of coherence. In order to escape the conceptual constraints that erase stories that don't fit, Japrisot proliferates perspectives; he does not work for narrative closure and allows the story to emerge in different voices, each of which has a different stake in, and a different take on, the events. Japrisot's narrative is multi- rather than uni-vocal; the nation/community is heterogeneous, not homogeneous—peopled by individuals who live in very different relation to dominant cultural narratives. Unlike the account of the war in the various history texts, the narrative of the war presented in the novel is more complex, incorporating rather than erasing contradictions; it is neither linear nor predictable, offering the messy details that reflect the confusions and blind spots of the time without forcing them into a tightly unified mold. In accounting for the motors of change, the novel looks to contingency, not destiny. Japrisot seems to be searching for a form appropriate to his material that might also articulate a set of protocols for history writing.

These are not the protocols that have informed the writing of *manuels scolaires*. Although efforts at historical revision in both the 1920s–1930s and in the 1990s did produce quite different narratives from the models each sought to resist, while the details of the narratives changed, the revised accounts remained, finally, embedded in a historical project that left them on a deeper level untransformed. Both in the earlier period and more recently, the reform of school texts attempted to re-form history: to make the story less bellicose; to make the nation less nationalist. On the level of content, there were intense debates as authors struggled over competing cultural and political agendas. For example, religious educators confronted secularists; pacifists opposed nationalists; conservatives challenged Marxists. In spite of these differences, however, many of the underlying assumptions about the form and commitments of the historical narrative were shared. As we have seen, old revisions and new continued to produce a discourse on France—the maternal fatherland—that was grounded in notions of familial love and patrimony, that erased differences, and selected out material that would challenge the overriding teleology of continuity. Old revisions and new unfolded around specific understandings of a latent destiny that each would articulate and realize by correcting or improving the story of the past.

In effect, history was supposed to be "fixed." But this "fixing" did not so much repair a deficient history as produce a historical fixation. "Fix" in its primary meanings refers above all to stability, if not to a kind of petrified rigidity:

Fix (verb): to place or fasten securely; to put into a stable or unalterable form, as: . . . to kill and keep a specimen intact for microscopic study; to prevent discoloration of a photographic image by washing or coating with a chemical preservative; to direct (the gaze, for example) steadily; to establish definitely; . . . to become stable or firm, to harden; . . . to decide or agree on; . . . to prearrange the outcome by unlawful means.[56]

What we have been looking at is the fixing of history, the hardening of the narrative around particular themes: the nation in Lavisse's case; the ideal of pacific cooperation, of *euroenthusiasme*, in the 1994 text. In producing a thematized narrative organized by the essential unities of a persistent and destined European-ness, the *euromanuel* authors are in fact Lavisse's heirs. "History" in this mode emerges, at best, as a fantasy or, less benignly, as an instrument that contributes to the confusion between the past and the present, between a mythologized national memory and national history.

In both the 1920s–1930s and the 1990s, the fixing of history produced an account of the past that is fundamentally ahistorical. The articulation of a "prearranged outcome" flattened alternative trends and possibilities, and suppressed discontinuities which are, by contrast, deeply threaded through the past. Struggles over the nature of the nation and the meaning of citizenship *are* the stuff of history; the present was *not* predestined, but rather the result of deliberate action, contestation, and contingency. The power and fascination that the past holds for us in the present lies precisely in its challenge to understand why this happened, in this way and not that. Implicit in Japrisot's novel is the recognition that to give up a tightly coherent story does not necessarily yield incoherence, but may enable a more nuanced, layered account, a more capacious history—one more attuned to the multiplicities of the past, to the differences among historical actors, to the exclusions and silences of more unitary accounts, to the ruptures and realignments that remake the contours of historical possibility.

I have called this final section a coda—that is, a more or less independent passage concluding a composition—and used the license offered by the standard of "more or less" to wonder how Japrisot's novel might speak to the

---

56. *American Heritage Dictionary.*

problem of historical writing. Historians do not write imaginative fiction; but perhaps they might take from Japrisot his simultaneous engagement with the process and the product of history writing. Like any good mystery writer, he withholds resolution of the plot, cultivating complexity while avoiding early closure. (In fact, Mathilde continues to add documents to her mahogany box decades after she has solved the mystery.) In its structure and content, the novel suggests a vision of history that organizes *and* exceeds memory, refusing to conflate the two. It also preserves the otherness of the past—its difference from the present—opening a perspective on disjunction that precludes facile continuities. By attending to these concerns, historians may be able to resist the desire to fix history, producing in the end more adequate accounts of the past—and, I would suggest, more effective ways to understand the challenges of the present.

Department of History
Wesleyan University

Name Index

Abdul Aziz, Shah of Delhi 484
Abdul Qaiyum, Sahibzada 482, 485, 487
Abid, Mohammed 486
Addison, Christopher 178
Adedeji, Sergeant Major 563, 566
Agulhon, Maurice 390
Akhmatova, Anna 51
Albert, King 381
Alberts, S.F. 505
Allen, Keith xviii, 125–47
Allen, Victor 565
Allenby, Edmund 378, 380
Anderson, Benedict 58, 60
Andrew, C.M. xxii, 465–77
Anfimov, A.M. 48
Angell, Norman 221, 241, 248
Archer, Robert 571, 572
Arthur, Sir George 303
Aschheim, Steven E. 83
Asquith, H. Herbert xviii, 175, 187, 301, 302, 306, 307, 308, 312, 320, 425, 432, 433, 435, 437
Audoin-Rouzeau, Stéphane 588

Babra Mulla 484
'Bach' 390, 397, 400
Backhaus, G. 216
Baha, Lal xxii, 479–87
Balesi, Charles J. 280
Balfour, Arthur 185, 186, 310, 315, 433, 434
Balibar, Etienne 584
Barbusse, Henri 583
Barnby, Earnest 216
Barnett, Correlli 150
Barrère, Camille 35
Barrès, Maurice 291
Batocki, Adolf von Tortilowicz 129, 137
Bartov, Omer 70
Bauer, Max 444, 445, 446, 455
Bäumer, Gertrud 138, 139
Beaverbrook, Lord 175
Becker, Annette 588
Becker, Jean-Jacques xvii, 588
Bédier, Joseph 326–37 *passim*, 340, 345, 347, 349, 352, 353, 355
Beharrell, George 179, 180, 183
Beldiman 118

Belloc, Hilaire 426
ben Ali Charbi, Rabah 267
ben Arrar, Mahmoud 261
ben Haya, Ahmed 274
ben Mohamed, Allal ben Hossaine 266
Bennett, Edward N. 345
ben Omar, Hamidi ben Allal 266
ben Sliman, Mena Brahim 267
Beringer, J. 560
Bernhardi, Theodore von 336
Berthelot, Philippe 32, 34, 39
Bertie, Sir Francis 33
Bethmann-Hollweg, Theobold von 102, 109, 116, 118, 133, 354
Beyers, C.F. 490, 491, 493, 495, 496, 497, 498, 499, 500, 501, 502, 503, 504, 505, 506, 507, 508, 509
Beynon, Sir Wiliam George Lawrence 487
Bezuidenhout, Colonel 498, 501, 506
Bismarck, Otto von xii, xiii, 18, 71
Bissinger, Soldier 330
Bloch, Marc 408
Bochkareva, Mariia 52, 53
Bodkin, M. McD. 207
Bonaparte, Napoleon 30, 400, 424
Bonar Law, Andrew 185
Bond, Brian xi
Bonner, P.L. 533
Bonnier 39, 40
Bonzon, Thierry 126, 129, 139
Booth, George 187
Boraston, J.H. 301
Borel-Clerc, Charles 407
Botha, Louis xxii, 489, 490, 493, 494, 495, 496, 501, 502, 503, 504, 505, 507, 509, 532
Bottomley, Horatio 206
Botrel, Théodore 393, 394, 395
Boukay, Maurice 410
Boulanger, Georges 29
Bousquet, Louis 401, 407
Bowley, A.J. 180
Boyer, Jean 419, 420
Boyer, Lucien 406, 407
Bradshaw, Granville 216
Bratianu, Ion 90, 92, 93, 94–7 *passim*, 98, 100, 101–9 *passim*

Brentano, Lujo 327
Briand, Aristide 30, 31, 32, 467
Brion, Hélène 403
Brogden, Gwendoline 206
Brownlee, W.T. 527
Brubaker, Rogers 58, 60
Bruce, Robert B. xix, 287–99
Bruno, G. 579
Brusilov, Aleksai A. 106
Buchanan, Sir George 45, 46, 49
Burian, Count Istvan 102
Bussche, Baron Hilmar von dem 94, 97, 99, 104
Butt, Clara 206

Caillaux, Joseph 310
Callwell, Sir Charles 306, 307, 313
Cambon, Paul 34
Canti, Lise 393
Carol I, King of Romania, 89–90 *passim*, 93, 94, 97
Carroll, Lewis 593
Cecil, Lord Robert 28
Chailley-Bert, Joseph 471, 474
Chamberlain, Austen 483, 569
Chaplin, Charlie 79
Charteris, John 317, 318
Chauvet, Louis 420
Churchill, Winston xx, 185, 301, 306, 320
Cimbala, Stephen J. xiv, 3–25
Cingo, W.D. 528
Claretie, Léo 408
Clemençeau, Georges xvi, 35, 276, 407, 468, 469
Clive, Lieutenant-Colonel 376
Cohen, Adolf 136, 137
Cohen, William B. 257
Conan Doyle, Arthur 199
Conrad von Hötzendorff, Franz xiii
Constantine, King 29
Cope, J.P. 200
Cope, Mrs 200–201 *passim*
Costinescu, Emil 92, 98, 100, 104
Cousturier, Lucie 280
Cowans 175
Cromer, Lord 303
Cross 571
Curzon, Lord 314, 569
Czernin, Ottokar 94, 97, 104, 108

Daladier, Edouard 476
Dales, H. 519
Danilov, Iurii N. 6, 7, 8, 13–14 *passim*, 47
Darwin, Leonard 199
Davenport, T.R.H. xxii, 489–511
Davidson, Sir John Humphrey 379

Davis, Belinda 126, 129, 139
Davis, Natalie Z. 254
Dean, Martin xvii, 221–51
de Beauvoir, Simone 404
de Castelnau, Noel J. 290
Decaux, Alain 578
de Fontenay 36
Defosse, Soldier 331
de Gaulle, Charles 578
Deimling, Berthold von 452, 453
de la Rey, Jacobus H. 491, 492, 493, 494, 496, 497, 498, 500, 509
Délcassé, Théophile 33
Deleting, Louise 265
Delouche, Frédéric 589
Deltheil, Joseph 411
de Margerie, Pierre 32
Derby, Lord 184, 187
de Roquefeuil, Pierre 29
Déroulède, Paul 393
Deschamps 586, 587
Deschanel, Paul 408
des Vallières, Jean 379, 381
Dewar, G.A.B. 301
de Wet, Andries 500
de Wet, C.R. 490, 494, 496, 497, 498, 502, 503, 504, 505, 506, 507, 508
de Wet, Piet G. 499, 500
Dewey, P.E. xvii, 149–73
Deyrmon, Jean 398
Diagne, Blaise 471
Dinuzulu, King 526
Djavid Bey 116, 120, 121
Djemal Pasha 115, 117, 118, 120, 121, 122
Dobrorol'skii *see* Dobrorolsky
Driant, Emile 290
Dobrorolsky, Sergei 13, 16, 56
Doda Jan, Mulla 484
Dodd, Major 487
Dorgelès, Roland 414
Duara, Prtasenjit 58
Dubas, Marie 418
Dubost, L-J. 291
Du Cane, J.P. 428
Duchêne, Albert 466
Duckman, Sir Arthur 187
Duff, Beauchamp 483
Duisberg, Carl 445
Duncan, Patrick 490, 491, 503
Durkheim, Emile 328
du Toit, S.J. 509
Dutton, David J. xvi, 27–43, 363
du Vivier de Streel, E. 471, 473
Dwinger, Edwin E. 812 *passim*

Ebbinghaus, Christof von 341, 342
Eberlein, Lieutenant 330, 333, 349
Edmonds, Sir James 320
Ehrlich, Paul 327
Einem, Karl von 454
Eliach, Yaffa 79
Eller, Regine 131, 132
Elliott, Sir Francis 28, 36
Ellis, Sir Charles 187
Enver Pasha 113, 114–15, 117, 118, 119, 120, 121, 122
Erickson, Edward J. xv
Esher, Lord 187, 199, 303
Estienne, Jacques 295

Fahlenstein, Soldier 330
Falk, E.M. 566
Falkenhayn, Erich von 69, 105, 109, 287, 288, 296, 445, 448, 449, 451, 453, 454, 456, 457, 458, 460
Farrow, Reuben W. 215
Fauchère 470
Fauser, Captain 342, 343
Feldman, Gerald 125, 126
Ferdinand, King of Romania 97, 105
Ferry, Jules 578
Filipescu, Nicolae 92, 94, 95, 97, 98, 99, 101, 103
Fischer, Emil 448
Fischer, Soldier 329, 344
Fisher, John ('Jackie') 185, 426
Fitzgerald, Charles Penrose 91, 199
Flammer, Max E.W. 337, 338, 341, 344
Flandin, Pierre-Etienne 469
Foch, Ferdinand 17, 288, 296, 364, 407
Förster, Paul 329
Fouché, Leo 490, 491, 492, 497
Fourie, Jopie 508, 509, 510
Fowler, Sir Henrt 187
Franck, James 452
Franz Ferdinand, Archduke xii, xiii, 10, 89, 97
Franz Joseph, Emperor xiii
French, David xix, 301–21, 363, 367, 432
French, Sir John 306, 308, 309, 311, 312, 370, 375, 428
Fribourg, André 474
Fried, Alfred 350
Fussell, Paul xxiii

Gaede, General 351
Gallieni, Joseph S. 291
Gambetta, Léon 18
Gapon, Father 62
Garvin, J.L. 434
Gauthier 586, 587

Gay, Peter 394
Geddes, Eric C. xviii, 175–88 *passim*
Gellner, Ernest 58, 60
George V, King 34, 480, 483, 518
Geyer, Michael 424, 428
Gibbs, Philip xx
Giers, M.N. 121
Gilbert, Georges 288
Girard, Lieutenant Colonel 292
Gleich, Lieutenant-Colonel 343
Glucksmann, André 577
Gobineau, Arthur de 257
Goga, Ocatavian 92, 103
Golovin, Nikolai N. 15
Göttsche, NCO 330
Gough, Lord 319
Gouraud, Henri 410
Grandmaison, Louis Loyzeau de 17, 288
Greenhalgh, Elizabeth 363, 364, 365–6 *passim*, 367, 368, 369, 373, 374–6 *passim*, 378, 379, 386, 387, 388
Gregorowski, Judge 501
Gregory, Adrian xviii
Grey, Sir Edward 30, 306, 424
Grieves, Keith xviii, xix, 175–90
Grimme, Hubert 331, 332, 333
Groener, Wilhelm 106
Grosse, Moritz 329
Grundlingh, Albert xxii, 513–39
Guchkov, Aleksandr 63
Guesde, Jules 258
Guillebaud, C.W. 135
Gullace, Nicoletta F. xvii, 191–219
Gumede, J.T. 523
Gupta, Partha S. 570

Haase, Bruno 128, 130
Haber, Fritz 327, 447–8 *passim*, 449, 451, 452, 453, 454, 455
Habibullah Khan, Amir of Afghanistan 479–80 *passim*, 482, 483, 484, 486
Haeckel, Ernst 327
Hahn, Otto 452
Haig, Sir Douglas xx, 29, 180, 181, 187, 301, 303, 311, 312, 313, 315, 316–19 *passim*, 320, 321, 364, 366, 367, 374–88 *passim*, 424, 436
Haldane, Lord 307
Halil Bey 117, 118, 120, 122
Hall, Richard C. xiii
Hallam, Basil 216
Hamilton, Sir Ian 371
Hancock, Sir Keith 569
Hankey, Sir Maurice 28, 30, 175, 301, 306, 312, 434, 435

Hardinge, Lord 479, 480, 481, 482, 483
Hari, Mata 403
Harris, J. William 253
Hauptmann, Gerhart 327
Havel, Václav 59
Haywood, A.H.W. 563
Hegel, Georg W.F. 336
Henig, Ruth xiii
Henri IV, King 587
Herr, Frédéric G. 290, 296
Herriott, Edouard 38, 39
Hertz, Gustav 452
Hertzog, James B. 489, 490, 491, 494, 502, 503, 506, 507, 509, 510
Heyl, Hedwig 138
Hindenburg, Paul von 69, 94, 109, 131, 297, 423, 424, 450
Hitler, Adolf 447
Hohenborn, Alfred W. von 446
Hollmann, Professor 328, 331, 333
Hollweg *see* Bethmann-Hollweg
Horne, John xix, 323–55
Horvath, General 552
House, Colonel Edward 570
Huau, Alphonse 410
Hudson, Geoffrey xxii, 541–55
Hügel, Friedrich von 455, 456, 458, 459
Humann, Hans 114, 121
Humperdinck, Engelbert 327

Ianushkevich 13–14 *passim*, 16
Ilse, Emil 451
Ionescu, Take 92, 94, 95, 97, 98, 99, 103
Iorga, Nicolae 91
Isaac, Jules 586
Ishii, Viscount 545

Jagow, Gottlieb 116, 120
Jahn, Hubertus 49
Japrisot, Sébastien 579, 593, 594, 595, 596
Jellicoe, Sir John 184, 185
Jingoes, Jason 516, 517, 519, 522
Joffe, Adolphe 555
Joffre, Joseph J.C. 17, 108, 288, 289, 290, 294, 308, 309, 310, 311, 313, 316, 318, 336, 364, 368, 370, 371, 372, 374, 377, 378, 379, 380, 381, 382, 383–4 *passim*, 386, 399, 407, 429, 444
Johnson, R.W. 571, 572
Johnston, Harry 570
Johnstone, William 517
Jones, Henry A. 197
Jones, J. 214
Jonnart, Charles 469, 471

Jordan, Sir John 548
Joubert, P.J. 497, 498, 499, 500
Jouhaux, Léon 263, 264

Kadalie, Clements 530
Kallaway, Peter 534
Kalmikov 553
Kamera, Kande 280
Kanya-Forstner, A.S. xxii, 465–77
Karakhan, Leo 554
Kathen, Hugo von 455, 457, 458, 459
Katzenellenbogen, S.E. 514, 533, 571
Kemp, J.C.G. 490, 491, 494, 495, 496, 497, 498, 501, 502, 503, 504, 505, 507
Kernahan, Coulson 199, 200, 201
Kessel, General 133
Keynes, John Maynard 432, 436
Khired Bey 486
Kiggell, Sir Launcelot E. 319, 376
Killingray 571, 572
Kitchener, Lord 175, 177, 178, 180, 191, 302, 303, 304, 305, 307–10 *passim*, 311, 314, 316, 317, 319, 320, 367–73 *passim*, 376, 377, 383, 386, 387, 425, 426, 430, 434, 435, 436, 437, 482, 483
Kitson, Frank 575
Klemperer, Victor 75
Knox, Sir Alfred 45, 54
Knox, Philander C. 544
Kock, General 501
Kocka, Jürgen 126
Kolchak, Aleksandr V. 553
Körsten, Alvin 136, 137
Kramer, Alan xix, 323–55
Krietzmann, Lieutenant 329
Krivoshein, Aleksandr 53
Krumeich, Gerd 588
Kuchernigo, Ivan 50, 51
Kuropatkin, A.N. 62
Kuttner, Max 331, 333, 352, 353

Lagarde, Paul de 71
Lang, Andrew 420
Lange, J.H. 490, 491, 492, 495, 505
Larsen, Karl 333
Lavisse, Ernest 328, 577, 579, 580–81 *passim*, 583, 589, 591, 595
Lawrence, Bill 209
Lawrence, Jon xvii, 221–51
Lawrence, T.E. xi
Leclos, Grégoire 415
Lecoq 35, 38, 39
Lee, Arthur 178, 184
Lehning, James R. 61

Lenin, Vladimir, I. 48, 552
Leopold II, King of Belgium 472
Le Roy-Lewis, Herman 180–81
Lestang, Mr 278
Letanka, D.S. 524
Lettow-Vorbeck, Paul von xi
Lever, Sir Hardman 187
Levy-Rathenau, Josephine 138, 139
Leygues, Georges 31
Liebenberg, P.J. 496, 497, 502, 505
Liggett, Hunter 360, 361
Lih, Lars 59, 60
Lloyd George, David xvi, xviii, 30, 175–7 passim, 179–83 passim, 184, 186, 187, 235, 302, 306, 307, 308, 315, 316, 317, 320, 427, 428, 432, 433, 434, 437, 524, 570
Loos, Reserve Lieutenant 343
Louw, A.S. 503
Lucaciu, Vasile 103
Ludendorff, Erich 69, 109, 131, 133, 139, 294, 297, 423, 424, 444
Lukin, Sir Henry 500
Lutard, Charles 470
Lutz, Ralph H. 324
Lyautey, Louis-Hubert 473

Mabathoana, P. 516
MacDonagh, Michael 200, 213, 215
MacDonogh, Sir George 309
Macey, David 62
McKenna, Reginald 216, 315, 431, 432, 433, 434, 435, 436, 437
Mackensen, August von 450, 456
Mackenzie, Compton 28, 29
Macleod, Jenny xii
MacOrlan, Pierre 415
Maginot, André 473
Maiorescu, Titu 104
Makoliso, D.S. 518
Malan, Daniel F. 510
Mallet, A. 586
Mallet, Sir Louis 115
Mandel, Georges 476
Mangin, Charles xxi, 280, 468, 469, 470
Mann, Thomas 80
Marder, Professor 184
Marghiloman, Alexandru 92, 98
Marie, Crown Princess of Romania 93, 94, 97
Maritz, S.G. 490, 491, 494, 495, 496, 497, 498, 499, 500, 502, 503, 504, 507
Marshall, George C. 359
Marwick, Arthur 192, 533
Mason, A.E.W. 202, 204
Matthews, James K. xxi, 557–66

Maurice, F.B. 312
Max, M. de 393
Mdlombo, E. 518
Memmi, Albert 257
Messimy, Adolphe 468
Meyer, Captain 341
Meyer, Jacques 297
Michaelis, Georg 129, 137
Migeod, F.W.H. 559
Millandy, Georges 410
Mille, Constantin 91
Millerand, Alexandre 371
Mills, Jack 211
Milner, Lord 175, 489, 569
Mir Mast, Jemadar 486
Missbach, Soldier 330
Mitchell, David 192
Mitchell, Thyra 211
Mitterand, François 578
Modiakgotla, Doyle 520
Mohapeloa, R. 516
Mokwena, M. 518
Molife, L. 521
Moltke, Helmuth von (the Elder) 5, 18, 19, 338, 424
Moltke, Helmuth von (the Younger) 4, 339, 348, 445
Montagu, Edwin 180
Montéhus, Gaston 393
Montorgueil, Georges 410
Moon, David 57, 58–62 *passim*
Moran, G.W. 558
Morgan, J.H. 334
Moritz, Soldier 334
Moss, George L. 257
Moukhtar Pasha 115, 116, 118
Muller, C.H. 495, 503
Müller-Öestreich, Ilse 138
Murray, Sir Archibald 303, 306, 310, 314
Mvabaza, L.T. 524

Napoleon III, Emperor 468
Nash, Sir Philip 180
Nasrullah Khan 479, 483, 486
Naumann, Friedrich 327
Neilson, Keith 363, 369
Nenninger, Timothy K. xx, 357–61
Nernst, Walther 445
Newana, S.M. Bennett 520
Ngoja, J.D. 524
Niamatullah Khan 485
Nicholas, Grand Duke 309
Nivelle, Robert 294, 297
Nkabindi, S. 526

Nora, Pierre 390, 578, 581

Obaid Ullah Sindhi 486
Oliver, F.S. 175
Oliver, Sir Henry 182, 183
Orczy, Baroness 205
Ossowski, Wladyslaus 347, 354
Ouvrard, Eloi 400
Oxenham, John 196
Ozouf, Jacques 582
Ozouf, Mona 582

Page, W.H. 570
Painlevé, Paul 40
Palavicini, Johann von 119
Palitsyn, General 15
Patterson, D.K. 207
Perrings, Charles 571
Perrot, Michelle 258
Pershing, John J. 357, 407
Pétain, Henri Philippe 287, 288, 290–91 *passim*, 293–7 *passim*, 405, 411, 417
Peterson, Colonel 452, 455
Pezold, Professor von 337, 338, 340, 344, 348, 353, 354
Philipp, Soldier 329, 334, 343
Philpott, William xx, 363–88
Picot, François-Georges 467
Pienaar, J.J. 495, 496, 497, 498, 499, 500
Pipes, Richard 46, 47
Pirouet, Louise 574
Planck, Max 327
Poincaré, Raymond 34, 254
Poirier, Léon 411
Poklevsky, S.A. 90, 96
Polin 397, 408
Polivanov, A.A. 56
Pope, Sir William 447
Posholi, M.L. 518
Postgate, Raymond 158
Pratap, Barakatullah 485
Pratap, Mahendra 485, 486
Preller, Gustav 509
Princip, Gavrilo xiii
Prior, Robin 363
Pritchard, S.M. 519
Privas, Xavier 408
Purseigle, Pierre xii
Putkamer, Captain von 341

Rabelais, François 335
Ralitane, L. 525
Rasafimanjary, Emmanuel 274
Rathbone, Richard xxi, 567–75

Rawlinson, Sir Henry 319, 437
Raynal, Sylvain-Eugène 296
Rearick, Charles xxi, 389–422
Reinhardt, Max 327
Renaudel, Pierre 271
Rennenkampf, P.K. 7
Rennles, Caroline 218, 219
Renoir, Jean 415
Renouvin, P. 27
Repington, Charles à Court 304, 370
Reynaud, Paul 476
Rhodes, Cecil 569
Richard, Major 291
Richert 354
Riddell, Lord 185, 186
Riezler, Kurt 354
Ringer, Fritz K. 337
Ritter, Professor 109
Robert, Camille 407
Robert, Jean-Louis xvii, 221–51
Roberts, Lord 91
Roberts, Mary L. 272
Robertson, Sir William 28, 303, 310, 311, 312, 313, 314, 315, 317, 319, 320, 379, 430, 433, 435, 436, 437
Rodzianko, Mikhail 53, 59
Roediger, David 281
Röntgen, Wilhelm 327
Roos-Keppel, Sir George 481, 482, 483, 484, 485, 486, 487
Roselius, Ludwig 98, 99
Rosenhainer, Ernst 81
Roskill, Captain 184
Rothacher, Anton 350
Roux, Edward 520
Rude, George 252
Runciman, Walter R. 315, 431
Rupprecht, Crown Prince of Bavaria 453, 454
Rutherford, Ernest 447

Said Halim, Prince 113, 118, 121, 122
Samsonov, V. 7
Sanborn, Josh xv, xvii, 45–67
Sarment, Jean 413
Sarrail, Maurice xvi, 28, 29, 30, 37, 38, 39, 40, 43
Sarraut, Albert 475
Saxton, Alexander 281
Sazonov, Serge 5, 10, 13–14 *passim*, 16, 95, 96, 101, 108, 119, 121
Scheepers, Gideon 509
Schiemann, Theodor 71
Schiller, Friedrich 75
Schlieffen, Alfred von 18
Schmoller, Gustav von 327

Scholtz, G.D. 491, 494, 495, 497
Schuster, Edwin 135
Scott, C.P. 434
Scotto, Vincent 403
Seeckt, Hans von 456
Seely, J.E.B. 301
Seitz, Theodor 499, 500
Selborne, Lord 314
Semenov, Grigory M. 553
Semina, Khristina 51
Seregny, Scott 61
Shapiro, Ann-Louise xxiii, 577–96
Sheffield, Gary xi, 363
Showalter, Dennis E. xiv, xv, 69–87
Simm, Erich 127, 133, 135, 136, 137
Simon, Henri 467
Simon, Sir John 431, 434
Simonsohn, Georg 126, 127, 130, 133–7 *passim*, 138, 139, 141
Smith, Leonard 58
Smuts, Jan C. xxii, 489, 495, 502, 506, 507, 509, 569
Snowden, Phillip 301
Snyder, Jack 17
Souchon, Wilhelm 111, 112, 114, 115, 116, 119, 120, 122
Spies, S.B. 513
Sprösser, Captain 342
Stamer, Dr 340, 341
Steglitz 125
Stenger, Major-General 330, 333, 350
Stere, Constantin 92
Stern, Fritz 588
Stevenson, James 187
Steyn, Pierre 506, 507, 508
Stirby, Prince Barbu 97
Stopford, F.W. 305
Stovell, Tyler xvii, xviii, xxii, 251–83
Strachan, Hew xi, xx, 423–39
Stratchey, John St L. 312
Stürmer 108
Sukhomlinov, Vladimir A. 6, 15, 16, 52
Summers, Ann 571, 572
Sun Yat-sen 547, 550
Svechin, A.A. 14–15
Syed Ahmad Shahid 484
Sykes, Mark 467
Sylvester, A.J. 177
Symonds, H. 210

Talaat Bey 113, 117, 118, 120, 121, 122
Tappen, Gerhard 451, 457, 458
Tappen, Hans 446, 448
Tavernier, Edouard 32

Teinert 499, 500
Terrier, Auguste 466
Theweleit, Klaus 83
Thomas, Albert xviii
Thomas, Evan 183
Thompson, E.P. 252
Tilly, Vesta 206
Timm, Carl 132
Torrey, Glenn E. xvi, 89–109
Townshend, Sir Charles 431
Travers, Timothy 312, 363, 424, 426, 428
Treitschke, Heinrich von 336
Trenet, Charles 420, 421
Trigger 500
Trumpener, Ulrich xv, xix, 111–22, 441–61
Tuan Ch'I-jui 549
Tuchman, Barbara xii
Tunde, Baba 560, 565

van Rensburg, Siener 492, 493
Van Vollenhoven, Joost 469
Veiel, Lieutenant 353
Veizelos, Eleftherius 29
Verhey, Jeffrey xvii
Verzhkhovskii, D.V. 48
Vince, P.C.S. 213–14 *passim*
Vincent, C. Paul 139
Visser 349
von Heydebreck, Joachim 500

Wali-ullah, Shah 484
Walshe, Peter 525
Wangenheim, Hans von 114, 116, 117–18, 119, 120, 121, 122
Warwick, Peter 513
Wason, Cathcart 216
Wcislo, Francis 61
Weaver, J.M. 517
Webb, Beatrice 307
Weber, Eugen 57, 60, 61
Wedel, Prince Karl von 118
Weindling, Paul J. 83, 84
Weir, Lord 187
Wermuth, Adolf 126, 129, 135, 136, 139, 140
West, Sir Glynn 187
Wieland, Lothar 325
Wildman, Allan 58
Wilhelm, II, Kaiser 287, 421, 586
Willard, Frances 200
William II, Kaiser 80
Williams, M.J. 320
Wilson, Sir Henry 307, 310, 367, 407
Wilson, Trevor 324, 363
Wilson, Woodrow 139, 524

Winter, Jay xxiii, 588
Woodward, A.M. 203–4, 551
Woolf, Virginia 193
Wrigley, Christopher J. 178
Württemberg, Duke Albrecht of 451, 453, 457, 459

Xabanisa, A.K. 520
Xenopol, A.D. 91
Xuong, Cang 267

Yarde Buller, Sir Henry 30

Yearsley, M. 192
Yuan Shih-k'ai 547, 548, 549

Zaionchkovskii, A.M. 48
Zhilinski 15, 16
Zibi, Z.F. 518
Zimmermann, Arthur 115, 116, 119
Zimmerman, Dr 350
Zola, Emile 335
Zuckerman, Larry xix
Zweig, Arnold 75

For Product Safety Concerns and Information please contact our EU
representative GPSR@taylorandfrancis.com
Taylor & Francis Verlag GmbH, Kaufingerstraße 24, 80331 München, Germany

www.ingramcontent.com/pod-product-compliance
Lightning Source LLC
Chambersburg PA
CBHW081141290426
44108CB00018B/2405